Studies in
Nuclear Terrorism

Edited by
Augustus R. Norton
and Martin H. Greenberg

Studies in
Nuclear Terrorism

G.K. Hall & Co. Boston, Massachusetts

Will Have the Bomb?'' from *International Security*. Mason Willrich and Theodore B. Taylor, ''Nuclear Theft: Risks and Safeguards'' from *Nuclear Power, Issues and Choices,* copyright 1977 by the Ford Foundation, permission of Ballinger Publishing Company. Lloyd Norman, ''Our Nuclear Weapons Sites: Next Target of Terrorists?'' from *Army Magazine*, June 1977, copyright by the Association of the U.S. Army. Bruce G. Blair and Garry D. Brewer, ''The Terrorist Threat to World Nuclear Programs'' from the *Journal of Conflict Resolution* 21 (1977):3, with permission of the authors. Bernard L. Cohen, ''The Potentialities of Terrorism'' from *The Bulletin of Atomic Scientists* 32 (1978):6, copyright 1978 by the Educational Foundation for Nuclear Science. David Comey, ''The Perfect Trojan Horse,'' same source as Cohen, supra. Michael Flood, ''Nuclear Sabotage,'' same source as Cohen, supra. Ted Greenwood, ''Discouraging Nuclear Proliferation in the Next Decade and Beyond: Non-State Entities'' from *Nuclear Proliferation: Motivation, Capabilities, and Strategies for Control*, copyright by the Council on Foreign Relations, permission of McGraw-Hill Book Company. Martha C. Hutchinson, ''Defining Future Threats: Terrorists and Nuclear Proliferation'' from *Terrorism: Interdisciplinary Perspectives*, copyright 1977 by the John Jay Press. Brian M. Jenkins, ''The Potential for Nuclear Terrorism,'' with permission of the Rand Corporation. David Krieger, ''What Happens If . . . ?'' from the *Annals of the American Academy of Political and Social Science*, vol. 430. R.W. Mengel, ''Terrorism and New Technologies of Destruction: An Overview of the Potential Risk'' from *Disorders and Terrorism: Report of the Task Force on Disorders and Terrorism*, 1976, permission of the author. Robert K. Mullen, ''Mass Destruction and Terrorism'' from the *Journal of International Affairs* 32 (1978): 1, by permission of the journal and the Trustees of Columbia University. Augustus R. Norton, ''Nuclear Terrorism and the Middle East,'' permission of the author. Nuclear Energy Policy Study Group, ''Nuclear Terrorism'' from *Nuclear Proliferation and the Near-Nuclear Countries*, permission of Ballinger Publishing Company. Forrest Frank, ''Nuclear Terrorism and the Escalation of International Conflict'' from *Naval War College Review* 29 (1976) :2. Louis René Beres, ''International Terrorism and World Order'' from *Stanford Journal of International Studies*, permission of the author. Robert H. Kupperman, ''Facing Tomorrow's Terrorist Incident Today,'' permission of the Law Enforcement Assistance Administration. ''Appendix 2: Licensed Nuclear Facilities,'' from *An Act to Combat International Terrorism, Hearings Before the Committee on Governmental Affairs*, U.S. Senate, 95th Congress, 2nd Session, 1978, S.2236. ''Glossary'' from *Nuclear Proliferation and Safeguards*, Office of Technology Assessment of the U.S. Congress, 1977.

Library of Congress Cataloging in Publication Data

Main entry under title:

Studies in nuclear terrorism.

  Bibliography:
  Includes index.
  1. Terrorism—Addresses, essays, lectures. 2. Atomic weapons—Addresses, essays, lectures. 3. Atomic warfare—Addresses, essays, lectures. I. Greenberg, Martin Harry. II. Norton, Augustus R.
HV6431.S78   301.6'33   79-18574
ISBN 0-8161-9010-0

This publication is printed on permanent/durable acid-free paper
MANUFACTURED IN THE UNITED STATES OF AMERICA

To Deanna and Sally

Contents

Preface

One measure of the far-reaching concern that the prospect of nuclear terrorism has generated is the multifarious sources in which serious treatments of the problem can be found. Exemplifying the unique sort of fission that occurs when a public problem attracts wide attention, analyses and discussions of nuclear terrorism have appeared in the journals of the social and natural sciences, in legal and military journals, in think-tank prognoses, in government documents and congressional hearings, in popular magazines, as well as books, newspapers, and the electronic media. What we, the editors, have attempted to do is pull together the best of these scattered works and offer them in a convenient and accessible format. Were this not to be done, many of the materials in *Studies in Nuclear Terrorism* would remain relatively inaccessible to scholar and layman alike, for very few libraries and research centers could offer all of the materials included herein.

With many of our colleagues in the academic world, we share a number of pet peeves about edited collections. All too often, such books appear to be slapdash efforts thrown together with far too little care and minimal concern for the reader. We have attempted to avoid as many of these irksome pitfalls as we might, while not being so naive as to presume that we have found the perfect formula. One of the first questions that we confronted was whether we would offer excerpts of the selected contributions or publish in toto. With very little hesitation, we decided that suffering some redundancy across treatments was a small price to pay for the greater benefit of having an unexpurgated version of the contribution. Many of the selections that follow are controversial, and the interpretation of the problem by some writers is going to be judged starkly incorrect by some readers, but each of the contributions is the product of careful scholarship and deserves to be judged in the form originally presented.

Each selection is preceded by a brief introductory note by the editors. These notes are not intended to serve as comprehensive summaries of the selections but instead are intended to highlight their significance, as well as any particularly insightful or controversial arguments. For those perusing the volume, the introductory notes serve to put each article in perspective. For those unacquainted with nuclear physics, nuclear reactor technology, and weapons construction, Appendix 1 is intended to provide a brief primer on the technologies. In addition, the glossary defines a number of technical terms.

Many aspects of the nuclear terrorism debate are, to put it mildly, contentious. Indeed, the very likelihood of nuclear terrorism is a matter of considerable debate, turning not only on questions of technical feasibility but on the very attractiveness of nuclear weapons to the perpetrators of terror-violence. However, perhaps what separates those of us who believe that the threat has been somewhat exaggerated from those who take a rather more alarmist view is less important than the point of intersection: that all of us can indeed conceive of circumstances in which it might happen, and that shared conception is horrific enough to justify our best efforts to insure that we understand the problem. To that final objective, we hope that this book is at least a small contribution.

This preface would not be complete if we failed to thank those whose efforts helped to make this book possible. In particular Mary Grace Smith, our editor, and Deborah Pokos and the staff at G. K. Hall. Finally, a very special note of thanks to our wives, who have cheerfully suffered that special brand of sacrifice that comes from being partners with two men who habitually have their noses stuck in books and their minds involved with far too many projects simultaneously. Naturally, however, we must make the customary disclaimer that we alone share with the contributors the responsibility for what follows.

AUGUSTUS R. NORTON
Monterey, California

MARTIN H. GREENBERG
Green Bay, Wisconsin

Foreword

"Terror is nothing other than prompt, severe, inflexible justice, and thus it is an emanation of virtue." These words of Maximilien Robespierre, the arch apostle of the Reign of Terror, remain as relevant today as they were during the bloodiest years of the French Revolution. Whether government inspired or state directed, whether individually motivated or group sponsored, whether national or international, terrorism requires victims. Ideological terror, whatever the source, demands justifications. Not surprisingly, motive and victim are inextricably intertwined in terrorist mythology. Political terrorists of all kinds have fervently embraced the Marxian credo that the end justifies the means. And for many, the use of terror for terror's sake has become an end in itself. "Apparently, we are able to distinguish clearly between man and beast," observes former West German Chancellor Willy Brandt, "but we are unable to see the line that goes straight through some men and makes them part man and part beast."

Terrorism is not a particularly new phenomenon. Its record is a long and bloody one, and its historical roots stretch all the way back to ancient civilizations. However, the way that terrorism is being implemented in the contemporary world is indeed new. Growing alienation among the young, violent political philosophies, and modern technology have been key ingredients in the spread of current terrorist activities throughout the globe. A rebirth of nineteenth-century nihilism has recreated what André Malraux once termed "the brotherhood of death" in *Man's Fate,* his great novel on revolutionary terrorism. Although recent terrorist techniques are both innovative and constantly changing, the vocabulary of terror-violence is much the same. Voices of destruction uttered by the "People's Will" still echo from the past: "We'll create political unrest," one of Fëdor Dostoevski's pathological nihilist revolutionaries boldly proclaims. "Don't you believe we can do it? We'll cause such a mess that everything will go flying to hell."

According to Central Intelligence Agency estimates, global terror-violence is receding, possibly due to increased national security measures. Another interpretation, debatable at best, is that terrorism is a cyclic phenomenon and that the current period represents a down cycle. Yet little more than two years ago, the CIA predicted widespread international terrorist activity. Whatever the reasons for the ebb and flow of terror-violence, it may well be argued that terrorist acts have become so commonplace throughout the world that ordinary hijacking or bombing incidents no longer have any real impact upon the policies at which they are directed. Thus, although the actual number is in decline, the nature and intensity of the specific act has become more severe and more dramatic as a way of recapturing media and popular attention. The kidnap-murder of Aldo Moro by the Red Brigade in Italy and the hijack-killing of thirty-four tour bus passengers near Tel Aviv by the PLO bear witness to escalation in the degree of harm perpetrated by terrorist organizations.

One of the major problems in evaluating the terrorist threat is the lack of agreement on what constitutes a terrorist act and over who justifiably can be called a terrorist actor. As of the present moment, there is neither a universally accepted legal definition nor even a commonly agreed-upon non-technical terminology, aside from the criminalizing of aerial hijacking by international treaty and convention. As long as a significant portion of the world community is willing to acquiesce in the liberationist slogan that one man's terrorist is another man's freedom fighter, confusion and politicization will continue to blur the issue and to forestall meaningful remedies.

The contributions to this volume indicate that although there is clear and convincing evidence that terrorism poses a serious threat to minimum world public order, there is nonetheless substantial disagreement over what constitutes the essence of that peril. For one thing, a legal as well as a typological difference exists between national and international terrorism, the latter being distinguished from the former by association of an international element with the act, the actor, or the target-victim. Terrorists come in all shapes and sizes. The two major typologies are state or governmental terrorism and individual or group terrorism. Most of the analyses contained in this study stress the individual and group threat, but no one can gainsay state power as the ultimate nuclear peril.

Psychiatrist Frederick Hacker has divided individual and group terrorists into three distinctive categories: crusaders, criminals, and crazies. There may at times be an overlapping, and supreme determination of the will provides a linkage among all three. "What distinguishes a revolutionary [terrorist]," Leon Trotsky pointedly asserted, "is not so much his capacity to kill as his willingness to die." The word *fedayeen* translates as "self-sacrifice," and the PLO commandoes have made fanaticism an integral part of their revolutionary personality. Terrorist politics has cataclysm as its world view. Destruction becomes not only a way of death but a way of life. "We are not of this world," declares one of Albert Camus's terrorist ideologues. "Our share is blood and the cold rope."

Much has been made during recent years of the use of terrorism as surrogate warfare. Both the Rand Corporation's statements on terror-violence and the report of the National Task Force on Disorders and Terrorism stress the possibilities and the probabilities of terrorist actors' carrying out unofficial government policies in an age where nuclear technology restricts or inhibits more conventional means of armed conflict. However, these studies also take note of a potential nuclear threat posed by the terrorists themselves. As far back as 1967, the AEC Ad Hoc Advisory Panel on the Safeguarding of Special Nuclear Material warned of "terrorist or criminal groups clandestinely acquiring nuclear weapons or materials." The consequences of such activity are no longer unthinkable but, in the view of physicist Theodore Taylor, are eminently·predictable. Just as with the biblical injunction that those who live by the sword perish by the sword, so does Taylor believe that those who live by the bomb may well destroy themselves by that very instrument.

Does this mean, then, that terrorism, or nuclear terrorism, represents the ultimate weapon? If so, should humankind resign itself to its inevitable fate? If not, what in fact can be done? And what of other terrorist modalities—whether biological, chemical, advanced weaponry, or homemade explosives? The overriding issue, unarticulated though it may be, is how to determine a credible threat from an empty boast or a flamboyant gesture.

If there is one thing that can be said with certainty about nonstate terrorist actors, it is that they are unpredictable. For them, variety has been the spice of destruction. Within the past several years, terrorists have desecrated the Versailles palace, have seized Dutch commuter trains, have threatened to poison urban water supplies, have allegedly infected Middle Eastern fruit shipments, have used Soviet SA-7 heat-seeking missiles against commercial aircraft, have attempted to steal an atomic submarine, have threatened the North Sea oil platforms, and even contemplated kidnapping Pope Paul VI. Anyone can be a terrorist actor, as demonstrated by the wheelchair hijacker of a Yemeni airliner. During 1975-1976, there were eight major explosions at French nuclear installations, and in the preceding five years a score of actual or attempted arson incidents occured at U.S. nuclear installations. Although the contributors to this book may not entirely agree, several would probably support Richard Falk's observation that "with sufficient money and will power, it is no more difficult to obtain enriched uranium or plutonium than it is to buy bulk quantities of heroin."

If, as Brian Crozier suggests, terrorism is a technique "for demolishing a State," then nuclear terrorism is quintessentially war against the state. The Aldo Moro kidnap-murder, the highly discriminate assassination of anti-terrorist prosecutors and judges in Germany, Italy, and Latin America, and the indiscriminate attacks upon innocent civilians in Ireland, Israel, and Rhodesia demonstrate beyond any question that the primary function of terror-violence is to destroy the credibility of state authority. Indeed, the proposed African U.N. self-determination resolution of October 20, 1978, would effectively legitimate terror-violence for all national liberation struggles.

Dr. Robert Kupperman, chief scientist for the United States Arms Control and Disarmament Agency, has frequently noted that the first successful nuclear threat may also be the last. Once macroterror becomes credible, then the world has left us no place to hide. Significantly, existing international atomic energy safeguard agreements are minimal at best. The NATO Permission Action Link System (PALS), a protective network of coded locks on nuclear warheads stored in Western Europe, has proven to be an effective deterrent to nuclear theft and unwarranted use. But PALS is merely a regional multilateral agreement carefully incorporated into a wider military security pact. The International Atomic Energy Agency (IAEA) has really no control, and its proposed safeguards mechanism, as Dr. David Krieger points out, is simply an inventory accounting technique. In March 1976, Secretary of State Henry A. Kissinger indicated his concern over the lack of cooperation and control in the international nuclear arena, but his proposed solution was only an international convention to establish some sort of minimal security standards. "What guarantees are there," asks historian Robert Paxton, "that supra-national institutions must grow?" Or that international agreements must work?

Even though sabotage of a nuclear facility or theft of a nuclear cargo are much more likely than someone's creating a usable bomb from purloined nuclear materials, the danger of either event's occurring at some future date is no longer mere hypothetical conjecture. With an increasing number of nuclear devices, atomic power plants, and radioactive materiel, the odds that someone will either disrupt or steal something dangerous have expanded from the realm of the possible to the perimeter of the probable. Recognition and implementation of disaster theories are now acknowledged formulas for global survival. We are slowly but surely reaching the level where terrorist actors have motive, means, and opportunity for what Dr. Brian Jenkins has termed "serious nuclear violence."

An ominous warning of the state of terrorist technology occurred just in the past year when Italian security forces discovered an electronic monitoring center of the Red Brigade, which contained equipment far more sophisticated than that supplied to the Italian Army. Who is to deny that at some future date scientists of great skill and questionable ethics may sell their talents to terrorist groups or to terror-promoting governments? And what of misguided scientific idealists who place their knowledge and techniques in the hands of terrorist ideologues? Given the nature of the human condition, the likelihood of such an event is not small.

On the other hand, there are those scholars and analysts who argue that, based upon past performance and present reality, the terrorist threat is more apparent than real. Psychiatrist Lawrence Z. Freedman, among others, queries: "Why does the whole world get upset by five or six people being killed by terrorists when 46,000 people get killed on American highways every year?" Historian Walter Laqueur writes of "the futility of terrorism" and argues that "compared with other dangers threatening mankind, it is almost irrelevant." In a microsense, their reasoning is at least debatable, but the possibilities of macroterror reduce the argument to scholastic disputation. The horror of modern terrorism and its awful consequences, as well as the source of its strength, in the words of psychiatrist Frederick Hacker, is that "everybody is a potential victim." Terror-violence truly affects all humankind. According to Nobel Laureate Albert Camus, "On both sides, a reign of terror, as long as it lasts, changes the scale of values." To ignore his warning is an invitation to catastrophe.

Unfortunately, just as terrorism can be construed as war against the state and civilized society, so combating terrorism is likewise war, and in the struggle to control its deadly force, civil liberties may emerge as yet another casualty. An unhappy consequence of security management is that efforts to control terrorism on the part of democratic, pluralistic societies must inevitably result in a diminution of civil liberties. That, of course, is a prime terrorist objective. Therefore, the issue is really at what cost can terror-violence be restrained. On a microlevel, tolerating terrorism is a costly decision, but the price may well be one that society can afford to pay. On a macrolevel, however, the price becomes a Hobson's choice—survival and authoritarian controls or mass destruction and Armageddon. Since terrorism is often the last refuge of the hopeless cause (witness the Basque nationalists, the Croatian secessionists, and the South Moluccans), one cannot depend upon a rational utilization of a credible threat.

Obviously, no one has yet provided an effective answer to hard questions that must be raised. And so far, there has been a genuine reluctance within the world community to face up to the real issues. Ignorance is not strength in the Orwellian sense but instead invites disaster. The essays contained in this important volume, even if they do not provide solutions, at least identify those issues that must be resolved. The choices still lie before us, but time is of the essence. Our terror decade is a time of testing. If nuclear terrorism becomes a reality, then the trial of civilization as we know it will have reached the final judgment. And there will be no victors.

ROBERT A. FRIEDLANDER
Ohio Northern University
College of Law
Ada, Ohio

Introduction

Augustus R. Norton

"Terrorism is an arm the revolutionary can never relinquish."
—Carlos Marighella[1]

"To the destruction of what is."
—The Professor[2]

The liberal governments of this world have increasingly come to find themselves attempting to cope with the extraordinary explosion of demands—both legitimate and illegitimate—that defines contemporary politics. For most of those who object to this or that policy, dissent takes constitutionally—or at least tacitly—acceptable forms. However, for a small segment of those rejecting not a policy or a particular government but rather a regime and "established legality" itself,[3] the language of dissent is violence, and the blunt instrument for its expression all too often is terrorism.[4]

Whether inspired by revolutionary ideals or the so-called logic of anarchy, terrorists of today have inscribed themselves indelibly in the consciousness of policy makers and citizens alike. Although pursuing widely variant objectives, the myriad subnational organizations, anarchists, and misfits of this planet have found one indisputable common ground for agreement: the utility of terrorism as a tactic for the achievement of a number of goals, including publicity, fund raising, or simply praxis.

To date, terrorism, whether at the hands of *fedayeen* extremists or Italian anarchists or other terrorists, has been more important as a headline grabber than as a destroyer of human life. This is all the more evidence of the quintessence of terrorism—symbolic violence for psychological and political effect.[5] For example, the world total of 375 deaths resultant of terrorist actions in 1974 (the record year to date) is considerably less than the U.S. highway fatalities for any recent year (1976 fatalities, for example, totaled 46,700).[6] Yet it is the terrorist extravaganza, not the carnage of the highway, that holds our attention. In human terms, the destruction wrought by terrorists has been appalling, and yet they have touched directly only the lives of very few. But as the world becomes inured to the murder of a head of state, to the slaughter of innocents who happen to be born of one nationality or another, to the maiming of those who respect a pope rather than an archbishop, and to those who die because they happen to be at the wrong place at the wrong time, will the "restraint" of today's terrorists give way to ever greater carnage wreaked by tomorrow's terrorists?[7] Does the prologue obscure the future? Is there a mushroom-shaped cloud in our future, compliments of this or that extremist? Such a prospect—the decision by terrorists to utilize nuclear weapons—is the focus of this introduction.

I

Terrorism has been likened to the theater by a number of keen observers of the terrorist phenomenon (Brian Jenkins of the Rand Corporation may have originated the metaphor). Following the theater metaphor, a serious question is raised concerning this prospective variant of macroterrorism: the nuclear.[8] Is it likely that the world will witness a mode of terrorism that stresses audience participation, or at least enlarges the cast, to levels never before experienced? This sort of question should be approached from a number of different perspectives in order to arrive at an acceptable (albeit tentative) understanding of the problem; however, before examining the pertinent points of inquiry systematically, it will be useful to gain some perspective on the problem by citing several of the analyses that have been completed to date.

Largely because of the enthusiastic and incessant efforts of Theodore B. Taylor, a physicist and former U.S. nuclear weapons designer, it is now widely believed that the civil nuclear fuel cycle has several keen vulnerabilities to the theft or diversion of nuclear explosive devices. Such devices would be crude nuclear devices with possible yields on the order of 0.1 kiloton (KT), a figure that has been revised downward from the 1KT and higher estimates that were widely circulated several years ago.* Such a crude nuclear weapon would not satisfy a military planner but would represent an awesome increase in the firepower available to terrorist groups or, for that matter, criminals. Obviously, this is not a prospect to be taken lightly; however, the magnitude of the problem is anything but a matter of common agreement.

While many academics-cum-consultants have only recently discovered the prospect of the unorthodox use of nuclear weapons by subnational groupings or foreign agents, the problem has actually been recognized since the be-

---

*KT=1,000 tons of TNT; thus 0.1 KT equals the explosive blast of 100 tons of TNT.

ginning of the nuclear age. For example, the Jeffries Report written at the Metallurgy Lab of the University of Chicago in 1944 discusses the possibility of a political group's unleashing a nuclear blitzkrieg by smuggling its weapons in commercial aircraft and secreting them in anticipation of the beginning of the attack.[9] In a similar vein, Vannevar Bush, writing in 1949, discussed the possibility that a bomb might be hidden in the hold of a ship.[10] In *The Absolute Weapon,* written in 1946, Bernard Brodie writes of the "new potentialities which the atomic bomb gives to sabotage."[11] Or Harold Urey, cited by the *New Republic,* December 31, 1945, said: "An enemy who puts twenty bombs, each with a time fuse, into twenty trunks, and checked one in the baggage room of the main railroad station in each of twenty leading American cities, could wipe this country off the map so far as military defense is concerned." More recently, Roberta Wohlstetter wrote of the "superficial sense of *déjà vu* which affects any look at the possibility that some subnational group or even an individual entrepreneur might use nuclear terror."[12] (Her article is reproduced in this book.)

Yet more than three decades have passed since the explosion of the first nuclear device, and as with the apocalyptic musings concerning nuclear war, nuclear terrorism is still, thankfully, a matter of conjecture rather than history. Why? We can look to several explanations. Brodie, for example, points out that "the bomb itself is a highly intricate and fairly massive mechanism. . . . Not one which can be slipped into a suitcase." But, even as he recognized in 1946, a simpler device could perhaps be developed (though one that still was dependent upon the same principles of physics). Nor might we be very comfortable with the tradition of a lack of experience with nuclear terrorism, for as Thomas Schelling has observed, "Of course, this could be one of those traditions that, being absolute, is discredited at the first violation."[13] We need to determine whether the "absolute tradition" will be abandoned. The route to that answer is the determination of discontinuities, as well as continuities.

Perhaps to this stage in the nuclear age, there has been a simple lack of motivation, skill, or even publicity concerning the possibility of nuclear terror. Perhaps no self-respecting terrorist had given the idea any thought. Indeed, "sometimes the genie must be pushed out of the bottle," by those who most want to protect us.[14] Or, as some authorities hold, it might just be that the technical means are only now becoming widely available, and at a juncture in the chronicle of terrorism when terrorism itself may be becoming more gruesome. The following factors should be considered:

1. Contemporary terrorism has emerged as a major and oft-used tool for the weak to defeat the strong. "Public protest by bomb and by bullet rather than by ballot has become and all-too familiar symbol of the last decade."[15]

2. As Wohlstetter suggests, the socialization of contemporary terrorists has included exposure to military strategies that coolly weigh
the destruction of millions of civilians, as exemplified in the so-
called countervalue targeting strategies.[16] This brand of "humanism"
is captured nicely by John Newhouse, who in describing the countervalue doctrine, observes, "Killing people is good, killing missiles is
bad."[17] Furthermore, any inhibition to aggression that might result
from face-to-face contact between victim and attacker has been precluded by the impersonal nature of the technology of modern
warfare.[18]

3. The spread of nuclear technology in the form of civil nuclear power
programs, and in particular the dispersion of technologies necessary
for the production of bomb-making material, has made the basic
materials more accessible. Most important is the sale of reprocessing
technologies, which provide the capability of separating plutonium
produced during normal reactor operations from the irradiated
(spent) fuel rods removed from the reactor to states with somewhat
unstable political systems.[19] Such sales have been made by Germany
to Brazil and by France to Pakistan.

4. The Atoms for Peace program, which in 1965 "led to declassifying
10,000 United States Atomic Energy Commission documents . . . ,
and over half a million by 1972," increased the open literature
immensely.[20] Many such documents would be of great assistance to
those concerned with nuclear weapons design and fabrication. As
one U.S. Department of Energy official commented recently: "With
the advent of terrorist threats, it seems possible that much unclassified information in the nuclear area may be useful to terrorists."[21]

5. The large numbers of personnel who have been or are employed in
atomic energy industries increases the pool of skilled labor that
might be tapped to produce an illicit bomb. One estimate puts the
total requirement for trained engineers by the international nuclear
industry at 115,000 by 1980.[22] It is frequently suggested that at
least a few of the technical experts might "desert" to the terrorists.
There is one reported case of a highly placed German, Dr. Klaus
Traube, who had "access to all blueprints for nuclear power plants
in West Germany," who was dismissed from this position as a result
of extended contacts with terrorists.[23]

6. Finally, the proliferation of books, articles, studies, monographs,
and speeches intended to warn us of the problem has also alerted
(and challenged) terrorists to the possibility. As Wohlstetter notes,
"It is even barely possible—as those who have recently warned us
recognize—that advertising the technical feasibility will raise the
probability."[24]

II

More than any other work, the Ford Foundation study by Mason Willrich and Theodore Taylor, *Nuclear Theft: Risks and Safeguards,*[25] has prompted the heightened public attention[26] to the possibility of nuclear terror. Taylor in particular has crusaded to alert the public of the alleged ease with which even one technically competent individual might fabricate a crude nuclear device.

Nuclear Theft has spawned a predictable spate of journal articles, monographs, and popular treatments (and in fairness, this book, too). Even the field of fiction has begun to capture the theme, although there has been little creative movement beyond the potboiler.[27] J. Bowyer Bell's comment on this facet of the "terrorism" phenomenon is well to the point. (Bell is himself the author of four recent books on terrorism and revolution.)

> Inevitably, it appears that the analysis of terror will continue to be
> a growth industry regularly supplied with additional spectaculars
> by the practitioners. The prospect of all these essays and articles
> dense with notes, and survey books and monographs on obscure
> bombers, should strike terror in the mind of the common reader.[28]

In an attempt to avoid being intimidated by the sheer volume of literature on the subject, a useful approach is to locate central tendencies in the literature. Although much of the serious nonfiction on the question of nuclear terror differs significantly in content and emphasis, it is possible to identify two distinct tendencies, or schools of thought, that encompass the major points in contention. The "realists' school" examines motives, feasibility and historical evidence; the "faith bloc" seems to accept the likelihood of nuclear terrorism as a matter of fatalistic faith, or at least as a concession to expert opinion.[29]

The faith bloc literature characteristically proceeds as follows: the possibility of acquisition of fissile materials, hence nuclear explosive devices, provides the motive for terrorists to find or compile the capabilities to carry out the threat of nuclear terrorism.[30] Following this line of reasoning, we might conceive of the prospective nuclear terrorist as a mountain climber who will climb the plutonium precipice simply because it is there.

This tendency to proceed from the feasibility of acquisition to a presumptive motive was recognized by Wohlstetter:

> Arguments for paying more attention to nuclear terrorism pro-
> ceed by showing mainly that it would be *feasible* for a lone in-
> dividual or a small group to steal or make and deliver a crude
> weapon, that there might be *some motive,* and that it would be
> *terrible* if it happened. This demonstration may be enough to
> warrant greater care in nuclear safeguards, but it does not offer

> much of a basis for judging the probability of such an event. . . .
> But in any case, the analysis of possible motives is generally
> rather thin and not much attention has been devoted to the
> viewpoint of the terrorist, the alternatives they have, and their
> psychological and political pathologies.[31]

This stress upon the acquisition element, which is characteristic of the faith bloc, is particularly evident in the work of Theodore Taylor and even more so in analyses by David Rosenbaum, David Krieger, Forrest Frank, and Louis Beres.

The difficulty with this acquisition-oriented approach is that it presents the problem of nuclear terrorism as if it were discrete from the rational decision-making framework likely to be used by the prospective terrorist; however, the two elements are intertwined rather than independent of one another. Ignoring the consequences and the objectives of an act of terror for the terrorist is to risk misunderstanding terrorism itself. As David Fromkin reminds us, terrorism "achieves its goals not through its acts but through the response to its acts":

> In any other such strategy of violence, the violence is the be-
> ginning and its consequences are the end of it. For terrorism,
> however, the consequences of the violence are themselves merely
> a first step and form a steppingstone toward objectives that are
> more remote.[32]

Thus, whether nuclear terrorism is indeed a viable "mega-threat" turns on technical feasibility plus the likelihood that terrorists will want to make the attempt given the possible favorable and unfavorable consequences of the act and their own objectives.[33]

We are not presuming, by the way, that terrorists will be guided by rationality in the normative sense. Paul Wilkinson is probably correct in his warning: "It would be a great mistake to assume that political terrorists will conform to some minimum standard of rationality and humanity."[34] We are concerned, however, with rationality in the utilitarian sense—that is, in the context of instrumental, goal-oriented behavior—and thus we distinguish the political terrorist (and the criminal, for that matter) from the psychopath whose vicarious enjoyment of destruction as an end in and of itself is irrational except in the strictest mechanical sense. For the rational actor, including the terrorist, goals exist beyond the act.

These points are not new to some whom we identify with the faith bloc, but they tend to denigrate such factors in the face of the assumption that terrorists will "do it." Thus, Louis René Beres acknowledges the trade-off between costs and benefits as follows: "No less than states, terrorist groups chose between alternative courses of action by assessing the perceived consequences of each course in cost-benefit terms."[35] But Beres, like many others, does not believe that the current costs are sufficient to deter terrorists from a nuclear strategy. This is an important divergence and one to which we will return.

Proceeding within the schema employed by the faith bloc, the matter of acquiring or constructing a nuclear weapon is the key point of interest. Therefore, the question of technical feasibility needs to be addressed. The following sorts of questions will lead the inquiry in the right direction: How difficult is bomb construction? How many people might we expect to find on a bomb-building team? What skills must the fabricators possess? How long would the project take from start to finish? How long after the fissile explosive material is obtained (stolen or diverted, for example) might the bomb be ready for use?

Beres appears to be the most optimistic (or perhaps pessimistic) in addressing the complexity of the technology that must be conquered. He asks, "How difficult is the design of a nuclear explosive?" and answers, "Not very." In fact, "Nuclear weapons are relatively easy to make."[36] Similarly, William Epstein, in a widely read book about nuclear proliferation, informs his readers that "it is not very difficult to make a bomb."[37] We need not be considered overly skeptical to ask, "Relative to what?"

These answers are unsatisfactory. For more precision, we can turn to Forrest Frank, who gives us cause to gaze suspiciously at that earnest college student who spends his days in the chemistry lab, the physics classroom, or under the vast geodesic domes of our engineering schools: "The amount of expertise needed to construct a bomb is perhaps no greater than that derived from college physics, chemistry, and perhaps engineering."[38] Or we might turn to David Rosenbaum, who believes that the skills necessary for the construction of a bomb are quite common:

> People with the skills needed to build crude nuclear weapons are
> easily found in the general technical community. Someone with
> the experience in calculating fast neutron systems would be use-
> ful, as would a physical chemist and an explosives expert. There
> are thousands of people with appropriate skills in physical chemis-
> try and explosives. Thus, most established organizations,
> given enough time, should be able to acquire appropriate people.[39]

The technical barriers to nuclear weapon construction are not that high, according to Willrich and Taylor: "It is difficult to imagine that a determined terrorist group could not acquire a nuclear weapon manufacturing capability once it had the required nuclear weapon materials."[40] Furthermore, Taylor has consistently held that just one person could accomplish the task.[41] Following Taylor, it is worthwhile to take note of one "do-it-yourselfer" who produced a bomb design—only a step along the way to weapons capability—

and was featured in the Public Broadcasting System program "NOVA." This celebrated MIT student was offered as proof that the threat of nuclear terror was real indeed. The message of the "NOVA" program was that bomb design and construction are relatively simple, and to substantiate the claim, a Swedish scientist favorably evaluated the student's blueprint for the program. Alas, the view of the scientist was rather more restrained than the unwary television viewer might have concluded from listening to the edited broadcast. Roberta Wohlstetter, quoting a letter from the scientist, shows that the student's efforts were rather more a qualified success than a resounding victory:

> a. design of the bomb was primitive; b. several essential features were forgotten; c. the student might not survive the fabrication of the bomb; d. should he survive, the probability that the bomb would go off upon "pressing the button" would be less than 50%; e. should a nuclear reaction start, the explosion yield would be very small. The probability that the device would yield as much as a 0.1-1kt would be very small; f. if a group of qualified scientists or a professional defector were granted more time and better means, including the possibility to undertake experiments, the bomb would be much better.[42]

J. Carson Mark, a celebrated physicist long involved with military-related nuclear activities, was called upon by the Senate Committee on Government Affairs in March 1978 to evaluate yet another amateur design derived from unclassified sources. Mark did not foreclose the possibility of a successful bomb-construction effort, but he did find several problems with the design at hand:

> There is not in [the individual's] work, in my view, sufficient awareness of some of the difficulties . . . in actually realizing the apparatus to perform in the way which he has said it would need to perform or that it would perform. This, of course, doesn't prove anything; because it remains true that I suppose [the designer], and certainly several people thinking as carefully as he has thought, could bring into reality such an apparatus.[43]

Clearly, one would be foolish to deny that a group of intelligent individuals could successfully design and construct a nuclear weapon, but it would seem that there has been some denigration of the sophistication required. This reminder is especially important considering that most terrorists—although well educated, with at least some university training being the norm—have pursued studies in the humanities and the social sciences rather than the exact sciences.[44]

Perhaps the core of the matter was best captured by an unidentified commentator in *The Curve of Binding Energy* (a popularized treatment of Theodore Taylor's views), who commented: "[Taylor] seems to think that anyone could do it, but that is not so. If you wanted to make a bomb, you would need a Ted Taylor."[45]

It is now becoming clear that the scientific community is considerably more skeptical about the ease of building a nuclear bomb than Taylor and Mark are. One authoritative view is offered by the Nuclear Energy Policy Study Group, which recently completed a major study, sponsored by the Ford Foundation. The group concluded:

> The difficulty of designing, planning, and constructing a crude
> weapon from reactor-grade plutonium should not be under-
> estimated.
>   After extensive planning, many months of intense work would
> be involved to produce a weapon. Even in a well-planned effort,
> there is a good chance that the weapon would fail to detonate
> or that the group would suffer fatal accidents during its construc-
> tion. Prospects for success would be somewhat enhanced if ter-
> rorists could operate freely enough within a society to test the
> high explosive parts of the weapon.[46]

This view is shared by Robert Kupperman, the chief scientist for the Arms Control and Disarmament Agency, who states: "Although terrorists could conceivably obtain materials and technology to manufacture a crude fission bomb, this is a difficult and dangerous task—they are more likely to turn to readily available chemical or biological weapons."[47]

Despite some of the more restrained authoritative analyses of the problem, the supposed ease of making a nuclear explosive device is still widely accepted as expert opinion, with scarce attention directed to evaluating such a conclusion. Some of the enthusiastic advocates of the faith bloc present a series of scenarios that might stretch the imagination of even the Saturday matinee crowd. Take, for example, a scenario offered by Rosenbaum:

> A nuclear facility near a metropolitan area could be captured by
> a terrorist group which threatened to cause an explosion re-
> leasing large amounts of radioactive material into the atmosphere.
> If the facility contained more than a WQ [weapon quantity] of
> *easily usable* SNM [special nuclear material], they might,
> given sufficient time, even construct a nuclear explosive on the
> site. Properly used, such an explosive could greatly increase the
> amount of radioactive material dispersed and the area over
> which it was dispersed.[48]

Leaving aside methods of access to the site, motives, size of the group, and other deatils, we must ask the following:

1. What is "easily usable SNM?" Reactors in commercial use do not use high enriched (weapons grade) uranium, and military facilities present difficult (though not insurmountable) problems of access.[49]

2. If the reactor at the facility uses MOX (mixed oxide fuels containing plutonium), and none in current or planned operation will, the plutonium would be in the form of pellets or slugs loaded into fuel rods.[50] If a fresh reload was standing by, the terrorists would have to disassemble the fuel rods and chemically process the fuel pellets to extract the plutonium. This is not an insurmountable task, but it requires a portable laboratory of some sophistication.

3. If a fresh reload is not available, the fuel rods in use will be highly radioactive, ("hot") and quite dangerous if not handled with the proper remote-control equipment and shielding.

4. The irradiated (spent) fuel rods will be stored in a cooling pool. They are self-protecting in the sense that they are very hot and quite lethal to the unprotected. Will the terrorists arrive with their own remote-control apparatus in tow?

5. How will the terrorists separate the plutonium from the spent fuel? Will they reprocess on site? (Even Taylor admits that the reprocessing threshold is significant for terrorists.)[51] It is appropriate to note J. Carson Mark's comments on just one of the laboratory procedures that the illicit bomb maker might confront—in this case, reducing plutonium oxide or uranium oxide to plutonium or uranium in metallic form. Although he allows that there are handbooks that provide the information for the processes in question, the procedure would not be easy for the inexperienced.

> It must be realized that these [the handbooks] are really in the nature of cookbooks. It is as if I should have Julia Child's book here in my hand and, reading carefully line by line, expect to come out with a galantine. It takes more than those instructions. It takes experience and it takes a feeling, really quite a broad awareness, to go from the kinds of statements available in the plutonium metals handbook to achieve plutonium metal.
> It is often claimed that this is an easy, straightforwardly available process for an inexperienced individual to follow. I think that statement is usually made by people who have never done it.[52]

6. How long will the weapon fabrication take? Many discuss bomb design and construction in time frames of months or longer. The Nuclear Energy Policy Study Group refers to "months of intense work."

7. What are the security officials and forces doing while the weapon is being fabricated? Is it reasonable to expect that the terrorists will hold them at bay for the months necessary to construct a device?

Clearly, Rosenbaum's assumption is that bomb fabrication is a simple and speedy process. This does not go too far beyond Taylor's comments. In a 1977 article, Taylor asserts that terrorists with the expertise can be within "days or even hours" of weapons capability; all they have to do is complete the process.[53]

We have already noted that Taylor speaks in terms of a 0.1 KT yield from a crude nuclear bomb. In their enthusiasm, many of those writing on the subject have greatly increased the possible yield. Epstein, for example, writes about a 15 KT bomb at one point[54] and of a weapon in the megaton range at another.[55] Rosenbaum presents a casualty estimate of one million people (Wall Street on a business day) based upon a 20 KT weapon. (Curiously, Rosenbaum's estimate is based on a letter from Taylor, who himself estimates the weapon would be in the subkiloton range.)[56] Krieger, by contrast, offers a panoply of targets, some more realistic than others, for which the terrorists might consider their bomb appropriate: "Terrorists could threaten the destruction of any number of key targets, including a nation's capital city, a major dam, or even a nuclear power generating station."[57]

Such speculation on likely targets should be weighed against the damage estimates that Taylor and Willrich provide for a 0.1 KT weapon (a yield often argued to be within terrorist capabilities). It should be understood from the onset that weapons yield is probabilistic, and even government specialists can do no better than predict the likely yield. The error in the yield of a small crude weapon might be as high as one order of magnitude. With this in mind, we note the following figures: a 0.1 KT weapon would produce radiation fatalities to a range of nearly five hundred meters, it would create at least moderate structural damage as far away as three hundred meters, and it would cast fallout perhaps as far as one kilometer away. If the weapon were only 0.01 KT, the ranges would be more than halved; similarly, they would be approximately doubled for a 1 KT weapon.[58] The damage would be awesome with such targets as the Sears Tower or the World Trade Center, vulnerable indeed to a well-placed weapon. Yet it must also be acknowledged that the destruction of a city or a nation is far out of the reach of any nonstate nuclear terrorist.

III

Several authorities posit that nuclear terrorists could place a modern society such as the United States or Canada peculiarly at risk since the "logic of deterrence" is not relevant to the threat. Thus, the threat of nuclear retaliation would be futile against the elusive terrorists.[59] Notwithstanding the fact that many terrorists "have many of the vulnerabilities of governments," it is hard to understand why the posited asymmetry receives such prominent attention.[60] Can we explain the phenomenon of aircraft hijacking by virtue of the fact that the states victimized may not counter by hijacking terrorist flag carriers? To deter someone from doing something does not require counteraction in kind. In order to deter a terrorist who is not already dissuaded by organizational costs from the nuclear path, it would seem that one would want to impose the prospect of unacceptable and credible costs (punishments such as capture, death, or destruction of the organization, for example) and not nuclear retaliation. Furthermore, can it be inferred that where terrorists would be vulnerable to nuclear attack that the logic of nuclear deterrence should be brought into play? Obviously, no. Careful consideration yields no other conclusion.

IV

It is frequently posited that terrorist groups might be provided a nuclear explosive device—for a number of reasons—by the authorities of a state (typically a radical one). However, it should be noted that there is something of an analytical problem here. Albeit the problem may be somewhat amorphous, it is nonetheless important; specifically, at what point does government-sponsored terrorism cease being perceived as the action of an organization and instead begin to be perceived as the policy of the state? The line is not easily drawn; however, it is probably drawn at the nuclear level at least. This is a key point since states that sponsor terrorists are subject to a range of coercive measures, which may not be effective against terrorists. For this reason, it appears that the likelihood that nuclear weapons will be transferred to a terrorist group has been rather overdrawn.

Rosenbaum, for example, posits that the U.S.S.R. might provide a nuclear weapon to terrorists.[61] This totally ignores the fact that the Soviets have been most conscious of precedent in international affairs (for example, hesitation on the issue of Jewish emigration from the U.S.S.R.) and furthermore have not been entirely supportive of terrorism (as distinguished from "revolutionary violence").[62]

David Krieger, arguing along similar lines, admits that stealing nuclear weapons from a government would be likely to be difficult "unless the power of the revolutionary force approached that of the government," but

> far simpler would be to convince a sympathetic government to
> give one or more weapons away. We can imagine, for example,
> another Middle Eastern nation clandestinely creating nuclear
> weapons in the same way Israel is purported to have done and
> then turning some of them over to a terrorist group.[63]

There are a few obvious problems with such supposition. First is the matter of risk for the donor who would be foolish to deliver the weapon(s) unless the transfer could be forever secret. Second is the faulty analogy provided; a state that is developing weapons "in the same way as Israel" would not allow for the confirmation of the existence of its weapons but would foster the suspicion as to their existence (as Israel does with great skill). Maintaining secrecy in such circumstances is probably not possible. Similar objections can be raised to Krieger's assertion that "the nuclear weapon may be given to the terrorist group as payment for other activities the national leader wants accomplished. Such an agreement would most likely be secret." For how long?[64]

We may not be in total agreement with Ted Greenwood when he argues that "all states have an interest in maintaining a taboo against non-state possession of nuclear weapons and in punishing and suppressing its violators."[65] But most states share such an interest, and for those that do not, the cost of nonconformity could be dear indeed.

V

It has been argued to this point that the goal-oriented behavior of terrorists may reflect unsavory motives and tactics but that such behavior is nonetheless instrumental in form. What remains is to examine the types of considerations that are likely to influence a decision by terrorists to attempt a resort to nuclear weapons. Rather than presuming a motive for a terrorist group to seek a nuclear capability, the terrorists' moral, purposive, and ideological underpinnings must be taken into account. The variables and concepts to be surveyed are depicted in Figure 1.

IDEOLOGICAL CONSIDERATIONS

There is certainly no consensus among those who have thought seriously about the terror-violence problem as to the fruitfulness of studying the ideological underpinnings of this or that terrorist group. On the one hand are those like Paul Wilkinson who argue that the failure to examine terrorists' ideologies is a "fatal flaw" in most analyses.[66] On the other hand is Arnold Beichman, for example, who argues that such an approach is likely to plow a fallow plot: "With possible exceptions such as the PLO and the IRA, terrorist 'programs' are nonexistent, therefore, nonnegotiable. *There is no way of studying terrorist ideology in any meaningful way.* [Emphasis added.]"[67]

Some accommodation between these two polar extremes is probably wisest. It is doubtlessly true that some terroristic groups simply do not betray any discernible ideology beyond the most facile parroting of a Sartre, a Marcuse, or a Marighella. Admittedly then, there are those, much like the

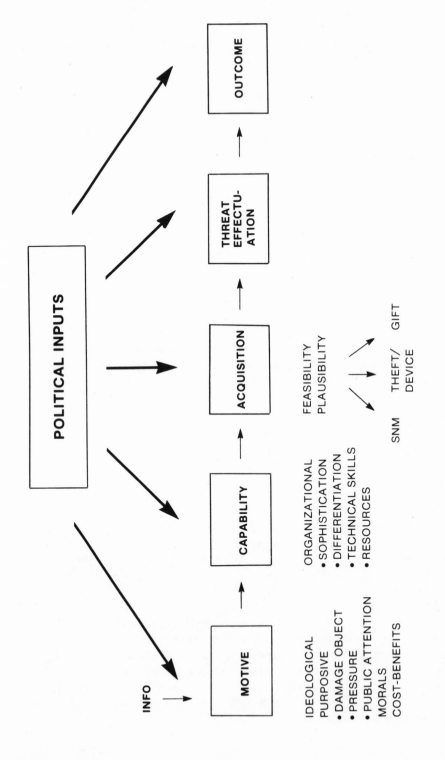

Figure 1.

characters in Paul Theroux's *Family Arsenal,* who engage in terrorism for the thrill. And yet, respective ideologies may provide an injunction for particular types of terrorist actions. For example, Bernard K. Johnpoll, in his very competent treatment of terrorism in the United States, discusses the theoretical basis for violence put forth by Johann Most, the nineteenth-century anarchist who argued that terror was "the only means available for overthrowing the oppressive system and making the new Utopia secure.

> Peripherally, Most and his followers argued that terror was essentially less oppressive than the continuation of the present system, that at least as many persons had died under the present system as would die during a period of terror, and that death from privation under the present system was far worse than death by assassination. This was to remain, with some modification, the basic philosophic argument for terror in the United States.[68]

Most's philosophy of violence should be contrasted to that of Sartre, who would present us with a milieu of perpetual (albeit "liberating") terror. For Sartre, notes Paul Wilkinson:

> Any killing or cruelty committed in the name of revolution is its own justification: the end justifies the means, the means justify the end; terrorism becomes an addiction, an obsession, a way of life, and the act of murder a sacramental duty.[69]

Alternately, a number of terrorist groups have espoused theories of violence or ideologies that do not justify the killing of innocents, or at least provide an impelling injunction to minimize deaths.[70] Some terrorists, at least, have agreed with Camus: "No cause justifies the death of the innocent." As Thomas Thornton noted in his influential article:

> The terrorist must always have the distinction between *apparent* indiscrimination and *actual* indiscrimination clearly in mind, if he is to succeed. As a general rule, it may be said that terror is most effective when it is indiscriminate in appearance but highly discriminate in fact.[71]

Many terrorists would agree that no cause justifies the *unnecessary* death of the innocent, although necessity and innocence are often oddly construed. This injunction is reinforced by ideology for some, but it is likely to be a strategic consideration as well, given the importance of the maintenance of at least a minimal base of support or sympathy (whether coerced or genuine). Thus, even if the ideology that inspires (or merely justifies) the terrorist abets the gratuitous destruction of the innocent, strategic considerations operate against senseless slaughter, particularly on the scale that we contemplate in the macroterror context.

PURPOSIVE ASPECTS

Closely related to the ideological considerations is an examination of the purposes for which an act of terror-violence has been committed. For the political terrorist, we expect to find a purpose that transcends the act itself, although this purpose is more likely to be pronounced in the case of groups such as the Palestine Liberation Organization than the latter-day nihilists typified by the Red Brigade. For example, when Fritz Trufel, a Baader-Meinhof gang member, said that "it is better to bomb a store, than to run one," it was obvious that any objective beyond destruction was quite obscure.[72] Naturally, one confronts considerable ambiguity when considering groups that pursue destruction per se, since their damage objectives may represent the earliest stirrings of a terror campaign for political objectives or merely the spasmodic flailing of the disaffected against a society that they have come to abhor. The difficulty is not so great, however, when the tactics chosen are more clearly associated with discrete objectives. Here, of course, we refer to pressure/coercive objectives and publicity objectives.

Even where there is considerably more ambiguity than heuristic models or taxonomies might imply, it is still important to attempt this distinction between tactics and objectives because it allows us to identify those whose terrorism is purposeless, those who seek objectives that presuppose the destruction of the existing political and social systems, and those whose aims presuppose only some restructuring of the political system. Following the categorization offered by Conor Cruise O'Brian, it is frequently the millenarian groups (typically of an anarchistic or a nihilistic bent) who conceive of tactics amorphously, only vaguely justifying them as a means toward the "destruction of what is," while secessionist-irredentist groups (the PLO and the IRA are examples) seek concrete objectives—frequently in the form of incremental concessions—beyond the tactics of terror violence that they employ.[73] It is the secessionist-irredentist terrorists who are most concerned with the attentions and the concessions of those whom they attack. This is not to say that millenarians do not seek publicity or carry out horrendous acts of coercion; rather it is to point out that the millenarians' "utopian" objectives presuppose the co-identity of terror and liberty, a position that allows minimal compromise and scant accommodation. The situation is not nearly so stark with those who seek less than a millennium.

Certain categories of targets are likely to be perceived as desirable objectives ipso facto among both types of terrorists, but the destruction of the masses would not be so perceived. For the absolutist, as well as the secessionist-irredentist, the murder of large numbers of civilians is simply unattractive. Notwithstanding the risks for the organizations, very little is to be gained by killing many, so long as the death of a few is newsworthy. As Brian Jenkins has asserted, "The objective of terrorism is *not* mass murder." "Terrorists want a lot of people watching and a lot of people listening, not a lot of people dead."[74] The difference between the murder of a few innocents and genocide is so obvious that those who would see a relationship between the two can only be ignoring the very dynamics of terrorism. Thus, an objection must be raised to Paul Wilkinson's following proposition: "If any individual life is expendable in the case of 'Revolutionary Justice' or 'Liberation' so may hundreds, even thousands, of lives have to be 'sacrificed.'"[75] The quantitative difference between the one and the other is so massive as to signify a qualitative distinction between assassination and murder, and mass murder. This is a distinction that has not gone unrecognized. As R. Mengel notes, "The terrorist that would resort to the direct application of new technologies causing uncontrolled, indiscriminate casualties and damage has not appeared."[76]

Targets more clearly identified with an offending government are likely to be more acceptable under "desirable objective" rubric. Thus, al-Fatah is likely to see the destruction of an Israeli military installation as a good in itself. Especially when dealing with targets of high symbolic value, however, it is usually more productive to threaten damage and make a suitable and proportionate demand rather than to destroy the target and receive nothing—save publicity—for the effort. Pathologically, coercion tends to replace destruction. Frequently, a terrorist organization will begin its career with a destructive act (or series of acts) in order to establish its credibility and then attempt to achieve subsequent objectives through coercion. In large part, the "infantile" acts such as bombing are simply easier, requiring far less in the way of sophistication and organizational skills, as well as fewer risks. Attacks by the Puerto Rican FALN against corporate and financial institutions in the United States probably illustrate this evolution in its (extended) infantile stages, while the Irgun of mandatory Palestine exemplified the "mature" coercive stage, as the activity of the *fedayeen* organizations frequently do today. It is also frequently the case that destruction of a given target may be symptomatic of near or total failure. Such acts may be structured as retaliation or retribution or simply frustration (the assassination of Martin Schleyer in the fall of 1977 is an example).

Terrorism is theater; it is intended to be effective and affective beyond those who are central players. Accordingly, a major objective of the terrorists' coercive attempts will be to apply adequate pressure in order to bring about a change of policy, prevent an undesired change, or otherwise achieve important concessions. For example, the *fedayeen* hijacking of a Dutch KLM airliner on November 25, 1973, had the purpose of forcing the Dutch government to change its pro-Israel stance. The Dutch concession—tailored to meet the terrorists' demands and save the airplane and passengers—was to stop formerly sanctioned aid for Soviet Jews emigrating through Holland to Israel.[77] The Dutch concessions were intended to prevent damage; if the aircraft had been precipitously destroyed, there would have been no reason to so concede.

In addition to the preceding factors, which are more or less associated with concrete demands or objectives, it may often be the case that the terrorists want, more than anything else, to call attention to their existence. Thus, the search for the attention of the public figured very strongly in the actions of the *fedayeen,* particularly the PFLP, in the interregnum between the 1967 and the 1973 Middle East wars. This objective of gaining attention salience is also explained by the need to maintain organizational vitality and recruitment and to enhance the images of respective terrorist groups in regions where there are contending groups. This latter aspect is keenly illustrated by the rush to claim credit for successful terrorist operations.

MORALS

It might appear at first ironical to associate morals and morality with terrorism; however, historically there has been such a link. Unfortunately, the link, by several indications, has been broken. The political code that marks off the official from the citizen is no longer in place. "Randomness is the crucial feature of terrorist activity" according to Michael Walzer.[78] The moral standard exhibited by the Russian revolutionaries who plotted to kill Grand Duke Sergei in the early part of this century is now conspicuous by its absence. New Left revolutionaries are not wont to join the Russian anarchists of earlier days in saying, "Even in destruction, there's a right way and a wrong way—and there are limits."[79] Instead we are more likely to hear that "morality, like politics, starts at the barrel of a gun."[80] (But note that although a gun can be the tool of indiscriminate murder, it is not inherently an indiscriminate weapon.)

This is a disturbing discontinuity that clearly implies that morality is not likely to be a hindrance to macroterror. This being said, it must be recognized that when the history of terrorism is surveyed, it is the instances of mass killing that suggest themselves, not because they are the norm, but rather the exceptions that prove the rule. The rule is that terrorists avoid mass killings not out of moral fervor or altruism but because such tactics poorly serve their purposes and may even be—in fact usually are—counterproductive. "The group that used or threatened to use nuclear terror might murder its own cause in the process."[81]

COST-BENEFITS RATIO

Benefits (rewards) are never valued absolutely by the typical terrorist but relative to the prospective cost of their attainment. As with many of the other aspects of our heuristic model, this factor will not only be operative at the motive stage but will continue to be influential throughout the model. Particularly with the case of nuclear weapons, the terrorist is likely to be sharply conscious of the risks (costs) associated with their acquisition and utilization.

Several levels of risks are likely to affect any cost-benefit calculation; these range from risks to the individual terrorist to those that have an impact upon the organization. At the individual level, the terrorist is not always inclined to participate in risky operations—hence one explanation for the widespread use of bombs by terrorists. Despite stereotypes to the contrary, terrorists have in large part avoided high-risk operations, leading R. W. Mengel to discuss the "nonsuicidal nature of terrorism."[82] Mengel perhaps overdraws the generalization, but he is far closer to being correct than many who might take the contrary view. Brian Jenkins has perhaps best captured the role of risk in terrorists' calculations when he observed: "Terrorists rarely assaulted facilities when there was a high probability that they might be defeated before they gained entry, but they were willing to assume high risks after they had gained entry and barricaded themselves."[83] The implication that Jenkins's remark holds for nuclear power facilities is obvious.

We have already made several comments as to the organizational risks that a macroterror strategy might hold the perpetrators. However, there are several additional organizational costs that should be expressly stated. First, for successful terrorist groups, terror reaches a point wherein further terrorism becomes counterproductive. As Thornton notes: "If the terrorists already enjoy a high level of active support, terror will not only be wasteful of energy and moral authority but may have a negative effect by endangering the orientation of those already included within the insurgents' activities."[84]

Second, terror might well become too successful in the sense that terrorism could serve as an inadequate surrogate for action on a wider scale. This is both a practical concern and an ideological dictum that is likely to be most influential for those who hew closest to a Marxist line. This possibility was recognized over sixty years ago by Leon Trotsky, who wrote:

> In our eyes, individual terror is inadmissible precisely because it *belittles the role of the masses in their own consciousness,* reconciles them to their powerlessness, and turns their eyes and hopes toward a great avenger and liberator who some day will come and accomplish his mission.[85]

Finally, it is difficult to conceive of any attainable terrorist objective that could not be achieved with a more efficient and less costly use of organizational assets than the nuclear gambit would require. There is clearly a limit to what a terrorist group could demand in the context of blackmail. The point is quickly reached when the concession demanded grossly exceeds the implement of coercion.

CAPABILITY AND ACQUISITION

The two factors are closely linked. When the aspects of capability are considered, the concern is essentially with the organizational characteristics of the group in question. Thus, the focus is upon the sophistication of the group in terms of the differentiation of intragroup skills, the level of technical skills evidenced, and the resources—both internally generated and externally provided—available to the group. Thomas Schelling, the esteemed strategist, offers the Jewish terrorist organizations as the prototype for the type of sophistication and skills that the group must possess.[86] Such a prototype is not today emulated by any known terrorist group. Furthermore, "Non-state entities are likely to use a nuclear weapon in inverse proportion to their ability to obtain one and . . . those most able to acquire nuclear weapons would probably use them, if at all, in a manner calculated to minimize destruction."[87]

The question of acquisition turns on the application of the group's capabilities. Thus, in the present case, questions must be pondered concerning the feasibility of the group's constructing a nuclear device, given its capabilities. For those groups without the capability of constructing a nuclear weapon (all or nearly all of them), the plausibility of certain techniques of acquisition becomes important—specifically, the provision of fissile explosive materials or even an intact device or, alternately, the theft of a device.[88] As noted earlier, there are acute problems for the aspiring nuclear terrorist with each mode of acquisition.

THREAT EFFECTUATION

This refers to the operationalization of the threat, which may range from a hoax to the actual detonation of a device. The terrorist will be concerned with the credibility of his threat and the security of his forces prior to, during, and after the threat is carried out (if necessary). None of these matters is insubstantial.

Nuclear terror may be associated with a negative threat. Specifically, instead of demanding that something be done, the terrorist might withhold his weapon as long as certain actions will not be taken.[89] In fact, it is precisely this possibility that strikes many, particularly of the realist school, as the most serious nuclear terror threat. Such a shift from coercion to dissuasion would make it far easier for the victim-government to concede to the terrorist's demands, since it would merely be a matter of not doing something rather than undoing something already accomplished.

Such a tactic could be keenly effective were the threat to be made secretly. "It would probably look more like diplomacy than terrorism."[90]

> The conceding state could avoid a public announcement that it "caved," while the terrorist group could maintain its base of international support, especially where the support is contingent upon peaceful vis-a-vis armed struggle.[91]

OUTCOME

This refers to the terrorist's expectations as to the results of his act, as well as the actual or predicted outcome. From the terrorist's perspective, the analysis of outcome is analytically indistinguishable from the purposive aspects of the motive. In actuality, the outcome is beyond the control of any single actor or group of actors. Thus, an important segment of the terrorist's analysis must be the likely effect of an undesirable outcome. That is to say, if the threat fails or is thwarted, what will the resultant effects be upon the terrorist actors? Must the possibility of death, torture, or imprisonment be considered? If so, are the terrorists willing to accept such a possibility? Probably not; "terrorists do not usually engage in activity that involves the risk of confrontation, capture or a fight to the death."[92]

Furthermore, the terrorist may also contemplate the possibility that his actions may result in far more widespread damage than may have been desired. "The new transnational television terrorists want media exposure, not exposure of the masses to radio-active fallout."[93]

VI

The thrust of this analysis is not to dismiss glibly the possibility of nuclear terrorism but to critique that which has been produced to date on the subject and to offer a more precise investigation than has been customary. By highlighting the disincentives and technological problems that will inhibit a resort to macroterror of the nuclear sort, it is possible to identify more starkly those actors to which the negative factors are not likely to be controlling. Thus, rather than perceiving the world population of terrorists as wholly comprised of aspirants to nuclear status, it is now possible to discriminate between the nonaspirants (the vast preponderance) and the aspirants. And, as J. Bowyer Bell observes, "The mix of motive, military and technological skills, resources and perceived vulnerability simply does not exist."[94]

For the foreseeable future, we can be thankful that the nuclear terror problem is more likely to engage intellectuals than terrorists. This is not a justification for complacency, however; we must be constantly alert to the threat and especially thankful to those who, like Theodore Taylor, provided impetus for us to insure that nuclear materials are treated with the respect that they deserve. As Yehezkel Droz reminds us, the problem must be taken seriously (and we should add, considered carefully):

> Those who regard such possibilities as too science fiction-like to deserve serious consideration should be reminded that science fiction is in a crisis because so many ideas which thirty or forty years ago were considered as pure science fiction have been realized. Therefore, the possibility of noncountry units getting hold of a few primitive nuclear devices is one which should be taken seriously, though it is less probable than the possibility of crazy countries achieving a limited nuclear capability.[95]

The likelihood of nuclear terrorism is the controversial question debated within this book. The optimism, if one can rightly use *optimism* in this context, is the result of a careful, and one should hope, accurate examination of the problem. To this point, it may be correctly asserted that those terrorists who are most desirous of adding the adjective *nuclear* are probably the least capable, while the most capable groups—all secessionists-irredentists—would lose rather than gain from such a tactic . . . but the future holds no guarantees, and it is here that the controversy lies.

Notes

1. Carlos Marighella, *Minimanual of the Urban Guerrilla,* reprinted in *Urban Guerrilla Warfare,* Adelphi Paper Number 79 (London: International Institute for Strategic Studies, 1971), p. 36.
2. A character in Joseph Conrad's *The Secret Agent* (Garden City, N.Y.: Doubleday and Company, 1907), p. 249.
3. The phrase *established legality* is from Herbert Marcuse, whose work has justified, if not in part inspired, the terrorism of the radical Left. The appropriate quotation follows: "An opposition which is directed, not against a particular form of government or against particular conditions within a society, but against a given society as a whole, cannot

remain legal and lawful because it is the established legality and the established law that it opposes." Marcuse, *An Essay on Liberation* (Boston: Beacon Press, 1969), p. 66.

4. This does not mean, however, that terrorism has become "more practical and *legitimate* [emphasis added]" as Bruce G. Blair and Garry D. Brewer argue in "The Terrorist Threat to World Nuclear Programs," *Journal of Conflict Resolution* 21 (September 1977): 379-403.

5. "Terror is a symbolic act designed to influence political behavior by extranormal means, entailing the use or threat of violence [emphasis omitted]." This important definition is from Thomas P. Thornton, "Terror as a Weapon of Political Agitation," in *Internal War: Problems and Approaches,* ed. Harry Eckstein (New York: Free Press, 1964), p. 73.

6. Edward F. Mickolus, "Statistical Approaches to the Study of Terrorism," in *Terrorism: Interdisciplinary Perspectives*, ed. Yonah Alexander and Seymour Maxwell Finger (New York: John Jay Press, 1977), pp. 213-214, and the National Safety Council, annual statistics, Washington, D.C.

7. According to Martha C. Hutchinson, "The lessons of the past indicate that the trend toward greater harm will continue." See "Defining Future Threats: Terrorists and Nuclear Proliferation," in *Terrorism,* ed. Alexander and Finger, p. 304. See also Robert H. Kupperman, "Facing Tomorrow's Terrorist Incident Today" (Report Prepared for the Law Enforcement Assistance Administration, Washington, D.C., October 1977), p. 50.

8. Radiological weapons and sabotage of nuclear facilities are excluded from the present inquiry for defensible reasons. First, radiological weapons are analytically indistinguishable from other gruesome agents of the chemical and biological genre, and they should therefore be so considered. This is not to say that the threat resultant of the possibility that such agents can find their way into terrorists' hands is less important than the terrorist nuclear bomb variant, but only that such a threat should be considered discretely from the atomic bomb issue. Second, as to the exclusion of attacks upon and sabotage of nuclear facilities, such tactics more properly belong to a discussion of attacks upon high-value targets or inherently dangerous facilities. For a rather different view, see Michael Flood, "Nuclear Sabotage," *Bulletin of the Atomic Scientists* (October 1976): 29-36.
An important discussion of radiological, chemical, and biological options for terrorists can be found in Robert K. Mullen, "Mass Destruction and Terrorism," *Journal of International Affairs* 32 (Spring-Summer 1978): 63-89.

9. Formally known as the "Prospectus on Nucleonics," submitted to Arthur M. Compton on November 18, 1944. Reprinted in Alice Kimball Smith, *A Peril and a Hope* (Chicago: University of Chicago Press, 1965).

10. Vannevar Bush, *Modern Arms and Free Men: A discussion of the Role of Science in Preserving Democracy* (New York: Simon and Schuster, 1949), pp. 137-157.
11. Bernard Brodie, *The Absolute Weapon* (New York: Harcourt Brace, 1946), p. 46.
12. Roberta Wohlstetter, "Terror on a Grand Scale," *Survival* (May-June 1976): 98. Wohlstetter also reproduces additional statements of foreboding.
13. Thomas Schelling "Who Will Have the Bomb?" *International Security* 1 (Summer 1976): 80.
14. Augustus R. Norton, "Nuclear Terrorism and the Middle East," *Military Review* 56 (April 1976): 11.
15. Robert A. Friedlander, "Sowing the Wind: Rebellion and Violence in Theory and Practice," *Denver Journal of International Law and Policy* 6 (Spring 1976): 83. See also Friedlander, "Terrorism and Political Violence: Do the Ends Justify the Means?" *Chitty's Law Journal* 24 (1976): 240-245.
16. Wohlstetter "Terror on a Grand Scale," p. 100.
17. John Newhouse, *Cold Dawn: The Story of SALT* (New York: Holt, Rinehart and Winston, 1973), p. 176.
18. See, for example, Paul Wilkinson, *Political Terrorism* (New York: John Wiley, 1974), p. 135.
19. See, for example, Albert Wohlstetter et al., *Moving Toward Life in a Nuclear Armed Crowd?* (Los Angeles: Pan Heuristics, 1976).
20. Wohlstetter, "Terror on a Grand Scale," p. 100.
21. U.S. Congress, Senate, Committee on Governmental Affairs, *An Act to Combat International Terrorism, Hearings* before the Committee on S. 2236, 95th Cong., 2d sess., 1978, p. 280.
22. Lewis Dunn, "Nuclear 'Gray Marketeering,' " *International Security* (Winter 1977): 109. In n. 7, Dunn cites unconfirmed reports to the extent that two hundred European nuclear engineers "cognizant of plutonium reprocessing technology presently are consulting in less developed countries."
23. *New York Times,* March 1, 1977. Dr. Traube's alleged contacts were with Hans-Joachim Klein, who participated in the December 1975 terrorist raid on the OPEC meeting in Vienna, and Mehdi Khanbaba-Theherani, a left-wing Iranian extremist leader. An interesting twist to this episode is the *San Francisco Chronicle* report of August 17, 1978, which indicated that Klein is being protected by the Israeli secret service in a Negev Desert kibbutz. This latter report has not been otherwise confirmed.
24. Wohlstetter, "Terror on a Grand Scale," pp. 99-100.
25. Mason Willrich and Theodore Taylor, *Nuclear Theft: Risks and Safeguards* (Cambridge, Mass.: Ballinger Publishing Company, 1974).
26. Naturally, private attention to the problem has become quite intense as well. Brian Jenkins, for example, notes that "about 40 percent of the Rand Corporation's total research on terrorism has dealt with the

question: Will terrorists go nuclear?" See "Research Note: Rand's Research on Terrorism," *Terrorism* 1 (1977): 89. The scope of classified research on the problem is alluded to by Kupperman, "Facing Tomorrow's Terrorist Incident Today."

27. See, for example, *Ultimatum: Pu 94* by Uri Dan and Peter Mann. (New York: Leisure Books, 1977). Reportedly the late Congressman Ryan finished a first-rate novel with a nuclear terror theme prior to his tragic death. *San Francisco Chronicle,* November 27, 1978.

28. J. Bowyer Bell, "Trends on Terror: The Analysis of Political Violence," *World Politics* 29 (April 1977): 488.

29. Forrest Frank, for example, has said: "My own view is that nuclear terrorism is probably inevitable." We need not be Hegelians to believe that history will end, but man's epoch consists of a number of lifetimes. If such predictions are to have any meaning, they must be tied to some specific and relevant time. It is futile, or at least not useful, at this point to argue that some event will occur in history. Frank, "Nuclear Terrorism and the Escalation of International Conflict," *Naval War College Review* 29 (Fall 1976): 15. Similar objections can be raised to C. L. Sulzberger, who stated in the *New York Times,* October 22, 1977: "Once—and it is inevitable—a modern terrorist group gains possession of even a crude nuclear device, nobody can foresee how it will be used." Or we might consider Willrich and Taylor, *Nuclear Theft,* p. 169, who state: "One wonders how in the long run nuclear power industries can develop and prosper in a world where terrorist activities are widespread and persistent. *For if present trends continue, it seems only a question of time before some terrorist organization exploits the possibilities for coercion which are inherent in nuclear fuel* [emphasis added]."

30. These concepts are explained and applied below. Talia Ben-Gal of the University of Chicago deserves credit for this formulation. Ben-Gal participated in the early drafting of this chapter in 1977.

31. Wohlstetter, "Terror on a Grand Scale," pp. 99-100.

32. David Fromkin, "The Strategy of Terrorism," *Foreign Affairs* 53 (July 1975): 692-693.

33. "Mega-threat" is drawn from David Comey, "The Perfect Trojan Horse," *Bulletin of the Atomic Scientists* 32 (June 1976): 33-34.

34. Paul Wilkinson, *Terrorism and the Liberal State* (New York: John Wiley, 1977), p. 49.

35. Louis René Beres, "International Terrorism and World Security," *Stanford Journal of International Studies* 12 (1977): 141.

36. Beres, "The Nuclear Threat of Terrorism" (Paper Presented to the Thirteenth North American Peace Science Conference of the Peace Science Society [International], Cambridge, Mass., November 10-12, 1975).

37. William Epstein, *The Last Chance* (New York: Free Press, 1976), p. 268.

38. Frank, "Nuclear Terrorism and Escalation," p. 13.

39. David Rosenbaum, "Nuclear Terror," *International Security* 1 (Winter 1977): 142-143.

40. Willrich and Taylor, *Nuclear Theft*, p. 115.

41. See, for example, Taylor's contribution to *Nuclear Proliferation: Motivations, Capabilities and Strategies for Control*, Ted Greenwood, Harold A. Feiveson, and Theodore Taylor, eds. (New York: McGraw-Hill, 1977), "Alternative Strategies for International Control of Nuclear Power" (with Harold A. Feiveson), pp. 125-183, esp. p. 136.

42. Wohlstetter, "Terror on a Grand Scale," p. 103. Another celebrated amateur, John A. Phillips, has recently published *Mushroom: The Story of the A-Bomb Kid* (New York: Morrow, 1978).

43. Committee on Governmental Affairs, *Act to Combat International Terrorism*, p. 259.

44. Charles A. Russell and Bowman H. Miller, "Profile of a Terrorist," *Military Review* (August 1977): 21-34. Iranian and Turkish terrorists tend to be exceptions at one extreme, since they tend to be educated in technical fields (in particular engineering); at the other extreme is the Provisional IRA, which has an almost negligible component of intellectuals.

45. John McPhee, *The Curve of Binding Energy* (New York: Ballantine Books, 1973, 1974), p. 122.

46. Report of the Nuclear Energy Policy Study Group, *Nuclear Power Issues and Choices* (Cambridge, Mass.: Ballinger Publishing Company, 1977), p. 305.

47. Kupperman, "Facing Tomorrow's Terrorist Incident Today," p. 11. On this point, see also Norton, "Nuclear Terrorism and the Middle East," and Mullen, "Mass Destruction and Terrorism."

48. Rosenbaum, "Nuclear Terror," pp. 144-145.

49. Troublesome loopholes in weapons security procedures have been exposed, however. See Joseph Albright's series in the *Atlanta Journal-Constitution*, January 8, 15, 22, 1978.

50. The exclusion of plutonium-based fuels is resultant of President Carter's decision of April 7, 1977, not to proceed with plutonium reprocessing in the United States. See *New York Times*, April 8, 1977.

51. Taylor, in *Nuclear Proliferation*, p. 140.

52. Committee on Governmental Affairs, *Act to Combat International Terrorism*, p. 257.

53. Taylor in *Nuclear Proliferation*, p. 140.

54. Epstein, *Last Chance*, p. 263.

55. Ibid., p. 268.

56. Rosenbaum, "Nuclear Terror," p. 145. Rosenbaum tends to exaggeration, or at least hyperbole: "a crude nuclear device as the perfect terrorist: a chance to hold an entire nation hostage," pp. 152-153. If that is possible with a 0.1 KT, or even a 20 KT weapon, the United States and the Soviet Union have been wasting their money for years. Taylor himself often varies his data. For example, the level of enrichment in the isotope U^{235} necessary to have weapons suitable material is

variously given as over 10 percent, over 20 percent, over 30 percent, or over 50 percent.

57. David Krieger, "What Happens If . . .? Terrorists, Revolutionaries, and Nuclear Weapons," *Annals of the American Academy of Political and Social Science,* no. 430 (March 1977): 50.

58. Willrich and Taylor, *Nuclear Theft,* p. 23.

59. See, for example: Greenwood, Feiveson, and Taylor, *Nuclear Proliferation,* p. 138, and Krieger, "What Happens If?" p. 50.

60. Wohlstetter et al., "Nuclear Armed Crowd?" p. 171. The quote is drawn from a section written by Harry Rowan.

61. Rosenbaum, "Nuclear Terror," p. 146.

62. The Soviets' reluctance to support terrorism has been a major stumbling block in U.S.S.R.-*fedayeen* relations. The interested reader may consult Augustus R. Norton, *Moscow and the Palestinians* (Miami: Center for Advanced International, 1974).

63. Krieger, "What Happens If?" p. 47.

64. Norton, "Nuclear Terrorism and the Middle East," p. 7; Mullen, "Mass Destruction and Terrorism," p. 85: "Such employment could very likely precipitate countermeasures of such severity as to topple the government associated with the act."

65. Ted Greenwood, "Non-State Entities," in *Nuclear Proliferation,* ed. Greenwood, Feiveson, and Taylor, p. 102.

66. Wilkinson, *Terrorism and the Liberal State,* p. 96. It should be noted that the term *ideological aspects* is being used to encompass ideology, creeds, systems of thought, and programs. This usage diverges from that of Edward Shils, for example, who distinguishes ideology from the other patterns of belief (see Shils's contribution on ideology in the International Encyclopedia of the Social Sciences); however, it is consistent with the formulations of other sociologists, most notably Karl Mannheim.

67. Arnold Beichman, "A War Without End," *American Spectator* 11 (April 1978): 21.

68. Bernard K. Johnpoll, "Perspectives on Political Terrorism in the United States," in *International Terrorism: National, Regional, and Global Perspectives,* ed. Yonah Alexander (New York: Praeger Publishers, 1976), p. 34.

69. Wilkinson, *Terrorism and the Liberal State,* p. 77.

70. The *Narodnaya Volya,* the Russian anarchist group active in the late nineteenth century, is an example.

71. Thornton, "Terror as a Weapon of Political Agitation," pp. 81-82.

72. Cited by Jillian Becker, *Hitler's Children* (Philadelphia: J. B. Lippincott Company, 1977), p. 89.

73. Conor Cruise O'Brian, "Liberty and Terrorism," *International Security* 2 (Fall 1977): esp. p. 58.

74. Brian Jenkins, "International Terrorism: A Balance Sheet," *Survival* (July-August 1975): 158. "A credible threat, a demonstration of the

capacity to strike, may be from the terrorists' point of view often preferable to actually carrying out the threatened deed, which may explain why, apart from the technical difficulties involved, terrorists have not done some of the terribly damaging and terrifying things they could do, such as poisoning a city's water supply, spreading chemical or biological agents, or other things that could produce mass casualties."

75. Wilkinson, *Terrorism and the Liberal State*, p. 203.
76. R. W. Mengel, "Terrorism and New Technologies of Destruction: An Overview of the Potential Risk," in *Disorders and Terrorism* (Washington, D.C.: Law Enforcement Assistance Administration, 1976), p. 458.
77. *New York Times*, November 26, 1973.
78. Michael Walzer, *Just and Unjust Wars: A Moral Argument with Historical Illustrations* (New York: Basic Books, 1977), p. 197. For the "political code," see the chapter on terrorism, pp. 197-206.
79. From a character in Camus's *The Just Assassins* in Caligula and Three Other Plays, trans. Stuart Gilbert (New York: Viking Publishers, 1958), p. 258.
80. *New York Review of Books*, August 24, 1967.
81. David C. Gompert et al., *Nuclear Weapons and World Politics: Alternatives for the Future* (New York: McGraw-Hill, 1977), p. 251.
82. Mengel "Terrorism and New Technologies of Destruction," p. 460.
83. Committee on Governmental Affairs, *Act to Combat International Terrorism*, p. 565.
84. Thornton, "Terror as a Weapon of Political Agitation," p. 74.
85. Leon Trotsky, "On Terrorism," November 1911, reprinted in *Leon Trotsky: Against Individual Terrorism* (New York: Pathfinder Press, 1974), p. 7.
86. Schelling "Who Will Make the Bomb?" p. 84.
87. Greenwood, "Non-State Entities," p. 104.
88. See: Norton, "Nuclear Terrorism and the Middle East"; Dunn, "Nuclear 'Gray Marketeering' "; and Dunn, Paul Bracken, and Barry J. Smernoff, *Routes to Nuclear Weapons: Aspects of Purchase or Theft* (Croton-on-Hudson, N.Y.: Hudson Institute, April 1977).
89. Schelling, "Who Will Have the Bomb?" p. 85.
90. Ibid., p. 86.
91. Norton, "Nuclear Terrorism and the Middle East," p. 9. Kupperman concurs on this point; see "Treating the Symptoms of Terrorism," *Terrorism* 1 (1977): esp. pp. 41-45.
92. Mengel, "Terrorism and New Technologies of Destruction," p. 460.
93. J. Bowyer Bell, *A Time of Terror: How Democratic Societies Respond to Revolutionary Violence* (New York: Basic Books, 1978), p. 121.
94. Ibid.
95. Yehezkel Dror, *Crazy States: A Counterconventional Strategic Problem* (Lexington, Mass.: Lexington Books, D. C. Heath and Company, 1971), pp. 52-53.

Part I

Across the Nuclear Divide: Perspectives on the Past, Present, and Future

Roberta Wohlstetter

Terror on a Grand Scale

*Much of the commentary and analysis of the nuclear terrorism question is
notably ahistorical in emphasis, depending as it does on the vulnerabilities
resulting from modern technology. Wohlstetter provides an antidote to such
contributions by tracing the problem to the earliest days of the nuclear age
and highlighting the developments that combine to create the current concern. Although she takes a restrained view of the problem, she does find
cause for disquiet, particularly in light of contemporary examples of careless
slaughter of innocents by terrorists.*

A historian looking at discussions about the dangers of the spread of nuclear
weapons to more nations and what we might do about it may get a sense that
plus ça change plus c'est la même chose. As for the dangers, reactions to the
first Chinese tests in 1964 included forecasts of the immediate spread to
additional countries such as Mexico. Knowledgeable American officials in
1966 expected India to explode a device in a matter of months unless the
United States guaranteed her nuclear protection. And that was the third wave
of alarm. The first wave—immediately after Hiroshima—included predictions
by scientists in the Manhattan Project that half a dozen countries would get
the bomb within two or three years, and some expected the Soviet Union to
be fourth in line. The next big wave of alarm at the end of the 1950s foresaw
as many as twenty additional countries getting nuclear weapons in the
following decade. So the alarm caused by India's "peaceful nuclear explosion" may merge in the reader's mind with each of these previous alarms.
We have been there before. There has been some spread. But (we may tell
ourselves) it has not been as bad as we expected. The remedies proposed, also
familiar, tend unfortunately to lose urgency. The recurring crisis is almost
comfortably recognizable.

The same superficial sense of *déjà vu* affects any look at the possibility that
some subnational group or even an individual entrepreneur might use nuclear
terror. Here at least no spread has occurred. Yet we've had plenty of
premonitions. During World War II James Conant and Vannevar Bush worried
about an insane or careless laboratory technician setting off a nuclear device,

and immediately after the war this possibility had become common gossip. George Orwell recorded that "At any moment, so the rumour went, some lonely lunatic in a laboratory might blow civilization to smithereens, as easily as touching off a firework."[1]

In a memorandum to President Truman of 25 April 1945, Henry Stimson predicted that "the future may see a time when such a weapon may be constructed in secret and used suddenly and effectively with devastating power by a wilful nation or group against an unsuspecting nation or group of much greater size and material power. With its aid even a very powerful unsuspecting nation might be conquered within a very few days ..."[2] Edward Condon later explained in detail the methods by which saboteurs, acting on their own or as special agents of a hostile power, could either smuggle in a bomb piece by piece, or secrete a whole bomb inside some ostensibly innocent item of cargo (such as a filing cabinet or an upright piano). "A target to be safe," he writes, "must be surrounded by a sanitary area of at least a mile in radius, all known to contain no suspicious man or thing. Any house can be as dangerous to its surroundings as the greatest of powder magazines. Twenty thousand tons of TNT can be kept under the counter of a candy store."[3]

Killing Civilians

This was not all wild imagining on Condon's part. He was proceeding from two actual wartime cases: the Black Tom explosion in New York harbour in 1916, which blew up some freight cars and a barge *en route* for the armies of the Czar of all the Russias; and the sabotage by Britain of the heavy water plant in Rjukan, Norway, during World War II (Norway being then under the control of Germany). These clandestine bombs did substantial damage and though they may also have done collateral harm to civilians, they were exploded in war materiel and facilities. They were, however, in Condon's phrase, "small-time" compared with the nuclear sabotage that concerned him. The Hiroshima weapon destroyed an area about a hundred times as large as that razed by the biggest non-nuclear block-buster. Inevitably its detonation moved the "side-effects"–killing people–to the centre of attention. This completed a process of loosening constraints in the killing of civilians which had started early in the war, when it became obvious that the inaccuracy of available weapons was enormous. The British, for example, learned to expect that only one quarter of their bombs would fall within an area of 75 square miles around the aiming point, and in September 1941 they planned a force of 4,000 bombers to drop 75,000 tons of high explosives a month in hundreds of thousands of bombs. Nuclear weapons then appeared as a way to cover with a few weapons, rather than thousands, the huge uncertain area where the bombs might fall. To devastate so large an area suddenly with a single weapon, of course, administered an enormous shock and gave the A-bomb from the start the aspect of terror—"a very big bang," said Oppenheimer, but not a useful military weapon.

The prevailing view immediately after Hiroshima took the line that the A-bomb was essentially a destroyer of cities—needed therefore only in modest numbers and in any case too scarce for use against smaller or less valuable targets. Yet their spread, it was argued, would tend to make equal the power of small and large countries. But why only countries? If a very few bombs usable against cities could raise a small nation to the level of a great power, what effect might one or two have in the hands of a subnational group?

In fact initial and some later discussion of the Bomb may be said to have treated governments like terrorists, rather than the other way around. When government officials began to measure how many weapons were "enough" in terms of the number of civilians they would kill, they were giving legitimacy to the sort of violence we normally associate, justly or unjustly, with terrorists. For a terrorist rather than a government to use a weapon of mass destruction would be an innovation in quantity rather than quality.

When we speak of a weapon of mass destruction here, we refer to one that would kill thousands of people, and possibly tens or hundreds of thousands. (This seems to be the range envisaged by recent writers on nuclear terrorism.) The deaths caused by any single guerrilla act in the past have been numbered in tens—the greatest number endangered, for example, in a hijacked 747 has been a few hundred. (Governments fighting guerrillas have conducted *campaigns* that have killed large numbers in reprisals, but never in one blow: the French in Algeria in 1945 killed about 15,000 Muslims in Setif in reaction to the death of about 100 Europeans.)[4] A rapid review of recent bombings or kidnappings in the Middle East, which today seems the most likely place for terror on a grand scale, reveals that the highest numbers of hostages were taken at Qiryat Shemona in Israel, with 18 civilians, and more than 80 children held in the town of Maalot. The highest casualties in random shooting in crowded places (in incidents such as that at Lod Airport) resulted in 25 killed and 70 wounded.[5] These actions were master-minded by two extremist Arab organizations, the Popular Front for the Liberation of Palestine (PFLP) and the Popular Democratic Front for the Liberation of Palestine (PDFLP), and it may be that their desperate character and doctrine are consistent with fewer qualms about large numbers of enemy deaths.

But how likely is it that terrorist tactics will eventually include the use of a weapon of mass destruction as we have defined it? Arguments for paying more attention to nuclear terrorism proceed by showing mainly that it would be *feasible* for a lone individual or a small group to steal or make and deliver a crude weapon, that there might be *some motive,* and that it would be *terrible* if it happened. This demonstration may be enough to warrant greater care in nuclear safeguards, but it does not offer much of a basis for judging the probability of such an event. It is even barely possible—as those who have recently warned us recognize—that advertising the technical feasibility will raise the probability. But in any case, the analysis of possible motives is generally rather thin and not much attention has been devoted to the viewpoint of the terrorists, the alternatives they have, and their psychological and political pathologies.

Prospects for Nuclear Terror

The fact that we have been talking in the same way about nuclear terror for some thirty years, and that there has yet been no public indication that terrorist groups are interested, does not of course mean that we will never witness a successful nuclear terrorist attack in the future. No matter how strong the impression of *déjà vu,* a great many things have changed since the immediate post-war period:

1. International terrorism has increased.
2. The casual weighing by officials and academics of the value of nuclear weapons in terms of people killed may have deadened our sensibilities over the years.
3. The number of civilian power and research reactors has greatly increased and is planned to rise further, along with the capacity to separate plutonium usable in explosives, thus creating more opportunities for diversion, theft or possibly seizure in internal war.
4. The number of countries capable of exploding a nuclear device in the period 1980-5 is also apparently on the increase. More serious is the fact that several countries thought most likely to follow suit are not those next in line in general technological or scientific prowess, but rather the less-developed, politically unstable countries— for example, Argentina, Brazil, Pakistan, and even Libya. This type of political context raises the probability of terrorist use of nuclear weapons considerably. The governments of some of the newly-rich countries, like Libya, might even be interested in sponsoring a foreign or international terrorist faction in the manufacture, theft or use of nuclear explosives.
5. Information on the technology of weapons materials and bomb manufacture has spread much more widely during 1975. The Atoms for Peace programme of 1964 led to declassifying 10,000 United States Atomic Energy Commission documents in the following year, and over half a million by 1972. All this before the Freedom of Information Act. Many weapons designers at the Livermore or Los

Alamos laboratories in the United States insist on the growing ease of manufacture of a primitive weapon, and point out that the number of workers leaving the atomic energy industry for other jobs is increasing with time.

6. Finally, commendable efforts to publicize the need for better safeguards against nuclear terror have inevitably further disseminated information on the way to make a bomb and where to get materials for it. Perhaps more important, their spectacular coverage in the media has helped create an audience expectant for news about this new quantum jump in threats. And a good many writers on subversive warfare have observed that terrorists tend to play up to an audience; that publicity is one of their goals.[6]

Building a Bomb

The arguments on the feasibility of theft, design and manufacture of nuclear weapons have been belaboured enough to make it clear that the operations involved are by no means impossible. Dr. Theodore Taylor has recently estimated that under conceivable circumstances one person who possessed about one normal-density "fast" critical mass of fissionable material and a substantial amount of chemical high explosive could design and build a crude fission bomb. By a crude fission bomb he means one that would be likely to explode with a yield equivalent to at least 100 tons of high explosive, and that could be transported in an automobile.[7]

This sort of bomb, though only 1/100 the yield of the Hiroshima bomb, could nonetheless wreak enormous havoc. At very low yields deaths from a nuclear explosion result primarily from prompt radiation, which declines more slowly with diminishing yield than blast and other major weapons effects. Rough calculations indicate that a 0.1 kiloton (KT) bomb would kill about 37,000 people in Cairo and about 9,000 in Tel Aviv.[8] By contrast the fatalities caused by the 1,000 lb high explosive warhead will be in the low tens for Tel Aviv, and for Cairo in the high tens, in proportion to its higher population density.

A more critical question, however, in estimating the likelihood that such an attack might be attempted, is the matter of motives or incentives. If some individual or group intends that much harm to so many people, there are other weapons of mass destruction which have been around for at least as long a time (some 30 years), namely biological weapons, which could be obtained more readily and put into use with smaller risks, lower costs, and more modest technical resources. The damage which may be caused by certain biological weapons, measured in numbers of deaths, can be on the same vast scale as those caused by a crude atomic device, and their use by terrorists would be quite as unprecedented. The fact that they have not yet been used—although the use of chemical poisons on a small scale has been contemplated—has some relevance in assessing the likelihood that there will occur the right conjunction of motive, skills, and resources to bring about a disaster of nuclear size.

So we must determine those characteristics of nuclear weapons that might make them more attractive to subnational terrorist groups than other alternatives. Are the big bang and the blast effects likely to be important to the terrorist, in addition to the capacity for indiscriminate mass deaths? Do most terrorists want all these effects, or any of them in this extreme?

Selectivity and Discrimination

There are some brilliant paranoids of a highly organized sort to whom nuclear terror might appeal and who might be able to serve as leader of an appropriately composed pathological group. Fortunately this sort of individual appears to be rare and he would have to bring together followers with some fairly exotic technical skills. The lone individual who could bring the whole thing off without followers is even rarer, if he exists at all. But have political terrorist factions expressed or exhibited a serious interest in indiscriminate destruction on a mass scale? The Latin American experience suggests the opposite. The tactics of both urban and peasant guerrillas there, in theory and in practice, have been generally selective and discriminate, and they have been able to get what they want with traditional weapons. If the goal is assassination, it is hard to beat a rifle for accuracy at long range; for taking hostages, it is hard to beat a hand gun for ease of concealment. In terms of objectives, the targets have been largely symbolic, and often foreign. Latin American guerrillas have kidnapped or killed certain elements of the indigenous population tagged as capitalists or local agents of North American imperialism, but they have usually tried to avoid harming their own people. This is not to say that their own people are completely safe from harm. When it is possible to teach that collaboration with the enemy will bring punishment, the guerrilla will not hesitate to make an example by maiming or killing those he deems guilty. In the Cuban revolution the indiscriminate use of violence—bombs in department stores and cinemas—was tried and abandoned, because it turned the general public against the 26 July Movement.

There are, however, some political groups that are less concerned about discrimination and reprisal, and that can afford to use indiscriminate violence without harming their own people. Certain Palestinian terrorist organizations and the Irish Republican Army (IRA) fit this pattern. When these groups operate in England or in Israel, it is almost a case of the bigger the blast the better since the destruction will occur in enemy territory. Reprisal against them is difficult, since their membership is dispersed and their headquarters mobile. The Palestinian terrorist groups can perhaps escape retaliation even more easily than the IRA, since only 20 per cent of the Palestinian population is in camps, and the rest distributed among many countries. Their doctrines also tend to make them more desperate and careless of their own lives.

Yet much evidence suggests that technical feasibility and a lack of concern for their own lives and those of others are not enough. In the complex politics of the Middle East, Arab governments have imposed various constraints on the *fedayeen,* if only to avoid Israeli reprisals for acts of terror that are miniscule in comparison with nuclear violence. It will be recalled that President Sadat went along tacitly with suppression of the *fedayeen* in Jordan at one time, and the *fedayeen* in turn are not anxious to lose the support of their financial backers. The push towards making the PLO respectable displays an element of political calculation by some *fedayeen* organizations as well as Arab governments. Some *fedayeen* organizations are in fact branches of Arab governments—in Syria, for example— and the intelligence organizations of some Arab states (not to mention Israeli intelligence) have the ability to monitor much of this activity which they do not directly control. The manufacture of nuclear explosives is a substantial enterprise, far more subject to detection and identification than the use of a small laboratory to produce a bacterial seed culture in quantity and maintain it in a virulent state; and while theft of nuclear material or hijacking a nuclear cargo may be more in the *fedayeen* line, there are indications that Arab states other than Libya and Algeria are not inclined to lend their support.

The PLO news file in Beirut indicates PLO interest in nuclear weapons for the Arab states; not for itself. The PLO reacted to Israeli President Katzir's declaration in December 1974, about Israel's potential nuclear capability, by calling on the Arab nations to take Israel's threats seriously and to carry out their own atomic research programmes with the aid of friendly countries.[9] Its official weekly journal speculated that the threat was another sign of Israel's conventional weakness, and that an isolated and frightened Israel was trying to terrify the world.[10] But it made no appeal to PLO followers to try to steal or manufacture a bomb. After India's first nuclear explosion in June 1974, Abu Ayyad—at that time the second man in *Al-Fatah*—publicly stated that claims that Palestinians could acquire or manufacture an atomic bomb were simply based on fantasy, and were put forward by "opposing circles" to hurt the Palestinian cause.[11] Sensitivity to Arab disapproval of such a course seems clear.

One way or another then, terrorist political factions have operated within constraints that have curbed even less spectacular violence than the destruction of tens or hundreds of thousands. But two qualifications are in order, one about the kind and the other about the extent of terrorist violence, which might affect a sober estimate about the future of nuclear terror. First, while terrorist groups are seldom merely lunatics, we may be witnessing a new style of terror. The random killings of recent times are, as Michael Walzer has suggested, quite distinct from the calculated limited murder of political personalities that began in the 19th century.[12] The elements of calculation, limit and political purpose do seem to have degenerated in the activities of terrorist groups. The murders of the "Manson Family" in California proceeded from eccentric political beliefs. But even the more familiar political ends—return to a homeland or unification of split territories—sometimes involve a means like the Red Army terror in Lod Airport, a careless slaughter of innocents that may indeed be an omen of the sort of random killing we see in nuclear destruction. Second, while it is true that no one has used the available biological weapons, this does not mean that terrorists will not use them or nuclear ones in the future. Research has indicated a glimmer of interest in massive terror among terrorists.

Revolutionary literature contains a few signs of interest in poison gas, but nothing that would cause destruction of the extent we are talking about.[13] In Argentina the seizure, and in France the bombing of nuclear power plants have been attempted, but even in these two countries, there has been no mention of the use of nuclear explosives in a guerrilla struggle for power. Without exception those who have been predicting such use and announcing their alarm to the press are Western physicists and political scientists—not terrorist organizations.[14]

In the *fedayeen* literature in Arabic available in the United States there are numerous references to Israeli and Arab non-nuclear military strategies and to guerrilla tactics of the PLO in the cities and campus of the Gaza district. But a search revealed only one reference to the *fedayeen* use of nuclear explosives, and that was by a Western scientist.[15]

Responses

How then should governments react to the spectre of nuclear terrorism? There is space here only for some summary observations.

1. If terrorist groups do not show a persistent and total disregard for discriminateness, then governments may be said to have even less use for nuclear or other mass-destruction weapons as a counter. As Robert Oppenheimer noted in 1946: "They are not police weapons. They are singularly unsuited for distinguishing between innocent and guilty or for taking even crudely into account the distinction between the guilt of individuals and that of peoples."[16] In general an indiscriminate reaction is badly suited to governments, especially democratic governments facing internal or trans-

national disorder. In dealing with such threats (and any other threats) we should search for methods that are capable of preserving things we value.

2. Precision-guided weapons are going to become increasingly available to governments, and some of these will fall into the hands of terrorists. But they would seem to add less to the terrorists' arsenal than might be expected. Many of them cannot be carried by a man, and even require advanced delivery and launch systems. Those that are hand-held, like the SA-7, might bring down a passenger plane, but that would seem a blunt instrument for terrorists—a case of using a precise instrument for indiscriminate effects. For purposeful terrorists, taking the passengers and the plane hostage would seem much more suited to their goals. For those who kill almost without purpose, an SA-7, or the like, would not be a massive change in scale.

3. It is important to distinguish between technical improvements—in weapons, reconnaissance and control—that permit a sharp focus and discrimination, and those that simply increase the area of wholesale destruction. For example, even in countering terror, technology can reduce the vulnerability of our society by "homing in" very precisely on the offending activity, and in a way calculated to preserve the safety and privacy of individuals. To choose one modest example, improvements in techniques using X-rays enable travellers to get their suitcases past inspection without the embarrassment of opening them and exposing their contents. Similar recent improvements in X-ray devices permit examination of envelopes for letter bombs, without disclosing the writing inside. But the point has wide applications to choice among technologies; we should not talk about "new" or "high" technologies wholesale, but rather with discrimination. For counter-terror in particular, technologies that gather and use information precisely are essential for a legitimate government. Precision here is of course not simply a technical matter. We must think rigorously of what we are aiming at and for what purpose.

Notes

1. George Orwell, *In Front of Your Nose 1945-1950.* Vol. 4 of *Collected Essays, Journalism and Letters of George Orwell*, Sonia Orwell and Ian Angus (eds) (New York: Harcourt, Brace, Jovanovich, 1968): 'You and the Atom Bomb' (19 October 1945), p. 7.

2. Grodzins and Rabinowitch, *The Atomic Age* (New York: Basic Books, 1963), p. 33.

3. 'The New Technique of Private War', in Dexter Masters and Katherine Way (eds.), *One World or None* (New York: McGraw-Hill Book Company, 1946), p. 40.

4. Nathan Leites and Charles Wolf, *Rebellion and Authority* (Chicago: Markham Publishing Company, 1970), p. 112.

5. *Terrorism: Hearings before the Committee on International Security,* House of Representatives, February 27-August 13, 1974, *passim;* and its Staff Study, August 1974 (USPGO, 1974).

6. This last point is rather different from the one sometimes expressed, where the author realizes the danger of releasing technical information, but feels that this has to be traded off against the improvements in safeguards likely to result. The point here is that this attention in the literature magnifies the potential pay-off for the terrorist, gives him a motive and lends additional value to the deed.

7. Interview with Theodore Taylor, 23 November 1975.

8. I am indebted to Gregory Jones for these calculations, using the *Encyclopedia Britannica* as a source for population density in these two cities, and the following missile systems and ranges: *FROG*–72km, *Scud B*–300km, *Jericho*–450km, and *Lance*–72km. In the absence of unclassified data on the median inaccuracy (CEP) of any of these missiles, assume that the CEP is less than 1,000m and greater than 100m. Also assume that the conventional payload of each is 1,000 lb of high explosive and the nuclear payload is one 0.1 kiloton device. For each city double the population density in order to reflect the greater concentration of people in the central part of the city: Tel Aviv–9,800 persons per square kilometre; Cairo–39,200 persons per square kilometre.

9. Abu-Allutf (Farouk Kaddoumi), "Foreign Minister" of the revolution and head of the Political Bureau of the PLO, in *An-Nahar* (a Lebanese daily), 7 December 1974.

10. *Filastin Al-Thawra,* 15 December 1974.

11. *Al-Dastour* (a Lebanese periodical), 8 July 1974.

12. "The New Terrorist," *The New Republic,* 30 August 1975.

13. For example, "Spray Can Nerve Gas on Munich Airport Lift,' *International Herald Tribune,* 28 January 1971; "Arab Plan for Chemical War," *Dagens Nyheter,* 30 September 1968, reporting an Arab Pharmaceutical Congress that pledged support of the PLO and urged training in BW warfare; and "Terrorists Use of Gas Feared," *Washington Post,* 13 May 1975, reporting the theft of 53 bottles of mustard gas from West German ammunition bunkers, allegedly by the Bader Meinhof gang.

14. For example, Professor Tom Kibbie, Professor of Theoretical Physics at Imperial College, London University, was one of 40 scientists who called for strict government control of nuclear power stations in a letter to *The Guardian,* 7 January 1975. He envisaged terrorist theft of radioactive waste as it left the power stations. In America E. L. Kinderman, David Rosenbaum, Mason Willrich, and Theodore Taylor have been alerting us to the problems of terrorist theft for some time. The most publicized reference has been of course the "Nova" project

at MIT, designed to test Dr. Taylor's theory that a person of modest technical know-how, working with available library references, could design a workable nuclear device. Dr. Jan Prawitz of the Swedish Ministry of Defence was reported as saying that this particular design, if constructed, might or might not go off. The message that is getting across on radio, television and in the press in America and Europe, however, is not the qualification that lies in the phrase "if constructed," of the Delphic tautology "might or might not," but the fact of the relative availability of materials for the clever thief, the simplicity of design, and ease of construction. That message does not represent Dr. Prawitz's sober view. He pointed out that (*a*) The design of the bomb was primitive. (*b*) Several essential features were forgotten. (*c*) The student might not survive the fabrication of the bomb. (*d*) Should he survive, the probability that the bomb would go off upon "pressing the button" would be less than 50 per cent. (*e*) Should a nuclear reaction start, the explosion yield would be very small. The probability that the device would yield as much as 0.1-1kt would be very small. (*f*) If a group of qualified scientists or a professional defector were granted more time and better means, including the possibility to undertake experiments, the "bomb could be much better . . . " (From a letter to the author of 16 July 1975).

15. This was found in an article reprinted (with some changes) from the French periodical *l'Express,* in the major Cairo newspaper, *Al Ahram.* In the 28 February 1975 issue Jaqueline Khoury reports an interview under the banner headline "*Fedayeen* Organizations Throughout the World Can Make the Atom Bomb: A Warning from an American Scientist." The scientist in question was Theodore Taylor. Her article ends with the following remarks: "Nuclear armament, and the danger of the use of nuclear weapons by the *Fedayeen* in *fedayeen* operations are the most dangerous problems on the international scene, more dangerous than the shortage of food supply" *Al Ahram* has a wide readership both inside and outside Egypt. It seems clear that somewhere among the Palestinians the seed of the idea of the technical feasibility of a *fedayeen* nuclear attack may have been planted. Whether this, or any other idea for the terrorist use of a weapon of mass destruction, takes root is another question. (I am indebted in my search of the *fedayeen* and related literature to George Keushguerian, Zalmay Khalilzad, and Augustus R. Norton.)

16. J. Robert Oppenheimer, *Atomic Explosives* (1946), reprinted in *The Open Mind* (New York: Simon and Shuster 1955), pp. 10-11.

Thomas C. Schelling

Who Will Have the Bomb?

Schelling's lucid article addresses the nuclear terrorism question as an aspect of nuclear proliferation rather than of political terrorism. He finds that state actors are far more likely proliferators than are terrorists. In fact, he sees the task of weapons construction as beyond the capability of today's terrorists. He posits that the Jewish terrorists of mandatory Palestine may be proto-typical for the type of organization that would be capable of the task. His comments upon the deterrent uses to which terrorists might employ nuclear weapons are both provocative and original.

The question is as interesting as the answer. What do we mean by "having" the bomb? Who has it now?

Does India have the bomb? Most of us would answer yes. Why do we answer yes? Because India exploded a nuclear device—call it a bomb. Do we know that India actually possesses another one? No. Does it matter? Probably not. Therefore, when we say that India has the bomb we do not mean literally that India possesses another nuclear explosive. In fact, it matters little whether India happens to have assembled a second device and has it all ready to explode.

But if we do not literally mean that India possesses an actual bomb when we say that India "has the bomb," what is it that we do mean?

We mean a mixture of things. First, India unquestionably disposes of the technical knowledge with which to produce a nuclear explosive, having proven that by exploding one. Second, we expect that though India may not be rich in explosion grade fissile material, India either has or can acquire enough explosion-grade fissile material to make some more explosive devices. And we may mean, too, that India has gone through the rites of passage—has celebrated its nuclear status by declaring to the world, by way of actual explosion, that it not only *can* explode a nuclear device but dared to and did.

What about Israel? Israel has not performed the ceremony of nuclear demonstration. (The Treaty on the Non-Proliferation of Nuclear Weapons [NPT] defines a "nuclear-weapon state" as one that "has manufactured and exploded" a nuclear weapon or explosive device prior to the cutoff date of

January 1, 1967. Whether explosion is a test of possession or a test of willingness to explode, it is nonetheless part of the acknowledged definition. Mere Indian manufacture and display would not have fitted the definition.)

At the end of 1975 it became known that Israel wanted to purchase some American ground-to-ground missiles. Objections were voiced that the missiles might carry Israeli nuclear warheads and that indeed the missiles might be intended specifically for that purpose. To allay any such fears (or perhaps to confirm them), an Israeli spokesman indicated that Israel would be willing to incur a formal commitment not to install nuclear warheads on any such missiles. The proposal could hardly be construed as a ringing declaration that Israel already had, or could promptly acquire, the nuclear warheads that it would agree not to install; but it did remind us that, although a nation cannot get into the nuclear club without both making and exploding some nuclear device, not every nation that has access to nuclear weapons of its own construction will necessarily go through the initiation ceremony to join the club.

It can also remind us that the main significance of nuclear weapons is not their parade-ground display but the possibility of their being used. The inhibitions on actually using nuclear weapons are surely so strong that most governments would consider military use only in a grave emergency. And any government that was actually ready to use nuclear weapons would probably be a government that would not be much further inhibited by an explicit earlier promise not to.

To fabricate nuclear weapons under government auspices, there are two crucial ingredients. One is the fissile material, uranium or plutonium of sufficient enrichment or purity. The other is people with the requisite engineering knowledge and skill. With the likely worldwide growth of nuclear electric power, most countries of any size, possibly all of them, will eventually have within their national boundaries reactors that produce plutonium as an intended or an unintended by-product. (A good-sized power reactor produces plutonium in amounts equivalent to a couple of dozens of nuclear bombs per year.) The chemical separation of plutonium out of the spent reactor fuel is a process that will be within the industrial capability of most nations, even the industrially undeveloped nations, especially if foreign companies are available to do it on contract. And the actual design and fabrication of a nuclear bomb is authoritatively asserted to be a task that any nation with a moderate industrial capacity can do without outside aid.* The best universities on this side of the Iron Curtain, possibly on both sides, are

*Hans A. Bethe, Bernard L. Cohen, and Richard Wilson presented a statement to the National Council of Churches on January 28, 1976, in which they reassured us that it is impossible for a single person to make a bomb. "At least six persons, highly skilled in very different technologies, would be required to do so, even for a crude weapon."

perfectly willing to train nuclear scientists and engineers from any country that will pay their tuition. Countries that do not participate in the Treaty on Non-Proliferation may pursue a genuine or feigned interest in PNEs (Peaceful Nuclear Explosives), and there is no guarantee that in doing so they will observe the same technological secrecy that heretofore has appealed to the nuclear-weapon states. In another ten or fifteen years it is unlikely that many countries will lack the technology and the personnel for making nuclear weapons out of indigenously produced fissile materials.

So there we have it. In a terribly important and terribly dangerous sense they will practically all have the bomb. By "they" I mean governments. By "have the bomb" I mean that at any time one of those governments decides to explode a nuclear bomb it will be able to do so, with some lapse in time—and of course, for most of them, with some breach of treaty, contract, or widely accepted standards, and with some possibility of punitive action. But even the United States, or France, or China—that is, the weapon states—will be bound by strong inhibitions and sometimes by treaty; and even for the weapon states there would be some lapse of time between the decision to use nuclear weapons and their actual use, especially if the use were anything other than the firing of permanently alert strategic weapons.

Until recently, having or not having nuclear weapons appeared to be, and was treated as, a question of yes or no. From now on it will make more sense to describe a country's nuclear-weapon status not with a yes or a no but with a time schedule. The answer will be a chart, giving the number of weapons of certain energy yields and certain physical characteristics that could be available after elapsed hours, days or weeks from the decisions to assemble them.

For many countries this is the way we describe armies. Does Switzerland have an army? In one sense the answer is no. Except in a military emergency or during the seasons of intensive training, Switzerland doesn't actually possess an army. What it has is a capacity to mobilize troops rapidly, and the best description of the Swiss army is not what one would get by an instantaneous census on a randomly selected day but a schedule relating manpower and firepower to elapsed hours from the moment of call-up. The governments of most countries in another decade or two will "have" nuclear weapons in much the way that Switzerland "has" an army.

Whether this is saying anything important or not will depend of course on whether the lead time to actual assembly of weapons in working order is measured in hours, days, months, or years. The longest delay might be measured in months if a country had taken no preparatory steps to acquire an inventory of weapons-grade uranium or plutonium. But if those preparatory steps, which would not need to be contrary to the Treaty on Non-Proliferation, had already been taken, either as continuing peacetime policy or after a crisis had begun to gather on the horizon, the rest of the mobilization would be a matter of weeks at most, more likely days, possibly hours. A useful comparison might be the time it would take the United States to airlift a division of troops overseas, or to mobilize the National Guard. Only a country that had deliberately eschewed any preparation that might enhance its capability for mobilizing nuclear weapons would need as long, from the moment of decision, as it would take the United States to pass a new draft law and train recruits and transport them with their gear to where they were needed.

There are two things to emphasize about this coming state of affairs, and it is important to emphasize them without making them seem to contradict each other or to detract from each other. The first is simply that unilateral access to indigenously produced nuclear weapons will have "proliferated," if I may use that somewhat inappropriate word. In terms of actual military nuclear readiness, the prior possession or even prior detonation of a nuclear explosive is not going to be a great watershed. It will continue to be significant but not decisive. A government that has never even authorized the rehearsal assembly of a nuclear explosive device, fissile material and all, may be able to get its hands usefully on more bombs quicker than some other government that actually has a few in storage, or that actually has them in delivery vehicles that might not be in the right place or of the right kind at the moment it became urgent to get them ready.

The second thing to emphasize is that this does not make any less important, and perhaps not any less effective, the kinds of institutional arrangements and safeguards and treaty obligations and contractual commitments and precedents and traditions that for several decades have constituted the kinds of arms control that became known during the past decade as the anti-proliferation movement. The emphasis has to shift from physical denial and technological secrecy to the things that determine incentives and motivations and expectations. The fact that a government could get its hands on nuclear weapons doesn't mean that it would. For years there have been governments, maybe a score of them, that had jurisdiction over the physical facilities and the personnel with which to construct nuclear weapons. As far as we can tell, they either found it good policy to resist the temptation to mobilize those nuclear resources, or they were not tempted.

The most severe inhibitions are undoubtedly those on the actual use of nuclear weapons, not on the possession of them. We have no good measure of how strong those inhibitions are, because, with the possible exception of two or three stages in the Korean War there has not been a military emergency that came close to putting those inhibitions to the test. But the fact itself that the weapons have not been used in more than 30 years, even if not a measure of the strength of the inhibition, undoubtedly contributes to it. Of course, this could be one of those traditions that, being absolute, is discredited at the first violation.

"Inhibition" has to be understood to include fear, especially the fear of retaliatory use of nuclear weapons against a first-user. It includes also a variety of sanctions and reprisals that may be directed at countries that violate treaties and contracts and understandings, and it includes the risk of disassociation on the part of protectors and allies that condition their help on a country's continued acceptance of non-nuclear status.

The worst of these fears and inhibitions would of course not apply to mere acquisition or display of nuclear weapons. But if the main purpose of *having* them would be to be able to *use* them, the disincentives to use them should detract from the advantages of their possession.

The decisive inhibitions, then, will always be those on the actual use of nuclear weapons. By far the worst consequences of their possession would be the use of them. Possession itself can be mischievous; and the stronger the perceived limitations on the usefulness of nuclear weapons, the stronger will be the considerations militating against acquisition.

There is a stronger way to phrase this. A government that would actually use nuclear weapons if it had them, and could get them, would get them. No inhibition on mere possession could survive a decision to use them. In ordinary times, when a country is not fighting for survival or for its vital interests, when it would not be using nuclear weapons if it had them, the incentives to possess them can be overridden by many kinds of inhibitions, including treaty obligations. And most of those inhibitions on possession *per se* should contribute to the reluctance to use them. But in an emergency, the ultimate safeguard has to be the reluctance to use them.

In these conditions—and we are probably talking mainly about the 1990s—possessing or not possessing some nuclear weapons, or having it known or not known that a country possesses some nuclear weapons, will not decisively differentiate countries as it may have done in the past. The difference will seem greatest when it doesn't matter much. When nothing is at stake except mere possession, those that have crossed the Rubicon will be sharply distinguished from those that have not. But when weapons really matter, and when capabilities to get weapons can be mobilized,the decisive considerations are likely to be similar for the countries that already have some and for the countries that don't quite have them yet. These considerations are the expected consequences of using them, not of just having them.

This does not mean that the weapon states and the non-weapon states will be in anything like the same nuclear status. Being able to produce some nuclear weapons on short notice would not make Panama look like the United States. But in an acute military crisis between Panama and a neighboring country, or between Panama and Cuba, or Panama and the United States, the nuclear aspects of the crisis should be not wholly dissimilar in the case of a Panama known by demonstration to have a few nuclear weapons and in the case of a Panama known to be without them but able to acquire them promptly.

Who Else Will Have the Bomb?

The reactor fuel that is presently used for the production of electric power is not an explosive material. It is uranium that has been enriched in the isotope U-235 from the naturally occurring percentage of .7 percent to 2 or 3 percent (or, in reactors that use "heavy water" instead of plain water as the moderator, not enriched at all). Not only is this low percentage of U-235 incapable of an explosive chain reaction, it cannot at present be further enriched except by an expensive process in very large establishments embodying advanced engineering technology. There is no danger that any-body will steal the stuff to make bombs, any more than people can mine and refine uranium ore in the myriad locations in which it naturally occurs and proceed with the complex task of making a bomb. That stuff is harmless.

What has caused alarm in recent years, and serious discussion of hijacking and theft and the possibility of nuclear bombs in the hands of political terrorists or criminal extortionists, is what comes out of the reactor after it has "burned" the uranium fuel to produce steam to make electricity. Some of the U-238, which constitutes 97 percent or so of the uranium in the reactor fuel, is converted to plutonium in the fission process that produces heat. The plutonium is itself fissionable, and indeed a part of the plutonium that is produced within the reactor fissions right there in the reactor along with the U-235 and contributes some of the energy that goes directly into steam and electric power. When the spent fuel is removed from the reactor, as it periodically is for replacement with fresh fuel, there remains about a third of the U-235 together with plutonium. The amount of plutonium, measured in energy potential, is equivalent to something like a fifth of the U-235 that burned to produce the plutonium as a by-product.

Once this plutonium has been chemically separated from all the other materials present in the spent fuel it can be used directly to produce energy in either of two ways. It can be made into fuel assemblies and fed back into reactors like the one that produced it. And it can be used as the explosive material in a nuclear bomb. The chemical process by which it is extracted from the highly radioactive spent fuel is not an easy one; but it is far less demanding than is uranium enrichment, and can presently be done on a much smaller scale.

There is controversy about whether it is going to be economical to recycle plutonium as a reactor fuel. But the recycling may prove economical; governments may wish to promote the technology even if it is not currently economical, to enjoy a reduced dependence on foreign fuel supplies and to be abreast of the technology at the time when recycling does become economical; and the recycling of plutonium is an "innocent" way to acquire a national inventory of potentially explosive plutonium and the capacity to produce more in a hurry. And because not every step in this "nuclear fuel cycle" will be done at central locations under continuous heavy armed guard, there is a possibility of theft or hijacking of the kind of material of which nuclear bombs can be made.

There is also the possibility that a maverick government, not party to the Non-Proliferation Treaty and willing to flaunt the generally accepted rules, and not afraid of a nuclear or other boycott, might actually sell plutonium with no questions asked. It seems unlikely, but not out of the question.

So there is the possibility that persons or organizations other than national governments might acquire the wherewithal to produce an atomic bomb. Does this mean that future terrorists, for motives either personal or political, will hold cities hostage, rather than just airplanes full of people?

It has to mean that they could. But at this point we probably should be a little more careful in estimating how easy it may be to construct nuclear weapons in the years ahead.

As a national enterprise with government support it is not going to be difficult, ten or fifteen years from now, even in comparatively non-industrial countries, to produce nuclear bombs. But compared with smuggling guns into an airport and shooting up an airplane full of passengers, the nuclear trick will be orders of magnitude more demanding. Remember the estimate given above: as a bare minimum, six highly skilled individuals possessing exactly the right skills, and very likely a good number of reliable employees to help with the job. Furthermore, in the absence of direct technical assistance they would have to do the job from the ground up. They must work together as a disciplined technical team over a protracted period, with access to computers, to a technical library, perhaps to metallurgical and other laboratory facilities, and probably to outside consultants. Even recruiting the initial six or more would be quite an enterprise, with some number of qualified people being approached who didn't want to participate, or who couldn't get away from what they were already doing, or who turned out to lack the skills that somebody thought they had. The people must either disappear or maintain contact with their normal lives and places of work while participating in the project. They will have wives or husbands. In addition to the menu of scientific and technological skills they must collectively provide, they have to be able to work productively together as a disciplined team, believing in the project and exercising skills in clandestine cooperation that may be as rare as the technical skills they bring to the enterprise. Unless they are simply paid huge amounts of money, they will probably want to be part of the organization that uses the bombs, or at least to have some veto over what is done with the enormous things they produce.

And so forth. Surely it can be done, and it needn't be quite as fantastically organized as it might be in a James Bond movie. But it is something altogether out of the league of the terrorists and separatist movements and liberation armies that have held our attention for the past seven or eight years. Perhaps the modern equivalent of the Jewish terrorist organizations that were active in Palestine in 1946 and 1947, with claims on money and Nobel Prizes, would be the kind of organization that might make itself into a small non-national nuclear power. But the potential number of such organizations is probably small compared with the number of nations that actually exist, and they might better be thought of as a special kind of mini-state. While they would be additional to the individual nations that we may already have counted as dangers to world peace, they would be very much like nations in the way they set their goals and conducted their diplomacy. At least, they won't be blowing up San Simeon with nuclear explosives.

The Prospects for Nuclear Terrorism

The organizations most likely to engage in nuclear terrorism will be national governments. Passive terrorism on a grand scale we call "deterrence." When it is directed at us, rather than at our enemies, we call it "blackmail." At the small end of the scale of magnitude would be an organization possessing only a few weapons, or claiming to possess them or believed to possess them, weapons that might be clandestinely emplaced where they could do, or threaten to do, horrendous civilian damage in the interest of some political cause. But that is probably the image that would fit one of those small nations that might have a small supply of nuclear bombs or a small capability to produce some in a hurry.

Actually, a suggestive model of nuclear terrorism is the one case in history that occurred. There was a government that felt a dreadful urgency to bring a bitter and costly war to an end and that had a couple of nuclear weapons of a kind that had never been fully tested. It considered announcements, demonstrations in uninhabited locales, use against military targets, and even a devastating attack on a population center. It couldn't be altogether sure that either bomb would work; a demonstration might be an embarrassing failure, and even if successful would half deplete the arsenal. Undemonstrated threats of some novel super-weapon would suffer the usual problem of credibility. In the end it was decided that only a massive unexpected shock had any hope of causing the necessary changes in the Japanese government. And then an unopposed weather reconnaissance aircraft introduced nuclear terror into our world.

In quick succession the second one was dropped on another city, emptying the arsenal.

All of that was done by people who believed their cause was just; who believed they were saving lives, even Japanese lives, if the gamble worked; who thought they had considered all the options and received the best advice; and most of whom afterwards were generally satisfied that they had done the right thing. Never again will a government, in using or considering the use of nuclear weapons, enjoy the luxury of knowing that it alone in all the world disposes of such dreadful things. Otherwise, the American model may not be a bad prototype for imagining what nuclear terrorism might someday be like. (This is another one of those predictions that we all hope can never be matched against experience.)

What is likely to be more widespread is the passive kind of terrorism that is called "deterrence." According to my dictionary, to deter is "to prevent or discourage (someone) from acting by means of fear, doubt, or the like." The Latin means to frighten *away from.* Compared with efforts to compel action through nuclear intimidation, encouraging *inaction* tends to be easier and quieter. Deterrent threats often go without saying. When they succeed they go untested. They do not involve deadlines. The terms usually do not involve quantities and degrees. (Don't do that, at all, ever!) There is no need for overt submission by the deterred party. Deterrence can be reciprocal. And the desired response—continued inactivity of some particular kind—is usually the kind of decision that a target government finds it easiest to agree on, and to implement.

The most passive deterrence of all would be just letting it be known, perhaps through an innocent leak of information, that a government or other organization simply had nuclear weapons, letting every potential addressee of this "deterrent threat" reach his own conclusions about what kind of misbehavior, if any, might provoke nuclear activity. A degree more active is the threat that specifies what action by what parties is under nuclear proscription, and what kind of nuclear response is to be anticipated. Especially if the threat is being extended, say, to cover a third party, the explicit statement is required, together with whatever ritual or preparatory actions are required to make the threat believable. A much more active, and undoubtedly more persuasive, deterrent threat could be directed at a type of misbehavior that involved overt preparation or some protracted operation, and would take the form of actually using a nuclear weapon against the victim the moment he begins his adventure, with repeated use as long as he keeps it up or as long as the bombs hold out. This method might appeal to a terrorist organization that chose to remain anonymous, or that acted on behalf of a friend or client that couldn't acknowledge the "help," or didn't want it.

Some of the more dramatic acts of terrorism that we have read about in recent years have been initiated by individuals or small groups that had more passion than perseverance, more interest in getting attention than in getting results. They did not appear to be well-articulated pieces of a grand strategy in furtherance of a major objective. Most of them do not seem to have involved careful planning by large numbers of thoughtful people. But an organization that had the brains and the money and the teamwork and the discipline to bring off the successful construction of a nuclear bomb would have plenty of time and plenty of reason to think carefully about how to use this potential influence, this dreadful threat that may be as diplomatically unwieldy as it is enormous. Furthermore, if they can make one bomb they can probably make two or more, and will be motivated to plan what to do next if the threat succeeds. Or if it fails.

They may have the time, the money, the motivation and the imagination to study strategy as well as bomb design. While they may have an urge to engage in some apocalyptic histrionics, they were probably mobilized by some cause they believed in. So we should expect them to do a more professional job not only in the way they coerce the behavior they want but in selecting the behavior to be coerced and the victims who, directly or indirectly, can bring it about.

That means that the "nuclear blackmail" that might be practiced by a non-governmental organization, by a front organization set up by some government, or even by a government, would be more effective than the small acts of individual terrorism that may first come to mind. It would probably look more like diplomacy than terrorism. It might be attached to a cause that half the world, or the other half, considered a just cause. The strategists might be responsibly concerned to avoid harm to innocent bystanders (but equally aware of the long tradition of nuclear-weapon states, which threaten nuclear destruction to the people whose leaders misbehave). And they might be no more transient in world politics than most liberation movements, governments in exile, or ethnic communities.

The most plausible "nuclear terrorism" on the part of a non-governmental group may be the kind that is almost indistinguishable from the traditional nuclear deterrence practiced by the United States and some other countries. It would be a threat of nuclear reprisal against some overt military action or against abetment of some military enterprise. The victims would be selected for their complicity in the enterprise and the targets would be related as directly as possible to the military enterprise itself. It could be on behalf of some victim country that enjoyed a good deal of sympathy, and it could be against the kind of military action that has already been the object of nuclear threats by the United States and the Soviet Union. A 30 years' tradition, acquiesced in by most American and Soviet spokesmen, that the appropriate targets of nuclear deterrent threats are people and their homes and their workplaces might make it especially easy for some smaller organization to look cleaner and more businesslike by announcing targets that were obviously military—airfields, ports, troop concentrations, and the like, that symbolized the misdeed for which this was reprisal. Careful selection of both the deed to be punished and the target to be struck could endow the threat with both credibility and sympathy. An especially effective threat would be one that demanded the non-performance of an action, or the cessation of some initiated action, that depended on the cooperation of so many people with different interests that there was bound to be somebody around who could stop it or sabotage it or veto it or focus the blame in such a way that those who could still carry out the deed didn't want to. (Examples are treacherous, but I propose the threat of a nuclear bomb on airfields in third countries that permit landing and refueling of aircraft bringing troops or weapons into a theatre of military operations from a country that is considered an aggressor or an outsider.)

Some Problems of Control

The chances are good that most countries, perhaps all of them, will accept safeguards against the diversion of nuclear energy from peaceful uses to nuclear weapons. The NPT requires the acceptance of International Atomic Energy Agency (IAEA) safeguards, but so do the several bilateral agreements under which countries that are not parties to the NPT have imported reactors and other facilities. And in his testimony March 9, 1976, to the Senate Committee on Government Operations the Secretary of State reported some success in developing among the main nuclear suppliers a "common set of standards concerning safeguards and other related controls associated with peaceful nuclear exports."

No foreign government or international organization could physically prevent a government from making any use it wished to make of the nuclear equipment and material within its jurisdiction, except by launching a military attack against it. But not many governments, if any at all, will want to jeopardize their nuclear future by violating treaty commitments or bilateral agreements or commercial contracts in a way that will lead the main nuclear suppliers to embargo fuel, parts, reactors, technical assistance, and anything else the country needs to import for nuclear energy. In the absence of an emergency so serious that governments would abrogate treaties and risk being outlawed as nuclear renegades, the network of institutional arrangements of which the NPT is the centerpiece gives promise of being effective.

There remain at least two kinds of risks. One is the theft of explosive nuclear materials. While most of the terrorist groups that might be moved to steal plutonium in some chemical form are not the kind that would know what to do with it after they had stolen it, a group that did know how to use the stuff might be able to launch a commando-like operation in a selected country or to offer a suitable amount of money, no questions asked, for high-grade nuclear explosive material. Someday it may be necessary to do a better job spoiling the black market for plutonium than has been possible with the black market for heroin. Maybe the intergovernmental cooperation will be a little more nearly unanimous.

A more serious problem will be a country's own armed forces. Two of the most common activities of military forces in many parts of the world are to fight among themselves—half the Army against the other half, or the Army against the Navy—and to depose civilian governments. Even in NATO, four governments have been subjected to severe military revolts; in three the revolts succeeded, usually without united actions by all the armed forces. New regimes that impose themselves by force or by other illegitimate means often fear, and with reason, outside intervention. They are often in a mood to denounce or at least to question the international commitments of the regime they deposed. They have little reluctance to violate civil rights and property rights. Their first task is to disable opposition and to entrench themselves militarily and otherwise. And if there is plutonium as well as gold in the vaults of the national bank, it may be put to some potentially more effective use without qualms by the new government.

If the government has qualms, in the noise and confusion of a small civil war the IAEA monitoring system can at least be disturbed long enough to let somebody get away with the nuclear stuff. It might even be that when the troops are initially deployed to the Presidential palace, to the national television station and the local airport, a fourth contingent will be sent to scoop up whatever fissile material is in a transportable form. This may be the strongest argument that a government would have for not allowing plutonium or highly enriched uranium to exist in readily usable form. It is hard to imagine keeping the location secret from senior officers in the armed forces, especially after they have taken power. But when Moslems are fighting Christians within the country, or officers fighting enlisted men, the Navy fighting the Army or French paratroopers marching on Paris, even those who would find plutonium an embarrassment may have to race for it and fight for it simply to keep it from falling into the wrong hands.

Some dangers are better not talked about, but not this one. If the time comes to grab the plutonium, nobody is likely to neglect it merely because, due to the reticence of arms controllers, it never occurred to them to capture it. But even those who expect to seize power by force may have the good sense not to want dangerous nuclear materials to be up for grabs in the event of civil disturbance or military revolt.

It is a useful exercise to speculate on how different the course of events might have been in Lebanon in late 1975 and early 1976 if that country had had an indigenous capacity to reprocess reactor fuel and to extract plutonium, even a small pilot plant. Who would have guarded the facilities? Who would have destroyed them, from nearby or from afar, at the risk of spreading deadly plutonium locally to keep bomb material from falling into mischievous hands? What outside country might have invaded if the spoils of war would have included a nuclear-weapon capability, even only to deny that capability to some other greedy neighbor? What neutral outsiders might have been invited in by the President or the Prime Minister, to guard or to abduct the dangerous stuff; and would all parties have willingly cooperated with the removal of such an awful prize, or would that have added merely one more armed group fighting its way to the cache? There may be some useful international understandings and procedures to be worked out for that kind of emergency. One thing is certain: in years to come there will be military violence in countries that have sizable nuclear power industries.

A tantalizing control problem will arise with respect to countries that do have, or are believed to have, nuclear weapons. The dilemma is this. Little as we like them to have nuclear weapons, if they are going to have them we would like them to have the best technical safeguards against accidental or unauthorized detonation, and possibly—though this is a tricky one—against military attack. At the same time we shall not want to reward countries that make nuclear explosives by offering them our most advanced technology to safeguard against misuse, especially if some of the most effective safeguards would be in the design of the bomb itself. We have all heard of remote electronic locking devices; there may be some crucial design aspects that could keep a bomb from exploding unless it were in some predesignated condition and that would spoil the bomb if the mechanism were tampered with. There must be ways of making the bomb with the fissionable material recognizable, even after explosion, and ways of making it easier to locate if lost or to follow if carried away. And if the weapons were to be installed in missiles or aircraft or on board ship or were to be hauled around for emplacement as land mines, there may be American technology and experience in the fusing of weapons and other characteristics of the entire weapon system that would reduce the likelihood of unauthorized or inadvertent firing, or theft or capture.

The recipient of any such technical assistance would have to be a country that had never ratified the NPT, or having ratified, had withdrawn pursuant to Article 10 or had abrogated or denounced the treaty. Reading the treaty gives me no hint to its legal interpretation on whether help in bomb safety could be provided, but it is probably not the legal interpretation that would be controlling. Done bilaterally this would be a suspect activity. Broadcasting the technology would certainly violate the treaty. Discreet bilateral transfer might be accomplished but, at least to the recipient of this sensitive technology, such evident complicity might be interpreted as tacit cooperation or approval, especially if it were not yet acknowledged that the country to whom we slipped the prophylactics had taken the decision yet.

The resolution of this dilemma is probably to append this problem to the more general problem of physical security against loss or theft or sabotage of dangerous nuclear materials of all kinds. Ideas and experience relevant to the problem of bomb safety, even if not engineering designs, can probably be gotten across undramatically and without challenge if there is at least a reasonable pretense that the measures are of wide security application. (An alternative solution is to let the French do it.)

And Now for the Good News

Think back 25 years. The Prime Minister had just flown to Washington to obtain assurances for his Parliament that President Truman would not let nuclear weapons be used in Korea. Russia had stunningly exploded a bomb, years before it was thought Russia would be able to. Our deterrent force was the propeller-driven B-36. Suppose I had been asked then to write something called, "Who Will Have the Bomb?" And suppose I had accurately answered that question for the ensuing 25 years.

This is how I might have replied.

There are going to be thousands of nuclear bombs on airbases and hundreds, probably thousands, on aircraft carriers and smaller naval vessels in port and at sea. Nuclear weapons are going to be available to a variety of short- and medium-range ground-to-ground missiles, antiaircraft missiles, and even artillery. They are going to be in Germany, Greece, Turkey, Okinawa, and probably the Panama Canal Zone. Some will be intended for airplanes to be flown by foreigners, and these weapons will be physically located so that in a hurry they can be available to foreign aircraft.

We are going to fly B-47s over Western Europe and the adjacent ocean loaded with big nuclear bombs, and a little later on we are going to fly B-52s to the North Pole and back with them. There is going to be a "Cuban" missile crisis, and in the course of it B-47s alleged to be accompanied by nuclear weapons, possibly with the nuclear weapons on board, will be photographed on the runway at Logan Airport in Boston. There are going to be two military revolts in Greece while American weapons are located on Greek military bases; and Greece will be on the brink of war with another NATO country, Turkey, that is also going to have American weapons on its military bases.

The number of bombs produced in America is going to reach the tens of thousands, and they are going to be transported all over the United States and a lot of the world, in the custody of thousands or tens of thousands of people, most of them enlisted men. The French are going to supply nuclear weapons to their bomber force and then move into the production of tactical weapons. Dozens of nuclear-armed submarines belonging to at least four nations are going to be continuously cruising the oceans, the weapons as well as the boats presumably under the complete physical control of a few officers who will be hermetically sealed in their vessels for months at a time.

Some of you would think I was out of my mind. Some would think I was exaggerating to cause alarm. And some would think, sadly, that my prediction might be right. But on the next part you would agree that I was deluding myself.

Because then I go on to say that in 25 years not a single one of these bombs will go off accidentally. Not a single one will be detonated by a demented military officer. Not a single one will be captured by foreign spies and used to defend Yemen against Egyptians or Cypriot Greeks from Turkish mainland forces. Not a single one will be captured by a domestic fanatic and used to avenge an assassination or to coerce the release of some prisoners. Not a single one will be known to have been sold by its guards or transport crews to foreign governments, to the Mafia, or to rich expatriate businessmen sought by the Internal Revenue Service and the Securities Exchange Commission.

A bomber will crash in Spain, rupturing a bomb and spreading its contents over some countryside and dropping another one in the water near a beach resort, but the Air Force will clean up the mess on land and our Ambassador will go swimming to reassure the Spaniards that their water is safe.

Nor will any awful things have happened with French or British or Russian or Chinese weapons, so far as we know.

And most important of all, there will have been no nuclear weapons fired in warfare.

Part II
Terrorist Acquisition of Nuclear Weapons: Readymade or Homemade?

Mason Willrich
and Theodore B. Taylor

Nuclear Theft:
Risks and Safeguards

In this chapter from their influential study for the Ford Foundation, Willrich and Taylor discuss the technology and the materials that would enable a few persons (or even one person) to construct a crude fission bomb or a radiological weapon. Their analysis has been the most important impetus for the many studies—both pro and con—of the nuclear terrorism question.

Overview

The first question we must explore is whether a successful theft of nuclear materials from the nuclear power industry would pose a genuine threat. Could some of the materials used as nuclear fuel in the power industry be used in weapons? Are these materials present in the industry in forms and quantities that are practical for the illicit manufacture of bombs? If a thief succeeds in making a nuclear weapon from these materials, how much damage might he cause?

Every educated person already knows the single most essential fact about how to make nuclear explosives: they work. Before the first atomic bomb exploded in the Trinity test near Alamogordo, New Mexico, in 1945, no one knew for certain that it would work. There was a possibility that the kind of fission chain reaction which had been sustained in the Chicago pile could not be accelerated to produce a large explosion. Indeed, some of the Los Alamos weapon design group strongly suspected that Trinity would not explode. A "pool" of yield estimates made before the test ranged from little more than the yield of the high explosive used to trigger the nuclear explosion to several tens of kilotons. (A kiloton is a unit of energy equal to the energy released by the explosion of one thousand tons of TNT. A megaton corresponds to the energy released by exploding one million tons of TNT.) The actual yield, close to twenty kilotons, was significantly greater than most of the estimates made before the test.

The certainty that an idea will work in principle is a large step toward finding ways to carry it out. During the twenty-eight years since the Trinity test much has happened to make it easier to design and fabricate a nuclear explosive, and to provide a high degree of confidence that the design will be successful. The first fission explosives built in the USSR, the United Kingdom, France, and China apparently worked quite well. A number of nuclear explosives with design features very different from the Trinity device, including the bomb exploded over Hiroshima, worked well the first time they were used or tested.

Ever since the successful test of the "Mike" device at Eniwetok in 1952, it has been known that fission explosions can be used to initiate thermonuclear explosions with yields in the megaton range. All governments that have developed fission explosives have also successfully developed high yield thermonuclear explosive devices. Less than three years elapsed between China's first detonation of an A-bomb and its first test of a thermonuclear explosive device—compared to seven years for the U.S., four for the USSR, five for the United Kingdom, and eight for France.

Until 1954, most of the information required for the design and construction of fission chain reacting systems, both reactors and fission explosives (A-bombs), was classified. A large body of this information was declassified in conjunction with President Eisenhower's "Atoms for Peace" speech before the United Nations on December 8, 1953, the enactment of the Atomic Energy Act of 1954, and the first international Conference on the Peaceful Uses of Atomic Energy at Geneva in 1955. Subsequent further declassification and public dissemination of new information of this type has been extensive.

In the initial draft of this book that was circulated to reviewers, we included in this chapter a rather extensive set of references to unclassified technical publications that would be available to a fission explosive design effort, particularly one with the objective of making a compact, efficient explosive with a reasonably predictable yield. The entire draft, including the references, was also submitted to the U.S. Atomic Energy Commission (AEC) for formal classification review and was determined to contain no classified information. Nevertheless, a number of the reviewers recommended that the set of references for this chapter and some of the text not be included in the published form of this book. They believed this information, though obtainable by a systematic literature search, would provide more assistance to an illicit fission explosive design team than would be prudent to collect together in one publication. We have made appropriate deletions in the published version. We believe, however, that the concern about the republication in a book such as this of certain unclassified information and references supports the central point we will develop: if the essential nuclear materials are at hand, it is possible to make an atomic bomb using information that is available in the open literature.

To give the reader some idea of the detail in which fission explosive design principles are described in widely distributed publications, and also to provide a point of departure for other parts of this chapter, we present below a rather extensive quotation from the article about nuclear weapons in the *Encyclopedia Americana*[1] by John S. Foster, a well-known expert on nuclear weapon technology and formerly Director of the Lawrence Radiation Laboratory in California and Director of Defense Research and Engineering in the Department of Defense:

> . . . It must be appreciated that the only difficult part of making a fission bomb of some sort is the preparation of a supply of fissionable material of adequate purity; the design of the bomb itself is relatively easy . . .
>
> *Fission Explosives*—The vital part of fission explosives is the fissionable material itself. The two elements commonly used are uranium and plutonium. Each of these elements can exist as isotopes of several different atomic weights according to the number of neutrons included in corresponding nuclei, as in U-232, U-233, U-234, U-235 . . . U-238, Pu-239, and Pu-240. Not all of the isotopes of these elements are suitable for use in a nuclear explosive. In particular, it is important to use a material with nuclei that are capable of undergoing fission by neutrons of all energies, and that release, on the average, more than one neutron upon fissioning. The materials which possess these properties and can be made available most easily in quantity are U-235 and PU-239.
>
> The immediate consequence of a nuclear fission is:
> U-235 or Pu-239 + neutron + 2 fission products + 2 or more neutrons (average) + 2 gamma rays (average)
>
> The total prompt energy release per fission is about 180 million electron volts. This means that the complete fissioning of 1 kilogram (2.2 lb) of U-235 or Pu-239 releases an energy equivalent to about 17,000 tons of chemical explosive.
>
> *Critical Mass*—However, 1 kilogram of U-235 or Pu-239 metal, which is about the size of a golf ball, will not explode by itself. The reason for this is that, if one of the nuclei is made to fission the neutrons produced would usually leave the metal sphere without causing a second fission. If, however, the sphere contained about 16 kilograms (35.2 lb) of Pu-239 (delta phase) or fifty kilograms (110 lb) of U-235, the mass would be critical. That is to say, for each fission which occurs, one of the neutrons produced would on the average cause a further fission to occur. If more material were added, the number of neutrons in the assembly would multiply.
>
> The mass of fissionable material needed to achieve a critical

mass is also determined by the type and amount of material
placed around it. This external material, called a tamper, serves
to reflect back into the fissionable material some of the neutrons
which would otherwise leave. For example, the presence of a
tamper made of U-238 one inch thick around a sphere of plutonium reduces the mass required to produce criticality from 16 kilograms to 10 kilograms (22 lb).

To produce a nuclear explosion, one must bring together
an assembly which is substantially above critical, or supercritical. For example, suppose that by some means a mass of
material equal to two critical masses is assembled, and a neutron
is injected which starts a chain reaction. Within two millionths
of a second or less, the energy developed within the fissionable material will cause it to explode and release a nuclear yield
equivalent to several hundred tons of high explosive. The actual
yield depends on the particular characteristics of the masses
and types of materials involved.

Initiation of the Explosion—Because a supercritical assembly
naturally tends to explode, a major aspect of the design is related to the way in which the material is brought together. The
simplest form involves a procedure by which two or more pieces,
which by themselves are subcritical, are brought together. One
can imagine, for example, a hollow cylinder inside of which two
cylindrical slugs of fissionable material are pushed togesther by
chemical propellant. While such an approach can be used to
provide a nuclear explosion, a considerable mass of fissionable
material is required. Nuclear explosives involving considerably
less fissionable material use a technique by which the nuclear
material is compressed, or imploded.

A simple picture of this so-called implosion technique can be
gained by imagining a sphere of fissionable material and tamper
which is slightly below critical. Under these conditions, a neutron
born in the central region of the fissionable material has almost
an even chance of producing a fission before it leaves the metal. If the
assembly is now compressed to twice the original density, the
radius is then reduced to about 8/10 of its initial value. A
neutron leaving the central region under the compressed conditions must pass through atoms which are more closely spaced
by a factor of two, although the total distance is reduced only
20 percent. Consequently, the chance of causing a fission is
actually increased by approximately 2 X 0.8, or 1.6 times. The

assembly is now obviously very supercritical, although only one critical mass was used.

The trick, of course, is to compress to several times normal density the mass of fissionable material and tamper. This requires pressures above 10 million pounds per square inch. Such pressures can be developed through the use of high explosive. The nuclear core could be placed in the center of a large sphere of high explosive. Compression of the fissionable material is attained by lighting the outer surface of the high explosive simultaneously at something like 100 points spaced roughly evenly over the surface. This procedure produces a roughly spherical, in-going detonation wave which, on striking the metal core, provides the necessary compression to lead to a nuclear explosion.

This encyclopedia article presents a description of the general principles for the design of nuclear explosives. In addition, information originally classified but now in the public domain includes: the measured and calculated critical masses of various fission explosive materials* in various types of tampers or reflectors; the nuclear properties of materials used in fission explosives, and practically all information concerning the chemistry and metallurgy of plutonium and uranium.

A fission explosive design team working in 1973 thus has available to it, in the unclassified technical literature, considerably more of the relevant information, with one possible exception, than was available to the Los Alamos designers when the Trinity device was tested. The exception is experimental and calculated data related to the actual performance of the non-nuclear components of specific bomb assemblies. The mathematical and experimental tools one needs to acquire such data, however, are extensively described in the technical literature on nuclear reactor engineering, on high explosive technology, and on the behavior of materials at very high pressures and temperatures.

It is generally known that fission explosions can serve as a trigger to ignite

*We define "fission explosive materials" to mean those materials that, without further chemical processing or isotope separation, can be directly used as the core material for fission explosives. We define "nuclear weapon materials" to mean those materials that can be used as the core material for fission explosives after chemical conversions involving processes much simpler than chemical reprocessing of irradiated nuclear materials or isotope separation. Hence, fission explosive materials is a narrower term than nuclear weapon materials. As we shall see, these two categories of nuclear materials are the primary concern of this study.

thermonuclear fuels such as deuterium or tritium (which are variant forms of hydrogen, the lightest element). When the atomic nuclei of these light elements fuse together, huge amounts of energy are released. A considerable amount of the information that is needed for the design and construction of thermonuclear explosives (H-bombs) has been made public, especially the results of intensive unclassified work in the United States and other countries on controlled thermonuclear (fusion) reactor systems. The basic design principles for thermonuclear explosives, however, remain classified. How long the "secret" of the H-bomb will be kept out of the public domain is speculative. There are thousands of people who know and understand the basic principles from personal experience working within the security classification systems of the five nations that have tested H-bombs, and their number continues to increase. Further unclassified development of controlled thermonuclear power concepts is also bound to make access to classified information less important to an H-bomb design team as time passes. As a result, it seems reasonable to conclude that the H-bomb "secret" will not be kept from public view through the end of this century.

Since, however, it is impossible to discuss fission-fusion explosives in any detail in an unclassified publication, we have concentrated our attention on fission explosives in this book. Furthermore, as long as some kind of fission explosion is required to ignite the thermonuclear fuel in an H-bomb, the controls to prevent illicit use of fission explosive materials have a direct bearing on the control of illicit production of H-bombs. Finally, the damage that could be inflicted by fission explosions provides, we believe, sufficient justification for effective safeguards designed to prevent theft or illicit production of fission explosive materials. The possibility of pure fusion explosives is discussed briefly at the end of this chapter.

Nuclear materials do not necessarily have to explode to cause severe damage over large areas. Some radioactive materials, including many that are produced in nuclear power reactors, are among the most toxic substances known. Radiological weapons that would disperse fission products or other radioactive materials have been seriously considered for military use. We have no evidence, however, that any government has found such weapons to be sufficiently effective compared to chemical or biological warfare agents and other weapons (including nuclear explosives), to include them in military arsenals. Nevertheless, we have considered several types of radiological devices that might be used by terrorists or other non-governmental groups—or perhaps even by individuals—to expose large numbers of people to radiation or to cause the evacuation of urban areas or major industrial facilities. We have given particular attention to possibilities for dispersing plutonium since that material is present in large quantities in nuclear power fuel cycles and is exceedingly toxic if breathed into the lungs in the form of very small particles.

Resources Required to Make Fission Explosives

OBJECTIVES

The time and resources required to design and make nuclear explosives depend strongly on the type of explosive wanted. It is much more difficult to make large numbers of reliable, efficient, and lightweight nuclear warheads for a national military program than to make several crude, inefficient nuclear explosive devices with unpredictable yields in the range of, say, one hundred to several thousand tons of ordinary high explosive. This is one reason why experts in the design and construction of nuclear explosives often disagree with· each other about how difficult it is to make them. Those who have worked many years on the development of nuclear warheads for ever more sophisticated nuclear-tipped missile systems often base their opinions on their own experience, without having thought specifically about nuclear explosive devices that are designed to be as easy to make as possible. Unlike most national governments, a clandestine nuclear bomb maker may care little whether his bombs are heavy, inefficient, and unpredictable. They may serve his purposes so long as they are transportable by automobile and are very likely to explode with a yield equivalent to at least 100 tons of chemical explosive.

Thus, aside from the essential fission explosive materials, there is a wide range of resources required to make different types of nuclear explosives for any of a variety of purposes and under diverse circumstances. In view of this situation, we concentrate in the following parts of this chapter on a discussion of the *minimum* time and resources required to make a fission explosive with a yield that could be expected to be equal to at least a few tens of tons of high explosive.

FISSION EXPLOSIVE MATERIALS

A material must have certain characteristics to be usable directly in the core of a fission bomb. First of all, it must be capable of sustaining a fission chain reaction. This means the material must contain isotopes* that can be split or

*An element such as uranium or hydrogen occurs in a number of different "isotopes." This means that different atomic nuclei of the element may contain different numbers of neutrons, although the number of protons in the nuclei and the number and arrangement of the electrons revolving around the nuclei will be the same. The numbers of protons and electrons bound together largely determine the chemical properties of the element, which will be basically the same regardless of the isotope involved. However, different

fissioned by neutrons, releasing in turn more than one neutron as a consequence of fissioning. Second, the average time between the "birth" of a neutron by fission and the time it produces another fission, called the neutron "generation time," must be short compared to the time it takes for pressure to build up in the core. Too much pressure early in the chain reaction can cause the core to expand sufficiently to become sub-critical, i.e., to lose so many neutrons by leakage from the surface that the chain reaction cannot be maintained. Third, the critical mass and volume of the fission explosive material must be sufficiently small so that the size and weight of the mechanism for assembling more than one critical mass—whether based on the "gun" or "implosion" design—will be small enough to suit the purposes of those who want to use the fission bomb.

The quantities of fission explosive materials that would be required to make nuclear explosives, and the problems an illicit bomb maker would face in using them, depend on which fission explosive materials are involved. The distinctive characteristics of each fission explosive material must be understood in order to determine where in the nuclear power industry the key materials are to be found, to assess the specific risks of nuclear theft, and to decide which safeguards measures are appropriate in particular circumstances. We shall briefly summarize some of the most important characteristics of plutonium, uranium that is highly enriched in the isotope uranium-235, and uranium-233. All three of these materials are or will be used in large quantities as nuclear fuel to produce electric power, and all three can be used, separately or in combinations with each other, to make fission explosives.

At the outset, it is useful to bear in mind that, of the three basic constituents of the nuclear age, neither plutonium nor uranium-233 occurs in nature in significant amounts, and uranium as it occurs in nature contains less than one percent uranium-235.

Plutonium.

Plutonium is produced in nuclear reactors that contain uranium-238, the most abundant isotope of natural uranium. Neutrons released in the fission process are captured in uranium-238, forming uranium-239. This radioactively decays, with a half-life* of about twenty minutes, to neptunium-239,

---

isotopes of the same element may have very different nuclear properties. Hence, certain isotopes of uranium, a very heavy element, are likely to split or fission when struck by a neutron, while some of the isotopes of hydrogen, a very light element, are likely to combine or fuse together under certain conditions. Both fission and fusion reactions convert mass into energy.

*The half-life of a radioactive isotope is the average time required for half of a given quantity of the isotope to decay and form some other isotope.

which subsequently also decays, with a half-life of a little more than two days, to form plutonium-239. This isotope of plutonium is relatively very stable, with a half-life of more than 24,000 years. It is the plutonium isotope of greatest interest for use as the core material in fission explosives.

Another isotope that is made in nuclear reactors, plutonium-240, is also important to our discussion. A plutonium-239 nucleus occasionally captures a neutron without fissioning, to produce plutonium-240. Plutonium-240 cannot be fissioned by neutrons of all energies. This isotope, instead of fissioning, is more likely to capture another neutron, resulting in plutonium-241. Thus, plutonium-240 tends to act as a "poison" in a chain reacting system and it cannot be used, by itself, as the core material for a fission explosive.

Plutonium-240 has another property that is important to a bomb designer seeking to use plutonium made in power reactors. It occasionally fissions spontaneously, without being struck by a neutron, and in so doing, releases several neutrons. The neutron production rate resulting from spontaneous fission may be sufficient to influence the chain reaction. Under some conditions, one of these neutrons might start a fission chain reaction in the core material of a fission bomb before the core is assembled into a highly compressed, supercritical state. This might cause the bomb to "predetonate" and release considerably less energy than it would if the start of the chain reaction had been further delayed.

The relative amount of plutonium-240, compared to plutonium-239, increases with the length of time the plutonium is exposed to neutrons in a nuclear reactor. In typical power reactors now in operation in the United States, plutonium-240 accounts for 10 to 20 percent of the plutonium in the fuel assemblies when they are removed from a reactor for reprocessing. This concentration is sufficient to make the presence of plutonium-240 an important consideration in the design of a fission bomb. But it does not prevent the plutonium produced in nuclear power reactors from being usable in fission bombs that would be very likely to produce explosions in the kiloton range.

Another characteristic of plutonium that has considerable importance in the construction of a nuclear explosive is that, with proper precautions, it can be handled safely. The products of plutonium-239 and 240 radioactive decay are primarily helium nuclei called "alpha particles." These particles have very small penetrating power, a millimeter or less in human tissue, compared to the very high energy x-rays, or "gamma rays," that are emitted in large numbers by many other radioactive isotopes. Plutonium-241 primarily emits electrons, or "beta rays," which also have very little penetrating power. And the spontaneous fission neutrons produced in plutonium-240 are too few to constitute a radiological hazard. As a consequence of these characteristics, plutonium can be a severe radiological hazard only if it is retained inside the human body, especially in the lungs.

Airborne plutonium particles, small enough to be barely visible, are among the most toxic substances known. Inhalation of particles the size of specks of dust and weighing a total of some ten millionths of a gram is likely to cause lung cancer. A few thousandths of a gram of small particles of plutonium (taken together, about the size of a pinhead), if inhaled, can cause death from fibrosis of the lungs within a few weeks or less. As long as it is not breathed in or otherwise injected into the bloodstream or critical organs, however, large quantities—many kilograms—of plutonium can be safely handled for hours without any significant radiological hazards. Therefore, plutonium that is being processed must be always kept inside some kind of airtight container such as a plastic bag or one of the increasingly familiar "glove boxes" that are standard equipment in laboratories that handle highly toxic materials. In short, plutonium must be handled with considerable respect.

The optimal chemical form of plutonium to use in a fission bomb is generally the pure metal. Metallic plutonium occurs in several different "phases" with different densities. So-called "alpha-phase" plutonium (which has nothing to do with alpha particles) has a density about nineteen times greater than water at normal pressure, while delta-phase plutonium is about sixteen times more dense than water. The critical mass of a sphere of dense alpha-phase plutonium-239 inside several inches of beryllium metal (an especially good neutron reflector) is about four kilograms and about the size of a baseball. The critical mass of a sphere of delta-phase plutonium that contains percentages of plutonium-239, 240, and 241 typical of plutonium made in today's nuclear power reactors is about eight kilograms when it is inside a several-inch thick reflector of steel or copper (neither of which is as good a neutron reflector as beryllium).

Plutonium oxide, which is used as fuel material in some types of nuclear power reactors, could also be used directly in a nuclear explosive. The oxygen in plutonium oxide, which has the chemical formula PuO_2, affects the ability of the plutonium to sustain a rapid chain reaction in several ways. The oxygen takes up space, thereby reducing the number of atoms of plutonium per cubic centimeter. This tends to increase the critical mass, since a neutron must travel further than it would in plutonium metal before making a fission. But oxygen atoms are much more effective than the much heavier plutonium atoms in slowing down neutrons by billiard-ball type collisions. In the language of nuclear engineers, oxygen is a neutron "moderator." Since the probability that a neutron will cause a fission in plutonium-239 tends to *increase* as the neutron slows down, this effect of the presence of oxygen (or some other moderator) tends to *decrease* the critical mass. But the increase in fission probability resulting from slower neutron velocities cannot compensate for the effect of the decreased concentration of plutonium atoms contained in plutonium oxide, so that the net effect is that the critical mass of the oxide is somewhat greater than that of plutonium metal. When well compacted, plutonium oxide has a critical mass that is about one and a half times as large as the critical mass of metallic plutonium.

A particular number of assembled critical masses of plutonium oxide will also explode less efficiently than the same number of critical masses of metallic plutonium. The reason is that the neutron generation time is longer in plutonium oxide than in the metal, since the average distance between plutonium atoms is greater and the neutrons are generally moving more slowly. Consequently, if plutonium oxide is used instead of the metal, less energy would be released by the time the buildup of pressure in the core caused it to expand to the point where increased leakage of neutrons from the core would cause the chain reaction to stop.

An illicit bomb maker who possessed plutonium oxide would have two options. Either he could use it directly as bomb material and settle for a bomb that was somewhat inefficient, or he could go to the trouble of removing the oxygen so that he would need to use only about two-thirds as much plutonium and would achieve a higher explosive yield. Whichever way he chose, however, the bomb maker would have to be extremely careful always to keep the plutonium inside airtight enclosures, and to monitor all steps in the process with some kind of radiation detector to make sure he never accidentally assembled a critical mass.

The processes for converting plutonium oxide to metallic plutonium are described in detail in widely distributed, unclassified publications. Moreover, all the required equipment and chemicals can be purchased from commercial firms for a few thousand dollars or less. We find it credible that a person with experience in laboratory chemistry and metallurgy could assemble all the required information, equipment, and chemicals, and safely carry out all the operations needed to reduce plutonium oxide to metal in a clandestine laboratory in a few months.

The preceding discussion is based on the assumption that a bomb maker would have acquired plutonium oxide before it had been mixed with other oxides. When plutonium oxide is used in nuclear power reactors, it is often intimately mixed with an oxide of uranium that is slightly enriched with uranium-235. Whether or not such an oxide mixture could be used, even in principle, as the core material for a fission bomb depends on the relative concentrations of plutonium and uranium. Mixed uranium-plutonium oxide fuel suitable for use in the kinds of power reactors now operating in the United States has much too low a concentration of plutonium (in the range of 1 to 5 percent) to make the fuel material directly usable in a fission bomb. The processes necessary to extract the plutonium from such a mixture, in the form of reasonably pure plutonium oxide, are less complicated than those required to reduce plutonium oxide to metallic form, and they are also thoroughly described in unclassified publications. Once having separated the plutonium oxide from the uranium oxide, an illicit bomb maker would have the same choice we previously described.

Mixtures of plutonium and uranium oxides suitable for use in the kind of "fast breeder" reactor now under intensive development could, in principle, be used without further chemical separation as core material for a fission bomb. In order to produce the same explosive yield, however, the amount of plutonium required would be at least several times greater than if the plutonium oxide were separated. Thus, the additional effort required to separate the plutonium, at least as the oxide from the plutonium-uranium mixture used in breeder reactor fuel, would generally be worthwhile.

After plutonium has been produced from the uranium-238 in a reactor, it is extracted from spent fuel at a fuel reprocessing plant. It is then in the form of a liquid plutonium nitrate solution. Plutonium nitrate solution can sustain a fission chain reaction; in fact, the minimum critical mass of plutonium in solution is considerably smaller than the critical mass of metallic plutonium. This is because hydrogen atoms in the solution are very effective in slowing down the neutrons, thereby increasing the chances they will cause fission. Under some conditions, the critical mass can be as small as a few hundred grams. However, unlike the oxide, plutonium nitrate solution cannot be used directly in the core of a nuclear bomb. The reason is that the neutron generation time of the plutonium in solution is much too long. The solution would form steam bubbles that would disassemble the bomb before the nuclear energy had built up to explosive proportions.

Plutonium nitrate solution is not difficult to convert to usable form. It is easier to make plutonium oxide from plutonium nitrate solution than it is to separate mixed oxides in order to reduce plutonium oxide to metal. A solution of sodium oxalate, a common chemical, added to plutonium nitrate solution, will form a precipitate of plutonium oxalate which is insoluble in water. The plutonium oxalate can be separated from the solution by simple filtration and then heated in an oven to form plutonium oxide powder. As long as the steps are carried out with small batches of plutonium—a few hundred grams at a time—there is no danger of accidentally forming a supercritical mass. The person performing these operations would, of course, have to take the precautions mentioned above in order to keep from getting significant internal doses of plutonium.

High-enriched Uranium

Natural uranium contains 99.3 percent uranium-238 and about 0.7 percent uranium-235. Uranium-238 cannot, by itself, sustain a fission chain reaction under any conditions. Nearly pure uranium-235 (more than 90 percent U-235), on the other hand, is very suitable for making fission explosives. A given number of critical masses of uranium-235 will explode with lower efficiency and, generally, a somewhat lower explosive yield than the same number of critical masses of plutonium-239.

The spherical critical mass of uranium-235 at normal density, which is close to twenty times the density of water, is between about eleven kilograms and twenty-five kilograms, depending on the type of neutron reflector that surrounds it. This is about three times the critical mass of alpha-phase plutonium-239. Without any reflector at all, the critical mass of uranium-235 is slightly more than fifty kilograms.

Unlike plutonium, uranium-235 is not particularly toxic. No radiation shielding or protective coverings are necessary to handle it safely in quantities less than a critical mass. Uranium-235 does not fission spontaneously at a significant rate, thus releasing neutrons that might prematurely initiate a nuclear chain reaction before a weapon assembly has become highly super-critical.* The critical mass of uranium-235 in the form of oxide (UO_2) or carbide (UC_2), which are forms used as fuel in some types of nuclear reactors, is about 50 percent greater than the critical mass of the metal. Either the oxide or the carbide can be used directly as the core material for a bomb. The steps required for converting uranium oxide to metal are similar to those for the conversion of plutonium oxide, except that the safety precautions are much less stringent. Generally speaking, uranium is easier to convert from one chemical or physical form to another than is plutonium.

Uranium-235 must be "enriched" above its concentration in natural uranium in order to make it usable as the core material in a fission bomb. The degree of enrichment required is difficult to define with any precision. Below an enrichment level of about 10 percent (i.e., the fraction of all uranium atoms that are uranium-235 in a mixture of U-235 and U-238 atoms is equal to 10 percent), uranium cannot be used to make a practical fission bomb, even though it can be used with a neutron moderator to sustain a "slow" fission chain in a reactor. This is basically for the same reasons that a solution of plutonium nitrate cannot be used to make a nuclear explosion.

At enrichment levels above 10 percent, the situation becomes complicated. The critical mass of metallic uranium at 10 percent enrichment, with a good neutron reflector, is about 1,000 kilograms, including 100 kilograms of contained uranium-235. Though very heavy, this would still be a sphere of only about a foot and a half in diameter. At 20 percent enrichment, the critical mass drops to 250 kilograms (fifty kilograms of contained uranium-235), and at 50 percent enrichment it is fifty kilograms, including twenty-five of uranium-235. At 100 percent enrichment, the critical mass of uranium-235 is about fifteen kilograms, and about the size of a softball.

*Uranium-238, however, does spontaneously fission at a rate that, though roughly 1,000 times slower than plutonium-240, can under some circumstances affect the course of a chain reaction in a fission bomb.

It is probable that some kind of fission explosive with a yield equivalent to at least a few tens of tons of high explosive could be made with metallic uranium at any enrichment level significantly above 10 percent, but the required amount of uranium-235 and the overall weight of the bomb is reduced dramatically as the enrichment is increased to about 50 percent. Since most nuclear power reactors use uranium fuel that is either enriched below 10 percent or above 90 percent, we are primarily concerned with uranium enriched above 90 percent. Unless otherwise noted, we use the term "low-enriched uranium" to mean uranium enriched above its natural concentration, but below 10 percent; "intermediate-enriched uranium" to mean uranium enriched between 10 percent and 90 percent; and "high-enriched uranium" to mean uranium enriched above 90 percent.

Natural or low-enriched uranium in the form of a gas, uranium hexafluoride (UF_6), can be further enriched in an isotope enrichment plant in order to obtain high-enriched uranium. After enrichment, the gas can be liquified under pressure for storage and shipment. Uranium hexafluoride is relatively easy to convert to uranium oxide or metal.

Two methods for enriching uranium that have been highly developed are gaseous diffusion and gas centrifugation. As far as we know, gaseous diffusion is the only method that has been used thus far for large scale separation of uranium isotopes. Many important details of the gaseous diffusion isotope separation process remain classified. It is well known, however, that it requires very large amounts of electric power (enough to meet the needs of a U.S. city with a population of several hundred thousand), and large capital investments (of the order of hundreds of millions of dollars, at least) in complex equipment and huge facilities.

As far as we have been able to determine, the performance characteristics of gas centrifuge techniques for uranium isotope separation have not been discussed in detail in the unclassified literature. It is generally claimed that the electric power and capital investments required for a gas centrifuge plant would be substantially lower than for a gaseous diffusion plant. But gas centrifuge systems are extremely complex. They require very many individual centrifuges which must be designed to exceedingly close physical tolerances.

A third method for uranium enrichment would make use of laser beams to stimulate atomic or molecular transitions in U-235 (but not in U-238). Laser techniques have recently received considerable attention, and may conceivably lead to large reductions in the cost and complexity of uranium isotope separation in the future. At the present time and for at least a few more years, however, isotope enrichment facilities for converting either natural or low-enriched uranium to high-enriched uranium will be extremely costly and complex, and probably beyond the reach of any but the highly industrialized nations.

High-enriched uranium hexafluoride is too dilute to use directly in any practical type of fission bomb. It is easier to convert the fluoride to uranium oxide than to metal, but both conversions could be carried out, conceivably in a clandestine laboratory, using chemicals and equipment that can easily be purchased commercially. High-enriched uranium hexafluoride is likely to be less attractive to a nuclear thief than the oxide or metal, but it is likely to be considerably more attractive than low-enriched or natural uranium.

Uranium-233

This isotope is produced in nuclear reactors that contain thorium. When a neutron is captured in thorium-232, the isotope of thorium that occurs in nature, it forms thorium-233. This radioactively decays, with a half-life of about twenty minutes, to protactinium-233, which subsequently also decays, with a half-life of about a month, to uranium-233. This isotope is relatively very stable, with a half-life of about 160,000 years. The critical mass of uranium-233 is only about 10 percent greater than the critical mass of plutonium, and its explosive efficiency, under comparable conditions, is about the same as plutonium. It is much less dangerous to work with than plutonium.

In ways that are analogous to the production of variant forms of plutonium in a uranium-fueled reactor, several other isotopes of uranium, besides uranium-233, are formed in a reactor that contains thorium. Some of these, such as uranium-234, act as a dilutant, thereby increasing the critical mass of uranium-233 about ten to twenty percent. None of these isotopes, however, fission spontaneously at a rate high enough to affect the course of a chain reaction during assembly of more than one critical mass in a fission bomb. In this respect, uranium-233 is similar to uranium-235.

One of the uranium isotopes formed in reactors that contain thorium is uranium-232. This decays through a rather complicated radioactive chain to form several isotopes that emit gamma rays, a particularly penetrating form of radiation. Uranium-232 is not separated from uranium-233 at a nuclear fuel reprocessing plant, the chemical properties of different isotopes of the same element being practically identical. Uranium-233, as used in the nuclear industry, will therefore contain enough uranium-232 (typically several hundred parts per million) to require concrete or other types of gamma ray shielding to protect workers in plants that routinely handle large quantities of the material. These gamma rays do not necessarily present a dangerous hazard to an illicit bomb maker who is working, without any shielding, close to kilogram quantities of uranium-233. However, the total time of direct, close-up exposure to the material must be limited to several dozen hours in order that the cumulative dose of gamma rays received amounts to no more than about a dozen chest x-rays. Although such exposure within a few months or less is considerably greater than that permitted workers at nuclear facilities, it might be of little concern to an illicit bomb maker.

Uranium-233 is much less dangerous to breathe or ingest than plutonium, but it is more dangerous in this respect than uranium-235. People working with unconfined uranium-233 could simply take the precaution of wearing masks designed to filter out small particles, and of making sure they do not work with the material when they have any open wounds. Alternatively, they could take the same precautions as those required for handling plutonium.

Since the chemistry and metallurgy of uranium-233 are practically identical to those of uranium-235, its conversion from one form to another requires the same processes. As is the case for plutonium or high-enriched uranium, the oxide or carbide forms of uranium-233 could be used as core material for fission bombs. Similarly, this would require about 50 percent more material, and produce a somewhat lower yield than if metal were used in the same type of bomb.

"Strategically Significant" Quantities of Fission Explosive Materials

Our discussion so far may have suggested to some readers that the minimum quantity of a fission explosive material required to make some kind of fission bomb, sometimes called the "strategically significant" quantity, is roughly equal to the spherical critical mass of that material, in metallic form, inside a good neutron reflector, or tamper. This is not the case. The amount required depends on the particular type of fission explosive in which it is used.

If the material is to be used in a gun-type of fission explosive, which becomes supercritical when more than one critical mass is assembled at normal density, the additional amount depends on the desired explosive yield. In his *Encyclopedia Americana* article, Foster states that a nuclear yield equivalent to several hundred tons of high explosive will be released if a mass of material equal to two critical masses is assembled and a neutron is injected to start the chain reaction. The actual yield depends on the particular characteristics of the masses and types of materials involved. On this basis one might argue that, to be on the safe side with regard to protecting nuclear materials from theft, the "strategically significant quantity" of a material should be its critical mass, as a sphere of the material in metallic form, inside a thick tamper of beryllium. We have chosen this arrangement because it corresponds to the lowest critical masses of fission explosive materials that are given in published reports. For plutonium, high-enriched uranium, and uranium-233 these masses are, respectively, about four, eleven, and four and one half kilograms.

If, on the other hand, the material is to be used in an implosion type of fission bomb, the amount required may be significantly lower than these quantities. Materials that are compressed above their normal densities have a lower critical mass than when they are uncompressed. In the special case when both the core and the reflector are compressed by the same factor, the critical mass is reduced by the square of that factor. Thus, when a spherical core and reflector assembly that is initially close to one critical mass is compressed to twice its initial density, it will correspond to about four critical masses. The dependence of the densities of heavy elements on their pressures and temperatures (their "equations of state"), and the pressures that can be achieved in various types of chemical explosive assemblies are described in unclassified publications. But this information alone does not tell one how high are the compressions that can actually be achieved in practical implosion systems. The reason is that the compressions achieved in an actual device depend, in detail, on how the device is designed. In particular, the compression achieved depends on how close the implosion is to being perfectly symmetrical.

Therefore, the minimum amount of fission explosive material required to make a reasonably powerful implosion type fission bomb depends on how much the bomb maker knows, on his ability to predict the detailed behavior of implosion systems during the implosion and the chain reacting phases, and on the skills, equipment, and facilities at his disposal for building the device.

One might argue that, to be on the safe side again, a strategically significant quantity of plutonium, high-enriched uranium, or uranium-233 should be defined as the smallest amount that could reasonably be expected to be used in a fission bomb designed by the best experts in nuclear explosive technology. Even if such quantities were defined, they would be highly classified. Nevertheless, the issue of what should be considered as a strategically significant quantity of fission explosive material for purposes of developing an effective system of safeguards against nuclear theft is one that recurs at various points throughout this study. Suffice it to say at this point that it is an important policy question for which there can be no purely technical answer.

SKILLS AND NON-NUCLEAR RESOURCES REQUIRED TO MAKE FISSION BOMBS

As a result of extensive reviews of publications that are available to the general public and that relate to the technology of nuclear explosives, unclassified conversations with many experts in nuclear physics and engineering, and a considerable amount of thought on the subject, we conclude:

Under conceivable circumstances, a few persons, possibly even one person working alone, who possessed about ten kilograms of plutonium oxide and a substantial amount of chemical high explosive could, within several weeks, design and build a crude fission bomb. By a "crude fission bomb" we mean one that would have an excellent chance of exploding, and would probably explode with the power of at least 100 tons of chemical high explosive. This could be done using materials and equipment that could be purchased at a hardware store and from commercial suppliers of scientific equipment for student laboratories.

The key persons or person would have to be reasonably inventive and adept at using laboratory equipment and tools of about the same complexity as those used by students in chemistry and physics laboratories and machine shops. They or he would have to be able to understand some of the essential concepts and procedures that are described in widely distributed technical publications concerning nuclear explosives, nuclear reactor technology, and chemical explosives, and would have to know where to find these publications. Whoever was principally involved would also have to be willing to take moderate risks of serious injury or death.

Statements similar to those made above about a plutonium oxide bomb could also be made about fission bombs made with high-enriched uranium or uranium-233. However, the ways these materials might be assembled in a fission bomb could differ in certain important respects.

We have reason to believe that many people, including some who have extensive knowledge of nuclear weapon technology, will strongly disagree with our conclusion. We also know that some experts will not. Why is this a subject of wide disagreement among experts? We suspect that at least part of the reason is that very few of the experts have actually spent much time pondering this question: "What is the easiest way I can think of to make a fission bomb, given enough fission explosive material to assemble more than one normal density critical mass?" The answer to this question may have little to do with the kinds of questions that nuclear weapon designers in the United States, the Soviet Union, the United Kingdom, France, or the People's Republic of China ask themselves when they are trying to devise a better nuclear weapon for military purposes. But the question is likely to be foremost in the mind of an illicit bomb maker.

Whatever opinions anyone may have about the likelihood that an individual or very small group of people would actually steal nuclear materials and use them to make fission bombs, those opinions should not be based on a presumption that all types of fission bombs are very difficult to make.

Effects of Nuclear Explosions

Even a "small" nuclear explosion could cause enormous havoc. A crude fission bomb, as we have described it, might yield as much as twenty kilotons of explosive power—the equal of the Nagasaki A-bomb. But even much less powerful devices, with yields ranging down to the equivalent of one ton of chemical high explosive, could cause terrible destruction.

A nuclear explosion would generally produce considerably more damage than a chemical explosion of the same yield. A nuclear explosion not only releases energy in the form of a blast wave and heat, but also large quantities of potentially lethal penetrating radiations (gamma rays and neutrons) and radioactive materials that may settle over a large area and thereafter lethally irradiate unsheltered people in the "fallout" area. The relative importance of these different forms and effects of nuclear energy in producing damage depends on the size of the explosion, the way the explosive is designed, and the characteristics of the target area. Radiation released within a minute after the explosion (so-called "prompt" radiation) tends to be more important in small explosions than large ones. The total amounts of prompt radiation released in two different nuclear explosions with the same overall explosive yield may differ, by a factor of ten or more, depending on how the bombs are designed. The relative importance of the effects of fallout, compared to other effects, depends on the local weather conditions, the nature of the immediate environment of the explosion, and the availability of shelter for people in the vicinity of the explosion. A nuclear explosion in the air generally produces less local fallout than a comparable explosion on the ground. The damage produced by the blast wave from an explosion also depends on the topography of the immediate surroundings, and on the structural characteristics of buildings in the target area.

We can illustrate such differences by a few examples. A nuclear explosion with a one-ton yield in the open in a sparsely populated area might produce slight damage. But the same explosion on a busy street might deliver a lethal dose of radiation to most of the occupants of buildings, as well as to people along the streets, within about 100 meters of the detonation. A nuclear explosion with a yield of ten tons in the central courtyard of a large office building might expose to lethal radiation as many as 1,000 people in the building. A comparable explosion in the center of a football stadium during a major game could lethally irradiate as many as 100,000 spectators. A nuclear explosion with a 100-ton yield in a typical suburban residential area might kill perhaps as many as 2,000 people, primarily by exposure to fallout. The same explosion in a parking lot beneath a very large skyscraper might kill as many as 50,000 people and destroy the entire building.

To give the reader some idea of the distances within which various types of damage might be produced by nuclear explosions of different yields, we have prepared the estimates presented in Table 1. These estimates are only rough approximations for the reasons given above.

Prompt radiation released during or very soon after the explosion can be in two forms, gamma rays and neutrons, both of which can easily penetrate at

Table 1. *Damage Radii for Various Effects of Nuclear Explosions as Functions of Yield*

| Yield (High explosive Equivalent) | 500 REM Prompt Gamma Radiation | 500 REM Neutrons | Radius for Indicated Effect (Meters) | | | | |
			Fallout (500 REM Total Dose)*	Severe Blast Damage (10 psi)	Moderate Blast Damage (3 psi)	Crater Radius (Surface Burst)	Crater Radius (Underground Burst)
1 ton	45	120	30-100	33	65	3.4	6.7
10 tons	100	230	100-300	71	140	6.8	13.3
100 tons	300	450	300-1,000	150	300	13.6	26.5
1 kiloton	680	730	1,000-3,000	330	650	27	53
10 kilotons	1,150	1,050	3,000-10,000	710	1,400	54	104
100 kilotons	1,600	1,450	10,000-30,000	1,500	3,000	108	208
1 megaton	2,400	2,000	30,000-100,000	3,250	6,500	216	416

*Assuming one-hour exposure to fallout-region, for yields less than 1 kiloton, increasing to twelve hours for 1 megaton.

least several inches of most materials. Gamma ray and neutron dose levels can be stated in terms of the REM, which is related to the Roentgen, a unit often used for measuring x-ray dosages. A radiation exposure of about five hundred REM of either gamma rays or neutrons absorbed over a person's entire body (a so-called "whole body" dose) would kill half the people so exposed within a few weeks or less. A radiation dose of about 1,000 REM would kill almost all the people exposed. The prompt radiation is released so rapidly that there would not be time for people in the vicinity of the explosion to take cover in shelters or behind buildings.

Delayed radiation from the fallout of a nuclear explosion could deliver lethal doses to people who remain in the open where radioactive debris has settled long enough for them to receive a total dose of roughly 500 REM. The ranges of distances indicated in Table 1 for radioactive fallout are based on the assumptions that the wind velocity in the area is about five miles per hour, and that exposed people remain within the area for one hour, for yields less than one kiloton, increasing to twelve hours for a yield of one megaton. These distances are the most uncertain of any shown in the table, since they depend strongly on the local weather conditions, the amount and characteristics of the surface material that would be picked up in an explosion's fireball and later deposited on the ground, the extent to which people would be able to take cover or leave the area quickly after an explosion, and many other factors.

The distances indicated in Table 1 for severe and moderate blast damage and cratering are considerably more predictable than the distances for severe damage by radiation. A peak overpressure of ten pounds per square inch would be likely to cause very severe damage to almost all residential and office buildings, and moderate damage to heavily reinforced concrete buildings. Three pounds per square inch would cause severe damage to wood frame residential buildings.

To summarize, the human casualties and property damage that could be caused by nuclear explosions vary widely for different types of explosions detonated in different places. Nevertheless, it is clear that under a variety of circumstances, even a nuclear explosion one hundred times smaller than the one that destroyed Hiroshima could have a terrible impact on society.

Radiological Weapons

PLUTONIUM DISPERSAL DEVICES

We have already stated that plutonium, in the form of extremely small particles suspended in air, is exceedingly toxic. The total weight of plutonium-239 which, if inhaled, would be very likely to cause death by lung cancer is not well known, but is probably between ten and 100 micrograms (millionths of a gram). Even lower internal doses, perhaps below one microgram, might cause significant shortening of a person's life. The total retained dose of plutonium that would be likely to cause death from fibrosis of the lung within a few days is about a dozen milligrams (thousandths of a gram). All these estimates, particularly those related to shortening of life from lung cancer, are uncertain, partly because the responses of different individuals to the same doses of plutonium are likely to vary considerably. For purposes of this discussion, particularly for comparisons with other toxic substances, we assume that fifty micrograms of plutonium-239 represent a "lethal" dose, i.e., the amount that would be very likely to cause eventual death if it were internally absorbed.

In terms of the total weight of material that represents a lethal dose, plutonium-239 is at least 20,000 times more toxic than cobra venom or potassium cyanide, and 1,000 times more toxic than heroin or modern nerve gases. It is probably less toxic, in these same terms, than the toxins of some especially virulent biological organisms, such as anthrax germs.

The amounts of plutonium that could pose a threat to society are accordingly very small. One hundred grams (three and one half ounces) of this material could be a deadly risk to everyone working in a large office building or factory, if it were effectively dispersed. In open air, the effects would be more diluted by wind and weather, but they would still be serious and long-lasting.

The quantities of plutonium that might produce severe hazards in large areas are summarized in the very crude estimates presented in Table 2. To estimate the areas within which people might be exposed to lethal doses inside a building, we assume that dispersed plutonium is primarily plutonium-239 in the form of an aerosol of finely divided particles distributed uniformly in air throughout the building. We also assume that exposure of people to the contaminated air is for one hour, that ten percent of the inhaled particles are retained in their lungs, and that, as stated earlier, the lethal retained dose of plutonium is fifty micrograms. These conditions might be achieved by carefully introducing the plutonium aerosol into the

Table 2. Lethal and Significant Contamination Areas for Release of Air Suspensions of Plutonium Inside Buildings

Amount of Plutonium Released	Inhalation Lethal Dose of Suspended Material (area in square meters)	Significant Contamination Requiring Some Evacuation and Cleanup (area in square meters)
1 gram	~500	~50,000
100 grams	~50,000	~5,000,000

intake of a building's air conditioning system. This might be quite difficult to do in many cases.

An area of 500 square meters (about 5,000 square feet) corresponds to the area of one floor of many typical office buildings. An area of 50,000 square meters (about 500,000 square feet) is comparable to the entire floor area of a large skyscraper. Even a few grams of dispersed plutonium could pose a serious danger to the occupants of a rather large office building or enclosed industrial facility.

The areas in which plutonium contamination would be significant enough to require evacuation and subsequent decontamination are roughly estimated to be about 100 times the areas subjected to a lethal dose. About a dozen grams of plutonium dispersed throughout the largest enclosed building in the world might make the entire building unusable for the many weeks that would be required to complete costly decontamination operations.

The dispersal in large open areas of plutonium with lethal concentrations of radioactivity is likely to be much more difficult to carry out effectively than dispersal indoors. The height of the affected zone would be difficult to hold down to a few feet. Even a very gentle, two-mile-per-hour breeze would disperse the suspended material several kilometers downwind in an hour. This would make it extremely difficult to use less than about one kilogram of plutonium to produce *severe* radiation hazards. With a few dozens of grams of plutonium, however, it would be relatively easy to contaminate several square kilometers sufficiently to require the evacuation of people in the area and necessitate a very difficult and expensive decontamination operation.

After the plutonium-bearing particles settled in an area, they would remain a potential hazard until they were leached below the surface of the ground or were carried off by wind or surface water drainage. As long as the particles remained on the surface, something might happen to draw them back into the air. Contamination levels of about a microgram of plutonium per square meter would be likely to be deemed unacceptable for public health. Thus, in an urban area with little rainfall, a few grams of plutonium optimally dispersed out of doors might seriously contaminate a few square kilometers, but only over a very much smaller area would it pose a lethal threat.

So far in our discussion, we have considered only plutonium-239, the isotope of plutonium that is produced in the largest quantities in nuclear reactors. Plutonium-238, which is also made in significant quantities in some reactors, is considerably more toxic than plutonium-239. Its half-life for emitting alpha particles is only about eighty-seven years, instead of about 25,000 years; one gram of plutonium-238 therefore emits alpha particles at approximately 300 times the rate that plutonium-239 does. As a result, the lethal dose of plutonium-238 is about 1/300 of what it is for plutonium-239. We mention this because plutonium-238 has been used in radioisotope-powered nuclear "batteries," and is being seriously considered for use in power supplies for heart pumps in people suffering from certain types of heart disorders. As much as sixty grams of plutonium-238, the equivalent in toxicity of almost twenty *kilograms* of plutonium-239, may be in each such heart-pump battery. This is enough material to produce serious contamination of hundreds of square miles, if dispersed in the form of small particles.

A variety of ways to disperse plutonium with timed devices are conceivable. These would allow the threatener to leave the area before the material is dispersed. Any plutonium contained inside such a device would not be a hazard until it was released.

People who absorb lethal but not massive doses of plutonium would not sense any of its effects for weeks, or perhaps years. The presence of finely divided plutonium in an area could be detected only with sensitive radiation monitoring equipment. Such equipment is now only used to monitor the presence of plutonium or other dangerously radioactive materials in nuclear installations. Except in such installations, therefore, people would not know they were exposed until they were told, either by those responsible for the threat, or by someone in authority who happened to detect the plutonium with instruments.

We are not aware of any successful non-military attempts to use chemical, bacteriological, or radiological poisons to contaminate large areas. Whether any such means will be used in the future for criminal or terrorist purposes is, we believe, an even more speculative question than whether nuclear explosives will be so used. Many types of potentially lethal poisons are no more difficult to acquire than chemical high explosives. However, high explosives are being used with greater frequency and in increasing amounts by terrorists and extortionists, while we have found no evidence that they have ever used poisonous agents. The practically instantaneous, quite obvious destruction that is produced by an explosion apparently better suits the purposes of terrorists and extortionists than poisons that act more slowly and subtly, but that are at least as deadly. Unlike other poisons, however, plutonium can be used either as a poison or as explosive material. Accordingly, a threat using a plutonium dispersal device could conceivably be followed by a threat involving plutonium used in a nuclear explosive.

OTHER TYPES OF RADIOLOGICAL WEAPONS

As part of our research for this study, we considered, in some detail, the effects that might be produced by dispersing radioactive materials other than plutonium, or by purposely pulsing various types of unshielded nuclear reactors to destruction without achieving a real nuclear explosion. We conclude that neither type of weapon would be as effective as a plutonium dispersal device or a low-yield fission bomb.

Spent nuclear reactor fuel and the fission products separated from reactor fuels at a chemical reprocessing plant are, potentially, extremely hazardous if dispersed in a populated area. But they would also be very dangerous to handle in sufficient quantities to pose a threat to a large area because they emit highly penetrating gamma rays, thus requiring heavy shielding to protect thieves or weapon makers. In short, plutonium would be easier to use for destructive purposes than radioactive fission products.

If a nuclear reactor core were pulsed to destruction, it would release a comparatively small amount of energy equivalent to, at most, a few hundred pounds of high explosive from a device weighing several tons. It would also release amounts of radiation and radioactive materials that would be very small compared to a low-yield nuclear explosion unless the reactor had been operated at high power levels for some time before use as a weapon. Under such conditions, it would have to be transported in heavy shielding and would pose even greater handling problems than stolen spent nuclear reactor fuel. Generally speaking, therefore, it would be easier to make and use a fission bomb than to make and pulse a nuclear reactor core in a way that would produce damage on the scale of a fission bomb.

Pure Fusion Explosives

A pure fusion explosive would be a device that would not require any fission "trigger" to initiate explosive thermonuclear (fusion) reactions in very light hydrogen isotopes such as deuterium and tritium. There is considerable discussion in the unclassified literature concerning the possibility of developing this type of explosive. No successful development has yet been announced, and we have no reason to believe it has taken place.

Recent papers suggest that it may be possible to use intense laser pulses to implode small "pellets" of deuterium and tritium (and possibly pure deuterium) in such a way as to cause the pellets to explode. The concept is described in the context of its possible use for the generation of electric power. Very small thermonuclear explosions would be confined, possibly with magnetic fields, and the explosion energy would be extracted to produce electricity.

Intensive research and development on such systems is under way in AEC laboratories and at least one industrial laboratory. Some people working on laser-induced fusion suggest that the scientific feasibility of the concept may be successfully demonstrated within a year or two. There is considerable controversy, however, about when the practicality of laser-induced fusion may be demonstrated. Whether or not laser-triggered fusion could be developed into practical and transportable nuclear explosives with yields equivalent to or greater than tons of chemical high explosives is not revealed in the unclassified literature, and the answer may well be unknown.

In any case, we do not believe that pure fusion explosives could be made clandestinely in the foreseeable future without highly sophisticated equipment and exceptionally highly skilled and experienced specialists.

Notes

1. John S. Foster, "Nuclear Weapons," Encyclopedia Americana, Volume 20, pp. 520-522, Americana Corporation, New York, 1973. Reprinted with permission of the Encyclopedia Americana, copyright 1973, The Americana Corporation.

Lloyd Norman

Our Nuclear Weapons Sites: Next Target of Terrorists?

One of the oft-discussed routes to nuclear weapons status by terrorists is the theft of an intact device. In this informative and informed article, Norman draws extensively from an interview with the Defense Department official charged with the security of nuclear weapons sites. Security procedures are outlined, as are the safety devices that preclude unauthorized use of nuclear weapons. It is conceded that a highly skilled perpetrator might be able to disassemble and reconstruct even a weapon equipped with security devices, thus pointing up the key importance of site security. Fortunately congressional and public interest has spawned significant improvements in the security of nuclear weapons.

With the threat of nuclear blackmail by international terrorists now a real possibility, the U.S. Defense Department is taking steps to beef up security at the some 1,500 nuclear weapons-storage sites it maintains around the world. Especially vulnerable, either to a terrorist grab or to enemy ground attacks, are the more than 100 such sites in NATO Europe—where the United States keeps about 7,000 tactical weapons—and those in South Korea, where about 1,000 warheads are reportedly stored.

If even one small nuclear weapon from this stockpile, each with an explosive yield of one kiloton (equivalent to 1,000 tons of TNT), fell into the hands of a terrorist group or a criminal mob, the world would quake as hostage under the threat of nuclear murder.

"We are living in probably the wildest period in history when we have to be prepared for the one-in-a-million possibility that a zealot or someone with a deranged mind could get hold of an atomic bomb from somebody's stockpile or from a weapon in the field or while it was being transported," said Joseph J. Liebling, deputy assistant secretary of defense for security policy. He is an internationally known expert on military security matters and strategic technology trade control.

"Safeguarding our nuclear weapons against theft or assault is getting high priority these days because of the possible threat," Mr. Liebling said. "The

Defense Department in fiscal 1978 is planning to add 20,000 more troops to improve the security of nuclear weapons-storage sites and about $400 million is being spent on anti-intrusion sensors, warning systems and hardening the sites.

"We are moving the quick response troops to hardened control centers on the sites so they can react fast to warning from a security patrol or the sensors."

The storage sites are usually concrete-and-steel underground "igloos" surrounded by double anchor-chain fences with sophisticated sensors (IDS, or intrusion-detection systems) which react to noise, magnetism, movement or seismic effect (earth tremor). The igloos are flood lighted at night and constantly guarded. Besides the guards at each site there are "reaction" or alert forces in nearby hardened buildings ready to defend the site when the alarm sounds.

The troops guarding the sites are called "dedicated"; they are specially selected for the assignment and they have to pass tough physical and mental reliability tests.

"We have to operate under the assumption that there could be an attempt made to penetrate a nuclear weapons site by terrorists or criminals," said Mr. Liebling. "Thus far we have not been able to identify or trace any attempts to break into a site to terrorists or criminals. Some attempts have been made to climb a fence or to cut a fence, but the possible intruders were frightened away. They may have been pranksters or people bent on some mischief, but they were not determined or sophisticated enough to go through with the attempted break-ins."

Mr. Liebling said that terrorists who want world attention and who are driven by some political cause would be most likely to plot the capture of atomic bombs. He suggested that they might employ criminals in their operations, but ordinary professional criminals probably would not take the risks of nuclear theft.

"The threat from terrorists is very significant," he said. "They have taken hostages, they have hijacked airplanes to propagandize their cause and now, with sophistication of terrorists far greater than ever, they may go for an atomic bomb.

"They have some highly trained people. These are fanatics motivated by an ideology. Their objective is to gain world attention for their cause, and what's more significant or terrifying than a nuclear weapon? It is frightening to contemplate what leverage they would have against a government by threatening catastrophic devastation.

"Thus far, there has been no incident of any penetration or attempt to enter a nuclear site to obtain weapons by any specific terrorist organization."

Secretary Liebling said he could not discuss intelligence studies that might identify terrorist groups who might make such an attempt. His refusal may have been prompted by the reluctance of intelligence agencies to disclose whether they are maintaining surveillance over political extremists.

"Modern technology has added to the sophistication of the terrorists' methods and techniques," Mr. Liebling said in a recent talk. "Weapons like the small, man-portable missile, the Russian SA-7 or the Redeye [infrared antiaircraft missile], which are particularly dangerous in the hands of terrorists, could be available through the black market or irresponsible governments.

"It is perhaps inevitable that more of these [types of] weapons will fall into the hands of terrorists. It has added to our vulnerability by providing the terrorists with targets of increasing attractiveness, and an assault upon them will draw the attention of the press, will embarrass the government, will be used for blackmail and will wreak havoc with the populace.

"I have in mind nuclear installations, public utilities and refineries, uranium enrichment plants, chemical plants, for example, as well as facilities and installations in support of national defense. Terrorist attacks on such facilities would be chaotic. With horrifying regularity these people who are desperate in their political aims are escalating to find the world stage they need to champion their cause."

So far, added Mr. Liebling, terrorists have taken the path of least resistance and gone after fairly easy targets like airliners, trains, people and buildings.

"These reckless people, because of their desire for world attention, may at any time decide to attempt an incident that could severely affect the national security of the United States," he said.

The secretary said that in response to this possible threat the U.S. government has launched "a massive program involving technology and research to adopt standardized sensors and intrusion-detection devices." Studies are being made of fencing, lighting, sensors using sound, magnetism, pressure, television and seismic devices for detecting intruders. The nuclear sites are protected by standard nine-gauge, two-inch-square chain-link fences with underground braces and a barbed-wire Y at the top. Cutting the wire or digging under it sets off an alarm.

The double-perimeter fence is monitored in some places by guards in a tower and by a control center that watches the detection systems. These patrols are augmented by the quick-response forces: specially trained military police or security troops who have passed emotional stability and reliability tests as well as the usual physical and mental tests. Secretary Liebling said they are given special instruction in guarding nuclear weapons sites.

The quick-response troops are equipped with armor vests, M16 rifles, M60 machine guns and M79 grenade launchers. They can be rushed to the atomic weapons "igloos" by jeep or helicopter if the site of the penetration is some miles from the control center. These ready troops can be augmented, if necessary, by combat forces from nearby military posts.

"In one drill the local command deployed a battalion of troops by helicopter in a matter of minutes," Mr. Liebling recalled.

As chairman of the Defense Department's physical-security review board, which sets uniform policy and standards for safeguarding military installations, Mr. Liebling said the board found that "our security concept for the protection of nuclear weapons required updating and that standardized safeguard criteria were necessary."

Concepts of the 1960s and earlier were "man-oriented," he said, depending upon sentries in the protected area to detect intruders. Intrusion-detection devices were used to determine attempted penetrations into storage areas. The studies showed that a more effective system would emphasize electronic equipment to alert the system to an attempted intrusion, with the manpower being used primarily for response forces.

The detection devices would be posted around the perimeter to give early warning. Security troops would be dispatched quickly from the control center that monitors the television and other detectors. Guards who were used previously to patrol the fences are now assigned to the tactical-response forces that can be deployed with a heavier concentration of firepower in the area under attack. Armed roving patrols augment the detection system.

Aside from terrorists and criminals, Secretary Liebling was asked, what security measures are available to guard nuclear weapons overseas from a takeover by the host government or by a revolutionary force that overthrows the government? Or, what happens if communist forces roll over an area that has U.S. nuclear weapons-storage sites?

For these worst-case situations, chairman Liebling said cryptically, "We have contingency plans, but those are not my responsibility. We are concerned with safeguards against theft, unauthorized access, or attempts to damage or destroy nuclear weapons by criminals or terrorists or some irrational person. A large-scale military attack is a separate problem."

A nuclear weapons expert said that "in an extreme situation we have contingency plans that provide for destruction of the weapons if they are in imminent danger of capture. We have the materials and procedures for destruction."

Defense Department directive No. 3224.3, on physical security equipment research, refers to "anticompromise emergency destruct (ACED) as a means which will prevent the recovery of national security information and material under emergency or no-notice conditions. With due regard for personnel and structural safety, the ACED system shall reach a stage in destruction sequences at which positive destruction is irreversible within 60 minutes at shore installations, 30 minutes in ships, and three minutes in aircraft, following a decision to destruct."

That's the last resort, for example, were an ally to suddenly turn on us and try to grab our nuclear weapons.

The nuclear weapons expert, asked if a terrorist could use a readymade captured or stolen atomic bomb, said, "It depends on whether it is an old-type weapon or a new one. The old ones might be taken apart by someone with expertise and he might be able to separate the pieces and reconstruct them. He could not detonate the bomb itself, however, because he would have to know the precise voltages and the necessary settings for that bomb.

"If he broke into a nuclear weapons igloo he might be confronted by various packing cases and he would have to assemble the components. The weapons are constructed in such a way that they contain internal safeguards against unauthorized use or misuse. It takes two people with the proper instruction to arm the weapon.

"The newer nuclear weapons are more sophisticated. They are controlled by a so-called PAL—permissive-action link. If certain actions are not taken in the proper sequence, the link won't be closed and the bomb won't work. Some weapons have numbered dials like a safe and two men have to set the dials correctly before the weapon is armed.

"Without the permissive-action link the bomb is a dud. It won't explode with nuclear force. You might set off an explosion of the chemical explosives, but that would not trigger an atomic explosion. It requires very exact timing of the explosion to get the critical mass for nuclear fission."

A sophisticated terrorist organization with competent engineers might be able to dismantle a stolen atomic bomb and rebuild it and possibly make it work, but the odds appear to be against that happening.

If the ready-made bomb is relatively new—fabricated in the late 1960s or later—it probably has the coded permissive-action link, one of the requirements ordered by President John F. Kennedy. The terrorists would have to obtain the ultra-secret codes to make the bomb go. And that would be highly unlikely unless they had some insiders to help.

The possibility of an insider in a nuclear weapons area being involved with a terrorist or criminal group cannot be discounted, but defense officials said measures have been tightened to "screen out" people who might be unreliable. The "human reliability" program was designed to do this, and so far, officials said, "There has been no lapse that has exposed any weapons to unauthorized use."

As an example of the screening-process results, the former Joint Atomic Energy Committee of Congress in 1975 disclosed that the U.S. Army in Europe, from April, 1972, to March, 1973, disqualified 213 enlisted soldiers (no officers) out of some 14,000 persons involved in handling nuclear weapons (which included 2,450 officers, 11,520 enlisted soldiers and 36 American civilians).

Of the 213 dropped by the reliability tests, 83 were for drug abuse, 18 for alcohol abuse, 52 for undesirable performance of duty, 26 for disciplinary problems, 12 for mental disorders and 22 for character traits (indebtedness, dishonesty or improper conduct).

The U.S. Air Force, from July through 31 December, 1972, disqualified one officer and 134 airmen out of 9,140 persons in the nuclear weapons program in Europe (including 1,470 officers and 7,670 airmen). Of those disqualified, 28 airmen were dropped for drug abuse; the others were rejected generally for medical or psychiatric reasons or both, the Air Force told the joint committee.

The U.S. Navy command in Europe told the committee that in 1972 four sailors were disqualified for nuclear weapons duty—two for "personal beliefs," one for drug abuse and one for disciplinary reasons.

The rejection of "unreliable" GIs for the nuclear weapons program was prompted by fears that troops involved in drugs, heavy indebtedness or other improper conduct would be vulnerable to blackmail or bribery by foreign agents trying to gain access to nuclear weapons.

Four years ago, Sen. John O. Pastore (D-R.I.), who retired last year, and Sen. Howard H. Baker (R-Tenn.) visited "special ammunition sites" (atomic weapons storage) in Europe because they were concerned. Sen. Baker said later "that nuclear weapons in NATO were vulnerable to terrorist attack and that some of these weapons were located in areas where they were susceptible to being overrun in the event of surprise attack." Their report, censored for security, was made public in April, 1975.

Senators Baker and Pastore urged at the time that the number of storage sites (described generally as more than 100) in Europe be reduced and security tightened at those remaining. The Defense Department told the senators in April, 1975, that 20 percent of the nuclear weapons sites had been closed during the two years since 1973 and that another ten to 15 percent would be closed by 1976.

Sen. Pastore in his 1975 statement said that the "Defense Department has taken steps to improve the security and protection of nuclear weapons in NATO" in the two years after their inspection in 1973. He said, however, that despite "considerable improvements" more needed to be done and he recommended that even more sites be closed and that the number of weapons in Europe be reduced, especially where their usefulness "is highly questionable."

He noted that some nuclear weapons for 155-mm and eight-inch guns were stored near the forward defense line only about ten miles away from Soviet or Warsaw Pact troops who might overrun them. He also observed that "nuclear weapons sites appeared to be vulnerable to terrorist attacks; that certain nuclear weapons sites appeared to be particularly vulnerable to surprise attack by communist forces, and that certain nuclear weapons might not be usable in the event of war."

The senators, in their comment, said that "today a new threat has emerged. In recent years, terrorism has become a means to achieve political ends." Their survey showed that "meticulous checking" of visitors to nuclear weapons sites would detect impostors but would be useless against terrorists who would try to shoot their way into a site.

The senators recalled that at one site (not identified for security reasons) the nuclear weapons were stored in the basement of a building with offices not guarded by a double-perimeter fence. A guard had been assigned to the entrance ramp to the basement only on the very day the senators visited the area. On an earlier visit, in November, 1972, the steel door to the basement was open and "it appeared that terrorists could probably at least reach the basement door without detection."

Emergency-destruction demolitions for that site were located about a 25-mile round trip from the barracks building where the nuclear weapons were stored. If the nuclear weapons had to be destroyed before they fell into hostile hands, it might take as long as an hour to deliver the explosives needed to destroy them.

In another instance, the senators learned that nuclear weapons for quick-reaction-alert fighter-bombers had to be moved on a public road about 300 yards, exposing them to possible capture. They also noted that the nuclear sites are easily identified because of the spotlights that are kept burning all night. They said that local newspapers and a communist magazine had identified the locations of some of the sites.

The senators noted that suspected intruders had been fired upon at two weapons sites but that none had been apprehended. They suggested that these suspects were probably trying to "case" the weapons areas.

Pentagon officials said more determined and organized terrorist efforts to steal a ready-made nuclear weapon cannot be ruled out. But they said safeguards at nuclear storage sites in Europe and elsewhere have been tightened substantially since the congressional inspections four years ago.

"With the improvements now under way the security at the sites should deter virtually any break-in attempt," one official said.

Bruce G. Blair and
Garry D. Brewer

The Terrorist Threat to World Nuclear Programs

The key contention of this controversial chapter is that the attraction that has been focused upon the terrorist threat to commercial nuclear facilities has obscured the serious vulnerability of nuclear weapons in the hands of the military and particularly the possibility that terrorists (or others) might seize or gain control of a Minuteman ICBM *(intercontinental ballistic missile). Blair and Brewer argue that these vulnerabilities result from a number of loopholes in site and technical security procedures, thus raising even the awesome specter of the unauthorized launch of a nuclear-tipped missile. They conclude with a number of recommendations, which they argue would reduce the vulnerability of the Minuteman and other nuclear-weapons systems.*

The Setting

In this decade, terrorism has grown from an esoteric aspect of aggression and violence to a predominant means for international and intranational conflict resolution.[1] It appears likely that as the smaller nations and weaker specialized interest groups of the world acquire the technology of modern war, both conventional and nuclear, they will increasingly turn to terrorism—just as the Palestine Liberation Army has done in the Middle East, as the Irgun and Stern Gang previously did against the British Empire, as guerrilla groups in various Latin American countries do, and as the nineteenth-century eastern European revolutionaries did in order to bring down autocratic governments.

It is ironic that terrorist groups have been among the first to recognize that we live together in a planetary community, rather than a conglomerate of national communities. The nearly threefold increase in the number of nations that have come into being since World War II makes this appear to be the most nationalistic of times. However, most of the newer nations are caricatures, the products of historical accidents rooted in the imperialism of the last three centuries. These new nations often have little in common, and many have no viable resources.

Nationalism was perhaps the main social, political, and historical focus of the nineteenth century, but in the twentieth century we have become one planet. The consumption of irreplaceable elements by a relative handful of the human race affects the lives of all members of the race, as it always has; however, now the relationship is known and often felt strongly. Couple this realization with the knowledge that the great powers have within their power the ability to destroy both opponents of the moment and probably all of human society and one comes quickly to the few alternatives that exist to resolve conflict.

A main alternative is terrorism. Formerly, terrorism was the prerogative of the powerless; it was a technique whereby a few determined men and women could affect the destinies of large empires. This has changed. Now we see examples of the technique being used by virtually all elements of society.

Terrorism, in this global setting, has become a predominant form of confrontation between differing subcategories of societies which seek to overcome each other, regardless of size.

This essay concentrates on nuclear terrorism throughout the world—a form of terrorism potentially so devastating that it must be considered meticulously. Even though many might treat it as a very low probability event, the margin for error is thin.

Problem Dimensions

Borrowing from Willrich (1975: 12), terrorism is defined as "threats or acts of violence planned, attempted, or carried out by an individual or group with a specific political intent in mind." In the case of international terrorism, the definition is modified; such acts must fall "outside the accepted norms of international diplomacy and rules of war" (Jenkins, 1975: 11).

This definition is broadly construed, and it includes the covert orchestration of surrogate warfare by nations. In other words, terrorism may be conducted by individuals or groups acting solely on their own accord to achieve self-determined political objectives; terrorism may be secretly sponsored by other groups, organizations, or nations; or terrorism may be jointly undertaken by several parties pursuing overlapping objectives. Later implications of nation-state-inspired and -financed terrorism, an important but neglected dimension of the terrorist threat, are outlined.

Of the various forms that nuclear terrorism could take in the future, governmental policy and research have focused almost exclusively on the problem of terrorists manufacturing nuclear weapons from stolen fissionable materials. There are understandable reasons why this definition of the terrorist problem has evolved.

So stated, however, the terrorist problem is narrowly misspecified. The central objective of a safeguards policy should not be solely to prevent the illicit manufacture of nuclear bombs. Rather, it should aim at preventing terrorists from acquiring a real or apparent nuclear weapon *capability*.

This improved specification enables us to identify several sorely deficient aspects of present safeguards policy and research. In particular, only modest policy attention and no publicly available research address the prospect of terrorists stealing assembled nuclear weapons from military regimes. Also, the public record suggests that virtually no consideration has been given to the possibility of unauthorized individuals acquiring an apparent or real capability to detonate nuclear weapons at their storage location, to arm and launch tactical or strategic nuclear weapons, or to direct armed forces personnel to execute nuclear strikes against other nations. (Our concern extends to all nuclear powers, not just the United States.)

The possibility of any of these events has seldom been raised. Only a handful of skeptics has questioned the adequacy of military nuclear safeguards, and seldom has any hard evidence been advanced in their support.[2] Krieger (1975: 28) expounds the prevailing view:

> stealing an assembled nuclear weapon from a nuclear weapon
> nation would be the most difficult and the least likely route for
> terrorists to achieve a nuclear weapon capability. . . . Additionally,
> there are reportedly sophisticated lock systems on the weapons
> themselves to prevent military weapons from being utilized by
> other than authorized personnel.

The view that military nuclear weapons are today immune from theft or misuse contrasts sharply with views held, at least in the United States, in the 1950s and early 1960s. The security and safety of nuclear weapons were controversial issues during that period, although earlier debate centered on the question whether safeguards were adequate to prevent the accidental or unauthorized use of nuclear weapons by armed forces personnel rather than nongovernmental terrorists. Such concern all but disappeared by the mid-1960s, and attention shifted to the development of safeguards for commercial nuclear power plants in the United States. Several factors contributed to this reorientation.

First, policy makers and the public received repeated assurances from military quarters that highly reliable weapons safeguards had been implemented—measures that in fact were so reliable and effective as to be "fail-safe."[3] Defense Department officials maintained that the chances of a U.S. nuclear weapon exploding were "so remote as to be negligible (Phelps, 1961). The development of supposedly "fail-safe" designs doubtless bolstered the public credibility of the military's risk assessment, but confirmation came from other observers as well. After completing a comprehensive study of military safeguards, Larus (1967: 42) was able to report:

> Today there is only a very slim possibility that a faulty com-
> munications signal, a mentally deranged airman, or any other
> mishap could trigger a Russo-American nuclear exchange.

Simultaneously, the issue lost much public visibility as Soviet allegations that U.S. military practices risked a major nuclear accident or provocation abated.

Second, a series of dramatic events shaped the reorientation. An incident that attracted great attention, and which resulted in an abrupt awakening among policy makers to the threat of nuclear theft, was the loss in 1965 of over 200 pounds of weapons-grade materials from a Pennsylvania Atomic Energy Commission (AEC) fuel fabrication plant.[4] As a direct result of this discovery, a new AEC Office of Safeguards and Materials Management was established in 1967 and was charged with responsibility for formulating nuclear industry safeguards policy. In addition, the event led to the creation of an independent study group to assess the vulnerability of power facilities to acts of sabotage. The panel's 1967 report was the first serious consideration that terrorists might attempt to steal fissionable materials from nuclear facilities and marked the beginning of systematic research devoted to investigating terrorist threats to nonmilitary nuclear programs.

The literature since 1967 is not voluminuous, but several excellent studies exist. Unfortunately, the important but rather narrow range of issues on which these studies focus has helped foster the belief that theft of raw fissionable materials is *the* nuclear threat posed by terrorism.[5]

A third influence contributing to the shift in U.S. safeguards policy was, and is, the rapid proliferation of nuclear technology. In 1965, the nuclear power industry was nascent.[6] Today there are scores of nuclear plants in operation in the United States alone, and several hundred are planned or under construction (Gapay, 1975). As of December 1976, 229 reactors were operational or under construction outside the United States, and 240 more were planned or on order (Walske, 1977). The diffusion of nuclear technology throughout the world is accelerating, with the result that industrial safeguards are absorbing most of the public and official attention and resources.

The changing nature of nuclear technology is arousing even greater fears. If the new generation of fast breeder reactors becomes operational, the number of plutonium shipments between processing plants and reactors will increase dramatically, vastly complicating the task of transport security, which is already considered the weakest link in the present safeguards systems. According to one projection, assuming fast breeder reactors become a commercial reality, the amount of nuclear material in international transit each year will be enough to make 20,000 nuclear bombs (Gapay, 1975).

Finally, the upsurge in worldwide terrorism during the past decade affects perceptions of the threat of nuclear terror. More than the absolute level of terrorist incidents, the historical trend and the realization that terrorism is unchecked are alarming. A recent study made for the Energy Research and Development Administration (ERDA) found a sevenfold increase in terrorist incidents between 1969-1973 over the previous 1964-1968 period (HERO, 1974). A recent downturn in this trend is heartening, but one cannot feel comfortable about a situation in which the ebb and flow of terrorist activity have less to do with governmental control than with the self-restraint exercised by terrorists themselves.

Contrary to popular belief, terrorism is not confined mainly to Middle Eastern and Latin American settings. Indeed, according to ongoing work by Mickolus (1976), the Atlantic community has experienced more terrorism in terms of both incident location and nationality of victims than any other region of the world. Latin America is second, followed by the Middle East, Asia, Africa, and Eastern Europe. Although differing operational definitions of terrorism produce different results, the message is clear. Terrorism is an international phenomenon that has eluded effective governmental control.

Security problems posed by a burgeoning nuclear power industry are cause for genuine societal concern. However, as policy makers intensify the search for solutions with a view to shaping safeguards policy around a single prospect—terrorist theft of fissionable materials and construction of home-made nuclear devices—concern for safeguarding a large and ever-growing stockpile of the world's nuclear weapons continues to fade.[7] In our view, a thorough reexamination of the security of those weapons is long overdue.[8]

This recommendation stems in part from an evaluation we made of the technical and procedural safeguards for what may be the Western world's most well-protected nuclear weapons program—the Minuteman Intercontinental Ballistic Missile (ICBM) force in the United States. After presenting a brief overview of the Minuteman security program, major findings are summarized, and several recommendations are advanced. These findings are based on conditions which existed in the very recent past and which have recently undergone review by the U.S. Air Force and the Department of Defense. We have been apprised that appropriate action has been taken to correct any safeguards weaknesses. Although it is our position that general assertions of safeguards effectiveness are not sufficient, and that the burden of proof must be on those who assert the adequacy of remedial steps, the reader is cautioned against drawing specific inferences about the present situation from the evidence presented. In developing a case which underscores the need for a policy of continuous and thorough safeguards evaluation, we make no claims concerning the workings or weaknesses of current Minuteman safeguards. However, we do share the grave concern evidenced in the following remarks made in March 1976 by Congressman Ottinger:

From classified material I have seen, as well as from unclassified
briefings I have received from former high-ranking Defense Department personnel, all of which I hope this committee will
take the time and trouble to explore thoroughly, I have every
reason to believe that the protections are inadequate against
catastrophe by way of theft, sabotage, unclear and overextensive
delegation of authority, incompetence or incapacity of authorized
personnel, unauthorized use, weakness of communications and
command and control. [U.S. Congress, House, 1976: 13]

From what was publicly known as late as March 1976, it appeared quite
possible that strategic nuclear weapons could be compromised in various
ways.

Military Safeguards: Minuteman

The Minuteman is a three-stage, solid-fuel missile with an intercontinental
range, capable of carrying a one-megaton payload, and housed in a protected,
concrete and steel underground silo.[9] A silo is also protected by an elaborate
security system, consisting primarily of a fence surrounding the perimeter of
the silo, combination locks to gain access to the underground silo, and
sensitive electronic instruments. Under normal conditions, when all security
systems are functioning properly, physical intrusion that "breaks" the silo
perimeter either above or below ground is registered by instruments and
transmitted via cable to a computer visual display and readout located in an
underground Launch Control Center (LCC) several miles away.[10] In this
manner, two-man LCC crews monitor the security status of a ten-missile
flight simultaneously. Security violations reported by the crew result in the
dispatch of armed security police who inspect the site and silo for intruders
and evidence of unlawful entry.

There are five flights, hence five two-man LCCs, in a 50-missile squadron.
Since all missiles and LCCs are electronically interconnected, the "normal"
launch of any or all missiles in a squadron requires the cooperation of only
two crews—no more, no less. One LCC crew can launch any or all of a
squadron, but in this "abnormal" situation the launch is delayed
substantially, i.e., the missile lift-off reaction time is increased from about
eight seconds to a matter of hours.[11] The primary reason for this built-in
delay is to allow adequate time to "inhibit" an illicit launch command
generated by a single aberrant LCC. Indications of such an attempt are
automatically relayed via cable and computer to each LCC in the squadron,
and each LCC crew is trained and responsible for instructing the squadron's
missiles, through a computer command, to disregard the unauthorized
command.

Located in each LCC are two launch keys, one for each member of the crew, and the codes needed to authenticate presidential launch directives. Only the launch keys, not the codes, are *physical* prerequisites for generating valid launch commands, the purpose of the codes being exclusively that of authenticating an execution directive.[12] Contrary to popular belief, there are no mechanical "Permissive Action Links" (PAL) installed at LCCs to prevent cooperating crews from launching missiles without presidential authority. The implementation of a version of PAL (called the "Permissive Enable System") is underway, but there is only a meager store of evidence on which to define the program's scope and purpose and to base an appraisal of its quality.

Other sensitive information found in each LCC includes lock combinations to missile sites which are passed to authorized personnel on site for silo maintenance, targeting information for missile sorties in the squadron, and codes and message formats used to validate directives of various kinds, including war termination orders.

Carefully selected and highly trained crew members are the only personnel authorized to perform various ICBM system operations, and the security of the operation depends heavily on their professional integrity. Technically, crew members can launch a nuclear attack with or without approval from higher authority. Unless PAL or its equivalent forecloses this option, as many as 50 missiles could be illicitly fired. Moreover, unless adequate precautions were instituted, an even more drastic option would be available. Crew members could conspire in the formatting and transmittal of strategic strike directives, deceiving the full contingent of Strategic Air Command (SAC) LCCs, as well as higher authorities, into reacting to a spurious launch directive as if it were valid and authentic. Or they could render the U.S. strategic force virtually impotent by formatting and transmitting messages invalidating the active inventory of presidential execution codes. Finally, crew members could aid accomplices in stealing thermonuclear warheads from missiles on active alert. Such weapons are many times more destructive than any atomic bomb that might be constructed from stolen fissionable materials.

The public's abiding confidence in the probity of the professional officer corps assigned LCC responsibilities *is* well deserved; however, the margin for error for the proper functioning of the launch network is not as great as one might believe. Without stringent safeguards, a single aberrant individual could "unsafe" the arming mechanisms of an entire Minuteman squadron, or facilitate the theft or sabotage of nuclear warheads. Other acts of terror, except for the physical launch of ICBMs, would require the collaboration of only two individuals (one person in each of two separate SACLCCs). Four individuals (two persons in each of two separate LCCs in the same squadron) acting in concert could succeed in mechanically launching one or more missiles.[13]

If these nontrivial risks were ignored or inadequately addressed, the terrorist problem would be compounded in the case where access to the launch network is not stringently controlled. Given the enormous discretionary power held by *whoever* has LCC control, effective measures for denying LCC access to individuals or groups bent on carrying out an act of nuclear terror are self-evident security requirements.

In the recent past, such safeguards were poor or nonexistent. Military personnel, e.g., maintenance airmen, and civilian contractors who possessed minimal security credentials, were granted LCC access, and annually thousands of visitors holding no clearance whatsoever were permitted access to operational LCCs. In the interest of public relations, the Air Force permitted ready access to the Minuteman launch network by practically anyone desiring it.

Requests for visitor access were routinely processed and approved. The requesting party had only to provide a name and social security number, and authentication checks were not usually made. As a matter of course, checks of individual backgrounds or motives for requesting LCC access were not made either. Furthermore, within wide bounds, access was scheduled at the convenience of the requesting party, and the number of individuals in a party was limited only by the capacity of an LCC—about eight persons.

Once military personnel and civilians are allowed inside an LCC, responsibility for them falls squarely on the shoulders of on-duty crew members. The present situation parallels that which existed several years ago in the area of airlines security. Aircraft flight personnel are manifestly incapable of curbing hijacking incidents, and not until major changes in airport security were implemented was the incident rate reduced to tolerable levels. LCC crews are no more capable of thwarting launch network seizures than unassisted flight personnel are capable of foiling hijack attempts. Added to all this are the facts that no acknowledged procedures or rules exist to prevent or prohibit groups of military personnel and/or civilians from gaining simultaneous access to LCCs in the same squadron, and procedures, i.e., technical orders for arming and launching missiles, are unclassified and can be readily performed, especially if rehearsed in advance.

One must also recite the obvious point that silos and launch control centers are located in desolate reaches of the heartland. Reaction times to mount a counterterror offensive pinpointed at one or a few of these facilities would be measured in hours, not minutes or seconds.

Although the unfolding scenario contains all the ingredients of a nuclear disaster, the seizure of one or more LCCs would not necessarily lead to nuclear violence. Even if the most serious loopholes were not closed by newly implemented changes in security, terrorists might be unable or unwilling to consummate the nuclear options potentially at their disposal. But the mere seizure of control and the acquisition of a possible nuclear weapon capability would greatly enhance the credibility of any threats they might make. In responding to the threats of terrorists whose nuclear capability is even remotely plausible, authorities may feel compelled to accede to their demands as if the alleged capability were real.

Elaborate lock systems, personnel screening, e.g., crew security clearance and human reliability programs, and "no-lone-zones" notwithstanding, there is little reason to have confidence that Minuteman safeguards are inviolable. If this component of America's nuclear force, so often hailed as epitomizing reliable command and control, has been or continues to be far less than "fail-safe," then America's nuclear force as a whole is implicated. As noted earlier, it was just March 1976 when Congressman Ottinger was able to voice serious concern about the safeguards for all nuclear weapons programs—both strategic and tactical:

> Let us now turn to tactical weapons. The situation with respect
> to safeguards against theft, sabotage, seizure, dangerous dele-
> gation of authority, unauthorized use, incapacity or incompe-
> tence of those authorized and ineffective communications,
> command and control is many times worse with tactical than
> with strategic weapons—and we should bear in mind that the
> differentiation between tactical and strategic weapons today
> is mostly a matter of mission—many weapons classified as tacti-
> cal have destructive power many times that of the bombs we
> dropped on Hiroshima and Nagasaki. [U.S. Congress, House,
> 1976: 13]

Terrorist Objectives and Capabilities

Corrective action is required to shore up commercial *and* military nuclear safeguards. But the question remains, what programs should have priority and how much improvement is needed? The answers lie not only in identifying security defects, but in understanding terrorist objectives and capabilities.

Not much is known about these subjects, and even less is known about them in relation to the commission of *nuclear* terror, since the terrorist manufacture or detonation of nuclear weapons has never occurred. Given the present state of knowledge and the potential consequences of failure, one could assume that some fraction of the terrorist population, however minute, will seek a nuclear capability. On purely assumptive grounds, upgrading ill-protected or ineffectual security programs is justifiable.

The type of safeguards systems most appropriate for deterring or subduing terrorists should be designed with the following factors in mind:

1. Likely tactical objective, e.g., achieving a credible nuclear launch capability, weapons theft, force degradation.

2. Likely strategic objectives, e.g., punishment, concessions, fear and alarm, publicity.
3. Terrorist capabilities.
4. Pervasiveness of groups disposed to committing nuclear terrorism.

With respect to historical precedents relevant to the latter two categories, researchers are finding that: terrorists and terrorist groups are growing in number and widening the scope of their activities, they are well-financed and well-educated, there is an unprecedented extent of international cooperation, attacks against targets of wider variety and complexity are being mounted, more ingenious means of gaining access to and escape from these targets are being devised and used, and more sophisticated conventional weapons than ever before are being relied on.[14]

The relevance of these trends for nuclear terrorism is speculative. While terrorists may not cross the nuclear threshold in the near future, that eventuality is difficult to assess. Whatever the motive or unforeseen circumstances, little stands in the way of terrorists' acquiring a nuclear capability should they choose to do so. Certainly in the case of surrogate warfare, the benefit of a national resource base would expand terrorist capabilities to high and unprecedented levels.

If gaining nuclear capability is possible, what political ends might be served? Bearing in mind the speculative nature of this question, some preliminary "scenario sketching" might prove useful and insightful. If, for example, terrorists could surreptitiously acquire control of part of the Minuteman launch network, the strategic objectives listed in Table 1 might hold.

Of course, this list is not exhaustive. Furthermore, some of these objectives may be achieved through other means, including nonnuclear ones. For example, the theft of the warhead or guidance system of an ICBM might enhance the military status of another nation or some political faction, but it would do so at the risk of severe military or economic repercussions. It would not affect détente (unless the Soviet Union were believed responsible), and it certainly would not trigger a catalytic war or eliminate opposing armed forces. Finally, accomplishing a tactical objective may advance several strategic objectives simultaneously, and in other instances it may conflict with others.

Even this rough sketch of objectives reveals some important distinctions. First, with respect to the example scenario, the achievement of surrogate warfare objectives is facilitated by the actual use of nuclear weapons.[15] Threatened use of nuclear violence appears to produce few if any advantages.

In contrast, other forms of terrorism can be symbolically meaningful or produce instrumental benefits without recourse to actual detonation of

Table 1 Strategic Objectives

Surrogate Warfare	Terrorism
Actual Use of Nuclear Weapons	*Actual Use of Nuclear Weapons*
• Punish the U.S. or other nations	• Punish the U.S. or other nations
• Destroy détente	• Destroy morale; create fear and
• Elevate the military or economic power of other nations	alarm
• Eliminate opposing armed forces	
• Destroy morale; create fear and alarm	
• Initiate a catalytic war*	
Threatened Use of Nuclear Weapons	*Threatened Use of Nuclear Weapons*
• Create fear and alarm	• Create fear and alarm
	• Gain concessions
	• Publicity
	• Provoke repression
	• Build morale within terrorist movement

*By the mid-1960s, the catalytic war thesis was no longer seriously entertained because it was believed that the nuclear superpowers would be able to identify accurately the source of nuclear attack, or at least would restrain from retaliating until determining the source. This thesis requires close reexamination in an era of accelerating proliferation and possible nuclear terrorism.

nuclear weapons; in fact, the latter appears counter-productive. Actual use of nuclear force may serve as a punishment or fear-inducing objective, but it would not promote terrorist aims if social structures of potential value to them were destroyed. Unless the indigenous terrorist is a complete nihilist,

> total indiscrimination is not desirable, for the insurgents will wish to concentrate their attacks on specific targets of intent, social structures, and symbols, to achieve economy of effort and ensure the maintenance of those structures that are of potential value to them. They must therefore determine which structures are to be preserved, which structures are the most vulnerable to attack, and which are the most crucial in holding together the fabric of society they wish to split. Certain compromises will inevitably have to be made, but the optimum targets are clearly those that show the highest symbolic value and are dominated by symbols that are most vulnerable to attack. [Thornton, 1964: 81]

This position is less tenable in the case of international terrorism, where the destruction of social structures of target nations may be irrelevant or perhaps even desirable.

Recommendations

MINUTEMAN AND OTHER WEAPONS SYSTEMS

The deficiencies identified indicate that basic changes in Minuteman safeguards are required, changes that may also pertain to other strategic and tactical weapons systems. The following recommendations do not exhaust the creative possibilities, but they appear to be promising and deserving of further consideration and evaluation. They are listed in what we believe to be an order of comprehensiveness and probable effectiveness. Similar assessments are also needed of *all* nuclear weapons systems, and these assessments would doubtless evince similar lists of recommendations for improved security.

1. *Install Permissive Action Links* (PAL). In 1953, the installation of an electro-mechanical system called Permissive Action Link (PAL) was proposed for Polaris submarines, but it was never implemented. The time is now right to reconsider PAL's use in all tactical and strategic nuclear systems under U.S. control, including the Minuteman program (Panofsky, 1973). A U.S. initiative and demonstration of concern could set the pace for safeguards reform among allies and adversaries alike. (We must stress again the worldwide implications of the latent terrorist threat to such weapons.)

A PAL-type system would prevent the generation of execution commands unless a set of codes is previously inserted. These releasing codes would be known only at some level of command that is positive and secure, e.g., the National Command Authority (NCA) level, would constitute a *physical* prerequisite to weapon use, and would be transmitted along with presidential execution directives should a nuclear war erupt.

Although it would not reduce the risk of LCC seizures, in the Minuteman case, PAL would eliminate the possibility of unauthorized weapons launch and detonation by terrorists or aberrant military personnel, including crew members. PAL would also obviate the necessity for developing safeguards against the illicit formatting and transmittal of deceptive and spurious, but authentic-appearing, execution directives.

The risks of nuclear theft, possible unauthorized weapons arming, or strategic degradation would not be affected, however. Other more modest disadvantages of the proposed design include the cost of developing and installing mechanical devices and revising command and control procedures, and the limitations it might impose on the attainment of maximum readiness and reliability of the *weapon system*. The limitations appear minor. However, inasmuch as "military personnel and weapons engineers are reluctant to accept complicated and elaborate systems of safety control" (Larus, 1967:31), the suggested system will encounter strong resistance from defense quarters unless high standards of readiness and reliability are met. Meeting such standards demands elaborate testing of both the mechanism itself and its human factors effects.

A potentially major problem with the proposed system is the effect it might have on the reliability of the *command system* which links higher authority with dispersed elements of the strategic force. If the authority to order a nuclear attack were vested only at the NCA level, a well-executed Soviet strike could possibly neutralize the NCA and, with it, all retaliatory capability. Clearly, an optimal balance must be struck between weapons safeguards and weapons usability. If existing organizational and physical safeguards reflect the degree to which nuclear authority is decentralized or ambiguous, then policy has leaned too far in the direction of priming weapons for ready use.

The locus of nuclear authority ought to be vested as high up the chain of command as possible without placing the command system itself in jeopardy. Having fixed the level of command at which discretion with respect to nuclear weapons is sanctioned, all subordinate levels of command should be fully protected against any risk of nuclear terrorism. Finally, since the vesting of authority at any level below the NCA would blur the distinction between political and military control of nuclear operations, the public should be made aware of this fact and encouraged to debate whether a compromise of constitutional authority is permissible and, if so, under what circumstances.

2. *Expand preaccess screening of military personnel and extend the principle to nonmilitary personnel.* Preaccess screening might incorporate more rigid clearance standards, improved physical and procedural identification techniques, physical or electronic search procedures to prevent concealment of arms, and so forth. The obvious model is the airport security program. Among these possibilities, the expansion of investigatory requirements will be the most expensive in the long run. Also, any form of preaccess screening of civilians, especially involving information storage systems like data banks, has potential for abuse and warrants close scrutiny.

3. *Suspend visitor access.* This measure could be easily and inexpensively implemented and would *reduce* defense outlays. However, its impact on civil-military relations could be judged to be detrimental. The military is interested in enhancing public relations programs, not cutting them back. Likewise, the public generally wants information about military operations to remain as unfettered as possible. Since no classified information is compromised during civilian visits, a curtailment of visitor access might be interpreted as undue secrecy and suppression of the public's right to be informed.

The dilemma clearly reveals a distinction between categories of information dissemination. Sole reliance on classification is an exhausted form of protection, and the need exists to develop better methods for safely disseminating unclassified information.[16]

4. *Create and improve procedures for damage limitation resulting from nuclear terrorism.* One such procedure might be the creation of an

international forum for sharing knowledge and presenting proposals concerned with war termination.[17] This concern certainly falls under the purview of the U.S. Arms Control and Disarmament Agency (ACDA), which would logically represent the United States in communicating and negotiating substantive issues such as war termination. At the national level, a "no-first-use" declaratory policy might assist in rendering suspect any terrorist-originated launch directive.[18]

THE CITIZEN'S ROLE

Secrecy has probably engendered more public ignorance of the risk of illicit nuclear weapons detonation than of security problems arising in connection with the growth of commercial nuclear power. In either case, public input in the development of nuclear safeguards policy is effectively limited by classification's ubiquitous stamp.

5. *Improve public debate about nuclear safeguards.* We need to generate and evaluate alternative ways of structuring public debate so that safeguards issues are revealed as matters of political choice open to democratic control. What constitutes an acceptable safeguards posture is a political as well as an empirical question "that should not be decided in our society by any group of experts, no matter how well informed or intentioned" (Willrich, 1975: 15). Naturally, we must take into account the possible effects that a changed public role might have on the nature of the threat itself.[19]

6. *Facilitate a variety of policy research initiatives from concerned but independent analysts.* In addition to creating public unawareness of the need for safeguards reform and contributing to distorted priorities,[20] secrecy hinders independent research and evaluation by nongovernmental institutions and scholars. A major premise of this report is that classification and technical complications do not constitute an insuperable impediment to either analysts or terrorists; otherwise there would be little cause for concern over the purported terrorist threat. Ironically, the analyst who is not privy to classified information is at a marked disadvantage, because terrorist intelligence gathering is often more sophisticated and almost always less bound by ethics and law, i.e., the terrorist perhaps can and will penetrate the classification barrier. This might be especially true in the case of surrogate warfare, where state-sponsored terrorists possess certain classified information about the target country which is denied the well-intentioned analyst.

Secrecy also discourages the well-informed outsider from attempting to effect changes in safeguards procedures. The Committee for Economic Development (CED, 1974: 42) observes that

> [the outsider] is subject to being intimidated, if not discredited,
> by the allegation that there exists decisive information that contra-
> dicts him but to which he may not have access.

Perhaps more common, but equally effective, are refusals to confirm or deny assessments made by outsiders. This, at least, has been our experience. Although repeatedly assured that "appropriate actions" have been initiated as a result of our critique of Minuteman security, no substantive and comforting response on ameliorative procedures implemented has been forthcoming because of "the sensitivity of the information."

THE NEED FOR INSTITUTIONAL FOCUS

Because nuclear terrorism is rapidly becoming more practical and legitimate, we need to go beyond examining the efficacy of safeguards in the context of terrorist capabilities and objectives. We also need to look closely at the organizational, political, and economic factors that determine the shape of terrorist prevention policy more generally.

7. *Rationalize programmatic responsibility for safeguards.* U.S. nuclear programs possessing the problem dimensions defined in the beginning of this report include (1) nuclear *weapons* programs, including research and development, under Department of Defense and Energy Research and Development (ERDA)[21] jurisdiction and to a lesser extent monitored by several committees of Congress, and (2) nuclear *power* programs under the primary direction and supervision of private industry but regulated by the Nuclear Regulatory Commission (NRC), ERDA, and the Congress.

Other significant but less comprehensive responsibilities which overlap both categories of nuclear programs belong to the Department of State, FBI, CIA, Arms Control and Disarmament Agency (ACDA), and the Government Accounting Office (GAO).[22] But, so far, no agency has been formed to deal exclusively with the terrorist threat to U.S. nuclear programs, although several recommendations have been made to this effect.[23] The only government body whose sole responsibility is terrorist crime prevention is the Cabinet Committee to Combat Terrorism established by President Nixon in 1972. In the words of Hoffacker (1974), who chaired the Working Group under the committee: "This body is directed to coordinate interagency activity for the prevention of terrorism, and, should acts of terrorism occur, to devise procedures for reacting swiftly and effectively."[24]

Despite the considerable overlap of oversight responsibilities and the plethora of agencies involved to some extent in developing safeguards policy, terrorism remains "a major policy problem without an institutional focus anywhere in the U.S. government" (Willrich and Taylor, 1974: 100). This condition stems in part from the bureaucratic disorganization and lack of resolve that characterize nuclear energy policy generally (Symington, 1977).

International programmatic responsibility is also not well assigned. Since the United States has offered to subject its nuclear industry to International

Atomic Energy Agency-administered regulations, IAEA may eventually become involved in domestic safeguards programs. To date they have not. Indeed, the IAEA had but 67 inspectors in 1976 to cover the entire stock of the world's nuclear power plants; less than one-third of its budget, or about $37 million in 1975, went for inspections and other regulation efforts (Brewer, 1977: 353).

Part of the problem has to do with incentives. Insofar as traditional concerns of the military, weapons invention and acquisition, vie with terrorist prevention programs for attention and resources, then one should expect the latter to be slighted. Similarly, to the extent that the traditional concern of the nuclear power industry, production of energy, vies with terrorist prevention (and safety) programs for attention and resources, then one should also expect the latter to be slighted.[25] Both cases characterize the current state of affairs.[26]

Therefore, we should identify and remove conflicts of interest within and among agencies presently charged with safeguards responsibilities and, if necessary, establish an independent and capable locus of supervision and decision for all nuclear activities bearing on terrorism.

The terrorist threat to world nuclear programs is not obviated simply by eliminating military vulnerabilities, because the threat to commercial nuclear programs may persist, and vice-versa. Moreover, solutions directed exclusively at correcting deficiencies in one area may actually increase the threat to the other. Other things being equal, terrorists would likely challenge the least effective or reliable security network, and improvements made in one network might simply reorient, rather than reduce, terrorist activity. This complex interrelationship, if it exists at all, is best dealt with through central direction and coordination. At the present inchoate stage of terrorism scholarship, not much light has been shed on the relative attractiveness of military versus commercial nuclear targets. But it is important to register the likely existence of a complex relationship and to begin to think about what organizational arrangements would most sensitively balance military and commercial safeguards priorities.

RESEARCH NEEDS

8. *Stimulate general scholarship on terrorism in all its aspects.* We know less about all of this than we should. Basic research is needed to better understand the causes and functional forms that terrorism has taken historically and will likely take in the future. We need, for instance, to consider the common structural features of the act of terrorism: audience, terrorist, sponsor, victim, media, spectator, authorities, allies, and sanctuaries. We should also examine the separate phases of the terrorist act, which include the play of the game,

preparation, execution, climax, and dénouement. Such a structural framework, or its equivalent, could serve the very useful purposes of organizing much of the existing, fragmented case study literature on terrorism and of understanding terrorism's many forms and processes so that appropriate and effective preventative and ameliorative policies and procedures might be developed.

Conclusion

Although concern is mounting over the increasing vulnerability of every society to terrorism, public policy in this field is emerging piecemeal and in some respects not at all. Unfortunately, unlike some other policy problems, there is no latitude for experimentation and little comfort in the hope that effective safeguards policy can be developed through a process of trial and error or by "muddling through." In the case of nuclear terrorism, the consequences of policy failure are catastrophic.

Admittedly, the probability that various agents, foreign or domestic, will soon resort to tactics of nuclear terror is low. Even though the likelihood of nuclear wars erupting between the United States and its adversaries is also low, we continue to devote a substantial share of our national income to minimizing that risk. The logic of our strategic nuclear policy is clear. The prevailing view is that the risk of nuclear war is low because the United States responds vigilantly to nuclear threats posed by other nations.

The same logic does not appear in our policy response to possible nuclear terrorism. There is no terrorist prevention doctrine in effect comparable to strategic deterrence doctrine, nor is there an institutional focus for preventing terrorism that is in any respect commensurate with that which exists for deterring nuclear war. If the likelihood of nuclear terrorism is remote, it is not because anyone has made a comprehensive effort to prevent it.

As smaller and smaller groups of extremists and disaffecteds acquire more and more power to disrupt and destroy, governments are becoming harder pressed to counter them without resorting to numerous, oppressive restrictions and affronts to the general citizenry. The emerging world is an unstable collections of nations, ministates, autonomous ethnic substates, governments in exile, national liberation fronts, guerrillas, and shadowy but destructive terrorist organizations. We have not, on a national or international scale, come to realize this basic fact.

Notes

1. Dr. Lawrence Z. Freedman of the University of Chicago's Institute of Social and Behavioral Pathology has been extremely helpful in shaping the arguments and thoughts in this essay.

2. Representative Long and Senator Pastore concluded that U.S. military weapons sited were inadequately protected against nuclear theft—mainly overseas—and rerebuked the Department of Defense for not acting responsively to correct the deficiencies (Los Angeles Times, 1974). See Dumas (1976) for a treatment of other rarely aired deficiencies with the safeguards program. See also remarks of Senators Pastore and Baker (U.S. Congress, 1974a).

3. Although this term originally referred only to procedures for launching Strategic Air Command bombers, its meaning is now generic and encompasses all mechanical devices, authentication systems, and communications redundancies for ensuring command and control.

4. The quantity of enriched uranium "lost" was enough to produce several fission explosions. The investigation of this incident concluded that the lost uranium was probably inadvertently disposed of in the form of scrap. There was no evidence of theft.

5. Apparently, it has been forgotten that, in 1967, the Lumb Report made the following recommendation: "Safeguards programs should also be designed in recognition of the problem of terrorist or criminal groups clandestinely acquiring nuclear weapons or materials useful therein." (Reprinted in U.S. Congress, Senate, 1975: 567.)

6. A summary of the growth of commercial nuclear power is found in Willrich (1971), Donnelly (1972), Epstein (1976), and Willrich and Taylor (1974).

7. This exceptional view is articulated by Iklé (1973), who regularly injects concern for weapons safeguards into discussions of American deterrent capability.

8. Pursuant to the 1971 "Agreement on Measures to Reduce the Risk of Outbreak of Nuclear War between the U.S.A. and the U.S.S.R.," an official review is obligatory. Article 1 of this Agreement states: "Each Party undertakes to maintain and to improve, as it deem necessary, its existing organizational and technical arrangements to guard against the accidental or unauthorized use of nuclear weapons under its control!" U.S. Arms Control and Disarmament Agency, 1972).

9. None of the information contained in this discussion is classified. It is *entirely* within the public domain.

10. Military police are assigned to guard any silo that is not secure; a site is not secure if any security measure malfunctions.

11. This system capability enables one crew to execute their element of the strategic plan (SIOP) in the event that all other LCCs in the squadron are destroyed.

12. If an LCC crew is ever directed to execute the SIOP, the verification procedure involves checking the execution message against the codes they

possess and then verifying that another LCC received a valid and authentic message.

13. Three authorized LCCs cannot cancel an unauthorized launch command generated by any two LCCs acting in concert. It is possible, though much less likely, that a single unauthorized LCC could succeed in launching a missile squadron. For that to happen, it would require simultaneous technical failures, or negligence, in the four remaining LCCs.

14. HERO (1974) and Mickolus (1976) contain more detailed accountings of known terrorist activities and trends.

15. This proposition also applies to industrial nuclear programs. For example, a recent study conducted for the Nuclear Regulatory Commission (NRC) concluded that any fading of détente could make the Soviet Union more likely to attempt sabotage of U.S. atomic power plants (Wall Street Journal, 1975).

16. U.S. Arms Control and Disarmament Agency (1976) offers one promising vehicle for this intiative. Stockholm International Peace Research (SIPRI, 1975) is another.

17. Iklé (1971) and Keckskemeti (1958) supply the intellectual underpinnings for this concern. Kreiger (1975) discussed the issue from the perspective of nuclear terrorism. And Foster and Brewer (1976) synthesize current thought on war termination issues and difficulties.

18. The arguments for and against a "no-first-use" declaration are discussed in Russett (1976) and in U.S. Congress, House (1976).

19. There are numerous contradictory views on this issue to reconcile. For example, in a comment pertaining to shortcomings in nuclear weapons security, Senator Pastore expressed concern over "the effect public discussion of a matter of this nature would have upon those who might be stimulated in activities of terrorism" (Los Angeles Times, 1974). In contrast, Willrich and Taylor (1974:3) assert that secrecy "assumes that criminals are no more perceptive than the general public about [nuclear] opportunities."

20. The distorting effects of secrecy are cause for the following observation by De Volpi (1974: 30): "Nuclear reactors are being subjected to proper and necessary review [while] tens of thousands of nuclear weapons in the world have proliferated without significant public debate or environmental review."

21. Safeguards pertaining to unclassified aspects of nuclear power operations are NRC's responsibility. Responsibility for classified aspects of military weapons and industrial safeguards programs is charged to ERDA.

22. GAO has been active primarily in the area of industrial security. See U.S. General Accounting Office (1973) and Nucleonics Week (1974).

23. These proposals pertain only to nuclear power programs. See Willrich and Taylor (1974) and U.S. Congress (1974a: S6621). The Senate Committee on Governmental Operations has been and will continue to be concerned with structuring programmatic safeguards responsibilities. This committee has assembled a very useful compendium on a broad

range of issues bearing on nuclear terrorism (U.S. Congress, Senate, 1975).

24. The committee is chaired by the Secretary of State, and includes the Secretaries of Defense. Treasury, and Transportation, the Attorney General, the U.S. Ambassador to the United Nations, the Director of the FBI, and Presidential Assistance for National Security and Domestic Affairs.

25. For attitudinal differences among key actors involved in commercial safeguards reform, see the rigorous study by Brady and Rapoport (1973).

26. The topic is treated extensively in Brewer (1977).

References

Allardice, C. and E. R. Trapnell (1974). The Atomic Energy Commission. New York: Praeger.

Beres, L. R. (1974). "Guerrillas, terrorists, and polarity: new structural models of world politics." Western Pol. Q. 27 (December): 624–636.

Brady, D. and L. Rapoport (1973). "Policy-capturing in the field; the nuclear safeguards problem." Organizational Behavior and Human Performance 9 (April): 253-266.

Brewer, G. D. (1977). "Existing in a world of institutionalized danger." Yale Studies in World Public Order 3 (Spring): 339-387.

Committee for Economic Development [CED] (1974). Congressional Decision Making for National Security. New York: CED.

De Volpi (1974). "Energy policy decision-making: the need for balanced input." Bull. of the Atomic Scientists 30 (December): 29-33.

Donnelly, W. H. (1972). Commercial Nuclear Power in Europe: The Interaction of American Diplomacy with a New Technology. Washington, DC: Committee on Foreign Affairs, U.S. House of Representatives.

Dumas, L. J. (1976). "National security in the nuclear age." Bull. of the Atomic Scientists 32 (May).

Epstein, W. (1976). The Last Chance. New York: Free Press.

Foster, J. L. and G. D. Brewer (1976). "And the clocks were striking thirteen: the termination of war." Policy Sciences 7 (June): 225-246.

Gapay, L. (1975). "New laws are studied to protect shipments of deadly plutonium." Wall Street Journal (October 23).

HERO (1974). The Terrorism and Sabotage Threat to U.S. Nuclear Programs. Dunn Loring, VA: Historical Evaluation and Research Organization.

Hoffacker, L. (1974). "The U.S. government response to terrorism." Vital Speeches of the Day (January 7).

Ikle, F. C. (1973) "Can nuclear deterrence last out the century?" Foreign Affairs 51 (January): 267-285.

———(1971). Every War Must End, New York: Columbia Univ. Press.

Jenkins, B. (1975). International Terrorism: A New Mode of Conflict. Santa Monica, CA: The Rand Corporation and the California Seminar on Arms Control and Foreign Policy.

———and J. Johnson (1974). International Terrorism: A Chronology, 1968-1974. Santa Monica, CA: The Rand Corporation, R-1597-ARPA.

Kecskemeti, P. (1958). Strategic Surrender: The Politics of Victory and Defeat. Stanford, CA: Stanford Univ. Press.

Krieger, D. (1975). "Terrorism and nuclear technology." Bull. of the Atomic Scientists 31 (June): 28-34.

Larus, J. (1967). Nuclear Weapons Safety and the Common Defense. Columbus: Ohio State Univ. Press.

———(1965). "To reduce the possibilty of nuclear catastrophe." Bull. of the Atomic Scientists 21 (April): 33-36.

Lasswell, H. D. (1965). World Politics and Personal Insecurity. New York: Free Press.

Lawrence, R. M. and J. Larus [eds.] (1974). Nuclear Proliferation Phase II. Lawrence, KS: Allen.

Leachman, R. and P. Althoff (1972). Preventing Nuclear Theft: Guidelines for Industry and Government. New York: Praeger.

Los Angeles Times (1974). September 27.

McPhee, J. (1973). The Curve of Binding Energy. New York: Ballantine.

Mickolus, E. F. (1976) "Statistical approaches to the study of terrorism." Paper read at the Conference on International Terrorism. New York: Ralph Bunche Institute. City University of New York, June 9-11. [Also available from the Department of Political Science, Yale University, New Haven, CT 06520.]

National Academy of Science (1975). Long-Term Worldwide Effects of Multiple Nuclear Weapons Detonations. Washington, DC: NAS.

Nucleonics Week (1974). October 29

Panofsky, W. K. H. (1973). "The mutual hostage relationship between America and Russia." Foreign Affairs 52 (October): 109-118.

Phelps, J.B. (1961). "The danger of accidental war." Bull. of the Atomic Scientists 17 (April): 146-148.

Raser, J. R. (1973). "The failure of fail-safe," pp. 85-104 in K. E. Boulding (ed.), Peace and the War Industry. New Brunswick, NJ: Rutgers Univ. Press.

Russett, B. M. (1976). "No first use of nuclear weapons: to stay the fateful lightning." Worldview (November): 9-11.

Schlesinger, J. K. (1975). FY 1975 Report of the Secretary of Defense James K. Schlesinger to the Congress. Washington, D.C.: U.S. Department of Defense.

Schelling, T. C. and M. H. Halperin (1961). Strategy and Arms Control. New York: Twentieth Century Fund.

Stockholm International Peace Research Institute (1975) World Armaments and Disarmament: SIPRI Yearbook 1975. Uppsala, Sweden: Almqvist & Wiksell.

Symington, S. (1977). "The Washington nuclear mess," Int. Security 1 (Winter): 71-78.

Thornton, T. P. (1964). "Terror as a weapon of political agitation," pp. 71-99 in H. Eckstein (ed.) Internal War. New York: Free Press.

U.S. Arms Control and Disarmament Agency [ACDA] (1976). Arms Control Report. Washington, D.C.: USACDA, July.

———(1972). Arms Control and Disarmament Agreements. Washington, D.C.: USACDA, June 1.

U.S. Congress (1974a). Congressional Record (April 30): 56621.

———(1974b). Congressional Record (September 25). "Security of U.S. nuclear weapons in Europe. Remarks by Senators Pastore and Baker.

U.S. Congress House (1976). First Use of Nuclear Weapons: Preserving Responsible Control. Hearings before the Subcommittee on International Security and Scientific Affairs, Committee on International Relations, 94th Congress, 2nd Session, March.

U.S. Congress (1975). Peaceful Nuclear Exports and Weapons Proliferation: A Compendium. Washington, DC: GPO, April.

———(1974). U.S.-U.S.S.R. Strategic Policies. Testimony of Defense Secretary James K. Schlesinger before the Subcommittee on Arms Control, International Law and Organization, Committee on Foreign Relations, 93rd congress, 2nd Session, March 4.

U.S. General Accounting Office [GAO] (1973). Improvements Needed in the Program for the Protection of Special Nuclear Material. Washington, DC: GAO, November 7.

Wall Street Journal (1975). December 12.

Walske, C. (1977). "Nuclear electric power and the proliferation of nuclear weapon states." Int. Security 1 (Winter): 94-106.

Willrich, M. (1975). "Terrorists keep out!" Bull. of the Atomic Scientists 31 (May): 12-16.

———(1971). Global Politics of Nuclear Energy. New York: Praeger.

———and T. B. Taylor (1974). Nuclear Theft: Risks and Safeguards. Cambridge, MA: Ballinger.

Part III

Analyses of the Problem: Maximalists, Agnostics, Skeptics, and Others

Bernard L. Cohen

The Potentialities of Terrorism

Cohen concludes that it is too late to engage in a dialectic concerning the utility of nuclear power. The time for such a debate was twenty years ago. Furthermore, he finds that the terrorists' concerns about their personal safety would lead them to less complicated and less dangerous mass destruction weapons—poison gas, napalm at a sporting event, the destruction of a dorm, or the poisoning of water—but even these options are out of character with the past activities of terrorists. Finally, he sees yielding to terrorism as a special kind of tyranny, which society must avoid, for "to stand fast is a guarantee of eventual victory."

How come it took Indian, French, and other national programs thousands of scientific man-years and hundreds of millions of dollars to develop nuclear weapons while we are told that a bunch of terrorists could build a bomb with stolen reactor-grade (*not* weapons-grade) plutonium within several weeks for a few thousand dollars? The answer, aside from gross exaggeration in stories about the simplicity of such a project, is that the hypothetical terrorist bombs are "crude" and much less devastating, capable of blowing up a large building according to Theodore Taylor. They are devices for killing a few thousand people, not, as most people envision, for destroying a city.

But if a terrorist group wants to indiscriminately murder a few thousand people, they have many other options. To suggest a few, they could:

> Release a poison gas into the ventilation systems of large buildings.
> Discharge a load of gasoline or napalm (either by airplane or tank truck) on the spectators in a football stadium—lighted cigarettes would do the rest.
> Blast open a large dam; there are situations where this could kill over 200,000 people.
> Poison a city water or food supply.
> Attack a tanker carrying liquefied natural gas as it passes near a densely populated area; estimates for this range up to 50,000 fatalities.

Any imaginative person could add many more items to this list.

Let's see how terrorists might operate. They could issue demands with a threat that if these are not met, there will be a mass murder incident. They needn't specify what type of incident or where—so it would be almost impossible to take precautions. Wouldn't this be as effective for blackmail or terror as blowing up a building with a nuclear bomb? There is no limit to the number of such incidents they could perpetrate.

Unlike plutonium, the necessary materials are readily available and there are plenty of people with all the necessary know-how to carry out these plans. There may be a risk of some of the terrorists being captured, but that's no problem: their release could be added to the conditions for the next threat. In the nuclear bomb option, however, there is a very substantial danger to the perpetrators: more than a 50 percent death risk in the thievery, according to Taylor, and something like 30 percent in the bomb fabrication.

Perhaps we should start guarding against these non-nuclear threats, as in our current approach to the nuclear bomb problem. For starters, we could guard ventilation systems of large buildings. We must have a guard force capable of withstanding a well planned and competently directed surprise attack by 15 heavily armed men—that is the type of attack assumed in plutonium theft scenarios. This would surely require a guard force of thousands in every large city—and that's just to take care of item no. 1 on our list, and our list is far from complete. (It is estimated that a very adequate guard force for our nation's supply of plutonium in a breeder economy would consist of a few thousand men.)

Is it even necessary for terrorists to kill thousands of people for their purposes? Wouldn't killing a bus load of school children, or turning a theater into a blazing inferno be almost equally effective? How about kidnapping wives and children of Congressmen?

Clearly, guarding all these potential targets would be impossible. A large, well led, heavily armed group of terrorists striking at a time and place of their choosing can commit as much mass murder as suits their purpose, and no amount of guarding or police action can stop them. (Police have had some success in capturing irrational offenders or those who can be traced through personal motive, but gangland killers working "under contract" are seldom apprehended.) Terrorists have had this mass murder option for a very long time, and the added possibility of stealing plutonium to fabricate it into crude nuclear bombs capable of blowing up a building adds little to this capability.

We may well take solace in the fact that terrorists have never exercised this option even though it has been available to them for some time; in fact, they have never killed large numbers of people in a single episode. Perhaps they have more morality than we credit them with, or perhaps they are deterred by the loss of public sympathy that would ensue. A universally hated group could probably not last long in any society. But if terrorists should decide to employ mass murder, there can be only one answer: Society must learn not to yield to blackmail. To yield is to live under constant tyranny, whereas to stand fast is a guarantee of eventual victory.

But what does all this have to do with nuclear electric power? If theft of plutonium ever was an issue, it should have been debated in 1956 when nuclear power development began, not in 1976 after so much money and effort has been spent. As we have shown, there are, and always have been, many easier vehicles for indiscriminate mass murder than blowing up a building with a crude nuclear bomb.

It is clearly prudent to guard our plutonium very carefully as a deterrent to thievery, especially since this adds only about 1 percent to the cost of electricity, but making a major issue of it as a reason for stopping nuclear power is hard to understand. Isn't this just another example of nuclear critics looking hard for issues to support their emotionally-based dislike for nuclear power? With so many good, well-meaning people being taken in by this operation, what terrorists can do may be among the lesser of society's problems.

David Comey

The Perfect Trojan Horse

Given the risk of nuclear terrorism, Comey sees the growth of civil nuclear power programs as inimical to civil liberties in the United States. Comey holds that the terrorist threat is so severe as to "require us to alter our traditional views about citizens' rights and the police powers of the government." Given the problems associated with nuclear power, Comey would prefer to do without the "benefits" of nuclear power rather than suffer the resultant deprivations of liberty.

An American army officer in Vietnam once explained, "We had to destroy the village in order to save it." Will our democratic institutions here in the United States meet a similar fate if we choose to make nuclear fission plants our major source of energy? If so, the irony would be that while we have spent trillions of dollars defending ourselves against the communist nations so that Americans will not have to live under a totalitarian regime, we would have chosen an energy supply requiring security measures that will turn America into a garrison state.

It is becoming increasingly apparent that civil liberties and an extensive nuclear power program are not compatible, because sabotage of nuclear power plants or terrorist use of stolen special nuclear material are risks that require us to alter our traditional views about citizens' rights and the police powers of the government.

Russell W. Ayres, whose thoughts on this issue are unusually clear and precise,[1] has put it in a nutshell:

> To the extent that we have civil liberties at all today, it is because we have not had to ask questions like whether it is better to torture a suspected terrorist than to let a city go up in flames.[2]

A recent report prepared for the Nuclear Regulatory Commission by the MITRE Corporation was written by a panel of twelve of the country's top experts on sabotage and terrorism.[3] They pointed out:

Terrorist groups may find themselves in political situations where they feel they have nothing to lose by an act, no matter how outrageous. . . . Terrorists might sabotage a nuclear facility as an act of vengeance. Alternatively, they might attack and gain control of a nuclear facility and hold it hostage to destruction unless certain demands were met. These groups are certainly aware of the power which any sort of nuclear action would give them. By the strange logic of the world in which we live, it might also make them heroes to a substantial segment of the world, particularly if the target were the United States. This is certainly a type of threat which should be taken very seriously.[4]

The report concluded, not very optimistically, that

There is unlikely to be any single, simple answer which will assure us of complete safety against malicious action. The threat is intrinsically complicated, being linked to the ingenuity of the threatener. The response must be one of sensible, effective and efficient measures in depth. The fate of nuclear power in our country and the world hinges upon finding an adequate answer.[5]

Given the nature of the measures being considered as "adequate," it is obvious that our civil liberties are in grave danger. Three points need to be made.

First, even after the recent improvement in security regulations, nuclear power plants are vulnerable to sabotage or blackmail. While we have erected enormous air and missile defense systems to prevent the delivery of nuclear warheads from abroad to our large cities, we are now surrounding many of these same cities with nuclear reactors whose fuel cores contain a thousand times as many fission products as are released by a Hiroshima-sized weapon. The radioactive contents of these reactors can be spread over a large area by the use of *conventional* explosives easily obtained by terrorists or criminals. A nuclear reactor on the edge of a major city is the perfect Trojan horse.

Second, the nuclear industry has banked heavily on the Rasmussen report's estimates that the probability of a major nuclear plant accident is so small as to be negligible.[6] The report's authors ignored the sabotage problem, however, and when confronted, reply: "That makes no difference: no saboteur could cause any greater radioactive release than those we envisage in our report." The answer misses the point: perhaps the consequences of the accident do not change, but the probabilities of its happening certainly do. No longer is one calculating the chances of malfunctioning machines; one is guessing the probability of malfunctioning human beings. One does not have to be a psychiatrist to realize that probability is high: one need only read the newspapers.

Third, nuclear proponents often argue that plutonium is no more toxic than botulin, and that terrorists are much more likely to obtain and use such a chemical toxin. This misses the point made by the MITRE report: nuclear terrorism has far greater publicity value, and is more likely to be effective than any other known threat. Nuclear terrorism is a mega-threat. Security measures against it will escalate, therefore, since it provides

> the first national justification for widespread intelligence gathering
> against the civilian population. In the past, federal courts have
> taken a skeptical view of attempts to justify spying on national
> security grounds, but with the very real threat of nuclear terrorism
> in the picture, that justification is going to sound very convincing.[7]

The nuclear industry discounts such fears, of course. A spokesman for Commonwealth Edison recently stated that safeguards against nuclear terrorism "can be accomplished with no more social displacement than the guarding of gold."[8] A more apt comparison would be the social displacement involved in guarding American citizens of Japanese ancestry during World War II.

The nuclear industry's favorite taunt to its critics is: "Well, do you want to go back to candles?" That is hardly the choice we face, of course, but if it were, then I should rather read the Bill of Rights by candlelight than not have it to read at all.

Notes

1. See, for example, R. W. Ayres, "Policing Plutonium: The Civil Liberties Fallout," *Harvard Civil Rights–Civil Liberties Law Review,* 10:2 (Spring 1975), 369-443. (Reprints may be obtained for $3.00 from William S. Hein, Inc., 1285 Main Street, Buffalo, N. Y. 14209)
2. R. W. Ayres, quoted in Washington Post, Nov. 17, 1975. P. A24.
3. "The Threat to Licensed Nuclear Facilities (MTR-7022)," MITRE Corporation, McLean, Virginia, Sept. 1975, 210 pp.
4. MITRE report, pp. 137-138.
5. MITRE report, p. 164.
6. U.S. Nuclear Regulatory Commission, "Reactor Safety Study" (WASH-1400) (Washington, D.C.: The Commission, October 1975).
7. R. W. Ayres, quoted in Chicago Daily News, Nov, 29, 1975, p.3.
8. Chicago Daily News.

Michael Flood

Nuclear Sabotage

Rather than addressing illicit bomb construction, which is the wont of many other commentators, Flood examines a problem that he argues has been neglected: the possibility that a civil nuclear power facility might be the target of terrorists. Of particular interest are the tables accompanying the article, detailing past incidents involving nuclear facilities. (Readers may also wish to consult appendix 2, which offers a complete incident list for the United States.)

Violence is by no means a child of the twentieth century; it has a long history. However, the *volume* of violence in this century has undoubtedly increased. This century has already witnessed 100 million deaths caused by fellowmen—give or take 20 percent. Even allowing for increased population and changed circumstances, the last 75 years appear to have been the most violent period in history.[1]

Politically violent individuals have also always been a part of society, and their activities have been largely contained by the police or military. Today, things are different. These individuals have discovered a political lever which *will* move the System and they have begun exercising it to effect. The lever is terrorism: the use of coercive intimidation for political motives.[2] Terrorism is not new, but it has undergone refinement; it is no longer the blunt instrument that it used to be.

In the context of 100 million violent deaths in this century, political terrorism is irrelevant. The number of victims makes no statistically significant impact on the mortality figures. But as a tool for political demolition—and one that can be wielded by just a single individual—terrorism today has no rival in the textbooks of conventional military strategy. The rewards are high and the risks, paradoxically, relatively small. Indeed, the techniques of political terrorism and urban guerrilla warfare have proved so effective against the industrially advanced nations of the world that they are now being mimicked on an increasing level around the globe. The western democracies are unlikely to find refuge from terrorism outside of a police state; the wheels are already in motion.

In the continuing search for new dimensions in terror, for new targets and new vulnerabilities, I believe that terrorists will turn to nuclear power. Indeed, the initiative has already been taken. Nuclear installations have been threatened, bombed and sabotaged.

Unfortunately for the nuclear industry and, of course, neighboring populations, nuclear installations make attractive targets for terrorist blackmail.[3] They have enormous inventories of radioactive materials. And the fear of radioactivity adds a new dimension to terror. Nuclear power, in theory, offers Man great promise; but it invests individuals with a potential for extortion or destruction on a scale approaching that of a blitzkrieg. Sooner or later when a threat is not heeded, or a counteroffensive mishandled, many people will lose their lives. This is inevitable.

To appreciate *why* terrorists will turn to nuclear terror it is important to understand terrorist psychology. In addition to sophisticated munitions which extend their destructive capabilities, terrorists have acquired a sense of timing and a mastery of mass manipulative psychology. Unlike most western politicians, their campaigning is done directly with a gun—and with free television air time.

In the main, guerrillas are not primarily interested in slaughtering greater numbers of people, though the potential would certainly be there if they seized a nuclear facility. Terrorists seek to publicize their cause merely by holding a knife at society's throat. They want "a lot of people watching and a lot of people listening, not a lot of people dead."[4] Sometimes, perhaps in frustration, the knife slips.

When apparently indiscriminate terrorist violence does occur, it is violence for effect.[5] It is intended to seize the imagination of the media and the mass audience, thus exaggerating the strength of the movement (which may have fairly limited local support) and the primacy of the cause. As the American political scientist Brian Jenkins has stated: "The real targets of terrorist violence are not always the actual victims, but rather the intended audience; terrorism is theatre."[6] And nuclear terror makes gripping theatre.

The media have extended the terrorist's stage. Television, especially, has increased the *visibility* of violence and done more for terrorism than perhaps any other single factor. It has relayed the action as it happens, bringing all but the smell of blood and cordite into the living room—a far cry from the dispatches from the front which took days to arrive and appeared more fiction than fact when finally in print.

Before progressing further, we might ask why nuclear installations will be singled out for terrorist attention instead of other targets, such as oil refineries, chlorine tankers, ocean liners, etc. Arguably, other targets could be attacked with minimum personal risk to the saboteur and at a fraction of the effort. Why then the nuclear dimension? It is not enough to answer "because it is there."

This issue has been debated in the pages of the *Bulletin*;[7] the case is clearly summarized by DeNike:[8]

> Critics of the radioactive-malevolence thesis . . . tend to attribute a remarkable rationality to aggressors—when it is convenient to do so. At other times they readily recognize the same characters as distraught killers. . . . [They overlook] the irrational in human nature.

In fact, the whole debate is now largely academic: nuclear installations *have* been attacked and terrorists *have* used or planned to use radioactive materials maliciously.[9]

No installation, so far as known, has yet been sabotaged in such a way as to release radioactivity; but it is all a question of time. These are the early days, the halcyon days of nuclear power. Some 20 nations have now invested in a nuclear future. Over 200 reactors have been built and are now operating, although mainly in a few countries. By 1980, however, the picture will be different; the number of reactors supplying power is expected to double.[10]

Nuclear facilities possess unique features which will attract the terrorist. They are, for example, highly prestigious targets—symbols of national progress—where an assault will draw the press and embarrass the government. An event involving "atomic terror" will make the headlines. The attack will not even have to succeed to send diplomatic ripples along the corridors of power. It was clearly the intention of the bandits who overran the Atucha station in Argentina to make the front pages (see Table 1).

As nuclear reactors are expensive to repair when damaged, especially if radioactive components are involved, the reactors could become the focus for *economic* sabotage. Electricity grids are a favorite target for saboteurs; and countless small, conventionally fueled units have been put out of action by guerrillas. Nuclear plants, which are massive and serve large areas, may challenge the ingenuity of saboteurs.

Those facilities designed and built by foreign nationals in developing (or even technologically advanced) countries may become symbols of imperialism. Their presence may suggest outside interference in national affairs and an intolerable degree of dependence on foreign expertise and materials. Prominent guerrillas, for example, in South America, have singled out North American firms, property and individuals for "reprisals."[11]

Militant individuals who object to a nuclear plant in their neighborhood may channel their anti-nuclear sentiment into direct action. An incident involving the release of radioactive material could stir up public hostility to nuclear power. The explosions in August 1975 at the Monts d'Aree reactor in France were said to have been a protest against the construction of nuclear plants in Brittany. The demolition of a surveying tower in the United States

Table 1. Attacks on Nuclear Installations or Facilities

Date	Installation	State of Operation	Person(s) Responsible	Possible Reason	Method	Damage
May 4, 1969	USA: Ill. Inst. of tech. reactor[8]	?	?	?	Pipe bomb found	?
Sept. 1970	USA: Point Beach Reactor at Two Creeks, Wis.[a]	?	?	?	Dynamite discovered	?
Dec. 7, 1971	USA: Stanford University Linear Accelerator in Calif.[b]	–	?	?	2 bombs	Heavy damage to electronic control equipment
March 25, 1973	Argentina: Atucha-1 reactor[c]	Nearly built	15 men from ERP[j]	Publicity	Overrun ; ERP flag raised	Damage light; no demands
Feb. 22, 1974	USA: 400 ft. nuclear survey tower in Montague, Mass.[d]	–	Sam Lovejoy	Anti-nuclear demo.	Unbolted the stays	Tower demolished
Aug. 27, 1974	USA: Pilgrim-1 reactor at Plymouth, Mass. [e]	Unit 1 at full power	?	?	Incendiary	Damage light; confined
May 3, 1974	France: Fessenheim reactor near Strasbourg[f]	Nearly built	Meinhof-Puig Antich Group[k]	Anti-nuclear demo.	2 bombs	Considerable damage after fire
May 27, 1975	USA: Zion reactor in Illinois[9]	?	?	?	2 shots apparently fired at security guards	No damage reported
June 6, 1975	France: Framatome (nuclear mfg.) main computer at Courbevoir[h]	–	Garmendia-Angela Luther commando	Anti-nuclear demo.	1 bomb carefully placed	Half input terminals destroyed
	Framatome workshops at Argenteuil[h]	–	"	"	1 bomb carefully placed	Valve testing shops damaged

| Aug. 15, 1975 | France: Monts d'Aree reactor at Brennelis[l] | Fully operating | Breton separatists | Anti-nuclear demo.; nationalism (?) | 2 bombs | Sufficient damage to close plant |

a. *International Herald Tribune*, March 20-21, 1976, p. 3.

b. Brian Jenkins, "Will Terrorists Go Nuclear" (see n.5).

c. *Applied Atomics*, 912 (March 28, 1973), 4.

d. H. Wasserman, "Trial of a Tower Toppler," *Peace News*, 1989 (Feb. 21, 1975), 8.

e. U.S. Atomic Energy Commission, Director, Regulatory Operations, Notification of an Incident or Occurrence No. OUO-8 Washington, D.C.: The Commission, August 1974); AEC, "Current Events, Power Reactors," Sept. 1974, p. 7.

f. *Times* (London), May 5, 1975.

g. John G. Davis, Acting Director, Office of Inspection and Enforcement, U.S. Nuclear Regulatory Commission, to James M. Cubie, *Congress Watch*, Jan 19, 1976.

h. *La Gueule Ouverte*, June 1975; *Undercurrents*, 12 (1975).

i. *Times* (London), Aug. 16, 1975, p. 3; *Nuclear News*, Sept. 1975, p. 134.

j. The Ejercito Revolucionario del Pueblo (ERP) of People Revolutionary Army is a combat wing of the Argentine Trotskyist Party.

k. To my knowledge this group had never been heard of before this incident; Puig Antich was an anarchist executed by the Spanish Government.

belonging to a nuclear company in Montague, Mass., was another violent demonstration against nuclear power.

One can even imagine a group of hallucinated or hysterical individuals attacking a facility to bring retribution on those who were "poisoning the water or killing the wildlife."[12] Other forms of psychotic motivation would depend on the nature of the delusional system involved. The intent may be to get one's name in the papers, to die spectacularly (and, perhaps, to take other lives at the same time) or, alternatively, to cause suffering or seek revenge. Sadistic motivation may result from a specific grudge against particular persons likely to be killed or injured in a nuclear incident.[13]

One of the reasons most commonly cited for an attack is blackmail. Once in control of a nuclear facility, insurgents would be in a convincingly powerful position, as David Comey has pointed out.[14] Protected behind reinforced concrete, they would be difficult to dislodge and could thus exert political and psychological pressure on a government. A counteroffensive would be unthinkable in view of the possible consequences. As Manning Muntzing, former Director of the U.S. Atomic Energy Commission, has conceded:

> A band of highly trained, sophisticated terrorists could conceivably
> take over a nuclear powerplant near a major city and destroy it in
> such a way as to kill thousands—perhaps millions—of people.[15]

Similar sentiments have been expressed by the U.S. General Accounting Office.[16]

One possibility that has been noted for the future is that terrorist groups may be employed as a means of engaging in *surrogate* warfare against other nations. Modern conventional warfare is becoming expensive and an increasingly unattractive mode of conflict.[17] Economic warfare has always been practiced; surrogate warfare is merely an extension of this. It may not be attractive to the major world powers (although their activities often appear to verge on it), but rather to smaller, belligerent nations.

When war threatens, nuclear installations become a national liability; they have been described in civil defense circles as a "Trojan Horse."[18] No surface facility could withstand bombardment by modern artillery. As one leading Finnish nuclear expert stated:[19]

> What happens in the case of war is rather difficult to discuss. It is,
> of course, being considered, but generally the feeling . . . is that in
> a state of war the criteria for safety of nuclear power stations would
> change.

Several countries with nuclear facilities have been involved in conventional wars or armed skirmishes (for example, India, Israel and South Vietnam), although no installations have as yet been attacked. All the countries which have adopted nuclear technology, however, are now encountering escalating terrorist activity; and some, like Argentina, also have serious internal problems. And the nuclear assets of a nation are a heavy responsibility not only when war is threatened but also during times of political instability and increased terrorist activity.

Unfortunately, the nuclear fuel cycle itself offers a range of potential targets for terrorists: uranium enrichment plants, fuel fabrication facilities, reactors (particularly the fast breeders), spent fuel cooling ponds, spent fuel reprocessing facilities (where the isotopes of uranium and plutonium are recovered from the raw wastes), as well as the high level liquid waste storage tanks.[20] As a rule, these installations and facilities are remotely sited and some require few personnel, especially at night.

The nuclear industry faces not only the saboteur with a pass or the saboteur with a gun but also the growing number of well-researched and credible threats by hoaxers. Such threats can cause a disruption in any industry (see Table 2). Security both inside and outside nuclear plants has been tightened; but the measures appear little more than a gesture. As the U.S. General Accounting Office stated:[21]

> ... security systems at licensed nuclear powerplants could not
> prevent a takeover for sabotage by a small number—as few, perhaps,
> as two or three—of armed individuals.

There seems little hope of present security forces' repelling an invasion by lightly armed insurgents; it would take a standing garrison of men—and that would be expensive and politically unattractive.

A malcontent inside any large industry presents a problem by virtue of his job skills. He may act alone, irrationally or in a calculated manner, with malicious intent. He may form part of a team, selling his services to an organization. He may well know precisely what to do to cripple an installation, even without carrying out a dramatic assault. His actions may cause anything from nuisance to calamity.

So far only a few reported incidents at nuclear sites have been positively associated with malice (see Table 3); most of these incidents occurred during industrial unrest or violent strikes. But unofficial reports of mysterious or deliberate damage to facilities circulate too frequently and consistently to be dismissed as mere gossip.

But whether or not it is a disgruntled employee, an amateur or a professional saboteur, sabotage to a very limited number of critical components—identifiable from the open literature—could disable enough safety systems through common-mode failure to lead to a core meltdown of the reactor and a containment failure.[22] Contrary to public opinion, effective sabotage does not need to follow the sequence of any stylized design-basis accident. Shaped charges, for example, which are extraordinarily powerful

Table 2. *Hoaxes and Threats to Nuclear Installations or Facilities*

Date	Installation	Hoax or Threat Received	Purpose
1966-1975	U.K.: facilities of British Nuclear Fuels Ltd. and U.K. Atomic Energy Authority[a]	23 threats and hoaxes received by staff	Various
1969-1976	USA: various facilities[b]	99 threats or acts of violence at licensed nuclear facilities listed by Nuclear Reg. Com.; 76 at facilities under ERDA's jurisdiction	Various
Oct. 1972	USA: fuel fabrication plant at Serrento Valley, Calif.[c]	Hoax: 3 canisters left in plant containing plastic explosive; personnel evacuated for 2½ hrs.; nothing found	To "show it can be done"
Nov. 12, 1972	USA: experimental reactor complex at Oak Ridge Nat. Lab., Tenn.[d]	Hijackers circled over installation and threatened to crash their plane; personnel evaculated, hijacker's bluff called	$10 million ransom
Dec. 15, 1972	Scotland: Dounreay reactor at Caithness[e]	Hoax: 2 parcels left; 1,500 workers evacuated; boxes at other sites	Nationalistic motives; work of the "Jacobites"
Summer 1974	USA: Zion reactor in Illinois[f]	Bomb threats received during industrial unrest; disgruntled employee blamed	?
Sept-Oct. 1974	USA: facilities of Bonneville Power Admin. in Washington and Oregon[g]	14 transmission towers dynamited and 6 demolished during negotiations over demands (extortionists later apprehended)	$1 million blackmail demand
Jan. 30, 1975	U.K.: Windscale reprocessing plant in Cumbria[h]	Telephoned threats of bombs	?

a. *Atom*, No. 233 (March 1976), p. 85. No figures given on numbers of threats to nuclear stations run by the Central Electricity Generating Board (CEGB).
b. *International Herald Tribune*, March 20-21, 1976, p. 2.
c. "Safety-Related Occurrences in Nuclear Facilities as Reported in 1972," ORNL-NSIC-109, Dec. 1973.
d. *Los Angeles Times*, Nov. 12, 1972.
e. *Guardian*, Dec. 15, 1972.
f. *Environment*, 16:8 (Oct. 1974), 21.
g. Armory Lovins and J. Price, *Non-Nuclear Futures: The Case for an Ethical Energy Strategy* (Cambridge, Mass.: Ballinger, 1975).
h. W. Patterson to M. Flood, Feb. 1975.

Table 3. Vandalism and Sabotage at Nuclear Facilities

Date	Installation	Damage
?	U.K.: Winfrith SGHW reactor in Dorset	Component (the calandria) seriously damaged after a compound of mercury, which was deliberately dropped into it, had amalgamated into aluminum base
March 1969- March 1971	USA: Lawrence Research Lab., Berkeley, Calif.[a]	7 separate arson attempts reported; damage not known
April 1970	U.K.: Berkeley reactor in Gloucestershire[b]	Wires controlling discharge machine cut by disgruntled employee
April 1970	U.K.: Wylfa reactor in Anglesey[c]	Gauges and dials smashed; electrical cables cut or removed; dozens of incidents of vandalism reported over 2-year period.
May 12, 1971	USA: Donner Lab., Berkeley, Calif. [a]	Arson attempt; damage not known
Nov. 4 1971	USA: Indian Point reactor in New York[d]	$5 to $10 million damage to equipment as result or arson by former employee
?	USA: Fort St. Vrain reactor at Platteville, Colorado[e]	Cables severed, and clogged helium pumps discovered
April 22, 1973	USA: General Electric, Knolls Atomic Power Lab., New York[a]	Suspected arson; damage not known
Nov. 2, 1973	USA: Turkey Point reactor in Florida[d]	100 off-site incidents of damage to equipment reported during strike; police alerted to rumor of sabotage to main generator
Summer 1974	USA: Trojan reactor in Ranier, Oregon[f]	Vandalism serious problem during construction; an intricate web of hand-shaped copper tubes smashed by hammer
Summer 1974	USA: Zion reactor in Illinois[g]	Valves and switches found in wrong position; other valves repeatedly failed; disgruntled employee suspected
April 4, 1975	USA: Point Beach reactor at Two Creeks, Wis.[a]	Telephone line cut by rifle or pistol fire
July 23,	USA: Nuclear Fuel Services West Valley, N.Y.[a]	Suspected arson in equipment storage barn; no further details

a. John G. Davis to James M. Cubie, Jan. 19, 1976.
b. *Daily Telegram*, April 30, 1970.
c. *Times* (London), May 11, 1970; *Daily Telegraph* (London), May 11, 1970.
d. W. B. Cottreil, "Protection of Nuclear Power Plants Against External Disasters," ORNL-NSIC-117, April 1975.
e. L. D. DeNike, "Unacceptable Security Deficiencies in the Draft EIR, Proposed San Joaquin Nuclear Project," memo to Los Angeles, Calif., Dept. of Water & Power, June 1975.
f. *Oregon Times,* Jan. 1975.
g. *Environment,* 16:8 (Oct. 1974), 21.

weapons, developed specifically for demolishing reinforced concrete, could be used to break through protective shielding, sever pipes and wires and smash safety devices or breach the containment dome. If a nuclear station's ultimate heat sink—the sea, a river or a lake—were cut off by the destruction of cooling water intakes, this could also lead to disastrous consequencès.

After much public debate the electric utility companies in the United States are now legally obliged to provide just two armed guards at each reactor site.[23] France reacted to a spate of terrorist attacks last year by strengthening fencing and alarm systems. Électricité de France has even built an artificial hill beside its Super Phénix fast breeder reactor site to discourage attacks from across the river.[24] In Britain, which has resisted arming its police despite the growth in violence, the government has taken the unprecedented step of arming the Atomic Energy Authority special constables at certain sites.[25] For as Dr. Franklin, Chairman of the Nuclear Power Company, explained:[26]

> It isn't good enough to rely on troops that could take hours to get
> to a nuclear site by helicopter—if the weather isn't foggy.

Perimeter fences have been floodlighted and alarm and communication links extended. The U.K. Minister of State for Energy, justifying the move in the House, commented: "It would be awful if we were considered to be a soft target, because that might invite some form of attack."[27] There is evidence to suggest, however, that the government is more concerned with the prospect of nuclear theft than with sabotage.

Public confidence in the nuclear industry, far from being strengthened by such measures, has been progressively undermined by a spate of incidents. Nuclear sites have been visited "unofficially" by various individuals. Besides the terrorists, who have committed acts of violence and who apparently had little difficulty in breaking through perimeter fences undetected, politicians, security agents, and other individuals testing the security system have entered nuclear installations unobserved or unchecked. One politician even carried a World War II bazooka past guards and detectors at a German site and presented it to the Director (see Table 4).

Utilities have had difficulty monitoring the coming and going of unauthorized people at the main gate. Incompetence and, on a few occasions, bad faith have marred the record. A dozen companies in the United States, for example, have been fined and many more reprimanded for failing to implement statutory security procedures (see Table 5). This has been seen by some as confirmation of the safeguards, but by others as failure. In the worst cases, U.S. companies were fined for failing to tighten security even after being warned. Other countries have been less forthcoming about official reprimands for poor security implementation. Security, however, even for nuclear-weapon stores, cannot be 100 percent foolproof. Black hat teams

Table 4. Security Breaches at Nuclear Installations and Facilities

Date	Installation	Purpose or Method of Entry
1957	U.K.: Calder Hall reactor in Cumberland	A rag stunt[a]
Nov. 18, 1966	U.K.: Bradwell reactor in Essex[b]	Theft of 20 uranium rods; reasons obscure
March 1971	U.K.: Springfield fuel fabrication plant[c]	5 uranium rods disappeared; stolen perhaps in transit or at the Wylfa reactor in Anglesey
Aug. 1971	USA: Vermont Yankee reactor[d]	Intruder wounded a night watchman before escaping
June 25, 1972	USA: New York University reactor[e]	Building broken into; no damage except door panel broken for access
March 15, 1973	USA: Oconee, South Carolina[f]	Break-in at fuel storage building; no material taken
Sept. 4, 1974	USA: U.S. Nuclear Corp., Oak Ridge, Tenn.[f]	Attempted fence breach
Feb. 23, 1975	USA: Nuclear Fuel Services, Erwin, Tenn.[f]	Fence breach; no theft
June 1975	Germany (FRG): Biblis reactor[g]	Werner Twardzig MP carried a Panzer-faust bazooka into the plant to present it to the Director
July 1975	USA: Brunswick reactor in North Carolina[h]	Guards failed to check identification badges of personnel entering the plant
July 1975	USA: Quad Cities reactor in Illinois[i]	NRC inspector entered plant through an open uncontrolled gate
July 2, 1975	USA: Kerr McGee Nuclear Corp., Oklahoma City[f]	Attempted forced entry
Aug 1, 1975	Canada: Pickering reactor in Ontario[j]	Morton Shulman MP entered the plant carrying a satchel; he was not checked at the gate or during his brief visit
Sept. 25 1975	USA: Mass. Inst. of Tech.[f]	Attempted forced entry
Jan. 27, 1976	USA: Three Mile Island reactor in Penn.[k]	Intruder scaled security fence and entered protected area; he later drove off without being apprehended

a. Students at many colleges and universities in Britain set aside one week each year—Rag Week—to help raise money for charity. Rag stunts are occasions for outbursts of boisterous of mischievous merrymaking.
b. *Daily Telegraph*, Nov. 19, 1966, *Guardian*, Nov. 21, 1966.
c. *Times* (London), April 1, 1971.
d. DeNike, "Radioactive Malevolence" (n. 9).
e. New York University to U.S. Atomic Energy Commission, June 26, 1972.
f. John G. Davis to James M. Cubie, Jan. 19, 1976.
g. *Not Man Apart*, 5:19 (Oct. 1975), 17.
h. U.S. Nuclear Regulatory Commission, *News Releases,* 1:33 (Sept. 23, 1975), 1.
i. U.S. Nuclear Regulatory Commission, *News Releases,* 1:35 (Oct. 7, 1975), 1.
j. *Toronto Star,* Aug. 6, 1975, p. A6.
k. U.S. Nuclear Regulatory Commission, *News Releases,* 2:12 (March 23, 1976), 1.

Table 5. U.S. Companies Fined for Non-Compliance with Security Regulations

Date	Installation	Company or Corporation	Offense	Fine* (dollars)
June-Sept. 1974	Dresden reactor in Illinois	Commonwealth Edison	a b c	$25,000[k]
Aug. 1974	Nine Mile Point reactor in New York	Niagara Mohawk Power	a	4,000[l]
Sept. 1974	Three Mile Island reactor in Penn.	Metropolitan Edison	a	3,500[m]
Sept. 1974	Maine Yankee reactor	Maine Yankee Atomic Power	a d e	7,250[n]
Oct. 1974	Surry reactor in Virginia	Virginia Electric & Power	a f	12,000[o]
Oct.-Nov. 1974	Fabrication facility in Attleboro, Mass.	Texas instruments	b	2,000[p]
Oct. 1974	Midwest fuel recovery plant in Ill.	General Electric	f g	6,000[q]
Nov. 1974	West Valley, N.Y. plant	Nuclear Fuel Services	f g	4,000[q]
Dec. 1974	Millstone Point reactor in Conn.	Northeast Nuclear Energy	a b d h	11,500[r]
July 1975	Quad Cities reactor in Ill.	Commonwealth Edison	i h	25,000[s]
July 1975	Brunswick reactor in North Carolina	Carolina Power and Light	a i j	7,000[t]
Jan. 1976	Three Mile Island reactor in Penn.	Metropolitan Edison	b	8,000[u]

*Some of these fines may have been altered on appeal.

a. Failure to control access, or to lock, or maintain surveillance over the entrance to restricted or secure areas of the plant.
b. Failure to implement security plans.
c. Failure to train guards and provide adequate communication between them.
d. Failure to properly document security procedures.
e. Failure to check into the background of guards.
f. Failure to maintain an adequate alarm system and intrusion monitors.
g. Failure to install barriers to protect against industrial sabotage.
h. Failure to provide sufficient perimeter lighting and fencing.
i. Failure to control access to the plant or check the identity of persons entering.
j. Failure to inspect vehicles entering the main gate.
k. U.S. Atomic Energy Commission, *News Releases,* 5:51 (Dec. 18, 1974), 6.
l. U.S. AEC, *News Releases,* 5:38 (Sept. 18, 1974), 4.
m. U.S. AEC, *News Releases,* 5:40 (Oct. 2, 1974; and 5:48 (Nov. 27, 1974), 8.
n. U.S. NRC, *News Releases,* 1:1 (Jan. 24, 1975), 2.
o. U.S. NRC, *News Releases,* 1:1 (Jan. 24, 1975), 3.
p. U.S. NRC, *News Releases,* 5:51 (Dec. 18, 1974), 2.
q. U.S. NRC, *News Releases,* 6:1 (Jan. 1, 1975), 2.
r. U.S. NRC, *News Releases,* 1:11 (April 16, 1975), 2.
s. U.S. NRC, *News Releases,* 1:33 (Sept. 23, 1975), 1.
t. U.S. NRC, *News Releases,* 1:35 (Oct. 7, 1975), 1.
u. U.S. NRC, *News Releases,* 2:12 (March 23, 1976), 1.

from U.S. Special Army Services have entered nuclear-weapon stores during Army exercises despite armed guards, electronic sensors and elaborate locks. And, "if the Army can do it, so could a well-organized terrorist group."[28]

Everything appears in the terrorists' favor. With local superiority of force and sufficient violence, guerrillas could overwhelm security personnel and enter by the front gate. In addition to the element of surprise, modern terrorists are likely to brandish a variety of sophisticated modern munitions, from wire-guided rockets and toxic gas to bazookas and mortars.[29]

A direct assault on an installation seems most probable; but other approaches, such as aerial bombardment, might prove as effective. An air-taxi or helicopter could deliver up to 1,000 pounds of high explosive. Several organizations have already hijacked and deployed light aircraft and helicopters in raids. In January 1974, for example, the IRA attempted to drop milk-churns packed with high explosive onto a police station in Strabane, Northern Ireland.[30] Many nuclear sites in Britain are within easy range of that beleaguered province; Windscale is just 100 miles from Belfast.

A more remote possibility is a kamikaze attack. A threat of this kind occurred in November 1972 to the Oak Ridge National Laboratory in the United States. The impact of a light aircraft might cause only superficial damage to an installation, assuming little fuel and no explosives aboard; but the impact of a larger hijacked aircraft, particularly its engines, would be another matter.

The nuclear industry is obviously concerned about these matters, not only because the potential consequences of an assault or bombardment could be so grave but also because the possibility of sabotage or nuclear theft makes the future of nuclear power look increasingly unattractive to the public. Indeed, this may partly explain the industry's reticence to discuss the hazard. A recent American study on terrorism and nuclear power concluded:[31]

> Given the present volatile character of the nuclear debate in our country, such an act [of sabotage] might cut off our nuclear power plant option.

Events in one nation will not go unnoticed in others. The report from the first disaster will ricochet around the world; but in which country, and when, will it first be heard?

Notes

1. Gil Elliot, *Twentieth Century Book of the Dead* (New York: Ballantine, 1972).
2. Paul Wilkinson, *Political Terrorism* (New York: Macmillan, 1974).
3. We shall not be concerned here with the likelihood of terrorists acquiring

nuclear weapons capability. This unpleasant prospect has been more fully discussed by Mason Willrich and Theodore Taylor in *Nuclear Theft: Risks and Safeguards* (Cambridge, Mass.: Ballinger, 1974).

4. Brian Jenkins quoted in New York Times, Oct. 18, 1974.

5. Jenkins, "Will Terrorists Go Nuclear?" discussion paper no. 64, California Seminar on Arms Control and Foreign Policy, Santa Monica, Ca., Oct. 1975.

6. Jenkins, "International Terrorism: A New Mode of Conflict," research paper no. 48, California Seminar on Arms Control and Foreign Policy, Los Angeles, Ca., 1975.

7. John Holdren, "Hazards of the Nuclear Fuel Cycle," *Bulletin,* Oct. 1974; Bernard L. Cohen, "Perspectives on the Nuclear Debate," *Bulletin,* Oct. 1974; Cohen, communication, *Bulletin,* Jan. 1975; Cohen, communication, *Bulletin,* Feb. 1975; L. Douglas DeNike, communication, *Bulletin,* Feb. 1975.

8. DeNike, *Bulletin,* Feb. 1975.

9. For a discussion of the dispersal of radioactive materials, see Willrich and Taylor (n. 3) and DeNike, "Radioactive Malevolence," *Bulletin,* Feb. 1974.

10. Stockholm International Peace Research Institute, "Preventing Nuclear Weapon Proliferation: An Approach to the Non-Proliferation Treaty Review Conference" (Stockholm: SIPRI, Jan, 1975).

11. See, for example, Carlos Marighella, "Minimanual of the Urban Guerilla," in Robert Moss, "Urban Guerrilla Warfare," Adelphi Paper No. 97, International Institute for Strategic Studies (London): The Institute, 1971).

12. Sandra Good and Susan Murphy, two members of the Manson cult, were recently convicted of conspiring to send 171 letters threatening death to executives accused of polluting the environment. The executives, "sentenced" by the "International People's Court of Retribution," were told that "Pacific Gas and Electric Company, the people who are poisoning the water, the people who are killing the wildlife, the people who are falsely advertising to the public—all of them will be butchered in their bedrooms because they are living off the blood of the little people." See *Undercurrents* (London), No. 13, November/December 1975, p. 4; "Name of Nuclear Figures on Manson 'Death List,' " *Nuclear News,* 18:13 (Oct. 1975), 38.

13. L. Douglas DeNike, "Nuclear Safety and Human Malice," unpublished paper, University of Southern California School of Medicine, 1972.

14. David Comey to M. Flood, March 1976.

15. M. Muntzing quoted in L. Dye, "Nuclear Energy: Great Hopes, Great Problems," Los Angeles Times, Dec. 17, 1973.

16. U.S. General Accounting Office, Comptroller General to Dixy Lee Ray, Chairman, Atomic Energy Commission, Oct. 16, 1974 (B-164105).

17. Brian Jenkins, "High Technology Terrorism and Surrogate War: The Impact of New Technology on Low-Level Violence," RAND Paper Series, P-5339, Jan. 1975.

18. David Krieger, "Nuclear Power: A Trojan Horse for Terrorists," in *Nuclear Proliferation Problems* (Stockholm: Stockholm International Peace Research Institute, 1974), pp. 187-198.

19. Palmgren, *Journal of British Nuclear Energy Society,* 13:1 (Jan. 1974), 120.

20. Spent fuel cooling ponds were singled out in 1974 by the U.S. General Accounting Office (n. 16) as a particular cause for concern. An explotion in the ponds could render an installation unusable; it could even cause a criticality incident by jamming fuel elements together (see Gadi Kaplan, "Bugs in the Nuclear Fuel Cycle," I.E.E.E. Spectrum, 12:9 (Sept. 1975(, 56. Liquid wastes continually generate heat which must be removed. Should the cooling connections be severed, or the tanks breached directly by shaped charges, a serious incident could occur. The possible consequences of such an incident are discussed in an Oak Ridge National Laboratory report (ORNL 4451) and by Kaplan (*I.E.E.E. Spectrum*). See also John Gofman, "Some Important Unexamined Questions Concerning the Barnwell Nuclear Fuel Reprocessing Plant," testimony before the Nuclear Study Committee, State of South Carolina, Jan. 7, 1972.

21. U.S. General Accounting Office (n. 16).

22. A *core meltdown* would occur if there was a failure in a reactor's cooling system that allowed the fuel to heat up to its melting point. A *containment* failure is a major release of fission products to the atmosphere as a result of the breach of the containment building following a core meltdown.

    With regard to a professional saboteur, it is interesting to note the following comment by a former U.S. Navy demolition officer, Bruce Welsh, testifying before the U.S. Joint Committee on Atomic Energy: "I could pick three to five ex-Underwater Demolition, Marine Reconnaissance or Green Beret men at random and sabotage virtually any nuclear reactor in the country. . . . There is no way to stop such activity other than to maintain a system of civil surveillance more strict than that maintained during the last war." See *Environment,* 16:5 (June 1974), 24. See also S. Burnham, et al., "The Threat to Licensed Nuclear facilities," MITRE Corp. study for USNRC, MTR-7022, Sept. 1975, p. 102; and Kevin P. Shea, "An Explosive Reactor Possibility," *Environment,* 18:1 (Jan-Feb. 1976), 6.

23. L. Douglas DeNike, "Terrorist Attacks on California Nuclear Power Facilities: A Threat Analysis," testimony to State of California Assembly Committee on Resources, Land Use and Energy, Nov. 19, 1975.

24. *Nuclear Engineering International,* 20:236 (Nov. 1975), 901.

25. The U.K. Atomic Energy Authority has armed special constables at the Dounreay, Windscale and Winfrith reactor sites as well as at their facilities at Harwell. See Atomic Energy Authority (Special Constables) Bill, Bill 70, *Hansard,* 906:57 (Feb. 26, 1976), 701

26. *New Scientist,* July 10, 1975.

27. *Hansard,* 906:57 (Feb. 26, 1976), 702.

28. Frank Barnaby, "A Problem of Protection," *New Scientist*, 66:951 (May 29, 1975), 494.
29. In April 1975 terrorists stole 3 liter bottles of mustard gas from German Army bunkers; and several cities, including Bonn and Stuttgart were threatened with a gas attack (Guardian, May 13, 1975). In March 1976, Austrian police arrested a four member gang that had produced a large quantity of a poison gas—DEP—which, if inhaled leads to death within 5 minutes. The gas, discovered in capsules, spray cans and bottles, was probably destined for the underworld (Ottawa Citizen, March 2, 1976).
30. Toronto Star, Feb. 9, 1974, p. A8.
31. Burnham, et al., MITRE study (n. 22).

Ted Greenwood

Discouraging Nuclear Proliferation in the Next Decade and Beyond: Non-State Entities

Although Greenwood does not foreclose the possibility of terrorists' aspiring to nuclear terrorism, he does find that the most capable groups are likely to be dissuaded by the tacit threats of retaliation, loss of prestige, and reprisal. Furthermore, he finds that terrorist-inflicted casualties have been relatively limited and indeed have been very far from the levels of wanton human destruction that many would associate with nuclear terrorism. His assertion that all states share an interest in maintaining the taboo against nonstate possession of nuclear weapons may be convincing but could stand further development in terms of policy implications and opportunities for diplomatic action.

Non-state entities acting independently, be they individuals or large, organized revolutionary organizations, and whatever their motivations, lack the legitimacy (both in the possession and use of force and in the control of territory) that international law and tradition afford to sovereign states. Thus they form a special category in the analysis of nonproliferation. Nuclear tests by a country on territory it controls, whatever the political implications, are not considered acts of belligerency. However, a detonation by a non-state entity anywhere except on the high seas would necessarily be on territory claimed by a sovereign state and would necessarily elicit severe retaliation and reprisals.

Just as states employ force or the threat of force for political purposes, so do organized groups of revolutionaries, guerrillas, and terrorists. Thus they can be distinguished, at least for analytical purposes, from criminals motivated by profit and from psychopaths who derive psychic gratification from violence. In fact, however, this distinction is not clear-cut. Small terrorist groups, such as the Japanese Red Army, the Symbionese Liberation Army, and the Baader-Meinhof Gang, act largely out of frustration and alienation. While being motivated by a diffuse political ideology, but lacking nationalistic orientation, they may actually have more in common with criminals and psychopaths than with large, nationally oriented groups such as the Palestinian Liberation Organization, the Irish Republican Army, the Tupamaros, or the Eritrean Liberation Front. All of these groups and individuals are of concern in thinking about non-state use of nuclear weapons. However, since the problems relevant to criminals, psychopaths, and small terrorist groups are quite different from those raised by large revolutionary organizations, they will be considered separately.

There is no need here to open the controversial issue of how various non-state entities might go about fabricating a nuclear explosive or precisely how difficult it would be to do so. Our concern here is more with motivation than with feasibility. Suffice it to say that obtaining weapons-grade material and fabricating even a crude nuclear explosive are reasonably difficult. They require substantial financial and technical resources, a capability for planning and coordinating complex activities, and sufficient cohesiveness and motivation to assure continuity of effort over an extended period of time. Assuming equal incentive, a sizable, organized group is much more likely to succeed than an individual or any small group except in the unlikely event that its members have extensive training in relevant technical areas.

Revolutionaries strive actively to destroy or topple an established political authority or to seek major political or territorial concessions. In doing so they might consider using nuclear weapons in conjunction with guerrilla, terrorist, or traditional military tactics.* Nuclear explosions might be used to disable or impede the operation of the government's deployed forces or to destroy important economic values or symbolic targets. They could also be used to intimidate; to attract attention to a cause; to undermine the legitimacy and authority of a government; to deter the carrying out of targeted activities; or to induce terror, fear, or alarm. They seem particularly attractive for the latter purpose because of the sheer extent of their concentrated power and the strong taboo against their use. The psychological impact of a nuclear explosion would be enormous and global no matter how few actual casualties were caused. There is probably no more dramatic or horrifying weapon of terror or more effective means of instilling fear of the perpetrating organization than a nuclear explosion. It would guarantee immediate, extensive, and continuing world attention.

Yet the power, destructiveness, and radioactive nature of nuclear explosives are potential disadvantages as well. An explosion in a populated area would result in large-scale and wanton killing. Even in their terrorist activities, revolutionary groups do not see killing as useful in and of itself. While people are frequently killed during terrorist attacks, the killing is usually limited, controlled, and calculated to serve one or more specific purposes. Mass killing would have no additional function beyond those served by conventional explosives. The immediate aims of terrorist acts (as opposed to the ultimate

---

*They might also consider seizing or damaging nuclear facilities or stealing nuclear material for reasons other than to manufacture weapons. While of great concern, such activities are not considered here.

objectives of terrorists) have been quite limited. Grand objectives simply cannot be achieved within the time scale of a single act of terror and may simply be unattainable. Governments will not destroy themselves or radically alter the societies they govern in direct response to threat or coercion, no matter how serious. To date, revolutionary terrorists have refrained from many very destructive acts they could accomplish without nuclear weapons. Presumably there has been no particular need or reason to do them.

Despite their revolutionary program and ideology, nationally oriented revolutionary groups have their own extensive stakes in the status quo which they would be loath to jeopardize by resorting to nuclear explosives. For instance, they seek international respectability as a means to legitimize their requests for political support and other aid. Groups engaged in protracted struggle include this endeavor as part of their revolutionary activities. Others may have time to establish respectability only after gaining power. In either case, any use of nuclear weapons that caused widespread destruction would seriously undermine claims to respectability and thus discourage states from granting recognition and support.

More important, any revolutionary group needs a base of support for sanctuary, supplies, and weapons. For groups operating within the territory controlled or claimed by the target government and relying on the support of the general population, a use of nuclear weapons that killed large numbers of people or destroyed important national values or symbols would risk alienating that support and inducing severe repression. The target government would surely gain significant popular support and possibly external aid for its efforts to suppress the perpetrating organization or retaliate against its supporters. Extreme tactics of torture and the unbridled use of military power would be condoned and assisted by the population as never before. Indeed, the likelihood of a popularly based revolutionary group surviving long after its first destructive use of nuclear weapons within the state it was seeking to control seems small. Even revolutionaries that do not rely on popular support (such as military dissidents) are not likely to use nuclear weapons against significant military or symbolic targets. No individual or group wants to achieve control of a nation in which the population and politically significant elites are so alienated that it is unable to govern.

Revolutionary or terrorist groups that receive sanctuary, protection, or significant resources from governments other than the one under attack would risk losing that support as well if they used nuclear weapons. All states have an interest in maintaining a taboo against non-state possession of nuclear weapons and in punishing and suppressing its violators. Sanctuary states in particular would view a nuclear revolutionary group within their borders as a threat to their own security. They would be similarly reluctant to assist the rise to power in a neighboring state of a group whose nuclear capability would make it that much more difficult to control or restrain. As the collapse of the Kurdish rebellion following Iran's withdrawal of support, the rapid decline in airline hijacking after the U.S.-Cuban extradition agreement in 1973, and the history of piracy have demonstrated, the loss of sanctuary and foreign support is fatal to terrorist or revolutionary organizations.

The one way that a revolutionary group might be able to use a nuclear explosive destructively to further its cause, yet not elicit overwhelming opposition from those it was seeking to govern, would be to direct it against an external power, perhaps the United States or Soviet Union, that was supporting the opposed government. The purpose would be to persuade the external power to cease its support. A crude weapon delivered in a boat to a harbor or coastal area would serve the purpose. Although such an operation might be conducted covertly, the revolutionary group could not expect to derive any coercive value from its action if it remained anonymous. Significant costs would therefore be incurred. First, the group's claim to international legitimacy would be jeopardized. Second, its own protectors might reduce or remove their support because of their reluctance to assist a group having nuclear weapons to become a sovereign entity. Third, the target state, particularly if it possessed a large military establishment, would probably redouble its efforts—whether or not supported by states in the geographical region in which the group operated—to eradicate the perpetrating organization. Nuclear use against either the Soviet Union or the United States could be expected to result in immediate and ruthless retaliation.

There are nondestructive ways in which a revolutionary group could use a nuclear weapon. These include detonations deep underground, deep in the ocean, in a remote and unpopulated area, and at high altitudes. Deep underground implacement is very difficult if even reasonable confidence is required that extensive venting will not occur. A deep ocean explosion would not vent but, like one deep underground, might not become publicized in the unlikely event that governments with appropriate detection equipment chose to suppress their intelligence information and succeeded in doing so. A remote land area that was accessible and was governed by a sovereignty that the revolutionary group was willing to affront could provide a relatively costless opportunity to demonstrate nuclear capability. Still, the explosion's long-range, long-term, unpredictable, and uncontrollable radiological effects could be expected to act as an enduring goad for revenge against the perpetrators. Perhaps the best way that a revolutionary group could demonstrate its nuclear capacity would be a high-altitude explosion. If sufficiently high, it would cause minimal fallout and no damage beyond retinal burns to those who looked directly at the fireball. With a careful choice of location, it could be very dramatic. There is ample evidence to suggest that obtaining an appropriate airplane would not be very difficult.

A revolutionary group that employed nuclear explosives in any of these nondestructive ways might avoid loss of legitimacy, loss of support, and

. severe retaliation; at least it might suffer them to a lesser degree. While nondestructive use might be linked to short-term objectives such as inducing terror or gaining publicity, it would be more fruitful as a component of a long-term political strategy. A revolutionary group with demonstrated nuclear capability could exploit nuclear threats against military or urban-industrial targets for coercive purposes. It might thereby be able to achieve political objectives short of overthrow of the opposed government or to exert significant influence on political events. Nondestructive use therefore seems to be the most serious threat from revolutionary groups in possession of nuclear weapons.

Nuclear incentives might be stronger and disincentives weaker for smaller, less capable terrorist organizations that are neither nationally oriented nor in any sense embodiments of the political aspirations of a religious, cultural, or linguistic group. Since they are neither motivated by a well-articulated political program nor tied to a geographical area, these groups (such as the Japanese Red Army or the Baader-Meinhof Gang) have much to gain and little to lose from publicity and the creation of panic. Almost all governments already are actively seeking their destruction. With less stake in the status quo than revolutionary groups with national aims, they might be more likely to use nuclear weapons destructively. Like either individual criminals or psychopaths or small groups of them, however, small terrorist groups generally would not have the resources or support—as nationally oriented revolutionary movements more often would—necessary either to obtain weapons material or, having accomplished that task, to fabricate an explosive. More important, the historical record suggests that even small groups of political extremists, criminals, and psychopaths do not generally perceive mass murder and widespread devastation as useful. Even though non-nuclear means to these ends have long existed, their use has rarely been contemplated seriously.

This discussion suggests that non-state entities are likely to use a nuclear weapon in inverse proportion to their ability to obtain one and that those most able to acquire nuclear weapons would probably use them, if at all, in a manner calculated to minimize destruction. When this analysis is considered with . . . observations about the degree of difficulty of making nuclear explosives and the extent of the incentives and disincentives to use them, it leads to the conclusion that the likelihood of nuclear destruction by non-state entities is quite small and that of any use only slightly greater. Nonetheless, this optimistic assessment does not mean that the likelihood is zero even for a very destructive explosion or that there is no cause for concern and appropriate caution. Indeed, while these conclusions seem to be reasonable extrapolations from the past, the future is as unpredictable in this respect as in any other.

There are several ways to keep the likelihood of nuclear use by non-state entities small or even to reduce it. Most important is to make stealing or otherwise obtaining a weapon or weapons material exceedingly difficult by adequately protecting all fissile material and particularly all weapons stockpiles. Guarding against large armed attacks would be very expensive, perhaps prohibitively so, but protection against the small groups and individuals that pose the greatest threat is less difficult. Nations in which there is a history of violent and socially disruptive struggles for power or in which terrorist groups have been able to operate with relative impunity pose the greatest risks. If they acquire civilian power facilities, stringent measures should be taken to reduce the chances that nuclear material can be seized under any conditions ranging from tranquility to extreme disintegration. Similar security measures will also be necessary if such states actually acquire nuclear weapons. Unfortunately, such requirements are easier to enunciate than to implement.

Governments could also try to anticipate which non-state groups are most likely to seek a nuclear capability and to suppress or dissuade them. For criminals, psychopaths, and small terrorist groups, suppression would be appropriate but has its limitations. Even an extensive intelligence capability may be unable to identify high-risk individuals or groups until they have acted. Some observers argue that the level of government surveillance or other sorts of intrusions into citizens' lives which would be necessary for potential nuclear terrorists to be recognized and suppressed would significantly undermine the foundations of democratic societies. Their claim is based upon assumptions and conclusions—about the ease of fabricating or stealing nuclear explosives and about the likelihood that someone will try to obtain weapons and will use them if successful—that are quite different from those reached in this analysis. There is indeed a limit to the degree of suppression possible and desirable in democratic societies and a limit to its effectiveness anywhere. However, these limits seem far beyond what is necessary to render the likelihood of nuclear terrorism very small. Indeed, the primary focus should be on protection of materials, not surveillance and suppression of potential terrorists.

The matter of identification and dissuasion is more complex for nationally oriented revolutionary groups. States are likely to support or oppose such groups for political reasons unconnected to nuclear potential. Changing a policy of opposition to one of support of a group because it seems about to launch a nuclear program would provide a major incentive for others to follow suit and would thereby expose states to easy manipulation and blackmail. It is not, therefore, either a useful or a likely method of dissuasion. Instead, states backing revolutionary groups would be well advised to make their support conditional on nuclear abstinence. While this position cannot be made formal by treaty or public statement, it nonetheless should and probably will be adopted and implemented subtly as a matter of pure self-interest.

Nuclear threats by non-state entities are a matter quite different from nuclear use. For nationally oriented revolutionary groups, the incentives and disincentives for employing nuclear threats would not be very different from those already discussed for nuclear use, although perhaps not as strong. The primary incentive would be the desire to coerce, extort, or terrorize. The primary disincentives would be the loss of legitimacy and support and the possibility of increased active repression.

But nuclear threats can be made by anyone (including criminals, psychopaths, and pranksters), for any purpose, with only a phone call or a letter. However, making the threat believable, whether to government officials or to the general public, is another matter. Under some circumstances, proof of possession of nuclear material or perhaps publication of a weapons design might be necessary. Yet even a totally unsupported threat that is well publicized might be all that is required to cause public alarm. The requirement would surely depend on the particular circumstances, including how the threat is made and how responsible officials and the media react. Although nuclear threats have been made in the United States and the Middle East and may very well be made again, none so far has been credible.

There seems to be little that can be done to prevent such threats except to minimize the expectation that they will result in benefit or personal gratification. For that purpose, the less discussion of threats the better, except when discussion focuses on states' determination to resist decisively. Since fashions seem to develop in the activities of criminals, psychopaths, and pranksters and since an important objective of terrorist threats, no less than of attacks, is publicity, governments at all levels should attempt to conceal the existence of a nuclear threat except, of course, if there is good reason to believe it is real. In this effort they should seek the understanding and cooperation of the media.

Reactions of resistance and minimal publicity may seem a lame prescription for deterring nuclear threats, but short of pervasive state surveillance of citizens' activities, there appear to be no alternatives. The reactions to and outcomes of the first few threats will strongly influence the frequency of subsequent ones. Protection and monitoring of fissile material is again critical; if sufficient confidence exists that no fissile material has been lost, nuclear threats will not be credible and cannot be real.

An international convention for the suppression of nuclear terrorism has been proposed, modeled after the Convention for the Suppression of Unlawful Seizure of Aircraft of 1971. It would be useful to the extent that it fostered the adoption of stringent physical security measures by all states, assured the denial of sanctuary to nuclear terrorists, and established a useful norm of national behavior. But its usefulness for deterrence would be limited. Those groups or individuals most likely to engage in nuclear terror or threat either are actively pursued anyway by national and international security organizations or would operate solely within the national borders of a single state.

More important are the encouragement of national governments' efforts to develop and employ very strict physical protection measures and the strengthening of the IAEA's role in assisting them. Adequate physical protection standards, no less than adequate safeguards, should be and are increasingly becoming a prerequisite to the sale of nuclear reactors or fuel-cycle equipment and technology. The recent nuclear suppliers' agreement included a provision requiring states purchasing nuclear facilities and materials to furnish rather stringent physical protection. Industrialized states with already large nuclear programs should lead the way by sharing technology and experience and, where necessary, by offering subsidies. Finally, the likelihood of social and political disorder that might so erode normal physical protection arrangements as to make access to weapons-grade material relatively easy for non-state entities should be seriously considered in decisions about which countries pose too high a risk for the transfer of reactors and other fuel-cycle facilities.

Martha C. Hutchinson

Defining Future Threats:
Terrorists and
Nuclear Proliferation

Hutchinson's analysis of contemporary terrorism leads her to the conclusion that the harm done by terrorists will continue to increase, and thus the possibility of nuclear terrorism is a real one. The essence of terrorism is said to be the willingness to accept risks in order to achieve political goals; such willingness prevails in this analysis. In addition, Hutchinson does not find that the prospect of mass casualties will deter at least some terrorists from employing nuclear weapons. Her concluding comments on the actions that governments may adopt to prevent nuclear terrorism, or failing that, to cope with nuclear terrorism, are likely to be of interest to even those who may object to her earlier conclusions.

George Quester has already defined the danger of what he called "micro-proliferation," the use of nuclear materials or weapons by non-governmental terrorist organizations.[1] We urgently need to think about how to deal with the possible intersection of two current lines of development in world politics: 1. terrorism, primarily a political phenomenon and 2. a growing dependence on nuclear energy, a technological phenomenon. Paradoxically, terrorism is usually considered as a "weapon of the weak," because groups who employ the extraordinary violence we label terrorism are resourceless by conventional standards. On the other hand, nuclear power is the hallmark and symbol of "super power" in international relations.

The specter of micro-proliferation or nuclear terrorism is an ambiguous and ill-defined danger that may exist in the future. As yet we have been alarmed only by hoaxes and warnings, but the fear that some incident of nuclear terrorism might occur is strong. How are we to assess the credibility and magnitude of such a future threat? Why does the threat exist? Exactly what is the danger we fear? What is the solution to the problem? What are governments doing to cope with the threat, and what sort of policies should they follow?

Why does the threat of nuclear terrorism exist? The threat depends upon the concurrence of two conditions: 1. growth of the civilian nuclear power industry and 2. its vulnerability to theft or attack by small groups. These conditions and the quantity and the quality of nuclear growth are permissive or enabling causes of nuclear terrorism. If commercial nuclear power were not spreading rapidly and widely, and if proliferation did not involve the acquisition of complete nuclear fuel cycles (not just power reactors), the threat might remain remote. However, nuclear growth has led to insecurity, and vulnerability is further magnified as the number of conspicuous and appropriate targets for terrorism increases. Until recently, we recognized the danger of the proliferation of international weapons, but encouraged the civilian use of nuclear energy for peaceful purposes. Now many nations perceive that any nuclear development constitutes a liability, not only for the developer but for the entire world.

Technically, the vulnerability of nuclear fuel cycles (or power systems) is due to the presence of "special nuclear materials," primarily highly enriched uranium and plutonium, in amounts that are "critical" enough to construct some kind of explosive device. Neither substance is used in the types of commercial power reactors built today, although they may be available in experimental or research reactors or weapons production.[2] However, plutonium is present in spent reactor fuel and is presently stored because reprocessing spent fuel into new fuel is not yet done commercially. Moreover, reactors of the future may use special nuclear materials as fuel; in fact, the liquid-metal, fast breeder reactor will produce more plutonium than it consumes, thereby providing its greatest utility. Reliance on plutonium for fuel may increase if a suspected natural uranium shortage develops. The most vulnerable aspects of the fuel cycle, in which highly enriched uranium and plutonium are found in basically usable form, occur in fuel reprocessing and fabrication and at uranium enrichment plants, and shipping and storage areas.[3] The projected spread of these facilities will of course increase vulnerability to terrorism on a global scale.

Predictions of future insecurity also depend on a substantial reliance upon nuclear power for the world's future energy needs. There are doubts as to the economic feasibility and the safety of nuclear energy, and the possibility exists that less risky and cheaper alternatives may be found. At present, however, there is no indication that the trend toward dependence on nuclear power will not continue.

Despite the limited amounts of special nuclear materials in contemporary fuel cycles, present nuclear facilities are vulnerable to terrorism. Since 1967, the risk of terrorism has been amply documented by governmental and private studies in the United States.[4] Despite greatly enhanced security precautions taken as a result of internal and external criticism, both the United States civilian and military programs (especially weapons located abroad) are considered insecure. Although it is almost impossible to acquire specific information on the security of foreign nuclear programs (no evidence exists of foreign public debates comparable to those in the United States), they are generally considered more vulnerable than United States programs. The recognition of present danger supports the assumption of enhanced insecurity in the future.

In explaining the existence of a threat of nuclear power, we need to ask ourselves what we mean by security *from* what and vulnerability *to* what? Terrorism, the systematic use or threat of extraordinary violence by non-governmental individuals to obtain political objectives, has.expanded in the post-war world. Terrorist exploitation of nuclear power would be a new tactical gloss on an old strategy; the basic causes and patterns of terrorism will remain fundamentally unchanged. The motivations which now inspire terrorism are not likely to disappear; in fact, they may increase. If political frustration and alienation grow, if terrorism continues to appear to be successful, available, and an easy way to satisfy grievances, then at some time the idea of nuclear terrorism will occur to those individuals who have been inspired by the convenience of machine guns and letter bombs, the vulnerability of air transportation, and the ease of kidnapping diplomats and businessmen.

That nuclear terrorism is likely to be a new means to old ends does not exclude the possibility of new motivations for terrorism. However, since the nineteenth century when terrorism against governments first became a technique of modern political protest and until terrorism spread from internal war to world politics, the causes of motivations for terrorist activity have remained relatively constant, while the permissive causes or opportunities for new forms of violence have grown. Recently, with the development of the mass communications media, the motives for terrorism have been diffused worldwide. Terrorism has almost become a respectable revolutionary strategy. The awareness that the discontent of others has found expression in terrorist violence encourages new terrorism. The publicity given to terrorism may make groups aware not only of strengths but also of grievances previously ignored. The communication of information about terrorism can create new expectations and new hopes. However, although new motives may enter the game, the phenomenon of terrorism remains basically the same.

Precisely what is it that threatens us? Why and how would a terrorist organization use or threaten nuclear violence? The number of possible scenarios of nuclear terrorism is undoubtedly infinite, but we can derive clues to the potential nuclear terrorist from past patterns of terrorist behavior and the special characteristics required for using nuclear power. We must, however, remain aware of the fearful inventiveness of the terrorists which makes future violence difficult to predict. Given the characteristics of terrorist groups, their usual purposes, and their methods, what would make nuclear power an attractive weapon for terrorists? If it was attractive, what might result?

The terrorist organization is by definition a non-governmental individual group with transnational organizational ties that cross national boundaries, an internal opposition movement, or a government bureaucracy acting independently, composed of military personnel or police. The factors which normally inhibit the conduct of government—responsibility to public opinion or organized interests, bureaucratic politics, reputation, or international legality or morality—would probably not constrain the actions of terrorists. Nor would terrorists, unless they represent a particular ethnic group or regional area, likely have a recognized geographic territory or national population against which a government could threaten retaliation.[5]

There are no ethnic or geographical restrictions on the origins of potential terrorist groups. In the past, groups have been organized in industrial as well as developing states and on all continents. Only in Communist states, excluding Yugoslavia, do we see no terrorism originating. Terrorism, like nuclear power, is becoming a world phenomenon.

In order to handle nuclear materials, to build some sort of explosive device, to seize a power plant, or otherwise to exploit nuclear power, some terrorists must acquire technical and scientific qualifications. The spread of knowledge is a largely uncontrollable transnational force, spurred by national ambitions for economic development and modernization. The skills of nuclear technology are a by-product of the diffusion of nuclear power. Since an American college chemistry student, using only publicly available information, was able to design a workable atomic bomb, technical requirements obviously will not pose a serious obstacle to the would-be nuclear terrorist. According to Theodore Taylor, construction of a nuclear explosive is no more complex than the manufacture of heroin.[6]

The terrorist group capable of stealing nuclear material, building a bomb, attacking a nuclear facility or shipment, or dispersing plutonium in a building, would not have to be extremely large. One person could conceivably build a very crude bomb; a team of about five technically proficient people could apparently build a bomb quite efficiently and safely.[7] The United States Atomic Energy Commission based its physical protection regulations on the arbitrary criterion of resistance to an armed attack of twelve to fifteen people. Undoubtedly, an exceedingly small organization could present a credible threat, especially if the group had connections with industry or government to simplify theft or attack.

However, nuclear violence would have to be a well-organized and carefully planned operation, much more so than past acts of terrorism (not that some acts have not been painstakingly planned and executed). The perpetrators would have to be a stable and cohesive group, capable of maintaining a conspiratorial unity for at least several months. If explosives had to be constructed from surreptitiously stolen materials, the operation would be quite time-consuming. For building a bomb, estimates range from a few weeks to over a year, depending on the number of people involved, their skill, experience, and resources, and the reliability and accuracy of the bomb. No matter what form it took, an act of nuclear terrorism could not be the result of a hasty or impromptu decision.

Financial resources would also be required by terrorists who intended to build a bomb. One estimate indicates that three or four people at an expense of $30,000 could in a year build a device that would almost certainly explode. A less reliable explosive could be devised by people willing to spend $10,000.[8] The necessary laboratory equipment is easily purchased at an unprohibitive expense for many existing terrorist groups, but nuclear terrorism need not require building a bomb.

Therefore, only a well-established and reasonably well-financed terrorist organization would be likely to detonate some kind of nuclear explosive, however crude. A less unified or well-provided group could mount less spectacular threats, such as attacking or seizing a nuclear shipment or plant or stealing and distributing plutonium; these threats would be more likely, because they are simpler to make. Nevertheless, no act of nuclear terrorism would be easy, and advance planning would be essential.

The most important characteristic of the potential nuclear terrorist is a willingness to take high risks. Any act of nuclear violence, including theft or sabotage, would be more risky in personal terms than any other form of terrorism, even given extensive proliferation and vulnerability. Most terrorists are apparently rational individuals, who undertake a campaign of terrorism, because the benefits to be gained exceed the estimated risks and costs. To calculate the cost-benefit ratio favorably, terrorists must feel competent about their abilities;[9] they must think that they have a chance of succeeding. Their success depends of what their goals are. Propensity for accepting risk is also related to the amount of their commitment to political values, which are also reflected in the nature of the objectives of the terrorist. Risk-taking is closely related to terrorist goals.

Regardless of the ideological bias of the terrorist group—revolutionary, nationalist, separatist, reactionary, anarchist—the objectives of terrorism can be conveniently categorized as 1. strategic and 2. tactical. Strategic goals are long-run, general, and often relatively imprecise. Tactical goals are short-run bargaining demands which are a means to strategic ends. The use of violence and threats for purposes of bargaining is a new development in the general pattern of terrorism.

The strategic aims of terrorism involve the disruption of the political status quo, on a national or international level. Terrorists seek to define and dramatize a cause through publicity. They do not necessarily want the approval of an audience of domestic or world public opinion; attention may be obtained at the expense of creating hostility. The terrorist group attempts to create insecurity and disorientation in the "enemy," who may be a government, a social class, or an entire national, social, or ethnic group.

Discrediting a government by demonstrating the impotence of the authorities faced with terrorist violence is a way of increasing instability. Provoking a government to unpopular and disruptive repressive measures can also be a part of the strategy of terrorists.

The tactical goals of terrorism are expressed in specific demands for definite concessions from governments or multinational corporations. Extortionate demands have included the payment of a monetary ransom, the release of prisoners, the publication of ideological statements, provision of food or medical supplies, safe transport to a country of asylum, and immediate and visible policy changes. Terrorists often demand acts of symbolic value in terms of their long-run goals.

The means selected by future nuclear terrorists will be logically related to their goals as well as to the accessibility of nuclear power. People who discount the risk of nuclear terrorism argue that because terrorists could obtain and use other equally destructive conventional explosives at much less cost, there is no reason for a nuclear threat.[10] Their argument overlooks the publicity value of the use of nuclear violence. If the present international prohibition on the use of nuclear force holds in the future, the political and psychological effects of even minor nuclear violence, although incomparable in physical destructiveness to strategic nuclear war, would be infinitely greater than the impact of conventional explosives. Similarly, the dispersal of plutonium would have consequences disproportionate to the actual number and timing of deaths caused.[11] The creation of emotional reactions out of all proportion to actual deaths or damage caused by violence is an essential characteristic of terrorism.

Skeptics also argue that because past terrorists have avoided large-scale explosions causing more than a hundred casualties, despite an ability to do so through conventional means, future terrorists will not want to risk incurring popular opprobrium and hostility by, for example, exploding a nuclear device in a city.[12] It seems naive to trust the good-will and humanitarian instincts of terrorists to prevent mass casualties. The argument, although ostensibly based on past experience, overlooks a definite trend toward greater destructiveness accompanying the availability of more sophisticated weapons and explosives. The lessons of the past indicate that the trend toward greater harm will continue. If in the future states have broken the prohibition against the coercive use of nuclear power, then terrorists would also be tempted to adopt comparable means of coercion. The effects and the effectiveness of terrorism must be seen in context. Nuclear war would drastically alter the context of terrorism by lessening the dramatic impact of nuclear terrorism and by making greater than conventional destructiveness necessary in order to impress an audience, especially a universal one.

Past terrorists have not avoided acts which might alienate many people. A single act of terrorism usually has many effects, depending on the identity and reaction of different audiences. Although terrorism is not generally indiscriminate, it may be indiscriminate against a targeted group. If the direct audience is the "enemy"—a social group hostile to the terrorists' aims—then mass casualties within that group would not necessarily be undesirable. Imagine, for example, a not implausible world in the future when the gap between rich and poor countries has grown rapidly. The anti-American, anti-imperialist, and anti-Western motives which have led to terrorism in the past are stronger, deeper, and wider. A terrorist group from a poor state might feel few qualms about causing additional American deaths that might increase their popularity in their poor, home state.

The means of terrorism are closely related to ends. Given the goals described, the methods of nuclear terrorism would fall into two types: 1. destructive, one-step acts serving primarily strategic goals and 2. complicated bargaining moves, implementing both general aims and specific demands.

Destructive terrorism is characterized by many casualties in an enemy group and less frequently acts of sabotage involving impressive damage. Bombings, often without prior warning, are common. Terrorists determined on using nuclear power could attempt theft and detonation of a nuclear weapon, theft of nuclear materials to construct and explode a bomb, sabotage of a nuclear facility or cargo to cause notable damage like the radioactive contamination of the surroundings or incapacitation of a plant, or theft and dispersal of radioactive or toxic substances like plutonium. Either overt or covert theft is possible, although covert theft would intensify the surprise effect of subsequent violence. Presumably groups aspiring to general national or international sympathy would select material targets to avoid human casualties. However, an organization seeking attention at any price or hostile to the audience to be affected (especially the people who would identify with or feel sympathetic toward the victims) would be insensitive to human deaths.

In bargaining during terrorism, a threat of violence is intended as the opening move in a give-and-take situation. Usually by seizing hostages, the terrorists attempt to acquire the status with which to bargain with a government or corporation. The seizure of hostages is an initial act of violence which makes the threat of further violence credible and gives the terrorists a means of rewarding a government or corporation if it accedes to the terrorists' demands. Terrorists who threaten nuclear violence if an ultimatum is not met must establish credibility, although the magnitude of the threat will be indisputable. Several ways exist to demonstrate the believability of a threat. First, nuclear material could be stolen overtly through an armed attack or in a manner that could subsequently be demonstrated to the authorities and to the public. On the basis of clear evidence of possession, a threat would probably be quite effective whether or not a bomb were actually constructed. If the time between theft and communication of a threat were long enough, the terrorists' claim of having built a bomb would be plausible. On the other hand, lengthening the period between theft and threat increases the risk for the terrorists if the government detects the loss of material. If plutonium were stolen, the problem of "critical time" would not exist.

Stealing enough material to build two bombs, or a large amount of plutonium, would be a difficult way to establish credibility of terrorists. The terrorists could explode, perhaps in an unpopulated area, a first bomb as proof of intent and determination. They might threaten to explode a second with worse consequences in order to deter pursuit from the authorities. A very small amount of plutonium could be dispersed in surroundings of low population density; then the magnitude of the threat might be escalated by communicating an intention to use additional plutonium in a crowded area next time. Bluffs are also conceivable.

Obviously a terrorist group could invent innumerable and various strategies and tactics, many of which need not involve the construction of an atomic bomb. What could the terrorists demand of governments? What concessions would be worth the risks of attempted nuclear extortion?

Bargaining demands could be symbolically related to nuclear power. A group could demand a halt to nuclear development. Other demands might be unrelated; while the potential violence would be extraordinary, the demands would not need to be. Since the United States has consistently refused to meet terrorist demands, a determined group might calculate that in order to force ordinary concessions, they would have to escalate their threat to nuclear dimensions. The United States has often been a third party target of transnational terrorism; terrorists have seized American hostages in a foreign country to force the host government to meet their demands. Nuclear terrorism to create coercion and bargaining is possible, but it does not seem necessary, because terrorists have been successful using conventional means.

Although destruction for immediate effect appears to be dangerous from the victims' point of view, bargaining during terrorism has its own perils. Once terrorists would announce a nuclear threat, especially publicly, tension would be acute. Terrorists evidently believe that they can control the risks inherent in a public situation of conflict, but the dangers of miscalculation or accident under pressure would be immense.

The major responsibility for coping with the threat of nuclear terrorism lies with governments. Not only are all matters of internal and external security the proper functions of government, but also the growth of nuclear industry has been promoted and regulated by governments in all countries. Consequently, nations bear some responsibility for the existence of the danger.

Preventing nuclear terrorism is not considered to be worth the cost of abandoning nuclear power as a source of energy. The question of a current policy response is framed around limiting, not halting, civilian nuclear development and improving physical security first. Governments are primarily concerned with controlling expansion and limiting vulnerability. They are also more interested in diverting nuclear power developed by the civilian sector to military uses than they are with the threat of terrorism.

Extensive criticism from inside and outside the United States government has made policymakers sensitive to the dangers involved in the civilian nuclear power industry. Frequent hoaxes and false alarms have publicized these dangers. Since 1973, the government has imposed stringent security requirements upon the nation's commercial licensees. These include design requirements for physical barriers, lighting, and exits, trained guards; security checks for personnel; detection procedures at exits; materials accountability for inventories; and an obligatory capability to respond to attacks and to establish liaison with government authorities. Transported nuclear materials have also received increased protection; armed guards ride with truck and train shipments and maintain radio communications *en route*. Military security has also been upgraded sharply in recent years; the Department of Defense budget in fiscal year 1976 provided $34 million for nuclear weapons security at Army sites in Europe.

Because both international interdependence and the nature of terrorist threat equalize state vulnerability, nuclear energy is a crucial foreign policy issue, dealt with on unilateral, bilateral, and multilateral levels, both formally and informally. The most visible interaction occurs in one formal institution, the International Atomic Energy Agency (I.A.E.A.), which has the dual responsibility of promoting the development of peaceful atomic energy and preventing weapons proliferation. To prevent diversion for military purposes, its authority to enforce safeguards on civilian programs was reinforced by the 1968 Non-Proliferation Treaty (N.P.T.) which requires non-nuclear weapon states signing it to submit to I.A.E.A. safeguards. Nuclear weapon states can export nuclear materials only under safeguards. Because not all nuclear weapon states are party to the treaty and since the successful Indian diversion of material for a bomb, some doubt exists as to whether the I.A.E.A. performs adequately.

While preventing weapons proliferation is one of the I.A.E.A.'s main responsibilities, preventing micro-proliferation is definitely a secondary task. Because of the sensitivities of sovereign states about internal security, the I.A.E.A. has no authority to enforce measures against non-governmental diversion or attack. In 1972 and in 1975, the I.A.E.A. convened experts to recommend physical protection standards for member states, but these recommendations are only guidelines; they are not binding. They merely symbolize the existence of concern among some of the I.A.E.A.'s 106 members.

The control of civilian nuclear exports is also the subject of international activity. However, the forum for international policymaking on exports is informal, and membership is restricted. No institutions have been created or treaties proposed, but a limited group of seven of ten supplier states met frequently in 1975 to establish what are essentially civilian non-proliferation agreements.

The initiator of the sudden activity by supplier states was the United States, which has the greatest responsibility in the area, because it is the supplier of seventy percent of all power reactors in operation or in order worldwide, with eighty percent of all foreign purchases financed by the Export-Import Bank.[13] Attempts at control by the United States have also been prompted by the same domestic criticism that led to the tightening of security at home. Since 1974, the United States has unilaterally required a determination of adequate physical security, including on-site inspection, before critical amounts of special nuclear materials may be exported.[14] The government also requires that spent reactor fuel be reprocessed outside the recipient country to reduce the danger of diversion or misuse of extracted plutonium. The United States refuses to export reprocessing or enrichment equipment or technology.

Policy-makers and industry in the United States are afraid that unilateral export restrictions weaken the nation's competitive position, since other states, notably West Germany and France, are less scrupulous in their export practices. These European suppliers will sell enrichment and reprocessing plants. An irony of international commercial competition in nuclear energy is that Framatome in France and Kraftwerk in West Germany are United States licensees and basically re-export American technology. Westinghouse owns forty-five percent of Framatome.[15]

After a controversial West German deal with Brazil, the seven supplier states, urged by the United States, agreed on mutual consultations during negotiations for foreign sales and on the imposition of strict controls on the end-use of nuclear exports.[16] This de facto cartel of exporters links the Soviet Union, Japan, and the West, including France which has not signed the Non-Proliferation Treaty, in a rather delicate combination of odd partners. Not only are their negotiations conducted in the utmost secrecy, but also their agreements will probably be limited in scope. For example, the United States proposal of regional nuclear fuel centers was rejected. However, informal policy coordination demonstrates that the common interest in preventing state and non-state proliferation can occasionally transcend political and economic rivalries.

There are many other ambitious proposals to prevent nuclear terrorism immediately. Recommendations can be grouped as they relate to controlling the spread of nuclear power, improving physical protection of nuclear materials, deterring terrorism with threats, and other "positive" methods to reduce the threat.

Controlling or limiting the spread of nuclear facilities would minimize the number of targets open to violence and would simplify the protection of them. One suggestion, favored by the Ford administration, encourages the United States to support commercial uranium enrichment and fuel reprocessing, because if ample supplies were available from the United States, other countries would not have the incentive to acquire indigenous facilities. Another idea is to concentrate nuclear functions by creating regional fuel centers internationally or "nuclear parks" on domestic levels. Reprocessing, enrichment, and fuel fabrication could be done in one location, minimizing transportation and assuring centralized control. The United States favors this idea, and the I.A.E.A. is currently concluding a study of the international feasibility of it. Another possible means of limiting civilian proliferation is the encouragement of alternative sources of energy. However, this option does not appear to be very attractive to policymakers or industry.

Direct improvement of physical protection could be accomplished through an international treaty requiring uniform standards, enforced by the I.A.E.A. The I.A.E.A.'s physical protection experts recommended a formal convention on international transportation safeguards. However, any expansion of the I.A.E.A.'s authority does not seem politically feasible. New responsibilities would be costly as well. On a bilateral level, supplier states could require that nuclear facilities be designed for security or that existing security practices be improved, as the United States requires. The bilateral imposition of safeguards seems to be the direction of current momentum, although it risks arousing the ire of recipient states; to be effective the imposition of safeguards requires the cooperation of all supplier states. Almost never mentioned is the possibility that the supplier countries could provide some kind of international financial assistance for their clientele, for whom security costs in addition to the high cost of nuclear power may be prohibitive. Because most commercial nuclear exports are government-financed, security assistance, without undue interference in local affairs, is possible. At least information on efficient plant design could be communicated at low cost to a recipient state.

Another means of preventing nuclear terrorism is through deterrence. Although physical protection measures may in some sense "deter" by making an act of terrorism extremely difficult and possibly more dangerous for the terrorists, deterrence means threatening punishment to a would-be terrorist if he commits a certain transgression. Specific deterrent measures, many of which have been suggested, would include imposition of the death penalty for any theft of special nuclear materials or for an attack on a plant or shipment. These measures improve a government's intervention capabilities. In the United States, specially trained military units respond to a terrorist attack. Globally, an international police force, perhaps under the auspices of the I.A.E.A., could be mandated to respond to terrorism.

Numerous problems are involved in relying on deterrence to prevent terrorism.[17] Theoretically, a strategy of deterrence depends upon shared standards of rationality between the potential initiator of a threat and the party wanting to deter the threat. When criteria of rationality differ, it is difficult for government policy-makers to perceive a terrorist threat accurately. In their study of United States policy on deterrence of limited conflicts, Alexander George and Richard Smoke found that decision-makers frequently underestimated their opponent's willingness to take risks.[18] Because knowledge and understanding of a terrorist's goals and values are more vague than perceptions of state behavior, a faulty analysis of the terrorist adversary is very likely. Governments tend to dismiss a terrorist's propensity to take high risks as irrational, but if terrorists are irrational, then no threat of punishment would deter them. If a government really wants to deter terrorism, then it must discover what kind of threat terrorists would interpret as punishment severe enough to make the terrorists rationally cease their terrorism.

An equally serious problem in implementing a strategy of deterrence is establishing the credibility of the deterrent threat. The strategic nuclear threat of retaliation against an aggressor's home population bears little correspondence to terrorism. A government threat to a terrorist usually involves personal harm or imprisonment and only secondarily involves the elimination of an organization as a political group or, perhaps more importantly, the destruction of the values or ideology which the terrorist believes his action supports. A terrorist may think that through his act, no matter what the future may be for himself or his comrades, the ideas he represents will continue to live.

The uncertainty of the implementation of a threat also weakens its credibility. Although the capture and punishment of a domestic terrorist may be certain, depending upon the state, international interdependence interferes with punishment of the transnational terrorist. To punish a hijacker or a hostage-taker, the United States must rely on the cooperation of other states to extradite or prosecute. Such dependence has proved unsatisfactory, and terrorists who operate transnationally probably feel sure that they may escape punishment. Consequently, unilateral deterrence cannot be effectively implemented, but mutual deterrence on a world scale is politically impossible.

Deterrence, which involves conflict and cooperation, also depends upon the adversaries' perception of a common interest that may be reflected in the outcome of a conflict. Both sides, the terrorists and the government, must compromise, but both must stand to gain something. The mutual aim of survival by avoiding nuclear catastrophe, which is at the heart of strategic deterrence, is missing. Perhaps the threats have not been horrible enough to make avoidance and survival reasons to compromise.

Terrorism may well be a threat that cannot be deterred. It is, however, dangerous to rely on deterrence as a protection against a threat of nuclear terrorism. Positive alternatives to deterrence would include maintaining an international climate of opinion in which the use of any form of nuclear weapons by states or non-states remains abhorrent and counter-productive. Another alternative, unfortunately utopian in present international relations, would be providing some peaceful means to at least recognize if not arbitrate political grievances. For example, an International Court of Justice could hear claims of non-states. Because the entire international community is now susceptible to the consequences of frustrations caused by the policies of each member, official repression which may inspire terrorism is no longer a purely domestic matter. Neither the responsibility for injustice nor its effects can be isolated. Because not all terrorism is caused by genuine political grievances, these positive proposals would not solve the problem entirely. However, the removal of one source of terrorism would diminish the imitation effect and would help remove the aura of revolutionary legitimacy which surrounds the use of terrorism.

Another area of government policy, a discussion of which inevitably sounds like a Dr. Strangelove, is contingency planning. If an incident of nuclear terrorism should occur and if all efforts at prevention and deterrence have failed, what should be the response of the threatened or attacked government? What should be the reaction of the international community? To cope with terrorist acts of either destruction or bargaining, advance planning for a coordinated response at all institutional levels of government, national and international, must be thorough and detailed. Plans should consider the proper authorities to alert at home and abroad; provisions for determining the credibility of the threat; means of reassuring or directing the population if necessary; and different policy options for various contingencies. The confusion and uncertainty in government and among the population following an unanticipated attack or threat would be immensely dangerous. Critics of a future "plutonium economy" fear that efforts to cope with nuclear terrorism will lead to serious deprivations of civil liberties.[19] An irrational and hasty response to terrorism might be more devastating than the terrorism.

Governments must learn to respond to a bargaining threat from terrorists. Refusing to negotiate would be extremely risky, and the consequences of a forceful response might be disastrous. In view of the magnitude of a terrorist threat, governments must develop skillful and well informed bargaining techniques. Attempts can be made to delay the implementation of a threat, to persuade the terrorists that execution of the threat would not be in their interests, or to offer less unacceptable alternative concessions to those demanded, including publicity. None of these bargaining attempts depend upon unequivocal surrender to terrorist demands, although governments must be prepared to consider the costs and benefits of total surrender.

Bargaining does not mean that a government must reward violence by agreeing to terrorist demands, which might indeed encourage future violence. However, a government must recognize that once a threat of nuclear terrorism is made public, choices are severely restricted, and the government may no longer be able to deny a reward to the terrorists. If terrorists actually want attention and recognition more than the specific concessions demanded, then an announcement of their threat has satisfied most of their ambitions, and the specific government response is insignificant except as it increases publicity. Governments must avoid the temptations of over-reacting. By under-reacting a government may gain bargaining leverage to persuade the terrorists that they do not want to take the mutually painful step of seeing their threat realized. Token concessions might have to be offered to allow the terrorists to retain their pride, but disaster could be avoided. Because terrorists may attempt to force a government to choose between capitulation and intervention, the government must try to increase the range of its available options.

Consideration of alternative responses to all types of nuclear terrorism is especially critical because of the potential effects of even a minor threat upon public opinion. Although popular reactions of widespread panic and terror might be avoided, the long-term results of nuclear terrorism might well be a strengthening of opposition to the use of nuclear energy and a serious loss of confidence in the government. It is psychologically conceivable that a population would blame their government for failing to protect them from terrorism more than they would blame terrorists for initiating violence.

The proliferation of both nuclear power and terrorism means that the two trends may merge at some future time. Nuclear terrorism is a political issue of high priority, yet study of it is under-developed. Understanding the significance and implications of this particular kind of violent conflict is an interdisciplinary endeavor, involving the coordination of data and insights from science and technology, psychology, sociology, and political science. Interdisciplinary research remains to be done. To explain the subject and prescribe policy responses in the area of politics, terrorism raises questions about the relevance of theories of political behavior and interaction. Traditional theories, which on domestic levels concentrate on "normal" political behavior and whch internationally concern state actions, do not encompass the phenomenon satisfactorily.

That threats may exist primarily in the future also complicates an assessment of the meaning of nuclear terrorism, yet the issue provokes thought about the ambiguities of the future world we are entering. What is the meaning of political power, if a small group of individuals can not only use a nuclear weapon but also seriously force a government to obey their wishes? What is the future of the nation-state in a world characterized by micro-proliferation? Is nuclear terrorism the kind of issue which should be handled by international institutions, or should it be left to unilateral national initiatives? What kind of economic, political, and technological developments will make micro-proliferation more or less likely? Defining the future threat of nuclear terrorism exposes inadequacies in both the theory and the reality of contemporary international relations.

Notes

1. "What's New on Nuclear Proliferation?" paper prepared for the 1975 Aspen Workshop on Arms Control; reprinted in U.S. Congress, House, Committee on International Relations, Subcommittee on International Security and Scienfitic Affairs, *Nuclear Proliferation: Future U.S. Foreign Policy Implications.* Hearings, 94th Cong., 1st Sess., Washington: G.P.O., 1975, pp. 476-99. See also: Hutchinson, Martha C., "Terrorism and the Diffusion of Nuclear Power," a paper prepared for the XVII Annual Convention of the International Studies Association, Toronto, Canada, February 25-29, 1976.

2. In 1974, 568 A.E.C.-licensed industrial facilities were authorized to process 1,041,000 pounds of plutonium or enriched uranium, but 99.8% of this material was used in 97 facilities, of which only 27 were considered vulnerable to theft. See: Senator Abraham Ribicoff's remarks in the *Congressional Record,* May 28, 1974, reproduced in U.S. Congress, Senate, Committee on Government Operations, *Peaceful Nuclear Exports and Weapons Proliferation,* Washington: G.P.O., 1975, 0. 497.

3. For an excellent discussion of the vulnerabilities of different types of fuel cycles, see: Mason Willrich and Theodore B. Taylor, *Nuclear Theft: Risks and Safeguards,* Cambridge: Ballinger Publishing Co., 1974.

4. See: list of reports, some classified, cited by Theodore B. Taylor in "Diversion by Non-governmental Organizations," in Mason Willrich, ed., *International Safeguards and Nuclear Industry,* Baltimore: John Hopkins Press, 1973, p. 177. The earliest public report was apparently the "Lumb Report," Ad Hoc Advisory Panel on Safeguarding Special Nuclear Material, *Report to the Atomic Energy Commission,* March 10, 1967, excerpts reprinted in *Peaceful Nuclear Exports,* pp. 563-72. The biographical study of Ted Taylor in *The New Yorker,* "The Curve of Binding Energy," XLIX, No. 41-43, Dec. 3, 10, and 17, 1973, also publicized the issue. Other critical studies are U.S. Comptroller General, Reports to the Congress, "Improvements Needed in the Program for theProtection of Special Nuclear Material." Nov. 7, 1973, and "Protecting Special Nuclear Material in Transit," April12, 1974, G.A.O., Reports B-164105, both in *Peaceful Nuclear Exports,* pp. 1170-1225; and the "Special Safeguards Study," the "Rosenbaum Report," done for A.E.C., placed in the *Congressional Record,* April 30, 1974, and reprinted in *Peaceful Nuclear Exports,* pp. 467-90.

5. Obviously some terrorist groups do have constituencies, which they may or may not represent accurately. For example, Israeli retaliation against Palestinian refugee camps is an attempt to strike at the terrorists' home base, but

governments cannot count on such circumstances, nor are the links between terrorists and constituency formally recognized.

6. There is substantial disagreement on the question of whether amateurs could build some sort of explosive device. See, however: Willrich and Taylor, Chapter 6, pp. 107-20; remarks by Senator Ribicoff in the *Congressional Record,* May 28, 1974, citing an A.E.C. experiment with two physicists, reprinted in *Peaceful Nuclear Exports,* pp. 491-97; and the transcript of NOVA's "The Plutonium Connection," *Congressional Record,* Vol. 121, No. 39, March 11, 1975, p. S3620.

7. See: E. M. Kinderman, "Plutonium: Home Made Bombs?" a paper presented at the Conference on Nuclear Public Information, Information-3, organized by the Atomic Industrial Forum, March, 1972, in *Peaceful Nuclear Exports,* pp. 25-26; and a statement by Theodore B. Taylor before the Subcommittee on International Finance of the Senate Committee on Banking, Housing, and Urban Affairs, July 15, 1974, in *Peaceful Nuclear Exports,* p. 983.

8. See: the New York *Times* interview with the student who designed the bomb for NOVA, Feb. 27, 1975, p. 12.

9. The A.E.C. noted that the terrorist's decision to attack a particular target will depend on how competent the individual thinks he is, which is a psychological factor difficult to judge objectively. See: *Proposed Final Environmental Statement* on the liquid metal fast breeder reactor, Dec. 1974, WASH 1535, Vol. IV, Section 7.4.3., excerpted in *Peaceful Nuclear Exports,* p. 605.

10. See for example: a statement by the manager of the A.E.C. safeguards program at Los Alamos, in Robert B. Leachman and Philip Althoff, *Preventing Nuclear Theft,* New York: Praeger, 1972, p. 275; and the I.A.E.A. Inspector General's statement to the New York *Times,* June 20, 1975, p. 8.

11. A gram of plutonium dispersed without warning in a building could cause seventy deaths, although not immediately. See: Bernard L. Cohen, "The Hazards in Plutonium Dispersal" (which discounts the danger), March, 1975, in *Peaceful Nuclear Exports,* especially pp. 1294-95, 1300, and 1302.

12. See: Brian Jenkins, "Will Terrorists Go Nuclear?" discussion paper No. 64, California Seminar on Arms Control and Foreign Policy, October, 1975.

13. See: U.S. Congress, Senate, Committee on Government Operations, *Facts on Nuclear Proliferation,* a handbook prepared by the Congressional Research Service of the Library of Congress. Washington: G.P.O., 1975, p. 198; also the New York *Times,* Aug. 17, 1975, p. 36.

14. These requirements were first implemented in sales to West Germany in 1975. See: U.S. Congress, Senate, Committee on Government Operations, *The Export Reorganization Act—1975,* Hearings, 94th Cong., 1st Session, Washington: G.P.O., 1975, pp. 74-75 and 227; and *Peaceful Nuclear Exports,* pp. 687-713.

15. The New York *Times,* Aug. 17, 1975, p. 36.

16. The seven major supplier states are Canada, France, the United States, Great Britain, Japan, the Soviet Union, and West Germany. See: the New York *Times,* Feb. 24, 1976, pp. 1 and 8.
17. Fred C. Iklé, Director of the U.S. Arms Control and Disarmament Agency, has cited "the core of the problem" as our reliance on deterrence: "Our principal approach in preventing the use of nuclear destructive devices, that is to say, the approach of nuclear deterrents [sic], would not be applicable to these threats, in all likelihood." Testimony in the Export Reorganization Act hearings, p. 12.
18. *Deterrence in American Foreign Policy: Theory and Practice.* New York: Columbia University Press, 1974, pp. 64 and 505.
19. See: statement on "The Plutonium Economy" and the supporting background report by a Committee of Inquiry chaired by Margaret Mead and René Dubos for the National Council of Churches of Christ in the U.S.A., September, 1975.

Brian M. Jenkins

The Potential for Nuclear Terrorism

Although conceding the technical feasibility of nuclear terrorism, Jenkins agrues that the question really comes down to intention, and political terrorists have never really "intended" mass murder. He dismisses organized crime as a possible nuclear terror actor (because of the likely societal reaction), as he does most of the "nuts" who might find such sensational terrorism attractive but lack the skills. The real risk is that nuclear terror may be attempted because of the adjective nuclear, *for an incident so named will garner wide and rapt attention. Thus, nuclear terror is posited to be more attractive as a threat than as an action.*

The possibility that criminals, political extremists, or individual lunatics might steal a nuclear weapon from a weapons storage site, fabricate a crude nuclear explosive device using stolen nuclear material, disperse toxic radioactive material, or create alarming nuclear hoaxes has become a topic of increasing public attention and concern. Even a relatively crude improvised explosive device, if successfully detonated, could have the destructive force of several hundred tons of conventional explosives, which is thousands of times the power of the largest bombs yet detonated by terrorists. It cannot be assumed that these possibilities have been ignored by existing or potential terrorists, or that they will not be considered in the future.

The rapid growth of a civilian nuclear industry, the likelihood of increasing traffic in plutonium, enriched uranium, and radioactive waste material, the spread of nuclear technology, all increase the opportunities for criminals or terrorists to engage in some type of nuclear action. There has been considerable debate about the difficulty—or the ease—with which criminals or terrorists might acquire nuclear material of weapons grade, design and fabricate a nuclear explosive device, acquire and effectively disperse radioactive material, or sabotage a nuclear reactor in such a way as to cause a core meltdown and a release of radioactive material. Present safeguards and security measures are considered by many to be woefully inadequate.

The implicit assumption that criminals or terrorists would see some utility in causing casualties of the magnitude that nuclear weapons would produce or see some other peculiar advantage in going nuclear merits some discussion. Whether or not terrorists will go nuclear has been the subject of a growing body of literature. Some is the product of sober analysis; the popular stuff borders on or is clearly sensationalism. Among the more alarming titles are: "Is There an A-bomb in Your Backyard?" "Better do as we say: This is an atom bomb and we're not fooling," and "Nuclear Hijacking: Now Within the Grasp of Any Bright Lunatic." Television offerings include "When Terrorists Go Nuclear," "A Do-It-Yourself A-Bomb," and "The Plutonium Connection." What conclusions can we draw from the research that has been done so far?

First, it can be done. A nuclear reactor probably can be sabotaged. Whether temporarily disabled or destroyed in such a manner that will result in a release of significant amounts of radioactive material and direct danger to the public remains an issue of debate. The notion that someone outside of government programs can design and build a crude nuclear bomb is a good deal more plausible now. In the beginning, the secrets of fission were closely guarded. However, much of the requisite technical knowledge has gradually come into the public domain. There also are a growing number of technically trained people in society who understand this material and who, without detailed knowledge of nuclear weapons design, theoretically could design and fabricate a nuclear bomb. It would involve considerable risks for the builders. Its detonation and performance would be uncertain. Its yield would be low, probably in the tenths of a kiloton range.

A former designer of nuclear weapons asserts that "under conceivable circumstances, a few persons, possibly one person working alone, who possessed about 10 kilograms of plutonium and a substantial amount of high explosive, could, within several weeks, design and build a crude fission bomb." Another expert suggests that "three to four individuals may comprise a more credible bomb-building scenario." They would need knowledge of nuclear weapons design, "a small machine shop, high explosives, some physical and technological ability, time [three to six months], space, and money." In addition, they would need "some chemical and high temperature chemistry capabilities for conversion of the SNM to a form suitable for core construction." A noted scientist, in a statement to the National Council of Churches, maintained that it was impossible for a single person to make a bomb. "At least six persons, highly skilled in very different technologies, would be required to do so, even for a crude weapon." That may put it beyond the grasp of any "bright lunatic," but the parameters of the debate are still significantly narrow. It could be done.

For a dispersal device, the technical and material requirements are much less. *Some* plutonium, or a quantity of some other available radioactive material, spent fuel for example, and a mechanism for dispersal would suffice. The principal impediment to building a nuclear bomb or filling a dispersal device is acquisition of the nuclear material.

The frequent use of reflective grammar—it could be done—is deliberate. There is a great difference between theoretical feasibility and someone actually attempting to carry out one of the actions described.

There are political extremists and criminal groups at large today that possess or could acquire the resources necessary to carry out any of the nuclear actions I have mentioned: sabotage a reactor, steal fissionable material and build a dispersal device or possibly even a crude nuclear explosive device. Some of the larger terrorist groups who might undertake such actions with or without the assistance or complicity of a national government, and organized crime, at least theoretically, have the option of acquiring a nuclear capability. There is general consensus on this. Arguments arise not so much in the area of theoretical capabilities, but rather in the area of intentions.

The historical record provides no evidence that any criminal or terrorist group has ever made any attempt to acquire fissionable nuclear material or other radioactive material for use in an explosive or dispersal device. Apart from a few incidents of sabotage in France and one incident in Argentina, political extremists have not attacked nuclear facilities. No criminal or terrorist group has demonstrated or claimed that it possesses fissionable material. If members of any such groups have ever discussed the option of going nuclear, I know of no such report. There have been bomb threats against nuclear facilities. There have been low-level incidents involving nuclear facilities or nuclear material—vandalism, token acts of violence, low-level sabotage, minor thefts of nonfissionable material. There have been nuclear hoaxes, most of which could easily be discarded as not credible. In sum, there is no direct historical evidence of any intentions on the part of the potential adversaries to carry out the actions of which they are theoretically capable. However, one ought to take little comfort in this fact. The lack of intelligence or of visible evidence does not mean that the option has not been discussed. Some group might move in this direction without providing clues or warning. We could first know about it when it happens.

There is, however, no inexorable linear progression that takes one easily from the currently identified spectrum of potential subnational nuclear terrorists to actual subnational nuclear terrorists, or from the nuclear incidents that have occurred thus far to nuclear actions of greater consequence. Terrorist groups, as we know them now, might be among future nuclear terrorists, but their acquisition of a nuclear capability would not be a simple escalation of what has been demonstrated in terrorist actions thus far. We can only say that terrorists have been active in the recent past, that there is an apparent increase in their technical sophistication, that they have demonstrated a degree of imagination in their choice of targets, that nuclear facilities and material theoretically could provide them with a dramatic backdrop or prop for any action, and that terrorists have shown a flair for theatrical actions. On the other hand, terrorists generally have not attacked well-guarded targets. They have generally relied on relatively simple weapons—submachine guns and dynamite—and the number of casualties normally associated with the detonation of even a crude nuclear device, or the dispersal of toxic radioactive material, is many times greater than the casualties that have occurred in any single terrorist incident. Terrorists have not yet gone to the limit of their existing nonnuclear capabilities. Acquiring a nuclear capability would represent a quantum jump, and upon close examination it is simply not clear what purpose taking that jump would serve.

It is an equally long conceptual jump from the present activities of organized crime to the notion of organized crime acquiring a nuclear capability. It would mean in effect that its leaders have decided to directly challenge the sovereignty of the nations in which organized crime's normal—and highly profitable—activities take place. This would require a fundamental change in the objectives of organized crime, whose members have sought to make money and to acquire political influence to protect their investments, but not to directly acquire political authority at higher levels or to invoke public or political reaction.

It is somewhat easier to imagine organized crime engaged in the theft of or illegal trafficking in fissionable material without seeking to acquire a nuclear capability. The annals of crime are filled with successful penetrations of well-protected targets to obtain precious commodities. For the immediate future, however, highly enriched uranium or plutonium are unlikely to be stolen for their intrinsic monetary value but rather for their strategic value as bombmaking material. They do not have the same marketability that gold or other precious metals have, and their theft is likely to be regarded in a totally different light by authorities. The loss of fissionable material probably would be viewed by government as a potential threat to the security of the nation, not simply as an economic loss. It would provoke a different level of response, perhaps applied in a state of national emergency, which could pose a serious threat to the very existence of organized crime as it now exists. It would require on the part of its leaders a change in their present goals and an acceptance of new kinds of risks.

That leaves the category of psychotic individuals operating alone usually, or occasionally in groups. Nuts are probably responsible for many of the low-level incidents and nuclear hoaxes that have occurred thus far, but most would not attempt to do something more serious than cause disruption. On the other hand, a few, if they had somehow acquired a nuclear capability, might use it. Lunatics have been the perpetrators of many known schemes of mass murder. Thus, in terms of intentions alone, psychotics are potential nuclear terrorists. In terms of capabilities, they are the farthest away from being able to acquire a nuclear weapon. To do so would require a quantum jump in their capabilities or an environmental change that made the task much easier to accomplish.

The history of the nuclear incidents that have occurred to date provides no convincing evidence of more serious incidents—the theft of a nuclear weapon or the detonation of a crude nuclear explosive device. Between 1969 and 1975, there were 288 recorded threats or incidents of violence at nuclear facilities in the United States; 240 of these were bomb threats; 22 were incidents of arson, attempted arson, or suspicious fires, many of them in office buildings where the Atomic Energy Commission rented space, or at university research facilities. Not included in the government's list of 288 incidents are several known cases of burglary involving nonstrategic nuclear material stolen from hospitals or research facilities. With the exception of two fires, one bombing, and an incident where a minute amount of plutonium was removed from a facility, possibly by an employee, none of the incidents could be called serious, and the exceptions were serious only in terms of property damage. Public safety was not imperiled. A night watchman was wounded by a fleeing intruder, the only known casualty. The perpetrators were found or suspected to be disgruntled employees, petty thieves, foes of nuclear energy, nuts, perhaps a few political extremists.

These incidents tell us that the nuclear industry is not immune to the bomb threats that have become commonplace in all businesses and industries, nor to arson, incidents of minor sabotage, nor an occasional bombing. Pacific Gas and Electric Company and Safeway Stores fare no better.

Several more serious incidents have occurred abroad. A uranium smuggling ring was uncovered in India. A nuclear reactor under construction was briefly seized by members of a terrorist group in Argentina. There have been several costly incidents of sabotage in France during the last two years. A 40-pound bomb was planted next to a reactor in Sweden. In Austria, an individual with a history of mental insanity contaminated several train coaches with radioactive material.

As the nuclear industry expands, we can expect the number of low-level incidents—bomb threats, pilferage, vandalism, minor sabotage—to increase proportionately. But there is no basis for predicting escalation to more serious incidents. Whether any of the current potential nuclear terrorists will decide to actually go nuclear remains an unanswerable question. We can identify potential adversaries and describe their objectives, their capabilities, and the likely modes of operation if they decide to go nuclear, but we cannot predict with any confidence whether any will ever make that decision. This leaves a vast area of uncertainty between what "can be done" and someone deciding to do it.

At this point, the discussion becomes theological. Arguments are advanced about the inherent malevolence of man or the perfectibility of social institutions. Whatever position one adopts must be accepted largely on faith for there is little direct evidence. The participants in the debate can be described in theological terms as well, for their viewpoints are not necessarily analytical; rather they are more like philosophical attitudes. There are "Apocalypticians" who subscribe to a kind of Murphy's Law of human behavior: "If something bad can be done, someone bad will do it." Given "the likely interaction of nuclear technology and the human predisposition to evil," wrote one author, ". . . it would seem that unacceptably great misuses of radioactivity cannot be prevented at acceptable cost in a world committed to fission energy." The Apocalypticians regard every incident of sabotage or theft involving any radioactive substance, however unclear in objective or minor in consequence, as evidence that more serious acts will inevitably follow. Criminals and terrorists *would* use nuclear means to threaten or cause mass destruction, *could,* and *inevitably will.* The Apocalypticians could turn out to be prophetic, but it is as prophets that they make their predictions.

At the opposite end of the spectrum are the disbelievers who scoff at the notion of serious nuclear terrorism. Noting the lack of serious nuclear incidents in a nuclear age now over 30 years old, they ask, "Where is the evidence?" There are also those who concede a potential, albeit remote, threat but who are positive about the perfectibility of man and his institutions, or who have a deep, abiding faith that science will find a way, that a technological solution to the problems of safeguarding and protecting nuclear material will be found.

I would describe myself as a prudent agnostic. I don't know whether terrorists will go nuclear, but the consequences if they were to do so may be so serious that society cannot afford to take a chance. Prudent agnostics argue for heavy security and suggest "Go Slow" approaches to crucial decisions such as the use of plutonium.

Let me digress for a moment and offer my own speculation as to why terrorists might go nuclear. In my view, the primary attraction to terrorists in going nuclear is not necessarily the fact that nuclear weapons would enable terrorists to cause mass casualties, but rather the fact that almost any terrorist action associated with the words "atomic" or "nuclear" automatically generates fear in the mind of the public.

Incidents in which terrorists have deliberately tried to kill large numbers of people or cause widespread damage have been relatively rare. Terrorists want a lot of people watching, not a lot of people dead—which may explain why, apart from the technical difficulties involved, they have not already used chemical or biological weapons, or conventional explosives in ways that would produce mass casualties. Mass casualties simply may not serve the terrorists' goals and could alienate the population.

Drawing attention to themselves and their causes, creating alarm, and thereby gaining some political leverage—which have been typical objectives of terrorists—could be achieved by undertaking relatively unsophisticated actions with a nuclear backdrop to add drama to the episode. Terrorists might do those things that demand less technical skill and risk on their part and also happen to be less dangerous to public safety, instead of attempting some of the more complex and riskier operations which potentially could endanger thousands of people.

Nuclear power, whether in the form of peaceful energy or weapons, is the most potent and, to many people, the most sinister force known to mankind. The words "atomic" or "nuclear" recall Hiroshima, not Indian Point. Any sort of nuclear action by terrorists would be assured of widespread publicity. It would instill fear and create alarm. Almost anyone who is believed to have a nuclear device or who has gained possession of a nuclear facility is a successful terrorist.

Terrorists may try to take advantage of the fear that the word "nuclear" generates without taking the risks of making the investment necessary to steal plutonium or highly enriched uranium and build a crude atomic bomb. A well-publicized hoax could be as alarming as actual possession of a real weapon, provided people have no way of knowing that it is a hoax. A well-publicized terrorist attack on a civilian nuclear facility, even if the terrorists failed in their intended mission, could be almost as alarming to the world as a terrorist success. While we cannot rule out the possibility of holding a city for ransom with a nuclear weapon, the assembly and detonation of a nuclear bomb appears to be the least likely terrorist threat.

Scenarios involving the deliberate dispersal of toxic radioactive material which could cause a number of immediate deaths, a greater number of delayed illnesses, and ultimately a statistical rise in the mortality rate from cancer among the affected population do not appear to fit the pattern of any terrorist actions carried out thus far. Terrorist actions have tended to be aimed at producing immediate dramatic effects, a handful of violent deaths. If terrorists were to employ radioactive contaminants, they could not halt the continuing effects of their act, not even long after they may have achieved their ultimate political objectives. It has not been the style of terrorists to kill hundreds or thousands. To make hundreds of persons terminally ill decades into the future would be even more out of character.

Nuclear terrorism seems more attractive as a threat than as an action. Possessing a nuclear device, it seems terrorists could demand anything. But the idea of nuclear blackmail has some weaknesses. It is not entirely clear to me how the enormous capacity for destruction associated with a nuclear weapon could be converted into commensurate political gains. Even with a nuclear device, terrorists could not make impossible demands. They probably could not permanently alter national policy or compel other changes in national behavior; to do so would require at a minimum that they maintain the threat and it is not clear how long this could be done without discovery or betrayal. They could not create a homeland, at least not without offering the victims of the blackmail a future set of hostages to retaliate against. They probably could not persuade a government to liquidate itself. They could not realistically expect to be given more nuclear weapons by claiming or even demonstrating that they had at least one. They could not easily collect billions of dollars ransom, even if it were paid.

They could make bizarre demands but beyond notoriety, how would these relate to the achievement of the group's goals? This pushes us to the lunatic fringe operating within a mind set totally alien to our own. Whether a large enough group composed of the people with the requisite skills for serious nuclear terrorism could be assembled to achieve utterly mad objectives, totally out of line with the means to be employed, is questionable.

The nuclear terrorists of the future may not arise from those candidates currently identified. There may appear individuals or new kinds of groups that have not yet been identified who might be more likely to use nuclear means to achieve their objectives. Threats to nuclear facilities or involving the malevolent use of nuclear materials may emerge on a different organizational or mental plane. Ten years ago, the members of the Lumb panel examining nuclear safeguards for the Atomic Energy Commission, identified "terrorists" as a potential threat to nuclear programs. They did not specify who or what they meant by the term "terrorist," and it is a little difficult to imagine today who or what they had in mind in 1967 since their report preceded the recent increase in terrorist violence. But in retrospect, their report was prophetic, for in the following decade terrorists in well-organized groups that operated internationally did become a significant problem. They are a new entity that has emerged as a major threat in the past decade, and although they have as yet given no indication of going nuclear, they potentially could. It is difficult to say now what new entities may emerge in the coming decade.

There is always the potentiality of the mad scientist working with some extremist group or on behalf of some bizarre cause applying his or her talents to fabricate a nuclear weapon. There is the possibility that some band of fanatical foes of nuclear energy could exploit the very vulnerabilities they decry in an attempt to turn society away from nuclear power or to achieve nuclear disarmament. We could see the entry of international terrorists into the realm of traditional crime, creating new international criminal entities. We could see members of an "embargoed" nuclear industry whose aborted careers or lost fortunes drive them to nuclear actions directed against society. The stuff of novels, perhaps, definitely speculation, not prediction, but the point is that there may in the future emerge nuclear terrorists of types we have not and cannot now identify.

My final conclusion is that the origin, level, and nature of the threat may change. Some individual or group may acquire a nuclear capability and successfully carry out some scheme of extortion or destruction that will inspire imitation. The probability of a second incident occurring, especially after a "success," would seem to be greater than the probability of the first. A terrorist group with the capabilities for acquiring a nuclear capability may be placed in a desperate situation that will begin to erode the political arguments against nuclear action. The political context may change. A war may occur in which nuclear weapons are used, inviting further use by nations and subnational groups. Plutonium could become more widely and easily obtainable owing to lack of adequate safeguards. New low technology enrichment techniques could emerge, making the production of fissionable material much easier, giving more entities the capability of producing weapons material. At some point in the future, the opportunity and capacity for serious nuclear violence could reach those willing to take advantage of it. We do not know where that point is or how close we may be.

David Krieger

What Happens If. . . ?
Terrorists, Revolutionaries,
and Nuclear Weapons

Krieger finds that the continuing expansion of peaceful nuclear technology will increase the possibility that tomorrow's terrorists will be armed with nuclear weapons. In addition, he argues the plausibility of a nuclear bomb's being provided by a sympathetic government, particularly in a Middle Eastern setting. His description of the problems that nuclear-armed terrorists might precipitate would rank such an event with history's greatest crises.

Terrorist and revolutionary activities spring from deep wells of social and personal discontent, and it seems unlikely that these wells will dry up of their own accord, or that social changes will soon cap them. Thus, we can predict with a high degree of certainty that terrorist and revolutionary activity will continue.

The Future of Terrorist and Revolutionary Activities

Terrorism is nongovernmental public violence or its threat performed by an individual or small group and aimed at achieving social or political goals which may be subnational, national, or international. Revolutionaries have the specific goal of bringing down a government, and to this end their actions may range from nonviolent to terrorist to organized military activities.

The victims of terrorist activity may be:

1. Victims of convenience (that is, easy targets) such as passengers aboard a hijacked airliner.
2. Newsworthy victims such as Olympic athletes.
3. Representatives of groups perceived to be exploitative, such as, diplomats, industrialists, politicians, or even tourists from a given nation.
4. Individuals or groups believed to provide an effective "bargaining chip." For example, any of the above could be held hostage in

order to extort money, have prisoners released, change government or corporate policies, and so forth.

Terrorists may also threaten inanimate objects. They may target social or
political symbols; for example, attempting to bomb the Washington
Monument or Independence Hall. They may also seek to control or destroy
vulnerable functioning technologies, such as computer centers,
communication systems, or power generating stations. Any of these events
could result in the death of innocent people who happened to be "in the
wrong place at the wrong time."

Terrorist activities seem to have increasingly taken on an international
character in the past decade. The U.S. State Department has published a
memorandum stating:

> ... since 1968 there has been a marked increase in international
> terrorism as a means for the attainment of political goals.
> Simultaneously, there has been a major development of in-
> telligence, training, financial and operational collaboration
> among terrorist groups in different parts of the world. . . . Tech-
> nological advances afford the terrorist opportunities he never
> had before: an instant world-wide audience . . . new types of
> weapons, a plethora of vulnerable targets.[1]

Thus, at least in the eyes of the State Department, international terrorism is
becoming better organized, with better financing and weapons, and plenty of
targets.

Based on past incidents, certain general motivations for terrorism can be
suggested:

1. To attain national or global publicity for a cause.
2. To achieve certain limited political and/or financial goals.
3. To demonstrate the weakness of an established government.
4. To manipulate a government into an unnecessary and discreditable
   use of force.
5. To create a situation where one can be hunted, killed, or put on
   trial with notoriety and excitement.

Motives range from clear political objectives to hazy quasi-suicidal
propensities. Globally, it would appear that there is a large body of persons
whose lack of sufficient satisfaction and excitement in their lives makes them
potential criminals or terrorists. We cannot say with certainty what catalysts
will convert individual dissatisfaction and thirst for adventure into political
terrorism. We can only suggest that we have no valid reason to believe that

the discontent from which terrorism arises will soon diminish or that terrorism will decline in the foreseeable future.

Revolutionaries may be defined as individuals and groups acting with the primary intention of bringing down a government and replacing the fallen government with one more in accord with their own value system. Revolutionaries may, of course, act from either a left or right perspective and may be comprised of poor and maltreated elements of society or of well-to-do and well-established elements discontented with government policies. In the latter case, national military forces or a branch thereof will often play a major role in overthrowing an existing government. Most Latin American nations, for example, are now governed by military regimes which forcibly supplanted preexisting governments. Naturally, a large, well-organized revolutionary movement, which included a trained military force could pose a greater threat to take possession of nuclear weapons or nuclear weapon materials than could a smaller, less powerful terrorist organization. Also, nuclear weapons may come into the possession of former revolutionaries who become legitimized by the assumption of power within a state and who persist in their revolutionary aims and aspirations, thereby transforming the threat from a national to an international one.

The Nuclear Dimension

It is the specific purpose of this paper to explore what may happen if terrorists and revolutionaries are able to develop nuclear explosive or dispersal capabilities. Thus far, only a few natioanl governments possess nuclear weapons, and each has taken strong (although possibly insufficient) precautionary measures to prevent their nuclear bombs or special nuclear materials which are convertible to explosives from falling into unauthorized hands.

Whether terrorists and revolutionaries of the future will be able to achieve a nuclear weapon capability depends upon several factors. These include:

1. The sympathies and political stability of regimes possessing a nuclear weapon capability.
2. Safeguards applied by regimes possessing uranium enrichment and/ or nuclear fuel reprocessing plants and their political stability.
3. The durability of safeguarding procedures for special nuclear material nationally and internationally over time.

At the present time, only five nations are acknowledged members of the nuclear weapon club: the United States, USSR, UK, France, and China. India tested what it described as a "peaceful" nuclear explosive in 1974, having created it with materials originally supplied by the United States and Canada for its nuclear power program. India's example illustrates how, under poor safeguards, nuclear electricity generation can lead to nuclear weapons.[2]

The stability of regimes possessing nuclear weapons is important, since opportunities for terrorists or revolutionaries to take possession of stockpiled nuclear weapons could arise as a result of a coup or revolution. The nations currently possessing nuclear weapons appear stable enough at present, but will this always be so? Imagine, for example, the government of China being unable to continue to assert control over the entire country after repeated, devastating earthquakes and factional struggles. A splinter group of army officers seizes control of a few nuclear missiles and (a) threatens to employ them against Japan unless a large sum is paid; (b) uses the weapons without warning against the USSR which is suspected of having caused the earthquakes in China by geological warfare; or (c) is convinced by a revolutionary student group to turn over the weapons to it to prevent capitalists from regaining a foothold in China.

Should there be a rapid proliferation of nuclear-weapon states, which at this time seems rather likely, future nuclear-weapon states may be less stable than current nuclear powers and thus more likely to lose their nuclear weapons to terrorists or revolutionaries. Nevertheless, of the various ways for terrorists or revolutionaries to gain nuclear weapons, taking them forcibly from a government would be relatively difficult unless the power of the revolutionary force approached that of the government. Far simpler would be to convince a sympathetic government to give one or more weapons away. We can imagine, for example, another Middle Eastern nation clandestinely creating nuclear weapons in the same way Israel is purported to have done and then turning some of them over to a terrorist group with whom its leader sympathizes. Or the nuclear weapon may be given to the terrorist group as payment for other activities the national leader wants accomplished. In either case, the agreement would most likely be secret, so that the national donor would not be held culpable for the terrorist use of the weapon. The situation could become even more confused and dangerous if the terrorist group claimed publicly to have received the nuclear weapon from an innocent party, thereby generating a retaliatory response against the innocent party. In certain cases, this could conceivably result in international war.

The above example, as with others, points out the difficulty of drawing a hard line between national goals and terrorist goals. In the future, as in the past, national leaders may work clandestinely to achieve certain goals through the activities of terrorist groups. Some of these goals may involve the use of nuclear weapons, and others may involve the trade of nuclear weapons for terrorist services rendered. Based on past performance, can we doubt that certain national leaders would be capable of such behavior? Moreover, we cannot safely dismiss the possibility that these leaders will eventually acquire nuclear weapons or that other leaders of this disposition will come to power in nuclear-weapon states of the future.

Nations possessing nuclear spent fuel reprocessing plants will have at hand the plutonium necessary for constructing nuclear weapons. Reprocessing plants will make it possible for nations possessing them to develop nuclear weapons or, depending upon the degree of safeguarding applied, for terrorists to obtain bomb-grade materials from the reprocessing facility. Since a certain amount of material is unaccounted for in processing, it is impossible to know with certainty whether it was, in fact, diverted. Uranium enrichment plants would offer less opportunity for diversion by terrorists or revolutionaries unless highly enriched uranium was being produced, and most enriched uranium for power plants is not weapons-grade.

It is widely acknowledged by the experts in this area that a sophisticated terrorist group would be capable of constructing nuclear weapons with information and equipment publicly available, once sufficient plutonium or highly enriched uranium had been obtained. Former nuclear weapons designer Theodore Taylor, for example, and his co-author, Mason Willrich, stated in their Ford Foundation Energy Policy Project study:

> It is difficult to imagine that a determined terrorist group
> could not acquire a nuclear weapon manufacturing capa-
> bility once it had the required nuclear weapon materials. In
> this regard, a terrorist's willingness to take chances with his
> own health and safety, and to use coercion to obtain informa-
> tion or services from others, should be contrasted with the
> probably more conservative approach of persons engaged in
> crime for money.[3]

Agreements are currently being pursued by France and West Germany to sell nuclear reprocessing facilities to less developed countries, including Brazil and Pakistan. The United States has opposed such technology transfers as promotive of nuclear weapons proliferation, but other nuclear exporting countries have not been ready to forgo the potential profits.

Regardless of the apparent present stability of national regimes acquiring reprocessing facilities, it remains impossible to assure that in the future such countries will not have leaders with terrorist sympathies or that, in the chaos of a civil war, nuclear materials would not fall into the hands of avowed terrorist groups. Similar considerations may be applied to nations with nuclear power facilities.

Nuclear power plants, while not prime potential sources of special nuclear materials, are major potential targets for terrorist attack; in effect, they are huge radiological weapons which terrorists could sabotage, spreading deadly radioactivity far downwind. We will discuss this possibility further in a separate section of this paper.

Safeguarding Special Nuclear Materials

A major factor in determining the ease with which terrorist groups may attain nuclear weapons will be the extent to which effective national and international safeguards over special nuclear materials are devised and enforced. The issue of nuclear safeguards became a subject of public and congressional concern in the United States largely through the persistent efforts of a former nuclear weapons designer Theodore B. Taylor. In his Ford Foundation study with Mason Willrich, it was argued forcibly that "without effective safeguards to prevent nuclear theft, the development of nuclear power will create substantial risks to the security and safety of the American people and people generally."[4]

Elsewhere in their study, the authors considered the possibility of terrorists gaining nuclear materials. They wrote:

> One wonders how in the long run nuclear power industries
> can develop and prosper in a world where terrorist activities
> are widespread and persistent. For if present trends con-
> tinue, it seems only a question of time before some terrorist
> organization exploits the possibilities for coercion which are
> inherent in nuclear fuel.[5]

The study by Willrich and Taylor was published in early 1974. Congressional interest was stirred, but little action was taken. In early 1976, the Director of the Nuclear Regulatory Commission's Division of Safeguards, Carl H. Builder, wrote a memorandum, which subsequently became public, in which he expressed concern that "... some or even many of our currently licensed facilities may not have safeguards adequate against the lowest levels of design threat [of theft] we are considering. . . ."[6] This level was defined as one insider and three outsiders. And the House Subcommittee on Energy and the Environment, in February 1976, summarizing testimony presented to it, noted that "although the witnesses differed on the severity of the threat, it is obvious there is insufficient security against threats the NRC considers plausible."[7]

Thus, more than two years after Taylor and Willrich called national attention to nuclear safeguarding inadequacies, the problems remain far from being solved. Taylor himself provided rather extraordinary testimony at the subcommittee hearings mentioned above. Rather than offering confident answers to safeguarding problems, Taylor indicated that he found himself faced with certain questions he was unable to answer after years of effort to do so. Specifically, regarding safeguards, he asked:

> What levels of risks of nuclear violence, whether caused by nations or criminal groups, are acceptable to society world wide, and who should decide what these levels should be? By what process is the worldwide public to be assured that international and domestic safeguards against purposeful nuclear violence will, in fact, be effective, in the sense that residual risks will be both known and considered acceptable by the public?[8]

Taylor's questions speak eloquently to the intractability of the problems of potential nuclear violence and nuclear safeguards. The safeguarding problems which Taylor was instrumental in raising seem further from solution now than when he initially raised them.

I have concentrated on U.S. safeguarding difficulties because it seems a valid assumption that if the world's richest and most technologically advanced nation cannot adequately deal with these problems, then other nations will be even more likely to fail. The supposed safeguards provided by the International Atomic Energy Agency (IAEA) are basically an inventory accounting system administered by the agency's small technical staff. The IAEA is able to recognize diversions after they occur, but is helpless to prevent diversions. It provides no physical security against diversion, nor does it have any capability to track down and recover diverted materials.

It appears that neither national nor international safeguards will prove adequate to prevent terrorists from going nuclear. In the following sections, we will consider what sort of world we may expect with nuclear armed terrorists.

What Terrorists and Revolutionaries Can Do With Nuclear Weapons

With a nuclear weapon at their disposal, the coercive leverage of a terrorist or revolutionary group is multiplied enormously. Terrorists could threaten the destruction of any number of key targets, including a nation's capital city, a major dam, or a nuclear power generating station. Nuclear threats against any of these targets could cause widespread panic and intense pressure on the government to accede to terrorist demands.

The government involved would be in the difficult position of not knowing with certainty whether the terrorists were bluffing. One wonders how much risk a government would take if the terrorists publicly presented a credible description and photographs of their nuclear weapon and a small sample of special nuclear material. As a matter of policy, the U.S. government refuses to negotiate for the release of Americans who have been kidnapped. Would it adopt a similar no-negotiation policy for the "release" of Americans who were in effect being held hostage by a nuclear bomb threat to New York or Chicago?

Nuclear terrorists would have the advantage of choosing whether or not to identify themselves for publicity purposes. But even while identifying themselves, they could remain unlocatable and thus untargetable for retaliation. This, of course, nullifies the basic premise of deterrence theory, namely that a nuclear attack can be prevented by fear of retaliation. Clearly, if terrorists cannot be located, they have no need to fear retaliation, and thus deterrence in this context becomes meaningless. Further, some terrorists may be assumed to be so alienated that they would not be deterred even if located and certain to die if they carried out their threat. Of course, a nuclear bomb could be detonated remotely, even in another city, by telephone signal.

An interesting variant of the above would be for the atomic terrorists to claim to be a group on which they desired to bring public enmity, or upon which they desired to inflict the retaliatory might of the threatened nation. When terrorists have deliberately misidentified themselves, one wonders whether or not national leaders would be capable of responding intelligently, under possibly panic conditions.

Were the terrorists to have more than one nuclear weapon, their position would be even more powerful. After they exploded one, it would be virtually impossible to reject their subsequent demands. Even if they had only one weapon which they used and bluffed a second weapon, it would be extremely difficult to attempt calling the bluff in the face of their already demonstrated capability and the likely overriding public sentiment to avoid further destruction at virtually any price. One successful nuclear extortion threat, or one actual nuclear bombing, would also undoubtedly instigate many similar threats. Distinguishing credible extortionists from hoaxers would increase in difficulty.

The sorts of situations we are now considering would very likely result in state-of-emergency declarations and the assumption of unlimited police powers by the threatened government. Responding to nuclear threats could undermine civil liberties and put democratic governments to their severest test.

Revolutionaries within a given nation would be unlikely to use nuclear tactics against a population center of their own people. They might, however, be willing to act against a military target or a government symbol. Revolutionaries could also act without identifying themselves if they perceived the action to be in their interest. Revolutionaries would probably be less inhibited in terrorizing a foreign government they desired overthrown. Theodore Taylor has pointed out that a nuclear weapon with a one-fiftieth kiloton yield (1,000 times less powerful than the yield at Hiroshima) detonated in a car on Pennsylvania Avenue would produce sufficient radiation to kill anyone above basement level in the White House, and that a one kiloton weapon (still 20 times less powerful than the Hiroshima bomb), if exploded just outside the exclusion area during a State of the Union message, would kill everyone inside the Capitol building.[9] Taylor states of the latter possibility:

> It's hard for me to think of a higher-leverage target, at least in the United States. The bomb would destroy the heads of all branches of the United States government—all Supreme Court justices, the entire cabinet, all legislators, and, for what it's worth, the Joint Chiefs of Staff. With the exception of anyone who happened to be sick in bed, it would kill the line of succession to the Presidency—all the way to the bottom of the list. A fizzle-yield, low-efficiency, basically lousy fission bomb could do this.[10]

The situation referred to by Dr. Taylor would involve no threat, no warning-simply the explosion, the death and destruction, and the ensuing chaos and panic. Terrorists or revolutionaries in possession of a nuclear weapon would have the option of exploding it without warning. Some groups might find this preferable both to avoid identification with the act and to avoid capture. By deliberately misidentifying themselves, terrorists might be able to catalyze domestic repression and/or international war.

Radiation Dispersal Devices

To construct a nuclear bomb requires either about 11 pounds of plutonium or about 45 pounds of highly enriched uranium. It also requires some expertise and at least several weeks of work by a small well-trained team. With lesser amounts of time, expertise, and plutonium, terrorists could prepare radiological weapons which could be used for extortion or contamination of chosen targets.

Plutonium is an extremely toxic carcinogen. In a study done by the U.S. Atomic Energy Commission, it was calculated that the release of 4.4 pounds of plutonium oxide as a fine powder would entail 100 percent probability of developing bone or lung cancer up to 1,800 feet downwind from the point of release, and a 1 percent risk as far as 40 miles downwind.[11]

The immediate impact in terms of deaths and recognizable injury would be far less with a radiological weapon than a nuclear bomb, but the psychological and economic impact of forcing the evacuation of a large area and the costly and lengthy decontamination procedures involved could make radiological weapons attractive to terrorist and revolutionary groups. Additionally, radiation dispersal devices would be far easier to prepare than a nuclear bomb, requiring only a basic knowledge of nuclear chemistry. Terrorists who threatened the release of plutonium oxide in a population center would have to be negotiated with seriously, particularly if they included a sample of plutonium with their threat letter. It would be virtually impossible for authorities to prevent the release of plutonium oxide when it could be done by simply attaching a leaking container of the material to a city taxicab or dropping it from the window of a tall building.

Dr. Edward Martell, a nuclear chemist with the National Center for Atmospheric Research, has stated: "In the not too unlikely event of a major plutonium release, the resulting contamination could require large-scale evacuation of the affected area, the leveling of buildings and homes, the deep plowing and removal of topsoil and an unpredictable number of radiation casualties."[12] The evident potential for creating the economic and social chaos—of forcing evacuation of a major city, say New York or Washington, D.C.—might prove a substantial lure for political terrorists in possession of plutonium. They might feel safer putting the diverted plutonium to immediate use rather than running the risk of organizing the talent and taking the necessary time to construct a nuclear bomb.

Radiation dispersal devices could also be used against more specific targets, particularly ventilated buildings. Feasible targets might include legislative chambers, stock exchanges, embassies, corporate headquarters, political conventions, power plants, and communication centers. Willrich and Taylor have calculated that the indoor release of one gram of powdered plutonium oxide could provide lethal dosages for inhabitants within a 500 square meter area and significant contamination requiring some evacuation and clean-up over a 50,000 square meter area. The indoor release of 100 grams of plutonium, about one-quarter pound, would give lethal inhalation dosages for 50,000 square meters and significant contamination over 5 million square meters.[13]

The above calculations are for an oxide of plutonium-239, the most common isotope of plutonium produced as a by-product of the nuclear fission process. A 1,000-megawatt light-water nuclear power reactor produces approximately 440 pounds of plutonium annually. A less common isotope of plutonium produced by the fission process is plutonium-238. This isotope decays at a rate approximately 280 times faster than plutonium-239, having an 87 year half-life rather than 24,400 years, and thus is approximately 280 times as toxic. Plutonium-238 is worthy of our attention, since it is being used to power cardiac pacemakers. Each pacemaker contains approximately one-quarter gram of plutonium-238. Extrapolating from the figures given by Willrich and Taylor, the one-quarter gram of plutonium-238 in a single pacemaker could provide lethal dosages over an indoor area of 37,500 square meters and provide significant contamination requiring some evacuation and clean-up to an area of 3,750,000 square meters. It would seem imprudent at best to dismiss the possibility of terrorists gaining a significant radiological weapon by the removal of an implanted nuclear heart pacemaker from a hapless victim, particularly when the recipients of nuclear pacemakers are periodically mentioned in the press.[14] At the present time, 20 such pacemakers are being manufactured and implanted monthly in the United States. A decision is pending on whether or not to proceed with nuclear heart pacemakers on a larger scale.

Since the major radiotoxic danger of plutonium derives from inhalation, sophisticated terrorists could theoretically contain the plutonium without hazard to themselves until they are ready to release it. If they chose to release it by time-bomb, they could be out of the area when the release occurred.

Douglas DeNike, a long-time scholar of nuclear terrorism, has painted this frightening scenario for the use of radiological weapons by terrorists:

> Perhaps the end will come with a whimper rather than a bang.
> Covert radiological warfare could cripple any nation without
> its immediate awareness. The downtown cores of the hundred
> largest American cities, for example, could be made unin-
> habitable by two foreign students on their summer vacation.
> The whole job would require roughly 100 pounds of power-
> reactor-grade plutonium or strontium-90 particles. A pound
> of either one, tied to the underside of a taxicab in a leaking
> container, would create an insidious cancer-induction hazard
> over several equare miles.[15]

While the health effects of the radiological contamination might not be felt for many years, the psychological and economic effects of announcing the contamination, as the terrorists would surely do, would be substantial, particularly if evacuation and decontamination were necessitated.

As with a nuclear bomb, the leverage of terrorists generally would increase after the initial terrorist release of radionuclides. It would be extremely difficult for officials of a threatened city to resist terrorist demands when another city had already been required to evacuate.

Nuclear Facilities as Targets for Terrorists and Revolutionaries

As we enter the fourth quarter of the twentieth century, nuclear power plants are being increasingly relied upon to supply electric power. While a majority of people probably continue to view nuclear power as a great technological achievement, a growing minority see nuclear power as a symbol of technological arrogance. It is becoming increasingly widely understood that a meltdown of a nuclear reactor core could result in the release of volatile radioactive materials which could take thousands of lives and cause billions of dollars in property damage. The amount of potential damage remains a hotly debated issue, but the most recent Nuclear Regulatory Commission (NRC) document on this issue, the "Reactor Safety Study" (Rasmussen Report), estimates a worst-case accident would cause 3,300 early fatalities, 45,000 cases of early illnesses, and $14 billion in property damage.[16] This study argues that the chances of a nuclear accident killing more than 1,000 people are extremely low, the likelihood of occurrence being once in a million reactor-years for 100 nuclear plants, about the same risk as this number of people being killed by a meteorite. The study, however, excludes consideration of intentional destruction of a nuclear reactor which could set the probability of a core meltdown at unity.

In 1972 airline hijackers threatened to crash a Boeing 727 into the Oak Ridge, Tennessee, nuclear installation. The site was evacuated, and the terrorists did not carry out their threat. James R. Schlesinger, who was at that time U.S. Atomic Energy Commission (AEC) chairman, commented on the incident that

> . . . if one intends to crash a plane into a facility and one is
> able to persuade the pilot that that is the best way to go,
> there is, I suspect, little that can be done about that problem.
> The nuclear plants that we are building today are designed
> carefully to take the impact of, I believe, a 200,000 pound air-
> craft arriving at something on the order of 150 miles per hour.
> They will not take the impact of a larger aircraft.[17]

A Boeing 747 is nearly twice as heavy as the aircraft the power plants are designed to withstand, and a smaller aircraft carrying conventional explosives would probably penetrate a reactor containment structure. This approach to radiation release would, of course, be suicidal, but demonstrably there are terrorists fanatical enough to sacrifice their lives for what they believe to be a greater goal.

There are simpler ways for terrorists to effect a radiation release at a nuclear power plant. A former U.S. navy demolition specialist testified before Congress that

> . . . as one trained in special warfare and demolition, I feel
> certain that I could pick three to five ex-underwater demolition
> Marine Reconnaissance, or Green Beret men at random and
> sabotage virtually any nuclear reactor in the country. It would
> not be essential for more than one of these men to have had
> such specialized training. . . . The engineered safeguards would

be minimally effective and the amount of radioactivity released could be of catastrophic proportions.[18]

A 1974 Government Accounting Office (GAO) survey of security systems at nuclear plants drew attention to the vulnerability of the spent fuel storage pools located at reactor sites. In a letter to then AEC Chairman Dixy Lee Ray, a GAO official noted:

> According to AFC and licensee officials, the used-fuel storage facility at a nuclear power plant is more accessible and vulnerable to sabotage than is the reactor core. Such a storage facility generally is an uncovered pool of water near the reactor. The highly radioactive used fuel does not have the same degree of physical protection as that provided to the reactor core by the reactor containment vessel.[19]

Terrorists might consider the spent fuel storage pool of a nuclear reactor as an inviting target. Dropping a waterproof bomb in this storage pool would probably result in high-level radioactive contamination of the power plant itself, making its evacuation necessary.

Nuclear power plants may justifiably be considered military equalizers. Locating a nuclear power plant near a metropolitan area gives terrorists or revolutionaries (or small enemy nations) a target which in effect can disrupt an entire city by radioactive contamination, necessitating precipitate evacuation. This concept of military equalizer is one which, to the best of my knowledge, no national department of defense has yet recognized. The GAO study referred to above also pointed out that at U.S. nuclear facilities "there has been no specific coordination with other Federal Agencies, such as the Department of Defense and the Federal Bureau of Investigation to protect against or respond to attacks by paramilitary groups."[20] Moreover, federal regulations specifically exempt the nuclear industry from responsibility for defending against sophisticated attacks on nuclear plants.[21]

Other areas of the nuclear fuel cycle could conceivably be targets for terrorist attack as well. These would include spent fuels being transported by rail or truck, and waste storage sites. In either case, a terrorist attack would involve the penetration of the transport cask with explosives and the consequent release of radioactive materials into the environment. This clearly would not be a strategy for terrorists or revolutionaries desirous of impressing a local population with their benevolence. Conceivably, though, the terrorists could perceive themselves as benevolent if they believed their action to be the only way to stop a dangerous technology (such as nuclear power) before industrial societies became too dependent upon it.

In the United States, between April 1969 and July 1976, there were 235 threats of violence or acts of violence toward nuclear facilities, and the frequency of such actions is increasing—there were 55 just in the first eight months of 1976.[22] As far as is known, none has yet succeeded in the loss of nuclear material or in causing damage to nuclear equipment or the general public, but the likelihood that one will soon succeed is not trivial.

Brief Scenarios for U.S. Policy-Makers

To give some idea of the difficulties which policy-makers may face in the future, let us consider the following brief scenarios.

1. A U.S. army base is destroyed without warning by a low yield nuclear weapon with no clues as to who is responsible.
2. The U.S. embassy in India is destroyed in the same manner.
3. A cadre of revolutionaries, including a nuclear engineer, take over a nuclear power plant and threaten to initiate a core meltdown if their demands for policy change are not met.
4. An American-owned factory in France is discovered to have been saturated with plutonium oxide, and threats are received that the same will happen to other American corporations if certain government policy changes are not made.
5. Japanese extremists divebomb an American nuclear reactor causing a core meltdown.
6. A German terrorist group threatens the nuclear bombing of an unspecified U.S. target in Europe unless the Netherlands releases certain political prisoners.
7. A multinational terrorist group, in possession of plutonium oxide, begins contaminating U.S. targets in Latin America and Asia, each time reiterating a demand for the United States to withdraw its nuclear weapons from Europe.

Conclusions

1. Nuclear or radiological weapons in the hands of terrorists or revolutionaries could provide a significant threat to any society, particularly urban and industrial societies.
2. Terrorists or revolutionaries can use nuclear or radiological weapons to extort money or extract political concessions from a government.
3. Once a nuclear or radiological weapon is used by a terrorist or revolutionary group, other such groups will be more likely to

threaten this approach and also more likely to be successful in having their demands met.

4. Since retaliation will be difficult if not impossible against possibly unlocatable and even unidentifiable terrorists or revolutionaries, it will be necessary to prevent any diversion of nuclear weapons or special nuclear materials anywhere in the world. As yet, no criteria have been established as to how nuclear safeguards can be assured for the present, let alone for a conceivable future with many more nuclear weapon and nuclear power states.

5. The threat of nuclear terrorism could precipitate restrictions on civil liberties. Policy-makers of the future will have to make some hard decisions in this area, particularly if nuclear power continues to expand as an energy source.

6. It is not inconceivable that nuclear terrorism could intensify international tensions and catalyze international wars, particularly if the terrorists are not identifiable or are misidentified.

7. The serious nature of the potential consequences of nuclear terrorism demands equally serious policy decisions by current government policy-makers. A starting point is an evaluation of the consequences of continued development and exportation of nuclear technology and a realistic assessment of how effective nuclear safeguards can be expected to be on a worldwide basis.

8. The solution to the problem of potential nuclear violence by terrorists or revolutionaries must be founded in a broad international context if it is to be effective.

Notes

1. Fahey Black, "Terrorism," *GIST* (Washington, D.C.: U.S. Department of State, March 1976).
2. In addition to the five nuclear-weapon nations and India, Israel is widely thought also to possess nuclear weapons developed from its nuclear reactors.
3. Mason Willrich and Theodore B. Taylor, *Nuclear Theft: Risks and Safeguards* (Cambridge, Mass.: Ballinger Publishing Company, 1974).
4. Ibid.
5. Ibid., p. 169.
6. Carl H. Builder, "Adequacy of Current Safeguards," Memorandum to R. A. Brightsen, U.S. Nuclear Regulatory Commission, 19 January 1976.
7. "House Subcommittee Chairman Calls for Improved Nuclear Security," Subcommittee on Energy and the Environment, House Committee on Interior and Insular Affairs, news release of 3 March 1976.

8. Theodore B. Taylor, Statement before the Subcommittee on Energy and the Environment of the House Committee on Interior and Insular Affairs, 26 February 1976.

9. John McPhee, *The Curve of Binding Energy* (New York: Farrar, Strauss and Giroux, 1973), pp. 221-22.

10. Ibid., p. 222.

11. "Generic Environmental Statement on Mixed Oxide Fuel" (U.S. Atomic Energy Commission WASH-1327, August 1974), vol. 4, p. v-48.

12. Edward H. Martell, cited in Roger Rapport, *The Great American Bomb Machine* (New York: Ballatine, 1972), p. 47.

13. Willrich and Taylor, *Nuclear Theft*, p. 25.

14. See, for example, "Government Owns Part of His Heart," *Santa Barbara News Press*, 26 February 1976. For a fictional account of nuclear terrorism with a cardiac pacemaker, see my story, "The Ordeal of Harry Dalton: A Parable for Our Times," *Science Forum*, vol. 8, no. 6 (December 1975), pp. 3-7.

15. L. Douglas DeNike, "Nuclear Terror," *Sierra Club Bulletin*, November-December 1975.

16. "Reactor Safety Study: An Assessment of Accident in U.S. Commercial Nuclear Power Plants, Main Report" (Nuclear Regulatory Commission, WASH-1400, October 1975).

17. Cited in *Mike Gravel Newsletter*, 31 October 1973.

18. B. L. Welch, Statement before the Joint Committee on Atomic Energy, 28 March 1974.

19. Henry Eschwege, letter to AFC Chairman Dixy Lee Ray, 16 October 1974, p. 2.

20. Ibid., p. 3.

21. IOCFR 50:13: "An applicant for a license to construct and operate a production or utilization facility, or for an amendment to such license, is not required to provide for design features or other measures for the specific purpose of protection against the effects of (a) attacks and destructive acts, including sabotage, directed against the facility by an enemy of the United States, whether a foreign government or other person, or (b) use or deployment of weapons incident to U.S. defense activities."

22. A complete listing of threats and acts of violence to licensed and unlicensed nuclear facilities may be obtained from the Energy Resources Division Administration and/or the Nuclear Regulatory Commission.

R.W. Mengel

Terrorism and New Technologies of Destruction: An Overview of the Potential Risk

Proceeding within a cost-benefits schema, Mengel finds that terrorists—particularly in the United States—are not likely to assume the high risks associated with "new technology terrorism" (in particular, nuclear, chemical, and biological terrorism). Alluding to a data base of more than forty-five hundred acts of terrorism, Mengel finds that terrorists are decidedly nonsuicidal, that they generally opt for "controllable weapons," and that their activities are reducible to patterns. Rejecting the lone-individual scenarios, Mengel asserts that high-technology terror is more appropriately a skilled team effort. He concludes with extended commentary and description of the law enforcement and incident-management aspects of the problem.

Introduction

Progress in technology on a worldwide basis, and particularly within industrialized nations, has advanced to the point where an individual or a group could perpetrate a terroristic act of catastrophic consequences. The purpose of this paper is to examine the broader aspects of this problem, to estimate its magnitude, and to identify the measures that local law enforcement authorities, governmental leaders, legislators, and the community as a whole might take to control high-technology terrorism. It is hoped that the material presented . . . will provide adequate information and recommendations that might serve as the foundation of interrelated policies and procedures for countering this potential threat.

History has been punctuated by acts of terroristic violence aimed at achieving such ends as radical changes in society, capitulation of government to specific demands, or simply the weakening of an incumbent authority. The issues of the time have ranged from undermining the Tsarist regime in 19th century Russia to those of the present day involving Palestinian liberation, Irish independence, and social change in Latin America. There is a multitude of issues in U.S. society today that provide the raison d'être for terrorist organizations . . . . The subject of this [article] is the use of new technologies of destruction—the illegitimate, unsanctioned use of weapons that are significantly beyond the current terrorist state of the art.

The heightened interest in the potential use of high technology by terrorists has been generated by the widespread and controversial issue of nuclear material theft. Growth of the nuclear power industry has raised the specter of stolen material and homemade bombs. For governmental officials, particularly local law enforcement authorities, and society in general, the problem goes beyond a nuclear safeguards system and the implications of its possible failure. The range of technologies available to terrorists and the potential consequences of its use are becoming progressively greater, to include deadly and often more exotic forms, such as chemical and biological agents, lasers, and precision-guided munitions.

The following discussion focuses on the full spectrum of high-technology weapons, including nuclear explosives, chemical poisons, and biological agents; the individuals who might become involved in their use; the motivations that cause these individuals to act; the resources necessary to employ high technology; the methods of employment; and control mechanisms. This brief paper is not intended to be a detailed examination of the problem, which would require far greater technical and behavioral discussions than space permits. Rather, it offers an overview of the many considerations involved in high-technology terrorism, providing insights into the complexity of the problem—a starting point.

The Concept of High-Technology Terrorism

DEFINITION OF HIGH-TECHNOLOGY TERRORISM

Any definition of high-technology terrorism is conditioned by the environment in which it is viewed. Transistorized portable radios and high-speed aircraft represent high technology in less developed countries. In modern industrialized states, fully automated factories, satellite communications, and laser beams are indicative of advanced technology. Even within any one society the extent of appreciation for technology may differ from group to group. Since the advent of the 20th century, and particularly in the period after World War II, technological advances have been so great that the gap between innovators of technology and the layman has grown steadily. This phenomenon is reflected in the ever-increasing disparity between the state of the art, or simply advanced technology, and the levels of the terrorist's application of them.

Throughout history terrorists have been capable of availing themselves of the technology of the day. Guy Fawke's use of 36 barrels of gunpowder in an attempt to blow up Parliament in 1604 is a good illustration. The Russian terrorists of the late 18th and early 19th century employed guns and explosives to undermine the Tsarist regime. However, as the 20th century has progressed, a marked change has taken place in that the technologies used by terrorists have not made the quantum jumps that technology as a whole has.

The apparent reasons for terrorists failing to remain abreast of technological innovations are quite complex, involving the motivation, education, and general background of the terrorist and the availability of advanced technologies. Crucial to the answer is the simple fact that terrorists have discovered that the more conventional methods of violence, explosives in particular, have been adequate for their needs. Whether in fact these less technologically sophisticated methods have resulted in victory or achievement of ends is a moot point. The key variables in limiting terrorist use of high technology appear to be the perception that traditional means are still effective and a general unwillingness to escalate to potentially greater levels of violence. To date, terrorists have considered plane hijackings, kidnapings, and bombings appropriate means to achieve desired ends.

Principal among the concerns of law enforcement and governmental officials are what forms of high-technology terrorist might be employed and what impact could be expected. The definition of high technology is best constructed by examining the dimensions of technology with respect to categories and limits. Technology taken alone, regardless of the category, is limited by more than hardware or even the sophisticated application of a device. It includes the organization necessary to conceive the idea and formulate the plan; the capacity to secure resources; and the organizational ability and mechanical expertise to construct, deliver, and employ the hardware.

Two categories of high technology are readily discernible and provide a convenient framework for studying this phenomenon. The first and less dangerous class in terms of potential consequences is that of improved current technologies. Within this classification are technologies that would represent advancement of means presently employed by terrorists. Central to this [discussion] is the second category of high technology—unfamiliar modes or new technologies not previously used by terrorists. Primary attributes that differentiate this class of technology from the first are that the technology itself is totally new in terms of terrorist application, and the societal consequences realized from the culmination of an act are at least an order of magnitude greater than those using conventional technologies. From this basic general understanding of high-technology terrorism it is possible to extend the discussion to specifics concerning each category.

Improved Technologies.

Evidence supports the contention that terrorists are not availing themselves of the present technologies. To date the most sophisticated weapons technology associated with terrorists has been the SA-7 Strella antiaircraft missiles. Several indications of intended use of these missiles have occurred, including the threats against Heathrow Airport outside London by IRA terrorists (1974) and the actual seizure of an unknown number of SA-7's in a Rome apartment occupied by Palestinian terrorists (1974). Although greater sophistication in planning, tactics, coordination, and group interconnectivity is apparent from such incidents as the attack on the Israeli Olympic team by the Black September Organization at Munich in 1972, few examples of the application of high technology can be cited. However, the increased liaison among terrorist groups and heightened awareness of the possible application of improved technologies pose the potential for escalation.

In examining the potentialities of terrorists employing this class of high technology, one is impressed with the fact that law enforcement will not be faced with a host of new problems, but only an extension of those that currently exist in combating terrorism. Analysis of terrorist activity over the past dozen years led to the postulation of two considerations with respect to improved technologies. First, there probably will not be a significantly large technological jump made at any single point; rather, incremental improvements on existing technologies will occur. For example, the use of precision-guided weapons would probably be preceded by the introduction of large-caliber, longer range rockets or mortars as terrorist weapons. Second, improvements on existing technologies will primarily affect law enforcement rather than the community as a whole. The changes wrought by advancing types of technology will not materially change the nature of terrorism, the ends to be achieved, or the means; nor is it likely that the patterns of target selection will be significantly altered.

Within the category of improved technology, the range of terrorist action is bounded in two ways: existing systems are improved upon or new systems with the same basic characteristics and capabilities are adopted for the first time; and the impact upon society in terms of destruction and death remains at essentially the same levels. At the more basic level, terrorists can be expected to employ explosives with greater destruction power in smaller quantities. Examples of other improvements along this continuum are: The introduction or upgrading of communications and jamming equipment; the use of remote control, even wireless command detonation units; the employment of wire-guided munitions; the development of computer models and simulations to anticipate law enforcement actions and to determine system vulnerabilities; and the use of advanced electronic systems to counter physical protection measures.

New Technologies

Within the technological environment in the United States there is a multiplicity of hazardous materials whose dangers are well known. For example, the result of an accidental nuclear power plant core meltdown is understood; the conditions posed by the accidental release of hydrochloric acid actually have been experienced; and the epidemic effect of certain foreign biological elements has been witnessed on numerous occasions. But the threat of intentional, malicious use of new substances designed to maximize their impact on society is a heretofore unapplied concept.

In the foreseeable future, new technologies that might be applied by terrorists appear to focus on the types of weaponry using nuclear, chemical, or biological materials. Although one might suggest technologies using other basic materials, this discussion of new technologies primarily restricts itself to these three. A discussion of more exotic technologies could include weather modification, high-energy lasers, fission weapons, and others. Any number of new technologies, such as precision-guided munitions, might emerge, but this [discussion] restricts itself to the technologies that seem to pose the most realistic potential for terrorist application in the near and midterm: nuclear, chemical, and biological.

Of these three, nuclear technology is the most significant in today's milieu because of societal attention. Society is becoming increasingly aware of the implications of the civil nuclear industry. The dangers of plutonium, in particular, and high enriched uranium, to a lesser degree, are extensively publicized. The nuclear is the newest of the three technologies, and as more nuclear material becomes available, potential for its illicit use increases. Nuclear technologies may be examined in terms of two general classes: fabrication of a homemade bomb (or stealing one) and construction of a dispersal device. Within each class, the chief variables are the type of radioactive material used, the amount of material required, and the size of the device.

Lethal chemical technologies are not new, but, aside from the World War I environment, their use has been limited. Although nuclear weapons have both antipersonnel and antimaterial capabilities, the primary characteristic of chemical weapons is their antipersonnel nature. In marked contrast to nuclear technologies, in which fabrication poses a greater difficulty than delivery, chemical technologies are rather easily developed, but actual delivery presents the most significant difficulty. Because of these delivery problems and the quantities of substances required, chemical technologies are potentially restricted to a much smaller scale in terms of application and casualty-producing effects.

There are many highly toxic substances usable for creating mass casualties whose components are commercially available to an apparently legitimate "front" organization. Three toxic chemicals exemplify the range of technologies available: the fluoroacetates, because preparation is relatively simple; the nerve gases, because they are so widely known; and botulinum toxin (BTX), because of its extreme lethality (although BTX is produced by a living organism, it is treated as a toxic chemical; its use does not depend on infecting the victim with the living organism, but is based on the ingestion or inhalation of the chemical substance associated with BTX). The ability of terrorists to employ chemical technologies is more dependent upon the target characteristics, the availability of the poisons, and the requirement for an effective delivery and dissemination means than upon the chemicals' intrinsic toxicity.

Biological technologies have a longer history than nuclear technologies and a somewhat shorter history than those involving chemical agents. Developed over the past 35 years by various nations, biological technologies are principally characterized by their antipersonnel nature and an inherent variability of effectiveness that makes their application unpredictable. Defined as living organisms, or infective material derived from them, that are intended to cause disease or death in man, animals, or plants, these agents range from the highly lethal anthrax and cryptococcosis to the moderately lethal pneumonic plague, from Rocky Mountain spotted fever and psittacosis to the mainly incapacitating agents such as undulant fever, desert fever, and tularemia. Unlike nuclear technologies, whose use is limited by the availability of material, and unlike chemical technologies, which are practically limited by delivery problems, biological technologies are quite adaptable to demonstration attacks on small, isolated targets, while retaining a capacity of a larger attack. The range of potential lethality within the spectrum of biological agents is indicative, in part, of the difficulty in preparation, delivery and dissemination problems, and resilience under differing environmental and meteorological conditions.

MAGNITUDE OF CONSEQUENCES OF TERRORIST HIGH-TECHNOLOGY EMPLOYMENT

The potential magnitude and resultant impact on the community of terrorist use of new high technology might strain or significantly undermine existing societal structures. Two general types of consequences for the community seem relevant to this discussion. The objective consequences can be measured in terms of casualties and damage, and the subjective consequences are concerned with the effects on the norms and values of society. By their very nature, subjective consequences are difficult to evaluate and project, and the almost complete absence of terroristic incidents involving nuclear, chemical, and biological technologies and the dearth of unclassified weapons' effects information leads to a situation in which much of the material in this area, even related to objective consequences, is imprecise and speculative.

Objective Consequences.

At the lower end of the threat range in terms of potential damage and casualties resulting from new technologies is the dissemination of chemical agents. Requiring the least amount of resources to manufacture of the technologies examined, the use of chemical agents would result in the fewest casualties because of the necessity for unique target vulnerability and the difficulty associated with dissemination. Four methods of dissemination appear plausible:

1. Covert contamination of foodstuffs or beverages with bulk agent:
2. Covert generation of lethal vapor concentrations in an enclosed area;
3. Covert dissemination of aerosols in an enclosed area;
4. Overt/covert attack in open areas.

The result of food or beverage contamination would be casualties to those using the commodity. Normal servings, such as a cup of coffee or an 8-ounce glass of juice or soda, would result in a lethal dose. Thus, the casualty rate is a function of how much of the contaminated foodstuff is consumed before discovery.

Vapor or aerosol dissemination of a nerve gas or BTX in an enclosed area could easily result in lethal doses to everyone at that location. As mentioned earlier, although chemical agents can be extremely deadly in small quantities, dissemination in large areas significantly reduces effectiveness and thus casualties. Dissemination problems increase geometrically with the size of the area and the ability to control the environment into which the agent has been introduced.

An attack on a selected outside population target is extremely sensitive to environmental conditions, the nature of the agent, and the form of attack employed. For example, a chemical bomb exploded in a busy terminal would undoubtedly kill hundreds; an attack on a stadium full of football fans using a low-flying crop-duster-type aircraft might kill thousands; aerosol dissemination by means of a smoke generator located in a van cruising the streets might kill tens of thousands. However, to accomplish an attack on an outside target as outlined above with only a moderate degree of success would require tens of gallons of agent and appropriate, although not necessarily ideal, environmental conditions. Even rudimentary calculations of casualties and other effects are extremely difficult to arrive at, and even they would be tenuous. On balance, it is clear that, if an attack is kept within what a terrorist group might reasonably undertake, the practicalities of chemical technologies would limit the resultant exposure to no more than a few thousand individuals at one time.

The least discussed and understood technology of the three presented is the biological, and yet it presents the greatest casualty-producing potential. As stated previously, biological technologies are difficult to assess because of the significant import of the environment and the general lack of experience in assessing effects. From what is known of these agents and their application, it is apparent that, with a commitment of technical expertise similar to that which nuclear weapon fabrication would require, the resulting casualty-rate potential is greater. The wide variety of biological agents outlined in the definition section offers myriad opportunities for the use of biological technology. For this reason, only the most lethal, anthrax and cryptococcosis, are considered below. Similar attack methods might be employed using the less lethal agents, with proportional reduction in casualties.

Using either anthrax or cryptococcosis, an attacker might simply drive through a medium-sized city using a truck-mounted dispenser. During spring or summer this type of apparatus would not raise questions in most locales. Anyone exposed for 2 minutes would probably inhale enough to be infected. Not all the victims would receive lethal doses, but the medical care problems associated with tens of thousands of cases of anthrax infection in themselves would be catastrophic for a community.

Smaller attacks could be successfully launched against large crowds that remain in enclosed spaces for 2 or 3 hours. The proliferation of domed stadiums has provided a series of ideal targets. For football and baseball games, these structures usually seat more than 70,000 persons. Using approximately 1 fluid ounce of either anthrax or cryptococcosis in aerosol form would result in the inhalation of an infective dose within an hour.

Nuclear technology represents a midrange threat in terms of casualties, but it is the most powerful with respect to damage or destruction of physical property. Unlike the use of chemical and biological technologies, terrorist employment of nuclear technologies would involve delivery problems that are relatively easy to solve. Far more difficult for the application of this technology are the acquisition of nuclear material and the fabrication of a weapon.

Simplest of the nuclear technologies to design and employ is the radioactive dispersal device. Although a wide range of radioactive materials, such as Cobalt-60, high enriched uranium, Cesium-137, Strontium-90, Iodine-131, and radium might conceivably be used in a dispersal device, the following discussion focuses on the most widely publicized and perhaps the most lethal radioactive material—plutonium. Whether employing a highly sophisticated dispersal mechanism or an uncomplicated bomb to send plutonium particles into the atmosphere, the results would be more in terms of casualties caused by cancer over a period of 15 to 30 years than immediate deaths. Without a complex medical explanation of the effect of plutonium on the human body, the extent of casualties can be examined as a function of the amount inhaled. If 12,000 micrograms (millionths of a gram) are inhaled, death will occur within 60 days; 1,900 micrograms, 1 year; 700 micrograms, 3 years; and 260 micrograms will cause cancer. For comparison, plutonium is approximately 10 times as toxic as nerve gas; anthrax is about 10 times more toxic than plutonium; and BTX lethality, measured in submicrogram quantities, is more than a thousandfold greater than anthrax.

However, these theoretical figures are somewhat misleading because they do not take into account the effects of environmental conditions on plutonium dispersal. Generally speaking, dispersal would be quite inefficient and the amount of plutonium inhaled would be small. For example, a daytime release of 1 kilogram of plutonium (approximately 2.2 pounds) would cover more than 2,000 square meters with a lethal dose potential. But the expected lethal dose received by persons in the area is one cancer for every 5 grams, or a total of 200 people. At night, this rate is increased threefold because of comparatively more stable atmospheric conditions. Dispersal within a building ventilating system would result in considerably more lethal doses for each gram of plutonium. In each case, the number of short-term (less than 60 days) deaths would be few, if any. Most of the victims would be unaware of the hazard because of the nature of plutonium and the lack of symptoms that might otherwise indicate the danger.

Once plutonium has been acquired, an alternative use might be the construction of a nuclear bomb. Few experts believe that one man in his basement is capable of building a nuclear device. Fabrication of a nuclear device is a time-consuming and risky task requiring highly skilled technicians. Given reasonable resources and talent, the yield of such a fabricated device would be 0.1 to 10 kilotons (KT). The range of the yield is highly variable, based on the expertise of the designer and the workmanship in construction of the weapon components. Assuming a surface burst of about 1 KT, using a truck as the probable means of delivery to the target, the damage in a downtown area of a major city would be in excess of 100,000 immediate fatalities from the blast and destruction totaling in the billions of dollars.

Damage produced by these weapons varies with the design and the yield of the weapon and the location of detonation. A demonstration explosion in a sparsely inhabited area might produce a few immediate fatalities and cause delayed casualties from fallout. A detonation in a small town or suburban area might destroy the community, but the actual fatalities would be in the thousands, not tens of thousands. Equally as significant as blast in causing casualties is the prompt radiation released by the explosion. The higher the prompt radiation, which is many times more dangerous to life than residual fallout, the greater the number of immediate and long-term casualties resulting.

Subjective Consequences

At a more abstract level of description, the subjective consequences of terrorist employment of new high technologies can be evaluated in terms of impact on the community. An incident involving chemical, biological, or nuclear technologies would certainly have significant ramifications for local and higher level governmental officials. But it will be public reaction that would drive, to a great extent, these officials. Thus, it is important to at least place these subjective consequences in perspective with respect to threatened incidents prior to the first actual use of new technologies and the possible impact of that first incident upon subsequent events.

There have been a number of threats over the past several years involving nuclear weapons or material, or other new technologies. Several radical publications have cited terrorist group threats to put LSD or other drugs in the water supply of cities. A 14-year-old boy, in Orlando, Fla. in 1970, threatened to blow up the town with an A-bomb unless a $1 million ransom was paid. The accompanying drawing he provided was convincing enough to raise serious questions. To date, none of these threats has been carried out, nor have communities been affected by the threats themselves. No mass evacuations have taken place, no extended searches have been undertaken, and no general curtailment of community life or individual liberties has occurred.

Communities have not been affected by threats involving new technologies, because in each instance the threat was either determined not to be credible or local decisionmakers made the conscious decision to treat the threat in generally the same manner as they treated conventional bomb threats in dealing with the community. The obvious drawback to this approach is that in the first actual instance many people might die. However, when weighed against the effects and costs of massive community action in response to every threat that seems credible, one can find merit in this style of response.

Once it is necessary to involve the entire community in countering threats of new-technology terrorism, the general fear level of the community will have been raised. Regardless of the outcome of that immediate threat, changes in society will have been wrought. Given the likely media coverage of a high-technology event, the effect of reacting on a community-wide basis would be experienced as a precedent by all local leaders involved with future threats, whether in the affected community or not. Equally as significant is the probability of an epidemic effect once it has been demonstrated that a threat resulted in a widespread reaction. As evidenced by event data on hijackings, bombings, and even kidnapings, often a rash of similar incidents or threats follows a widely publicized terrorist act.

Until a threat is actually carried out or a threat is permitted to impact on the community as a whole, it seems unlikely that any change in public fear will result. Although the nuclear safeguards debate has highlighted a full range of catastrophic dangers, there has been relatively little reaction from the public, including those communities in the vicinity of the 55 operational nuclear power plants. There is no evidence of a general exodus from plant areas or even any sign of shrinking property values. Once an incident occurs, changes in public fear will be primarily a function of the damage, casualties, and societal psychological impact. With respect to these functions, the principal fear in determining the subjective consequences of an act appears to be the distance from the target and the extent of media coverage. At this point it is impossible to judge societal reaction, because, to date, the world has not experienced a deliberate act that killed thousands of people, outside of war. But some insight might be gained from recent disasters and terrorist acts.

A Palestinian terrorist killed himself and 87 other persons aboard a U.S. commercial airliner in 1974 when he detonated a bomb while inflight off the coast of Greece. The incident was initially reported as an accident; the subsequent findings of a deliberately set bomb did not have any significant impact on aviation in general or on passenger volume in particular. In April 1974, a self-styled Atom Guerrilla sprayed railway compartment cars with radioactive I-131 in Austin, Tex., on two occasions. A total of six persons became ill with upset stomachs, but no hospitalization was required. Again, no recognizable impact occurred, even of a local character.

Two incidents in the United States resulted in significant consequences. The ALIEN bomber killed three persons at the Los Angeles Airport in late 1974 with an explosive device placed in a locker. This had the immediate but transient effect of reducing the use of that airport and led to increased security measures for all passengers. The bomber later threatened other incidents, causing public fear and an increase in local security measures. The LaGuardia Airport bomb explosion in December 1975 killed 12 persons and was the catalyst for Presidential action. The media coverage brought the incident to virtually millions of homes. As a result of this event new countermeasures have been instituted at airports, affecting every air traveler.

The incidents cited above point, as does the full weight of evidence derived from disaster and terrorism research in general, to several conclusions concerning subjective reaction. First, the local consequences of acts are far greater than the nonlocal consequences. Particularly with respect to the overall level of concern and fear, locales impacted upon directly by events have reacted by taking preventive measures. Nonlocal populations have reacted with sympathy and even bitterness, but implementation of new measures has been limited. Second, it is unlikely that public fear will increase until after an event occurs. Threats have not resulted in significant societal changes. Finally, assuming that an extrapolation from current experience to incidents involving new high technologies is valid, the communities subjected to new-technology terrorism will accept increased safeguards and the concomitant decrease in civil liberties. The paramount concern of society is to protect itself from known consequences. Society will seldom act until after some consequences have been demonstrated, particularly consequences of a local character, but society will be susceptible to changes in its norms, values, and structure once an event has been experienced.

Panic

Beyond the societal consequences mentioned, the question of panic merits attention because of the impact it can have on a community, both as an immediate phenomenon and with respect to longer term consequences. Panic is often discussed, but research and understanding of the subject are limited. For the purposes of this paper, panic is a human reaction to danger impelling the instinctive removal of oneself from the immediate danger area. This panic may be, in fact, the result of the loss of self-control caused by acute fear, or it may be a more orderly flight for the same reason. There are few instances in which communities, in part or as a whole, have fled in panic. For example, panic was not evidenced in either World War II atomic bomb attacks. Only limited, localized panic has been witnessed in the numerous tornado and earthquake situations. No evidence is available that portrays serious panic resulting from mere threats without accompanying action.

Of greatest importance to law enforcement and local authorities are those conditions that are most conducive to creating panic situations. Foremost, the threat must be sudden and unexpected, posing a danger that would be sufficient enough to cause immediate and intense fear. The threat must be direct and localized. Other factors contributing to panic include a population that believes there is a danger for which they are unprepared and which is beyond the capacity of normal behavior responses to adequately treat. Elements of novelty or incomprehensibility increase the tendency to panic. Confusion with respect to the general situation and specifics, such as escape, avoidance, and counteraction, directly impact on the likelihood of community panic. Finally, not only must the population be aware of their helpless situation—no escape routes, no information, bewildering uncertainty—but community leadership in the form of an authoritative, realistic response must be absent.

It is unlikely that these conditions could be successfully achieved by a terrorist, regardless of the nature of new technology selected for employment. Beyond the necessity of establishing the credibility of the threat without compromising himself, the perpetrator is faced with the problem of localizing the threat to specific segments of the population and successfully conveying that threat. These two elements of a panic situation would require at least some official assistance, in the form of coordination with the media. Any degree of official involvement will offset characteristics of panic, such as the unexpected or incomprehensible nature of an event and the resultant leadership void.

Even in a direct application action, it is unlikely that panic would occur. At worst, a sudden nuclear weapon detonation would tear apart a community. Probably some form of initial panic would result, but early action would be taken to implement preexisting contingency plans. Whether or not these would deal with the resultant damage is a matter of conjecture. But the authorities would be in control, exerting leadership, and countering the principal characteristics of a panic situation.

Other types of new technologies offer less of an opportunity for panic. Authorities would have time to respond to chemical and biological attacks by providing avoidance guidance and countermeasure instructions. Although the use of those technologies could present a completely unexpected action, the total uncertainty of the situation would contribute to the authorities' ability to control the populace. Because such employment would be new, any reasonable response from authorities would be accepted as correct and helpful, thus defusing the panic tendency. Only in the absence of governmental information, guidance, and leadership is the public prone to panic.

Although panic is rare, particularly in large segments of the population, there are cases of mass hysteria in localized situations. Over the years, instances of panic in hotel or restaurant fires have been noted. The possibility of this type of panic, isolated and localized but still potentially serious because of the potential for it to spread to other segments of the population, must be recognized and prepared for by local officials.

Up to this point, panic has been considered as a possible correlative to unique and catastrophic events. The question of panic takes on different dimensions after the first high-technology attack, although it must be explored in a more speculative vein. What would happen if terrorists elect to launch a campaign of incidents involving high technologies, and particularly new technologies? To date most of the literature deals with disasters that, at most, occur every several years. The compression of several events into a narrow timespan may well change community behavior, heightening the tendency to panic. The evidence of wartime bombing, the extended violence in Northern Ireland, and other high-intensity terroristic situations (e.g., Algeria between 1954 and 1957), however, all indicate that panic occurs only in isolated cases. Whether or not past experience would be reflected in high-technology terrorism situations is a point of contention that will only be settled when or if such a situation occurs. But at a minimum, governmental officials should be aware of the possible consequences of panic and the possible general, societal reaction to an intensive campaign of high-technology terroristic acts.

Throughout U.S. history, the citizens of this country have shown remarkable resilience in the face of adversity. One might attribute the lack of catastrophic, disastrous outcomes in the United States to advanced technology and communications. Regardless of the act, the populace has had at least a background appreciation of the type of disaster and the consequences involved. The abundance of portable radios and the rapid response of authorities have combined to minimize fear and limit panic. These same characteristics will play a significant role in future situations. It is incumbent upon local law enforcement and other governmental officials to take measures that will enhance their ability to provide adequate guidance to the population in situations where panic is likely.

Assessment of the Threat Potential of New Technologies

RELEVANCE OF CURRENT TERRORISM

The initial section of this paper outlined the different types of new high technologies that might be employed by terrorists and focused on those involving chemical, biological, and nuclear technologies. With these definitions as a reference point, a brief discussion of the objective and subjective consequences for society of new technologies was presented. A logical next step is to explore the threat as it appears to exist today, then outline a general method of analysis for examining the seriousness of the threat of high-technology terrorism as a whole, and finally, apply that methodology to the assessment of threats posed by new modes of high-technology terrorism.

In and of itself, technical capability does not provide an adequate basis for perpetration of a terrorist attack. There are a variety of strictly non technology factors that serve as preconditions for high-technology terrorism; among them are organization, group size, tactical methods, and intelligence capabilities. Equally significant, motivation must be present. The difficulty in assessing these necessary attributes arises from the dearth of incidents involving new technologies from which insights might be derived. To date very few incidents using chemical, biological, or nuclear agents have been undertaken, although a review of a few may be of interest.

Several instances of each type of new technology have occurred, but none with significant consequences. In 1970, a group of radicals attempted to blackmail an officer at the U.S. Army's biological warfare center into assisting in the theft of biological weapons. This plot was discovered when the officer requested issue of several items unrelated to his work. Two college students plotted to introduce typhoid fever bacteria into the Chicago water supply in early 1972. The culture was developed in the college laboratory and was to have been placed originally in water supplies throughout the Midwest. The circumstances surrounding discovery of the plot are unclear, but the organism selected would have been readily destroyed by normal chlorination.

Nuclear incidents are probably the most prevalent of all acts involving new technologies. The Orlando and Atom Guerrilla cases have been mentioned previously. Over the past 10 years, there have been a number of incidents in the United States in which small quantities of radioactive material were lost or stolen from hospitals and research facilities. None of the thefts has been of weapons-grade material or of other materials in an amount that would present a significant danger to large segments of the population. Several unsuccessful intrusions at U.S. weapons sites in Europe have been reported. And in Italy, neo-Fascist extremists plotted to introduce radioactive material into the water supply of selected cities in 1974. The plot was uncovered before any material was acquired.

These few incidents illustrate the application of new technologies by terrorists, but at a low level of technical sophistication. None achieved the level of potential outlined earlier. Thus, it is not possible to analyze and draw conclusions from past events with any degree of confidence. A different approach must be taken to assess the potential threat of new technologies. The current milieu of terrorism, employing conventional modes of destruction, provides a baseline from which extrapolation to the application of new technologies can be made. Quantification of conventional events lends itself to the systematic evaluation of past motives, targets, and resources. But for the assessment of the new-technology threat potential, one must move beyond past data and make subjective judgments.

The assessment of the use of new technologies with respect both to terrorists at large and to specific groups should combine the evidential and the judgmental. It is unlikely that the correlations that presently exist among motivations, objectives, and targets will change, regardless of the level of terrorism. A principal factor then becomes the ability to ascertain to what levels of violence a particular type of group will escalate to achieve its objectives. A type of group that has taken pains to avoid casualties in the past, probably will not be interested in creating the fatalities generally associated with adopting new technologies. Conversely, a type of group that has taken pains to avoid casualties in the past, probably will not be interested in creating the fatalities generally associated with adopting new technologies. Conversely, a type of group that has historically shown little regard for human life in the target area, such as a separatist movement, should be examined to determine whether it has escalated its terrorist acts and has collected the resources necessary for new-technology terrorism.

Current terrorist threat data and historical events do no more than provide insights. Once certain correlations have been made, it is necessary to move to the judgmental. Questions requiring subjective evaluation include: What persons, including terrorists and nonterrorists, are prone to employ new technologies; when will an attempt be made to use new technologies; what types of technology are most likely to be used; and what general and specific targets are likely to be attacked?

Prior to discussing the specific characteristics of the potential terrorist threat employing new technologies, a brief description of the method of analysis is warranted. Starting with a brief overview of the vulnerability of U.S. society to terrorist attack, the analysis then focuses on the specific characteristics of terrorists that might be indicative of those inclined to perpetrate acts using new technologies. The initial characteristic examined is motivation, which permits the later placing of other characteristics in perspective with respect to the force driving the perpetrator to act. Then the discussion shifts to the potential targets and the resources necessary to undertake new-technology terrorism. The final portions of the section address the modes of application for new high-technology terrorism and conclude with a summary of the characteristics that provides a total view of the discrete elements discussed previously.

Characteristics of Potential New-Technology Terrorists

VULNERABILITY OF MODERN SOCIETY

Because it is technologically developed, mobile, and wealthy, U.S. society offers the terrorist a variety of resources and targets that leaves little doubt concerning its vulnerability. The highly interrelated services necessary to keep a modern city alive offer countless opportunities to the terrorist. Accidental occurrences underscore the vulnerabilities of our society. The Northeast power blackout of 1965 and the New York City telephone exchange fire typify potential targets. In the former case, electric service to the Northeast section of the United States, including New York City, was totally cut off for hours because of a power grid problem. The telephone exchange fire in the spring of 1975 disrupted service to a large segment of New York City, in some cases for a week. Initially, police, fire, and other emergency services were completely cut off from telephone service, as were tens of thousands of individuals. Terrorists have not taken advantage of these vulnerabilities to date, but it is evident that it would be possible to disrupt society using conventional means only.

U.S. society contributes to its own vulnerability. There is no question that the technical skills and resources to embark on new-technology terrorism are available. The limiting factor has been, and will apparently continue to be, the ability of an extremist group to combine the necessary physical resources with technicians who are motivated to engage in an activity that could potentially kill thousands of people.

IMPORTANCE OF CHARACTERISTICS

The ability to understand terrorism and to structure responses is in large measure dependent upon an appreciation of the characteristics of the perpetrators. For this reason, the following sections will describe the more crucial characteristics: motivations, targets, resources, modes of employment, and risk and attractiveness of specific acts. The information presented in this discussion is drawn from the evaluation of over 4,500 worldwide terroristic acts of violence from 1965 to 1975. That data base contains the full spectrum of terroristic violence including hijacking, kidnaping, bombing, arson, armed attack, assassination, and psychological terrorism.

The detailed analysis of these events highlighted the significance of examining characteristics by providing insights into some of the myths that have been created concerning terrorism. By way of illustration, one of the principal findings refuted the oft-repeated warning of the intuitive analyst—that terrorist acts do not form a pattern but must be examined as individual acts. In fact, there are several discernible characteristics that typify various types of groups. Although each of the groups and incidents is not totally comparable, there is enough similarity to permit the acceptance of identifiable characteristics within group types. For example, issue-oriented groups, such as antiwar extremists, target symbols of the issue; U.S. black revolutionary groups target symbols of authority; separatist groups are indiscriminate with respect to inflicting casualties; and all groups are fundamentally nonsuicidal, with only a few willing to risk direct confrontation with force, such as Black September and the Japanese Red Army.

Many of the aspects of high-technology employment can be extrapolated from conventional terrorist acts. Whether target selection is indiscriminate or discriminate is highly relevant. Analogies may also be drawn between conventional and high-technology terrorism in the areas of motivations, tactics, and the collection and application of resources. An understanding of terrorist characteristics may assist law enforcement officials in determining credible threats, in successfully countering high-technology undertakings, and in providing the community with information essential for insuring timely recognition and identification of possible terroristic indicators.

MOTIVATIONS

The principal purpose of this discussion is to provide the reader with an overview of the motivational characteristics of terrorists. Although persons acting with other motivations might potentially employ high technology for their ends, the emphasis here is on the terrorist. As a basis for explanation and as a means of placing terroristic violence in perspective with respect to other forms of violent behavior, a framework of eight motivations has been developed. This framework is established by viewing motivations in general, then examining the more explicit components of stimuli and nature of the act, and finally describing each of the eight forms of violent behavior, with an extended presentation of terroristic violence.

There is general agreement among psychologists that motivations, including violent motivations, are internal factors that arouse, direct, and integrate a person's behavior. The nature of the motive may be described along two dimensions: the source of the stimulus to violence; and the degree of rationality in adjusting the means to the ends. These two components are the basis for determining the propensity of an individual to engage in new or unfamiliar modes of high-technology violence with its associated results.

In defining these motivations, it is necessary to briefly discuss two theoretical concepts that permit a reasoned categorization. First, all stimuli are either external or internal. External stimuli require some environmental cue to be activated, such as the nuclear power issue, food for the poor, unemployment, civil rights, or the war in Vietnam. These stimuli react on preexisting dispositions to internal motives. Internal stimuli are those that originate entirely within an individual or group psychology and do not require environmental cues. Either of these two stimuli may be rational or emotional; that determination is made on the basis of the rationality applied to approaching the ends desired. A final set of concepts involves the public or private nature of the act. In public violence, there is a societal reaction or an audience for a given event. Conversely, private violence has an internal benefit for the perpetrator, with no outside feedback necessary for the perpetrator to achieve a sense of fulfillment.

By combining these three sets of concepts—source of stimuli, rationality, and the nature of the act—one is able to isolate potentially real threats from those considered unlikely to be carried out, with respect to high-technology terrorism. Figure 1 provides a graphic representation of the eight forms of violent behavior that can logically be drawn from an evaluation of these factors and actual violent incidents.

Figure 1. Forms of Violent Behavior

Stimuli / Nature	Rational-Internal Stimulus	Emotional-External Stimulus	Emotional-Internal Stimulus	Rational-External Stimulus
Private	Criminal	Revenge	Pathological	Vigilante
Public	Terroristic	Protest	Sociopathic	Paramilitary

These eight forms are representative of the spectrum of violent behavior. Although terrorism is central to this [article], often the other seven forms of violent behavior are termed terroristic, gaining wide publicity for that reason. Furthermore, individuals or groups engaging in any of the forms of violent behavior may employ high technology to achieve their ends. The following offers a detailed discussion of terrorism and briefly treats the other forms of violent behavior.

TERRORISTIC VIOLENT BEHAVIOR

Terroristic violent behavior, as the principal focus of this paper and the most likely to involve high technology, is examined in somewhat greater depth than the other forms. Persons who engage in terroristic behavior have a variety of motivations, such as protest demonstration, disruption, revenge, and persuasion. At the core of terroristic behavior is the political nature of the movement and its goals. Thus, by definition, actions of terrorists are in some fashion related to the ultimate goal of effecting political change—the raison d'être for the organization's existence. The means of realizing respective terrorist motivations can be graphically depicted in four sets that run along a progressive continuum (Figure 2). The high specificity of demands entails that government or some other entity either perform, or refrain from performing, some act. Hijackers that bargain for the release of prisoners provide an example of this means. Other illustrations include the continuing power substation bombings in northern California by the Red Guerrilla Family, accompanied by demands for reduced power rates, and the release of the Harrises from jail, demanded after the explosions at the Hearst Estate Museum in early 1976, which was perpetrated by the George Jackson Brigade and the New World Liberation Army.

At the low end of the demands spectrum are those with much less specificity: the political statements. These demands are usually generalizations concerning society as a whole and are often represented as ends to be achieved through action. Examples of this type of demand are "freedom

Figure 2. Terrorist means

Specificity of Demands / Target Selection	High	Low
Discriminate	Bargaining	Political Statement
Random	Social Paralysis	Mass Casualties

for everyone" and "elimination of all forms of racism, sexism, capitalism, Fascism, individualism, possessiveness, and competition."

Highly discriminate targeting is usually associated with bargaining and political statements, and involves a relatively low level of actual violence. These targets are chosen for their readily identifiable connection with the opponents of the terrorists or because of the target's value and the willingness of the coerced parties to meet certain demands to regain or preserve it. Random target selection is most often the hallmark of those groups whose means are to create social paralysis or inflict mass casualties. Terrorists seldom resort to random target selection in the initial stages of their movement and terroristic activity. Rather, indiscriminate attacks are resorted to when neither bargaining nor political statements have been perceived as successful by the terrorists. Usually, random targeting is accompanied by an increase in the level of violence.

Experience demonstrates that social paralysis is usually associated with relatively high levels of specific demands. The random targeting that accompanies social paralysis is indicative of a group that has failed to achieve its ends through bargaining and political statements using less destructive violence. Terrorists who are motivated to employ social paralysis as a means usually do not care about publicity as a method of gaining popular support for their position. They appear to believe that the higher level of violence associated with social paralysis, through random targeting, enables them to achieve more specific demands. These activities bring the struggle directly to the anonymous citizen. The IRA attacks in London subways in mid-March 1976 are illustrative of the type of attack that terrorists so motivated undertake. In recent history, no U.S. domestic terrorist group has had these motives.

Means involving mass casualties are typically employed by a group at the conclusion of a failed revolution, during periods of intense frustration, or when support declines. Acts involving mass casualties express recognition by the group that:

1. The strength to use bargaining as an effective tool has been lost;
2. The public has been saturated with statement-related attacks; or
3. Popular support has been eroded either by attacks that caused social paralysis or by other terroristic acts in general

OTHER FORMS OF VIOLENT BEHAVIOR

Of these other seven forms of violent behavior, criminal, paramilitary, and vigilante behaviors are least likely to be motivated to employ high-technology violence, particularly new technologies. The motive of the criminal is financial gain, an unlikely result from the application of a new-technology attack. Vigilante-type groups are motivated by their perceptions of social justice and societal norms, and are not disposed to employ methods that are anomic to society. Paramilitary behavior is primarily motivated by adventuresome considerations. There is no indication that this type of violent behavior would motivate a group of individuals to employ high-technology terrorism. The lack of incidents involving this type of behavior constrains explanation and limits the utility of further elaboration.

Protest behavior is usually associated with groups who commit violent acts as a means of venting frustrations. These groups are likely to represent a faction of a larger organization that is protesting through legitimate means. Protest violence tends to be a spontaneous and relatively short-lived phenomenon. This form of behavior is often confused with issue-oriented terrorism, and, in fact, differentiation is often not possible because terrorist groups are radicalized splinter groups of protest movements in many instances. The motivation of these splinter groups is essentially that of bringing issues to the fore. This behavior is not conducive to motivations that would result in an attempt to use high-technology terrorism.

Revenge as a form of violent behavior is motivated by vengeance directed against the source of frustration or injustice. It is quite possible that high-technology violence might be of interest to an individual seeking revenge. Two factors, however, militate against the use of this level of violence. First, the target is usually very discriminate, and, second, revenge is a highly individualistic motivation that is unlikely to result in group formation; group formation is a practical prerequisite for most acts involving high technology.

Pathological behavior, like revenge, is highly individualistic. But the stimulus is internal, arising from some need for personal psychological gratification. Thus, the specific motivation of an individual may be any one of an infinite number. Persons acting on pathologically related motivations should be considered the most likely, apart from terrorists, to turn to high-technology violence. Considering the individualistic, private nature of this form of behavior, the chief inhibiting factor for this individual is the lack of resources and technical knowledge.

Sociopathic behavior may be either an individual or group phenomenon. Viewing society and its requirements for conformity as external stimuli for violence, sociopathic violent behavior may be motivated by thrill seeking, subculture group loyalty, or purely antisocial reasons. The category of sociopathic behavior requires a group psychology of collective arousal to consummate an act of violence. Although sociopathic violent behavior is basically antisocial and amoral, those involved in this type of behavior have not been disposed to employ the advanced methods of violence that the application of high technology would require.

TARGETS

The types of targets terrorists might attack employing high technologies are an important characteristic in assessing the potential threat. An understanding of target selection will provide a planning basis for local officials and higher governmental authorities. The application of historical data with respect to targets has validity because it appears that the nature of the motivations, the means, and the ultimate goals for terroristic behavior will not change. Hence, regardless of the specific targets one considers, it is likely that the process of target selection will remain essentially the same. Terrorists will probably select targets using the same fundamental criteria that have been applied in the past: targets have been lightly or totally unprotected and have offered the terrorist an opportunity to communicate a message at relatively low risk. Seldom are targets randomly selected, even those that appear to be indiscriminately chosen. Rather, targets are selected to convey some symbolic message or to graphically depict the total vulnerability of society to terrorist actions.

Targets such as power-generating stations, communication centers, fuel tank farms, refineries, bridges, tunnels, dams, transportation systems, and large office buildings could be considered potential targets for new technologies, particularly a nuclear explosion. Aside from low-level explosions at numerous power substations in northern California over the past 2 years and scattered incidents involving attacks on power transmission lines and office buildings, terrorists have not elected to attack the many vital targets in the United States. Most of the targets listed above would be susceptible to the employment of conventional high explosives with potentially devastating results. To facilitate further evaluation, potential targets of new technologies have been divided into two categories: property and personnel.

If the terrorist selects a form of new technology for an attack because of the target's resistance to conventional methods, then property targets will probably be large, relatively hard, and inaccessible to a direct attack using conventional munitions. If the terrorists desire to deny access through contamination, the use of a nuclear device is the only reasonable technology available.

People as a primary terroristic target are equally vulnerable to all three categories of new technologies: chemical, biological, and nuclear. A nuclear explosive device would have a devastating effect on a large crowd in the open. A nuclear explosion or biological agent used in the vicinity of a major outdoor sports complex would be maximized by the high density of population. Because of the impact of environmental conditions, however, dispersal technologies are most effectively applied in closed areas. Delivery of these agents into a subway system, large public building, domed sports stadium, or convention center would inflict thousands of fatalities.

Attacks through bulk foodstuffs or beverages (via dairies, meat processing plants, canning companies, bakeries, and soda and beer bottlers) offer the terrorist a means of attacking either particular groups or a broad cross section of society, depending on the specific facility attacked. Contrary to popular belief, the water supply is not a highly vulnerable target. For example, based on personal consumption as opposed to other uses and a 4 billion gallon reservoir, if each member of a community of 20,000 were to drink 16 ounces of water, it would require in excess of 14 billion lethal doses to deliver one dose per person. If the best suited chemical, fluroacetates, were used, it would require 600 metric tons. Any of the highly lethal biological agents are not effectively transmitted by water and would be further debilitated by the purification system.

RESOURCES

Without a doubt, the resources to commit any act involving known high technology are available in the United States. At the same time, all of the types and applications of high technology the terrorist might potentially employ are unknown because of the breadth of the problem and the absence of experience when uncontrolled high technology was adopted. Thus, much of this material is speculative and, in the interest of brevity, exemplary. To this end, each class of new high technology is examined separately, with the intent of providing insights rather than definitive descriptions of resources.

Chemical Technology Resource Requirements

Construction and employment of high technology involving chemical agents are not extremely difficult for a trained chemist or toxicologist. Using standard organic chemistry processes, any of the compounds listed previously can be manufactured. A consensus among the chemists queried is that one knowledgeable individual could legally purchase all the supplies and equipment necessary, and establish a laboratory operation that probably could produce more than 10 kilograms of toxic agent per year, depending on the specific type. Thus, for a few thousand dollars in supplies, extensive dedication in terms of time, and a small facility, a knowledgeable individual could have the basic ingredients necessary to kill thousands of people.

Probably more difficult and risky for the terrorist is the fabrication of a satisfactory dispersal device and actual dispersal. Although a myriad of methods for dissemination might be suggested, the opportunity for operational testing is limited. Thus, the attack would probably be the first full use of the device. Three to five persons would be necessary to set up the device and insure that it is working prior to departure. Information on the target, specifically building heating and air conditioning systems, is highly significant. Without some detailed information on the target prior to the attack and even without construction of the dispersal device, the probable success of the effort might be in question.

With respect to chemical technologies, a few points merit emphasis. First, one trained individual could make and employ chemical agents. However, for any one person to be knowledgeable in the technical aspects as well as the operational considerations of target analysis, methods of attack, placement of the device, security, and escape is extremely unlikely. Second, it is unlikely that a terrorist with the requisite tactical expertise would also possess the skills necessary to successfully manufacture chemical agents.

Although the most toxic chemicals have been discussed, numerous less toxic agents are available for use by the terrorist. Some of these agents are available commercially as insecticides. In attempting to achieve certain ends while restricting the level of violence, terrorists might well resort to these less toxic chemical agents. At a minimum, the shock effect of this technology would probably produce a societal reaction and recognition of the group.

Biological Technology Resource Requirements

Resources considered necessary and sufficient to develop biological agents and employ this technology are somewhat greater than those for chemical agents. The task is made more difficult by the nature of biological agents themselves. Several specific steps are required to manufacture this type of agent and then apply it to a target. These steps include the selection and acquisition of the seed culture, seed cultivation in ample quantities to meet target requirements, a means of keeping the agent virulent, and a method of effective dissemination.

To successfully develop biological technology, the most important resource is trained persons. The type of knowledge needed probably is beyond a biologist, necessitating the employment of both a microbiologist and a pathologist. This requisite expertise—the minimum staff capability—appears critical for the achievement of a biological weapon. Equipment is dependent upon the type of agent selected, but the extent of the facility and the accompanying cost would be somewhat greater than that for working with chemical agents and less costly than nuclear weapons fabrication.

Two principal problems still face the potential biological terrorist. An initial problem is the necessity to secure the biological seed culture, obtainable from one of three sources: a research facility, a medical laboratory, or a natural reservoir. The first two involve theft or diversion, while the third, and most secure source, requires the terrorist to sample, isolate, and identify the organism. Obviously, this latter method cannot be accomplished by the layman. Second, assuming there are adequate facilities to manufacture and maintain the completed quantities, the use of biological technology evolves around a practicable method of employment. Avoiding the detailed discussion of the difficulties and pitfalls of dissemination, it is adequate for purposes of this paper to state that overcoming the problem of the deterioration of the biological agent once it has been released requires extensive skills, even beyond those available to microbiologists and pathologists.

Examining the practicable adoption of biological technologies by terrorists leads to several conclusions concerning resources. It would take a highly trained individual with experience in microbiology, pathology, aerosol physics, aerobiology, and even meteorology to make a reasonable attempt at manufacture and employment of a biological agent. Thus, although it is possible for one individual to undertake this type of technology, it is highly unlikely that this will occur. A larger group of at least three to five members with a full range of capabilities, including training, tactics, technical knowledge, resources, and operational experience, is considered the optimal number required to perpetrate an act using biological technologies.

Nuclear Technology Resource Requirements

Nuclear technology is at the same time the most difficult and the simplest of the new technologies for terrorists to employ. On one hand, of the technologies explored, the dispersal of radioisotopes by wrapping a material, such as COBALT-60, with explosives is the easiest. Aside from acquisition of the radioactive material, which is relatively simple today, this type of device is quite uncomplicated, and employment presents no technical problems. Given the terrorists' willingness to accept a rudimentary device with little concern for dispersal patterns, one individual can achieve enough technological skill to steal the material, wrap it in explosives, set the charge, and detonate the device. Manufacture of a nuclear weapon, however, is another matter.

The initial problem faced by the would-be bomb maker is the availability of weapons-grade material. Theft or diversion of adequate amounts of material in themselves requires extensive resources in terms of personnel, equipment, and weapons. Diversion of material from an operating facility places minimal requirements on the perpetrator in terms of weapons and equipment, but at least one employee must be involved. Systematic diversion from a plant where material is processed and stored appears impractical because of the stringent security measures specifically designed to preclude such an incident. These same security procedures limit access to quantities of material adequate for weapons fabrication, eliminating the simple crime of opportunity as a source of sufficient material.

Theft of material by an overt or covert attack on fixed sites or the transportation system offers an opportunity to acquire the requisite quantity of nuclear material for bomb fabrication. But the resources considered necessary are well beyond most groups. Current security measures have been determined adequate to counter a theft by up to six armed personnel. In addition, intelligence requirements, familiarity with nuclear operations, handling expertise, and specialized nuclear equipment further complicate any attempt at material theft. Such thefts would be highly complex, requiring resources more extensive than the most sophisticated conventional criminal design, such as the Brinks Robbery.

Despite the testimony of a few nuclear experts on the one-man resource for nuclear weapon construction, it is apparent from the bulk of the literature that a one-man operation is not feasible. Once material is acquired, most experts agree that anywhere between 10 and 20 persons might construct a crude but reasonable weapon in 1 to 2 years. Staff for the project would have to include at least one competent nuclear physicist and a nuclear engineer. Other necessary support staff are a chemical engineer, a metallurgist, several technical personnel trained in general and specific nuclear laboratory procedures, explosives and nuclear materials experts, and possibly a precision metal worker. Facilities for this effort must, at a minimum, include laboratory accoutrements, nuclear handling tools and equipment, precision metal shop machinery, radioactivity monitoring gear, and adequate ventilation. The cost of the laboratory and associated equipment would probably be in excess of $50,000 to $100,000. Once the weapon is completed and mounted on transport or emplaced, however, resources for the employment of that particular device are minimal. One person can effect the initiation of any action using the weapon.

Although the above description addresses the resources necessary for weapons fabrication with a degree of assurance with respect to safety and success, the question of the absolute minimum is still unanswered. A group that does not concern itself with safety or the destructive characteristics of the resultant weapon could fabricate a weapon with four to six personnel with the following skills and equipment: a nuclear engineer and a nuclear physicist; explosives expertise; nuclear material handling equipment; and minimal laboratory facilities. Even were personal safety to be totally disregarded, which is a questionable assumption for a group of four to six persons, certain minimum equipment and knowledge is necessary to accomplish the task. Under the conditions outlined above, it is possible that those constructing the weapon would receive lethal doses of radiation because of the lack of safety features. Fewer resources in terms of knowledge and equipment would most likely result in the death of group members prior to completion of the project.

The preceding discussion has focused on the resources necessary to manufacture the three new high technologies from basic raw materials. For the terrorist, a simpler solution in many respects might be the theft of a weapon or device from some government facility. With respect to nuclear technology, weapons and weapons-grade material have been highly protected since the inception of nuclear technology. The proliferation of nuclear weapons, however, and the expansion of the commercial nuclear industry, which has a by-product of weapons-grade material, has significantly increased the opportunity for theft. Requiring less manpower and technical skill, theft of a weapon or weapons-grade material requires less manpower and less technical skill and is less difficult than the actual fabrication of a nuclear bomb.

Chemical and, to a lesser degree, biological weapons have been available for years both in the United States and abroad. Although ostensibly protected, these sites have been vulnerable to attack. In fact, in 1975 a quantity of mustard gas was reported stolen from a munitions storage site in France, allegedly by a terrorist group supporting the Baader-Meinhof Gang in West Germany. With respect to availability of these weapons, the U.S. policy of elimination of its biological weapons and reduction of chemical weapons stockpiles has significantly reduced the danger of theft. Further, following reports of storage site vulnerabilities, security has been appreciably improved at these sites in recent years.

By way of summary, the reader should understand that the employment of any of these technologies is not easy. This admonition is necessary because this discussion of resources has been abbreviated by design. The specialized talent required to construct each technology must be emphasized. Chemical and biological technologies have the advantages of essentially unrestricted data sources, relatively small resource requirements, the availability of key resources, and at least a limited opportunity to test the product. But recognition must be given to the fact that significant design and engineering problems exist, particularly with respect to dissemination.

On the whole, of those technologies examined, it appears that chemical technologies might be constructed most easily, but that they pose a somewhat ineffectual threat. Biological weapons might be constructed with a little more difficulty than chemical weapons, while posing a more significant threat. An equally great threat might be realized from nuclear technologies involving weapons-grade material, but the relative difficulty in obtaining the material and the subsequent difficulties of bomb construction raise questions of the overall practicality of selecting this new technology.

Moreover, there has been no evidence to substantiate that any terrorist group within the United States has the requisite resources and motivations to undertake an act of high-technology terrorism. Adequate resources, in terms of personnel and equipment as outlined above, have been available to a number of terrorist groups, but technical expertise and the resolve necessary to develop and employ high technology appear lacking. Although U.S. terrorist groups have failed to initiate any such attack in the past, apparently because requirements exceeded capabilities, the increasing sophistication of these groups may result in an organization capable and willing to engage in high-technology terrorism.

APPLICATION OF NEW TECHNOLOGIES

For the law enforcement officer, the legislator, the decisionmaker, and the community as a whole, discussions of the separate and distinct elements that compose new-technology terrorism are of obvious interest. Even more significant, however, each is concerned with the consequences of the combination of these characteristics. This section is designed to bring the earlier segments of the paper together and place the new technologies in perspective. It is apparent that two general modes of employment form an appropriate framework for this discussion: the direct application and the coercive threat of new technologies.

Direct Application

The direct application of new technologies involves an action with little or no warning. When warning is provided, it is not for bargaining purposes but as a means of limiting damage, causing panic, gaining publicity, or for other target-related reasons. For example, most U.S. terrorist bombings that would potentially endanger people have been preceded by a warning for purposes of limiting casualties. Direct application is undertaken by perpetrators who have determined that their purpose is best served by the use of the weapon itself.

A broad spectrum of high-technology direct applications might be employed by the terrorist, and the decision to use any one of them is based primarily on motivation and resources of the individual or group. At the lower end of the spectrum are the discriminate employment alternatives, which focus on the use of smaller, controllable quantities of the technology. In these instances, the primary objective would be the demonstration effect. Releasing a small quantity of a chemical or biological agent in a controlled manner to produce casualties within a selected target group is illustrative of this level of action. Similarly, the use of precision-guided munitions with a minimal amount of explosives exemplifies this mode of direct application.

At a higher level of damage, direct application of high technology has two salient features. First, as the potential consequences to the target or public increase, the degree of discretion in target selection diminishes. Although a PGM may be targeted against a police precinct headquarters, the high explosives will undoubtedly cause public casualties beyond the target itself. Second, and closely related to discrimination, is the proportional loss of control of the consequences as the level of action escalates. Chemical or biological weapons may well carry effects far beyond the intended target. Once agents are released, the attacker has lost control of events, with potential catastrophic results.

In the past, few attackers have selected targets indiscriminately, and even fewer have employed weapons that present problems of subsequent control after employment. Throughout their history, the Weather Underground has targeted areas where the likelihood of personal injury was minimal. In most cases, the Weather Underground telephoned a prior warning to further preclude casualties. It is evident from past events that terrorists, in general, seldom opt for direct application of technologies that cannot be controlled and for which the quantitative consequences cannot be determined to some degree prior to the attack.

The terrorist that would resort to the direct application of new technologies causing uncontrolled, indiscriminate casualties and damage has not appeared. This terrorist would have to combine the motivation necessary to inflict a high level of damage; the technical expertise and resources; and the willingness to sustain his commitment for an extended period of time. For certain types of new technologies, such as biological or nuclear weapons, the requirements, in terms of resources, organization, and group cohesion, are significantly increased because of the necessity to involve more than one person. Problems of technical expertise and resources may well be lessened by expansion of the group, but the problems associated with maintaining motivation and sustained group commitment increase in geometric proportions in relation to group size. One individual may well accept uncontrolled indiscriminate consequences, but it is not likely that any group of persons would be able to retain the organization with objectives of this nature.

Coercive Threats

Terrorist employment of new technologies as means of coercive threat is more likely than direct application. In this mode, the terrorist is able to exert considerable pressure while permitting avoidance or delay of the decision to actually use the capability. The range of possible coercive threats covers all of the new technologies discussed throughout this paper, as well as those involving more exotic and devastating means. It is difficult to provide a full range of illustrations of coercive threats to date because many of them are either classified or simply have not been publicized. But the 1970 Orlando, Fla., extortion, previously described, is typical of the coercive threats for money; and the 1974 A-bomb threat against the Capitol, in an attempt to gain $10 million of food for the hungry in the United States, exemplifies those threats used for improvements in social conditions and general political statements. The majority of the new technology threats have involved nuclear material, particularly bombs, and have been for extortion or explicit political concessions. None of these threats has been carried through. More interestingly, very few of the threats have been assessed as possibly credible.

Analysis of particular coercive threats using new technologies is best accomplished by examining each threat through four components. First, there is the actual or implied threat itself; second, the target or hostage; third, the demands; and fourth, the authorities involved with the threat and its verification. The mere fact of a threat, although it might indicate a perception on the terrorists' part that the coercive threat offers more than direct application of technology, does not necessarily signal a serious incident. Persons charged with response authority must assess the potential of the threat and the wide-ranging implications should it be carried out.

With respect to the threat itself, two principal factors relating to the characteristic of the threat, regardless of its context, are important in the overall process of its evaluation: the magnitude of the consequences if the threat is executed; and the credibility of the threat. In terms of the range of new technologies, these two factors cannot always be separated. The type of technology involved and the potential results of application may influence the determination of threat credibility. Nevertheless, each threat must be examined individually, and a judgment made as to its credibility.

It is necessary for officials to realize that an evaluative process must take place to reasonably determine the credibility of the threat. Each threat must be viewed in several steps. First, is the threat possible? Given the state of the art, the specified nature and scope of the threat, and the situation, is it possible in technical and theoretical terms to achieve what is threatened?

Second, the threat must be examined for feasibility. Because high technologies are new phenomena, the question of whether or not the threat can be believed may be unanswerable. Rather than attempting to answer it, officials must analyze if it is feasible to carry out the threat. Questions at this level focus on the nature and extent of resources and motivations. Third, the threat must be evaluated in detail to determine the practicality of the act. This determination centers on examining whether or not the threat is practical in terms of the organization threatening the act. In what is actually a refinement of feasibility analysis, officials must make a subjective determination based on the best information available. Finally, the process is completed through making a highly judgmental determination of the probability of the occurrence.

Only through a combination of these steps can officials assure themselves that each threat has been completely examined. Significantly, within a certain range, as the magnitude of consequences increases, the willingness to accept the threat credibility also increases. This phenomenon is the result of the decisionmakers' evaluation of the potential cost to the target and the community, and the escalated consequences of a wrong decision.

Until a threatened act of new high-technology terrorism is actually committed, it is unlikely that the approach to credibility evaluation outlined above will change. Following the first incident of actual violence using any of these new technologies, however, all other threats become more credible. And the more threats that are carried out, the greater the acceptance of relative likelihood will become.

In cases of new-technology threats, the target or hostage could significantly influence the decisionmaking process. The determining factor is the communication of threat facts to the hostages themselves and the size of the threatened group, perceived or actual. In small-group situations, akin to aircraft hijackings, it is unlikely that the group could influence decisions. The possible threat to a city of 100,000 people, however, may create an entirely different atmosphere for the decisionmaker. To date there are no events from which to extrapolate the consequences of hostage impact. In most nuclear threat cases the public was not informed, primarily because the threat was deemed not credible. If a threat using new technologies is carried out, the nature of the hostage will probably have greater impact on the decisionmakers than previously.

The character of any official response to a coercive threat will also depend on the nature of any demands accompanying that threat, and, in particular, on their reasonableness. Regardless of the threat magnitude, certain demands will not be met by authorities, either because of an inability to do so or because of a patent unwillingness to sacrifice that much. A $1 billion ransom, immediate unilateral disarmament, an end to all nuclear power plant construction, resignation of all Democrats or Republicans in Congress, and changes in laws are examples of demands that would not be acquiesced to by governmental authorities. If the perpetrator has been rational enough to arrive at the point of possession and threatens application of new technologies, however, a valid assumption would be that the terrorist has the rationality to keep his or her demands within acceptable bounds, or at least negotiate toward them. The use of a coercive threat must be recognized as a leverage mechanism, permitting a small group to exert inordinate pressure on the system, in relation to its size. Coercive threat demands are seldom the only or "best and final" offer, but rather are a prelude to negotiation.

Perhaps the most significant set of personnel in the coercive threat are the authorities involved. Law enforcement officers and governmental decisionmakers must make judgments concerning the threat and its credibility. The perceptions of this group with respect to the situation and its subsequent actions are the catalyst for the terrorists. Whether or not a coercive threat reaches fruition, or is even prematurely triggered, is the direct result of the authorities' actions.

The first task of decisionmakers—credibility evaluation—has already been discussed. Closely allied is the difficult, often impossible, task of threat verification, which requires the decisionmakers to combine scientific data and subjective judgments. The scientific inquiry provides the basis for determining the possibility, feasibility, practicality, and probability of occurrence of the threat. As one moves across the spectrum from possibility to probability, scientific data become less useful and subjective evaluations gain in prominence.

Unless indications of preparation for the future application of a new technology are detected during those preparatory stages, it is hard to verify most threats in a timely manner. Chemical and biological technologies can be developed in a small laboratory facility. Even the employment of nuclear material in a threat might be credible, because verification of missing minimal quantities of the material is not possible. The more secretive the organization making the threat, the greater the difficulty to be encountered in verification.

Successfully countering the direct application and coercive threat modes of high-technology terrorism is dependent upon well-planned and -executed control measures and timely and appropriate responses. Without these control and response measures, the ability of authorities to differentiate between hoaxes and realistic threats is severely handicapped. Understanding the range of characteristics of terrorists likely to employ high technology in achieving their ends is central to formulating effective control measures and response means.

SUMMARY OF TERRORIST CHARACTERISTICS

Prior to discussing control and response mechanisms, it is beneficial to summarize the characteristics of terrorists who might potentially use high technology. Although terroristic or other forms of violent behavior may result in the use of high technology, the adoption of high technology will be tempered by the objective of the group. An implicit point made earlier in the text should be clearly stated by way of summary—new modes of high-technology terrorism do not necessarily involve mass casualties or a high dollar value of destruction. But the physical resources, training, planning, overall organization, and risk involved in designing or acquiring and employing high technology are far beyond what most groups would be motivated to undertake. Two concepts are useful in summarizing those characteristics that indicate a willingness to explore, formulate, and initiate actions to use high technology: the elements of risk and attractiveness associated with actual attacks; and the nonsuicidal nature of the terrorist.

Addressing the nonsuicidal nature of terrorism first, an appropriate generalization appears to be that terrorists do not usually engage in activity that involves the risk of confrontation, capture, or a fight to the death. Despite highly publicized but isolated cases of suicidal terrorist attacks, such as the attack on Lod Airport, the Malot raid in Israel, and the siege and subsequent death of SLA members in Los Angeles, terrorists and most other perpetrators of violence do not have a death wish. Supporting this assertion is the fact that the over 2,500 bombings reported by the FBI Bomb Data Center in 1975 represent in excess of 95 percent of all U.S. terrorist activity. Bombing attacks, and terrorist activities in general, are usually covert actions against unprotected targets.

Closely associated with the nonsuicidal nature of terrorism is the terrorists' reluctance to engage in attacks that might result in confrontation. In examining over 4,500 incidents, no U.S. events occurred where a guard force of more than two or three men armed with sidearms were on duty. Cases where a small guard force was involved are few, less than 1 percent of the total. Equally as illustrative is the fact that over 60 percent of all bombs are placed outside the target: against a wall, on a windowsill, or against a door. These placements can be made easily with little risk of detection.

The second and most significant concept relative to terrorist characteristics is the risk and attractiveness of the intended attack. Either implicitly or explicitly, terrorists will examine the factors of risk and attractiveness in determining the nature of their attacks and the targets. Attractiveness represents the appeal of the target and the method of attack to be used. Primarily the terrorist is asking: What will be the gain in terms of achieving the goal of the organization? At the same time, the terrorist will consider the accompanying risks involved in accomplishing the act.

Risk is actually twosided: risk in acquisition and risk in implementation. In assessing the former, the terrorist must weigh the risk of acquiring the necessary resources to include personnel, skills, equipment, and material. High-technology terrorism, particularly chemical, biological, and nuclear modes, requires extensive risk in the acquisition phase. Not only are there extensive dangers of detection in accumulating resources such as nuclear material, but personnel safety is a constant concern, as are the strains placed on the organization by the requirement for commitment over an extended period of time.

Implementation risk is greater in high technology than in conventional terrorism because of the inherent characteristics of the technologies themselves. It is generally more difficult and risky to employ a chemical, biological, or nuclear device than to engage in other forms of terrorism. Resources, personnel, and organization, along with the target and mode of attack are key risk-determining characteristics. Probably most significant of the risks is maintaining the necessary degree of motivation among organization members. Unless the willingness and resolve to commit an act that may have catastrophic societal consequences can be sustained, the organization faces an increased likelihood of compromise.

The terrorist is least likely to become involved in a low attractiveness-high risk situation; but a high attractiveness-low risk situation is ideal. Terrorists normally opt for some point between the worst and ideal cases, trying to optimize each and still achieve their objective. As evidenced by the previous characteristics of terrorist attacks in general, and bombings in particular, terrorists will trade off attractiveness to reduce the risk factor. In high-technology terrorism, two points are evident with respect to risk:

1. When acquisition risk is low but employment risk is high, the greatest potential is for threat situations; and

2. When acquisition risk is high and employment risk is low, the greatest potential is for direct application.

Figure 3 provides a graphic representation of risk and attractiveness associated with high-technology terrorism. Regardless of the range of casualties and destruction, the risk of acquiring most high technology is far greater than the risk of acquiring conventional resources. Thus, where the risk in achieving the capacity to employ high technology is low, so is the ultimate attractiveness of the act. Only with high risk can a relatively high attractiveness be realized. But when resources are acquired at high risk, the

Figure 3. High-technology terrorism risk and attractiveness

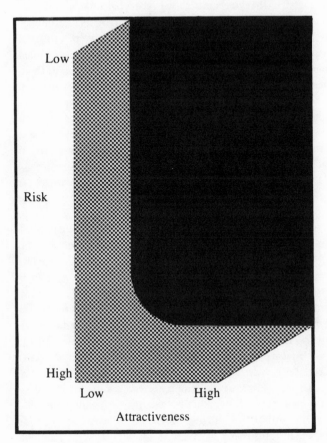

scale then curves sharply toward high attractiveness, indicative of the fact that once resources for an attack employing high technology have been obtained, nearly any desired degree of attractiveness can be attained. The initial risks of obtaining resources and successfully using them are so great, however, that few, if any, groups would be willing to attempt to cross the threshold of violence associated with high-technology terrorism.

Control of and Responses to High-Technology Terrorism

An understanding of the uniqueness of the phenomenon called terrorism is central to attaining even marginal success against the conventional or high-technology attacks. Both the current approach taken to combat terrorism and the dismal failure of governmental authorities to thwart actions are symptomatic of a system that does not recognize the nature of the threat. All too often, police and governmental officials refer to terrorists as criminals and approach the problem as if terrorists were acting out of criminal motivations. In general, authorities are ill-prepared to deal with conventional terrorism. More significantly, when terrorists employ the types of high technology discussed [here], local, State, and even Federal authorities will probably be incapable of fully coping with the situation. This final section initially addresses, in brief form, several shortcomings of the current system and postulates a series of control and response considerations that are applicable to various levels of law enforcement, to other official decisionmakers, and to legislators.

Introduction of high-technology terrorism will place additional strains on systems that are already facing rising crime rates, citizens' demands for better protection and effective government, and the economic realities of escalating costs. The ability of those systems to respond to the unique demands of high-technology terrorism is thus constrained by resources. Further, the inability to identify the official participants may also constrain response capacity.

Local officials will probably be principal participants in most high-technology terrorism incidents. In particular, local law enforcement will be the first to recognize an actual attack and, in the majority of the cases, the first to be notified of threats. The preponderance of the high-technology threats over the past 5 years have been received initially by local officials. Recognizing the secondary role that State and Federal agencies play in countering these threats, the following discussion emphasizes the local aspects of controls and responses to high-technology terrorism. Throughout this section . . . however, the authorities, jurisdictions, and functions of Federal, State, and multilocal organizations as they relate to those of local government are presented.

Two concepts of crucial importance in analyzing the current system for controlling and responding to high-technology terrorism are jurisdiction and authority. Often used without definition and interchangeably, the specific meaning of each is significant for understanding the problems that exist today. Jurisdiction refers to specific boundaries between entities and is primarily used in terms of lateral integration. Authority is used with respect to the horizontal relationships between organizations, particularly in describing local, State, and Federal roles and functions.

CURRENT SYSTEM CHARACTERISTICS

The current system for controlling and responding to high-technology terrorism can be viewed as a system of measures that provides a general overview of preparedness. The extent of planning is a general measure in that it reflects other system characteristics. It is not only necessary to examine local planning, but it is also useful to explore State and Federal planning as well. Other aspects of preparedness include resources, training, intelligence, and local, State, and Federal relationships.

Planning

To date, planning has generally been inadequate to meet the problem of high-technology terrorism. There has been little or no planning designed to specifically meet and respond to incidents involving high technology. This is particularly true at the local and State levels of government, and to a lesser degree within Federal agencies. In those cases where local and State disaster plans exist, they are plans for natural disasters. For example, along the gulf coast there are well-formulated plans to respond to hurricanes; in the Midwest extensive tornado planning has been accomplished; and earthquake response plans have been prepared in detail in California. These plans provide special systems for specific incidents, however, and fail to offer the responses necessary to counter high-technology terrorism attacks.

Despite the profileration of nuclear power plants and ever-increasing amounts of radioactive material used in society, very few locales have planned for nuclear emergencies created by failures in systems. Even fewer have considered those factors related to a terrorist-instigated act. Although an extensive improvement at the State governmental level is apparent with respect to peacetime nuclear emergencies, terrorism is still not adequately addressed at the State level either. Only recently has the Federal Government undertaken actions to plan for nuclear terrorism. Within the Energy Research and Development Administration, and to a lesser extent within the Nuclear Regulatory Commission, there has been contingency planning and agency responses have been formulated.

Unfortunately, the limited planning that has been done suffers from several shortcomings. The higher the level of planning organization along the local, State, and Federal continuum, the less likely it is that issues of vital importance to the local authorities will have been addressed. Although Federal and State planning contribute to local planning, it is unlikely that the plans are coordinated, and, more significantly, it is questionable that the contents are made known to other levels of government. Of greatest importance to the overall problem of high-technology terrorism is the fact that, aside from nuclear terrorism, other forms have not been addressed at any level of government.

Resources and Training

Resources may be categorized into two general types: physical and information. Physical resources deal with those resources that are tangible in nature, available to respond to and control incidents; information resources are those intangible assets such as training, procedures, and techniques—generally, learned material. A myriad of resources are available in times of crisis. These include official resources at the local, multilocal, and State levels; U.S. military and nonmilitary Federal resources; and resources available in the private community.

It is generally agreed that adequate physical resources are available to provide relief to the victims of high-technology terrorism. But specialized equipment permitting earlier intervention in high-technology incidents is lacking. The availability of equipment to handle chemical, biological, and nuclear situations is not widespread enough to insure adequacy of response.

The sufficiency of information resources is open to question. Over the years, many mechanisms have been created for the application of resources in disaster environments. Often these procedures have worked extraordinarily well, but in other instances there have been noticeable failures. The preceding discussion of current planning highlighted the problems of applying specialized individual disaster plans to high-technology terrorism situations. From a resources standpoint, one must question whether previously established preplanned mechanisms or rapidly generated *ad hoc* procedures will actually provide the needed physical and information resources under the uncertain conditions created by high-technology terrorism.

Another basic consideration is the training of those who might be confronted with high-technology terrorism. Most certainly the training provided for law enforcement officers significantly contributes to their ability to respond to crises generally, regardless of the specifics. New methods of response are recognized and understood and advanced equipment provides assistance in identifying problems and bringing outside expertise to bear on the situation quickly. But even though they are prepared to cope with general crisis situations, law enforcement personnel and decisionmakers are not trained to counter high-technology terrorism specifically. In fact, there is not general appreciation of the problem of terrorism. As previously stated, in most instances terrorists are viewed as common criminals, with identical training and operational procedures established for handling both terrorists and criminals. This serious weakness in training and in actual operational policies and procedures will result in a less than adequate response in those instances where high-technology terrorism is employed. The rather undistinguished record of law enforcement in apprehending terrorists is ample testimony to support the proposition that the training necessary to deal with this phenomenon is lacking.

Intelligence

One reason law enforcement has been ineffective in countering terrorism is that intelligence has generally been insufficient. The nature of terrorism—

covert acts undertaken by small groups of dedicated secretive individuals—is a major obstacle to successful intelligence activities. Compounding the problem of intelligence gathering is State and Federal protective legislation regarding invasion of privacy by governmental organizations, and the overall concern for individual privacy that has created the climate and controversy within which these laws were framed. Beyond constraining intelligence collection and use within any one jurisdiction or authority, the current milieu has also restricted dissemination and coordination of intelligence among local, State, and Federal agencies and between parallel organizations across jurisdictional lines.

By way of illustration, during the intensive search for the Harrises and Patricia Hearst, this group was stopped by a local law enforcement official. Not realizing the identities of this group, however, he conducted a license check and permitted them to leave. At the same time, other law enforcement agencies were actively gathering and evaluating information on this group. This episode demonstrates that often the line law enforcement officer is not provided with critical intelligence.

The current intelligence system does not have the capacity to effectively counter high-technology terrorism. A hypothetical example serves to highlight a major deficiency in the intelligence system. The theft of a highly infective biological culture from a Chicago research facility, the purchase of laboratory equipment in Cleveland, and the rental of an isolated facility suitable for a laboratory in Akron present an excellent portrait of a potentially dangerous situation. But the lack of intelligence exchanges and standardized procedures applicable to high-technology terrorism would permit this series of significant but seemingly unrelated activities to pass unnoticed.

Local, State, and Federal Relationships

Planning for high-technology terrorism is in a rudimentary stage and is characterized by problems of decentralized authority and resources, jurisdictional ambiguities, and deficiencies in provisions for intelligence collection and exchange. At each echelon of government, authority with respect to incidents involving nuclear material is explicitly governed by Federal statute, with many States having parallel legislation. Where chemical and biological agents are involved, however, there are no similar delineations of authority. Thus, in any incident the potential for the exercise of implicit prerogatives at all levels exists, even in cases where a situation might be better handled by another entity. For example, the local decisionmaker may insist on retaining control of the situation following the employment of a chemical weapon by terrorists. Because of the potential for direct impact on neighboring communities and the breadth of resources available to the State, this kind of division of authority may deny the affected locale the full benefit of available assistance. The issue of jurisdiction and authority is multi-dimensional, involving far more than the definition of local, State, and Federal relationships.

In the first instance, the question of jurisdiction arises within the local law enforcement agency. Particularly during that uncertain but crucial initial period, without planned procedures it is probable that intradepartment in-fighting will develop concerning control of the situation. The likelihood of this occurring appears to be proportional to the size of the department and the lack of prior planning. As the locale begins to request State resources, and the magnitude of the incident becomes apparent, questions relative to local and State authorities will evolve. Further, in the more serious attacks where required Federal assistance includes the use of military forces, a new problem in the apportionment of authority arises. Experience in the 1960's with major city riots raised several authority issues. In the riot context these have been partially resolved, but for the unique high-technology terrorism situation, little has been accomplished in addressing these questions.

Recognizing that the current system of law enforcement, decisionmaking, and legislation has failed to adequately address the question of high-technology terrorism as a unique and potentially dangerous phenomenon, it is necessary to formulate guidance that will contribute to rectifying the inadequacies as they now exist. The hypothetical nature of high-technology terrorism creates a dilemma in postulating control measures. The lack of an evidentiary basis makes the discussion more evocative than prescriptive in nature. From the foregoing description of present day preparedness, it is clear that action at all levels of government is required.

RECOMMENDATIONS FOR CONTROLS AND RESPONSES

The range of possible controls that might prevent, deter, or limit the employment of high-technology terrorism is similar to those outlined in the main body of this report. Because of the magnitude of potential consequences and the differences in certain components of the threat, however, it is worthwhile to detail those characteristics of high-technology terrorism that will in turn affect controls and responses. Throughout the preceding discussion of high-technology terrorism, there has been an implicit framework of five phases for each incident, comprising a life history of the event. These phases provide a conceptual means of understanding how far any one instance has gone; they offer a sequence in which control points may be identified and action taken, and, if significant numbers of incidents occur, they will contribute to the determination of the most effective allocation of resources by phase.

● Conceptualization of the basic idea—It is at this point that the perpetrator decides that conventional means of attack are inadequate. Because of the dissimilar nature of the types of high-technology terrorism, in all probability the terrorist initially determines the general character of the technology to be employed: chemical, biological, or nuclear. At least tentatively, the terrorist has weighed the risk and attractiveness factors, decided on the objectives to be achieved, and selected the general category of target. It is difficult to take control measures against this first phase because it is not feasible to directly impact on formulation of the idea. Certain general preventive measures, however, may assist in deterring an attack: hardening of likely targets; control of materials; systematic intelligence exchanges; publicized planning and citizen information programs; and generally, any measure that will reduce risk and attractiveness.

● Formulation of the group and attack planning—In all probability the group is already in existence; the decision to employ high-technology terrorism is an escalation in the group activity. The key to this phase and continuation into the other phases is the willingness of the group to accept the new threshold of violence. Data on past terrorist organizations indicate that the strain created within the group by escalation, particularly to extreme forms of violence, has caused the disintegration of many groups. This phase is indistinguishable from the first phase in terms of control measures, except that the factor of strain on the group may produce opportunities for direct intervention by authorities. In particular, disaffected group members may become available as informers.

● Fabrication/theft of a high-technology device—At this point the group must assemble adequate resources to implement its plan of high-technology terrorism. Only in this phase does the group intention surface. The resource requirements may necessitate expanding the group, either to provide a sufficient number of persons or to incorporate essential expertise into the organization. The danger of detection increases significantly in this phase because the terrorist group must interact with outside sources to collect resources, either through legitimate channels or by theft. Once again the principal actions for control are preventive, but the opportunity to infiltrate the group or to detect significant indicators is far greater in the third phase than in the first two phases.

● Application of the weapon—The fourth phase involves either the direct application of the weapon against a target or the use of the weapon in a coercive threat. Once this stage has been reached, the consequences will affect all aspects of the community. In this phase, control measures move beyond the essentially preventive, to the responsive. In addition to law enforcement agencies, decisionmakers, nonofficial community leaders, and outside official agencies become extensively involved in the processes. Response measures include activation of plans, coordination with other agencies, application of resources, and considerations of the potential of future incidents occurring. Primarily, these measures focus on limiting damages and allocating resources.

• Consequences of the action—The fifth, and final, phase in the framework developed to examine control and response to high-technology terrorism is the consequences of the action. In this phase, the terrorist is no longer principal; the focus shifts to governmental agencies, the attacked community, and society in general. The types of control measures implemented in this phase deal primarily with a continuation of those measures outlined in phase four and specific postattack plans and actions to restore normal community life.

It must be recognized, however, that the dearth of high-technology terrorism results in a degree of speculation with respect to control mechanisms. Without adequate historical data, the relative importance of any measures recommended is open to question. The following discussion attempts to be analytical, but in many cases the extrapolation from the known to the perceived outcomes of high-technology terrorism is purely hypothetical. The greatest utility of some sections of this discussion may be in surfacing issues and positing concepts in situations where the evidentiary basis is lacking. Suggestions for control and response measures are offered with reference to the five incident phases outlined above in a variety of categories: planning, resources and training, decisionmaking, local, State, and Federal relationships, intelligence, legislation, and constraints.

Planning

Central to effectively controlling high-technology terrorism is the implementation of a planning process, not only by local law enforcement but also by local decisionmakers, parallel jurisdictions, State and Federal agencies, and the community as a whole. Planning offers a connecting function that to some degree embraces all the other control mechanisms. Regardless of the specific control measure for high-technology terrorism, planning is essential. The uniqueness of high-technology violence necessitates prior consideration and planning for this phenomenon by all levels of government.

This [article] is intended to offer a starting point for planning by presenting the information necessary to gain an appreciation of the dimensions of high-technology violence and by outlining specific planning considerations. All law enforcement agencies and governmental units should develop contingency plans with respect to high-technology terrorism, either as a stand-alone set or in conjunction with other plans for implementation in terrorist situations. Primary planning responsibility should be vested in those organizations with response authority, but cooperation with other agencies is essential. The planning process itself must be either a comprehensive multiagency effort across jurisdictional and authority lines, or a series of single-agency plans that are integrated and coordinated with all potentially involved agencies.

Coordination and verification of plan elements should be effected with all agencies that might participate in response to high-technology terrorism. The degree of detail will be greater at lower levels, but each governmental unit must be aware of its role as perceived by others. Plans created in a sterile environment without interagency interaction will only lead to confusion and ineffective application. It is better to identify and clarify differences in the planning stage rather than during an actual incident.

The plan should provide detailed guidance on these aspects of high-technology terrorism:

1. Methods for identifying potential high-technology terrorism situations should be outlined to include the collection of indicators, assessment of the threat, and operational procedures specifically designed to thwart a developing threat. Basic to this phase of planning is the establishment of a workable threat-assessment methodology;

2. Methods for verification of threats, and procedures to rapidly evaluate direct application of high technology without warning, should be formulated;

3. Procedures for responding to a direct application or a coercive threat should be established. The roles and functions of the lead organizations, parallel governmental units, higher level government agencies, and nonofficial organizations should be defined. These procedures would identify responsibilities, authorities, and, most importantly, the systematic application of physical and personnel resources to a range of situations. This portion of the plan must identify the required resources and realistically consider the availability of internal and external resources to meet these requirements in the application and consequence phases of the incident. In particular, responses to coercive threats should provide detailed information concerning negotiations. Key personnel for a wide range of negotiation situations should be identified with explicit guidance relevant to lines of authority, coordination, roles, and responsibilities;

4. Specialized units, as outlined in the following section dealing with resources, should be defined and plans for organizational implementation detailed. Clear, concise procedures must be delineated to insure the rapid, smooth transition of organizational resources and functions to these units at the proper time. Multiagency planning in this respect permits organizations to plan this type of resource on a predictable basis and insures that a mechanism exists for implementation;

5. Alternative command and control structures should be established with predetermined conditions stipulated for activation of these mechanisms;

6. Specific guidance with respect to the media and public information should be formulated; and

7. Policies concerning the application of police powers during periods of

uncertainty following the employment of high technology should be established.

Plans should include detailed procedures to be followed by all organizations, regardless of their role. Policies and procedures that become operational when high-technology terrorism is detected should be specifically defined to include gradations of response tailored to the level of technology employed and extent of application. Other policies and procedures should be developed for coping with the consequences phase of high-technology terrorism. These include measures to preclude recurrence; emergency mechanisms as required; definitions of type and scope of outside assistance by class of incident; provisions for integration of outside assistance; and sequences for the restoration of order, services, and normal community life. Plans must be specific yet flexible. Regardless of the diligence exercised in planning, the application of any plan will ultimately be on a case-by-case basis. For this reason, it is essential that the plan be drawn to permit its successful implementation across the spectrum of high-technology violence. The characteristics of high-technology terrorism present a planning problem for government agencies. Currency in plans relating to high-technology terrorism situations is crucial. But the lack of information about this form of violence means that new information has greater importance than for other plans where detailed data are available. Those plans dealing with high-technology terrorism should be updated as often as possible, particularly in comparison to other, less perishable plans.

Beyond planning itself, a series of distinct but related controls and responses should be discussed. The next several segments . . . address these subjects, including: resources and training, decisionmaking, and local, State, and Federal relationships. Each of these generalized areas of control and response is examined, not only with respect to that subject in particular, but also as it relates to planning.

Resources and Training

All organizations are constrained in providing the requisite amounts of resources and training considered necessary to meet existing requirements. With respect to high-technology terrorism, the requirements for resources and training could be boundless. Those described herein, however, seem to be a prudent minimum for successfully identifying and responding to high-technology terrorism.

There must be recognition of the fact that different training is needed at different levels of authority. At the local level, on which the primary emphasis of this discussion rests, training in recognizing and responding to high-technology terrorism must be broad-based. At the same time, local specialization should not be encouraged because of the breadth of resources necessary to support such an effort. Local training should include four major elements that are essential in coping with high-technology terrorism. Each of these four is outlined below, with a brief description of what local responsibility should be.

1. The potential application of high explosives and new technologies (chemical, biological, and nuclear) requires that local officials be familiar with the basic characteristics of these technologies. This knowledge is necessary to permit preliminary identification and assessment of the nature of the attack. All local law enforcement officers should be trained in these characteristics, including: type of device, means of delivery, and possible location of the launcher or placement of the device;

2. Local officials should be trained in procedures and mechanisms for controlling and responding to high-technology attacks. First aid, immediate local actions, and countermeasures should be taught on a recurring basis, updating training as new characteristics of that type of terrorism are discovered and new procedures formulated;

3. A negotiation situation may be thrust upon any local official. Time constraints and other factors dictate that local officials should have enough training to undertake at least initial negotiations. Even though no two situations are alike, any potential negotiator can profit from this type of training. Specifics concerning the characteristics of negotiation situations and guidelines for negotiations should be developed and taught. Simulations involving not only local, but also State and Federal officials would provide excellent training and offer insights into the best techniques for negotiation situations;

4. All three elements of training listed either implicitly or explicitly require obtaining outside assistance from multijurisdictional, State, multi-State, and Federal agencies, and nonofficial sources. Because assistance comes from an array of organizations, local training should stress what agencies should be notified in what situations. As a general rule, when a jurisdiction is faced with a high-technology threat, the FBI should be contacted immediately. In cases where terrorists have employed high technology, local officials should notify the FBI to obtain Federal specialists as appropriate, and the State Governor's office to request activation of appropriate disaster measures.

Emphasis on training at the State level should be upon specialization to augment the capabilities of locales, as required. Specialized training should be oriented toward those services necessary to restore order and normal community life, to assist in preventing high-technology terrorism, and to provide appropriate planning coordination and integration. Multi-State specialist teams could provide many of those services normally viewed as a strictly State or Federal prerogative. Federal training should focus on those highly specialized areas, particularly in technical fields, such as a sophisticated detection system for locating radioactive material, where neither local nor

State governments have the information or the capacity to accomplish the job.

The type and amount of equipment acquired in anticipation of high-technology terrorism must, by the necessity of resource requirements, vary with the size of the law enforcement agency, particularly at the local level. At a minimum, however, each jurisdiction should have a basic chemical test kit and a radiological monitoring device. Beyond these, the examination of probability of use seems to indicate that local expenditures for additional equipment will not provide a return in relation to the cost. Sophisticated radioactivity detectors, infrared detection devices, artillery/mortar shell tracking radars, delicate chemical monitors, and other similar equipment are available through U.S. Government agencies as the need arises. Local officials should understand the procedures for requesting such Federal assistance.

Where both personnel and equipment are concerned, conservation of scarce resources is achieved through the employment of outside assistance. Each agency, however, should recognize the trade-offs in terms of timely response, potential for ineffective coordination, and interjurisdictional problems when outside assistance is sought and depended upon to fill existing voids. Regardless of the preplanning and operational relationships, capability is somewhat reduced by reliance on extraorganizational supplements for equipment and expertise. Most significant among the problems inherent in outside assistance is the extent and timeliness of integration into the existing framework. Many of these operational problems might be overcome by planning exercises, simulations, games, and actual field exercises.

Decisionmaking

The decisionmaking process is to a large extent connected with planning and, to a lesser extent, with training. Decisionmakers must have some preplanned basis upon which to build in crisis situations. Detailed planning assists the decisionmaker by permitting maximum time for actual decision while minimizing the time required for adjustments to that particular crisis. Training is necessary to insure that the decision process is a smooth-flowing sequence of events with minimal disruptions. Decisionmakers must have practice implementing the process, while contributors of information and supporting personnel must be trained in the preparation of timely responses in support of the decisionmaking process. Without planning and training, the decision process might flounder for lack of necessary information.

The most compelling aspects of decisionmaking in the event of high-technology terrorism revolve around the potential societal consequences of the act and the time available to make the necessary decisions. With respect to the conceptualization, planning, and fabrication phases of high-technology terrorism, the decisionmakers must be prepared to evaluate data and implement security and preventive measures. Prior to the first completed action with meaningful consequences, it is unlikely that any decisions affecting large segments of the community will be made. But in the aftermath of that first incident, decisionmakers will be faced with extensive public pressures to respond during this first phase of the decisionmaking process.

Following the direct application of high technology or as a result of consequences of a failure to thwart a coercive threat, the decisionmaker is faced with those tasks normally associated with other disasters. Although the stress will be greater because the deliberate nature of the act will create a general atmosphere of community fear, it is not unreasonable to assume that the majority of the decisions will follow previous patterns noted in disaster situations. These decisions can be, and already are, preplanned to a large extent. Decisions should be formulated in the planning stages, with flexibility to react to individual situations.

Critical for the decisionmaking process are those instances where a coercive threat has been received. In these situations, policies and procedures should be established to govern a range of decisions, including, but not limited to, those that involve the definition of negotiable issues and the conduct of negotiations. These policies and procedures should include:

1. Identification of decisionmakers and notification processes that include local, State, and Federal officials;
2. Initial responses to the full range of threats and demands;
3. Threat verification actions;
4. Procedures for evaluating the consequences of threatened actions;
5. Identification of the role of outside nonofficial participants;
6. Requirements for local, State, and Federal assistance;
7. Policies concerning negotiable demands and tailored responses;
8. Policies governing media coverage and news release;
9. Preventive actions appropriate for the threat; and
10. Disaster mechanisms should the threat materialize.

These are by no means all-inclusive. They lack the desirable detail with respect to planning for coercive threat situations, but offer insights into the more salient considerations. The principal advantage in planning and actually arriving at sets of predetermined responses is to focus on the problem. Increases in the magnitude and consequences of high-technology terrorism, however, carry a concomitant decrease in the validity and, perhaps, in the acceptability of preplanned responses.

Two factors significantly influence the decisionmaking process in stress situations. First, the essence of individuality cannot be captured in contingency plans, no matter how detailed. Responses of decisionmakers are situation-dependent. Thus, all planning must be flexible enough to permit incremental or even wholesale changes because of situational differences.

Second, time is the most crucial element in coercive threat situations. The likelihood of severe time constraints must be examined for their impact on planned decisions. For example, time restrictions may force decisions on other echelons sooner than anticipated. Time pressures may also require that decisions be made in the absence of information or without opportunities for detailed evaluations. Realizing there is never adequate time to respond to these situations, procedures and methodologies must be well thought out prior to incidents, unique problems and issues must be anticipated, and decisionmakers must be trained to respond in stress situations.

Local, State, and Federal Relationships

Most likely, high-technology terrorism will initially involve local officials, particularly law enforcement officials, with outside agency assistance evolving from that point. With respect to this type of terrorism, only in the case of nuclear material does the law clearly identify a role for the Federal Government. In addition, when any disaster of major consequence occurs, including a terrorist attack, the State Governor has the option of declaring martial law and using the National Guard or requesting Federal military assistance. Beyond these, there are no clearly defined situations where existing statutes would apply, relevant to high-technology terrorism.

The nature of most official relationships will, to a great extent, depend upon preexisting relationships, the type of incident, personalities, past experience, and recognition of the assistance that is available. For example, if intelligence is to be effective in countering the threat in the planning and fabrication phases of high-technology terrorism, exchanges of information must take place at all levels of law enforcement, including lateral exchanges between parallel agencies.

Once a coercive threat becomes apparent or direct application of a weapon is a fact, the problem of relationships between involved agencies increases significantly in complexity. Because new-technology terrorism may well affect areas that cross city, county, State, or even international boundaries, the possibilities of questions or even confrontations over prerogatives, authorities, and responsibilities are great. The complex nature and sophistication of these technologies may require the application of specialized skills and equipment that is available only at State and, more usually, Federal levels of government. For example, the military has the most advanced chemical and biological expertise and apparatus; expert nuclear bomb technicians are available within the Energy Research and Development Administration and FBI general laboratory support is unrivaled throughout the world.

A few points are worth mentioning.

1. In cases where there is no clear jurisdictional authority, or the potential for multijurisdictional impacts are present, all levels should endeavor to clarify and identify lines of authority and responsibility. Because the local level has the principal planning burden and will probably be the principal on-the-scene authority, it is at this level that discussions should be initiated;
2. Each level of authority should consider the total resources available from all sources in responding to high-technology terrorism, and should consider coordinating the use of these within an overall planning framework. Special skills and equipment should be identified, coordinated, and integrated into plan preparation; and
3. Nonofficial sources of skills and equipment should be identified and integrated into planning. These resources must be coordinated by local officials, stipulating under what circumstances these resources are to be used, when control passes to official authority, guidelines for use, and a set of overall terms and conditions covering such use.

Intelligence

Current law enforcement intelligence methods are inadequate for dealing with the existing and projected terrorist threats in the United States. The large above-ground movements with terrorist branches underground, such as the Black Panthers and the American Indian Movement, have, to a great extent, been replaced by small terrorist organizations with less than 10 members. Although evidence supports the thesis that some sort of loose network of groups exists, these groups are difficult to track and penetrate. The meaning for high-technology terrorism is plain: current methods of intelligence are insufficient.

In dealing with potential high-technology terrorism, proven intelligence methods should not be abandoned. It must be borne in mind that the intelligence systems under discussion here are specifically designed to counter high-technology terrorism; to function, these systems require an adequate existing system for generalized antiterrorism intelligence. For example, identification of terrorist groups is in the realm of general intelligence, but without it, other intelligence specifically related to high technology loses much of its importance. Continued reliance on general intelligence for purposes such as identification of groups and individuals and their modus operandi is the key to successful intelligence operations against high-technology terrorism.

Despite the importance of a general intelligence system, the need to develop specific intelligence related to high technology is apparent. A general indication of possible terrorist activity does not usually provide sufficient insights to ascertain the type of violence that is to be employed. The early detection and substantiation of possible high-technology terrorism is of paramount significance in light of the potential magnitude and consequences of such an attack. The following discussion focuses on specific high-technology indicators and two types of trend analysis—escalation trends and objective trends.

Examples of indicators that should be developed and evaluated include:

1. Theft of radioactivity monitoring equipment;
2. Theft or loss in shipment of a biological culture;
3. Theft of chemicals clearly associated with the manufacture of dangerous agents;
4. Theft of explosives and/or bomb components;
5. Purchase or theft of unique filters;
6. Purchase or theft of special handling equipment (e.g., protective clothing, isolation chambers, glove boxes);
7. Abduction of persons with high-technology backgrounds;
8. Rental of isolated facilities;
9. Purchase of laboratory equipment suitable for chemical, biological, or nuclear experimentation;
10. Suspicious purchases of chemicals;
11. Indiscriminate targeting by terrorists;
12. Increased acquisition of funds by terrorist groups;
13. Increased terrorist liaison and coordination;
14. Increased expenditures by terrorist-connected groups; and
15. Unexplained sickness or unusual diseases reported for treatment.

It is very doubtful that even three or four of these indicators would occur at any one locale. Thus, to be of utility in detecting potential high-technology terrorism, there should be a mechanism for information exchange. This type of activity is beyond the ability of local police to implement. But even at the local level, law enforcement agencies can create a liaison that will provide information exchange within the locale or regionally. Once these indicators appear, law enforcement and decisionmakers should initiate preplanned activities, consider required responses, and attempt to match the pattern of activity with other general intelligence indicators in order to establish the group involved and the nature of the threat posed.

One final intelligence technique merits discussion: trend analysis. In the past, police have examined the target patterns of terrorists and analyzed the possible future targets. Although it has not proven very successful in apprehending terrorists, the emphasis that this type of analysis places on selecting and protecting potential targets serves to focus on the increased security measures. A reasonable assumption is that this has in many cases deterred activities of terrorists by altering the risk and attractiveness evaluation of the terrorist.

Escalation trend analysis moves a step beyond target pattern evaluation, and addresses and builds on any sequence of acts committed by a single group. When taken as a whole, the characteristics of events may provide predictive indicators of future activity. Figure 4 is a duplication of terrorist means portrayed in Figure 2, with the addition of a directional arrow. Historically, terrorist activity has escalated through a series of steps, with each of the four means reflecting a higher plateau of violence—from bargaining to political statements to social paralysis to mass casualties. Application of this generalization might indicate when a terrorist group has or will escalate its activities. Equally as important, the failure of a group to change means and engage in more destructive terrorism is a signal either that, in the group's perception, their objectives do not merit more indiscriminate targeting and greater destruction or that resources are lacking to increase the level of violence.

A second type of trend evaluation—objective trend analysis—provides indications of the potential for a particular group to escalate to the employment of high-technology terrorism to gain specific objectives, without the escalation of means depicted in Figure 4. For example, a group may continue to be motivated to bargain for certain objectives, but be frustrated in attaining them using conventional terrorist tactics. Recognizing that more extreme means are inappropriate to their objectives, the only options open to the group are to abandon the quest or to seek greater leverage—an option satisfied by the use of high technology. Election of this latter option does not

Figure 4. Escalation of terrorist means

Specificity of Demands Target Selection	High	Low
Discriminate	Bargaining	Political Statement
Random	Social Paralysis	Mass Casualties

Source: Based on data supplied by the Rand Corp.

necessarily indicate the direct employment of high technology, but the likelihood of a coercive threat is significantly increased as the group's inability to achieve its ends and an unwillingness to escalate direct violence results in frustration. Tracking the attributes of individual groups and the incidents they perpetrate will provide at least a rudimentary indication of this type of trend and the potential for high-technology terrorism.

Legislative

With respect to the legislative measures that might be enacted to control high-technology terrorism, the temptation exists to at least outline a series of statutes that would enhance the efforts of law enforcement agencies and governmental bodies in dealing with the problem. Unfortunately, legislative prescriptions for this problem do not come easily. Three factors act to restrict the delineation of laws curbing terrorism in today's milieu:

1. The phenomenon of terrorism has defied adequate definition—one that would truly be viable in a legalistic sense; behavior that is perceived as terroristic by some people is perceived as psychopathological by others;
2. To date, laws specifically designed to combat terrorism in free societies have not in fact curtailed terrorism; and
3. Assuming that meaningful legislation could be written, the efficacy of undertaking security or preventive measures that might curtail civil liberties, while being of dubious value in the current threat environment, must be questioned.

At the same time, two facets of legislation applicable to high-technology terrorism deserve further consideration. In the first instance, there are a number of legislative enactments that might have a deterrent value. These statutes might well be enacted in today's environment as they do not directly affect individual civil liberties, but appear to have merit with respect to establishing desirable standards and guidelines. Such laws would:

1. Develop standards for protecting specific materials and items of equipment crucial to the manufacture of high-technology weapons;
2. Clarify jurisdictional questions and establish operational responsibilities governing direct application, coercive threats, and consequence situations; and
3. Provide specific legislative guidance governing the authorities of police and responsibilities of local and State decisionmakers in high-technology terrorism incidents.

In a future milieu where the threat of high-technology terrorism is a reality or a threat of increasing probability, legislative action may be not only required but demanded. Recognizing the admonitions stated earlier with respect to civil liberties, a legislative program should include the following additional considerations:

1. Provision of specific mechanisms for the exchange of intelligence information and indicators among all levels of government, including lead-agency designation;
2. Prescription of licensing procedures for the purchase and retention of special materials associated with high-technology terrorism; and
3. Establishment of specialized State, Federal, and regional units trained in high-technology terrorism countermeasures, including negotiations.

Civil Liberties

An examination of the consequences of the employment of high-technology terrorism creates questions concerning countermeasures and the ultimate abridgment of individual civil liberties. The potential for such abridgment is, in part, a function of the actions of local law enforcement; more importantly, however, it resides with the various State legislatures and the Federal Government. Conducting efforts to maintain individual civil liberties while protecting the community from high-technology violence requires considering the consequences of underreaction on the one hand, and the impact of overreaction on existing norms and values on the other. High-technology terrorist acts occur along a continuum of magnitude and consequences in which no one set of responses is appropriate for all cases. Thus, it is essential that potential responses be planned, weighing proposed countermeasures against the consequences of each act.

From the standpoint of law enforcement, the mere existence of a potential for high-technology terrorism does not in and by itself confer any special powers of search, seizure, detention, or other extraordinary legal means; the political realities in any community would make it difficult, if not impossible, to move beyond existing laws relating to individual rights so long as high-technology terrorism does not move beyond its first three phases: conceptualization, planning, and fabrication. Even the exercise of existing State prerogatives, such as declaring martial law, using military forces, and imposing local options such as curfew, appears unrealistic prior to the first meaningful attack that results in extensive injuries or destruction. Following the application phase and extending into the consequence phase of a high-technology terrorist action, it is likely that normal disaster measures, including those that affect civil liberties, will be promptly implemented.

Moreover, once high technology has been employed by terrorists, political constraints on new initiatives that impinge on civil liberties will be relaxed.

The immediate and perhaps extensive alteration of existing laws is to be reasonably expected. In addition, law enforcement will alter practices and procedures to meet new requirements for countermeasures. In addressing this problem, law enforcement officials and local, State, and Federal decision-makers and legislators should carefully weigh the merits of each new step that involves limitations on civil liberties.

Furthermore, in a series of events involving high-technology terrorism that reaches various phases but falls short of direct application and consequences, it is likely that officials will react with gradually escalating countermeasures. The implementation of incremental control measures most likely will result in an erosion of civil liberties, more gradual, but no less real than those that would follow a completed incident.

Several points warrant special attention by law enforcement and legislators considering countermeasures:

1. Regardless of the magnitude and consequences of any act of high-technology terrorism, future actions are still of low probability because of the difficulty in combining the requirements for resources, motivations, and opportunity;
2. The probability of future incidents of equal or greater consequences than the first act is inversely proportional to the magnitude of the first action;
3. The tendency toward overreaction appears to far outweigh that of underreaction, creating a real risk that civil liberties will be sacrificed for a minimal derived value in terms of societal protection; and
4. The greatest danger to civil liberties in the long term is that the evolution of control measures will erode individual rights incrementally. Individual measures may appear prudent and warranted at the time; the danger lies in the synergism of such measures.

In conclusion, it is worth noting a complex paradox. In any curtailment of civil liberties to counter high-technology terrorism, the measures taken should not be so extensive as to seriously impair democratic norms and values or the structures built on them. Even if terrorists do not succeed in reaching their particular objectives, they win when they provoke the system to restrict civil liberties drastically. At the same time, however, the values and structures that must be preserved in a response to terrorism are among the very factors that permit the terrorist to continue to operate.

ECONOMIES

The most salient issue in a discussion of economies and high-technology terrorism is the question: What is the value of countermeasures? How much money and other resources should local, State, and Federal governments spend to protect against a possible threat that obviously has a potential for consequences several orders of magnitude greater than any current threat, but a much smaller probability of occurrence? Indeed, will any moneys be spent to combat the threat of high-technology terrorism? The political and fiscal realities for local officials cause a common dilemma. How can moneys be spent on an unrealized potential threat when current problems such as drugs, prostitution, organized crime, street crimes, and even white collar offenses are greater than the capacity of society to deal with them? The choices are to be made by local leaders, whose deliberations must seriously question whether the economic realities of the modern community will permit expending resources on terrorism before the fact. Unfortunately, the magnitude of the threat and its possible societal consequences, however great, are difficult to portray in terms as urgent as everyday community problems such as school budgets, services, and conventional police protection.

The problems with economic balancing in designing countermeasures at all levels of government are far too complex to be effectively explored here. But a brief discussion of possible economical trade-offs and constraints in controlling high-technology terrorism at the local level is appropriate. To begin, it should be apparent that high-technology terrorism is more speculative than real. Chemical and biological technologies have been available for years and have never been employed. The necessary expertise and resources have evidently not combined with the unique motivation required to precipitate an act. And based on past terrorist behavior, the most likely future action will be the coercive threat. Thus, when ordering priorities for the expenditure of resources for measures to deal with high-technology terrorism, the item of first importance may well be those costs associated with threat situations, including verification procedures. The development of techniques and procedures for dealing with high-technology threats will also have secondary value, because they will apply also to hostage-bargaining and negotiation situations involving conventional threats.

A second priority for local expenditures might be to provide at least a minimal capability to conduct preliminary tests to determine the nature of an attack that used chemical, biological, or radioactive material. Although such an attack is a low-probability event, it is possible to achieve a crude but workable detection system at a small cost for those actions that have high societal consequences. Each police unit could maintain relatively inexpensive monitoring equipment and test kits. Although its use generally would be restricted to ascertaining the presence and identity of a substance, this equipment would enhance the opportunity for rapid detection and an appropriate response.

More difficult to evaluate in terms of economy and trade-offs is the attainment of a middle ground between a minimum capability and a fully independent local capability to cope with high-technology terrorism. At this time it would seem prudent for local agencies to expend resources to gain an understanding of the problem and to begin basic planning. Currently there is no overall system that specifically addresses controls and responses within the framework of the five phases of high-technology terrorism outlined above. How many resources should be allocated to each phase seems to be of key importance. Extensive expenditures to counter phases one and two (conceptualization of idea and formulation of the plan) appear to offer only minimal return because of the secretive nature of the venture at this stage. But moneys spent to detect fabrication (phase three) may result in deterrence and prevention. Expenditures for phases four and five (application and consequences) beyond basic planning and practical preparations for negotiation would be marginal at this time.

Especially significant to local law enforcement's consideration of resource allocation is that the unique character of high-technology terrorism demands that outside resources be applied to achieve even a modicum of success in combating it. The emphasis in resource allocation should be directed toward planning response requirements, defining availability of assets, (internal and external), and achieving their integration into an overall plan. Expenditures for sophisticated equipment to counter high-technology terrorism does not appear to be a necessary investment for local or even State governments. The concept of Federal reaction teams seems well worth pursuing from a resources point of view in the foreseeable future. These teams would offer locales a relatively timely response capability, while preserving local resources for the more important tasks of planning, negotiation, and establishing basic detection systems.

Conclusions

The preceding material has attempted to provide an overview of terrorism and new technologies of destruction. By the very nature of the subject, much of the paper has been more speculative and heuristic than definitive. It is difficult to fully verify all attributes given in the descriptions of high technologies. With respect to total casualties and destruction, it is difficult to define even the potential with precision. However, the discussion does place the likely impact of new technologies in perspective with respect to current terrorism in the United States.

Although the threat of high-technology terrorism encompasses a broad spectrum of malevolent acts, from relatively inconsequential radioactive releases to nuclear detonations and large-scale anthrax infections, the threats examined have been grouped in the upper limits of that range. In summarizing those threats of greater magnitude and societal consequences, it can be stated that, the probability of any group successfully combining the material resources, requisite skills, and motivations necessary to perpetrate an act using high technologies is extremely low. Even the theft of a suitable ready-to-use weapon, such as a precision-guided munition nuclear device or plutonium is not likely. Although probability is low, recognition must be given to the fact that, if an action is perpetrated using high technologies, the results could strain the very fabric of society. Casualties and damage might be several orders of magnitude greater than any terrorist attack of the past.

For these compelling reasons, new-technology terrorism and control mechanisms merit the attention of law enforcement officials, decisionmakers, and legislators at all levels of government. Particularly significant in this respect are the local law enforcement agencies and decisionmakers. In all probability, terroristic acts in the first instance will involve the local community. Local officials will be the first to encounter the attack, becoming responsible for initiating counteraction and response procedures. Examination of control measures here has centered on the local officials and emphasized the roles played by them.

In the discussion of the eight specific aspects of control, several key points have surfaced repeatedly. First, as an umbrella concept, planning is the principal factor in control. Without planning, other aspects of control will in all probability fail when implementation is necessary. Second, the resolution of jurisdictional issues cuts to the heart of effective planning, coordination, and response. Delineation of authorities and responsibilities laterally and vertically in local, State, and Federal relationships is essential.

Third, civil liberties must be considered wherever a possible conflict with safeguards arises. Above all else, the basic norms and values of American society and the structures within which they exist must be preserved. The dismemberment of these traditional democratic institutions, either as a reflexive reaction to a significant terrorist attack or incrementally, must be resisted. Fourth, regardless of the optimum, or even desirable, steps to combat the potential threat of new-technology terrorism, the economic and political realities of the community, the State, and, to a lesser extent, the Federal Government, limit any meaningful attempts to achieve positive action prior to a successful coercive threat or the direct application of new technologies. Issues of current concern dominate both the political and economic attentions of decisionmakers and law enforcement officials. The unknown, the unrealized, and the untried do not command the allocation of scarce resources.

New-technology terrorism represents an unknown, unrealized threat. But its potential nature should not delude public officials and private citizens into believing it cannot happen. Despite the limited resources available now and in the future, the risks of inaction mandate that this phenomenon be examined and evaluated and responses to it planned.

Robert K. Mullen

Mass Destruction and Terrorism

Mullen offers a unique discussion of the problem of macroterrorism. Rather than concentrating on scenarios, prospective perpetrators, or prescriptive measures, he offers an informed discussion of chemical, biological, and nuclear agents with mass destructive capabilities and then proceeds to identify the production and delivery considerations that will confront the macroterrorist. His presentation offers important evidence for those who agree with his conclusion that mass destruction threats from terrorists are "vanishingly remote." For those who would disagree, Mullen cannot be ignored in their response.

Introduction

The concepts of mass destruction and terrorism are ancient; what is relatively recent is a frequently expressed view that terrorists will acquire the means and motivations to exercise mass destruction. This paper examines that view in terms of the means of mass destruction which exist in a technologically advanced society, what broad properties characterize such means, the resources required by a terrorist or terrorist group to implement them, and the characteristics of terrorist adversaries who may be considered potential implementers.

This is a subject frequently marked by tendentiousness, with well regarded authors sometimes adopting apocalyptic views concerning an evolution of the level of terrorism from conventional violence to mass destruction. Given that the intensiity of terrorism has increased in a time in which technology is at once both more complex and more accessible, both of these factors sometimes appearing to insulate technology from the application of effective safeguards against misuse, such views are understandable, and evoke a certain sympathy.

One objective of this paper is to place the potential for mass destruction terrorism into a perspective tempered by recent and historical events relative to demonstrated terrorists' capabilities and motivations. In so doing, this discussion avoids Shultz' general category of "Establishment Terrorist,"[1] either in the sense of institutional terrorism, or terrorism applied by elements of governments, as in attempts or executions of coups d'état. The reasons for this are several. Not the least of these is that potential mass destruction establishment terrorism is distinctly different from potential non-institutional mass destruction. Establishment terrorism in the realm of mass destruction gets into questions of treaty obligations, stability of governments, international trade in sensitive materials, and other legal, economic, and political issues which are fundamental to any discussion of potential mass destruction establishment terrorism, but which bear only tangentially on such potentials outside of legitimate governmental bodies.

This paper considers the objectives of terrorism subsumed by Shultz' general categories of Revolutionary and Sub-Revolutionary Terrorism. Nihilistic terrorism, which seems to fall outside this taxonomy, is also considered.

The capability to inflict mass destruction has until relatively recent times been limited by technology. That is to say, killing large numbers of people used to be manpower intensive: a lot of people were required to do the killing. To be sure, throwing plague-ridden corpses over the walls of a besieged city, or into a city's water supplies, has in the past been a tactic used to sometimes devastating effect. These are exceptions, however, and of course their occurrences represented no technological advances, nor any appreciation for the mechanisms through which mass destruction resulted.

The development and subsequent refinement of nuclear, chemical, and biological weapons has resulted in the credible possibility that a single individual could develop a capacity of causing mass destruction.[2]

Prior to addressing the potential terrorist use of mass destruction weapons, however, their characteristics are discussed in terms of the materials and active agents of which they may be composed, resources required to develop a mass destruction capability, and the problems of dissemination of the active agents of relevant weapons.

The Terrorist Nuclear Threat

THE DEVICE

Much has been written about the availability of nuclear device design data in the open literature.[3] It is true. There appears to be sufficient material available in the unclassified literature to provide a potential bomb maker with enough information to fabricate a crude device that has some probability greater than zero of functioning in the nuclear mode. It has been estimated that such a device, containing a mass of fissionable material sufficient to produce a nuclear explosive yield of twenty kilotons (kt) TNT equivalent, could function in the range of 0.1 to 1.0 kt.[4]

The potential sources of strategic nuclear material (SNM) for the construction of a clandestine nuclear device are assumed here to be the nuclear fuel cycles for the several types of power reactors now operational. This SNM is, of course, plutonium; in particular plutonium-239 (^{239}Pu), one of several isotopes of this largely artificial element.

Although relevant, a discussion on the problems associated with recovering plutonium from spent reactor fuel, or the problems associated with overcoming safeguards designed to thwart attempts at theft or diversion of plutonium, once separated from such fuel, would perforce be a discussion of some length. Such discussion would furthermore tend to reinforce the author's conclusions. It is assumed, therefore, that the adversaries possess SNM in quantities they feel sufficient to construct a nuclear device.

Given that SNM is on hand for either direct use as core material for a clandestine nuclear device, or for conversion to a form so suitable, the additional resources required for the former include nuclear weapon design information, perhaps a small machine shop, high explosives, considerable physical and technological capability, time, space, and money. For the latter, all the above are required in addition to chemical and high temperature chemistry capabilities for conversion of the SNM to a form suitable for core construction. Depending on the nature of the basic nuclear material on hand, it has been estimated that in some instances, a clandestine nuclear device could be constructed by a single individual.[5] Three or four individuals may constitute a more credible bomb building scenario.

DIVERSION OF AN INTACT NUCLEAR WEAPON

At first appearances, the most direct means of acquiring a private nuclear capability would seem to be through stealing an intact weapon. There are mitigating conditions, however, which even in the event of the successful acquisition of a military nuclear device, could bound the possible range of subsequent events.

A diverted military nuclear device could be used directly in a terrorist nuclear threat if the adversaries had access to appropriate resources for arming and firing the device. Arming and firing a military nuclear device frequently involves a complex series of steps in the arming procedure, and can involve also command instructions from separate firing equipment. The design purpose of any particular weapon dictates, in part, the requirements for its arming and firing. To prevent accidental or unauthorized firing, protective systems called permissive action links have been devised to increase assurance that a nuclear weapon may be armed only by following a coded sequence of events which, in some weapons, is followed by another series of events which occur during the weapon's flight to its target, and which occur independent of human control, once they are programmed.[6] Some of these permissive action links which are independent of human control, once they are programmed, include terminal velocity, barometric, or radar actuated links, as well as others.

There is another class of nuclear weapon which, although possessing permissive action links, has none of the independent permissive action links characteristic of projectile, bomb, or missile warheads. This is the atomic demolition munition (ADM); nuclear devices intended for purposes quite different from other types of nuclear munitions.[7] The ADM does, however, require a coded signal for firing. Presumably, if such a device were diverted by a clandestine group possessing the coded arming resources, such a group could go to considerable pains to acquire the firing resources as well.

Alternatively, of course, the possessor of a stolen nuclear device could attempt to bypass the arming and firing circuits. There are safeguards against such attempts, however, involving such things as disassembly of the weapon or destruction of the core's potential to become supercritical.

Superficially, it might also seem possible that the adversary could use the core of the stolen weapon in a clandestine design. This seems only marginally credible, however, since nuclear weapons are exceedingly sophisticated, being constructed in such a manner that to function in the nuclear mode it is essential the geometries of the core and the high explosive be maintained. It is essential also that the detonation characteristics of the special high explosives also be maintained. This is to say, substituting one high explosive for another in all likelihood would lead to a nonnuclear chemical explosion upon detonation of the device.

The preceding notwithstanding, there may be some efforts on the part of clandestine groups to acquire a military nuclear device. Penetration attempts have occurred at facilities where nuclear weapons are stored.[8] Unauthorized possession of a military nuclear device would be a matter of grave concern. No matter that the group possessing the device may not be able to make it function. Mere documented possession could, under some circumstances, create considerable political strain leading, in some instances, to instabilities in the ruling power structure. Cleverly implemented and manipulated, such an event could also lead to serious international problems.

In summary, the clandestinely diverted military nuclear device could be more of a threat to various power elites than to the general public, since the terrorist possession of such a weapon does not automatically imply that it is functional in such hands with one exception. Disaffected elements of the military may, under some circumstances, have control over the requisite resources to actually carry through a clandestine nuclear threat with a military nuclear device to its ultimate end. Establishment terrorism scenarios, however, are not discussed in this paper.

The Clandestine Chemical or Biological Weapon

GENERAL

Chemical and biological weapons are generally perceived to be antipersonnel in nature, although there is ample evidence for the long-term area denial capacity of certain biological weapons.[9] This latter capacity, although of interest, is not germane to the principal issue of this paper, and will not be discussed further.

The antipersonnel effects of chemical and biological weapons are strongly dependent on the modes of their dissemination. This point is germinal to the relationship between the concepts of mass destruction and the potential clandestine use of chemical or biological weapons. The importance of marrying a potentially lethal agent to an adequate delivery system cannot be overestimated when the objective is mass destruction. The delivery system includes, of course, the means for getting the agent to the target area, but also includes the means for disseminating the agent once it is delivered.

The inherent differences between chemical and biological agents in their modes of action, preparation, toxicity, problems of dissemination, and other characteristics lead to a logical dichotomy; thus the characteristics of chemical and biological agents are treated serially, as are the mechanics of their preparation.

CHEMICAL AGENTS

There exists a staggering array of highly toxic chemical agents. Many of these are exotic chemical formulations; others not so exotic, but relatively uncommon nevertheless. For these and other reasons, the discussion will be limited to compounds considered to be extremely toxic and which are available as byproduct, or manufacturing chemicals; chemicals employed for agricultural purposes; and chemicals of acknowledged potential utility for producing large numbers of casualties (so-called poison gases and nerve gases), for which information on chemical preparation is available in the open literature. Even with such restrictions, the list of chemical agent candidates would be unwieldly. Two artifices have been adopted to circumvent this problem. The first is to discuss classes of compounds when it is possible to do so, rather than to treat extensively individual agents within such classes. The second artifice is less elegant. It is an arbitrary choice on what to include in the discussion and what to leave out.

Another factor that has influenced the nature of the discussion of chemical agents is the relative availability in the open literature of information concerning them. There are literally tens of thousands of professional papers, monographs, and books in this literature. A trained clandestine adversary has virtually at his fingertips, at almost any university library, all the information he would need to synthesize toxic chemical agents from raw materials or intermediates.

Fluoroacetic Compounds and Their Toxic Behavior

A large number of fluoroacetic compounds have been synthesized since the original preparation of fluoroacetic acid by Swarts in 1896.[10] The toxicities of fluoroacetic acid derivatives and the potential utility of them as chemical warfare agents were not appreciated until the 1930s. Since that time, a number of more toxic derivatives have been synthesized. For those interested, practically the entire literature on fluoroacetates, to about twenty years ago, has been summarized in one book.[11] This book discusses the chemistry, preparation, toxicology, lethal doses, and other characteristics of hundreds of fluoroacetates and related fluorine containing compounds.

Fluoroacetate compounds exert their toxic effect on living organisms by blocking essential energetic processes which preserve normal cell functions. Blockage of these processes leads to cell death and, ultimately, to the death of the organism. The speed with which these events occur after introduction of the agent into the system depends largely on relatively small differences in the chemical structures of the agents. That is, the toxicity of a parent compound may often be enhanced by making relatively minor changes in its atomic or molecular structure. Thus, fluorocarbons that differ only by one carbon atom may exhibit vastly different levels of toxicity.

There are no effective antidotes to fluoroacetate poisoning. Treatment consists of measures supportive of vital circulatory, respiratory and nervous functions. The problem appears to reside in the nature of the biochemical behavior of fluoroacetate compounds, which bind irreversibly with enzymes important in processes which supply energy to body cells.

Preparation and Utilization of Fluoroacetates and Other Fluorinated Hydrocarbons

Since there are fluoroacetate compounds available commercially, such as rodenticides, it is legitimate to ask why a terrorist, bent on mass destruction, would bother to prepare one. It would seem a simple matter to purchase or steal something like compound 1080, which is mostly sodium fluoroacetate. In fact, one cannot preclude such a possibility. However, if it is important that there are no outward indicators of an effort to employ a clandestine chemical weapon until it is time to do so, and if the terrorist wishes to inflict a higher proportion of fatalities per unit of material disseminated than is possible with some commercially available fluoroacetates, then the preparation of a fluoroacetate may be indicated. The chemicals and equipment necessary for such preparation are easily purchased; their purchase should not arouse any suspicions concerning their ultimate use; and as suggested above, fluoroacetate compounds with much greater specific toxicity than, for example, commercial compounds based on sodium fluoroacetate, may be prepared for use in chemical weapons.

The initial steps in fluoroacetate synthesis are quite simple and straightforward, and will yield materials directly utilizable as toxic chemicals. Such processes are outlined in moderate detail in undergraduate organic chemistry text books.[12]

Fluoroacetic acid and sodium fluoroacetate have LD_{50} doses (the dose fatal to fifty percent of the exposed population) of about two to ten milligrams per kilogram of body weight (2-10 mg/kg), when ingested. On the other hand, 8-fluorooctanol, 4-fluorobutyric acid, and 8-fluorooctanoic acid have LD_{50}'s in the range of 0.6 to 0.65 mg/kg.[13] The preparation of these compounds, while somewhat more difficult than that of the simpler fluoroacetates, would present no unique challenge to a trained chemist.

One kilogram (2.2 pounds) of 8-fluorooctanoic acid contains 5,000 potentially lethal doses. A single individual could easily produce several tens of kilograms of this material in a few weeks of part-time effort. Producing a million lethal doses is largely a matter of time. Having done that, however, does not imply an ability to produce even a small fraction of that number of fatalities. The reasons why this is so are discussed later.

Organophosphorus Compounds and Their Toxic Behavior

There is a huge number of organophosphorus compounds—one estimate places the number at well over 50,000.[14] Insofar as is known, the first was synthesized around 1854. It was tetraethyl pyrophosphate, which is still used as an industrial chemical known as TEPP; it is one of the most toxic of the organophosphates.

The organophosphates are in fact the most toxic of all chemical agents. Several of these are available commercially as insecticides. Parathion is one such. This particular insecticide received much publicity in the popular press due to the potential hazard it poses for agricultural workers, and due also to occasional mishandling which led to fatalities such as happened in Tijuana,

Mexico, some years ago when this agent was stored in a mill and contaminated flour which was subsequently consumed as bread.

Between the world wars, the synthesis of organophosphorous compounds for insecticidal purposes was pursued in Germany. In the mid-1930s, the general formula for these was patented as a contact insecticide. In accordance with the law as it then existed in Germany, all new toxic chemicals were to be submitted to the government for examination as possible agents of war. The organophosphates were thus quickly adopted by the military. Tabun and Sarin, compounds developed by the private chemical industry in Germany while investigating the insecticidal potentials of the organophosphates, were incorporated into the German military armamentarium.

Another organophosphate, diisopropyl fluorophosphate (DFP), was synthesized in the U.S. in the early 1940s and it found considerable use among biochemists who have used it as a taggant in mapping many biochemical and metabolic processes, especially those involved in certain enzymatic reactions. Although it is a poison—relatively mild by standards to be considered here—DEP has been produced in a clandestine laboratory for what would appear to be assassination purposes.[15]

A huge open literature on organophosphates exists in part due to military interest, but also because of interest in commercial and academic circles concerning the chemistry of this family of compounds which has considerable economic importance as insecticides, and because of interest which developed in the 1950s in basic research on nerve activity, in particular the electrochemical transmission of nerve signals, and the action of the enzyme acetylcholinesterase—an enzyme involved in the electrochemical phenomena which transmit signals from one nerve ending to another. Organophosphorous compounds block the action of acetylcholinesterase, interrupting the transmission of signals along nerve pathways.

As mentioned previously, the family of organophosphate compounds contains within it the most toxic of all chemicals. They are lethal, albeit in different specific weights, whether administered orally, whether they are respired, or whether they came into contact with the skin. It is said that in the past, careless crop dusters who allowed liquid Parathion to splash on their shoes died when the liquid penetrated the leather of their footwear and came into contact with the skin of their feet. Such tales may be apocryphal, but the toxicity of some of the organophosphates is impressive. It is known , for example, that extremely small droplets of some of these compounds, when they come in contact with the eye, are fatal.[16]

The toxicity of the previously discussed fluoroacetate compounds was expressed in terms of oral doses to humans. The picture is somewhat more complex when discussing the toxicity of organophosphates, however, since there are such a variety of them; their toxicities vary over one or two orders of magnitude depending on the species tested and route by which administered; chemical purity of the compound may be difficult to establish with certainty; and other factors that tend to make the toxicity issue somewhat less straightforward than that for fluoroacetates.

The LD_{50} for TEPP by the oral route is stated by Heath[17] to be in the range of 1.05 to 1.70 mg/kg, and by another authority, 2.4 to 7.0 mg/kg,[18] when applied on the skin. On the other hand, the oral LD_{50} for Sarin is in the range of 0.14 to 0.28 mg/kg.[19] Sarin is highly volatile, which may explain its relatively low skin dose toxicity as compared to TEPP (about 17 mg/kg).[20] This high volatility leads to some rather bizarre effects, however. Among these is that a very small quantity of Sarin dropped on the skin is likely to lead to a vapor concentration in the vicinity of the person on whom the Sarin was dropped which exceeds the LD_{50} inhalation dose for a single breath! That dose can be worked out from figures in one authoritative publication,[21] which indicates that the inhalation LD_{50} dose is 75 mg/min/m^3 (75 mg Sarin per cubic meter of air per minute). At normal respiratory rates, this is an LD_{50} dose of about 0.015 mg/kg.

Still more potent organophosphates are found in that group of agents commonly referred to as V-agents. The generic formula for the V-agents is widely known, and is:

$$R - P(O) \underset{SCH_2CH_2NP''_2}{\overset{OR'}{\diagdown}}$$

where the substituents R, R' and R'' are, in general, short chain aliphatics (non-aromatic hydrocarbons with 2-4 carbon atoms).[22] The agent VX is in this family, and its formula is regarded as secret, although it, and its method of preparation, has been published by the British Patent Office. Enough information has appeared also in the U.S. press to deduce both the formula and the preparatory routes to its manufacture.[23]

The toxicity of VX by the respiratory route is estimated to be approximately 15 times that of Sarin,[24] or about 0.001 mg/kg. VX is relatively nonvolatile as well, and it has been stated that 6 mg applied to the skin is lethal; which makes VX about 300 times more lethal than Sarin by this route.[25]

These figures should be taken as relative toxicities only. Even then, relationships between toxicities of different agents are difficult to quantify for a number of reasons, some of which were outlined previously. The important point to recognize is that the organophosphates which have been selected, studied, and stockpiled by various nations as chemical weapons, and which are in use world-wide as insecticides, are among the most toxic synthetic agents developed by man.

Death can come from a variety of causes resulting from the action of an organophosphate, and descriptions of the symptoms predisposing to death are not important here. Death from organophosphate poisoning may be so rapid that the afflicted individual may be entirely unaware of what is happening.

Preparation and Utilization of Organophosphate Compounds

A perpetrator of a mass destruction event, whose vehicle were to be an organophosphate could: (1) acquire a compound directly through commercial channels; or (2) explosively rupture a vehicle transporting such a compound. It is a credible thesis that an event of high consequence could be precipitated, or threatened, by explosively dispersing such an agent in an appropriate environment, or by stealing a truckload of it for purposes of extortion. Of course, the latter threat could be credibly precipitated with much less than a truckload quantity.

Organophosphates, which are less common or absent from normal commercial channels, could be manufactured in a clandestine laboratory. The greater the toxicity of the agent, of course, the less material may be required to accomplish the intended end.

For example, Sarin can be synthesized in a small laboratory in quantities sufficient to cause thousands of deaths, presuming efficient dispersal of the agent, for a modest investment in chemicals and laboratory supplies. The starting chemicals are available commercially, syntheses processes are in the open literature, and the appropriate laboratory ware available from almost any laboratory supply house. The preparative schemes (and there are several) for synthesizing 100g quantities of Sarin could be considered tedious; they do involve hydrofluoric acid, a difficult acid to handle, but these procedures are well within the capabilities of an organic chemist with some graduate training.[26] As, it may be added, are the procedures for the synthesis of Tabun,[27] an organophosphate more toxic than Sarin.

A variety of V-agents may be prepared with somewhat more difficulty than that required to manufacture Sarin. More steps are involved; the procedure more hazardous due to the nature of some of the intermediate products and the final product, but again the processes are well within the capabilities of a graduate chemist.[28]

The utility of the organophosphates as instruments of mass destruction would appear to be obvious. They would appear to possess, on a weight-for-weight basis, an inherent advantage over the fluoroacetates in their capacity to cause fatalities. On balance, that is indeed the case. There are, however, so many variables associated with effective delivery of a chemical for mass destruction purposes, as to make a straightforward comparison between the potential lethalities of fluoroacetates and organophosphates a most difficult proposition.

Biological Agents

GENERAL

There are some differences between biological and chemical agents which go beyond basic differences between living systems, or their products, and synthetic ones. For example, one may discuss chemical agents by whole categories, or families, if you will. Witness the previous remarks on fluoroacetates and organophosphates. Both are natural groups of chemicals and both contain thousands to tens of thousands of chemicals within each.

When discussing potential biological agents, however, the discussion is usually limited to a specific organism, or product of that organism. This is not quite true since there are different serological types of an organism which, for purposes of arranging in a systematic hierarchy, taxonomists may refer to as a single species. For example, six serological types of *Clostridium botulinum,* the bacterium which produces botulinum toxin, are known, but taxonomists recognize only the one species. (There are other species of *Clostridium,* of course, but that is not relevant to this point.)

There are also different strains, subspecies, or species, of particular genera of organisms which exhibit varying levels of toxicity. *Bacillus anthracis,* for example, is one of the most poisonous organisms known. Another species of *Bacillis, B. cereus,* is on the other hand quite harmless.

Biological agents are therefore discussed on individual species bases and not on the basis of properties shared in common with a large number of kindred compounds, as is possible with some chemical agents.

BOTULINUM TOXIN AND ITS TOXIC BEHAVIORS

Botulinum toxin is a neurotoxin produced by *Clostridium botulinum,* and is among the most poisonous of toxins known. One may argue whether it is more properly discussed under chemicals or biologicals, since it is not a living entity but is a toxin produced by a living organism. Since it is a natural product of the metabolism of a living organism, however, and not a synthetic chemical, I have elected to discuss it with the biologicals.

Botulinum toxin, of course, causes botulism. What may be less well appreciated, however, is the fact that while 5-10 milligrams or so of a V-agent, the most potent of the synthetic chemical agents of mass destruction, may be required to cause a human fatality, a few micrograms of botulinum toxin will do the same thing. In short, botulinum toxin is about a thousand times more toxic than the organophosphates, and a million times more toxic than any fluoroacetate.

With respect to the mechanisms of action of botulinum toxin; those mechanisms are not known in the detail that those of the fluoroacetates or organophosphates are known. Even the human LD_{50} for botulinum toxin is not precisely known. It is assumed to lie somewhere between less than a microgram (a millionth of a gram) and a few micrograms. One of the problems inherent in determining human LD_{50} doses for such small amounts of material is the fact that the amounts are so small. This in itself makes any quantitative assay, on a postmortem examination for example, virtually impossible. Further complicating that job is the chance that the victim ingested not only botulinum toxin, but live botulinum bacilli as well, which go on producing toxin in the body of the victim.

Extrapolation of the human LD_{50} dose from animal experimentation is not possible either, because of the peculiar manner in which various non-primate species respond to this agent. Some species respond in a straightforward manner in which the LD_{50} dose is a function of body weight; i.e., the heavier the animal, the greater the LD_{50} dose. In other species the LD_{50} dose may be independent of body weight. Figures for human LD_{50} doses by inhalation are published, however,[29] and correspond to a total LD_{50} dose to the human of about 0.3 micrograms, or about 5000 times more toxic than the organophosphate Sarin.

Like the organophosphates, botulinum toxin acts on the nervous system. Botulinum toxin blocks the transmission of nerve impulses, as opposed to the organophosphate action of preventing those impulses from being turned off.

This is, essentially, the state of knowledge today concerning the mechanisms of action of botulinum toxin. The victim of botulinum toxin poisoning, should that victim succumb, succumbs frequently to paralyses of the respiratory muscles—the victim suffocates.[30]

PREPARATION AND UTILIZATION OF BOTULINUM TOXIN

Clostridium botulinum, the bacillus which produces botulinum toxin, is found in soil virtually everywhere. One may, from a trowel full of dirt, culture *C. botulinum.* To be assured of getting a virulent form of *C. botulinum,* however, a bit more sophistication is required.

Botulism is, of course, an ever-present danger to the food industry. For that reason, public health agencies and the medical profession in general have long studied *C. botulinum,* developing procedures for isolating and culturing various species of clostridia (some clostridia cause gangrene or tetanus). Because of this interest, the open literature has long contained detailed descriptions of the isolation, culturing, and testing of species of *Clostridium.*[31]

A terrorist interested in preparing a culture of *C. botulinum* for purposes of extracting botulinum toxin could attempt to grow the organism rather than try to obtain a culture of it from, say, the American Type Culture Collection. Growing your own requires a certain amount of screening for the proper serologic type; assuming a terrorist would wish to maximize the lethality of a toxin, it is necessary that his *C. botulinum* be tested for serologic type. The processes for doing this are somewhat involved if the terrorist is insistent on maximum security, precluding the purchase of standardized anti-toxins for serologic typing: involved, but not unmanageable for the trained individual.

Once the proper serologic type of *C. botulinum* is identified, it may be isolated and grown under anaerobic conditions in pure culture, from which continuous production of toxin is possible. It may be desirable to purify and concentrate this product. Directions for doing so are in the open literature. With modest facilities, an individual could produce in a relatively short period several hundred thousand human LD_{50} doses of botulinum toxin.

There are risks associated with these procedures; self-contamination is possible if special precautions are not taken. It may be assumed, however, that an individual with the capability to prepare botulinum toxin is well aware of the health and safety risks involved, and will have taken appropriate steps to eliminate those risks.

The product may be of unknown toxicity, but in any case, could be a most toxic agent. The utility of botulinum toxin as an agent of mass destruction is enhanced by the fact it is highly toxic by inhalation or ingestion. Ultimately, however, as with all agents of mass destruction discussed in this paper, its utility for mass destruction purposes depends for the most part on an effective means of dissemination.

ANTHRAX AND ITS TOXIC PROPERTIES

We are now into discussing an agent which is clearly and unambiguously biological. This agent is a living organism—not a toxin produced from it. Furthermore, this agent is perhaps the most toxic substance within the capabilities of a terrorist to employ.

Anthrax bacilli are highly infective, particularly potent casualty producers, resistant in spore form to environmental factors of heat, moisture, cold and dessication. The bacillus occurs in cutaneous, intestinal, and respiratory forms.

A particularly insidious quality of anthrax poisoning is the fact that it must be treated before it is obvious what disease the patient has in order that a modest chance for survival can exist. Waiting to provide treatment until the symptoms are obvious virtually guarantees the patient will die within two to three days. It is sobering to note that even at Fort Detrick, where more elaborate safety measures were in force than in any other comparable facility in the U.S. (one may argue there was no other facility comparable to Fort Detrick when it was engaged in the production and investigation of biological agents), two employees died of anthrax in the late 1950s.[32] In its respiratory form, anthrax is frequently fatal within twenty-four hours.

The infectious mechanisms of anthrax are relatively well understood; however, the mechanisms through which toxicity is mediated are not well in hand. Along this line, if certain chemicals are mixed with anthrax spores and the mixture administered in concentrations which are not lethal when either the chemical or anthrax is administered singly, anthrax infections are nevertheless produced. Just why such synergism is displayed in these cases is not well understood.

The toxicity of *B. anthracis* seems to be mediated through a chemical factor produced by the bacillus which overwhelms defense mechanisms the body normally arrays against infections. The vegetative growth and reproduction of infective bacilli progress relatively unimpeded throughout the respiratory tract; the lymphatic and blood circulatory systems are rapidly invaded; and the infection widely disseminated to other organs throughout the body. The infection proceeds with uncommon speed, and death in 24 hours or less is not unusual. Although a number of vaccines are available, unless the disease is recognized very early, the utility of these vaccines for reducing mortality is minimal.

PREPARATION AND UTILIZATION OF ANTHRAX

Bacillus anthracis, like *Clostridium botulinum,* can be prepared in continuous culture. Prior to such preparation, however, a seed culture must be obtained. This should present only moderate difficulty to virtually anyone with a background in microbiology or a related discipline. University and public health research laboratories, pharmaceutical research laboratories, and other sources exist where a seed culture could be obtained under apparently legitimate circumstances. For maximum security, the terrorist may choose to acquire his seed culture from the natural environment in which *B. anthracis* lives. Procedures for sampling, screening, identifying, isolating, and culturing almost any biological organism of public health concern are published widely in microbiological texts and manuals, the sampling, care, and feeding of *B. anthracis* included. This organism would appear to be a good choice for a potential mass destruction weapon: once it is obtained in seed culture it grows rapidly and requires only moderate care, and readily forms spores.

Once a terrorist has obtained a seed culture, the organism may be grown in quantity by either continuous culture methods, or in batches. Again, generic directions for doing so are freely accessible in the open literature. Methods of mass culture of organisms closely related to *B. anthracis (B. cereus* and *B. subtilis*) have been discussed[33] and could be used by a terrorist to perfect techniques before attempting mass culture of the anthrax bacillus.

A terrorist has a number of options available for isolation and concentration of *B. antracis* from the culture medium. Simple centrifugation will separate the cells from the culture medium, which can then be suspended in a stabilizing medium and stored under refrigeration. Virulence of the stored cells could be maintained under such conditions for several weeks. Alternatively, it may be desired to maintain stocks in spore form, in which case the organism would be permitted to sporulate, then separated from culture, dried, and stored in the dark. Virulence could be maintained for years under these conditions.

Dispersal of deadly chemical or biological agents is frequently treated in the popular press as no more difficult than dumping the agent in a community water supply. So done, mass casualties are deduced to automatically result. Rarely could this be the case, however. The efficient dispersal of a potential agent of mass destruction could be a formidable problem for anyone contemplating such an act. Some of the difficulties associated with efficient dispersal of a toxic agent are discussed in the following section.

Dispersal of Toxic Agents

CHEMICAL AGENTS

In previous sections addressing the preparation and utilization of chemical agents, it was implied that relatively large quantities of materials could be produced with only moderate requirements. In general, this is true. It also can be misleading, however, to assume that a given quantity of agent is translatable to a capability to produce some number of deaths with that quantity. For example, if the objective of an individual were to produce, say 5,000-10,000 casualties, depending on the method of dispersal chosen, up to one million times this amount in LD_{50} doses may have to be produced. No matter what route of agent dissemination is chosen, losses during dissemination will occur. These losses are usually quite large: at a minimum, it may be assumed that 90 percent of the dispersed agent will not reach the intended target in doses sufficient to cause casualties. This is a very general statement, of course, and if the adversary were judicious in choice of target and method of dispersal, losses could perhaps be reduced.

Several methods of dispersing chemical agents may be considered. These include contamination of bulk food supplies; generation of gases in enclosed spaces with volatile agents; generation of aerosols in enclosed spaces with non-volatile agents; and dispersal with explosives.

The first three of these dispersal mechanisms are assumed would occur under covert conditions; the last, overtly. The number of scenarios for dispersal is virtually limitless. It is, however, doubtful that an adversary could under any conditions, with a high probability effectively target a group of people larger than a few hundred with any kind of chemical attack. If an adversary were to attempt an attack on a larger scale, such an attempt would likely be made out of ignorance concerning the logistical, dispersal, and material resources required to launch such an attack effectively. These requirements place the chemical mass destruction attack in the realm of a very large scale undertaking which, for a number of reasons, is not considered credible.

On the other hand, an attack with chemical agents on a select population of individuals, such as the inhabitants of an office building or large auditorium, is an attack which is manageable by a single individual. Whether one would characterize the result of such an attack as mass destruction is largely a matter of how one defines that term. Peacetime man-caused disasters (fires, explosions, etc.) that result in a hundred fatalities or more are quite rare. An event involving a chemical agent attack on a select population which resulted in several hundred deaths would be a significant event indeed, with effects extending far beyond the immediate tragedy. Although the clandestine chemical attack does not appear a viable method for producing very large numbers of fatalities, an event which resulted in a few hundred fatalities could certainly be categorized as an event of mass destruction.

BIOLOGICAL AGENTS

With the exception of botulinum toxin, the effective dispersal of biological agents is for the most part limited to aerosolization. Aerosols are, of course, suspensions of small particles in a gaseous medium. Not all aerosols that could be made up of pathogenic or toxic particles would, by the nature of their constituents, be necessarily harmful, however. That is largely due to the fact that the possible particle size range of an aerosol is rather broad, while the particle size range of aerosols which will effectively involve the human respiratory system is relatively limited.

This is a very simplistic explanation of the relationships of aerosol particles to the human respiratory system, and it is for the most part more appropriate to a discussion of non-living aerosol particles than to a discussion of living particles. (See the discussion on plutonium dispersal.) Aerosols made up of a virulent organism such as *B. anthracis* may be somewhat effective even if particle sizes are outside the range of those most effectively trapped by the respiratory system. The residence time of too small or too large particles (i.e., the time to clear these particles from the respiratory system) may be sufficient to permit their toxic factors to be released, or for the spores making up the particles to reproduce. Furthermore, particles cleared from the respiratory tree may be swallowed. *B. anthracis* is also toxic if the intestinal form is ingested.

A significant problem in the aerosol dissemination of almost any biological agent, is the survival of the agent long enough to infect the intended target. The mechanical stresses in the aerosolization process may kill a significant proportion of the pathogenic agent. Moisture in the air, sunlight, smog, radical temperature changes, and other factors may contribute to reducing, through death of significant numbers of organisms in the agent, the virulence of that agent. Thus, as with chemical agents, it is misleading to equate the number of LD_{50} doses an adversary may possess with the number of LD_{50} doses delivered, irrespective of a host of other problems associated with aerosol delivery, others of which are touched upon later with respect to the discussion on plutonium.

It is not in the objectives of this paper to go in depth into methods of aerosol delivery. No purpose would seem to be served by doing that. Suffice it to say that if an adversary possessed some basic understanding of meteorology, the biological characteristics of the agent he chose to employ, the requirements for and affects of aerosolization, was careful in the selection of the target population, and was aware of the various temporal and spatial conditions which would affect the aerosol dispersal of a particular organism, a significant threat could arise. That adversary could precipitate an event which, by anyone's definition, would be an event of mass destruction.

Recall further that spores of *B. anthracis* are quite resistant to many environmental factors. To illustrate, the Island of Gruinard off the coast of Scotland was used by the British in World War II for testing biological weapons. Anthrax was tested there, and it was estimated in 1967 that the island may remain infected with viable anthrax for one hundred years.[34]

To summarize, there appear no technological impediments to the mounting of a credible clandestine mass destruction threat with some biologicals; such would appear more difficult with potential chemical agents. The resources required to mount a credible mass destruction threat with a biological weapon are trivial compared to those required for a credible explosive nuclear threat.[35] A similar statement could be made for the nuclear compared to the chemical threat, but by any measure, it does not seem credible that a chemical threat could be mounted that could result in the magnitude of destruction potentially possible with nuclear or biological weapons.

It should not be assumed from the above that any value judgment is being made with respect to the mounting of any mass destruction threat. This is quite a separate question.

The Plutonium Dispersal Weapon—A Special Case

As implied earlier, the apparent simplicity of the aerosol device, in one form or another of ubiquitous household familiarity, has seemingly led to the assumption that aerosols themselves are easy to produce. Which in fact they are, relatively speaking, but uncritical acceptance of this tends to lead also to the assumption that effectively toxic aerosols of plutonium are also easy to produce.

The following observations on the toxic properties of plutonium are presented with a view towards placing the issue of plutonium dispersal, as employed in a radiological weapon, into some perspective. Since inhalation is the most sensitive route of entry into the body relative to the toxicity of plutonium, other modes of entry (ingestion or accidental injection) are not discussed.

Particles of small enough dimensions, and in large enough density in space and time to be classed as aerosols, possess a number of interesting characteristics which, in the past and current debates concerning the relationship of plutonium to some usually poorly defined capability to cause death or injury when introduced into the respiratory system, have by and large been ignored. There are, of course, scholarly exceptions to this generalization;[36] but these also seem to be ignored in present debate. The reasons for this are not altogether clear, since many of the principles required to perform adequate assessments of the behavior of aerosols in the atmosphere, in the respiratory system, and the expected toxicity of plutonium aerosols in particular, are relatively well in hand.

Aerosol particles behave differently in a relatively free aerodynamic environment, as in the atmosphere, than they do in the aerodynamic environment of the respiratory tree. It is important to possess at least a basic understanding of the behavior of aerosol particles in both environments before one can say much that is credible concerning the potential toxicity of a plutonium aerosol.

Producing an aerosol may be by one of several means. Aerosols may be generated aerodynamically, by centrifugal action, hydraulically, by vibration, or through electrostatic processes. The aerodynamic method is the most common. Here, however, a distinction must be made concerning the material from which the aerosol is generated. Aerodynamic generation of an aerosol from a liquid as, for example, from hydrated plutonium nitrate, involves forcing the liquid with high pressure air through a nozzle or other terminal device which breaks up the liquid into small particulates of the desired size. If, however, the starting material is solid as, for example, plutonium dioxide powder or plutonium nitrate crystals, the particulates must first be formed mechanically. Once formed, the particles are then propelled by air pressure (or some other gas) through an air pipe, hose, or some other delivery device.

Once the aerosol is formed, its behavior in the atmosphere is affected by processes which operate to greater or lesser degree to degrade the presumed desired performance of the aerosol.

In an external environment, effective distribution of an aerosol depends upon the height from which it is released, local air currents, density of suspended particles at an effective height for an effective period of time, particle size, and amount of starting material. These factors, and those mentioned previously, may provide some indication of the problems facing any terrorist who would disperse a plutonium aerosol in the open environment with the objective of causing large numbers of short-term fatalities.

Effective dispersal of a plutonium aerosol indoors is not without its problems either. It is generally accepted that the most efficient manner in which to disperse a plutonium aerosol into a building is via the air conditioning system. Frequently implicit in such scenarios is perfect mixing and ideal aerosol cloud stability within the building, since rarely does one ever find discussed any of the problems inherent in such a scenario. These include plating out of a significant proportion of the aerosol particles on the enormous surface areas of the air conditioning duct work of large buildings; the effect of air conditioning, especially humidification, on the aerosol particles; the effects of passive and electrostatic filters on the aerosol; and other factors, including many of those previously discussed, which in general would act to degrade the desired performance of a plutonium aerosol introduced into a building's air conditioning system.

Up to this point, no mention has been made of the dependency for effectiveness of a plutonium aerosol on the particle size distribution of that aerosol, i.e., the relationship between particle sizes and the characteristics of respiratory physiology. As a general statement it may be said that up to 25 percent of the particles inhaled from an aerosol, which are in the size range of 0.5 microns (millionths of a meter) to about 7 microns, will be deposited in deep lung tissue. Above 7 microns, the proportion of particles deposited in deep lung tissue declines sharply. Particles of less than 0.5 microns may be phagocytized (engulfed by cells specialized for removing foreign material), or actually move through the interstitial spaces between cells, and migrate out of the lungs.

Particle sizes of plutonium compounds found in nuclear facilities frequently fall within the respiratory size range, although particle sizes of plutonium in fuels for experimental reactors may be 2-3 times larger than the upper range indicated here.[37]

Before relating this information to the respiratory physiology of aerosol particles in general, and plutonium in particular, it is necessary to describe in a superficial manner the structure and characteristics of the respiratory system relative to particle deposition. For present needs, it is sufficient to divide this system into three zones: the nasopharyngeal, the tracheobronchial, and the pulmonary. The nasopharyngeal zone consists of the nose and that portion of the airway to the level of the trachea. This zone of the respiratory system will entrap approximately 80 percent of inhaled aerosol particles up to 7 microns in aerodynamic diameter, and larger yet proportions of particles above this size. These particles, after entrapment, are cleared from this zone in one-half times of a few hours to one or two days.

The tracheobronchial zone includes the airway from the trachea, through the bronchus and bronchi, to and including the terminal bronchioles. Some small fraction of aerosol particles are deposited in this zone by impaction, sedimentation, or diffusion in the case of very small particles. An anatomical feature of this zone is that it is both ciliated and contains mucous-secreting glands, which together clear the zone of deposited foreign particles in one-half times of thirty minutes to about one day, depending on particle size, point of deposition, and health of the individual.

The pulmonary zone is where functional gas exchange takes place in the lungs, and structurally consists of small sacs termed alveoli. Very few particles deposited in the alveoli exceed 7 microns in aerodynamic diameter. Residence one-half times in this zone can be long for insoluble particles, such as plutonium dioxide, and are frequently assumed to be on the order of 500 days.[38] One must say assumed, because clearance mechanisms from this zone are not completely understood. As might be expected, the pulmonary zone is the sensitive target area for a plutonium aerosol. It is in the pulmonary zone where pathological conditions induced by a plutonium aerosol can cause fatalities, given that enough material is deposited.

Which gets us, finally, to the question of plutonium toxicity. This issue has been confused by attempting to equate the toxicity of plutonium with a lethal substance such as nerve gas. It is a poor comparison, since nerve gases do not have to be inhaled or ingested to be lethal. Sarin, as previously noted a potent nerve gas, has gained a certain amount of popularity in terms of comparable toxicity vis-à-vis plutonium. It is lethal in milligram quantities. Under some conditions, a milligram or two dropped on the clothing, and soaking through to the skin where it may be absorbed, is a lethal dose. Microgram quantities striking the eye are lethal. On the other hand, a milligram or two of a plutonium aerosol, applied to external body surfaces only, is completely innocuous, as is a kilogram or two applied in the same manner. One may wish to make a distinction at this point between the radiobiological effectiveness of weapons grade plutonium versus reactor grade plutonium, but the distinction in this context would be academic.

The toxicity of plutonium, or any other material for that matter, is expressed in terms of some minimum amount which has some probability of causing a pathological effect. In the case of plutonium, as mentioned previously, this is a function of the mode of entry into the body, which is not true to the same extent of some other toxic substances. Selecting the most sensitive route of entry, through the respiratory system, plutonium toxicity becomes expressible in terms of that quantity of material, deposited in the pulmonary region of the respiratory system, that has a high probability of leading to short-term (one year, or less) fatalities. Experimentation on dogs indicates that this quantity, for insoluble plutonium, is about five billionths of a curie per gram of lung tissue. Death arises from pulmonary fibrosis.[39]

Making some extremely simplistic calculations, and extrapolating directly from the animal data, it may be shown that milligram quantities of insoluble reactor grade plutonium, deposited in the pulmonary region of the human lung, will cause a short-term fatality in that individual so exposed. Such calculations do not, however, take into consideration any of the previously mentioned physical factors which tend to degrade the performance of any aerosol; the environmental factors which affect the time and space occupancy characteristics of any aerosol; the physiological factors which require an aerosol to possess certain characteristics if it is to be effective; and other factors which make any attempt to cause numbers of short-term fatalities from a plutonium aerosol, an undertaking of great uncertainty.

Which is to say, calculations indicating milligram quantities of insoluble reactor grade plutonium are lethal are based upon data obtained on laboratory animals in strictly controlled environments, and under exposure conditions which ensured the pulmonary deposition of controlled quantities of plutonium oxide. One must recognize that any relationship between such environments, designed specifically to result in pulmonary depositions of aerosol particulates, and virtually any other environment into which an aerosol may be dispersed, is tenuous in the extreme.

Frequently seen statements that small quantities of plutonium, dispersed into undefined environments, in some undefined manner, and made without consideration of the problems involved in creating an aerosol, much less those of maintaining its integrity once discharged from the aerosol generator, causing thousands of deaths, are simply incredible.

If it were possible to confine one thousand people to a controlled environment in which each individual was, through a breathing apparatus specially constructed for the purpose, separately administered about one milligram of reactor grade plutonium oxide, it would only require about one gram of such material to cause short-term mortality in that population of individuals. Under any other conditions, the dispersal of an aerosol of reactor grade plutonium oxide, done with the objective of causing one thousand or so short-term fatalities, would have to be a brute force operation.

It is difficult to argue against the proposition that to cause one thousand short-term fatalities from the inhalation of an aerosol of reactor grade plutonium, it would require material in amounts up to a million times greater than that required to accomplish the same thing in a controlled environment such as that just outlined. That is, it would require some amount of material in the range of 1,000 kilograms, or one metric ton, to attempt the feat, and the outcome would still be uncertain because of the many factors which operate on all aerosols, and over which no control is possible. Conditions for dispersal may be selected to optimize the opportunity to create greater hazards, of course. There remain many variables, however, over which manipulation is possible only in a probabilistic sense. Thus, the outcome of a brute force plutonium aerosol attack of even incredible proportions could not be predicted with certainty.

In sum, the "poison gas" characterization of a plutonium aerosol must be put into a perspective appropriate to certain unavoidable physical and physiological prerequisites for the application of such material in a manner designed to cause short-term fatalities. In that regard, it may be useful to consider the fact that to have some probability of success in causing thousands of casualties in a military operation, even so-called nerve gas gases must be dispersed in quantities of hundreds to thousands of kilograms.

The plutonium dispersal weapon is, simply, not a weapon of mass destruction. This is not to minimize the other characteristics of such a weapon which include radiological contamination and the potential for causing life-shortening through induction of cancers in individuals 15 to 30 years following exposure. This is a separate subject, however, and one which also has seemed to suffer more than benefited from much of recent discussion.

Mass Destruction and Terrorism

This subject, among many other things, requires transcultural evaluations of motivational stimuli. In some instances such evaluations simply may not be possible. Motivation, as an aspect of modern human behavior, is increasingly difficult to assess in the traditional terms of an advanced industrial Western society. To the Western mind, recent terrorist acts frequently seem irrational.

The problem of assessing in rational Western terms the political and/or sociological aspects of a terrorist mass destruction threat is further complicated by the fact that such a threat is an extraordinary act: this kind of threat involves skills, values, and risks that are not encountered in more conventional forms of terrorism. Extrapolations of past terrorist activities to encompass the terrorist employment of a weapon of mass destruction may be misleading. Which is not to say that past terrorist activity should not be examined in an attempt to evaluate the motives leading to the consummation of such a threat. For better or worse, this past and continuing activity represents the only reservoir of human experience from which it is possible to develop a qualitative assessment of factors which could be predisposing to a mass destruction threat.

In the popular press, learned journals, books, and monographs, the potential relationship between terrorism, as it is increasingly practiced around the world, and a terrorist mass destruction capability has received considerable attention, particularly with regard to a potential nuclear threat. Analyses of terrorism found in the popular press often state that terrorists will ultimately acquire a nuclear capability (from civilian or military sources), and then be in a position to wield extraordinary powers of extortion or political blackmail.[40] Similar sentiments have been expressed in more learned works.[41] Recently, however, the assumptions that terrorists would acquire means for inflicting mass destruction as a natural evolutionary sequence have been attacked, largely on the basis of analyses of the raison d'être of terrorist movements.[42]

There is no question that, under appropriate circumstances, terror has proven to be both an effective and efficient psychological weapon. No other technique is as immediately available or offers as much return for relatively small investments as does selectively applied terror. Conditions are important, however, and, as Simpson puts it:

> . . . the competent practitioners of terrorism usually know how
> their actions will affect their enemies and what reactions they
> can expect from those not directly involved.[43]

Implied in Simpson's remark is the requirement that there be limitations to any terror campaign. Most authorities agree that non-institutional terrorism is a tactic of the weak. This being the case, in order for terror to be an effective tactic for coercion, terrorists must be able to make their constituencies understand what is being attempted, and let them know that there are penalties involved and that innocents will be spared to the degree possible.[44] The use of weapons of mass destruction could violate each of these criteria. Such weapons could kill or injure innocent people in very large numbers; the penalties would far exceed any accepted norms for conventional violence; and the terrorist message would likely be lost in the revulsion engendered by any such attack.

The recent shift in perspective—from perceiving terrorist movements as naturally progressing to a mass destruction, and in particular nuclear capability, to a more measured appraisal of those movements—has revealed some analytical superficialities in the earlier literature. Only recently have there been attempts to reexamine terrorist movements in terms of ultimate goals and objectives, insofar as employment of weapons of mass destruction within these movements is concerned. For example, a recent exhaustive search of the literature dealing with Arab terrorist *fedayeen,* which is replete with references to nonnuclear military and guerrilla strategies, has revealed only one reference to the possible *fedayeen* use of nuclear explosives. This reference arose in an interview with a Western scientist who discussed the potential ease of manufacture of a clandestine nuclear device.[45]

Historians and social scientists are beginning to point out that many terrorist organizations engaging in transnational terrorism are heavily subsidized by several governments: some are, in fact, governmental branches. This in itself might lead to caution in the employment of weapons of mass destruction, since such employment could very likely precipitate countermeasures of such severity as to topple any government associated with the act.

Terrorist organizations not aligned with any particular government would still be constrained from the use of mass destruction weapons by factors considered earlier: risking the lives of their constituencies, excessive penalties, and loss of sympathy for the movement. It is difficult to discern any set of conditions short of sheer desperation which would systematically and logically lead terrorist groups to the conclusion that it was in their interest to employ a weapon of mass destruction.

With respect to the potential desperate use of such a weapon, several observations may be made. Ignoring scenarios leading to desperate measures, of which there are many, there are several requisite steps which must be taken before the desperate use of a mass destruction weapon may be made. The principal one is the advance preparation of contingency plans which encompass such a strategy. However, it does not seem likely that an organization would plan in advance for its own final hours. It is not in the nature of such organizations to plan for apocalyptic events.

There is, of course, the frequently cited scenario of terrorists holding a city or government hostage for purposes of extortion by threatening the use of a weapon of mass destruction. As must be apparent, however, there is still much fertile ground to be plowed by purely conventional means of hostage-taking for ransom. This is not to say, of course, that there is no upper bound. Hostage-takers cannot, for example, demand more than can be paid; they cannot demand of a government more than the government's constituency is prepared to give. Nor can they demand the dissolution of a government, or even an effective major policy change, since such demands would tend to be unenforceable unless the terrorists could maintain a long-term enforcement capability, which seems rather unlikely.

Terrorists are undoubtedly aware of these considerations; the most capable terrorist organizations are politically astute. The more mass destruction weapon city- or government-hostage scenarios are examined, the more unlikely a proposition they seem to become.

What seems the most credible variation of this family of scenarios, however, is that in which a government might be held hostage for the release of political prisoners. In this case, there might be no money demand; the time for compliance could be relatively short; and once the demand was met, there would be no continuing requirement for the terrorists to maintain the threat. All of these factors work to the terrorists' advantage relative to all other city- or government-hostage scenarios which have had some currency in the past. This is not to say, however, that many other difficulties, both practical and political, do not stand in the way of perpetrating such a threat. Some of these have been discussed previously.

One of the questions that must be asked then, is what can transnational terrorists accomplish through the use of mass destruction terror that they could not accomplish with conventional military and guerrilla methods at less risk and cost, the almost certain increase in public abhorrence of such methods, and the potentially disastrous political reactions arising therefrom?

Insofar as indigenous terrorists are concerned, they would be under additional sets of constraints against the implementation of weapons of mass destruction. Since these groups operate almost entirely within their own countries, they must retain a reservoir of favorable public opinion in order to satisfy at least some of their objectives. Recent history shows several instances where conventional indigenous terrorist violence was curbed. Wohlstetter[46] points out that during the Cuban revolution, indiscriminate use of violence by the 26 of July Movement had to be curbed because of unfavorable public reaction. In Uruguay, the Tupamaros carried violence to a point that led to their virtual destruction. Violence perpetrated by the Tupamaros reached such proportions that the Uruguayan government finally acceded to its army's request for special powers to destroy the movement—which was done, although at a considerable and continuing cost to civil liberties.[47]

Another factor contributing to the speculation surrounding the potential terrorist use of a mass destruction weapon which needs to be examined are terrorist technological resources, and the employment by terrorists of other than conventional, non-crew-served weaponry. For purposes of this discussion, manpower resources are not considered to be limiting.

With respect to weaponry, it may safely be stated that conventional munitions such as small arms, including automatic weapons, bulk explosives, and hand grenades are freely available to terrorists.[48] Such munitions are known to move relatively freely between sympathetic governments and terrorist groups, and between terrorist groups which, not infrequently, share munitions.[49] As is well-known, other weaponry is also available to terrorists.

Shoulder fired missile launchers have, on rare occasions, been employed by terrorists, or terrorists have been apprehended with them in their possession.[50]

To the first point, it is apparent that some terrorist groups have always had available to them the conventional munitions of the day. Today, that means the latest in assault rifles, submachine guns, and other firearms, as well as sophisticated explosives in bulk, and man-portable military explosive devices such as hand grenades, demolition shaped charges, satchel charges, anti-personnel mines, and other devices. A somewhat surprising observation is, in spite of such availability, the last mentioned explosive devices are rarely used except in actions which may be supportive of civil wars or "wars of liberation." This observation bears on the following discussion.

With respect to the second point, we are frequently given to believe that less conventional weaponry is also available to terrorist groups more or less indiscriminately. That is to say, shoulder fired missile launchers, in part due to their widespread military use, high rate of manufacture, relative cheapness, and occasional use by terrorists, will come to be a primary weapon in the armamentaria of terrorist groups. This line of reasoning occasionally also extends to the future terrorist adoption of precision guided munitions such as the TOW, HOT Blowpipe, and other optically or wire guided missiles. One may, however, look in vain for even modest use of portable missile launchers which have been around for decades.

To be sure, there have been instances of such use,[51] but the incidence of use does not point to an evolutionary step in increasing terrorist violence mediated by special weapons. To the contrary, the munitions types employed by terrorists have remained somewhat static over the decades, with the only evidence of an evolutionary trend being the adoption by terrorists of more recent small arms and similar munitions as these become available. The numbers of incidents where rocket launchers are employed are rare, no matter in what terrorist cause they may be used. Moreover, their rate of use remains relatively constant. One therefore observes that the level of terrorist violence has remained over the years relatively static; only the frequency of incidents has increased in the past decade.

One resource that may be limiting to almost all terrorist groups who would perhaps otherwise engage in incidents requiring some technical sophistication, is technological skill. Although terrorist groups are frequently composed of literate, educated, middle-class individuals, these people are most often educated in the social sciences and the humanities. In fact, if one searches for terrorist groups possessing technological and physical science skills, such will be found only in two or three relatively small groups in the mid-East.[52] This fact seems to influence the nature of terrorist tactics and target selection. It also seems to bear on the effectiveness of many terrorist incidents where the possession of even moderate technical abilities could have had marked effects on the outcome of an incident. It would also seem to bear on the capability of a terrorist group to embark on the construction and employment of a weapon of mass destruction. [Such an undertaking, while in some instances requiring what the author would term only modest technological skills, are nevertheless levels of skill not apparent in terrorist organizations today or historically]. It appears very much as though terrorist groups are simply incapable of mounting a credible mass destruction threat, based on technological resource requirements alone.

What then are we to make of the terrorist mass destruction threat? Aside from the technological problems, which at this time do not appear to be insignificant insofar as terrorists are concerned, there remain the political and constituent factors to consider in any strategy to employ a weapon of mass destruction. It simply strains the bounds of credulity to conclude that noninstitutional terrorist violence will evolve to a mass destruction capability. The indiscriminate effects of a mass destruction weapon would, it seems, in and of itself discourage its use for all but highly parochial and discrete targets. Even in such instances as these, the weapon must be chosen carefully and designed specifically for the job at hand. Thus, biologicals may be ruled out for use because of difficulties in controlling the spread of the effects of some agents. The employment of a nuclear device may require a weapon designed to have effects restricted to the target. Given that it appears at present there may not exist any terrorist group with the skills requisite for building a crude nuclear device of unpredictable yield, it would seem that it is simply beyond terrorist capabilities to design a weapon with a yield predictable within acceptable error limits.

It is not irrelevant to observe that the capacity for a single individual to cause an event of mass destruction has existed for at least two generations. In that time we have seen numerous unsubstantiated tales of terrorist threats or attempts to employ chemicals or biologicals against society at large, or against specific elements of society. In that time we have also seen such tales concerning the clandestine nuclear weapon.

In that time we have also seen, however, a plot to employ typhoid bacillus in metropolitan water supplies,[53] the manufacture of diisopropyl fluorophosphate by a criminal organization, which packaged the DFP in aerosol cans for use as assassination weapons,[54] the theft of mustard gas from a disposal site in Europe,[55] and unconfirmed reports of attempts to steal anthrax bacillus from Fort Detrick.[56]

Thus, although the possibility of a credible terrorist mass destruction threat seems remote in the extreme, we are nevertheless faced with something akin to a conundrum. On the one hand the possibility of a threat appears too remote to consider that a credible one will occur in the foreseeable future. On the other hand, the potential consequences of such a threat are greater than most natural disasters. The latter fact appears to be the driving force behind most analyses of potential terrorist mass destruction threats, suggestions for regulation of sensitive industries and materials, and for the development of contingency planning in the event of a credible threat.

While the author takes exception with a good deal of current and recent past analyses of potential terrorist mass destruction threat capability, it is felt that more effort than has heretofore been expended needs to be spent on: examining how sensitive non-nuclear materials are handled in commerce; what levels of accountability exist for their possession or use; where bureaucratic responsibilities lie for manufacturing, transport, possession and use of sensitive substances; the nature of responsiveness of the various bureaucratic strata to a credible mass destruction threat; how a threat is communicated from the receiver to an identifiable agency with clear-cut responsibilities; how a threat assessment group is established to determine threat credibility; and on the development of sound crisis management policy[57] at various levels of government.

In summary, the potential terrorist mass destruction threat may be viewed as requiring various levels of technological skills depending on the nature of the threat. Requiring the greatest skills would be a credible threat involving a discriminate nuclear device. Considerably less skill would be required to precipitate a clandestine nuclear threat with a device of uncertain yield, and with some unknown probability of functioning in the nuclear mode. Fewer skills yet would be required to precipitate a credible mass destruction threat with either a chemical or biological agent. To date, such skills are felt to be beyond the capabilities of contemporary terrorist organizations.

These considerations are quite independent of political factors and constituent support following such use; indeed, the possibility of severe political consequences befalling such a constituency subsequent to such an event, forces one to the conclusion that the danger of non-institutional terrorist mass destruction threats are vanishingly remote.

This general conclusion needs to be qualified to the extent that the possibility such a threat could arise is also a function of geo-political, cultural, temporal, and economic factors. These cannot be considered in this paper. Therefore, while the general conclusion is felt to be a reasonable one, the same level of potential threat, while small, does not exist for all people and all nations.

But that subject is one of higher resolution than that treated here. It requires separate consideration.

Notes

1. Richard Shultz, "Conceptualizing Political Terrorism: A Typology," *Journal of International Affairs* (1978).
2. Mason Willrich and Theodore B. Taylor, *Nuclear Theft: Risks and Safeguards* (Cambridge, Mass: Ballinger Publishing Company, 1974); John McPhee, *The Curve of Binding Energy* (New York: Ballantine, 1974); Robert K. Mullen, *The International Clandestine Nuclear Threat, Clandestine Tactics and Technology* (Gaithersburg, MD: International Association of Chiefs of Police, 1975); *Idem, The Clandestine Use of Chemical or Biological Weapons, Clandestine Tactics and Technology* (Gaithersburg, MD: International Association of Chiefs of Police, in press).
3. Willrich and Taylor, op. cit.; McPhee, op. cit.
4. Willrich and Taylor, op. cit.
5. McPhee, op. cit.
6. Joel Larus, *Nuclear Weapons Safety and The Common Defense* (Columbus: Ohio State University Press, 1967).
7. U.S., Department of the Army, *Employment of Atomic Demolition Munitions (ADM) FM 5-26* (Washington, D.C.: Government Printing Office, 1971).
8. Jack Anderson, "Will Nuclear Weapons Fall Into The Hands of Terrorists?" *Parade,* Sept. 20, 1974; B. J. Berkowitz, et al., *Superviolence: The Civil Threat of Mass Destruction Weapons,* Adcon Corp. report A72-034010, Sept. 29, 1972 (Santa Barbara, CA: The Adcon Corp., 1972).
9. E. Langer, "Chemical and Biological Warfare," Science, 155 (1967); U.S. House of Representatives Committee on Government Operations, *Environmental Dangers of Open-Air Testing of Lethal Components* (Washington, D.C.: Government Printing Office, 1969).
10. F. Swarts, "Sur l'acide Fluoroacetique," *Bulletin of the Royal Academy, Belguim,* 31 (1896).
11. Frederick Lewis Maitland Pattison, *Toxic Aliphatic Fluorine Compounds* (New York: Elseiver, 1959).
12. Robert Thornton Morrison and Robert Neilson Boyd, *Organic Chemistry* (Boston: Allyn and Bacon, 1959).
13. Pattison, op. cit.
14. E. Chadwick, "Actions on Insects and Other Invertebrates," in *Cholineterases and Anticholinesterase Agents,* Vol. 15, *Handbuch der Experimentallen Pharmakologie,* ed. by G. E. Koelle (Berlin: Springer-Verlag, 1963).
15. "Australian Police Nab Poison-Gas Producers," *Ottawa Citizen,* March 2, 1976.
16. K. P. DuBois, "Toxicological Evaluation of the Anticholinesterase Agents," in *Cholinesterases and Anticholinesterase Agents,* Vol. 15, *Handbuch der Experimentallen Pharmakologie,* ed. by G. E. Koelle (Berlin: Springer-Verlag, 1963); D. Grob, "Anticholinesterase Intoxication in

Man and Its Treatment," in *Cholinesterases and Anticholinesterase Agents*, Vol. 15, *Handbuch der Experimentallen Pharmakologie*, ed. by G. E. Koelle (Berlin: Springer-Verlag, 1963).

17. D. F. Heath, *Organophosphorous Poisons* (New York: MacMillan, 1961).
18. U.S., Department of Health, Education and Welfare, *Clinical Handbook on Economic Poisons* (Washington, D.C.: Government Printing Office, 1967).
19. Grob, op. cit.; Heath, op. cit.
20. Stockholm International Peace Researach Institute, *The Rise of CB Weapons*, in Vol. 1, *The Problem of Chemical and Biological Warfare* (New York: Humanities Press, 1971).
21. Stockholm International Peace Research Institute, op. cit.
22. Stockholm International Peace Research Institute, op. cit.
23. Nicholas Wade, "Going Public with VX Formula—A Recipe for Trouble?" *Science*, 177 (1977).
24. Stockholm International Peace Research Institute, op. cit.
25. Stockholm International Peace Research Institute, op. cit.
26. P. J. R. Bryand, et al., "The Preparation and Physical Properties of Isopropyl Methylphosphono Fluoridate (Sarin)," *Journal of the Chemical Society (London)* (1960).
27. Bo Holmstedt, "Synthesis and Pharmacology of Dimethylamide-ethoxyphosphoryl Cyanide (Tabun)," *Acta Physiologica Scandinavica*, 25, Suppl. 50 (1952).
28. P. J. R. Bryand, op. cit.; Bo Holmstedt, op. cit.; R. Chosh and J. R. Newman, "A New Group of Organophosphorous Pesticides," cited in Berkowitz, et al., op. cit.; B. Holmstedt, "Structure-Activity Relationships of the Organophosphorous Anticholinesterase Agents," in *Cholinesterases and Anticholinesterase Agents*, Vol. 15, *Handbuch der Experimentallen Pharmakologie*, ed. by G. E. Koelle (Berlin: Springer-verlag, 1963); A. H. Ford-Moore and B. J. Perry, "Diisopropyl Methylphosponate," *Organic Synthesis*, 31 (1951); *Idem*, "Triethyl Phosphite," *Organic Synthesis*, 31 (1951).
29. Stockholm International Peace Research Institute, *The Problem of Chemical and Biological Warfare* (New York: Humanities Press, 1971).
30. Hans Rieman, "Botulinum Types A, B and F," in *Infections and Intoxications*, ed. by Hans Reiman (New York: Academic Press, 1969).
31. G. Hobbs, Kathleen Williams, and A. T. Willis, "Basic Methods for the Isolation of Clostridia," in *Isolation of Anaerobes*, ed. by D. A. Shapta and R. G. Board (New York: Academic Press, 1971).
32. Richard Dean McCarthy, *The Ultimate Folly: War by Pestilence, Asphyxiation and Defoliation* (New York: Random House, 1969).
33. I. W. Dawes and J. Mandelstam, "Biochemistry and Sporulation of Bacillus subtilis 168: Continuous Culture Studies," in *Proceedings of the Fourth International Symposium on Continuous Cultivation of Microorganisms*, ed. by I. Malek, et al. (New York: Academic Press, 1969); J. Ricica, "Sporulation of Bacillus cereus in Multi-Stage Continuous Cultivation," in *Proceedings of the Fourth International Symposium on*

Continuous Cultivation of Microorganisms, ed. by I. Malek, et al. (New York: Academic Press, 1969).

34. E. Langer, op. cit.

35. Mullen, *The International Clandestine Nuclear Threat,* op. cit.; Mullen, *The Clandestine Use of Chemical or Biological Weapons,* op. cit.

36. R. F. Phalen and O. G. Raabe, "Aerosol Particle Size as a Factor in Plutonium Toxicity," in *Proceedings of the Fifth Annual Conference on Environmental Toxicology,* Aerospace Medical Research Laboratory Report ARML-IR-125 (Wright Patterson Air Force Base, Sept. 24, 1974).

37. U.S., Atomic Energy Commission, *Liquid Metal Fast Breeder Reactor Program Environmental Statement, WASH-1535,* Appendix II-g (Washington, D.C.: Government Printing Office).

38. Phalen and Raabe, op. cit.; National Academy of Sciences/National Research Council, *Health Effects of Alpha-Emitting Particles in the Respiratory Tract,* Report to the Environmental Protection Agency, EPA 520/4-76-013, 1976 (Washington, D.C.: Environmental Protection Agency, 1976); D.S. Myers, "The Biological Hazard and Measurement of Plutonium," in *Proceedings, Radiological Defense Officers Conference* (Lake Tahoe, CA: California Governor's Office of Emergency Services, 1974).

39. J. F. Park, W. J. Blair, and R. H. Busch, "Progress in Beagle Dog Studies and Transuranium Elements at Battelle-Northwest," *Health Physics,* 22 (1972).

40. Thomas M. Conrad, "Do-it-Yourself A-Bombs," *Commonweal,* July, 1969; Aland M. Adelson, "Please Don't Steal the Atomic Bomb," *Esquire,* May, 1969; Lowell Ponte, "Better Do As We Say: This is an Atom Bomb and We're not Fooling," *Penthouse,* Feb., 1972; *Idem.* "The Danger of Terrorists Getting Illicit A-Bombs," *Los Angeles Times,* April 25, 1976; Robert A. Jones, "Nuclear Terror Peril Likely to Increase," *Los Angeles Times,* April 25, 1976.

41. P. A. Karber, et al., "Analysis of the Terrorist Threat to the Commercial Nuclear Industry," *Draft Working Paper B, Summary of Findings,* Report to the U.S. Nuclear Regulatory Commission, THE BDM Corp. Report BDM/W-75-176-TR (Vienna, VA: The BDM Corp., Sept., 1975); Miliaglo Mesarovic and Eduard Pestal, *Mankind at the Turning Point* (New York: E. P. Dutton, 1974); Brian Jenkins, *International Terrorism: A New Kind of Warfare,* Rand Corp. paper P-5261 (Santa Monica, CA: Rand Corp., June, 1974).

42. Brian Jenkins, "Will Terrorists go Nuclear?" (paper presented at California Seminar on Atomic Control and Foreign Policy, November, 1975); Roberta A. Wohlstetter, "Terror on a Grand Scale," *Survival,* 18 (1976); Bernard L. Cohen, "The Potentialities of Terrorism" (Mimeographed); Eric D. Shaw, et al., "Analyzing Threats from Terrorism," CACI-Inc., April, 1976 (Mimeographed).

43. H. R. Simpson, "Terror," *U.S. Naval Institute Proceedings,* 96 (1970).

44. N. Leites and C. Wolf, Jr., *Rebellion and Authority: An Analytic Essay on Insurgent Conflicts* (Chicago: Markham Publishing Company, 1970).

45. Wohlstetter, op. cit.

46. Wohlstetter, op. cit.

47. Brian Crozier, *Survey of Terrorism and Political Violence,* Annual of Power and Conflict, 1972-1973 (London: Institute of the Study of Conflict, 1973); Richard Clutterbuck, *Living with Terrorism* (London: Faber & Faber, 1975).

48. C. A. Russell, "Transnational Terrorism," *Air University Review,* 27 (1976); D. L. Milbank, *International and Transnational Terrorism: Diagnosis and Prognosis,* Central Intelligence Agency report PR 76 10031 (Washington, D.C.: Government Printing Office, 1976); S. Burnham, ed., *The Threat of Licensed Nuclear Facilities,* Report to the U.S. Nuclear Regulatory Commission, The Mitre Corporation report MTR-7022 (McLean, VA: The Mitre Corp., 1975).

49. Russell, op. cit.

50. Milbank, op. cit.; Burnham, op. cit.

51. Burnham, op. cit.; "2 Missiles Threaten Israeli Embassy," *Washington Post,* Dec. 13, 1977; "Philippine Terrorists Hit Oil Storage Tank," *Washington Post,* Dec. 13, 1977.

52. Charles A. Russell, Leon J. Baker, Jr., and Bowman H. Miller, "Out-Inventing the Terrorist" (paper presented at Terrorism Conference, Evian, France, June, 1977).

53. "Chicago Pair with Plot to Poison Midwest Water Supply," *Los Angeles Times,* Jan 19, 1972.

54. *Ottawa Citizen,* op. cit.

55. "Terrorist Use of Gas Feared," *Washington Post,* April 13, 1975.

56. Berkowitz, et al., op. cit.

57. Robert H. Kupperman, "Crisis Management: Some Opportunities," *Science,* 187 (1975); *Idem,* "Treating the Symptoms of Terrorism: Some Principles of Good Hygiene," *Terrorism,* 1 (1977).

Augustus R. Norton

Nuclear Terrorism and the Middle East

The Middle East is an often-mentioned setting for nuclear terrorism, with the fedayeen *(Palestinian terrorists) cited as the likely perpetrators. In this selection, Norton investigates the Middle Eastern case, with particular emphasis on the acquisition of nuclear weapons, the motivation for doing so, and considerations of threat effectuation. He finds a lack of motivation among the most technically capable* fedayeen *and a number of heretofore unrecognized problems for the terrorist bent on carrying out an act of nuclear terrorism.*

We live in a world in which yesterday's fantasy may well be destined to become today's or tomorrow's reality. The prospect of a nuclear explosive device in the hands of a subnational group and its subsequent use in an act of nuclear terror may be such a contemporary fantasy.[1] However, as with so many other posited consequences of nuclear proliferation, the specter of nuclear terrorism may be more frightening than its midterm probability. The purpose of this essay will be to discuss unemotionally the conditions which must be met or overcome by the prospective practitioner and to focus upon a subnational grouping which is considered a prospective perpetrator by some. Considered in this regard are the radical Palestinians—the *fedayeen*.[2] In the context of the Arab-Israeli zone and beyond, the *fedayeen* have earned a reputation as terrorists willing to make the ultimate sacrifice in the interest of effectuating their ultimate objective—the defeat of Jewish nationalism (that is, Zionism) and the establishment of the Palestinian state. After considering procurement conditions and tactical considerations below, this article will address "nuclear terror" as it may be applied in the Middle East by various (but not all) Palestinian organizations and, finally, the utility of nuclear vis-à-vis chemical or biological weapons.

II

There are doubtless few informed persons in the contemporary world who are naive enough to deny the existence of individuals or groups willing to resort to nuclear terrorism. Needless to say, however, the mere existence of such elements does not prove the case at hand. In order to justify the modifier "nuclear," nuclear terrorists must possess, or at least appear to possess, a nuclear explosive device (or perhaps a plutonium dispersal device).[3] This qualifier implies critical questions of access, capability and technical expertise. The possession threshold may be crossed by various methods, each with intrinsic advantages and disadvantages for the terrorist. A discussion of possession options follows:

The first and most obvious option is the theft of a device intact. A group lacking the expertise, funds or facilities with which to fabricate a device could well view theft as the only available means of procurement. The target of such a theft could be any of the several storage facilities in Western Europe or, though less likely, in the United States. Since free access to, and movement within, the countries involved would be a prerequisite, storage sites in the Soviet Union and the People's Republic of China are dismissed out-of-hand as relatively secure from the threat of nuclear theft.

U.S. tactical nuclear weapons present an interesting target for the terrorist. Certain of such weapons are compact with yields in the low and sub-kiloton (KT) range. The smaller varieties are projectiles intended for use with the standard 155mm howitzer. In the case of the smaller devices, they are easily handled by two men, or even by one strong man. Such weapons are reasonably efficient, although at the lower yields the radiation effects tend to dominate, while the larger yield weapons are more significant in their blast effects. In any event, the smaller weapons would enable the terrorist to be reasonably selective in terms of limiting collateral damage and precluding excessive innocent deaths. Such a tack, however, would entail penetrating the overt and passive defenses maintained by the United States and allied armed forces. Thus, seizing a complete device could well require a sizable quasi-military force with adequate weaponry, sophisticated mobility and an accurate intelligence-gathering apparatus. Once captured, the device even then might not be operational due to permissive action link (PAL) security devices which prevent the weapon from detonating in a nuclear mode, or from being successfully disassembled to remove the nuclear material. On balance, the possibility of the theft of a complete device would seem quite unlikely. In contrast to the other possession options, theft would be the option most easily discouraged by the United States since increasing security levels would directly affect the size and type of force adequate to the task.

III

A second method of crossing the threshold to procurement would be the theft of fissionable materials (that is, weapons grade material which may be used directly for a fission explosive device without resort to complex isotope separation procedures or chemical processing) or materials usable subsequent to chemical processing or isotope separation. In the first case, a competent physicist or perhaps a team of physicists and technicians might, in time, be capable of assembling a device using the unclassified literature available on the subject; at least such is the assertion of several of the publicizers of the threat.[4] Fortunately, however, procuring fissionable materials could prove far more difficult than stealing a device intact. Despite hyperbole to the contrary, acceptable materials are simply not readily available for the taking. With the exception of the high temperature gas reactor,[5] there is not a commercial reactor in current or projected use which utilizes weapons grade material. By the same token, and despite public belief to the contrary, there is not a reactor in current or projected use which produces fission explosive materials directly employable in a weapon without processing. The universe of possibilities is not exhausted, however, since weapons grade materials are available in the various centralized national weapons fabrication points. Since security measures at such locations, whether in the United States, the U.S.S.R., France or China, are obviously highly classified, one can only conjecture that the theft of materials from such a location would be at least as difficult as the seizure of an intact device.

A more serious danger, and the crux of the Willrich and Taylor thesis, is the prospect of the theft of materials from points within the reactor fuel cycle which, through various methods of processing, may be used in fission weapons. While there are technical and physical barriers complicating this approach, it must be considered a major security problem in light of anticipated reactor proliferation.[6] As with the proverbial chain, man's security against nuclear blackmail and terror will only be as strong as the least secure facility. It should be noted at this juncture, however, that the potential for such an occurrence is a future prospect rather than a present danger since its likelihood turns on the advent of reprocessing facilities and, later, the introduction of the breeder reactor. A summary elucidation of the light water reactor (LWR)—currently the most popular reactor type—fuel cycle is useful in understanding the dangers and the vulnerabilities.

The LWR uses fuel in the form of low-enriched uranium[7] which is contained in pellet form in fuel rods which are, in turn, combined to form fuel assemblies. A typical LWR will contain from 220 to 450 kilograms of low-enriched uranium, depending upon the variety of LWR. However, stealing the low-enriched uranium either prior to fuel fabrication or in pellet form in the fuel rods would still leave the thief with the awesome task of enrichment. Even if this monetary and technical barrier could be overcome, the enrichment process requires a facility of such scale that it would be hard to camouflage for the several months that the process requires, not to mention the construction time in preparation for enrichment which must be measured in multiples of months.

The reactor produces waste in the form of irradiated fuel which is contained in spent fuel rods. After removal from the reactor, the irradiated fuel undergoes a cooling period which lasts up to six months. The irradiated fuel is highly radioactive and extremely dangerous to handle. It is for all intents and purposes self-protective during the cooling period. Since one of the by-products of the fission process is plutonium 239—which was used successfully in the Nagasaki bomb—it is highly desirable from an economic and conservation standpoint that the irradiated fuel be reprocessed to separate out the plutonium which will then function as a substitute for a portion of the relatively scarce uranium in the fuel assembly. At the present time, there are no reprocessing facilities in operation in the United States and only a handful abroad; accordingly, irradiated fuel is being held in storage in anticipation of reprocessing.[8]

The reprocessing facilities will not produce plutonium in a form which the bomb manufacturer can use with certitude. Instead, the initial product will be plutonium nitrate which cannot sustain a fission reaction and is, therefore, not directly usable in an explosive assembly. The nitrate is, in turn, further processed to form the compound plutonium oxide. Whether the oxide will sustain a fission reaction long enough to provide explosive force is currently a matter of contentious debate within the scientific community. However, the possibility is strong enough that the plutonium oxide must be safeguarded to the same degree as plutonium metal—the bomb-making material. It is the oxide which will be used in reactors; there is no technical requirement for further processing the plutonium.

Needless to add, the potential terrorist gaining a quantity of the nitrate or the oxide could complete the processing to derive plutonium metal. While plutonium is extremely hazardous to handle, it is likely that the terrorist would settle for far less stringent safety precautions than prudence would call for and complete the processing. Alternately, the terrorist could assume that the plutonium oxide would serve his purposes and fashion a crude fission device that at least Willrich and Taylor believe will work.

Since readily usable active materials are not in transit or especially vulnerable at the present, the risk in the short term appears minimal. As reprocessing facilities come on line in this country and multiply abroad, the threat greatly increases. While the materials are self-protecting at some stages of the fuel cycle and of little utility at others, there are several critical points at which they must be zealously safeguarded. There can be little doubt that nations blessed with stable political environments and an awareness of the problem may institute the requisite security measures. If there is to be a real risk of nuclear terror, however, it will exist in nations not so fortuitously endowed. The recently announced sale of a complete fuel cycle to Brazil by Germany and the possibility of similar purchases by Argentina accent the problem.

Finally, the prospective nuclear terrorist will strike where the tools of his trade are most accessible. Therefore, the institution of increased safeguards must be an international rather than intranational endeavor.

IV

If the procurement opportunities for nuclear terrorists were limited to theft, it would be relatively simple to protect against the hazard merely by improving fuel cycle and weapons storage security. Unfortunately, the state system is replete with hostility and antagonism, and it is not at all inconceivable that fission explosive materials, or even an assembled weapon, can and may be furnished by a state actor. There would be a certain logic to such an act, especially if the transfer was intended to achieve some political end which the donor state could not achieve within its own resources.

The diversion of materials is not precluded, even by the International Atomic Energy Agency (IAEA) safeguards. The acceptance of a negotiated safeguard agreement with the IAEA is normally the *sine qua non* for international reactor sales. As many authorities have taken pains to establish, the IAEA procedures primarily function as an alert system to warn of a suspected—but not necessarily established—diversion. It is a political deter- mination on the part of the nuclear weapons states (NWS) as to what action will be taken if diversion *seems* to have occurred.

As will all international agreements, the IAEA safeguards contain a fair quota of loopholes. One gaping loophole is that a state could report the theft of materials to mask the transfer of materials. In such a situation, the probable action of NWS and other reactor suppliers could well be to demand that the state in question tighten its security after the fact. As with the barn, the horses would have already escaped. It is even possible that materials could be diverted and escape detection through the loophole known as the MUF (materials unaccounted for). The MUF is a percentage measure of the amount of materials which may be lost in the system. As Ryukichi Imai has stressed in his monograph, nuclear weapons are constructed from absolute amounts of fissionable materials rather than proportionate measures.[9] However, to hold a reactor to an MUF smaller than the amount of fissionable material needed to assemble one critical mass would impose far too stringent accounting standards. Therefore, a nation could divert adequate materials for the one or two weapons that would be needed to supply the nuclear terrorists and escape detection. Since a state could hardly be expected to claim meaningful nuclear weapons status on the basis of such a piddling arsenal, it could in this manner establish itself as a weapons power by proxy without increasing its vulnerability to the major nuclear powers.

While the diversion of fuel rods or irradiated fuel is relatively meaningless without the ancillary reprocessing or enrichment facilities, the events of the past two years have established that nations are content to disregard the laws of nuclear economics in favor of national chauvinism as expressed by the possession of the complete fuel cycle. While the purchase and construction of complete fuel cycles are uneconomical for states with a handful of reactors, both India and Brazil have emphasized the weight which developing nations assign to elements of national power and prestige. The sad result is the brutal fact that a nation capable of processing its own fuel also has the ingredients for nuclear weapons.

There are negative considerations for any nonnuclear weapons state (NNWS) or NWS which may consider providing materials or devices to a subnational group. Most obviously, relationships must be extremely stable to preclude the use of the weapon against the benefactor. Furthermore, any such state would have to be invulnerable to a meaningful retaliatory attack by the victim, or, alternately, the transfer would have to occur under the highest conditions of secrecy and without the possibility of an ex post facto link to the supplier. Naturally, there may be several states willing to accept retribution in the interest of a perceived higher cause. There are not many states which fill the latter category, but it only takes one.

A serious possibility in the Middle East is Libya under Gaddafi's leadership. Colonel Gaddafi has publicly expressed his willingness to buy a bomb, and he has displayed the requisite level of irrationality. On 2 June 1975, the sale of a 2-megawatt reactor to Libya by the Soviet Union was announced by the Arab Revolutionary News Agency in Tripoli. Significantly, part of the price extracted by the Soviet Union was ratification of the nonproliferation treaty,[10] but that does not prevent Libya from utilizing the loopholes assuming it also builds reprocessing facilities. Adding to the potential seriousness of the situation are the close links which Gaddafi has forged with the Palestinian rejection front. Hopefully, the possibility that a weapon would, in fact, be used by a movement like the rejection front would militate against even Gaddafi providing the weapon or materials.

Perhaps the most forceful argument against the provision of a nuclear device or fissionable materials to a subnational group would be the awesome precedent it would establish. All but the ethnically homogeneous states must pay heed to such a precedent.

In the section which follows, the identification of Palestinian elements which may be candidates for utilizing nuclear terrorism is established.

V

It is the contention of this writer that the numerous elements that are collectively subsumed under the term *"fedayeen"* are too often glibly viewed as monolithic. That the *fedayeen* are of anything but one mind is important to this discussion since resources and intraregional and extraregional support varies widely between the organizations; therefore, the probability of successful implementation of nuclear terrorism also varies. Two important variables distinguish the groups which are prone to such tactics from those which are not: first, the perceived prospect of a settlement in the Middle East including an Israeli state; and, second, the degree of change that must be evinced in the social structure of the Arab world for the respective movement to achieve its proclaimed objectives.

These two variables roughly distinguish those groups or groupings which are potential nuclear terrorists from those which are not. The groups which are loosely led by Yasir Arafat within the Palestine Liberation Organization (PLO)[11] fall within the latter category. The Arafat bloc has evidenced a degree of moderation not present in the more extreme groups. Certainly, any indications or signals of PLO (potential) moderation must be viewed in the shadow of the Savoy Hotels and Nahariyas that dot the landscape of the conflict. Yet Arafat and his followers are in a rather tenuous position in that they are vulnerable to threats from the Right and the Left by various *fedayeen* and theocratic organizations. Expectations of conciliatory statements are both unrealistic and devoid of a clear understanding of the Palestinian political milieu. Arafat and his fellow travelers must play to several audiences, and the script is concerned with an issue that has great and fundamental emotive appeal in the Arab world—thus, an inherent explosiveness which must not be ignored. The precarious position of Arafat makes him vulnerable to preemption, as it does others within the PLO leadership. Ergo, the exclusion of such a grouping from the potential nuclear terrorist categorization is subject to change, indeed rapid change at that. However, the exclusion, albeit temporary, is important since the PLO is by far the richest revolutionary movement in the world today,[12] the broadest based in terms of Arab state support and quite large in comparison to contending groups. [13]

The opposition to the PLO is provided by the so-called "rejection front" [14] which views any settlement entailing the existence of Israel as tantamount to surrender. This all-or-nothing mentality is personified in George Habbash, the leader of the Popular Front for the Liberation of Palestine, who believes that only through a complete social revolution in the Arab world may the Palestinian state be achieved. The rejection front views war with Israel as preferable to self-defined surrender of the struggle implied by the acceptance of Israel. Habbash and his followers share this analysis with Colonel Gaddafi. Assumedly, a war resultant of nuclear provocation would be more desirable than an unacceptable settlement or no settlement at all. Habbash, for example, has been quoted as follows:

> We want and look forward anxiously to a new war. . . . A new war is no danger to the Palestinian people. They can't suffer any worse than they have since the 1948 creation of Israel on their homeland.[15]

VI

Possessing a nuclear device could enable a subnational group to attempt to gain some political objective from its weapon or weapons, but mere possession will not ensure the success of the venture. There are critical tactical considerations which must be addressed, reconciled and, in some cases, overcome by the nuclear terrorist. By the same token, it behooves the potential victim to understand these considerations and to use them to his advantage if the time comes. Prominent among these tactical considerations are matters of threat credibility, security, delivery and target selection.

If the perpetrators seek to achieve some end beyond destruction of materiel or personnel per se, the threat to employ a nuclear explosive device must above all be credible. (If the objective is solely wanton destruction—that is, terror for terror's sake—then prior notice is unnecessary and even counterproductive.) Assuming the objective is a political or military concession by the victim, then the credibility of the threat becomes all important. Threat credibility may be enhanced as follows:

Since the theft of a weapon intact appears to be the only method by which the existence of the weapon could be conclusively established,[16] it would probably be necessary to convince the victim that a weapon does exist. Three methods of proof are apparent: First, the terrorists could allow the weapon to be examined, especially by an individual technically competent to pronounce on its effectiveness. The individual(s) would have to be known as both technically able and at least politically neutral reference the issue or issues at hand. While this method presents the fewest problems in terms of delivery, it presents the gravest security problems since the location of at least the sample could be compromised. Thus, as with the second and third options, the terrorist group would have to maintain a second weapon, or seem to, in a separate safe locale and be willing to accept retaliation both against the organization(s) and the country in which the sample was being maintained should compromise occur.

The second and third methods would be to detonate a demonstration weapon. These two methods vary as to the selection of target only. The weapon could be harmlessly detonated, perhaps in the Sinai in the Middle Eastern case, or it could be deployed against a materiel or personnel target for symbolic effect. In the former case, a movement concerned with "world public opinion" could temper the outcry while dramatically proving the validity of its threat. In the latter case, the loss of life and property would convincingly prove the group's resolve to employ a nuclear device ruthlessly. Naturally, the third method could well strengthen the resolve of the victim to retaliate, perhaps in kind. As a further complication, and applicable to the Middle East especially, each step to enhance threat credibility would increase the risk of states punitively preempting to prevent the eruption of a wider conflict.

Less dramatic, although much safer, would be the use of a graphic representation of a nuclear device. Such a method could well be convincing if used subsequent to the discovery that fissionable materials had been diverted or stolen. This method would not be appropriate if the active materials obtained required reprocessing not within the apparent capability of the movement. It is quite possible that a threat validated by graphic representation could result in a successful act of secret blackmail though for far lower stakes than one might envisage for the other methods. Thus, the conceding state could avoid a public announcement that it "caved," while the terrorist group could maintain its base of international support, especially where the support is contingent upon peaceful vis-à-vis armed struggle.

While nuclear blackmail, should it ever occur, will open a Pandora's box of horrors for the state actors of the world, it also makes the perpetrating group extremely vulnerable. It would become obvious to many that a group engaging in atomic terror is a threat to humanity and must be eliminated. Thus, the subnational must be doubly conscious of the security of its nuclear device or devices. Should the nuclear capability be destroyed or captured, the offending group will have lost its only meaningful defense. Security is a complex concern in this context since the weapon or weapons must be secure from direct or indirect preemption.

Direct preemption may be defined as the capture or destruction of the device by forces of the threatened state or a state that may be subject to retributive action as a direct result of the threat. Indirect preemption is defined as the application of coercive pressure, short of force, by the tacit or formal allies of the terrorists. Such pressure could be either the result of unacceptable risks or abhorrence of the precedent. For indirect preemption to succeed, the group would have to perceive its political future as bleaker should it carry out its threat rather than reneging.

Adequate security would require that the weapon(s) location be secret, or its means of delivery sufficiently mobile to preclude its detection. Alternately, the weapon could be maintained at a known location on the territory of a secure sponsor. In which case, the blackmail would be little more than a proxy act on behalf of the sponsoring state and qualitatively outside the realm of this discussion.

Implicit throughout this discussion is the capability of the terrorist group to deliver a device both to the demonstration site, if appropriate, and to the threatened locale. Since the type of weapons under discussion are of a relatively crude variety and not of the same genre as the sophisticated and compact weapons in the superpowers' arsenal, the devices will be of low yield and be relatively awkward. The configuration of missile warheads or nuclear artillery rounds is dismissed out-of-hand as beyond the capability of the fledgling bomb manufacturer. The more likely means of delivery will be a truck or cargo-type aircraft. Fortunately, both are prone to early detections, especially in the Israeli context.

It is with delivery considerations that the nuclear terrorist faces the most difficult choices. He will have no easy answer and will be most prone to detection and failure at this postprocurement stage.

To maximize limited radii of destruction, the weapon(s) must be either precision-delivered (which seems not to be possible) or delivered against a target large enough to make discrimination unnecessary. Considering the security-conscious Israelis, the easy choice may be to choose a target abroad (for example, a major Israeli embassy), but this raises the possibility of politically unfavorable collateral damage. Within the state of Israel, target disirability will tend to be proportional to increasing security, so the terrorist may be forced to choose a relatively insignificant target minimizing the impact of the threat and the act should it occur while still establishing the same perhaps self-destructive precedent. Once again, and fortunately, the terrorist would have no easy answers.

VII

Logically considered, any subnational group seeking the publicity and success that would seem possible with nuclear terrorism could readily turn to other sensational weapons which could easily duplicate, if not exceed, the potential of crude nuclear devices.

Specifically, the terrorist could choose biological or chemical weapons which are relatively simple to produce, require laboratory facilities far smaller than nuclear weapons and are far easier to deliver. Technology for their development is available, and costs are relatively low. The biological and chemical weapons offer a spectrum of effects which would allow the terrorist to be relatively selective in impact and to avoid the destruction of property. Most ominously, such weapons would be impossible to defend against for any meaningful period of time, and their use would be most difficult to detect before symptoms had time to appear. The point is not to promote the use of such weapons in lieu of atomic bombs, but to assert that the potential for their use has been there for some time. Yet they have not been used and for good reason. Any such weapon is not unilateral; retaliation is to be expected. The threat of retaliation, coupled with the moral constraints which characterize all but the most base of conflicts, have prevented their use to date.

While the prospect of successful nuclear terrorism in the Middle East or elsewhere is not a wholesome or reassuring thought, it appears far less likely to occur than the alarmists have led the public to believe. That is not to say that the alarmists have not provided a service, for indeed they have raised an issue which has increased the security consciousness of the American atomic energy establishment. However, it is interesting to note that the subject of nuclear weaponry in the Middle East has received little play in the Palestinian press and journals except in response to periodic reports of Israeli nuclear capability. In fact, the first major article to appear in recent years on the subject of illicit atom bomb production was an interview with Theodore Taylor that appeared in the Cairo daily, *Al-Ahram,* in early 1975. Sometimes, the genie must be pushed out of the bottle.

Notes

1. See especially Mason Willrich and Theodore B. Taylor, *Nuclear Theft: Risks and Safeguards,* Ballinger Publishing Co., Cambridge, MA, 1974, especially Chapters 2 and 6.
2. Several other Middle Eastern subnational movements may be candidates for employing "nuclear terror" as well, although the relative resources, capabilities and fiscal liquidity of non-*fedayeen* groups make the prospect less reasonable. For example, the South Yemenite-sponsored Popular Front of the Liberation of Oman and the Arab Gulf and remnants of the defeated Kurdish movement are possibilities. To a degree, the discussion which follows will apply to these and other such groups as well.
3. Willrich and Taylor, *op. cit.* p. 25, posit the following for example: "one hundred grams (three and one-half ounces) of this material could be a deadly risk to everyone working in a large office building or factory, if it were effectively dispersed."
4. *Ibid.,* especially Chapter 2.
5. The high temperature gas reactor will not see extensive use until post-1980, if then. By 1980, there will be five in operation in the United States based on current projections.
6. As many as 236 reactors may be operational in the United States by 1985 according to a report in the *New York Times* 29 June 1975.
7. That is, uranium which has been enriched to 2 to 3-percent U-235 (Uranium 235). In nature, uranium is typically composed of .7-percent U-235 and 99.3 percent U-238 which is not usable as a weapon. Uranium enriched to weapons garde contains 90 percent or more U-235. The enrichment process currently in use is highly complex and conducted at massive scale. The process known as gaseous diffusion is quite expensive with facilities in the billion-

dollar range. A less expensive system, the centrifuge, is technically more complex. Recently, the use of laser technology for enrichment has received wide play in the scientific community. However, the technique is still in its very early stages, with the Soviet Union and the United States announcing in April 1975 that it has worked at experimental scale. (The Israelis have a patent on a system using parallel technology.)

8. Due to a recent Nuclear Regulatory Commission (NRC) decision, a facility in Barnwell, South Carolina, will not come on line until 1978. The Barnwell facility will then be the only operating reprocessing plant in the United States although others are in various stages of planning, construction or redsign. The NRC decision was apparently prompted by the security concerns which underlie the current controversy. See, for example, *The Christian Science Monitor,* 23 June 1975.

9. Ryukichi Imai, *Nuclear Safeguards, Adelphi Papers,* Number 86, The International Institute for Strategic Studies, London, Eng., March 1972, pp.16 and 34.

10. Reported in the Arab Press Service (Washington) *Middle East Recorder,* June 1975, serial numbers 308 and 311, and Associated Press dispatch, 5 June 1975. The *Middle East Recorder* reports that the reactor may be later expanded to a 10-megawatt capacity (compare the Israeli reactor at Dimona which has a 6-megawatt capacity).

11. The Palestine Liberation Organization (PLO) is presently composed of *Al Fatah, Al Saiqah* and the Popular Democratic Front for the Liberation of Palestine.

12. The Arab Summit Conference at Rabat (1974) endowed the PLO with a yearly grant of $50 million.

13. Total strength of *fedayeen* organizations within the PLO may run as high as 20,000 as compared with a maximum of 5000 members for the rejection front.

14. The rejection front is composed of the Popular Front for the Liberation of Palestine, the Popular Front for the Liberation of Palestine—General Command and the Arab Liberation Front.

15. Cited in *The New York Times,* 12 February 1975.

16. U.S. "tactical" nuclear weapons carry a classified Federal serial number; therefore, competing claims of possession by several groups could be resolved by demanding the Federal serial number be provided.

Nuclear Energy Policy Study Group*

Nuclear Terrorism

This selection is from the comprehensive study, Nuclear Power: Issues and Choices, *sponsored by the Ford Foundation. Although concerned about inadequacies in the physcial security of nuclear reactors in this country and abroad, the authors find that the difficulties involved with designing, planning and constructing a nuclear weapon from reactor grade materials are considerable. Such a project would entail many months of well-planned efforts, with the attendant health risks and the final possibility that the device would not detonate. They find fewer problems for the terrorist bent on blowing up a nuclear reactor, although they point to some keen survival risks for the potential perpetrators.*

The past few years have seen an upsurge in the size, sophistication, and capabilities of terrorist groups around the world. Terrorist activities offer strongly motivated political or dissident groups a way to dramatize their causes and influence their adversaries. Modern communications enable terrorists to project their messages widely. Weapons of increasing sophistication are available to terrorists, including automatic weapons, modern high explosives, and even rockets and antiaircraft missiles.

For some years the possibility has existed that terrorists might attempt to steal nuclear weapons. The worldwide development of civilian nuclear power provides additional opportunities for terrorists—whether revolutionaries, nationalists, dissidents, or criminally motivated—to employ nuclear energy as a weapon. One is to acquire, from somewhere in the nuclear fuel cycle, the material with which to fashion a simple nuclear explosive. The second is to

*Spurgeon M. Keeny, Jr. (chairman), Seymour Abrahamson, Kenneth J. Arrow, Harold Brown, Albert Carnesale, Abram Chayes, Hollis B. Chenery, Paul Doty, Philip J. Farley, Richard L. Garwin, Marvin L. Goldberger, Carl Kaysen, Hans H. Landsberg, Gordon J. MacDonald, Joseph S. Nye, Wolfgang K. H. Panofsky, Howard Raiffa, George W. Rathjens, John C. Sawhill, Thomas C. Schelling, and Arthur Upton.

use a reactor itself as a potential radiation weapon, by threatening to take actions leading to core meltdown and breach of containment.

Terrorists might choose the nuclear industry as a target to exploit the mystique that surrounds nuclear energy and nuclear weapons. The threat of nuclear terrorism may be used to extort money, secure the release of prisoners, or publicize a particular cause. Whether terrorists are actually in a position to carry out their threats is probably less important than their plausibility. A group may be able to achieve its objectives with a hoax such as the one perpetrated by an Orlando, Florida, teenager whose claim to have a bomb was taken seriously for a time by local officials.

Some incidents have already occurred. In 1973, the Argentine Atucha reactor was temporarily occupied during its construction by a Trotskyist urban guerrilla group. In separate 1975 incidents, bombs were detonated at French nuclear plants at Fessenheim and Mt. D'Arree by as yet unidentified groups. In 1974, a meteorological tower at a proposed nuclear reactor site in Massachusetts was toppled by a saboteur protesting the proposed plant. On the other hand, no terrorists have yet credibly claimed to possess stolen nuclear materials, and no actual weapons have been stolen during a military coup, although U.S. nuclear weapons were located in Greece at the time of two successive military revolts.

The implications of terrorism are international in scope. Nuclear materials might be stolen in one country, fabricated into a weapon in a second, and used to threaten a third, in different parts of the world. Precipitation of a nuclear incident anywhere in the world could affect public acceptance of nuclear power in many countries. Radioactive clouds would not halt at national borders. The security of nuclear facilities everywhere is therefore of interest to the United States.

The possibility of nuclear terrorism poses difficult questions. What can the United States do, and what is it worth to keep nongovernmental groups from possession of nuclear weapons or materials? How should the United States respond to the threat or occurrence of terrorism? What legal and constitutional issues are thereby raised?

Decisions about civilian nuclear policy have an important bearing on the terrorist problem. If plutonium is not recycled, the opportunities for plutonium theft in civilian industry are essentially eliminated. Similarly, if the high temperature gas-cooled reactor is not commercialized, the amount of highly enriched uranium in commerce will be very small. Technologies which introduce weapons-grade materials into commerce are clearly undesirable from a security viewpoint.

As presently operated, the security system even in the American nuclear industry does not appear adequate to meet the potential threat of terrorism. Measures to strengthen security, at the local, national, and international levels, need to be carefully developed and vigorously carried out.

This chapter addresses the security of civilian nuclear facilities and those nuclear materials (i.e., plutonium, highly enriched uranium-235 and uranium-233) that might be used by terrorists to make weapons. It addresses theft of materials, the vulnerability of reactors to terrorist attacks, technical and institutional problems in prevention of terrorism, and the constitutional implications of governmental action in response to the terrorist threat. . . .

Theft of Nuclear Materials

Criminal or terrorist groups might seek to obtain nuclear materials to construct a crude nuclear explosive or conceivably to use the materials as radiological poisons.

The potential sources of such materials in the United States are under strict government control. These include government facilities for the production of highly enriched uranium and plutonium, and a handful of licensed commercial facilities involved in the transportation, storage, and use of materials in research, and in the nuclear weapons and nuclear submarine programs. Nuclear materials suitable for weapons are not now available in the commercial market and do not flow in commercial channels. Decisions on plutonium recycle, the future of the breeder, and construction of other reactors of all types have important implications for increasing or decreasing the opportunities available to unauthorized groups of individuals to gain access to dangerous nuclear materials.

Adequate security at U.S. sites alone will not eliminate the threat. If nuclear materials are in commerce in any country, their security will be of concern to the United States. It may prove simpler for terrorists to steal materials in one country and use them to threaten another.

AVAILABILITY OF FISSIONABLE MATERIALS

The vulnerability of nuclear installations to the theft or capture of materials by terrorist groups depends on the reactor types and the fuel cycles in use. The low-enriched uranium used in most commercial power reactors cannot be made to explode or be fashioned into a radiological weapon. Theft of spent fuel is also unlikely since it is extremely radioactive and can be handled only with special shielding and equipment. The heavy casks (30-100 tons) in which it is shipped further complicate theft. Thus, with the nuclear power technology presently in use and under construction in the United States, the danger of terrorist bombs from stolen American materials is minimal.

Plutonium reprocessing and recycle would increase the opportunities for theft. In a reprocessing or mixed oxide fuel fabrication plant, large quantities of plutonium will be on hand. Because of time lags and uncertainties in the inventory measurement system, employees might be able to steal small quantities of materials over an extended period without arousing suspicion. (To get the materials out of the plant, the thieves would also have to evade existing security systems including sensors capable of detecting small quantities of nuclear materials.) Another possibility is forcible theft by outside groups. Under current NRC security procedures and industrial practice, one cannot have confidence in the ability of plant security personnel to defend against a well-armed group until help arrives.

The LMFBR would pose problems like those of plutonium recycle for LWRs, but with much greater quantities and higher concentrations of plutonium. Less than 100 kilograms of fresh LMFBR fuel would yield enough plutonium oxide for an explosive.

An HTGR fuel plant would use large quantities of highly enriched uranium. But once fabricated into the HTGR fuel stacks, the uranium is highly dilute (about 0.4 percent by weight) and difficult to separate for use.

With plutonium fuels, or high enriched uranium, the weakest link in security would be transportation. A dispersed national and international nuclear industry will have large flows of nuclear materials within nations and across national borders. In addition to flows in military and experimental programs, terrorist targets could include shipments of highly enriched uranium from enrichment plants to fuel fabrication plants, shipments of highly enriched uranium or mixed oxide fuel from fuel fabrication plants to reactor sites, and shipments from reprocessing plants to storage sites and fuel fabrication plants.

In 1969-72, several incidents occurred in the United States where shipments of nuclear materials were misrouted in transit, lost for periods of time, or delivered to the wrong facilities. As a result, the AEC tightened regulations governing their transport (Title 10, Code of Federal Regulations, Section 73.30). These regulations apply to shipments of enriched uranium-233 and plutonium larger than two kilograms and highly enriched uranium-235 in quantities of five kilograms or more. There are no security procedures for shipment of smaller quantities of nuclear materials.

The 1973 revisions to transport regulations reduced the likelihood of, for example, a lone truck driver diverting a shipment of nuclear materials. The use of two-man driver teams, escorts, regular check-ins en route, etc., have reduced considerably the probability of employee theft in transportation. The regulatory changes did not eliminate the possibility that a small armed group could successfully hold up a truck and hijack its load of nuclear materials.

Neither the NRC nor any other federal agency directly regulates the carriers and transporters of commercial nuclear materials. NRC requirements are levied upon licensees who, in turn, have responsibility for assuring that common carriers and contract shippers meet the NRC standards. Transport procedures are not vastly different from those employed by armored car companies and other carriers that ship high-value cargo. Some criminal and terrorist groups have already demonstrated capabilities to defeat such precautions.[1]

CLANDESTINE FABRICATION OF WEAPONS

To fabricate nuclear weapons a terrorist group would have to obtain either plutonium or highly enriched uranium. The plutonium would have to be obtained in the form of metal or plutonium oxide since separation of plutonium from irradiated fuel would almost certainly be beyond the capabilities of a small group. Separate plutonium will only become accessible in commercial channels if plutonium is reprocessed and recycled.

The difficulty of designing, planning, and contructing a crude weapon from reactor-grade plutonium should not be underestimated. The final device would most likely consist of one or more subcritical masses of plutonium metal or oxide surrounded by other machined metal parts and a ton or more of high explosive. Mechanisms would be necessary to assure simultaneous detonation of the high explosive at various points so that the plutonium could be symmetrically imploded to form a supercritical mass. This requires a good design, very precise work, and microsecond-scale synchronization of detonation of the high-explosive charges. The process of fabricating the weapon under less than ideal conditions would present serious risks from accidental criticality leading to low-level nuclear explosions in addition to the general health hazard of working with plutonium without special equipment. These problems are not insoluble, but they do require substantial knowledge, planning, and extraordinary care in execution. A small group of even highly intelligent people is unlikely to have all the skills needed to carry out such a program successfully.

The yield of a simple device using reactor-grade plutonium would be substantially impaired by the presence of the isotope plutonium-240. Plutonium-240 builds up in reactor fuel used for extended periods as is customary in commercial reactors. Thus, a device which otherwise would have a yield equivalent to ten thousand tons of TNT would probably yield a few hundred tons.[2] This reduced yield is a consequence of the fact that plutonium-240 undergoes spontaneous fission to produce neutrons. The presence of these neutrons would initiate the chain reaction in the device as soon as it reaches criticality and cause it to disassemble before it became sufficiently super critical to produce a full yield. Although sophisticated designs might produce full yield despite the presence of plutonium-240, the complexity of such a device puts it beyond the capability of a small group.

The simple bomb that a group of terrorists might be able to construct with reactor-grade plutonium might still have a yield equivalent to a few hundred tons of TNT, unless some element of the system actually malfunctioned. This would be a factor of at least ten less than a comparable military weapon but would still be able to do terrible damage in a densely populated area. One has only to recall that the largest conventional bombs of World War II contained about ten tons of high explosives.

A weapon employing highly enriched uranium would present fewer fabrication problems than a plutonium weapon since it could make use of the so-called gun design in which two subcritical masses of uranium are brought together rapidly by gun powder within a container similar to a gun barrel. Such a weapon might have a yield equivalent of around ten kilotons (ten thousand tons of TNT). As with the implosion weapon, to obtain this yield it would be necessary to develop a complex neutron-injecting mechanism, a task of very different nature from the rest of the weapons problem. Simpler approaches to design might result in zero yield or an unpredictable yield anywhere between zero and ten kilotons. At present, there is little highly enriched uranium suitable for weapons in commercial channels, and there are no plans to deploy a reactor, such as the HTGR, that would utilize highly enriched uranium. However, there is considerable interest in the HTGR abroad, and this situation could change in the future.

The success of such an attempt to construct a nuclear weapon clandestinely would be critically dependent on the technical skills of the terrorist group. The chances of success would be increased if individuals with backgrounds in nuclear materials or weapons design, construction or handling, or individuals with experience with high explosives could be recruited. After extensive planning, many months of intense work would be involved to produce a weapon. Even in a well-planned effort, there is a good chance that the weapon would fail to detonate or that the group would suffer fatal accidents during its construction. Prospects for success would be somewhat enhanced if terrorists could operate freely enough within a society to test the high explosive parts of the weapon.

Attacks on Nuclear Reactors

Attacks on nuclear power plants pose a spectrum of potential consequences. At the low end are symbolic acts, perhaps even by disaffected employees. Such actions cause property damage but may not hazard lives, threaten radioactive release, or pose risks to the public. At the other end, a group that wanted to cause or threaten widespread damage could seize a reactor and damage it to precipitate a core meltdown and radioactive release. While other dangers are conceivable, such as an attempt to disperse spent fuel at storage sites, the consequences would be considerably less than a serious reactor accident.

The NRC has recently reviewed how terrorists might set in motion the sequence of events leading to a major reactor accident. The NRC concluded that the safety characteristics of reactors (massive containment structures, redundancy of safety systems) make it difficult to induce a radioactive release and that actions which might endanger the public could be carried out only by knowledgeable people with technical competence.

While it is true that safety features reduce the likelihood of a major incident, they cannot reduce it to an inconsequential level. In contrast with an accident where "defense-in-depth" deals with chance coincidence of malfunction, probabilities here must take into account *deliberate* simultaneous sabotage of reinforcing safety measures.

It is also true that it would require technically sophisticated and knowledgeable commandos to have a high probability of causing a large radioactive release. However, this does not pose an insuperable barrier to a group with time, resources, and determination. The flow of personnel through military nuclear programs and the growing international civilian nuclear industry provide a large pool of experienced manpower from which a group could seek assistance. Reactor personnel held as hostages might be forced to assist their captors under duress. The technical problems in blowing up a reactor would be easier than those in designing and constructing a nuclear explosive. Explosives could be carried by a few people into a reactor or other facility and could cause major damage. Shaped charges could severely damage main inlet pipes for cooling water. Automatic control and safety equipment could be destroyed. Even primary containment could be ruptured with conventional explosives.

One serious deterrent to nuclear sabotage is the likelihood that the terrorists would be killed or captured during the operation. The terrorists would have to operate openly since there is little chance they could clandestinely emplace explosives at the critical points necessary to disable a reactor. Having initiated a meltdown, they would either be the first victims of prompt radiation or would face likely capture if they tried to escape.

The NRC does not impose rigorous security requirements on reactor sites, fuel fabrication plants, or other facilities that do not possess strategic quantities of special nuclear materials. Industry is not required to protect such facilities against threats of the type that could be posed by "foreign enemies of the United States" i.e., international terrorists with paramilitary capabilities or by extension against similar threats from domestic groups.[3]

Reactors are usually protected by armed contract security guards who may be little more than watchmen and could not be counted on to hold off a well-armed team of attackers until assistance arrived. If local police do not arrive until the attackers have secured themselves in the reactor building (and perhaps taken hostages as well), the terrorists have time to set explosives or perform other preplanned acts. Local police units are rarely equipped or trained to deal with such contingencies.

The probability of such events can be reduced through increased security at reactor sites and more effective coordination of response at the local, state, and national level. Explicit measures should be prescribed for action that threaten widespread damage. While this is by no means a likely threat, the potential damage is such that a sizable investment is warranted.

If terrorists succeeded in defeating the "defense-in-depth" safety technique and initiated a meltdown, the consequences would be like those estimated for accidents, . . . although more severe consequences are possible for sabotage. In safety calculations, fission products are assumed to decay for several hours between core melt and containment breach. This essentially eliminates many shortlived fission products. Thus, if containment were breached at the outset as part of the sabotage operation, more radioactivity could be released, with possible increases in the number of prompt casualties.

Responding to Nuclear Terrorism

Many methods for upgrading security of nuclear facilities have been suggested. Some are technical improvements—inventory of materials, or defense of stages in the fuel cycle that might become targets. Others are improved security procedures and institutional arrangements. Although none of these proposals will solve the problem completely, some of them will make nuclear terrorism much more difficult to accomplish and thus hopefully deter it. Some proposals may create more problems than they solve.

TECHNICAL MEASURES

The security system can be alerted to potential thefts by improvements in the inventory and accounting systems to keep better track of nuclear materials flowing through facilities and reactors. If spent fuel is reprocessed, the currently used techniques to measure the plutonium and uranium content have a margin of error of about 1 percent. This discrepancy is termed "material unaccounted for" or MUF. MUF does not mean that material has been stolen or lost, but simply indicates the imprecision inherent in the measure of the inventory.

Other sources of MUF include scraps when plutonium or enriched uranium is compacted and machined into pellets for insertion in fuel rods. A small fraction of this scrap, about 0.5 percent, is unavoidably lost during processing. When nuclear materials are processed in liquid form, small amounts may remain in vessels and process lines. The NRC requires that these losses and discrepancies be within the NRC's estimated "limits of error" of material accounting techniques (LEMUF).

Current regulations require that a facility's inventory books be balanced to LEMUF standards every six months for reprocessing plants and every two months for all other facilities holding strategic quantities of nuclear materials. If small quantities of plutonium or highly enriched uranium were diverted over the course of several weeks, discrepancies might not be noted until months later. There are many difficulties with such scenarios. Thieves would still have to remove the material from the facility through various technical detection barriers that can be designed to be sensitive to extremely small quantities of plutonium. Such a barrier to physical removal would be equally sensitive, regardless of the amount of plutonium in the facility or the size of the MUF.

To combat this problem, the timeliness of material inventories and the accuracy of measurements can be improved. Real-time or near real-time computer-based systems might allow material balances at the end of each shift before workers had left the plant. Improved measurement could reduce the margin of error reflected in MUF. Improved timeliness in accounting and inventory could also supplement international safeguards for nations utilizing plutonium or highly enriched uranium in their fuel cycles.

A second countermeasure is to attach radioactive sources, emitting hard-to-shield radiation, to material shipments or certain areas in plants to discourage attempts at theft. This process, known as "spiking," could be utilized for detection, location, or denial of access.

Spiking could be applied to facilitate the detection of materials in a plant; to enhance their detectability if stolen; and intense sources could be attached to shipping canisters to produce extremely high-exposure doses that would incapacitate unprotected persons within a short time.

In a plutonium plant, spiking for detection would be feasible at little increased cost or hazard to workers. Spiking for location is also feasible, though this involves more substantial cost and some increased hazard to workers in an accident. Spiking shipments to deny access is feasible, but poses a dilemma. To pose a threat to potential thieves, the source would be so intense as to endanger the public in event of accident. If the current one hundred ton shipping cask was employed for shipping plutonium-bearing fresh fuel, the radioactive inventory (1-2 megacuries) of the spiked cask would be similar to a load of irradiated reactor fuel. One assessment of an accident involving spent fuel assumed that about 1 percent of the fuel would be scattered in a nonurban area (population density one hundred per square mile), causing 0.6 early deaths and three hundred latent cancer fatalities. If a spiked fresh fuel cask was opened and some of the cobalt sources were somehow dispersed, it could result in many times as much damage in a comparably populated area. Because of the attendant risks of accident or deliberate dispersal, spiking should probably not be the preferred method for the protection of nuclear materials.

There are many other improvements such as advanced security systems for identification and access control, and systems for continuous communication. At present, transporters of nuclear materials may be out of radio contact for periods of up to several hours during shipments. Continuous communications could be obtained by add-on capabilities to planned earth-orbiting satellites.

In general, all of these improvements are inexpensive. The total investment for the list of security options identified in the draft GESMO is a few hundred million dollars for the entire industry. Annual operating costs for the industry might be in the tens of millions of dollars, adding 1 or 2 percent to the cost of nuclear-generated electricity.

INSTITUTIONAL CONSIDERATIONS

The institutional response to terrorism encompasses preventive measures such as improved guard capabilities at reactor sites, better alerting and intelligence, and activities associated with response to a crisis once it is underway. Recognition of the need for upgraded security, and action to achieve it, has been slow. For industry, security and safeguards are additional burdens and expenses and there are few incentives to accept these costs unless required. The NRC has not moved rapidly on these issues and has been reluctant to specify in detail what the utilities should do about security. The NRC usually operates through the lengthy and sometimes indirect process of proposing rather general standards for public comment, modifying them, promulgating them, and finally inspecting and evaluating their implementation. The NRC does not have direct authority over critical elements in the security system, such as the contract guards employed by most utilities or the transport services used to ship nuclear materials.

A similar problem arises among federal, state, and local law enforcement authorities. The NRC has not expected industry to defend against armed threats, but government responsibility to do so is not clearly assigned. The NRC requires utilities to establish liaison with local law enforcement authorities, but these forces are often unresponsive or inadequately equipped. The NRC has little authority for dealing with other federal agencies. It is trying to alert local FBI agents to the potential hazards of nuclear terrorism, but such a campaign hardly assures an adequate federal response.

Federal authority to deal with nuclear terrorism is diffuse. Theft of nuclear materials is a federal crime; but an attack on a reactor might not automatically involve federal authorities, since it is not a crime under the Atomic Energy Act. Federal authorities might become involved if national defense statutes or the interstate commerce clause of the Constitution could be invoked.

Security could be improved by federal training, equipping, and regulation of privately employed guards. Legislative and administrative action is required to fix institutional responsibility, set adequate standards, and see that they are met. At minimum, the NRC or the Justice Department should have regulatory authority over the operation and training of guard forces at nuclear facilities. Local and state law enforcement cooperation with utilities and federal officials could be encouraged through mechanisms such as Law Enforcement Assistance Administration (LEAA) planning grants. In any event, an attack on a nuclear facility should be clearly designated a federal crime.

A more comprehensive measure would be the creation of a federal Nuclear Protective Force. The advantages of a federal force include uniform training, access to and authority to use a wide range of weapons, and a clear conception of mission and responsibility. The disadvantages include infringement on police powers of the state, layering of security bureaucracies, and the possible expansion of federal police powers at the expense of civil liberties. If a federal force was created, its mission should be limited to local, on-site security against criminal or terrorist action. The force should not have investigative or intelligence functions. A model might be the Executive Protection Service (EPS) which protects the White House grounds and foreign embassies in Washington, D.C., and has circumscribed powers.

Statistics on most terrorist activity (bombing, kidnappings, etc.) show a distinct increase in recent years. In airplane hijacking, however, the trend is sharply downward. International diplomatic efforts, coupled with security improvements and airports, appear to have reduced significantly the incidence of air piracy. Modest increases in security have bought a lot, even in the highly accessible airline industry. Though not all of the early hijackers were international terrorists, improved security has raised the threshold from something that a lone gunman could accomplish to a small-scale paramilitary operation. Moreover, while many hijackings had political overtones, nearly all nations found a common interest in countering a threat to international commerce, whatever the affiliation of particular hijackers. By the same token, modest improvements in security at nuclear facilities may substantially raise the threshold for theft, and there is a similar basis of mutual dependence and common interest among nations in preventing nuclear incidents.

The federal government appears to be poorly prepared to respond to an act or threat against a reactor or theft of nuclear materials. The responsibilities of the NRC, the FBI, ERDA, Civil Defense, and other federal agencies are not clearly defined, nor are the liaison procedures with state and local authorities in the event of an emergency. It is not even clear where the focus for information and decision in Washington would be.

A modest effort has been started under the auspices of the Cabinet Committee on International Terrorism chaired by the Secretary of State. However, nuclear terrorism, whether perpetrated by domestic or foreign terrorists, is different from other terrorist activities and merits separate attention. It involves a different set of agencies and should have a separate organizational focus.

Resolving this set of problems is independent of improvements in security for nuclear facilities and materials. Whether site security is provided by federal, local, or private guards, it is essential that the federal government be able to respond if local defense fails. There must be a recognition of the federal interest and role in a nuclear crisis and an effective chain of command. There must also be clarification of responsibilities and authority of many federal, state, and local agencies in a nuclear crisis. Finally, there should be contingency planning, including compilation of information on nuclear sites and transportation routes, inventories of federal, state, and local equipment and forces in different areas, what terrorists or saboteurs could and could not do, and the associated consequences.

U.S. actions are only part of the story. If plutonium or highly enriched uranium become items of international commerce, terrorists or criminals will go where they can get them. Materials or bombs will not necessarily be used against the country from which they are stolen. The United States should therefore use available bilateral and multilateral channels such as the IAEA to encourage adequate security standards and practices for nuclear activities and facilities abroad. The IAEA has published advisory guidelines on security at nuclear facilities but has not made acceptance of the guidelines a condition for IAEA assistance. The United States should urge a reconsideration of this policy by IAEA and propose security standards as an integral part of all future international agreements for peaceful future cooperation in nuclear energy.

Security and Civil Liberties

Preventive or responsive actions may impinge on civil rights and liberties of those employed in the nuclear industry, those living or working near nuclear facilities, and the general public. Civil liberties may be affected by activities designed to prevent terrorist incidents or by activities undertaken in response. Preventive measures could affect civil liberties by invading the privacy of employees as a result of personnel security check, and physical search, and by surveillance and domestic intelligence dealing with or anticipating antinuclear threats.

Restrictions on employees of the nuclear industry are part of any effort to increase security against terrorism. Such measures must be subject to constitutional guarantees. For example, physical search is subject to Fourth Amendment limitations. Use of devices such as magnetometers, which do not require intrusive physical search, has been upheld by courts in searches for airline and courtroom security. But frisk-type, "hands on" searches (absent probable cause) are of doubtful constitutionality.

Security clearances and personnel screening are subject to restrictions, e.g., membership in particular organizations may not be sufficient grounds to deny employment. The NRC may soon require security clearance for 30,000 employees in the nuclear industry. This should be compared to five million persons already subject to the government's security clearance program. As long as the procedures and standards for nuclear industry employees are carefully drawn, there need be no new cause for concern about civil liberties. Substantial protections for employee rights exist.

Problems could be posed by domestic surveillance to identify potential terrorists. Likely targets would include crriminals, terrorists, and possibly domestic dissidents. Surveillance of foreign nationals can be conducted under the national security authority of the President. Where U.S. citizens are involved, techniques such as electronic eavesdropping are subject to the Fourth Amendment requirement for a warrant based on probable cause. Wiretapping in domestic security cases is also regulated by the Omnibus Crime and Safe Streets Act of 1968, which spells out surveillance procedures and enumerates specific crimes in which surveillance is permitted. Wiretapping is permitted with a warrant in crimes relating to the Restricted Data provisions of the Atomic Energy Act and for crimes such as extortion and sabotage. However, theft and unauthorized possession of special nuclear materials, while a federal crime, are not crimes for which a warrant can be issued under the Act.

The use of informants or undercover agents is less well regulated in U.S. law. Use of informants per se has never been held to threaten constitutional rights. However, informants or undercover agents cannot contravene a citizen's constitutional protection in the course of their activities. Though in some cases recognizing a potential "chilling effect" on free speech, the courts have been reluctant to interfere in this area.

If a crisis is threatened or underway, the urgency may subject civil liberties to different pressures. The character of the risk can vary enormously. At the low end of the scale would be a company's response if a quantity of plutonium appeared to be missing at the end of a shift. Employees might be detained, searched without probable cause, or otherwise subjected to abuse of their liberties. At the other extreme, if terrorists had stolen nuclear materials, there might be calls to subject hundreds or thousands of citizens to blanket search, warrantless surveillance, forced evacuations, and detention and interrogation without counsel or probable cause.

Once the crisis is past, there is the risk that some tactics employed in the crisis might be carried over into routine operations or extended to other law enforcement problems. This tendency would be exacerbated if there was strong public sentiment that such a crisis should never be allowed to happen again, and widespread fear of society's vulnerability to nuclear terrorism. It is essential to protect against such spillover effects on civil liberties. There are trade-offs between physical security measures for the protection of facilities and materials and activities that might affect civil liberties. Where this is the case, additional investments in site protection and local security forces are preferable to expanded surveillance.

Well thought out and well understood guidelines and contingency plans for federal, state, and local law enforcement officials would minimize the confusion and panic in which ill-advised actions infringing on a civil liberties might be taken. Uniform response procedures should be developed and subjected to realistic testing by utilities in conjunction with appropriate authorities at all levels. Only through careful planning, testing, and evaluation in advance of a crisis can law enforcement officials assure that response procedures will not affect civil liberties.

Conclusions

The likelihood of nuclear terrorism is impossible to quantify, but the possibility must be taken seriously. If terrorists were to obtain reactor-grade plutonium, a small group of technically trained people might be able to build a bomb that might have a few hundred tons of explosive yield. If highly enriched uranium were available, the design and fabrication would be somewhat less complicated than for a plutonium bomb but the resulting yield would be unpredictable, and might well be zero. In any case, even in a well-planned effort, there is a good chance that the weapon would fail to detonate or that the group would suffer fatal accidents during its construction.

If plutonium is not reprocessed for recycle in LWRs or breeders, plutonium would not be available in the fuel cycle in a form suitable for use by a small terrorist group since reprocessing fuel elements would be beyond their capabilities. Highly enriched uranium is not now generally available in commerce for nuclear power reactors although this could change if new types of reactors are introduced. At present, both plutonium and highly enriched uranium would have to be diverted from national nuclear military programs.

An armed group could seize a reactor, damage it in such a way as to overcome safety measures, and precipitate a meltdown and radiation release. While this would not be a simple operation, it would not be beyond the capabilities of a knowledgeable, well-trained group willing to risk perishing. The consequences of such an act would be similar to those of a nuclear reactor accident.

Current physical security arrangements for both nuclear facilities and materials require strengthening. At a minimum, federal regulation and training of private security forces are required. Ultimately, the federal government may need to assume responsibility for physical security of materials and facilities against theft or sabotage.

Public authorities are poorly organized to respond to a crisis involving terrorist acts involving nuclear facilities or materials. The federal government should provide leadership and fix responsibility for dealing with terrorist acts. This should include coordination of action and information and assurance that local security forces (public and private) are properly trained and understand their roles. New legislation may be desirable to establish reactor attacks as a federal crime and provide authority for dealing with it.

Improved security measures can be introduced without endangering civil liberties. A potential problem does exist, however, and in establishing new procedures, care should be taken to avoid infringing on civil liberties. An actual crisis could create precedent-setting problems. This possibility puts an additional premium on improved physical security over key nuclear facilities and transportation activities to forestall such incidents.

Nuclear terrorism is a problem international in scope. The security of materials and facilities elsewhere has direct importance to the security of the United States. The United States should press for effective international standards and measures in nuclear export policies, discussions with other supplier countries, and in bilateral and multilateral arrangements with other countries.

Notes

1. Nuclear weapons and ERDA owned materials are transported under more strict security procedures in specially designed tractor trailers. The ERDA trucks have special armor plating, bulletproof windows and have HF and VHF communications and a radio telephone. The trucks are also fitted with special immobilization features. The trucks are escorted en route by a separate vehicle, which has redundant communications. Typically, there are four armed driver guards (two in each vehicle), who are ERDA security personnel.
2. The availability of weapons-grade plutonium would not necessarily improve the terrorist's chances of achieving a high yield. Unless the designer were able to construct a mechanism to introduce neutrons into the plutonium core at the exact moment of maximum criticality, the device would have a substantially reduced yield, or no yield at all. Develop-

ment of such a mechanism would additionally burden the capabilities of any small group. A continuous source of neutrons would result in a low yield for the same reason as would a high concentration of plutonium-240.

3. Licensees are not expected to defend against foreign enemies of the United States. The Atomic Safety and Licensing Board in a 1974 decision on the Indian Point reactor (Docket number 50-247) extended this exemption to include well-armed domestic threats. The Board concluded that licensees have no realistic means to disciminate between domestic terrorists and foreign enemies, and thus are not responsible for defending against either.

Office of Technology Assessment of the U.S. Congress

The Non-State Adversary

This selection is drawn from an informative study, Nuclear Proliferation and Safeguards, *prepared by the congressional Office of Technology Assessment. Proceeding from a useful review of terrorist activities, this chapter considers several of the nonstate adversaries that may attempt to acquire nuclear weapons: terrorists, criminals, and the mentally defective. Although the historical record does not disclose any individual or group efforts toward nuclear terrorism, the reader is advised to avoid taking solace in this fact, since our knowledge of potential adversaries is incomplete at best. The second part succinctly addresses the impact that nuclear safeguards may have upon civil liberties in the United States, presenting synopses of the three modes of confronting the question.*

The Nature of Non-State Adversaries and Their Acts

Nuclear non-state adversaries include those who might attempt to steal a nuclear weapon; to steal nuclear material to sell, ransom, or use to make a nuclear explosive or dispersal device; to purchase illegally, or smuggle, nuclear material, or otherwise participate in a nuclear blackmarket; or claim that they possess nuclear devices to extort concessions or cause alarm. The term also includes those who might undertake serious malevolent actions against nuclear facilities. They might threaten or actually attempt to sabotage a nuclear facility or transport vehicle, or seize termporary control of a nuclear facility.

These adversaries are often referred to collectively as criminals and terrorists, although all are criminals in that their actions would violate existing laws. The term criminal however, generally implies a purely profit motive while the term terrorist (in current usage) implies political objectives. The spectrum of potential nuclear non-state adversaries is much broader. It includes profit-minded criminals, political extremists, a dissident faction within a government, violent foes of the manufacture of nuclear arms or of civilian nuclear power programs, disgruntled employees of the nuclear industry, or individual lunatics. The actions that might conceivably be carried out by such individuals or groups range from hoaxes to the construction and detonation of a nuclear explosive device which could kill hundreds or thousands of people and deny the use of large areas of land. Strictly speaking, nuclear adversary actions should not include minor incidents (such as vandalism), although it is useful to study minor incidents for indications of trends in the direction of more serious aactions.

THE SPECTRUM OF POTENTIAL NUCLEAR ACTIONS

The non-state threat compromises a spectrum of potential actions, with varying degrees of difficulty to complete and varying degrees of consequences.

At the low end of this spectrum are bomb threats, nuclear hoaxes, and token acts of violence not aimed at producing serious casualties or damage. These in general pose little direct danger to public safety and require a minimum of skill, resources, and organization to carry through.

Further up the scale are actions such as low-level sabotage which could result in serious damage to a nuclear facility and could endanger onsite personnel, although they would not necessarily pose a threat to public safety.

At the high end of the scale are actions such as theft of weapons material followed by the construction of a nuclear explosive device, or sabotage of a reactor which succeeded in causing a core-melt and breach of containment. The sabotage of a reactor was judged peripheral to the subject of this report: the proliferation of nuclear weapons. Therefore, this report has not assessed the difficulty of reactor sabotage.

. . . Some clever and competent non-national groups could possibly design and construct a crude nuclear explosive having significant nuclear yield.

The effective design of security systems for nuclear facilities requires an understanding of the threat to be defended against. Defined threat levels can be used to gauge, as a first approximation, the difficulty of obtaining weapons material. Until recently, however, threat levels were not defined by the U.S. Nuclear Regulatory Commission (NRC). In January 1976, the NRC began a special review of the safeguards at 15 facilities licensed by it to possess significant amounts of highly enriched uranium or plutonium. In March 1976, the U.S. Energy Research and Development Administration (ERDA) began participating in the reviews. The threat levels defined for this review consisted of:

> An internal threat of one employee occupying any position, or
> an external threat comprised of three well-armed (legally obtain-
> able weapons), well-trained individuals, including the possibilities
> of inside knowledge or assistance of one insider.[1]

Of the 15 NRC licensed facilities involved in the safeguards reviews, 8 were judged adequate to withstand both the threats defined above.

More recently, NRC has required these facilities to begin upgrading their security to guard against an increased possible threat. This potential threat could involve a conspiracy of two or more insiders acting in collusion with an outside group of several attackers armed with automatic rifles, recoilless rifles, and high explosives. As part of the upgrading, full-field investigations and other security checks will be required for licensee employees who might effectively conspire to steal or divert weapons-grade material. . . .

In the section which follows, it will be seen that the nuclear incidents to date have all been low level.

THE RECORD OF NUCLEAR INCIDENTS*

Between 1969 and 1975, the AEC and then ERDA recorded 288 threats or incidents of violence in the United States directed at nuclear facilities or buildings or offices that were in some way related to nuclear activities. (This figure does not include nuclear hoaxes, of which there were 38 in roughly the same period. See the section on nuclear hoaxes below.) Of these, 240 were bomb threats; 14 were bombings or attempted bombings; 22 were incidents of arson, attempted arson or suspicious fires; and 12 were cases of forced entry or other breaches of security. There was, in addition, one possible case of diversion of a minute quantity of plutonium. A number of incidents were directed against university research facilities of Federal office buildings. There were no casualties. The ERDA list is apparently not complete. Moreover, it seems unlikely that no incidents took place before 1969. A case of low-level reactor sabotage resulting in considerable onsite damage is not contained on the list. In addition, a night watchman was reportedly wounded by an intruder at the Vermont Yankee plant in 1971. This was the only known casualty in an adversary nuclear incident in the United States. Several known thefts of radioactive material (but not radioactive waste or special nuclear material) do not appear on the list. (None of the material was used to endanger the public.)

There are no complete chronologies of incidents involving nuclear facilities or material elsewhere in the world. Those incidents that have been reported in the foreign press consist mainly of bomb threats, hoaxes, vandalism, low-level sabotage, a few thefts of low-enriched uranium, and one verified incident of non-lethal radioactive dispersal of material possibly stolen from a hospital.

*See appendix III, volume II of *Nuclear Proliferation and Safeguards* for details.

There have, however, been serious incidents of bombing and sabotage in Europe causing considerable damage to property. Demonstrations against the construction of new nuclear powerplants in West Germany, where antinuclear forces appear to have merged with extremist political movements, have resulted in violent confrontations with the police.

The combination of antinuclear elements with political extremists has led to violence in Europe where further violence and perhaps some escalation seems possible. There is no evidence in these incidents that any group has so far attempted to acquire plutonium, highly enriched uranium, or radioactive waste for use in an explosive or dispersal device.

Most of the nuclear incidents worldwide have been low-level and have not imperiled public safety. More such incidents can be expected as the nuclear industry expands. The record suggests that the nuclear industry will not be immune to the problems of bomb threats, low-level sabotage, and pilferage, which are common to other industries.

Publicity surrounding the incidents was not great, attracting international attention in only a few cases. The perpetrators included disgruntled employees, common thieves, political extremists, foes of nuclear power, and a few lunatics. Their motives included protest, greed, revenge, or desire for attention.

For the most part the perpetrators were individuals; a few consisted of small groups. The low-enriched uranium smuggling ring in India, involving contacts in at least three countries, showed the most organization. . . .

Although all nuclear incidents to date have been of a relatively minor nature, this gives no excuse for complacency in the future. The present record of nuclear incidents was assembled in an era of relatively few nuclear reactors. In the future, nuclear power will be greatly expanded, even in low-growth projections, and plutonium recycle may afford potential non-state adversaries a number of highly visible targets. This fundamental change, coupled with marked trends towards increased violence, makes the past an uncertain predictor of the future.

Moreover, in many developing countries, internal coups, guerrilla wars, insurgent movements, and military regimes are common. One can imagine, for example, how a military coup could involve a struggle for control of a nuclear reactor or, even more serious, a reprocessing plant with its stocks of separated plutonium. Another factor gives cause for concern in the Third World. Developing countries may not have the resources necessary to provide adequate security around their newly acquired nuclear facilities. Thus, as the nuclear industry expands into the Third World, as it is apparently going to do over the next several decades, these facilities may become more attractive targets for insurgent and terrorist groups.

ORIGINS OF INCREASED CONCERN ABOUT THE NON-STATE ADVERSARY

Although only minor nuclear incidents have occurred so far in the United States, public concern about the possibility of nuclear adversary actions, particularly nuclear terrorism, has been increasing in recent years. There appear to be a number of reasons for this. First among these are the rapid growth, actual and projected, of nuclear powerplants throughout the world and the projected use of plutonium as a fuel. Increased demands for energy in both the industrialized and developing nations and the impacts of the oil embargo in 1973-1974 spurred the development of nuclear power.

Concurrent with the expansion of nuclear power, a national environmental movement grew in the United States. In their criticisms of nuclear energy, many environmentalists have been giving increasing attention to the possibilities and consequences of deliberate malevolent actions by terrorists and criminals. Moreover, the great increase in violent crime and international terrorism, reported in detail by the mass media, have made malevolent acts seem more commonplace and closer to home. Expectations of violence are probably also increased by regular exposure to violence in fiction, particularly in movies and television. Finally, many of the events of the past 15 years have reduced public confidence in our social, political, and economic institutions. Whereas the citizens of the United States might have once accepted their leaders' statements that strong and sufficient measures were being taken to prevent nuclear adversary actions, the public now tends to be more skeptical of such assurances.

THE GROWTH OF INTERNATIONAL TERRORISM*

One of the reasons mentioned in the previous section for the growth of public concern about potential nuclear adversary action is the great increase in international terrorism.

Terrorism can be described as the use of actual or threatened violence to gain attention and to create fear and alarm, which in turn will cause people to exaggerate the strength of the terrorists and the importance of their cause. Since groups that use terrorist tactics are typically small and weak, the violence they practice must be deliberately shocking.

Terrorism has become an international phenomenon in recent years. Modern air travel provides terrorists with worldwide mobility, and mass communications provides them with a worldwide audience. New weapons have increased their capacity for violence, while society has become increasingly vulnerable because of growing dependence on complex systems

*See appendix III, volume II of *Nuclear Proliferation and Safeguards* for details.

and technology that can be exploited malevolently (e.g., nuclear energy, civil aviation).

During the last few years, small groups of extremists have repeatedly demonstrated that terrorist tactics can create international incidents causing national governments to negotiate before a worldwide audience.

In the presentation of data which follows, international terrorism is defined as terrorism that has clear international consequences. It includes incidents in which terrorists go abroad to strike their targets (as in the Lod Airport massacre), or select victims or targets because of their connections to a foreign state (as in the assassination or kidnapping of a diplomat), or attack international lines of communication and commerce (as in the hijacking of an airliner). It does not include incidents of domestic terrorism.

Since the late 1960's, international terrorism has been on a sharp upward curve, whether one measures such a curve on the basis of the number of terrorist incidents each year or on the basis of the number of casualties inflicted. (See figures 1 and 2.)

Figure 3, taken from an unclassified CIA report "International Terrorism: Diagnosis and Prognosis," breaks international terrorist incidents down into several categories. (The totals in figures 1 and 2, taken from data collected by the RAND Corporation differ slightly from the totals in figure 3, because of slightly different reporting criteria.) All told, more than 140 terrorist organizations—including a number of fictional organizations created to shield the identity of the true perpetrators of some particularly shocking or politically sensitive acts—from nearly 50 different countries or disputed territories have thus far engaged in international terrorism. About 1,000 persons have died in international terrorist incidents since 1968; another 2,000 have been injured. If the casualties of domestic political violence are added, the number of deaths may reach 10,000. For comparison, 20,000 persons are murdered every year in the United States.

Some observers have been encouraged by an apparent decline in international terrorism in 1976. However, figures 1 and 2 show that this apparent decline was not real; international terrorism rose in 1976. The *apparent* decline of international terrorism in 1976 can be explained by the fact that 1976 saw more assassinations and murders and fewer hostage incidents than the preceding year. Hostage incidents may be in the news for days or even weeks; murder is usually in the news for a day or two.

Although any forecasts about terrorism in the future are conjectural, some trends are discernible.

Although few terrorists have reached their stated long-range goals, terrorism has proved useful in getting publicity and occasionally obtaining some political concessions. The record to date might even be considered reasonably positive from a terrorist perspective. Terrorist groups have been notably successful in avoiding capture and escaping punishment.

Figure 1. Total number of incidents of international terrorism, 1968-1976

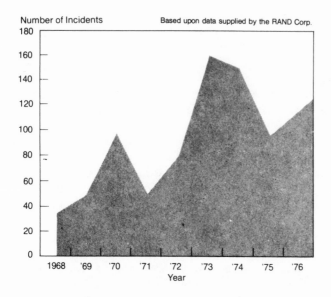

Figure 2. Total number of deaths in incidents of international terrorism, 1968-1976

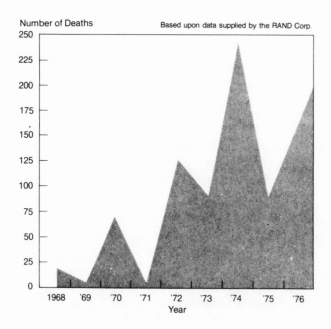

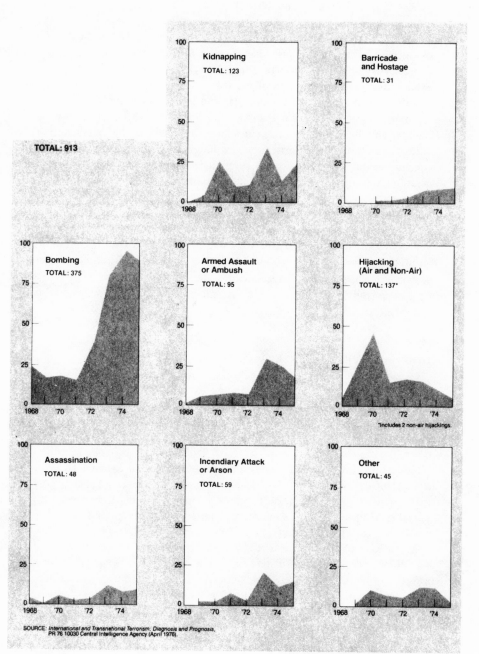

Figure 3. International and transnational terrorist incidents by category, 1968-1975

TOTAL: 913

Kidnapping
TOTAL: 123

Barricade and Hostage
TOTAL: 31

Bombing
TOTAL: 375

Armed Assault or Ambush
TOTAL: 95

Hijacking (Air and Non-Air)
TOTAL: 137*
*Includes 2 non-air hijackings.

Assassination
TOTAL: 48

Incendiary Attack or Arson
TOTAL: 59

Other
TOTAL: 45

SOURCE: *International and Transnational Terrorism: Diagnosis and Prognosis*, PR 76 10030 Central Intelligence Agency (April 1976).

With the exception of a number of bilateral agreements providing for a greater exchange of intelligence and technical assistance, the international response to terrorism has been relatively weak and ineffective.

Terrorists will remain highly mobile, able to strike targets anywhere in the world. Recent developments in explosives, small arms, and sophisticated man-portable weapons will provide terrorists with an increased capacity for violence. They appear to be getting more knowledgeable in their tactics, their weapons, and their exploitation of the media. They will continue to emulate each other's tactics, especially those that win international publicity. Terrorist groups appear to be strengthening their links with each other, forming alliances, and providing mutual assistance. One result is the emergence of multinational freelance terrorist groups willing to carry out attacks on behalf of causes with which they are sympathetic, or to undertake specific operations or campaigns of terrorism on commission from client groups or governments. Nations or groups unable or unwilling to mount a serious challenge on the battlefield may employ such groups or adopt terrorist tactics as a means of surrogate warfare against their opponents. Moreover, there are signs that some international and domestic terrorist groups are beginning to recruit individuals who are attracted to violence not for political ideals, but for money or the lure of a clandestine lifestyle.

Terrorism can be expected to persist and perhaps increase as a mode of political expression.

POTENTIAL NUCLEAR TERRORISM

There is substantial disagreement among experts as to the likelihood of terrorist attempts to acquire a nuclear capability. A nuclear capability would greatly increase their potential destructive power. The detonation of a crude nuclear device in a carefully selected, heavily populated area could kill tens of thousands of people.

The historical record shows that in no single incident in the past 50 years have terrorists killed more than 150 people, and incidents involving more than 20 deaths are rare. (See Figure 4.) This is not because of lack of capability. Terrorist groups could have acquired the means to kill many more people than they have, even by using only conventional explosives.

On the basis of the historical record and the theory of terrorism, it is not clear that causing mass casualties or widespread damage is attractive to a terrorist group. By using terrorist tactics, political extremists have created alarm, attracted worldwide attention to themselves and to their causes, compelled governments to negotiate and often grant concessions, while at the same time forcing governments to spend an unequal amount of resources for protection against terrorist attacks. Terrorists have contributed to the

Figure 4. Number of deaths per incident of terrorism involving any deaths, 1968-1976 (October 6)

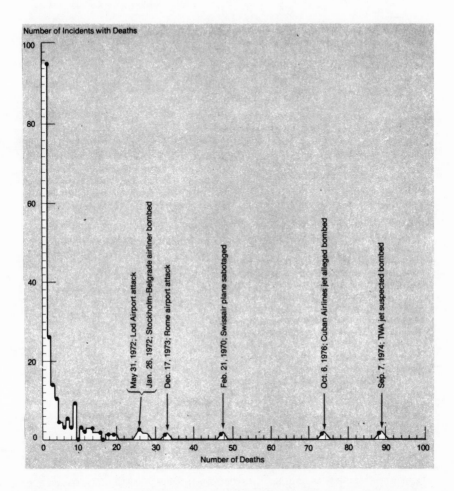

downfall of a few governments, aggravated North-South and East-West relations, kept the Palestinian question at the forefront of international concern, introduced strains in the Western alliance, and adversely affected the quality of life in many open or formerly open societies. They have achieved these results without resorting to mass murder.

Mass murder might actually be counterproductive. It might alienate sympathizers and potential supporters, provoke severe crackdowns that public opinion would demand and support, and threaten the survival of the organization itself. For these reasons, any scheme of nuclear destruction may create disagreement and dissension within the organization contemplating it, and expose the operation and the organization to betrayal. For these reasons, a number of experts have argued that mass murder appears unlikely to be contemplated by terrorists groups capable of making elementary political judgments.

However, there is no assurance that terrorists will continue to behave in the future as they have in the past. A desperate group might decide to strike one catastrophic blow.

Moreover, as Roberta Wohlstetter has suggested "... familiar political ends ... sometimes involve a means like the Red Army terror in Lod Airport, a careless slaughter of innocents that may indeed be an omen of the sort of random killing we see in nuclear destruction."[2]

In addition, it should be recognized that pure massive destruction would serve the goals of nihilistic groups, should they emerge in the coming years.

The primary attraction for terrorists to go nuclear may not be to cause mass casualties. Almost any nuclear action by terrorists would attract widespread attention. For example, if a terrorist group seized control of a nuclear power reactor or a nuclear weapons storage site, they would create a frightening situation and achieve worldwide publicity by the seizure alone. As another example, it might not be necessary for terrorists to actually design and construct a nuclear explosive device in order to achieve the effect they want. Extortion based on a credible nuclear threat would require less technical skill and risk but would still receive publicity, inspire fear, and, possibly, succeed in obtaining concessions.

In addition, ... even nuclear explosions need not be equated with mass slaughter. The detonation of a nuclear explosive at any one of a number of important sites at a time when very few people would be about could have a stunning effect, while minimizing the number of deaths.

The whole area of motivations, incentives, demands and negotiations, in the area of nuclear blackmail by terrorists (and other non-state adversaries) deserves systematic examination, which it has not received. At present, the published literature contains only speculations about the types of demands terrorists can, cannot, and are most likely to make. Many of these speculations are extremely ingenious, but their main focus is on the terrorist nuclear action itself; few attempt to come to grips with the much harder question of how a terrorist group could exploit the enormous leverage a nuclear device would give to effect a commensurate irreversible political change.

ORGANIZED CRIME AS A POTENTIAL NUCLEAR NON-STATE ADVERSARY

In this discussion, organized crime means an organization dedicated to illegal activities; its existence transcends any single act; the organization survives its members. Organized crime should be distinguished from individual groups of criminals that organize themselves to carry out specific crimes.

Whether organized crime should be considered a likely nuclear non-state adversary remains a matter of debate. . . . L. Douglas DeNike concludes that it is credible that organized crime would engage in nuclear activity:

> Armed with plutonium or high level waste, organized crime might demand Federal assurances of non-interference with their operations. Punishment for non-cooperation might be the loss of Washington, D.C. as a habitable center. Nuclear thieves could demand large sums of cash, control over policy or special concessions from national governments.

Considering the possibility of theft of nuclear material, the MITRE study concludes:

> They (organized crime) are interested solely in acquiring more money and power for themselves. . . .They are involved in almost all the highjacking that goes on in the United States, and have been able to exert considerable control over substantial parts of industry, labor and government. Their business is often international and they have long-standing and secure links in Europe, the Middle East, Latin America, and the Far East. There is little question that, for a sufficient amount of money, members of organized crime would take a contract to acquire special nuclear material for another party.

Other experts disagree that nuclear extortion or theft would be a likely activity for organized crime. This point of view has been summarized by Brian Jenkins:

> . . . one should be cautious about over-estimating the attractiveness of engaging in nuclear extortion or trafficking in fissionable material to the criminal underworld, especially to organized crime. . . . organized crime is a conservative, service-oriented industry. It provides gambling, prostitution and narcotics. The profits from the provision of these services are good and, perhaps more important, *steady*. . . .
> There is a willing market for such services, and despite the social harm they cause, they may not be perceived by the public as a direct threat to individual or collective security. Indeed, the existence of organized crime depends a great deal on tacit public acceptance or at least indifference and therefore it has tended to avoid criminal ventures—for example, in this country kidnappings for huge ransoms—that are likely to arouse public anger. Nuclear blackmailing would bring tremendous heat on the organization and provoke crackdowns

that could interrupt the flow of large steady profits from more socially acceptable crimes.[5]

There is, however, one area of consensus within the debate. No one who
has commented on the topic seriously believes that organized crime lacks the
resources, skills, patience, or force necessary to steal special nuclear material
or engage in an illicit international trade of material. The deterrents, if they
exist, would possibly lie in fears by the leaders of organized crime that such
actions would provoke public outrage and lead to severe responses that would
seriously damage organized crime's other profitable enterprises. If organized
crime attempted to deter such counter-measures with a nuclear threat, it
would mean, in effect, that the leaders of organized crime had decided to
challenge the sovereignty of the nations in which their normal activities take
place. This would require a fundamental change in the objectives of organized
crime, which typically up to now has sought to make money and to acquire
political influence to protect its investments and operations but not to
directly acquire political authority at the highest levels or provoke political
reaction.

At the same time, even those who believe that the risks to organized crime
of involvement in nuclear theft or nuclear extortion probably exceed the
perceived benefits, appear to find it credible that if a worldwide market for
nuclear material develops, and if the price is right, organized crime (perhaps
without becoming directly involved in the theft of nuclear material) might act
as a fence or broker for the stolen goods. Plutonium or uranium could be
stolen or fenced for their monetary value as commodities, that is, as reactor
fuel or, in the case of low enriched uranium, as feed for dedicated
facilities. . . . There are some indications that theft of low-enriched uranium
for reactor fuel may have already happened in India. . . . Thus, as nuclear
power spreads worldwide, and especially if plutonium comes into widespread
use as a reactor fuel, it is possible that organized crime might become
involved in all aspects of black and gray markets in nuclear material as
commodities. Such a development would be extremely dangerous. It is
difficult to see how such a market could for long resist developing into a
market for plutonium as bomb material.

Some observers argue that organized crime would not get involved in a
black market in plutonium for bombs (or in assembled nuclear weapons), for
the same reasons, discussed above, that they would not be likely to attack
nuclear facilities or engage in nuclear extortion. Thus, organized crime might
also steer clear of trading in special nuclear material as commodities, if they
perceived the commodities market and the bomb market as closely
linked. . . .

NUCLEAR HOAXES; PSYCHOTICS

A *nuclear hoax* is defined as a threat to *detonate a nuclear explosive* or to *disperse radioactive material* when the threatener lacks the capacity or the dedication to carry out the threat. No such threat to date has been judged credible, and no perpetrators have had the capability of which they boasted; therefore all have been classed as nuclear hoaxes. There have been 38 nuclear hoaxes between 1970 and 1976. . . .

Hoaxes demonstrate that there are people who are thinking about using nuclear material to cause harm or as the coercive basis of a threat. It is not clear how many hoaxers, if they had access to nuclear material, would choose to mount a real threat rather than a hoax. There continue to be many conventional bomb hoaxes even though dynamite is easy to come by. However, the interpretation of the available data, both nuclear and non-nuclear, suggests that there are those who would carry out a real nuclear threat if they had the nuclear material and the capability to use it.

It appears, from a study of hoaxes, that psychotics may be more attracted to nuclear threats than politically or criminally motivated persons. Psychotics may also be responsible for many of the low-level nuclear incidents that have occurred so far. Most psychotics would probably not attempt to do anything more serious than cause disruption. On the other hand, lunatics have been the perpetrators of many known schemes of mass murder. Thus, some psychotics would have the will to carry out the most destructive of nuclear adversary actions. In terms of actual capabilities, however, they of all the categories of potential nuclear non-state adversaries are usually the least competent. However, there are some brilliant psychotics who have technical knowledge and skill. If one such also has the will to cause destruction and has access to weapons material he would constitute a formidable adversary.

ASSESSMENT OF THREAT CREDIBILITY

It is a vital and potentially difficult problem to distinguish a hoax from a real threat—that is, a threat backed up by capability and determination.

The FBI by Federal statute is the lead investigative agency in all cases where threats are made involving radioactive material. The nuclear aspects of threat assessment have been delegated to ERDA.

Current assessment of a nuclear threat consists of both a technical evaluation of the alleged nuclear device by ERDA and a behavioral evaluation principally by the FBI, of the threat message and the context in which it originated. So far, no perpetrators have backed up their allegations of a nuclear capability by any sort of evidence.

The usual approach has been to rule out the possibility of a credible threat. If the assessment found that the threat was not credible, an assumption was usually made that it was a hoax. Positive criteria for establishing that a threat is in fact a hoax are being developed.

At this time, a great deal of emphasis is placed on evaluating technical aspects of the threat and accounting for the supplies of special nuclear material. However, even if all U.S. special nuclear material could be perfectly accounted for, a foreign source of special nuclear material could be used in a threat mounted in the United States.

The cost of evaluating, investigating, and reacting to nuclear threats is not insignificant. An increasing number of persons are acquiring information and technical expertise in nuclear matters. If a person very knowledgeable about nuclear matters were to initiate a hoax it would be difficult to negate its credibility from a technical and behavioral assessment alone. In such cases, the ability to assess the adversary's dedication to carry out the threat would be critical.

If the time should come when an adversary of verified capability presents a credible threat, then the ability to assess motivation, intent, and dedication will be essential if it is decided to establish communications.

SUMMARY

There are probably groups at large in the world today that possess or could acquire the resources necessary to become nuclear adversaries, if they wanted to. That is, they might be able to sabotage a reactor, steal fissile material, build a dispersal device, or possibly even a crude nuclear explosive device. Presently these include organized crime, certain terrorist groups who might undertake such actions with or without the assistance or complicity of a national government. Arguments arise less in the area of theoretical capabilities, but more in the area of intentions.

The historical record provides no evidence that any criminal or terrorist group has ever made any attempt to acquire fissile nuclear material or radioactive waste material for use in an explosive or dispersal device.

One ought to take little comfort from this fact, however. The lack of intelligence or visible evidence does not mean that the option has not been discussed; that some group might move in this direction without providing clues or warning. It is disquieting to realize that, in the past, most new terrorist groups have not been detected before their first terrorist act.

There is no logical progression that takes one easily from the existing pool of potential nuclear non-state adversaries to actual nuclear non-state adversaries, or from the nuclear incidents that have occurred to nuclear actions of greater consequence. Terrorist groups, as they presently exist, might be among future nuclear non-state adversaries, but their acquisition of a nuclear capability would not be a simple escalation of what has been demonstrated in terrorist actions thus far.

It is also a long conceptual jump from the present activities of organized crime to their acquisition of a nuclear capability.

Some authors of nuclear hoaxes have manifested desires of becoming nuclear non-state adversaries but none have demonstrated the required capabilities, and it is not certain that all hoaxers, even if they had access to nuclear material, would be anything more than hoaxers. In terms of intentions alone, some psychotics are potential nuclear non-state adversaries. In terms of capabilities they, of all the categories of potential nuclear non-state adversaries, are usually the least competent. To acquire a nuclear capability would require a quantum jump in capabilities for the vast majority of psychotics or an environmental change that would make the task much easier to accomplish.

Whether any of the current potential nuclear non-state adversaries, or other as yet undefined adversaries, will decide to actually go nuclear, cannot be answered at this time. Potential adversaries can be identified, their objectives, their capabilities, and the likely modes of operation if they do decide to go nuclear can be described.

There is left a vast area of uncertainty between what can be done and what will be done. The area of uncertainty could be reduced if society had a better understanding of the possible motivations and utilities of nuclear action to potential adversaries; not how society assesses its utility, rather how potential adversaries might. Although a growing body of literature on terrorism exists, much less is known about how they reach their decisions to do or not do something, how they weigh the various factors involved, how they judge risks and benefits. Likewise, in the area of crime little is known how organized crime would address a decision in this area, nor is it known if the issue has ever come up.

The nuclear non-state adversary may not arise from those groups currently identified as potential nuclear non-state adversaries; there may already be, or there may appear in the future, new kinds of adversaries, or special subclasses of existing adversaries, that have not yet been identified who might be more likely to use nuclear means to achieve their objectives. Threats to nuclear facilities or involving the malevolent use of nuclear material may emerge on a different organizational or mental plane. In the past decade, international terrorists have become a significant problem. They are a new entity which has emerged in the past decade, and although they have not yet given any indication of going nuclear, they could transform into entities that might. It is difficult to say now what new entities may emerge in the coming decade.

The origin, level, and nature of the potential nuclear non-state threat may change. Among the current adversaries, new tactics may be invented to effectively exploit the leverage that a nuclear capability would give and achieve a goal commensurate with the threat. If an individual or group successfully carried out a scheme of nuclear extortion or destruction, other individuals or groups would probably imitate the act. Thus, the probability of a second incident occurring, especially after a success, would seem to be greater than the probability of the first. The growing ties among international terrorist groups, referred to earlier in this chapter, increase the possibility of imitation.

The political context may change. Terrorists with the capabilities for acquiring a nuclear explosive may be placed in a desperate situation that will begin to erode the political arguments against nuclear action. The potential profits could become so enormous that organized criminal groups could be attracted to the nuclear industry. A war between two small nuclear powers may occur in which nuclear weapons are used, inviting further use by nations and subnational groups. Plutonium could become widely obtainable if adequate safeguards and physical security are not implemented, giving more entities the material with which to construct nuclear explosives.

Finally, the entire subject of adversary actions involving massive threats or destruction has apparently only started to receive systematic study. The imaginative use of chemicals or biological agents or even conventional explosives as the basis of a massive threat has apparently not caused much concern in the public mind, although such materials may be more easily obtainable than nuclear material and require less skill to cause large loss of life. The origins of the nuclear age may have much to do with this; the word nuclear recalls Hiroshima, not PeachBottom. Nevertheless, although the concentration on potential non-state nuclear violence to the neglect of other forms of potential mass violence may be strictly speaking irrational, it may be intuitively correct. If non-state adversary groups with the will to threaten or carry out large-scale violence do appear, they may choose nuclear means, even if it is somewhat more difficult, because they understand the public fascination and fear, and know that the nuclear threat or act will have the greatest impact.

Civil Liberties Implications of U.S. Domestic Safeguards

Civil liberties issues have recently moved to a prominent position in the public consideration of nuclear power development. The growth of concern over the impact of nuclear power on civil liberties would probably have occurred even without consideration of plutonium reprocessing. As incidents of non-nuclear terrorism have mounted worldwide there has been an increased program to guard nuclear facilities against possible sabotage. Such increased security measures raise some issues of civil liberties impact, but the development of plutonium recycle and other nuclear technologies using material that could, if diverted, be made into nuclear explosives has set off the current debates.

Plutonium reprocessing offers the greatest opportunity for potential non-state adversaries—terrorist groups, profit-oriented criminal organizations, deranged persons, and disaffected employees of nuclear facilities—to obtain special nuclear material. Therefore, this section devotes its major attention to the civil liberties impact of safeguard measures necessary to prevent the theft of plutonium and to effect its recovery if stolen.

To analyze the potential impact of plutonium recycle on civil liberties, this section will:

1. Provide a brief framework of all civil liberties concepts.
2. Describe the most likely size of a plutonium recycle industry in the near future.
3. Analyze possible safeguard measures for such an industry and discuss their civil liberties implications.
4. Present three widely held positions about the acceptability of civil liberties risks in a plutonium-safeguards program.
5. Provide observations on the underlying assumptions and relative strengths and weaknesses of these three positions.

A BRIEF FRAMEWORK OF CIVIL LIBERTIES CONCEPTS

U.S. society regards protection of individual freedom and limitations on the exercise of Government power as fundamental tenets of the Republic. Some civil liberties interests, such as the right of religious belief and exercise, receive very broad, near-absolute status; other civil liberties interests, because their exercise has impact on public health and safety, the rights of others, or national security, have to be defined and applied by balancing competing social interests or conflicting civil liberties claims. The rise of new social and economic settings, new technologies, and complex urban life also requires constant adaptation of the civil liberties concepts framed in the 18th century Bill of Rights.

What distinguishes U.S. society from many others, including some other democratic systems, is the belief that protection of civil liberty is so central to moral, political, and legal values that serious limitations on liberty should always be shown to be clearly necessary; that measures having such effects should be kept to the minimum required in a given circumstance; and that U.S. courts will weigh the need for such measures and are empowered to declare unconstitutional any laws or executive actions which transgress basic liberties.

In the context of plutonium recycle safeguards, the two aspects of civil liberties which would be most directly involved are *free expression* and *fair procedure*.

Free expression involves the guarantees of free speech, press, assembly, association, religion, and privacy protected by the First Amendment to the Federal Constitution and its State counterparts. Fair procedure, or due process, involves the standards by which Government investigatory activity should be conducted and the procedures under which Government makes formal determinations about individuals, in both administrative proceedings and criminal trials.

While courts play a central role in defining and enforcing constitutional rights in the United States, it is also tradition that the legislatures and executive branches of Federal and State governments are expected to be, and often have been, strong guardians of the citizen's liberty. This means that debates over the civil liberties implications of Government programs such as plutonium recycle are policy matters for elected officials and the public to consider. What is good civil liberties policy, therefore, is not merely a matter of what the courts may have held to be constitutional law in prior-related situations. It is also what elected officials and the American public believe to be the best balance between liberty and other social interests in a particular context. This public responsibility is especially important in situations—of which plutonium recycle is one—where it may be unlikely that the courts will pass judgment in the early phases. . . .

Potential terrorist threats to obtain and use nuclear, chemical, or biological weapons pose especially knotty problems of civil liberties policy. Since dangers to human life and public safety could be great, safeguards against such activities must be strong and effective if public confidence is to be preserved. Yet safeguard measures which would sweep so widely as to curtail basic liberties for substantial numbers of people or for broad sectors of public life could move our society toward the kind of garrison-state environment that political terrorists hope to force upon democratic nations to undermine the vitality of their social orders. Walking the line between underreaction and overreaction is the goal of democratic societies, and careful examination in advance as how to draw that line is the context in which we must examine both the decision to develop and safeguard a plutonium industry and the likely impact of various safeguard measures on civil liberties.

THE MOST LIKELY SIZE OF A PLUTONIUM RECYCLE INDUSTRY
IN THE NEAR FUTURE

When the consideration of civil liberties and plutonium recycle first arose during 1974-76, critics and supporters based their arguments on projections that envisaged a very large plutonium recycle industry in the next 25 to 50 years. By the year 2020, these early projections indicated that there would be some 60 plutonium fabricating and reprocessing plants and 2,000 reactors in the United States, an extraordinarily large number of shipments per year of special nuclear materials between fabricating plants, reprocessing plants, and storage sites; and a plutonium work force of over 1 million persons.

Official and unofficial projections have been scaled sharply downward during the past year. [Table 1], drawn from the Generic Environmental Statement on the use of Mixed Oxide Fuel (GESMO), indicates the current projections of components for a light water reactor industry using uranium and plutonium recycle. GESMO estimates that in 2000, 27,000 people would be employed in the fuel cycle and 55,000 people in the nuclear electrical power industry. Of these people, a maximum of 20,000 persons in the fuel cycle would be in positions requiring clearances, 13,000 of which would require full-field investigations.[6]

The size of the employment force needed to transport special nuclear material between fabricating and reprocessing plants has become a matter of uncertainty rather than firm projection. If the decision were made to colocate fabricating and reprocessing plants, this would eliminate the need for shipping pure plutonium offsite. Coprecipitation of plutonium oxide and uranium

Table 1. The Projected LWR Industry, 1980-2000* with U and Pu Recycle

LWR Industry Components	Number of Facilities		
	1980	1990	2000
LWR's*	71	269	507
Mines**	416	1,856	4,125
Mills	21	56	77
UF$_6$ Conversion Plants	2	4	5
Uranium Enrichment Plants	3	3	5
UO$_2$ Fuel Fabrication Plants	6	6	7
Reprocessing Plants	1	3	5
MOX Plants	1	3	8
Federal Repositories for Storage	0	2	2
Plutonium Shipments in metric tons**	5 tons	273 tons	1,170 tons
Commercial Burial Grounds	6	6	11

*From Table S-10 of Final GESMO NUREG 0002. Vol. 1 Summary.
**From Page XI-35 of Final FESMO NUREG 0002.

oxide at the reprocessing plant would also eliminate transportation of pure plutonium.

The size and distribution of a plutonium industry is now seen as much smaller than when the civil liberties impacts were first examined, and several major technological aspects remain either uncertain or are open to choice rather than being technologically determined. How this affects the civil liberties problems will be discussed later.

SAFEGUARD MEASURES FOR A PLUTONIUM INDUSTRY AND THEIR CIVIL LIBERTIES IMPLICATIONS

Current Federal law forbids the unauthorized possession of special nuclear material or efforts to obtain it illegally. Extensive personnel and physical security programs are used in military nuclear facilities, and in Government shipments of special nuclear material. The NRC's recent announcement of its intention to install a clearance program for employees of private nuclear reactors has already been noted. There are comparable personnel and physical security programs outside the nuclear industry to safeguard sensitive facilities (gold depositories, intelligence facilities); to screen out dangerous objects (airports scanning for weapons); and safeguard shipments of valuable or dangerous objects (bank currency shipments, nerve gas). This leads some commentators to conclude that plutonium safeguards would differ only in degree and not in kind from protective programs that our society already employs.

However, other commentators point to the extremely high level of harm that would be done if a nuclear diversion and explosion were successful (in numbers of deaths and long-term radiation effects), and to the immense public fear of nuclear explosion that a blackmail threat itself would generate. They conclude that these risks are so great that a plutonium safeguards program would have to be different in kind, not merely degree. It would have to be far more intense, permanent, and put more people outside the plutonium industry under preventive or responsive intelligence than anything presently in force.

There are several important points of agreement between these two views:

1. If plutonium recycle is initiated, there would be a genuine need for high-security measures. In other words, this would not be an instance where responsible critics would allege that there was no need for any strong measures, as they denied the presence of security risks serious enough to justify passage of the Alien or Sedition Laws in the 1790's, the Palmer round-ups of aliens in the 1920's, or the Joseph McCarthy investigations of the 1950's.

2. In the general public debate over broad police powers of arrest, search and seizure, some argue that work should be done on the underlying problems that cause high crime—such as unemployment or racial discrimination—rather than allow police to use intrusive or harsh techniques. In the case of potential threats against plutonium plants, however, there are no real prospects in the foreseeable future of adopting national or international policies to remove the causes of all political terrorism, individual derangement, or criminal conspiracies, thereby obviating the need for high-security measures.

3. No complete technological solution is available, or is foreseen, that could entirely eliminate the need for other safeguards measures which could raise civil liberties issues. For example, the machine scanners used in airport searches have made it unnecessary to require pat-down searches of millions of air travelers, thus providing a technological measure of acceptability to the courts and the public. However, searches to recover plutonium, if diverted, could not presently be accomplished by radiation detection alone, and it would be necessary to use some measures that would have potential for violating civil liberties.

Having noted these areas of general agreement among observers of the safeguards problem, the types of safeguards used in the past in high-security contexts are described and their civil liberties implications discussed. These can be grouped under four headings: employee screening; material production; threat analysis; and recovery measures.

1. *Employee screening* ranges from minimal national agency name checks and questionnaires asking for detailed personal histories to full-field investigations asking neighbors, former employers, and associates about the background, loyalty, character, and life style of applicants for employment. Screening may also entail the use of polygraphs to measure physical and emotional responses to questions about suitability characteristics (use of drugs, thefts, lying about previous activities or the use of psychological tests to investigate emotional and mental instability. All of these techniques could be directed at identifying employees who might use their position to steal or sabotage nuclear material. There are serious civil liberties concerns over both the standards of conduct employed in such screening (such as current denials of sensitive employment to homosexuals) and the verification techniques used (polygraphs and psychological tests, which have been attacked as both unreliable and as invasions of privacy).

2. *Material protection* involves measures to control access to or misuse of special nuclear material. Some of these—such as mechanical detec-

tion of radioactive material, inspection of hand-carried items, and
personal identity checks—do not raise serious civil liberties issues.
Other techniques, such as visual or audio surveillance of workers on
the job or pat-down searches (frisking) of individuals entering or
leaving an area do raise civil liberties issues.

3. *Threat analysis* would involve efforts to obtain advance warning of
diversion or sabotage attempts, or to guide recovery efforts should a
successful diversion take place. Overt intelligence checks of potential
assailants usually entail investigative techniques such as background
inquiries, checks of law enforcement intelligence files, and physical
surveillance. Covert intelligence measures may include electronic surveillance, surreptitious entries, use of informants and undercover
agents, mail openings, and similar methods. While overt intelligence
techniques may be both necessary and acceptable if limited to genuine potential terrorists, the classic civil liberties danger in such activity is that the investigative net is cast too widely, and covers large
numbers of ideological dissidents. The overt intelligence techniques
also raise this danger, exacerbated by the covert nature of the privacy-
invading methods. Whether covert techniques are used under administrative controls or are subject to either judicial or legislative committee supervision, bears on the degree of potential injury they will
inflict.

4. *Recovery measures* are potentially the most dangerous to civil liberties. At the low end of the spectrum in potential harm are quaran-
tines of the facility, full-scale searches of personnel, and searches of
surrounding areas by mechanical (radioactivity) detectors. At the high
end of the spectrum, should other measures fail, could be large-scale
roundups of suspects, room-by-room physical searches by hand,
wholesale evacuation of populations from target areas, censorship of
the press, and harsh interrogation of persons strongly believed to be
members of the diversion groups or who know the location of
stolen material.

With this brief overview of the kinds of measures involved in safeguard
programs, the following section discusses the estimate of civil liberties risks
and trade-offs in the context of three main positions about plutonium and
civil liberties developed over the past few years.

THREE POSITIONS WIDELY HELD IN U.S. SOCIETY AS TO THE
CIVIL LIBERTIES RISKS OF PLUTONIUM RECYCLE

The positions described below have been constructed from an analysis of
public statements made by industry representatives, scientific and legal

experts, executive-agency officials, members of Congress, public-interest groups, and similar commentators. . . .

Position One: A Plutonium Economy Would Require Such Extensive Safeguards and Curtailments of Civil Liberties That Its Creation Would Jeopardize Free Society in the United States.

This position makes a number of key assumptions:

a. The presence of hundreds of thousands of pounds of plutonium in reprocessing plants or in transit—when 20 pounds would be enough to make a nuclear explosive, and with prevailing conditions of domestic and international terrorism—poses a situation so perilous to public safety that only a far-reaching zero-risk safeguards program would be sufficient to protect the public. Therefore, that kind of sweeping safeguard program is the one to envisage.

b. The immense potential consequences of a nuclear diversion from inside or an assault from outside would probably lead the courts to uphold sweeping preventive intelligence measures. The courts would be even more likely to decline to interfere if Government took Draconian measures in response to a blackmail threat or nuclear incident. The release of intelligence agencies and security investigators from constitutional limits would not only be harmful in itself but would also be likely to stimulate surveillance and dossier-building in non-nuclear fields.

c. Even if a safeguards program were originally set up with strong civil liberties protection written into legislation or executive orders, public reaction to foreseeable incidents of diversion and blackmail, and certainly to any successful explosion, would lead to the dropping of such limitations and the adoption of a maximum security program. Thus no safeguards program can be expected to stay limited as a plutonium economy continues for any length of time.

d. The growing political movement opposing nuclear power will produce protest demonstrations focused on highly visible targets such as fuel-cycle facilities and transportation. This will require harsh protective responses and produce serious confrontations.

e. Giving industrial security forces and corporate managements a role in collecting data and managing security programs about employees would be harmful to sound employer-employee relations.

f. Given these likely consequences, and the fact that alternative energy sources such as coal or solar power require no such safeguard measures, proponents of plutonium recycle must prove to Congress and the public that no other energy sources or conservation programs can be developed to meet American energy needs, even at higher but not unbearable economic costs.

Based on these assumptions, Position One concludes:

1. On civil liberties grounds alone, Congress should reject plutonium recycle.
2. The United States should not export plutonium technology. This is partly to diminish the threat of diverted plutonium being smuggled into this country by terrorists, thus creating the need for extensive customs-search procedures. It is also urged in order to avoid having the United States export a technology that would inhibit the evolution of greater civil liberties in developing nations.

Position Two: Safeguards Can Be Adopted for a Plutonium Industry That Would Be Both Effective Against Threats and Acceptable in Terms of Civil Liberties.

Position Two proceeds from the following primary assumptions:

a. Operators of military and commercial nuclear facilities have been managing safeguard programs successfully for decades; adapting these to the new scope and requirements of a plutonium economy would therefore represents an expansion of present operations, not a totally new venture.

b. It is unacceptable for a strong society such as the United States to let potential threats from a few terrorists, criminals, or disturbed people deprive the American economy and the public of badly needed energy supply. Nuclear power is economically competitive with other sources, capable of safe use, and environmentally sound. The need to safeguard nuclear power facilities is no more a reason for rejecting nuclear power than potential threats against other vulnerable facilities, such as natural gas facilities, dams, city water reservoirs or subway systems constitute good reason to close them down.

c. Whether the size of a plutonium work force would be 20,000 or 1 million, it is justified to set clearance standards for persons who choose to work in that industry. This deprives no one of her/his rights to pursue gainful employment, even in the nuclear field, as there will be many other nuclear research and operating facilities beside the commercial plutonium industry. The same justification of voluntary choice with advance knowledge is presently seen to justify other personnel security measures in highly sensitive operations outside the nuclear field.

d. The intrusions into personal liberties of workers, community residents, and diversion suspects that would take place if a diversion were detected or a nuclear blackmail threat made—awesome as those situations are—are really no different than if nerve gas or a highly dangerous bacteriological agent were stolen from a civilian or military site. In all such cases, preliminary investigation by professionals would establish the credibility of the danger, negotiations would be weighed, and a response pursued appropriate to the situation. There is simply no way a democratic society can *eliminate* the possibility of such episodes.

e. Regarding intelligence-gathering about potential diverters, there is a need for obtaining intelligence about terrorist organizations and other groups whose actual conduct indicates that they might use nuclear means of violence. Legislation and regulations would carefully spell out the operational limits of such intelligence programs, both as to the range of groups on which data would be collected and the methods used to do so.

Based on these assumptions, Position Two reaches the following conclusions:

1. After full public participation in a rule-making proceeding addressing both safeguards requirements and civil liberties considerations, the United States should proceed with a plutonium licensing program.
2. The United States should also proceed with sales of plutonium recycle facilities abroad, under a safeguards program that would meet both U.S. and IAEA standards.

Position Three: An Acceptable Program of Plutonium Safeguards Is Possible But Only If American Society Is Willing to Run Some Permanent Risks of Diversion in Order to Keep Civil Liberties Risks at a Low Level.

These assumptions underlie Position Three:

a. To adopt a zero-risk approach to safeguards, or even to speak of holding threats to negligible proportions, is to ensure that the civil liberties costs of such a program will be unbearably high. Once it is assumed that reducing threats to near zero is the objective, managers of a safeguards program would be driven to adopt highly dangerous techniques of personnel security and preventive intelligence.

b. Instead of this standard, there should be adoption of a standard that would trade-off some *small* risks of diversion against *heavy* risks to basic civil liberties. Americans should see the creation of a reasonable, efficient, and freedom-respecting network of safeguards as the approach to plutonium security.

c. This would mean deliberately rejecting some widely proposed techniques of personnel screening, employee monitoring, and preventive-intelligence gathering on anti-nuclear groups, not merely because many of these techniques are of doubtful effectiveness but because their civil liberties costs are too high. In balancing slightly greater risks of diversion against very heavy risks to basic freedoms, the decision would have to be made to protect freedoms.

d. A least restrictive alternative test can be applied to each component of a safeguards program. As a recent report to the Nuclear Regulatory Commission put it:

We think it vital that such a "least restrictive alternative" approach be the keystone of the NRC's approach to the selection and shaping of safeguards measures. In approaching a particular safeguards problem, the Commission should evaluate the impact on civil liberties of each of the ways of solving that problem. The factors to be considered in evaluating the impact of various safeguards measures on civil liberties should include the following: (1) the extent of the intrusion on personal liberties; (2) the frequency and pervasiveness of the intrusion on civil liberties (Will it be part of a daily routine or will it only occasionally be employed? Will its effects be temporary and limited or long lasting?); (3) the number and types of individuals affected (employees in nuclear plants, members of suspected terrorist organizations or dissident groups, "innocent" members of the public); (4) the likelihood that a particular safeguards measure will actually be employed; and (5) the likelihood that the same or similar invasions of civil liberties will take place even if the safeguards measure under consideration is not employed.[7]

e. For plutonium recycle to go forward, such a set of fully articulated trade-offs would have to: be set out as the philosophy of a safeguards program; be tested before the public in a variety of hearings and proceedings; be fully accepted by the commercial firms and Government regulatory agencies most directly concerned; be written explicitly into legislation and implementing regulations; be subjected to firm annual reporting duties and legislative reviews; and have procedures created for both administrative appeals and judicial review.

f. It would be especially important to a proper safeguards program that the Nuclear Regulatory Commission not simply turn over to the discretion of the FBI the conduct of preventive intelligence for plutonium security, or leave the decisionmaking responsibility in a recovery effort or diversion response to ad hoc developments among Federal, State, and local officials. These activities, because they are among the most important for civil liberties, should be defined and supervised by the NRC, possibly with a congressional oversight role.

g. Holding to this line would involve continually reaffirming the bargain in the face of probable low-level and possible high-level incidents. This would mean that the American public would have to hold the line of moderation, refusing to let itself be stampeded by demagogues, and forcing sufficient public supervision to prevent the program being subverted by secret government.

Based on these assumptions, Position Three draws the following policy conclusions:

1. Congress should go forward with a full-dress review of the need of plutonium recycle to meet America's future energy demands, and of

whether this process can be made environmentally and physically safe. If the answer to these inquiries is yes, then Congress should receive from NRC a fully worked out plan for safeguards, which then would be publicly reviewed and implemented.

2. Position Three takes no stand on the desirability or civil liberties risks of selling plutonium technology abroad.

Observations and Comments on the Three Positions

The effort to isolate key differences among the three major positions obviously produces some rigidity in stating premises and conclusions. Someone may share one or more premises of a position without reaching the same final conclusion as the advocates of that position. For example, a person may believe that the voluntary nature of employment in a plutonium industry justifies personnel clearances without concluding that it justifies more intrusive techniques, such as polygraph examinations. Also, the differences between Position One (which would forgo plutonium recycle because of civil liberties concerns) and the other two positions (which would go forward with plutonium recycle with different steps to solve civil liberties problems) are clearly more marked than the differences between Positions Two and Three.

There is also a sense in which each of the three positions outlined is partially right.

1. Position One points correctly to the dangers of so much plutonium being handled in a world of terror and mishap; the public pressure that could be created to use Draconian safeguards measures; and the highly optimistic assumptions as to unbroken national responsibilities and moderation on which both Positions Two and Three rest their faith.

2. Position Two reminds us that the year 2020 will come gradually, allowing a plutonium economy to develop slowly; safeguards could therefore be developed step by step, modifying the technology, physical locations, plant design, shipment procedures, and many other elements as it went along.

3. Position Three suggests persuasively that it has been a traditional feature of American pragmatism to resist either/or choices, seeking ways to trade off one set of risks against another to preserve both liberty and order.

It is helpful also to examine the effect of some altered assumptions of safeguard approaches on these positions, and some of their weaker points.

1. The concerns of Position One about diversion of special nuclear material during transportation would be greatly reduced if colocation

of reprocessing and fabrication facilities or coprocessing (without co-location) completely eliminated transportation of weapons material. Similarly, concerns about assaults by outsiders would diminish if facilities containing material usable in weapons were convincingly designed to prevent removal of weapons materials even by a large, heavily armed band. Such successful defenses for colocated facilities could reduce or eliminate the need for offsite security measures such as surveillance and dossier-building on members of the public. Finally, if the number of people in the plutonium industry who would be subjected to on-job surveillance were very limited in number (such as several tens of thousands), the number of people affected is less than presently exists in the defense industry or other sensitive private activities. It is not clear, however, what number of employees must be affected in order to reach a point of civil liberties concern; some people would regard 20,000 as an acceptable number for such intensive security measures; others might accept only lower numbers.

2. The assurances contained in Position Two would be disputed by many knowledgeable persons. It is not *proven* that the past and present safeguards system has been totally successful. Because of the significant amounts of unaccounted for material accumulated over the last 20 years, the possibility that diversions have already occurred cannot be dismissed. However, none of this material has ever been involved in a weapons threat. (Note that all weapons threats received to date have been hoaxes. . . .) Nor is it clear that Position One is correct in saying that an expanded plutonium industry merely represents a difference in degree, not in type. In cases where a plutonium facility becomes a major or dominant employer in a community, there is less freedom of choice for residents as to whether they accede to the security restrictions or refuse to work at the facility. In small rural communities the company-town syndrome may appear, making it difficult for employees to resist extensive security measures.

3. As for Position Three, past experience with security officers makes many persons doubtful about the possibility of containing a security program to least restrictive security procedures. Security personnel are prone to seek tighter measures; professionally, they tend to seek foolproof techniques that threaten infringement of civil liberties. Even with tight internal security and strong perimeter defenses, it is likely that security personnel would want to employ positive intelligence (e.g., surveillance and informers to identify potential attackers or critics). Also, the addition of ombudsmen or public advocates to the system to protect against unwarranted security intrusions is subject to the well-known danger that constant proximity to security pro-

cesses render them too sensitive to the needs of the security forces. Finally, Position Three may be ignoring the resulting effect of a successful diversion if followed by major threat or actual casualties. It is not clear that the original limited safeguards system contemplated by Position Three would survive the pressures of an outraged public determined to prevent any further incidents.

In trying to decide which one or combination of these views is right and therefore should be used in policymaking, it should be recognized that this is not a problem that can be put to the tests of either logic or empirical investigation. The reality is that each of these positions rests, fundamentally, on sociopolitical judgments as to how the U.S. Government and public opinion have dealt in the past with threats to national security (real or assumed); how Government and commercial security forces would be likely to carry out a safeguards program; how much privacy, dissent, protest, and cultural diversity our civil liberties traditions demand or our society should encourage; and how the American public would probably respond to diversions, blackmail threats, or a nuclear explosion, in terms of its shocked post-incident attitudes toward the scope of safeguards measures.

There is also no good decision guide in the way other industrialized democracies are dealing with the plutonium recycle issue. In Britain, for example, the debate over plutonium and civil liberties is in almost exactly the same stage as in this country. There is support in British Government documents, parliamentary reports, commercial industry materials, and civic group literature for each of the three positions outlined above.

In conclusion, the choice between the total ban on plutonium advocated by Position One and the acceptance of plutonium recycle by Positions Two and Three (though with different conceptions of how to conduct a safeguards program) is likely to be made on a total package basis by U.S. society, not on the basis of the civil liberties considerations alone. Indeed, the civil liberties aspects really tend to reinforce the existing orientations of each of the main contending parties debating the value and risks of plutonium recycle as an energy source.

The single most important conclusion suggested by this review is that if a plutonium industry as described earlier in Table 1 were to be pursued in the near future, steady attention would need to be paid by Congress, the executive agencies, public-interest groups, and the courts to the way in which safeguards are defined, administered, monitored, and reviewed. Keeping a plutonium safeguards program consistent with civil liberties would become an important, continuing task of those who cherish American freedom.

Notes

1. NUREG-0095/ERDA 77-34; Joint ERDA-NRC Task Force on Safeguards (U) Final Report July 1976; Unclassified Version; p. ii.
2. Roberta Wohlstetter, Terror on a Grand Scale, *Survival*, May/June 1976.
3. Douglas DeNike, Radioactive Malevolence, *Bulletin of the Atomic Scientists* (February 1974).
4. *The Threat to Licensed Nuclear Facilities, MTR-7022*, p. 95, The Mitre Corporation, September 1975.
5. Brian Jenkins, "Will Terrorists Go Nuclear?," Paper #64, California Seminar on Arms Control and Foreign Policy, Santa Monica, October 1975.
6. In March 1977, the Nuclear Regulatory Commission announced a proposed rule to require 4,000 employees in 63 private nuclear reactors to get a security clearance requiring full-field investigation, and 2,000 employees in such plants to get the equivalent of a "confidential" clearance, requiring a name check against national agency files. This program is aimed primarily at protecting against reactor sabotage.
7. Timothy B. Dyk, Daniel Marcus, and William J. Kolasky, Jr., *Civil Liberties Implications of a Safeguards Program for Special Nuclear Material in the Private Nuclear Power Industry*, a report to the Nuclear Regulatory Commission, October 31, 1975.

Part IV
Coping with the Threat

Forrest Frank

Nuclear Terrorism and the Escalation of International Conflict

After rehearsing the new familiar vulnerabilities that combine to create the threat of nuclear terrorism, Frank provides some interesting preliminary commentary on the possible effects that an act of nuclear terrorism might have on international relations. Proceeding from a position that views nuclear terror as an act possessed of (inherent) ambiguity, he sees considerable risk that the act could precipitate interstate conflict. The risks range from crises resultant of retributory acts to a catalytic war.

The dangers posed by the proliferation of nuclear weapons among nations of the world to international security have long been recognized by analysts of political and military affairs.[1] Problems for international security posed by terrorist acts have also been examined.[2] Recent analysis, however, has focused on the nexus of these two different threats to international security—terrorist acquisition and possible use of nuclear explosive devices, radiological weapons, or attacks on various nuclear facilities and installations.[3] Few studies have examined the problems arising from incidents of nuclear terrorism, choosing instead to focus solely on the feasibility or probability of nuclear terrorism. These studies have resulted in significant improvements in efforts to protect physically nuclear materials and nuclear weapons stockpiles, particularly those under U.S. jurisdiction.[4] However, the problem of limiting the escalation of conflict arising from terrorist acts in which nuclear explosive devices, radiological weapons, or attacks on nuclear facilities are employed remains to be considered. This paper addresses this problem. Hopefully it will initiate scholarly discussion and analysis.

The views expressed in this article are solely those of the author and in no way do they necessarily represent the views of either the International Division or the Comptroller General of the United States.

Defining Nuclear Terrorism

Nuclear terrorism can be defined as the unauthorized use or attempted use of nuclear explosive devices, use or attempted use of nuclear materials, or attacks or attempted attacks on nuclear facilities and installations for extortionate purposes. The victim of nuclear terrorism may be an individual, a group of individuals, an organization, or a government. The primary actor on whom the burden of response to nuclear terrorism will fall, however, is the government of a nation on whose territory nuclear terrorist acts are committed. Governments rather than individuals, groups of individuals, or organizations will assume primary responsibility for response because of the scope and magnitude of the effects nuclear terrorist acts may have on individuals, property, and the entire fabric of society.

Four distinct types of nuclear terrorist acts can be considered: overt threat to use nuclear explosive devices or radiological weapons, or an overt threat to attack a nuclear facility; use of nuclear explosive devices; use of radiological weapons; and attacks on nuclear facilities housing nuclear weapons, peaceful nuclear explosive devices, nuclear fuel cycle processes and materials, or nuclear weapons fabrication processes and materials.

How likely is nuclear terrorism? The answer to this question depends on several factors; however, three factors seem particularly significant. The first factor is the amount of expertise needed to fabricate or otherwise acquire nuclear explosive devices or radiological weapons or to attack various nuclear facilities. The amount of expertise needed to fabricate a nuclear explosive device varies in inverse proportion to the fissionability of material available. No expertise is required to assemble a nuclear explosive device if it can be stolen intact from the arsenal of a nuclear weapon state or a state possessing "peaceful nuclear explosive devices." Considerable expertise is necessary to fabricate a nuclear explosive device from uranium highly enriched in isotope 235 or 233 or from plutonium. Vast amounts of expertise as well as considerable capital equipment and other economic resources are required to fabricate natural uranium isotope 238 into a nuclear explosive device.

It is important to bear in mind that a terrorist trying to construct a nuclear explosive device does not operate under the same rigorous performance constraints that bound the efforts of a military weapon designer. After all, "a clandestine nuclear bomb maker may care little whether his bombs are heavy, inefficient, and unpredictable. They may serve his purposes so long as they are transportable by automobile and are very likely to explode with a yield equivalent to at least 100 tons of chemical explosive."[5] While the amount of expertise needed to construct a bomb is perhaps no greater than that derived from college physics, chemistry, and perhaps engineering, the amount of expertise needed to construct a simple device for dispersing radioactive material is even less. Any container capable of dispensing liquid radioactive waste under pressure would be sufficient; pouring liquid or particulate radioactive materials into air-conditioning systems of large buildings or into urban water supplies might also represent highly effective methods of dispersing some radioactive materials.

The amount of expertise needed to attack a nuclear facility depends, in very large measure, on the kind of facility to be attacked. Some facilities such as nuclear weapons fabrication plants are heavily guarded and would require a sizable force of terrorists for there to be much chance of a successful attack. Other installations such as nuclear fuel fabrication plants, nuclear power reactors, spent nuclear fuel reprocessing centers, critical assemblies used in research, and various installations using radioisotopes in research, industrial processes, or medical treatments might require very little military-type expertise to be successfully overcome.

The second factor bearing on the likelihood of nuclear terrorism is the accessibility of nuclear materials to potential nuclear terrorists. There are many radioactive substances that might be suitable for use as radiological weapons. These are materials that could be acquired from scientific supply houses, industrial materials wholesalers, and other types of industries catering to the research, teaching, and quality control market. Most, if not all of these substances, however, are not suitable for use in nuclear explosive devices.

There are relatively few materials that can be taken off the shelf of a chemical supply house or a nuclear facility and fabricated into a nuclear explosive device. Most of these materials are not widely distributed or used outside the nuclear power or nuclear explosives fabrication industries. These materials include the following: uranium enriched to 90 percent in isotope 235 or 233; plutonium; plutonium nitrate in solution; enriched uranium isotope 235 hexafluoride; high-temperature, gas-cooled reactor graphite-coated fuel particles; fuel elements for light water reactors using plutonium; plutonium oxide and depleted uranium oxide pellets used as fuel for liquid metal fast breeder reactors, and critical assemblies used in physics research on college campuses and in industry.[6] Most, if not all, of these materials are regulated by international safeguards when transferred from a nuclear weapon state to other states; the U.S. Government also imposes standards of physical security on installations handling these materials as well as other materials that could, with additional processing, be fabricated into nuclear explosive devices.[7] Other nations employ similar systems of physical and accounting safeguards to minimize the likelihood of theft or misuse of these nuclear materials. Limiting access to these materials by various methods significantly reduces the likelihood that terrorists will be able to acquire materials which could be fabricated into a nuclear explosive device. Unfortunately, access to materials that could be used in radiological weapons is often not well regulated by national or international safeguards.[8]

The third factor that figures prominently in calculating the likelihood of nuclear terrorism is the motivation of individuals and groups employing terrorist tactics to achieve their political and/or economic objectives. While our definition of terrorism has excluded psychotic or neurotic behavior, deranged individuals might also employ nuclear explosive devices, radiological weapons, or attack various nuclear facilities as a result of their illnesses. One analyst has prepared a list of potential terrorists and the motivations underlying their behaviors:

Possible Malefactors

1. Foreign governments and their agents, acting under orders.
2. Sub-units of foreign governments and their agents or military forces acting with or without official sanction.
3. Individuals or groups engaged in domestic subversive activity: extremists, terrorists, nihilists.
4. Criminals—highly organized, loosely associated, or individual.
5. Psychopaths, severe neurotics, and psychotics, harboring sadistic, homicidal, or suicidal motives.
6. Mercenaries in the pay of others, or who need the money to pay off debts, support a heroin addiction, etc.
7. Disgruntled employees seeking to sabotage an installation for revenge, or out of casual vandalism.

Motives for Nuclear Malfeasance

1. International enmity or rivalry.
2. Sectional or factional enmity, such as civil war, terrorism.
3. Desire to create panic or interrupt electrical power, either for its own sake or secondary to some other design, such as looting under cover of darkness, etc.
4. Desire to establish credibility of later threats of repetition, demands for blackmail payments, etc.
5. Desire to obtain special nuclear materials for bombs.
6. Desire to obtain radioactive waste materials for terror, homicide, blackmail, or resale. Motives 6 and 7 may also subsume the desire to control such materials in order to secure immunity from persecution or prosecution for the thieves or for others as stipulated in threats to the authorities.
7. Sadistic motivation—merely to cause suffering. This might take the form of a specific grudge against particular persons likely to be killed or injured in a nuclear incident, such as employer, spouse, rival, etc.

8. Suicidal/homicidal motivation—to die spectacularly, take other lives at the same time.
9. Publicity motivation to get one's name in the papers, or to publicize some specific cause (a frequent motive for aircraft hijacking and terrorism).
10. Psychotic motivation. This can take various forms, depending on the nature of the delusional system involved.[9]

One might add to this list the theft or possible use of materials by accident of opportunity. Clearly, recent experience in the Middle East, in Northern Ireland, in Japan, in the United States, in Western Europe, and in Latin America illustrates the willingness of individuals to use extreme, extortionate violence to attain their political and/or economic objectives.

In calculating the likelihood of nuclear terrorism, at least these three factors must be simultaneously evaluated. Merely because an individual has expertise in the design of nuclear explosive devices and may have access to materials that could be used to fabricate such a device, he may not be motivated to become a nuclear terrorist. Indeed, I suspect that a potential nuclear terrorist first would consider using nuclear materials or attacking nuclear facilities, then he would acquire the necessary expertise to fabricate a nuclear explosive device, construct a radiological weapon, or attack a nuclear facility. Finally, he would seek out the appropriate materials to carry out such plans.

Reasonable people may reach different conclusions about the net threat of nuclear terrorism. Some may conclude that the threat is not very great; others may conclude nuclear terrorism is imminent. My own view is that nuclear terrorism is probably inevitable. We have already witnessed several terrorist or terrorist related incidents involving nuclear materials.

At least one attempt has been made to extort money from government officials by an individual threatening to destroy a city with a homemade, thermonuclear bomb. The attempt was thwarted by good police work, not because the design of the bomb accompanying extortion notes was considered defective by government officials.[10] Unknown individuals disseminated radioactive materials normally used in medicine aboard an Austrian train in April 1974, causing much concern if not substantial property damage and casualties among railroad passengers.[11] Concern over possible theft of nuclear weapons has mounted in the United States over the past few years as various shortcomings in the physical security of U.S. nuclear weapons have been revealed. In 1974, reports reached the press that a Nike-Hercules antiaircraft installation outside Baltimore had been broken into in an apparent attempt to steal nuclear weapons thought to be stored at that installation for use in air defense.[12] During the period, 1973-1975, members of Congress investigated the security of U.S. nuclear weapons stored overseas.

Senator Symington, commenting on U.S. nuclear weapons stored in Korea, reported that we "were not being as careful with our nuclear stockpile in the Far East as we are in Europe."[13] The European situation was termed "critical" by Senators Pastore and Baker in discussions with Defense Secretary Elliot Richardson upon their return from an inspection of the U.S. European nuclear weapons stockpile.[14] While many of these deficiencies were corrected in the eyes of critical Senators,[15] the U.S. Government intends to continue its efforts to upgrade the security of nuclear weapons stored at home and abroad to the tune of $230 million over the period, July 1975 through September 1977.[16]

In addition to these problems, there have been several known threats against nuclear facilities such as nuclear reactors or uranium enrichment plants.[17] The crash of a B-52 bomber some 20 miles from a nuclear power reactor plant in South Carolina[18] raised the specter of a terrorist flying a "kamikaze" mission into a nuclear facility. David Krieger quotes then Atomic Energy Commission Chairman Dr. James Schlesinger, appearing on a radio question-and-answer program, discussing this subject with typical bluntness and candor:

> If one intends to crash a plane into a facility and one is able
> to persuade the pilot that that is the best way to go, there is,
> I suspect, little that can be done about the problem.
> The nuclear plants that we are building today are designed
> carefully to take the impact of, I believe, a 200,000 pound
> aircraft arriving at something on the order of 150 miles per
> hour. It will not take the impact of a larger aircraft.[19]

Krieger notes that a Boeing 747 "weighs about 365,000 pounds and travels considerably faster than 150 miles per hour."[20] Thus, even nuclear power plants protected by very strong physical security on the ground might be vulnerable to air attack by kamikaze pilots or remotely piloted vehicles.

We have witnessed only a few incidents resulting in minimal property damage, little loss of governmental prestige, and minimal international conflict. What will happen, however, if a terrorist group succeeds in stealing nuclear materials, fabricates a bomb, and actually detonates it? Furthermore, what will happen if the terrorists steal materials from one country, fabricate a bomb in bases on the territory of a second country, and detonate the bomb on the territory of yet a third? What will the government victimized by a nuclear terrorist act do? How will other nations respond to the nuclear terrorist incident and the countermeasures taken by the victim government? We turn now to a consideration of the physical effects and political consequences of nuclear terrorism.

The Effects of Nuclear Terrorism

There are several physical effects that would result from the detonation of a nuclear explosive device, the dispersal of radioactive material, or the attack on various nuclear installations in which radioactive material was released. Use of nuclear explosive devices by terrorists would result in the same types of damage caused by military use of nuclear weapons. Dispersal of radioactive material might cause many of the same problems associated with the effects of radioactive fallout from atmospheric nuclear weapons tests or the long-term consequences of the use of nuclear weapons. Attacks on various nuclear installations resulting in the release of radioactive materials might cause a broad range of physical effects ranging in severity from little more than small spills of radioactive material following accidents involving U.S. nuclear weapons in the midair collision of a B-52 bomber and a tanker over Spain[21] to the kinds of damage envisioned as the result of a nuclear reactor core meltdown with simultaneous failure of the emergency core cooling system[22]

Terrorist detonation of a nuclear explosive device would cause damage and casualties as a result of four specific forces: blast, thermal radiation, prompt nuclear radiation, and long-term nuclear radiation. Additionally, disruption of communications and malfunctions of electronic equipment might occur as the result of electromagnetic pulse. The severity of these effects would depend on a number of factors, including the following: yield of the explosion; types of materials used in the fabrication of the device, height of the device above ground at the time of detonation; prevailing wind and weather conditions at the time of detonation and for a period of hours thereafter; relative hardness of the target area; and the amount of relief, rescue, and medical aid immediately available to survivors of blast and thermal effects.[23]

The effects of terrorist use of radiological weapons are far more difficult to predict. Such effects would depend in very large measure on the kinds of radioactive materials dispersed, the pattern of dispersal, and the length of time individuals are exposed to radioactive materials. Use of radiological weapons, in addition to possibly causing casualties, would result in the contamination of a wide range of physical resources including land, water supplies, buildings, and capital equipment. These effects would also occur as a consequence of radioactive fallout generated by the detonation of a nuclear explosive device. Dispersal of radioactive material might not cause casualties; however, it would necessitate expensive, time-consuming, disruptive decontamination efforts.[24]

Attacks on nuclear facilities intended to cause the release of radioactive material into the atmosphere are perhaps the most difficult forms of nuclear terrorism to evaluate in terms of physical effects. The nature of the work being carried out at the installation to be attacked, the kind of materials and processes used in the facility, the difficulty in bypassing redundant safety features built into the facility, the ability of the facility effectively to contain released radiation within its physical structures or on the site, and the degree of physical protection against direct attack are all important variables that affect the physical effects of terrorist attacks on nuclear facilities. While overcoming these obstacles to the release of radioactive material into the biosphere during a terrorist act is a major task, Theodore B. Taylor reminds us that criminals have been eminently successful in attacking heavily fortified buildings and vaults in recent years:

> In the last fifteen years more than two dozen major thefts
> from modern alarmed vaults wired directly to a protective
> agency have been reported. Alarm systems connected only to
> the door of the secured place have been circumvented, and
> comprehensive alarm systems have been successfully discon-
> connected. Burglars have used diamond-tipped steel drills,
> acetylene torches, twenty-millimeter antitank guns, thermic
> lances, explosives, and other highly specialized equipment to
> penetrate cement-filled doors, steel-reinforced concrete vault
> walls, steel vaults, and steel vault doors as much as two feet
> thick.[25]

Taylor argues, in effect, that nuclear facilities are vulnerable to attack by highly organized, well-equipped terrorists just as are Brinks armored trucks, large bank vaults, and other "secure" installations.

A broad set of qualifications must be introduced in trying to estimate the effects of an attack on a nuclear facility that results in the release of nuclear or radioactive materials into the biosphere. The location of the facility in relation to large concentrations of civilian or military personnel is obviously important in estimating casualties. The weather at the time of the incident and for a period of hours thereafter is also an important factor. The extent to which the site of such an attack was cut off from outside assistance would also affect the number and extent of casualties, as would the reaction of individuals displaced by preventative or rescue and relief efforts. Mass panic arising from fear, hasty and poorly planned evacuation of areas, unconfirmed rumors, et cetera, could claim large numbers of lives through accidents, coronaries, and the withdrawal of medical services by overworked, frightened, and perhaps injured medical personnel.[26]

The ability of terrorists to acquire and use nuclear explosive devices or radiological weapons, or to attack successfully nuclear facilities causing the release of radioactive material into the biosphere may lead to wild speculation about the number of casualties in various scenarios. While numbers are somewhat hard to pin down, there are many factors which influence the severity of casualties resulting from blast, thermal radiation, prompt nuclear radiation, and long-term radiation. The types of materials used, weather, distribution of radioactive materials, length of exposure to radiation sources, and the reaction of the victims of nuclear terrorist acts all bear on the severity of the physical effects of nuclear terrorism. The physical effects of nuclear terrorism, in turn, may substantially affect the political consequences of nuclear terrorism. We turn now to a consideration of this aspect of the problems posed by nuclear terrorism.

The Political Consequences of Nuclear Terrorism

There is a variety of political consequences arising from incidents of nuclear terrorism that affect governments of many states in addition to the government of the state victimized by nuclear terrorist acts. While the latter is necessarily faced with the most difficult choices in responding to and coping with the effects of nuclear terrorism, a number of factors very quickly bring other governments into contact with the political fallout of a nuclear terrorist act. While the broad range of specific acts of nuclear terrorism and the incalculable number of potential targets make it impossible to detail all the possible consequences of nuclear terrorism, analysts should try to understand those types of consequences or actions that would be particularly important in controlling the escalation of international conflict following an incident of nuclear terrorism.

There are at least four major types of consequences or actions that merit attention. First, we should consider how the government of a victimized state will react to the nuclear terrorist act. Second, we should examine how other states will perceive the victim's actions and reactions to nuclear terrorism. Third, we must consider the actions of the government of the state ravaged by nuclear terrorism toward other states. Finally, we should contemplate the broad systemic consequences of nuclear terrorism for international relations generally.

The government of a state which is attacked by nuclear terrorists in any of the four broad types outlined above is immediately confronted with several problems. It must determine if a threat to use nuclear explosive devices or radiological weapons or to attack nuclear facilities is credible, or it must verify the actual occurrence of a terrorist act. Second, it must identify the most probable perpetrators of nuclear terrorism independently of various claims of responsibility. Third, it must cope with a variety of domestic problems generated by nuclear terrorism. Casualties must be treated; the homeless resettled; property, buildings, capital equipment, and farmland must be decontaminated; and the faith of citizens in their government's ability to protect them must be restored.

The actions taken by the government of a state ravaged by nuclear terrorism directed solely within its own territory to cope with nuclear terrorism may nonetheless precipitate major international crises leading to international conflict. A number of actions taken in the absence of confirmation that nuclear terrorist acts have occurred are ambiguous; given the presence of latent or manifest conflict between two nations or two sets of nations, these actions might be interpreted as preparations for war. For example, evacuation of cities, censorship of news, drastic changes in patterns or modes of internal communication, suspension of regular commerce, declarations of martial law or changes in civil police procedure, limited or general military mobilization, or redeployment of military forces-in-being might all be reasonable steps for a government trying to cope with nuclear terrorist acts to take. Each of these measures or a combination of such measures might also be perceived as preliminary preparations for war.[27] This interpretation seems especially likely in those cases where previous real or alleged incidents of terrorism have precipitated reprisals by the victimized state against its neighboring states or other states thought to have been responsible for the initial terrorist act.[28]

The government of a state trying to cope with nuclear terrorism might also undertake a variety of nonmilitary and military measures against one or more other states. Likely targets of these actions include states thought to have supplied nuclear materials to terrorist groups; states assumed to have harbored nuclear terrorist groups before and/or after commission of terrorist acts; states thought to have supplied nuclear terrorists with nonnuclear supplies, technical resources, expertise, or money. The government of the victim state might turn to other states for the extradition of any individual alleged to have been involved in the nuclear terrorist incident. States might also seek international cooperation and assistance in identifying the sources of nuclear materials used in the fabrication of nuclear explosive devices or radiological weapons. Claims for indemnification of individuals, organizations, and governments suffering personal injury and property loss as the result of nuclear terrorism might be filed against various states, including nuclear materials supplying states as well as nuclear materials recipient states.

The use of military force in response to nuclear terrorism by the victim state cannot be overlooked. Military force could be deployed against the same wide variety of states noted above. The range of military actions that could be undertaken could vary greatly from minimum efforts to close the border between the victim state and its neighbors to more drastic actions. These actions might include some or all of the following: interdiction of terrorist infiltration routes; attacks on terrorist base camps; embargo or blockade of states aiding terrorists or permitting terrorists to operate from their territories; attacks on the civilian population of other states roughly equaling the destruction caused by a nuclear terrorist act; destruction of other states' nuclear facilities; or even a full-scale invasion and occupation of other states in reprisal for nuclear terrorism.

It is clear that acts undertaken by the victim state toward other states would have profound effects on international order. The military actions described above would be sufficient to unleash a major war, depending on the states directly involved and the strength of their respective alliance systems. Incidents of nuclear terrorism involving materials nominally under international safeguards would automatically raise very serious questions about the reliability of International Atomic Energy Agency (IAEA) safeguards on nuclear materials. IAEA inspection of national nuclear materials accounts, the primary safeguard against diversion of nuclear materials, that fail to detect the diversion of nuclear materials subsequently thought to have been used in the commission of a nuclear terrorist act may raise very grave questions about the entire safeguards system. Such questions once raised would be very hard to quiet, hence weakening the IAEA's ability to perform its critical function of verifying the Nuclear Nonproliferation Treaty.[29]

Nuclear terrorism may also raise a number of problems relating to the obligations assumed by the nuclear weapon states in their adherence to the Nuclear Nonproliferation Treaty—Security Council Resolution 255, (19 June 1968).[30] The nuclear weapon states might find themselves in a position of direct confrontation with one another because of demands on the part of the government of the state attacked by nuclear terrorists for assistance. Furthermore, use of nuclear terrorism by a group claiming the status of a state, i.e., a liberation movement, might cause major political problems in relations among the nuclear weapon states, as well as between the nuclear weapon states and nonnuclear weapon states.

Successful nuclear terrorism might also give rise to more general security problems without regard to actions undertaken by the victim state. All states would become concerned about nuclear terrorism and might undertake actions that could easily be misinterpreted by other, potential adversaries. Successful nuclear terrorism in one part of the world might be an invitation to terrorists in other parts of the world to use nuclear explosive devices, radiological weapons, or attacks on nuclear facilities as an effective, spectacular means of achieving political and economic objectives. Government leaders might conceivably be faced with a new set of dominoes—nuclear facilities, sources of radioactive materials, or sources of fissionable materials.

In surveying the political consequences of nuclear terrorism, it becomes clear that nuclear terrorism creates problems which, in turn, may be more destructive over the long term than the act of nuclear terrorism itself.

Initiation of hostilities between two or more states as the result of a catalytic nuclear terrorist act ought to be an outcome over which great efforts would be expended in an effort to avoid it. Unfortunately, little attention has been paid to the problem of limiting the escalation of conflict arising from nuclear terrorism. We now turn to some possible steps that might be taken unilaterally, bilaterally, or multilaterally by nations of the world to avoid the "worst case" outcome of a nuclear terrorism incident.

Limiting the Escalation of International Conflict Arising from Nuclear Terrorism

Nuclear terrorism can be analyzed in traditional arms control terms with considerable improvement in understanding of the problems to be solved. The objective in developing mechanisms to cope with nuclear terrorism is to reduce the likelihood of war and, failing that, to minimize the effects of war should it occur.

Nuclear terrorism is an inherently ambiguous event. Thus, there is a need for all parties—states, international organizations, and terrorists—to verify many different aspects of terrorism. In addition to verification, there is a need to develop a set of incentives and penalties, as well as a means of enforcing these incentives and penalties to discourage the escalation of international conflict as the result of a nuclear terrorist act. There is also a need to detect attempts to employ nuclear terrorism so that appropriate, nonescalatory countermeasures can be taken. Let us examine each of these problems momentarily.

The state attacked by nuclear terrorists has several distinct verification problems. First, it needs to determine whether or not it is under attack by terrorists, by unauthorized action by regular military forces of another state, or by a clandestine military operation mounted by another state. The government of the state under nuclear terrorist assault must also verify the use of nuclear-explosive devices, radiological weapons, or the successful attack on nuclear facilities so that it may undertake appropriate decontamination actions as well as mobilize necessary medical and relief personnel.

Other states, too, have a vested interest in confirming the identity of nuclear terrorists. Some states may find themselves committed to military action by treaty or executive agreement unless it can be established that their ally, the victim of a nuclear terrorist act, is not under an authorized military assault from another state. States with nuclear weapons or peaceful nuclear explosive devices may also be very concerned about the identity of nuclear terrorists as well as the source of nuclear materials because of their concern about possible breakdowns in command and control over their own nuclear weapons.

Potential adversaries of the victim of nuclear terrorism require verification of a number of acts. First, they too need to verify that nuclear terrorist acts are committed by terrorists and not agents provocateur on the one hand, or that alleged nuclear terrorist acts are not simply a pretext for the victim to initiate hostilities against one or more potential adversaries on the other. Second, potential adversaries of the victim state need confirmation of nuclear terrorism incidents to interpret what are otherwise ambiguous events in the victim country. Other countries neither aligned with the victim nor potential adversaries require verification of nuclear terrorist acts so that they may be able to assist in the management of crises by refusing havens to alleged nuclear terrorists, providing rescue and relief supplies and personnel, and offering their good offices to mediate disputes arising between the government of the target state and other states it feels are responsible for nuclear terrorist acts.

In addition to coping with the problems of ambiguity inherent in real or alleged acts of nuclear terrorism, in the domestic responses to nuclear terrorism, and in the international responses to nuclear terrorism, attention should be paid to the development of mechanisms that militate against both domestic and international escalation of conflict arising from incidents of nuclear terrorism. One set of possible remedies addresses some of the underlying motivations for escalation on the part of the victim state. Another set of possible remedies looks at the problem of limiting the scope and magnitude of escalation in the event of nuclear terrorism.

There are a number of factors that would tend to encourage the government of a state ravaged by nuclear terrorist acts to lash out at real or imagined enemies in an effort to cope with the problems raised by nuclear terrorism. One of the incentives to lashing out would be to apprehend and bring to justice those individuals directly responsible for nuclear terrorist acts. An arrangement providing for the prosecution or extradition for prosecution of individuals alleged to have participated in nuclear terrorism analogous to the Convention for the Suppression of the Unlawful Seizure of Aircraft[31] may be a useful measure in the management of crises arising from nuclear terrorism. While this kind of guarantee of prosecution may not deter terrorists, it may discourage states from kidnapping alleged nuclear terrorists on the territory of other states and forcibly returning these individuals to the victim state for prosecution.* Such actions might cause very serious problems

---

*The kidnapping and forcible extradition of Adolf Eichmann from Argentina to Israel in May 1960, resulted in a considerable increase in tensions between those two states until August 1960, when the two governments agreed to

for the relations among the states directly involved in the "forcible extradition" of alleged nuclear terrorists.

Agreement in some form might also be reached to provide for the compensation of individuals suffering injury or property loss as the result of nuclear terrorism. Such an agreement might contain a flat limitation of liability comparable to the Price-Anderson insurance arrangement for the U.S. nuclear industry;[32] it might have provisions for sharing of costs among all nuclear materials supplying and receiving nations. If some mechanism could be developed to minimize the financial losses incurred by governments, private citizens, and various economic entities as the result of nuclear terrorism, the government of the state injured by nuclear terrorism might be better able to resist internal public opinion and bureaucratic pressures to resort to the use of military force to redress the grievances of its citizens against other states.

Some form of agreement to procecute or extradite individuals accused of participating in nuclear terrorism and another agreement to provide compensation to the victims of nuclear terrorism may take some escalatory pressures out of nuclear terrorism from the perspective of the victim. Neither agreement, however, will do much to aid in the verification or detection problems alluded to earlier. Here, there are some recent developments worth noting that augur well for improved international capability to detect nuclear terrorism.

Earlier in this paper, it was observed that limiting access to nuclear materials seemed to be the easiest, surest way to reduce the likelihood of nuclear terrorist incidents. An agreement was concluded among the seven major nuclear materials supplying nations—the United States, the Soviet Union, the United Kingdom, Canada, France, and the Federal Republic of Germany—imposing a variety of physical safeguards on nuclear materials supplied to other states under agreements for cooperation safeguarded by the IAEA. While the exact content of the agreement has not been made public, newspaper accounts suggest that the kind of physical protection demanded would be sufficient to improve greatly the likelihood of detecting attempts to steal nuclear materials in transit from supplier to recipient as well as from stockpiles of materials already in the hands of the recipient nation.[34]

National intelligence networks relying on both national technical means of verification and a variety of other human assets and analytical techniques may be able to aid in the verification of attempted or successful acts of

---

drop the matter of forcible extradition. The issue did arise during Eichmann's trial when the defense challenged the competence of the Israeli court to try Eichmann because of his extralegal extradition to Israel.[33]

nuclear terrorism.[35] The critical problem is the distribution of intelligence data from one country to another in a manner that does not compromise intelligence sources and methods, but nonetheless permits all concerned to verify nuclear terrorist acts, domestic reponses to such acts, the possible attempt at nuclear terrorism, and other related actions.[36]

The use by the International Civil Aviation Organization (ICAO) of intelligence data on possible airplane hijackers provided by member nations may be a useful model on which to base a similar scheme of intelligence data sharing. Apparently, when a national intelligence organization detects a possible airplane hijacking attempt, it alerts the ICAO. The ICAO in turn distributes this information directly to all member nations. Thus, member states are alerted to the dangers of airplane hijackings without any one nation's intelligence sources and methods being unduly compromised.[37]

Another possible approach to the problem of verification of nuclear terrorist acts and various domestic actions taken by the victim government might be "verification by challenge" as formulated in the Biological Weapons Convention.[38] There is no formal on-site inspection or other verification of the destruction or diversion "to peaceful purposes . . . of all agents, toxins, weapons, equipment, and means of delivery . . ." of bacteriological (biological) methods of warfare.[39] However, there are provisions for verification in the event a nation believes another is engaging in questionable acts. Article VI provides:

(1) Any State Party to this Convention which finds that any other State Party is acting in breach of obligations deriving from the provisions of the Convention may lodge a complaint with the Security Council of the United Nations. Such a complaint should include all possible evidence confirming its validity, as well as a request for its consideration by the Security Council.

(2) Each State Party to this Convention undertakes to co-operate in carrying out any investigation which the Security Council may initiate in accordance with the provisions of the Charter of the United Nations, on the basis of the complaint received by the Council. The Security Council shall inform the States Parties to the Convention of the results of the investigation.[40]

Verification by challenge would be particularly useful in better understanding the actions of the government of the state trying to cope with the aftermath of nuclear terrorism. Other states would already have some information based on diplomatic reports; verification of nuclear terrorism by challenging specific domestic responses would be beneficial in clarifying ambiguous acts without necessarily forcing potential adversaries to take actions which the victim state would regard as hostile.

Clearly, verification of nuclear terrorism could not be handled exactly the same way as verification of biological weapons manufacture or stockpiling. There would be many objections to the use of the U.N. Security Council as the primary investigating organ. Some kind of *ad hoc* arrangement drawn from governments allied with the state victimized by nuclear terrorism, the victim state's potential adversaries, and states nominally "nonaligned" in the context of the possible dispute with technical support by the International Atomic Energy Agency's office of the Inspector General might be a more appropriate verifying force. However, if the burden for verifying incidents of nuclear terrorism can be removed from the shoulders of the victim government and its potential adversaries, the chances of managing crises successfully are probably enhanced.

There are a number of other areas that might lead to conflict that will eventually have to be addressed. Time and space permit only a cursory description of the problems yet to be addressed.

First, how are nuclear materials recovered from thefts, unsuccessful attempts at nuclear terrorism, et cetera, to be handled? Who shall pay recovery costs? Who shall insure that these recovered materials are adequately accounted and safeguarded so that they do not become the source of second or third order nuclear terrorist weapons?

Second, how shall existing safeguards be enforced? The present IAEA safeguards system merely requires that evidence of safeguard violations be presented to the Board of Governors—22 national representatives—who may act as they deem fit. Might the world be somewhat better off if a clear schedule of penalties for violation of international safeguards be established?

Third, what is the future role of the IAEA to be in any scheme of nuclear materials safeguarding and the coping with problems of nuclear terrorism? The IAEA has become more and more reluctant to take a vigorous leading role in developing physical security standards, procedures, and technology, alleging it lacks the budget and manpower necessary to accomplish these tasks. What changes, if any, in the Statute of the International Atomic Energy Agency might be in order so that it could be a more vibrant force in helping nations cope with the aftermath of nuclear terrorist acts?

Finally, what additional steps should be taken to enlarge the scope of national and international safeguards on nuclear materials? Some might argue that a large number of materials that could be used in a variety of terrorist weapons are presently beyond the scope of national or international safeguards. Given the magnitude of the risks these materials pose to international order, might this be the time to develop safeguards on radioactive elements used in industrial research, nuclear medicine, college teaching, and other places that might be diverted to terrorist use?

These questions lead us directly to the need for an agenda of actions that can be taken over the next few years.

An Agenda for Action

The problem of nuclear terrorism will go away only when the more general problem of terrorism has been solved. Thus, it is necessary to consider a number of unilateral, bilateral, and multilateral steps that can be taken to minimize the likelihood of escalation of conflict arising from incidents of nuclear terrorism.

Clearly, one of the most important and perhaps most easily accomplished tasks is to restrict vastly the worldwide supply of materials from which a fission nuclear explosive device could be fashioned until such time as stringent physical security standards are developed, put in place, and enforced by suppliers of nuclear materials. The January 1976 agreement referred to above is clearly a step in the right direction.

Second, I believe there is a need for a unilateral declaration on the part of the United States on the seriousness of nuclear terrorism. Such a statement should, in my view, include a call for a policy of "no safe havens" for nuclear terrorists, preferably to be codified in an international treaty.

Third, I believe there needs to be a concerted effort to initiate international discussions on ways to minimize the escalation of conflict arising from nuclear terrorism. While the conclusion of additional agreements providing worldwide communications modeled after the United States-Soviet "Hot Line Agreement" would be useful, I think it is very important that we not lose our perspective on technology. Nuclear technology has a habit of failing; it can be made to fail. I believe we need to look beyond technological "fixes" to the problem of nuclear terrorism and deal with the "people" problem terrorism implies.

At the same time, we should be alert to the dangers some remedies to the problem of nuclear terrorism may pose to civil liberties, freedom of information exchange, and freedom of movement of peoples across international frontiers. A balancing of the rights and interests of many diverse groups must take place; hopefully it will take place before we must cope with incidents of nuclear terrorism that result in severe escalation of international conflict.

Notes

1. For some early public discussion of the dangers of nuclear proliferation, see "The Baruch Plan: Statement by the United States Representative [Baruch] to the United Nations Atomic Energy Commission, June 14, 1946," in U.S. Department of State, *Documents on Disarmament 1945-1959* (Washington, D.C.: U.S. Govt. Print. Off., 1960), vol. I, pp. 7-16. For analyses of the dangers of nuclear proliferation presented during the 1950's and 1960's, see National Planning Association, *The*

Nth Country Problem and Arms Control (Washington, D.C.: National Planning Association, 1960); Leonard Beaton, *Must the Bomb Spread* (Baltimore: Penguin Books, 1966); and William B. Bader, *The United States and the Spread of Nuclear Weapons* (New York: Pegasus, 1968).

2. An excellent summary of current and past research on the problem of terrorism edited by Yonah Alexander was recently published by Praeger. The study, entitled *International Terrorism: National Regional and Global Perspectives* (New York: Praeger, 1976), has an outstanding bibliography.

3. See, for example, the following studies and articles: Robert B. Leachman and Phillip Althoff, ed., *Preventing Nuclear Theft: Guidelines for Industry and Government* (New York: Praeger, 1972); Theodore B. Taylor, "Diversion by Non-Governmental Organizations," in Mason Willrich, ed., *International Safeguards and Nuclear Industry* (Baltimore: Johns Hopkins University Press, 1973), pp. 176-199; M. Willrich, "Nongovernmental Nuclear Weapon Proliferation," and D. Krieger, "Nuclear Power: A Trojan Horse for Terrorists," in B. Jasani, *Nuclear Proliferation Problems* (Cambridge: MIT Press for the Stockholm International Peace Research Institute, 1974), pp. 168-186 and pp. 187-200; Mason Willrich and Theodore B. Taylor, *Nuclear Theft: Risks and Safeguards* (Cambridge: Ballinger, 1974); and Martha Crenshaw Hutchinson, "Terrorism and the Diffusion of Nuclear Power," a Paper Prepared for Delivery to the XVII Annual Convention of the International Studies Association, Toronto, Canada, 25-29 February 1976.

4. See, for example, regulations for the handling of special nuclear materials promulgated by the Atomic Energy Commission on 5 December 1973; 15 November 1974; and regulations on the packaging of radioactive material for transport promulgated by the Atomic Energy Commission on 22 June 1974. These are reprinted in U.S. Congress, Senate Committee on Government Operations, *Peaceful Nuclear Exports and Weapons Proliferation* (Washington, D.C.: U.S. Govt. Print. Off., 1975), pp. 332-355; see also Nuclear Regulatory Commission rules and regulations governing the physical protection of nuclear plants and materials promulgated in 1975 reprinted in *ibid.,* pp. 356-361.

   The U.S. Government recently extended its physical protection requirements of domestic nuclear facilities to include materials and facilities exported to other countries. See, for example, the Associated Press story, "U.S. Adopts New Requirements for Export of Nuclear Knowhow," *San Jose Mercury-News* 21 February 1976.

5. Willrich and Taylor, p. 10.

6. *Ibid.,* p. 54.

7. United States Nuclear Regulatory Commission Rules and Regulations, Title 10, Chapter I, Code of Federal Regulations, Parts 70, 71 and 73, reprinted in *Peaceful Nuclear Exports and Weapons Proliferation.*

8. See, for example, materials to be subjected to international safeguards described in International Atomic Energy, *Safeguards* and *The Struc-*

ture and Content of Agreements Between the Agency and States Required in Connection with the Treaty on the Non-Proliferation of Nuclear Weapons, reprinted in *ibid.,* pp. 732-788.

9. Douglas DeNike, "Nuclear Safety and Human Malice," mimeographed paper, University of Southern California School of Medicine, 1972, quoted by Krieger, pp. 195-196.

10. Timothy Ingram, "Nuclear Hijacking: Now Within the Grasp of Any Bright Lunatic," *Washington Monthly,* June 1973 reprinted in *Peaceful Nuclear Exports and Weapons Proliferation,* pp. 32-33.

11. "Austria Seeks 'Atom Guerrilla,' " Reuter, *San Jose Mercury* , 23 April 1974; also Thomas O'Toole, "Fear of Nuclear Theft Stirs Experts, AEC," *Washington Post* , 25 May 1974.

12. Thomas O'Toole, "2 Break-Ins Suggest Thieves Eye A-Arms," *Washington Post,* 28 July 1974.

13. Ingram, p. 37.

14. "Security Review at Certain NATO Installations," *Congressional Record,* vol. 121, No. 68, 30 April 1975, pp. S7184-S7189, especially pp. S7185-7188.

15. *Ibid.,* p. S7184.

16. Donald Rumsfeld, *Annual Defense Department Report, FY 1977* (Washington, D.C.: U.S. Department of Defense, 1976), p. 86.

17. Ingram, p. 34.

18. United Press International, "B-52 Explodes Near A-Plant," *San Jose Mercury,* 4 September 1975.

19. James R. Schlesinger quoted from transcript of "Meet the Press," in a *Mike Gravel Newsletter,* 31 October 1973, by David Krieger, "Terrorists and Nuclear Technology," *Bulletin of the Atomic Scientists,* vol. 31, No. 6, June 1975, p. 32.

20. *Ibid.*

21. See Phil Goulding, *Confirm or Deny* (New York: Harper & Row, 1970), pp. 23-51.

22. For detailed and critical analysis of the effects of a reactor core melt-down see the following: U.S. Atomic Energy Commission, *The Safety of Nuclear Power Reactors and Related Facilities* (Washington, D.C.: U.S. Atomic Energy Commission, WASH-1250, June, 1973); U.S. Atomic Energy Commission, *Reactor Safety Study: An Assessment of Accident Risks in U.S. Commercial Power Plants* (Washington, D.C.: U.S. Atomic Energy Commission, Draft WASH-1400, August 1974).

   See also Joel Primack and Frank von Hippel, "Nuclear Reactor Safety," *Bulletin of the Atomic Scientists,* vol. 30, No. 8, October 1974, pp. 5-11; Norman C. Rasmussen, "The Safety Study and Its Feedback," *Bulletin of the Atomic Scientists,* vol. 31, No. 7, July 1975, pp. 25-28, and U.S. Congress, House Committee on Interior and Insular Affairs, *Oversight Hearings on Nuclear Energy—Overview of the Major Issues* (Washington, D.C.: U.S. Govt. Print. Off., 1975).

23. See the following for discussion of the effects of nuclear weapons: S.

Glasston, ed., *The Effects of Nuclear Weapons, 2nd Edition*, (Washington, D.C.: U.S. Govt. Print. Off., 1962); U.S. Congress, Senate Committee on Foreign Relations, *Briefing on Counterforce Attacks* (Washington, D.C.: U.S. Govt. Print. Off., 1975) and *Analysis of Effects of Limited Nuclear Warfare* (Washington, D.C.: U.S. Govt. Print. Off., 1975); *United Nations, Effects of the Possible Use of Nuclear Weapons and the Security and Economic Implications for States of the Acquisition and Further Development of These Weapons* (New York: United Nations, 1968).

24. See, for example, problems encountered in decontaminating Eniwetok Atoll described in U.S. Congress, Senate Committee on Armed Services, *Military Construction Authorization Fiscal Year 1976* (Washington, D.C.: U.S. Govt. Print. Off., 1975), pp. 399-436.

25. Taylor, "Diversion by Non-Governmental Organizations," p. 190.

26. See U.S. Defense Atomic Supply Agency, *Proceedings of the Third Interdisciplinary Conference on Selected Effects of a General War* (Washington, D.C.: Defense Atomic Supply Agency Information and Analysis Center, 1971), especially pp. 92-224.

27. See, for example, Barbara Tuchman, *The Guns of August* (New York: Dell, 1962), for an excellent description of events and perceptions of Europe's leaders leading to the outbreak of World War I.

28. For further discussion, Robert Jervis, "Hypotheses on Misperception," *World Politics*, vol. 20, No. 3, April 1968, pp. 454-479; Irving Janis, *Victims of Groupthink* (Boston: Houghton Mifflin, 1972); and Joseph de Rivera, *The Psychological Dimension of Foreign Policy* (Columbus: Charles E. Merrill 1968).

29. See for further discussion, Paul C. Szasz, "International Atomic Energy Agency Safeguards," in Mason Willrich, ed., *International Safeguards and the Nuclear Industry*, pp. 73-141; W. Hafele, "NPT Safeguards," and J. Prawitz, "Arguments for Extended NPT Safeguards," in *Nuclear Proliferation Problems*, pp. 142-167.

30. J. Goldblat, "The UN Security Council Resolution of 19 June 1968 and the Security of Non-Nuclear-Weapon States," *ibid.*, pp. 236-241.

31. "Convention for the Suppression of Unlawful Seizure of Aircraft," in U.S. Congress, Senate Committee on Foreign Relations, *Aircraft Hijacking Convention* (Washington, D.C.: U.S. Govt. Print. Off., 1971), pp. 93-96.

32. See, for example, section 2(i) and section 170 of "The Atomic Energy Act of 1954, Public Law 83-703 as amended" in U.S. Congress Joint Committee on Atomic Energy, *Atomic Energy Legislation Through 93rd Congress*, 2nd Session (Washington, D.C.: U.S. Govt. Print. Off., 1975), pp. 5 and 71-80. See also U.S. Congress, House Committee on Interior and Insular Affairs, *Oversight Hearings On Nuclear Energy*—The Price-Anderson Nuclear Indemnity Acts (Washington, D.C.: U.S. Govt. Print. Off., 1975).

33. See Isser Harel, *House on Garibaldi Street* (New York: Viking, 1975),

for an account of the Israeli Government's kidnapping and forcible extradition of Adolf Eichmann from Argentina to Israel and the subsequent diplomatic furor over the summer of 1960. Hanna Arendt commenting on this aspect of the Eichmann case in her book, *Eichmann in Jerusalem* (New York: Viking, 1963, 1964), observes that Argentina might not have been as willing as it was to forget about the kidnapping of Eichmann had Eichmann been an Argentine citizen. "He had lived there under an assumed name, thereby denying himself the right to government protection, at least as Ricardo Klement (born on 23 May 1913, at Bolzano—in Southern Tyrol—as his Argentine identity card stated), although he had declared himself of 'German nationality.' And he never invoked the dubious right of asylum. . . . All this did not make Eichmann stateless, it did not legally deprive him of his German nationality, but it gave the West German republic a welcome pretext for withholding the customary protection due its citizens abroad." (page 240).

34. United Press International, "7 Nation Nuclear Pact Set," *San Jose Mercury,* 30 January 1976.

35. Dr. Fred C. Iklé, Director of the U.S. Arms Control and Disarmament Agency underscored the value and importance of national intelligence systems in a speech reprinted in the *Hackensack,* N.J. *Record* entitled "How Will We Know Who Bombed Us?" 14 February 1975.

36. The importance of protecting sources and methods of intelligence was underscored by Arms Control and Disarmament Agency Director Iklé in his advocacy of legislation to make such information privileged. See transcript of *Meet the Press,* vol. 19, No. 31, 3 August 1975, pp. 4-5.

37. "Security Bulletin (RIS: SE-1600-19) ASE-73-3," in U.S. Congress, House Committee on Interstate and Foreign Commerce, *Anti-Hijacking Act of 1973* (Washington, D.C.: U.S. Govt. Print. Off., 1973), p. 306.

38. "Convention on the Prohibition of the Development, Production and Stockpiling of Bacteriological (Biological) and Toxin Weapons and on Their Destruction," in U.S. Arms Control and Disarmament Agency, *Arms Control and Disarmament Agreements* (Washington, D.C.: U.S. Govt. Print. Off., 1975), pp. 118-124.

39. *Ibid.,* p. 119.

40. *Ibid.,* pp. 119-120.

Louis René Beres

International Terrorism and World Order: The Nuclear Threat

This selection explores the factors underlying the argument that the prospect of nuclear terrorism is both credible and perilous. Beres attributes this acute threat to easy terrorist access to nuclear weapons, the contemporary changes in the terrorists' "political code," and the tendency for terrorism to be condoned or at least tolerated within the international system. Beres offers three basic responses to attenuate the threat: technical changes to render the nuclear materials less accessible, international agreements to control traffic in nuclear goods, and attempts to change the behavior of the terrorists. The last proposal is the most controversial, for such attempts at behavior modification at the group level may conceivably backfire.

I. Introduction

As residents of an endangered planet, we have grown accustomed to omens which kindle the apocalyptic imagination. Among such omens, the continuing threat of nuclear catastrophe looms large. The urgency of this threat is underscored by a new and frightening path to nuclear destruction—the use of nuclear explosives or radioactivity by terrorist groups.[1]

In view of this threat, the following essay will explore the factors underlying the argument that the prospect of nuclear destruction by terrorists is both credible and perilous. The threat appears imminent primarily as a result of three developments: (1) the increasingly easy access of terrorist groups to nuclear weapons, nuclear power plants, and nuclear waste storage facilities; (2) the special nature of terrorist groups as actors in world politics; and (3) the global trend toward tolerance of terrorist activity. After considering these three basic developments, a conclusion is offered that suggests strategies to halt the prevailing drift toward nuclear terrorism. Such strategies, it will be argued, must be cast in terms of the technological, political, and social dimensions of the problem of nuclear terrorism.

II. The Technological Problem:
Terrorist Access to Nuclear Weapons

A. OBTAINING FISSIONABLE MATERIAL

Mankind's high-velocity drift toward a nuclear Armageddon is no longer confined to the risk of war between the United States and the Soviet Union. Today, with more than fifty major terrorist groups operating in the world,[2] the most likely scenario of nuclear destruction has become one involving terrorist activity.

This shift in the perceived locus of threat from war between the superpowers to terrorist use of nuclear weapons is borne out by a number of important developments.[3] Foremost among these developments is the increased availability of nuclear weapons, either by theft of assembled systems from military stockpiles and production facilities, or by self-development from nuclear materials pilfered from nuclear power plants.[4] In the case of theft of an assembled weapon, determined terrorist operatives might direct their attention to any of the tens of thousands of nuclear weapons now deployed across the world, in more than seventeen different countries.[5] Unfortunately as the number of national members in the so-called "nuclear club" grows, such terrorists are likely to have a significantly enlarged range of possibilities for stealing nuclear weapons.

How difficult would it be to accomplish such a theft? According to the *Defense Monitor,* a publication of the Center for Defense Information in Washington, D.C., "U.S. Army Special Forces exercises have shown that nuclear weapons storage areas can be penetrated successfully without detection despite guards, fences, and sensors. Their example could obviously be followed by a daring and well-organized terrorist organization."[6] These fears are shared by several Congressmen who investigated the problem of U.S. nuclear weapons security overseas during the period 1973-75. Upon their return from an inspection of the U.S.-European nuclear weapons stockpile, Senators Pastore and Baker termed the situation "critical."[7] Even if this particular situation is improved quickly and dramatically (an improvement that is expected to cost at least 250 million dollars),[8] terrorists could still direct their attention to the presumably less secure arsenals of other nuclear powers.

In the case of self-development from basic nuclear materials, terrorist groups would require both the materials and the expertise to fashion them into an explosive device or radiation dispersal implement. According to a substantial number of specialists in the field, however, it would be relatively easy for groups to fulfill these requirements.[9]

As the available supply of fossil fuels continues to be depleted, a growing number of states can be expected to turn to nuclear power for energy needs. This turn represents a preeminent source of danger from terrorist use of nuclear weapons because the by-products of fission in the nuclear plant are the basic material for a fission bomb or radiation dispersal device.[10] Although nuclear technology is becoming available to less developed countries, the threat of nuclear materials theft in the immediate future is apt to be confined to the major industrial powers. These highly industrialized countries are producing large amounts of fissionable materials, thus increasing the opportunities for terrorists to exploit the weapons possibilities associated with nuclear fuel.[11]

Terrorists would not find it difficult to get their hands on substantial amounts of fissionable materials.[12] According to Mason Willrich and Theodore Taylor, co-authors of a special report on the problem to the Energy Policy Project of the Ford Foundation, the extant system of safeguards in this country is so inadequate that terrorists will inevitably be able to surreptitiously remove the essential fissionable materials from nuclear power plants.[13] Indeed, even if appropriate steps to improve nuclear safeguards are taken in this country,[14] genuine protection of such materials from terrorist groups must be *global* in scope. After all, American safeguards do not secure us or anyone else against nuclear weapons fashioned from materials stolen abroad.[15]

Moreover, Willrich's and Taylor's concerns about nuclear materials safeguards are shared by several experts in the field. A recent task-force report to the Energy Research and Development Administration (E.R.D.A.) concluded that public alarm about nuclear materials is justified, and that nuclear materials are most vulnerable while in transit.[16] The Director of the Enrico Fermi Institute at the University of Chicago has become so pessimistic about terrorist theft of nuclear materials as to conclude that there is "essentially no escape from the road leading to nuclear disaster."[17] A recent discussion group report on "Nuclear Theft and Terrorism" issued by twelve leading experts expresses concern about "weak links" in national and international safeguards that could enable terrorist thefts of nuclear materials.[18] Recent remarks by N.R.C. (Nuclear Regulatory Commission) Commissioner Victor Gilinsky concede that we must tighten our security control over nuclear materials.[19] And political scientist Forrest R. Frank has expressed particular concern about access to materials that can be used in the manufacture of radiological weapons.[20]

B. TECHNOLOGICAL EXPERTISE

The second requirement which a terrorist group would have to satisfy in order to fabricate its own nuclear weapons is expertise. In this connection,

Willrich and Taylor tell us that "the design and manufacture of a crude nuclear explosive is no longer a difficult task technically, and a plutonium dispersal device which can cause widespread radioactive contamination is much simpler to make than an explosive."[18] Since as early as 1954, declassification and public dissemination of information about the design of fission weapons has been extensive. Terrorists who are determined to construct a nuclear explosive or radiological weapon are unrestrained by the rigorous performance requirements which constrain the efforts of professional weapons engineers.[22]

What could a terrorist group do once it obtains the necessary plutonium? According to nuclear physicist Ralph Lapp, a dedicated band of bomb makers, comprised of skilled scientists and technicians, might fashion "a modestly effective implosion bomb."[23] Alternatively, such a group might use its plutonium in the form of a radiation dispersal device, a much simpler matter technically.[24]

Experts generally agree that terrorists could easily use plutonium for radiation dispersal implements. Forrest R. Frank, who has studied the problem in great detail, argues:

> While the amount of expertise needed to construct a [nuclear] bomb is perhaps no greater than college physics, chemistry, and perhaps engineering, the amount of expertise needed to construct a simple device for dispersing radioactive material is even less. Any container capable of dispensing liquid radioactive waste under pressure would be sufficient; pouring liquid or particulate radioactive materials in air conditioning systems of large buildings or into urban water supplies might also represent highly effective methods of dispersing some radioactive materials.[25]

Dr. Frank's views are corroborated by a substantial number of A.E.C. and N.R.C. studies, including one which states that a scattering of only 4.4 pounds of plutonium from an elevated release point would expose anyone within 1800 feet downwind to a high risk of bone or lung cancer.[26]

Terrorists might make use of the growing nuclear energy industry in still another fashion by sabotaging nuclear plant facilities. This sort of an attack could yield extensive death and property damage via radiation release; a 1973 A.E.C. estimate suggests that an accident involving reactor core meltdown could precipitate 45,000 deaths, 100,000 injuries, and 17 billion dollars in property damage.[27]

Although the chances of accidental reactor meltdown are generally believed to be extremely small, the case is quite different with respect to *deliberate* reactor meltdown. Testifying before the Joint Committee on Atomic Energy in March, 1974, a former U.S. Navy Underwater Demolitions officer stated that any three to five underwater demolition or Green Beret officers could "sabotage virtually any nuclear reactor in the country." In such actions, he continued, "the amount of radioactivity released could be of catastrophic proportions."[28] Moreover, it is well-known that a calamitous reactor core meltdown might be precipitated by kamikaze-type plane crashes into nuclear facilities. Today's nuclear plants are unable to withstand the impact of large aircraft.[29]

These frightening views of nuclear plant security are supported by other expert opinions. In 1974, after present security regulations had been put into operation, the General Accounting Office stated: "License and A.E.C. (Atomic Energy Commission) officials agreed that a security system at a licensed nuclear plant could not prevent a takeover for sabotage by a small number—as few perhaps as two or three—of armed individuals."[29a] A recent study prepared by the Sandia Corporation concluded: "It appears that a sufficiently determined and able group could perform acts of sabotage which could endanger the safety of the public surrounding the plant."[29b] And one high N.R.C. official said recently: "Several people with high explosives who really know how to use it can probably go through a nuclear facility like butter."[29 c]

In order to appreciate the urgency of the situation, these views of nuclear plant security must be coupled with the understanding that there already have been at least 175 instances of violence or threats of violence against U.S. nuclear facilities since 1969.[30] Several dangerous incidents have also occurred outside of the United States. In 1975, two bombs exploded at a nuclear plant being built near Fessenheim, France. An extensive fire ensued, but the reactor itself did not melt through its protective shielding. In 1973, terrorists armed with automatic weapons and hand grenades attacked a nuclear plant near Buenos Aires. Although there was surely no lack of opportunity, they made no effort to damage the reactor itself.[31]

III. The Behavioral Problem: Terrorist Inclinations to Nuclear Weapons Use

Although the increasing accessibility of nuclear weapons and nuclear power plants represents the most important reason behind the fear of nuclear terrorism, a number of other developments warrant mention. These developments concern the intrinsic behavioral features of terrorist groups themselves rather than the highly destructive weapons technologies upon which they might draw.

A. DEVELOPMENT ONE: THE ORIENTATION TO VIOLENCE OF MODERN
TERRORISTS

Today's terrorist groups exhibit an orientation to violence that seems to be a
phenomenon of all modern warfare: they no longer operate according to a
code of honor which distinguishes between combatants and non-combatants.
Engaged in what Michael Waltzer describes as "total war against nations,
ethnic groups, and religions,"[32] their selection of victims is often unaffected
by considerations of age, sex, or innocence. As a result, the age-old terrorist
processes of political killing or assassination have been augmented in recent
years by the killing and wounding of a great many people whose individual
ties to the grievance at issue are either marginal or nonexistent.[33]

Two factors explain this recent development. First the apparent randomness in selecting targets is designed to foster fear on the part of anyone who is
aligned against the terrorists. If the alleged enemies of terrorists are made to
feel that *everyone,* not only statesmen and political figures, is a proper object
of terrorist violence, then fear and terror may become exceptionally
widespread. From the point of view of the terrorists, the resultant conditions
of dread and uncertainty are desirable since they serve to detach the
individual from his customary social supports.

In the second place, by rendering the arena of conflict coextensive with the
boundaries of the planet itself, terrorists expect to focus worldwide attention
on their demands. Publicity is a preeminent concern of terrorist groups. By
exploiting the capabilities of a sophisticated global communications system,
they hope to evoke the kind of interest and concern which can bring their
goals to fruition. This kind of exploitation, they believe, requires a pattern of
violence that is self-consciously indiscriminate.

Has the shift in targets been helpful or harmful to terrorist objectives?
While the particular effects of this doctrine clearly vary from one context to
another, nowhere have they included even the realistic promise of a genuinely
lasting success. If anything, the willingness of modern terrorists to sacrifice
virtually anyone for the sake of expediency has been inexpedient. Opposition
to terrorism has generally been stiffened rather than stifled, and
counterterrorist measures now demonstrate the same relentless cruelty as the
terrorism which brought these measures into being. It appears, therefore, that
modern terrorist groups—in spite of their rejection of any sort of humane
"rules of the game"—have no better chance of producing genuinely lasting
successes than did their predecessors.[34]

Nevertheless, viewed from the standpoint of probable nuclear terrorism, the
absence of terrorist inhibitions in applying maximum force to virtually any
segment of human population could have the most serious implications. The

shift in targets suggests that terrorists now see themselves engaged in a "no holds barred" situation wherein the amount of suffering to be inflicted is limited only by the availability of weapons resources. With this in mind, the expansion of the arena of conflict that characterizes modern terrorism implies a high probability of nuclear weapons use (should such weapons be obtained) or nuclear power plant sabotage (should access be realized).

B. DEVELOPMENT TWO: THE RELATIVE INSENSITIVITY OF MODERN TERRORISTS TO RETALIATORY THREATS

The name of one terrorist group *Fedayeen*, means self-sacrificers. It is a meaning of particular significance because many of today's terrorist groups, not only the *Fedayeen*, often are willing to risk their lives for activities which feature only a minimal chance of ultimate success. In other words, because terrorists seem willing to risk more to gain less,[35] the "deadly logic" of deterrence has been effectively redefined. Terrorist groups are now much less sensitive to threats of retaliatory destruction than might ordinarily have been presumed.[36]

The most significant implication of this behavioral characteristic[37] of terrorists is that if they should obtain access to nuclear explosives or radioactivity, the implicit calculus of benefits and costs due to use of these weapons would be relatively unfavorable to the general population.[38] In effect, this means that orthodox threats of deterrence might not have decisive bearing on the terrorist's decision of whether or not to employ nuclear tactics. While the strategy of deterrence is not altogether inapplicable to terrorist groups, its utility is contingent upon the possession of an assured capability and willingness to wreak a reprisal so devastating that it threatens the terrorist group's survival.

C. DEVELOPMENT THREE: THE TREND TOWARD GROWING COOPERATION AMONG TERRORIST GROUPS

Heightening the nuclear threat of terrorism is the growing cooperation now manifest among terrorist groups. Such cooperation, based more upon calculations of common advantage than upon ideological affinities, is indicated by such cases as the weapons training of Venezuelan terrorist Illich Remirzed Sanchez in Lebanon by the Popular Front for the Liberation of Palestine (P.F.L.P.); the weapons training of the Japanese Red Army movement in Lebanon; the establishment of joint training programs and arms transfers between the Turkish People's Army and Black September; and the training of United States Weathermen, Irish Republican Army members, and

representatives of Nicaragua's *Sandanista* movement in Palestinian camps.[39]
Additional evidence of terrorist collaboration can be detected in the demand
by Black September operatives in Munich for the release of German
insurgents who had been involved in killings of German policemen, and in the
more recent example of Palestinian and German skyjackers using hostages
from an Air France flight to secure the release of fifty-three assorted
colleagues, ranging from Melchite Catholic Archbishop Ilarion Capucci, to
Japanese Red Army member Kozo Okamoto, to agents of the
Baader-Meinhof gang.

Perhaps the most notorious example of terrorist cooperation is the ongoing
liaison between the P.F.L.P. and the Japanese Red Army. It was this terrorist
alliance that brought on the Lydda Airport massacre at Tel Aviv in May 1972.
There, three members of the Red Army—trained in Fedayeen camps and
provided with false passports by P.F.L.P. agents—killed twenty-six persons
and wounded eighty.

Moreover, the recent Red Army attack on the American Embassy offices in
Kuala Lumpur points to a continuing link between the two groups. In
between the 1972 airport venture and the Malaysia attack, mixed Red
Army-P.F.L.P. squads hijacked a JAL flight (July 1973) and attacked the
Japanese Embassy in Kuwait (February 1974). In September 1974, a Red
Army group commandeered the French Embassy at The Hague and obtained
the release of both P.F.L.P. and Red Army agents.

It seems unlikely that the existence of terrorist cooperation signals the
beginnings of a genuine, system-wide organization of terrorists. The intrinsic
informality of terrorist activities and the heterogeneity of terrorist ideologies
and objectives mitigate against such an organization. Nevertheless, a pattern
of cooperation has been established which is nurtured and sustained by a
number of national leaders such as Libya's Qaddafi. While this cooperation
has not always produced success, the terrorists surely have no viable
alternative. Without such cooperation, their transnational ventures would
cease altogether.

What are the implications of such cooperation for nuclear destruction by
terrorists? First, inter-terrorist cooperation greatly increases terrorist
opportunities for acquiring nuclear weapons. This is especially the case when
acquisition takes the form of self-development and design from "raw"
fissionable materials since cooperation greatly increases opportunities for
both capital and expertise. Second, cooperation among terrorist groups is
likely to facilitate the proliferation of "private" nuclear weapons throughout
the world, creating a network whereby such weapons can be exchanged and
transmitted across national frontiers. Third, cooperation between terrorists is
apt to spread the "benefits" of advanced training in the use of nuclear
weapons and the techniques of nuclear power plant sabotage. Fourth, and
finally, terrorist cooperation is likely to provide such reciprocal privileges as

forged documents, and safe havens, which are essential for both pre-attack preparations and post-attack security.

IV. The Contextual Problem: Tolerance and Support of Terrorism

Ironically, while terrorists are engaged in "total war" with selected nations, religions, and ethnic groups, much of the world tolerates their activity, or even supports it enthusiastically.

Consider a very recent example: In the wake of the recent Israeli commando raid in Uganda which freed 105 hostages taken by pro-Palestinian skyjackers, African members of the Security Council proposed a resolution to condemn the raid as a "flagrant violation" of Uganda's sovereignty. The Ugandan supporters also refused to participate in the vote of a rival resolution under joint American-British sponsorship that would have condemned airline hijacking in particular and terrorism in general.[40]

This tolerance and support of terrorism can be explained in terms of two different political groups. In one, sympathy for terrorist goals is so great that there is very little concern for proportionality between these goals and the means adopted for their implementation. In another, fear of terrorists is so great that tolerance of their demands, or even capitulation to them, is judged necessary for survival.

This tolerance and support of terrorist groups suggest that they will be able to increase their strength and to step up their activities with little or no fear of concerted interference. Should such an opportunity be seized upon, two alternative scenarios can be foreseen: on the one hand, the combination of sympathy and fear that sustains the milieu of tolerance and support may lead the way to terrorist successes without the need for nuclear "assistance"; on the other hand, this same combination may encourage development of a nuclear weapons and nuclear sabotage capability that is ultimately threatened or resorted to by terrorists because they believed it to be necessary. To avert the second probable outcome, steps will have to be taken that would necessarily impair prospects for the first as well. Such steps will have to aim at a restoration of concern by current sympathizers for proportionality between the ends and means of terrorist action, and at a systemwide (preferably U.N.-directed) commitment to make use of all available counterterrorist measures.

At the present time, such steps seem unlikely to succeed. For some terrorist sympathizers, terrorist objectives are presumed to be of such overriding importance that no act of violence designed to maximize those objectives, however heinous, can be regarded as immoral or unreasonable. For other terrorist sympathizers, the issues of morality and reasonableness are overshadowed by the presumption that terrorists, however inadvertently, work in the sympathizers' own interests. As a result, any systematic attempt to launch a concerted assault on international terrorism is bound to exclude the participation and cooperation of a significant number of states.

V. Conclusion

This paper has considered three basic problems concerning the threat of nuclear terrorism in the world system. Taken together, these technological, behavioral, and contextual problems indicate a high probability of such terrorism taking place. Unless the rate of our descent toward terrorist use of nuclear technology is quickly and surely altered, we are likely to be confronted with unusually destructive conditions on a planetary scale.

How can such an alteration be accomplished? And what are the chances for success? The basic options involve technological, political, and social changes.

With respect to technological changes, governments can take decisive measures to guard against both the theft of assembled weapons and fissionable materials and the sabotage of nuclear reactors. Pursuant to some of the steps not being taken by the United States at military and industrial levels, worldwide efforts need to be undertaken to implement such essential safeguards as heavy containers, vaults, barriers, locks, alarms,[41] remote surveillance, and armed guards.[43] New and more imaginative protection systems can also be explored. For example, one promising area involves the utilization of quick-hardening plastic foam which is effectively impenetrable and can be sprayed into storage vaults in case of attack.[43] An even more basic step would be to limit the number of sites where plutonium is processed or stored and to reduce transportation between these sites. This could be accomplished by grouping several power stations together with the chemical-reprocessing and fuel-fabrication plant in a common nuclear "park" with limited access.[44]

Since the safeguarding of nuclear materials must be carried out internationally, steps must be taken to limit the spread of nuclear technology and nuclear materials throughout the world, and to tighten up international inspection safeguards. This requires pressing forward with the idea of regional, multinational nuclear fuel centers designed to minimize the number of the world's plutonium production plants, and enlarging the international inspections system to keep pace with the worldwide growth of nuclear power.[45]

Today, the Treaty on the Non-Proliferation of Nuclear Weapons (N.P.T.) appears on its surface to be the most suitable instrument by which these steps might be implemented. In fact, however, there is little cause for optimism here. The I.A.E.A. (International Atomic Energy Agency) associated with the

N.P.T. represents neither an effective instrument of international enforcement nor a viable mechanism of international inspection.[46] In view of this situation it is unlikely that the I.A.E.A. could influence states to conclude that the probable benefits of multinational nuclear fuel centers and strict international inspections would exceed the probable costs.[47]

It is with this understanding that David Lilienthal, the first Chairman of the Atomic Energy Commission, called recently for an immediate, unilateral American embargo on the exportation of nuclear reactors, nuclear technology, and fissionable materials until such time as effective international controls can be brought into being.[48] While Lilienthal's plea is certainly well-intentioned, a number of basic problems remain unresolved. Why, for example, should such a unilateral embargo be undertaken without reasonable assurances of support from other major suppliers? Why should such a unilateral embargo help to bring about effective international controls? Precisely what kinds of controls ought to be implemented? How might they be established, enforced, and modified?

Unless the United States could succeed in convincing other national suppliers of nuclear technology that an American embargo would signal the beginning of an effective, worldwide moratorium on sales of pilot plutonium reprocessing plants,[49] it is unlikely that such an embargo would be imitated by other supplier states.[50] The prevention of future nuclear deals requires more than unilateral American action. It requires broad understanding among all major supplier states that the prospective costs of the "every man for himself" dictum in the business of transnational nuclear shipments are out of all proportion to the prospective gains.

The major impediment blocking the development of such an understanding is the so-called "tragedy of the commons," which arises when individual states decide that a particular course of action is preferable only if most other states reciprocate. From the standpoint of halting commerce in nuclear technology and materials, the tragedy of the commons refers to the difficulty in securing an effective moratorium agreement among *all* supplier states so long as each supplier state is uncertain about the good intentions of every other supplier state. Unless each potential moratorium participant believes that its own willingness to cooperate is paralleled by every other potential participant, the supplier state is apt to calculate that the prospective benefits of compliance are exceeded by the prospective costs.

How can the conditions be created whereby each supplier state would entertain such a belief? The answer is essentially a political one: Only by creating a global agency of general authority which is generally perceived to be both willing and able to render the costs of noncompliance unacceptably high. What is required, therefore, is a significantly greater degree of international cooperation than can be accomplished within the context of any conventional treaty arrangement. Such a degree of cooperation can be brought about only through the erection of a genuinely supranational agency that is endowed with the means to ensure broad compliance.

Nothing is more futile than an attempt to control the spread of nuclear technology and materials through conventional treaty processes. No treaty can succeed by opposing general considerations of peace and security to the particular impulses of commercial interest. An agreement without provision for affecting the prospective costs and benefits of compliance, as Pufendorf once noted, makes "no addition . . . . to the obligation of the natural law, that is, the convention does not add anything to which men were not already bound by the very law of nature, nor does it make the obligation more binding."[51]

Regrettably, it seems unlikely that supplier states would be willing to submit to the required diminution of their extant sovereign-authoritative prerogatives that an effective supranational organization would require. As a consequence, these states are apt to remain prisoners of the tragedy of the commons and to permit an already dangerous situation to become even worse. Notwithstanding its apparent desirability, therefore, the infeasibility of a "world authority" approach to the problem of nuclear terrorism means that we have to look elsewhere for a solution.

Where shall we look? Perhaps our greatest hope lies in changing the behavior of the terrorists themselves. The best long-run solution in this regard seems to be removing the causes which occasion terrorist disaffection in the first place. As Walter Laqueur has pointed out, however, there will always be grievances that are used to indict the state or the world system and to justify strategies of terrorism. Moreover, even if such grievances were soluble in principle, they would certainly not yield to treatment in the short run.[52]

However, there *are* three strategies that can be followed in the short run to inhibit the use of violence by terrorists. First, steps ought to be directed toward convincing terrorists that their prevailing inclinations to violence are manifestly ineffective. This can be accomplished only by the repeated demonstrations of states that they will not submit to intimidation. Such a prescription is easier said than done, of course, and will surely require short-run sacrifices accompanied by considerable individual pain and suffering.

Second, steps can be taken to render terrorist actors more responsive to threats of deterrence. Although terrorist actors are generally apt to tolerate substantially higher levels of death and injury than states, there *is* a threshold beyond which certain costs become intolerable. No less than states, terrorist groups choose between alternative courses of action by assessing the perceived consequences of each course in cost-benefit terms. While such assessments are bound to be fairly rough and imprecise, their use suggests that counter-terrorist measures can succeed once the threshold of unacceptable damage is understood and the terrorist population has been identified and isolated.

Finally, steps can be taken to impede the growing cooperation among terrorist groups. These steps would include a broad range of options, including infiltration of terrorist organizations to gather information about their intergroup ties, improved border checks throughout the world, expanded use of the media to publicize patterns of terrorist cooperation, and separate negotiations with selected terrorist groups to destroy their bonds and atomize their operations.

Should such steps begin to be implemented, major strides will begin to be taken toward reducing the threat of nuclear terrorism. In the coming years, however, the outlook for success with these steps is clouded by the understanding that state actors in world politics are divided in their feelings about terrorists. The resultant lack of systemwide interest in dealing with the problem of terrorism may have the most grievous consequences for counterterrorist strategies, since it ensures a continuing measure of safety and support for terrorist causes.

In principle, the surest path to success in limiting the dangers of nuclear terrorism would involve a unified opposition by states to terrorism. But as this kind of opposition is assuredly not forthcoming, at least in the next few years, it will remain the responsibility of certain individual states, acting alone or in combination, to obstruct global terrorism. Functioning within the context of a "self-help" system of international law, these states, cognizant of their responsibilities in a decentralized world system, are the only realistic hope for preventing nuclear terrorism. To sustain this hope, they must commit themselves as completely as possible to the sorts of steps that have just been outlined.

Notes

1. The extant list of paths includes intentional strikes by one nuclear state against another; intentional strikes by a nuclear state against a non-nuclear state; nuclear accidents; and the unauthorized use of nuclear weapons.
2. This paper draws no distinctions between different terrorist groups in terms of the legitimacy or reasonableness of their claims. Rather, the paper rests upon the assumption that every terrorist group, however reasonable or unreasonable its rationale, has the potential to precipitate extraordinary levels of global instability.
3. *See* 4 The Defense Monitor 8 (No. 2, Feb. 1975), a publication of the Center for Defense Information. The point is made that "we are more

likely to become casualties from nuclear terrorist attacks than from attacks by other countries."

4. In this context, the term "nuclear materials" refers to plutonium, highly-enriched uranium, and uranium-233.

5. For example, the United States alone maintains an arsenal of approximately 7000 tactical nuclear weapons in Western Europe. The United States also has tactical nuclear weapons in Asia (approximately 1700 in South Korea, Philippines, Guam, and Midway), on board U.S. Navy combat ships (approximately 2500), and in the custody of selected Army, Navy, and Air Force units in this country (approximately 10,800).

6. The Defense Monitor, *supra* note 3, at 8. In his forthcoming book, The Assault on NATO, British investigative reporter David Lewis relates that the Soviet KGB once used espionage and blackmail to penetrate NATO security in 1976 and to steal a complete Sidewinder air-to-air missile.

7. *See Security Review at Certain NATO Installations*, 121 Congressional Record S7184-S7189 (No. 68, Apr. 30, 1975). *See also Nuclear Theft and Terrorism*, Sixteenth Strategy for Peace Conference: Discussion Group Report (Oct. 1975).

8. *Id.*

9. *See* Mason Willrich & Theodore Taylor, Nuclear Theft: Risks and Safeguards 115 (Cambridge, MA: Ballinger, 1974). *See generally Nuclear Theft and Terrorism, supra* note 7; William Epstein, The Last Chance: Nuclear Proliferation and Arms Control (New York: The Free Press, 1976); Frank, *Nuclear Terrorism and the Escalation of International Conflict* (paper presented to the Annual Meeting of Midwest Political Science Association, Chicago, Ill., May 1, 1976); Krieger, *Terrorists and Nuclear Technology*, The Bulletin of the Atomic Scientists XXXI, No. 6, (June 1975); Lapp, *The Ultimate Blackmail*, The New York Times Magazine 31 (February 4, 1973).

10. At this time, nuclear material from which nuclear explosives might be fabricated exists in approximately 30 countries. By 1985, it is expected that nearly 50 countries will have at least one nuclear power plant that can produce sufficient plutonium each year for at least several dozen nuclear explosives. *See Nuclear Theft and Terrorism, supra* note 7.

11. In principle, prospective nuclear thieves could direct their energies to the acquisition of U-235 as well as plutonium. In fact, however, this would pose a much more staggering task because the uranium fuel would have to undergo the vastly difficult process of enrichment before it could be used in a nuclear explosion. In its available form it would not be "weapon grade" material. Moreover, the uranium fuel used in the extant water reactors is only negligibly radioactive, and would not be suitable for use as a radiological weapon.

12. Only some eleven to twenty pounds of plutonium are needed to construct a crude explosive device. Moreover, only three and one-half ounces are needed to make a radiation dispersal device capable of killing thousands.

13. *See* Willrich & Taylor, *supra* note 9. The Atomic Energy Commission and the nuclear power industry were at one time unable to account for *thousands of pounds* of nuclear materials that could be fashioned into explosives or dispersal devices. Burnham, *Thousands of Pounds of Materials Usable in Nuclear Bombs Unaccounted For,* New York Times 26 § 1 (Dec. 29, 1974). Safeguards to prevent theft or diversion of fissionable materials were the responsibility of the A.E.C. until January 1975. Thereafter, pursuant to the Energy Reorganization Act of 1974, the A.E.C. was divided into E.R.D.A. or Energy Research and Development Administration, and N.R.C. or Nuclear Regulatory Commission. The N.R.C. will face a difficult task in accounting for nuclear materials. According to a recent article in The Christian Science Monitor: "Accounting for nuclear materials is a laborious and cumbersome process. It involves measurements of small quantities of nuclear materials per month. Each measurement has an unavoidable uncertainty. Therefore, after thousands of measurements, the total uncertainty can become very large." Salisbury, *Keeping Track of Nuclear Materials—Or Else,* The Christian Science Monitor 6 (Jan. 13, 1976).

14. Steps to correct some of the most atrocious deficiencies in the American safeguards system were taken pursuant to a report by the General Accounting Office to the Congress in November 1973. *See Improvements Needed in the Program for the Protection of Special Nuclear Material,* Comptroller General of the United States, General Accounting Office (June 1974).

15. The Mitre Corporation, acting as consultants to the N.R.C., has reported that "There is little question that, for sufficient amounts of money, members of organized crime would take a contract to acquire special nuclear material for another party." Plutonium and highly enriched uranium are now worth about $10,000 a kilogram. *See* Jones, *Danger of Nuclear Terrorism Likely to Increase,* Los Angeles Times 1-4, § 2 (Apr. 25, 1976).

16. *See* Salisbury, *How Modern Science Prevents Nuclear Theft,* The Christian Science Monitor 6 (July 14, 1975).

17. *See* Press, *Atomic Bomb Developers Warn of Nuclear Dangers,* The Christian Science Monitor 13 (Dec. 23, 1975).

18. *See Nuclear Theft and Terrorism, supra* note 7.

19. *See* Gilinsky, *NRC Safeguards and Related Issues* (remarks made by Commissioner, U.S. Nuclear Regulatory Commission, before the Institute of Nuclear Materials Management, New Orleans, LA, June 18, 1975).

20. *See* Frank, *supra* note 9.

21. Willrich & Taylor, supra note 9, at 1. A crude nuclear explosive made from pilfered plutonium would probably have a yield in the range between several hundred and several thousand tons of high explosive. If such an explosive were detonated in a crowded metropolitan area, as

many as 10,000 people might be killed directly while tens of thousands might suffer severe fallout problems. *See Nuclear Theft and Terrorism, supra* note 7, at 35.

22. *See generally* Frank, *supra* note 9.

23. *See* Lapp, *supra* note 9.

24. There is little danger that plutonium would be taken from a working nuclear reactor because of the extreme radioactivity of the reactor fuel and the extraordinary difficulty of the required operations. However, plutonium *might* be stolen from the chemical reprocessing plant (after radioactive fission products have been removed), the fuel-fabrication plant, or the transportation system between the plant and the reactor where refabricated fuel elements are installed. *See* Bethe, Cohen, & Wilson, *Comments on The Background Report: On the Plutonium Economy—A Statement of Concern* (paper presented to the National Council of Churches, Jan., 28, 1976). In spite of its toxicity, processed plutonium—which is usually fashioned into small pellets the size of a rubber eraser on a pencil—would not endanger the thief as long as the metal did not come into contact with an open wound or reach his lungs.

25. Frank, *supra* note 9 at 3-4. *See also* Willrich & Taylor, supra note 9, at 25. The nuclear energy industry takes issue with this conclusion. In a "position paper" appearing in a recent Fortune magazine, John W. Simpson, Director-Officer of the Westinghouse Electric Corporation and Chairman of the Energy Committee, states the following: "The release of plutonium in an enclosed area—as say in a building's ventilating system—would have a limited effect from a terrorist point of view. The filters and ducts would prevent a substantial amount from being circulated in the system. Hence use of plutonium as a radiological weapon would be effective only in the immediate vicinity of the point of release and that area can be decontaminated." Simpson, *Nuclear Energy and the Future*, Position Paper #5, Managing and Safeguarding Wastes and Fissionable Material, Fortune 138 (May 1975).

26. *See* Generic Environmental Statement of Mixed Oxide Fuel described by Jones, *supra* note 15, at 3, Section II, col. 1.

27. *See* Atomic Energy Commission, The Safety of Nuclear Power Reactors and Related Facilities (Washington, D.C., 1250, June 1973). Experts in a discussion group concluded that the prospective costs of reactor core meltdown are still apt to be considerably less than the costs associated with other destructive uses of nuclear technology. According to the *Discussion Group Report* issued by Chairperson Theodore B. Taylor and Rapporteur William J. Lanouette: "There was consensus among the group that if a terrorist group managed to take control of a nuclear power station, and caused the core to melt and release a substantial fraction of the radioactivity through the containment structure, the worst conceivable physical consequences would still be less than from a low-yield nuclear explosion in a highly populated area, or the

effective dispersal of a kilogram or so of plutonium throughout a very large office building." *See Nuclear Theft and Terrorism, supra* note 7, at 35.

28. *See* B. L. Welch, *Statement Before the Joint Committee on Atomic Energy* at 32. According to the Mitre Corporation's recent report to the Nuclear Regulatory Commission, terrorists, foreign nations, and organized crime elements might collaborate to sabotage nuclear facilities.

A study done for the N.R.C. by the B.D.M. Corp. of Vienna, Va., however, concludes that organized crime is not apt to pilfer fissionable materials because "a market does not exist for special nuclear materials today." *See* Burnham, *Nuclear Agency Is Reported to Oppose Special Force to Combat Terrorist Attacks at Facilities,* New York Times 11, (Jan. 12, 1976). The B.D.M. study also found that between 1966 and 1975, at least 21 incidents took place in which some individual or group attacked a nuclear facility.

29. Jones, *Nuclear Reactor Risks—Some Frightening Scenarios,* Chicago Sun-Times 12 (Apr. 30, 1976).

29ᵃ. *Id.*

29ᵇ. *Id.*

29ᶜ. *Id.*

30. This information was disclosed by the U.S. Energy Research and Development Administration, Division of Safeguards and Security, to Mr. James M. Cubie of Congress Watch, an organization associated with Ralph Nader, in a letter dated 26 January 1976. I have received and reviewed a copy of this letter and the attached listing of threats or acts of violence with regard to Energy Research and Development Administration (E.R.D.A.) unlicensed nuclear facilities.

31. *See* Jones, *supra* note 15.

32. Walzer, *The New Terrorists,* 173 The New Republic 12-13, No. 9 (Aug. 30, 1975)

33. While assassination remains a strategy of modern terrorism, the incidence does seem to have decreased. There were more killings of leading statesmen during the 1890's than at the present time. *See* Laqueur, *The Futility of Terrorism,* Harper's 99, 103 (Mar. 1976).

34. *See* Laqueur, *supra* note 33, at 99-105.

35. The optimal level of sacrifice, of course, is one in which the losses incurred in any particular operation are no greater than the losses that are essential to the success of that operation, and in which the losses pose no threat to survival of the group itself.

36. This disadvantage is exacerbated when retaliatory strikes are precluded because of difficulty in *locating* the terrorist targets or in *separating* them from "non-combatant" populations.

37. As examples of this characteristic, one can consider the actions of Arab terrorists who, in April 1974, seized an apartment building in northern Israel and were ultimately killed; the actions of the S.L.A.members who preferred death to incarceration during the widely-publicized California shootout in May 1974; the actions of the two Red Army terrorists who

killed themselves during the attack on Israel's Lod International Airport on May 30, 1972; the attempted suicide of a Baader-Meinhof terrorist in the West German Embassy in Stockholm after the Bonn Government's refusal to capitulate to the group's demands in April 1975; and the self-inflicted death by hunger of Holger Meins of the Baader-Meinhof group in 1974.

38. While dead terrorists may be useful per se as martyrs, the principal advantage of terrorist willingness to die "for the cause" (a characteristic, incidentally, which is not always operative and which varies from group to group), is the heightened insensitivity to orthodox threats of retaliation. Moreover, there is a point at which martyrdom itself may lose its value to the movement and become counterproductive—i.e., the point when the presumed morale-boosting benefits of the ultimate sacrifice are offset by the manpower-depleting costs of death.

39. See Fisk, *The World's Terrorists Sometimes Are United*, New York Times 3, Section E, col. 3 (Aug. 17, 1975); Alexander, *Some Perspectives on International Terrorism*, 14 International Problems 24, 27, No. 3-4 (Israel, Fall 1975); and Wolf, *Black September: Militant Palestinianism*, 64 Current History 5, 37, No. 377 (Jan. 1973).

40. See discussion of United Nations debate on terrorism Dugard, *International Terrorism and the Just War*.

41. Safeguards expert Theodore Taylor is in the forefront of those urging more extensive detection and alarm systems—systems in which monitors detect fractions of an ounce of nuclear materials when they are taken outside designated areas. Notwithstanding the importance of such systems, however, a number of highly sensitive nuclear facilities have yet to adopt them. For example, simulated attackers were able to reach the front door of the Nuclear Fuel Service Plant in Irwin, Tennessee, without sounding an alarm about 50 percent of the time. *See* Salisbury, *supra* note 13.

42. The Nuclear Regulatory Commission is now considering special training for Army Special Forces units to prepare them for situations wherein terrorist groups have secured a nuclear facility. *See* Burnham, *supra* note 28, at 11.

43. Research on this strategy is now underway at Sandia laboratories near Albuquerque. *See* Salisbury, *How Modern Science Prevents Nuclear Theft*, Christian Science Monitor 6 (July 14, 1975).

44. Wilson, *Where Did We Put That Nuclear Reactor?* New York Times 21, col. 2 (Jan. 3, 1976). Mr. Wilson is a specialist on nuclear safety and Professor of Physics at Harvard University.

45. Such enlargement requires both the capability to deal with a larger number of annual inspections (presently the International Atomic Energy Agency conducts 450 inspections a year in 33 countries) and the authority to inspect *all* nuclear plants built with a supplier's technology is subject to inspection.

46. *See* Mason Willrich, Perspective on the N.P.T. Review Conference (Occasional Paper No. 7, The Stanley Foundation, 1975). In addition to the

problems involved in the inspection of signatory states' facilities, there
is the overwhelming problem of non-signatories. At this time, Egypt,
Japan, and Switzerland have not yet ratified the N.P.T.; and Argentina,
Brazil, Chile, China, France, India, Israel, Pakistan, Portugal, South
Africa, and Spain have not yet signed. The implications of this condition for international stability are as ominous as they are obvious.
47. The feasibility of inspection is especially doubtful because of the continuing pattern of staunch Soviet opposition.
48. Testimony before the Senate Government Operations Subcommittee,
January 19, 1976.
49. The projected end of such a moratorium could coincide with the effective
implementation of regional nuclear fuel centers and viable international
inspection standards.
50. Curiously, Lilienthal himself believes that if the United States undertook
such a unilateral embargo, the other supplier nations would also cease
their exports. *See* Burnham, *U.S. Export Ban on Nuclear Equipment
Urged by Former Atomic Energy Chief*, New York Times 2, col. 1 (Jan.
20, 1976). Lilenthal's testimony was presented before the Senate
Government Operations Subcommittee, January 19, 1976.
51. *See* Pufendorf, *On Manner of Settling Disputes in a State of Natural
Liberty*, De Jure Naturae at Gentium Libri Acto 562 (New York:
Oceana, 1964).
52. *See* Laqueur, *supra* note 33, at 103.

Robert H. Kupperman

Facing Tomorrow's Terrorist Incident Today

This important report by the chief scientist of the Arms Control and Disarmament Agency reviews and summarizes the results of extensive research funded by the Law Enforcement Assistance Administration. Kupperman takes a wide view of macroterror, including nuclear, biological, and chemical variants, as well as other significantly disruptive acts (such as terrorist interdiction of electrical grids). Special consideration is devoted to target hardening, policy choices (including co-optation), incident management, and damage limitation. An appendix summarizes several of the more impressive recent efforts at event modeling and adversary description.

Introduction

Highly industrialized nations—especially those which place a premium on competition and market efficiency—are fragile in the sense of their vulnerability to catastrophe. Commercial aircraft, natural gas pipelines, the electric power grid, offshore oil rigs, and computers storing government and corporate records are examples of sabotage-prone targets whose destruction would have derivative effects of far higher intensity than their primary losses would suggest. Consider the recent New York blackout. Disproportionately high damage occurred—nearly uncontrolled looting and arson, resource shortages, and a further loss of already low public confidence. Suppose, instead of its two-day span, the blackout were to have lasted just three days more. Understanding that the City would have been paralyzed, it is not difficult to invent stark—possibly realistic—scenarios: looters would run wild, fires starting at random, and jittery National Guardsmen shooting into crowds of panicked people; food and water would become scarce, the food spoilage being nearly total; the sanitation system would collapse, the spectre of disease becoming an overriding concern; and the rats, which outnumber the people, would be close to achieving a permanent victory.

The point is that "nature," with the aid of human inefficiency, produced the two-day siege; but a trained, quite small paramilitary force could take the

City of New York—or any large metropolitan area—off-line for extended periods of time.

Thus far our experience with terrorism is limited to diminutive acts. Even so, the world was riveted to the TV screen when the Munich killings occurred in 1972; and it was blind luck that the Hanafi Muslims did not choose a more interesting target. Because we are implicitly willing to accept the human and political losses, we are prepared to handle the "Hanafi" assaults; but a slight upward deviation from the projected pattern of familiar incidents could bring about terrible hardships. Thirty years ago terrorists could not have obtained extraordinary leverage. Today, however, the foci of communications, production and distribution are relatively small in number and highly vulnerable—and the media balance themselves on tightropes, doing their jobs of reporting the news, yet being perilously close to inciting further terror.

Terrorism of any form is disturbing. But its theatrical attraction[1] diminishes as the audience becomes inured by repetition. Unfortunately, the terror-organism adapts to this changing environment. The crux of the matter is *instability*: a slight change from a familiar mode of attack can panic an otherwise bored public.

There is little point in describing the multiplicity of possible "choke points." Most are obvious, and the rest should not be made public. It is also foolish to make confident probabilistic estimates of terrorist trends, for we can extrapolate only from scant data. Yet there are useful, qualitative statements to make, none of which is reassuring. Further, because strategic planning of large organizations (whether governmental or private) often exists in name only, it is impossible to predict responses to terrorist assaults other than to suggest that their handling may be ad hoc.

If the obvious targets are examined, it is clear that terrorists need not resort to using nuclear bombs or biological agents to bring about devastation.[2] At root is the increasingly nihilistic character of transnational terrorist groups and their resources—they are well trained and ruthless, and they have money and technical assets. Western nations, even the United States, are ill prepared to cope with any form of warfare other than conventional military response. A clever terrorist who understands the potential failure modes of government can inflict grievous harm, possibly more harm than war. Unless governments take basic precautions, we will continue to stand at the edge of an awful abyss.

The purpose of the LEAA grants was to study the management and technology aspects of nationally disruptive acts of terrorism. Were governments convinced that the erosive effects of terrorism would not exceed those of the Lod Airport massacre, the LaGuardia bombing, the Hanafi incident, or a raft of assassinations and kidnappings, this report would be unneeded. The world would adapt, accepting the threat as it does the statistics of disease and automobile accidents. Eventually the disease cycle would reach a natural boundary, the threat entering into a dormant, spore phase. Unfortunately, no such guarantee exists. On the contrary, there are qualitative trends toward increasing levels of violence and disruption. Focusing upon the higher-order act, the report surveys the technology of counterterrorism, discusses incident management needs, and recommends ways to lessen the risks of nationally disruptive acts.

Threat Assessment and Risk Taking[3]

The assessment of the threat of terrorism relies on intelligence techniques—observing known or suspected terrorists and, when feasible, penetrating their organizations. Unfortunately, the task of keeping up with terrorists in this fashion is overwhelming, for it is virtually impossible to tell when a formerly obscure or inactive group will suddenly spring into prominence. (The incident of March 1977 in which Hanafi Muslims terrorized Washington with three separate sieges illustrates this point.) On the other hand, terrorism which is widely advertised in advance may never take place, at least in part because of the intense counter-efforts prompted by that advertisement.

Terrorist acts force the generation of their own countermeasures, as airplane hijackings led to screening of air passengers. Though politically explosive incidents still occur, the problem becomes a *quantitative* one, and countermeasures will be improved and developed until the probability of success for the particular form of terrorism appears tolerably small.

The first occurrence of a new mode of terrorism, however, usually appears as a *qualitative* problem, and it can present a grave problem if it has not been anticipated. We must therefore attempt to "out-invent" terrorists, assessing as yet unexploited technical possibilities and devising countermeasures.

Qualitative errors in threat assessment are potentially more destabilizing influences upon national policies toward terrorism than are quantitative mistakes in estimating the frequencies of familiar types of attacks. While avoiding actions that could cause widespread alarm, we must also avoid the contrary extreme of believing that because a certain type of incident has never yet occurred, it is therefore unlikely to occur in the future.

WHO ARE THE TERRORISTS?[4]

It is not always an easy matter to distinguish the terrorist from the criminal or the psychotic. Normally the terrorist is associated with a political cause, ostensibly engaging in extortion, assassinations and bombings for more noble reasons than the criminal. People who combine their intensely held beliefs with an imperative to commit acts of violence are to be found in a wide variety of places.

There are Italian and South American groups who have made a lucrative business of kidnapping executives and obtaining sizable ransoms. There are, of course, the PLO and its splinter organizations which may function as surrogates of Libya and other Arab countries. The Japanese Red Army, beside being leftist-leaning, is both violent and suicidal. Nihilists, such as the Red Cells in Germany and the predecessor Baader-Meinhof gang, have committed a number of despicable acts and they attract well-educated members who are often the offspring of wealthy parents. In the United States there are a number of terrorist groups: the FALN which supports Puerto Rican independence and uses fairly sophisticated bombs; the Weather Underground which is predisposed to blowing up buildings (and, at times, themselves); the American Indian Movement of Wounded Knee notoriety; and various small groups such as the Symbionese Liberation Army that sprang into fame when it abducted Patty Hearst.

Terrorism, often viewed as a means to a political goal, is becoming an end in itself. Today, terrorists recognize the dilemma they pose to democratic governments restrained by moral and legal principles in countering their activities. They also understand and exploit the inability of bureaucracies to respond quickly to new and complex problems. Despite a dearth of significant political success, they have achieved many operational cops. These, along with the historical precedents of Cuba, Algeria, and other areas in which terror tactics played an important role in toppling governments, have led some terrorist groups to subordinate divergencies of political objectives to a pervasive and general nihilism.

Although few terrorist groups have yet focused systematic attacks on non-human targets, this may become a more attractive alternative as we become inured to assassinations, bombings and hostage-taking. Incidents such as the attacks on mass-transit ticket machines in West Germany, power facilities in California, broadcasting studios in Spain and Argentina and nuclear power plants in France, Argentina and Spain may foreshadow more extensive, nationally disruptive acts. The technology requisite for such attacks is readily available.

Throughout the world, as well as one can count, there are some fifty terrorist groups of varying sizes having in all about 3,000 members. Of these groups only four or five, amounting to several hundred terrorists, constitute the primary transnational threat. But the "several hundred" is the tip of an iceberg, there being several thousand sympathizers who form the infrastructure of international terrorism. The "several hundred" is the action corps. These people have trained together in North Korea and Lebanon. They know each other well. They plan and execute operations jointly. Being highly organized and having the support of governments such as Libya and South

Yemen, they have little difficulty obtaining automatic weapons and they have used modern surface-to-air rockets as well as antitank weapons. (At Rome in 1973, five Palestinians were caught attempting to shoot down an El Al commercial jet with SA-7s; a similar attempt was made in Nairobi in 1976; and at Orly in 1975 a Palestinian damaged a Yugoslav aircraft with an antitank weapon.) In sum, "they have their act together."

In 1975 Austrian authorities arrested three entrepreneurs who were synthesizing nerve agents for sale to terrorist groups. Well-engineered barometric bombs and bombs with delayed fusing mechanisms have been used by terrorists. German terrorists have threatened to use mustard agents against civilians; and it is no secret that many governments—and some subnational groups—are anxious to get their hands on a nuclear weapon.

When we consider the abundance of targets and the cohesiveness of relatively small groups of well-trained zealots, their use of sophisticated weaponry, and the ease with which they could extort governments, we are forced to ponder the future with alarm.

THE POTENTIAL FOR PHYSICAL DAMAGE

In preparing to cope with terrorism it is important to comprehend the potential physical damage terrorists could inflict and the resources they would require to accomplish it. Although derivative societal effects may, in some instances, outweigh physical damage, techniques intended to minimize physical damage may be the only key to lessening the total trauma. Decisions such as those concerning possible concessions to terrorists and the extent of emergency services required to deal with the results if a threat is carried out are obviously crucially dependent on an understanding of both the possible physical effects and the resources available to terrorists.

In terms of fatalities, conventional weapons such as machine guns and small bombs constitute the least threat. They can produce tens or hundreds of casualties in a single incident. Chemical weapons such as nerve agents constitute a substantially greater threat, being capable of producing hundreds to thousands of fatalities. A small nuclear bomb could produce a hundred thousand casualties, but biological agents—both toxins and living organisms—can rival thermonuclear weapons, providing the possibility of producing hundreds of thousands to several millions of casualties in a single incident.

The physical effects of terrorist weapons also depend upon their targets. An antitank weapon weighing less than ten pounds might puncture several feet of reinforced concrete in the center of a major city and still cause relatively minor damage. The same weapon used against key components of the nation's electrical power grid could cause a regional blackout.

Conventional weapons and high explosives are universally available. Even such sophisticated "conventional" weapons as the man-portable Soviet SA-7 surface-to-air rocket and RPG-7 light antitank weapon have proliferated beyond control. Various commercially available insecticides are highly effective nerve agents. Although terrorists could conceivably obtain materials and technology to manufacture a crude fission bomb, this is a difficult and dangerous task—they are more likely to turn to readily available chemical or biological weapons. Despite the great toxicity of biological agents, their efficient delivery requires considerable technical sophistication.

THREE LINES OF DEFENSE

If a nation could know beforehand "where, when and how," a terrorist assault might be thwarted; however, there are gaps to be bridged between an intelligence coup and operational victory. The value of intelligence is neither uniform nor easily predictable. Knowing for example that a certain terrorist group has a high propensity for violence may suggest a greater allocation of collection (warning) resources rather than of substantial operation (reactive) assets. Yet, during a delicate hostage-barricade matter even such "soft" assessments of cultural and behavioral traits are valuable. We need to know if the captors are likely to murder the hostages, what behavioral patterns delimit rescue attempts, and so forth. In other words, *damage limitation*—may depend upon intelligence data, but the needed precision of these data depends on their applications.

The perennial dilemma of an aggressive intelligence apparatus is how to match its activities to the needs of its clients. Although there is often close collaboration between the users of intelligence and its collectors, little analysis of the relative worth of various types of collection activities may have been done. For this and other related reasons, our understanding of terrorism may suffer from stunted thought. It is easy to raise doubts about the effectiveness of intelligence efforts, but having advance information about an impending terrorist assault is surely preferable to being caught totally unprepared. *Intelligence is the first line of defense.*[5]

The *second line of defense* is contained in an idea that is simple but often expensive to implement: to *harden the target,* building "high-pass filters" which block the admission of the amateurish terrorists and increase the costs to the more talented as well. Limitation of access through physical means and controlling the accessibility of dangerous devices and materials is necessary. Fences, guards, various sensors, closed-circuit television, metal detectors, tags for explosives, secure communications means, etc. are elements of a growing *counterterrorism technology.* While vulnerability is reduced, and the costs for both sides are increased, it is not clear what the "cost-benefit ratios" are.

Deterrence of future terrorist acts, though a subjective matter, is undoubtedly enhanced by reducing target vulnerability.

Finally, even the best intelligence and physical security efforts will sometimes fail, and governments will be forced to manage crises produced by terrorism. To minimize the trauma resulting from such acts, governments must behave efficiently. Organizational arrangements, management information and communications systems, sources of expert help, specialized military assets, emergency medical, food and power generation supplies, and clear delineation of legal and administration authorities must be developed ahead of time. Policy-level officials should have practice in making the sorts of decisions they may face.

Severe risks to civil liberties are ever present—if nothing is done to prepare and an incident does occur, governments may resort to repression on a broad scale. If governments overreact prior to a major incident, they may become subject to ridicule and charged with alarmism. Finally, if a major incident does take place, it is crucial that government meet the crisis squarely, and in a way to assure the public that reasonable and thoughtful action has been taken. Preparedness measures to meet terrorism must be neither isolated nor unexercisable; rather, they should fit within routine activities of government, ensuring an ability to mobilize resources at time of strain.

Hardening the Target [6]

Hardening the target has prophylactic value. It entails denying terrorists access to arms and explosives as well as denying them access to their intended targets. The objective is to make the potential terrorist act so difficult that the amateur is defeated and the professional finds the cost too high. Thus "hardening the target" is synonymous with establishing barriers, some of which are managerial and the others are physical. The physical methods of hardening are to reduce the terrorist's ability to damage a specific installation; and for networks, such as the electric power and communications systems, to increase the number of critical nodes. Here, we consider two types of barriers: (a) denial of means, and (b) security devices and procedures.

The rapid pace of modern technology has permitted significant improvements to be made in methods for detecting devices and materials suitable as terrorist instruments and in methods for preventing access to potential terrorist targets. None of the present or anticipated devices has a long-range detection capability. None of the present and anticipated barrier concepts is impenetrable. Sensors are most useful in preventing terrorism by making it difficult for potential terrorists to obtain and transport arms, explosives, as well as chemical, biological, and radiological agents.

DENIAL OF MEANS

The most effective preventive measure is to deny terrorists the means to strike, but our basic political, social and economic values make this an unattainable goal. Much can be done in a technical way, however, to limit opportunities without taking repressive actions which would alter the very nature of our government. (Indeed, the terrorists' objectives may include goading the government into such unpopular acts.)

Tightened controls over access to commercial explosives through regulation of purchases and improved procedures to bar thefts would be of some use, but the wide availability of constituents (such as fertilizers) suitable for clandestine manufacture of high explosives makes it impossible to deny high explosives to terrorists. A capability to detect such explosives would help provide some protection to selected targets which are either particularly vulnerable or particularly valuable.

A number of techniques for automatic detection of the characteristic vapors given off by many explosives are under active development. There is considerable variation among explosive compounds in the amount and detectability of vapors emitted, but the most common ones emit detectable vapors. The two most useful and promising detection methods are specially trained dogs (which are expensive to train and manage) and *electron-capture vapor detectors*. Neither of these is completely satisfactory. The broad utility of such detectors in preventing a wide range of terrorist threats indicates that their development and procurement should receive priority.

Another technique for combating the use of explosives in terrorism is impregnating detonators with distinctive chemicals at the time of manufacture so that the presence of an explosive can be detected easily. If widely advertised, this technique has a deterrent value. Of related value is the tagging of explosives with "coded" microspheres. While not aiding detection, tagging can be of immense value to the investigatory phase after a terrorist bombing has occurred.

The case of small arms is parallel to that of high explosives. Despite all that may be done to limit access, terrorists can almost certainly obtain them while only a relatively small number of potential victims can be protected by detecting devices. While technical measures can serve to frustrate the marginal terrorist and protect key targets, they will not eliminate the problem.

Metal detectors, such as those used to screen passengers before boarding airliners, have become familiar. These detectors are useful in locating small arms. X-ray machines are presently used to inspect airline carry-on baggage. Their increasing use for inspection of checked baggage and cargo is expected but the interpretation of X-ray shadowgraphs of large volumes of luggage will be tedious and imperfect. Developing and acquiring contrast enhancement and automatic pattern recognition attachments could be especially useful.

The situation with heavier armaments is rather different, for few sources of supply exist and the level of technology required virtually precludes clandestine manufacture. On the other hand, protection against them is virtually impossible. The key to thwarting terrorist use of these weapons thus lies in denying them access. The chances for such a policy are fairly good. Although sophisticated ground-to-air and antitank weapons are widely dispersed in the hands of various national troop units (and significant quantities have found their way into clandestine arms traffic), this traffic is somewhat vulnerable to interdiction. Increased customs vigilance, new physical devices and better procedures for tracking and locating stolen weapons appear to be the most promising measures to limit terrorist access to them.

In the United States measures have already been taken to protect US military stocks and to screen baggage and cargo entering the United States. The possibility of tagging military stocks in order to place them under stricter control has been investigated. Although there are a number of promising principles, each has some drawbacks. Further development is needed to determine if an acceptable method is possible and, if so, what costs and operational problems might be encountered.

Intelligence, inspection and tagging are necessary but inadequate means to disrupt the clandestine arms traffic in advanced, man-portable weaponry. Weapons like the Soviet SA-7 surface-to-air missile and the Soviet RPG-7 antitank weapon are already in the hands of terrorists. International agreements are needed to limit distribution as well as to set physical security and "trackability" standards for them. In addition to international agreements, we must examine the question of their true military need. Heavier, jeep- or truck-mounted surface-to-air rockets might fulfill military requirements while denying the terrorist ease of weapons transport and operation. Admittedly, this thought is ironical when the typical goal of fixed weapons performance at minimum weight or cost is considered. Yet, Sweden has adopted this philosophy in the design of its RBS-70 SAM, a bulky, tripod-mounted system which would be difficult to conceal.

Chemicals of great toxicity are so widely used in farm and factory that preventing access to such agents by potential terrorists is an unachievable goal. Moreover, the potential targets are so diverse and the mode of attack can be so subtle that protection does not seem possible either. At best, chemical detectors could interdict selected chemicals or give warning of an attack. It may be possible to further reduce this threat by developing and using sensors capable of detecting trace amounts of hazardous substances. Since it is nearly impossible to remove all traces of some agents from the outside of a sealed container after filling, trace detectors could be useful. A considerable amount of development is still needed because there are many potential toxic chemical agents.

There are numerous hazardous biological agents which could suit a terrorist's purposes. Unlike chemical agents, however, they are not generally available on a commercial basis. Although bacterial cultures can be obtained in many ways, isolating and subculturing the desired organisms can be a time-consuming, technically sophisticated matter. Sources of pure cultures of the more virulent pathogens are rather limited and hence would be easier to control. The existing controls over access appear to be loose and only limited knowledge is required to breed a large amount of bacteria from a minute sample. As with chemical agents, protection of possible targets from biological attack is extremely difficult and the particular measures which can limit the effects of an attack depend on rapid diagnosis of its nature. Here there is an opportunity for technological innovation.

The techniques for control and detection of nuclear materials are much better than those for chemical or biological agents. Improvement, however, would be difficult and expensive for much has already been accomplished. Fissionable and radioactive materials, such as could be used to construct crude nuclear weapons or cause a significant radioactive hazard, come from very limited sources and are strictly controlled. Denying access to such materials to unauthorized personnel has been a major concern of governments since the advent of the nuclear age.

Fissionable materials are guarded by the most sophisticated technical systems and are undoubtedly the most difficult materials for a terrorist to obtain in significant amounts. Should he succeed in doing so, however, protection of potential targets would be at least as difficult as with the other modes of terrorist attack. Moreover, the mere explosion of a crude nuclear bomb in a desert area by a terrorist group would cause panicky public reaction and form a basis for extreme demands.

SECURITY DEVICES AND PROCEDURES

In the absence of specific intelligence about terrorist plans, the task of preventing terrorism falls upon such general purpose measures as fences, guards, alarms, and the screening of passengers and luggage at airports. There can be no guarantee that skillful terrorists will not circumvent such measures, but their use can discourage all but the most talented and determined. To be effective even to this extent, however, these barriers must be ubiquitous. If they are not, terrorists will simply shift their operations to unprotected targets. Potential air hijackers, for instance, will board planes at airports where security is known to be lax. (The Entebbe terrorists boarded the Air France plane at Athens, then a known weak point in the airport security system.)

Because they must be applied universally to all the potential targets to be effective, these preventive measures must be relatively inexpensive when the number of targets to be protected is large. This would tend to rule out a high level of technological sophistication in measures to prevent terrorism except in isolated instances where a few extremely vulnerable targets exist. A technology directed against a broad spectrum of possible terrorist activities may be economically feasible in situations where few opportunities of relatively great vulnerability exist, but even in such a case the necessary broadness of the measures militates against use of high technology countermeasures to specific threats. A device which could detect remotely a wide variety of poisons, explosives and drugs with moderate reliability might be useful in screening airline passengers if its cost were reasonable. Installing a single-purpose cobra venom detector at each airport, on the other hand, is ludicrous.

Access to potential terrorist targets can be made more difficult by erecting fences and barriers; using intrusion sensors; and increasing the effectiveness of guard forces. Many existing defenses were designed to be effective against the curious interloper or petty thieves. While any barrier serves a useful purpose by excluding the less determined potential intruders, defenses against a determined, well-equipped terrorist group must be sophisticated and strong to have significant value.

The chain link galvanized steel fence, sometimes topped with a few strands of barbed wire, is probably the most common perimeter barrier. If it is backed up by a guard force, it is quite effective against casual and even some determined intruders. Intruders using wire cutters, ladders, or even heavy vehicles can penetrate such barriers. Nevertheless, a well-maintained, well-lighted, and well-patrolled chain link perimeter fence is probably the first priority as a defense against saboteurs. When such a perimeter is frequently patrolled or monitored by closed-circuit TV or intrusion sensors, it can be effective against surreptitious attack.

The category of intrusion sensors spans a wide variety of uses. Among the less sophisticated devices are the widely-used door switches, conductive tapes, and photo-electric detectors used for home, store, and factory alarm systems. At the high end of the spectrum are sensors developed for the war in Southeast Asia, sensing vibration, sound, and heat. Experience with these devices has shown that they are very useful for sounding the alarm, but they must be accompanied by quick investigation and a backup guard force. Furthermore, alarms are often installed with inadequate attention given to protecting the alarm system itself. Although intrusion sensors can increase the effectiveness of a guard force, they require continual testing for malfunctions and other weaknesses.

Closed-circuit television (CCTV) has become fairly widely used to expand the surveillance area of a guard force. The cost and reliability of such systems have been improved so that we may anticipate their increasing use. The number of cameras that can be monitored effectively by a single guard is limited.[7] Moreover, cameras can be blinded in a number of ways.

US Sinai Support Missions[8]

There are a great many examples of installations using advanced sensor systems, but the Sinai effort is possibly the best known application.

The US established and operates an early warning system in the Sinai, which is intended to monitor the approaches to the Mitla and Giddi Passes. The system uses advanced types of intrusion sensors (acoustic, seismic, etc.) emplaced in arrays to detect all intrusions. Further, there are devices designed to monitor the sensor fields; these include day-and-night imaging systems to determine the nature of the intrusion.

Fundamental Policy Choices

On the face of it, governmental policy should prohibit concessions to terrorists. This posture may indeed be appropriate when the lives of a handful of individuals are threatened. However, the policy of "no substantitive bargaining with terrorists" would be reevaluated in the event that society was threatened with mass destruction of lives and property. Indeed, should the destruction of a major city be considered a real possibility, the government would have little choice but to consider major concessions, concessions that could potentially undermine its ability to govern.

PRECONDITIONS FOR BARGAINING

In the case of "intermediate" terrorism (downing commercial aircraft, sabotage of power or communications facilities, and other nationally disruptive acts), we are not dealing with the kind of threat that could permanently cripple the nation or irreparably rupture the foundation of modern society, but neither are we dealing with the kind of threat that can be dismissed out of hand as unworthy of substantive negotiation. We must therefore attempt to strike the difficult balance between a willingness to make meaningful concessions and an unwillingness to bargain at all.

Although often of nihilistic basis, we must assume that terrorist violence is the product of people with rational (to them) political or financial goals. We are thus led to a fundamental policy question that must be resolved: while we may or may not understand the specific aims of a particular terrorist group, what kind of concessions would we be willing to make in the event of an "intermediate" terrorist threat?

Before attempting to outline a defense, it is essential that we identify the ramifications we fear most. The immediate physical damage is a lesser danger than the impact the incident might have upon our socio-economic structure. The greatest dangers arise from the persistent secondary effects. For example, should a terrorist group be successful in destroying a jumbo jet at takeoff, the institutional and psychological effects could be far more significant than the actual destruction. In some cases, such as attacks upon electric power or communications networks, the secondary effects upon society could approach those of "mass destruction."

In light of this potential, our preeminent goal is to "decouple" the secondary effects from the primary incident. If both potential terrorists and government become convinced that "intermediate" acts of violence need not have far-reaching societal repercussions, we would be in a far better position to exclude strategic[9] concessions from consideration. However, if government becomes panicky and overreacts to a terrorist incident, what can government expect of the media and the public?

It cannot be too strongly emphasized that strategic capitulation must be excluded from the bargaining table. If it appears that extortionists can command political and financial power by threatening us with serious assault, the impetus for others to attempt similar ventures could become irresistible. Success begets success!

BARGAINING WITH TERRORISTS [10]

The least difficult variety of extortion to accede to is that involving a financial demand without any political or institutional implications. This is more or less common in the private sphere. Although we could expect it to reach greater proportions when directed against a government, it would probably not deal a crippling blow to national sovereignty. In such a case, the government might attempt to protract negotiations in an attempt to locate the extortionists. If it were unable to do so because of a strict time limit imposed by the extortionists, it might be preferable to pay at least a portion of the demand rather than to test their willingness to carry out the threat. The success of politically motivated terrorists may also attract criminal groups to the lucrative opportunities for extortion.

Threats requiring a change in government policy are a different matter. They are decidedly unconventional because they cannot be levied against an individual or group but only against an official decision-making body of a legitimate government. Accession to such a threat could undermine that government's domestic and international credibility. However, even within the context of political extortion, there is a broad range of possible demands and an equally broad range of possible response.

For example, a terrorist group may present the target government with a list of required incremental policy shifts, shifts that could plausibly occur over a period of time within the context of administration policy. In such a case it might be possible to negotiate without overtly undermining national sovereignty. In the long run it might be possible to thwart the extortionists' designs as the government learns about their operations; but in the short run the government might attempt to bargain and be forced to accede—partially or in full.

The target government would face a much more serious problem if the terrorists announce their threat to the public or if the media somehow became aware of it. (The problem of maintaining secrecy about the threat could be exacerbated by a terrorist group demanding a dramatic and immediate shift in policy that could not possibly occur within the context of the Administration's programs.) Once it becomes apparent that a small group can force a legitimate government to alter its domestic or foreign policy, there is evidence that a "bandwagon" effect could be significant. Other fanatic groups might quickly realize that they too could enter the arena of political power by resorting to threats of major consequence. Should the threat become public or should there even be rumors of the threat in the press, widespread panic could result. Because we have never faced this problem in the past, and thus have no experience in coping with it, one can only speculate about the impact that a distraught public might have upon government officials responsible for making crisis decisions. It is quite possible, however, that the pressure to accede (or not to accede) to any and all terrorist demands would be enormous, thus further constraining the target government's options.

Although maintaining secrecy while bargaining would certainly be preferred, some terrorist groups might consider it advantageous to publicize their threat. Publicity would make them more visible and might also cause a panic-stricken population to exert pressure upon the authorities to comply with terrorist demands. This problem could be further complicated if the terrorists imposed a strict time limit upon negotiation. In such a situation, if the authorities were unable to convince the terrorists to lessen their demands or to convince them that great violence would not further their cause, the target government would have to make the ultimate decision—accede to their demands, either partially or in full, or test their willingness to carry out their threat.

When the target government is dealing with a terrorist group that seeks a permanent stake in the international system—such as the PLO—the chances for *cooption* (endowing the terrorists with resources they will be forced to protect in bargaining) and *confidentiality* are reasonably high. Because the group wants to be a part of the system, it would gain little by making it impossible for nations already in the system to accede to their demands. Such groups want to be coopted.

By contrast, nihilists may believe that terror is in their interest. Because they despise the established order and have no desire to become a part of it, the target government may not be able to convince them to maintain confidentiality. Their tactics alone may preclude the possibility for maintaining secrecy. Consider a scenario in which the terrorists overrun a nuclear weapons storage site and are subsequently surrounded by military forces. Such a case could not be kept confidential and it would require the authorities to cope with the threat in public. In this case, the major political damage would already have been done once the terrorists were successful in taking over the storage site.

Although the publicity factor might complicate matters in one sense, this scenario presents fewer bargaining and logistical problems than do many others. In this case, the threatened area could be evacuated, intelligence operations could be limited because the culprits are surrounded, and the area of potential physical damage is identified in advance. In this classic barricade setting, the authorities might refuse to negotiate at all, finding it preferable to mount a full-scale attack against the terrorists. The biggest concession to these terrorists that could be considered is their *initial* safe passage out of the area.

In the above cases, bargaining possibilities might be greatly increased if the extortionist demands remained secret and if the group itself had a desire to be coopted. Many times this is clearly impossible. Nevertheless, because secrecy and cooption may represent the target government's best chance to limit damage, they should be considered as bargaining objectives when the use of force cannot succeed. Therefore, because cooption is a strategy that the government may need to consider when negotiating with terrorists threatening national disruption, let us examine the philosophical premises and tactical procedures for implementing this strategy.

1. The target government must be able to convince the terrorists that, should they insist upon public humiliation, negotiation may be impossible.
2. In order to make this strategy operational, the target government must be willing to consider some concessions. Without them it might be impossible to prevent the terrorists from publicizing their threat in order to bring public pressure to bear upon the government.
3. By conceding in part, the government must demonstrate that the terrorist gains could be lost in escalating violence. If they obtain assets that a target government can retaliate against, the target government

then acquires a hostage. Once the terrorists have a stake in the system, their desire to destroy it may fade away.

4. Cooption of terrorists is designed to promote a situation of deterrence, not friendship. (Indeed, if at any time during or after the negotiations it becomes possible for the government to disarm the terrorists, such a course of action would be "fair play.")

5. There remains the possibility that terrorists may refuse to negotiate or that they may negotiate only to gain publicity and intensify the drama. In such an event one must attempt to preempt.

Incident Management and Damage Limitation

The first two lines of defense can fail. Enough advance information may not be obtained in order to thwart a terrorist attack. Also, if it is worth the cost, any physical security system can be defeated. Thus we come to the last line of defense, the efficient management of the incident, including the "clean-up" phase. All that lies between a full loss of public confidence in government, possibly chaos, and government's saving of face is the public's perception that government did all it could. The truth may be irrelevant.

Just how would we respond to an extortion or assault? Our actions to date are mixed. For the small hostage incident we have developed behavioral techniques that seem to work well. For the bigger events, such as the LaGuardia bombing, government fibrillated, the incident having escalated to open Presidential involvement within hours of the explosion. In the case of the Croatian skyjacking, our no-concessions policy eroded. At the hijackers' insistence, their propaganda message was published and leaflets were airdropped over London. And in the Hanafi matter, it was hard to tell who were the heroes—the police, the psychiatrists, or the Muslim ambassadors? Somehow, whether by muddling through or by using honed behavioral tools, a massacre was avoided. Over the past five years there have been various nuclear weapons extortions, all of which were handled competently by the FBI and ERDA. Fortunately, the threats were amateurish. The "Philadelphia fever" does not appear to have been a terrorist act; yet it was mysterious, frightening the public and forced the Bellevue Stratford Hotel out of business.

There are many terrorist objectives and an even greater variety of potential terrorist acts. We shall confine ourselves to a discussion of those situations where timely crisis management action is possible and productive. Crisis management techniques can be effective when a terrorist's preliminary actions have not obviated the need for further governmental action to limit damage. These techniques can be usefully applied to the hostage-barricade situation, politically motivated hijackings of aircraft, trains or ships;

economic or institutional hostages (e.g., seizure of nuclear power stations, sabotage of electric power grids, elements of the Federal Reserve System, etc.), and threats of mass destruction including nuclear, chemical or biological extortions. In these instances the terrorists have not fully engaged their ultimate destructive potential, providing government with several options, including bargaining with the terrorists and limiting damage in the event that bargaining attempts were unsuccessful.

The mere existence of a capability to counter a terrorist action or to limit and repair the damage done is worth little if that capability cannot be exercised in a controlled way. Most large nations possess enormous inherent capability. The problem is mobilizing it in face of terrorist attack and, moreover, doing so in a manner consistent with the legal, ethical and political constraints of the particular society.

Whether a threat, a convincing demonstration followed by a threat, or an outright assault, fear and confusion will take hold: What should one do first? How should government respond? Who is in charge? Who are the terrorists? What are the hostages—a few people or a planeload, a major city, or the electric power grid? What sort of weapons do the terrorists have—pistols, submachine guns, explosives, or weapons of mass destruction? Can government meet their demands? Are they *thinkable;* e.g., the payment of money or the release of specified prisoners? Or are the demands so outrageous that they cannot be met by government; e.g., the imposition of a capital levy that would reduce the wealthiest to a level of, say, $100,000?

The willingness to execute a threat, the assessment of the terrorists' technical competence and resources, and the discerned costs and benefits attributable to both government and terrorists are inextricably interwoven. Government's flexibility is limited by the demands themselves, the tough-mindedness of an established policy to deal with terrorists, the personal strength of a Chief Executive and the forethought that has gone into organizational and other contingency planning to meet such crises.

The balance of this chapter is devoted to a discussion of assessing threat credibility, organizing government to deal with a terrorist-caused crisis, contingency planning, developing management information systems, applying gaming techniques, and limiting damage should terrorists attack. These topics are components of the management machinery needed to implement the "last line of defense."

JUDGING THE CREDIBILITY OF A THREAT

Having been threatened with massive violence or national disruption, what actions should we take to minimize the short-term dangers to the "organism"? No study can adequately treat this question, for no amount of forethought can relieve the President of having to make "seat of the pants" judgments if the risk of catastrophe is perceived. Even though predictive models cannot be built, the problem can be bounded. At a minimum the credibility of the threat must be assessed and the penalties for failure understood.

Credibility assessment is a complex matter requiring intelligence as well as behavioral and technical information. If the PLO were to threaten to use nerve agents unless their demands are met, the credibility question might center about their resolve to execute the threat rather than trying to verify the existence of the nerve agent. By contrast, if less well-catalogued terrorists were to make comparably difficult demands, interest in analyzing their motivation would not be lost, but concern would center about determining their technical ability to carry out the threat.

Credibility is not a static phenomenon; intelligence and behavioral factors play influential roles as each act of the drama is improvised. Unlike the conditioning experience of movie-going, the tragic fact is that the "good guys" do not always win, even in the end. We may have to settle for probabilistic outcomes, uncertain shades of gray.

Alone, a credibility assessment may not be useful; rather, the assessment must be linked to a class of possible actions government might take in response to the threat. Moreover, cost is measurable in different ways; there are monetary and political costs, risks to human life because of panic created by a federal action, costs in terms of losses of civil liberties, jurisdictional disputes with state and local governments; and, at the extreme, the destruction of the organism itself, whether through miscalculation of the opponent or by government's own hand.

It is not difficult to imagine the simplest act causing panic; e.g., using specialized equipment to search for a hidden nuclear bomb. If the equipment were too obvious, the attempt to locate the "weapon" could cause widespread panic, especially if the search were centered in a major city.

A Crude Taxonomy

The credibility of a threat might be judged by a ranking scheme: the base of the scale might start with obvious hoaxes and crank calls. Ascending the scale we might label events involving multiple messages, ongoing communications with the terrorists, and definite evidence of the terrorists' ability to inflict great harm. At the high end of the scale there might be demonstration attacks and finally the execution of the full threat, such as the detonation of a nuclear weapon. To each of these events there would correspond a set of actions and their costs. Thus, for example, at the low end of the credibility spectrum there should be little source for jurisdictional disputes with state governments; and at the top of the scale state governments may be only too happy to turn the problem over to the federal government. In this case we may find that government's largest costs occur in the mid-range of the credibility scale. The same may be true of the public affairs issue. By contrast, however, the cost of disaster relief peaks at the high end of the scale. Although the measurements would be highly subjective, it would be useful to set up a taxonomy based on credibility and cost indicators. From this we could derive some crude policy guidelines. We will discuss a way of measuring costs and benefits in the appendix.

Intelligence Collection

In order to deal successfully with terrorist extortion, the government must obtain good intelligence, efforts which include terrorism trends and the more difficult matter of monitoring the day-to-day dynamics. Special attention must be given to assessing their technical sophistication.

In the event of a mass destruction threat the intelligence community would be called upon to perform monumental tasks of supplying background information on the terrorists, locating their weapons and assessing their capabilities and intentions. Research and development efforts into such areas as nuclear, chemical and biological agent detection equipment must be an integral part of our intelligence collection capabilities. Obviously, new and innovative approaches to these problems are essential.

Technical Assessment

The technical estimation of threat-credibility may be quite difficult. Designs and some details of nuclear devices that, in principle, can be made to work exist in the open literature. Unless there exists some obvious flaw in the design that can be readily identified by nuclear weapons experts, it may take considerable time and effort to determine whether a specific design is viable and, if so, whether it would have a yield of a few tons or a few kilotons. Given the fascination of popular writers and the media with this subject, in the years ahead more information about nuclear weapons design will be publicly available. The evaluations of such threats may rely principally upon the accountability of nuclear materials to determine whether plutonium or highly enriched uranium has been diverted.

Unlike special nuclear materials that are maintained under rigorous inventory control, virtually all biological and chemical agents can be obtained easily. If biological or chemical threats were made, the extortionist group could submit a sample of the agent. The technical evaluation of the threat would then hinge on the terrorists' ability to disperse the agent.

Behavioral Assessment

After a threat is verfied to be authentic, crisis managers will be concerned with formulating steps to meet the emergency. At some point in this process a critical behavioral analysis of the threatening group's motivation, intention and capability must be made, either intuitively by decision-makers on the spot, or with the assistance of specialists.

Although each terrorist and each incident are unique, behavioral techniques may be the only means of prediction. Ideally, predictions become more accurate as more background data become available. From such intelligence, behavioral scientists make initial judgments about the motivations, capability, and intentions of terrorists as well as their probable responses to various negotiating tactics.

While there is no distinct "terrorist personality," researchers have produced profiles of those who commit acts of terror. These include, with overlap, the psychotic, the psychopath, and the political ideologue. Because behavioral scientists have dealt with these personalities in other contexts, there is a substantial data base that may be applicable to terrorist activities.

There is a compelling need for additional research on the behavioral aspects of terrorist threats.

ORGANIZATION OF GOVERNMENT AND CONTINGENCY PLANNING[11]

Typically, authority for dealing with various aspects of a terrorist incident is dispersed over a number of government departments and jurisdictions in a manner which is well suited to handling day-to-day concerns but which may impede efforts to deal with a crisis. To maintain public confidence that the government is reacting capably, it is important not to resort to unnecessarily alarming emergency measures and to handle things through channels—up to a point. At a certain level of public concern, on the other hand, handling things "through channels" may appear callous or stupid and the public will be more reassured that everything possible is being done if the Chief Executive is visibly involved. This is a very fine line to walk, and fraught with hazards for the Chief Executive who is suddenly thrust into the midst of a developing situation.

To overcome this problem, we suggest that the primary organizational arrangements for dealing with terrorist incidents remain fixed along traditional law enforcement and diplomatic lines, but that a small group at the highest level of government, and having the confidence of the Chief Executive, be given both the responsibility of monitoring emergent crises and the authority to coordinate and expedite government actions when necessary. With such an arrangement the Chief Executive should be able to participate in management of a major threat in an informed way, to the degree he desires, and with the amount of public visibility which seems appropriate.

Because public alarm is often the terrorist's objective, the perception of the governments's reaction by the press and the public can be of utmost importance. Maintaining "business as usual" where possible, and facilitating a smooth transition to high-level coordination and management when necessary, seems the surest way of reassuring the public as well as deserving their confidence.

A straightforward terrorist attack may pose impressive problems for the government's disaster-relief agencies and for those concerned with tracking down and prosecuting the criminals. A major attack might even warrant the sort of high-level coordination described above. A threat of national disruption, however, presents a much more complicated set of problems. As we have discussed earlier, the first of these is the credibility of the threat. This is an extremely delicate matter, especially in the case of chemical, biological and nuclear threats. Being too easily alarmed can lead the government into hasty, foolish actions which can serve the terrorist's ends with no further need for action on his part. Being too phlegmatic can lead to tragedy if a valid threat is ignored. As we emphasized beforehand, rapid access to the requisite expert advice from appropriate scientists is crucial to making informed judgments of the credibility of exotic threats, but advice from behavioral scientists may also help to determine the credibility of particular threats. The high-level monitoring group we suggest could serve to buffer the government from overreaction to negligible or unevaluated threats as well as to expedite response to a threat deemed valid.

The same organizational idea is the model for the national security community; the National Security Council Staff serves as the buffer mechanism between the President and the major actors. Preparations to manage the effects of a nationally disruptive terrorist act are part of civil emergency preparedness, a program which may exist in name only.

Contingency Planning

The initial steps in organizing to combat terrorism are those of planning and of delineating responsibility. Within the executive-level group we have suggested as desirable, clear lines of responsibility must be drawn and plans developed. To assure smooth functioning in time of crisis, however, the organization must be exercised so that it can develop routines. The senior advisers we envision can scarcely be expected to engage frequently in such exercises, but aides familiar with their interests could do so. Moreover, a small staff drawn from the agencies most likely to be involved in terrorist incidents, and serving as liaison with those governmental agencies, should be established. The staff would conduct exercises aimed at developing smoothly working routines. These should involve collaboration with the other levels of government, local officials, and other interested parties to resolve the difficulties posed by sample terrorism scenarios. The emphasis should be placed on finding ways to draw on needed resources and to arrive at decisions in a crisis atmosphere. The objective would not be to prepare for specific crises but to develop modes of operation and an awareness of the available resources, how to get access to them, and the logistics problems involved in using them. In conducting such exercises an awareness of required resources could gradually be developed. It would be possible to experiment with the use of various forms of information networks, computer-assisted searches and automatic checklists of factors relevant to decisions, and the relative utility of various forms of data bases concerning terrorist groups. As the process proceeded, the effective modes of operation should become understood and the requirements necessary for coping successfully with a variety of terrorist groups and incidents should become clearer. The design of such exercises must be worked out in advance with great care in "blackboard exercises" by the staff. They should be designed to serve as a useful model of reality without becoming so complicated that they confuse more than instruct.

While computer-assisted decision aids can be of considerable value, they do not replace the artful crisis management team. However, when we deal with giant logistical problems, such as the delivery of emergency services including health care; or if we are plagued with major resource interruptions, such as communications or electrical power failures, sophisticated computer aids and large management inventory systems are indispensable. Such systems should be intelligently designed—and thus meet the needs of the crisis manager—or they will grow cancerously.

Gaming is an extension of the "case-method" of research. For the small-scale hostage event we already have a sizable amount of data. Techniques to handle these events are emerging. In fact, there are several successful training programs dealing with the behavioral and tactical aspects of hostage-barricade situations. (The FBI National Academy and the New York City Police Department are prime innovators in this area.) However, when there is no data the "cases" must be simulated. Obviously, simulations do not replace live experiences, but it would be difficult to find a sane person who wants to experience the management problems of mass destruction terrorism. Gaming should prove to be indispensable for training and planning and may prove to be as valuable during an actual incident.

Simple heuristic models, on-line displays that ask the right questions and set forth a protocol of "dos" and "don't" are indispensable. An on-line listing of pertinent experts must be immediately available. These and other informational aids are crucial tools for the President and the crisis team.[12]

A considerable amount of effort is required to construct the models, data bases and management information systems needed for effective crisis management. The path is largely unchartered.

Media Relations

Media—newspapers, magazines, radio and television—are star actors in a terrorism play. The media can emerge as forces for good, limiting the derivative societal repercussions of an attack, or the media can incite terror. Media coverage cannot be eliminated, nor would that be desirable in free societies. If the media were not to cover terrorist events, terrorists might commit even more acts—or escalate the level of violence—in order to attract public attention.

When exercises are conducted it would be worthwhile to ask representatives of the media to participate in them. Otherwise the "games" would suffer from an obvious lack of reality and not serve as teaching or learning devices for government or the press. Any attempt by a democratic government to unilaterally dictate a code of ethics for the media would be a serious mistake. Such a code must emerge from within. Openness and understanding of each other's roles in dealing with incidents of terrorism are essential if the terrorist is not to succeed in turning a relatively small attack into a circus.

CONSTRUCTING THE "GAME"

We have argued the case for a crisis management team having immediate access to the President or, in the alternative, a civil emergency preparedness organization that can perform the crisis management function for terrorist incidents as well. Further, we have argued that problems of crisis management are sufficiently complex—and possibly amorphous—to warrant "playing games" in order to better structure the tasks of incident management and train future crisis managers. At this juncture it is appropriate to set down some thoughts about constructing "games," understanding that no method of gaming is fully defensible.

Among the more obvious tasks, we must establish a skeletal crisis management organization, "Red" and "Blue" Teams, as well as a system for refereeing. Further, to make the exercises concrete, representative scenarios must be chosen. Above all they must *appear* to be tractable. Thus, a mass destruction terrorist attack killing hundreds of thousands of people, followed by political demands and a threat to kill millions, is an impossible case. Such scenarios are far enough removed from reality to make the "game" unattractive to potential players.

The objectives of gaming include training, but an inclusive concept of setting forth clear definition of the tasks confronting government is the encompassing goal. We realize that the "game" should be played at the highest levels of government; but this is probably an unrealistic expectation. The initial versions of the "game" are likely to be primitive: scenarios will be chosen, messages simulated, and the crisis team will attempt to communicate with the operating elements of government.

Initially, referees should not attempt to give numerical scores—they should point out the lessons-to-be-learned, defining the managers' tasks more clearly, noting their failures and, when possible, suggesting practical means to solve some problems quickly. For example, if we were to decide to concede partially, and if a great deal of money were required, how could the money be gotten quickly? How should we deal with a recalcitrant state government holding "political" prisoners? When should the leadership of the Congress be consulted? Are government's operations centers adequately "netted," one not operating independently of another but all being under central control? What sorts of experts will we need quickly—technical, behavioral, medical, political, public relations? Etc., etc.?

It seems that a requisite for belonging to the crisis management team is knowledge of the bureaucracy—and, hence, access to the right people. Moreover, there are some obvious skills that should be embodied in the crisis management operation: politics, international relations, technical knowledge, law, military, public relations and law enforcement. The crisis management team (here, the "Blue Team"), which is likely to be headed by the President at a time of crisis, should be regularly led by a ranking official, for the team must appear to have clout, it being the interface between policy and operations.

The "Red Team"—the pseudo-terrorists—need not be as elaborately equipped. In fact, the composition of the "Red Team" should be scenario-dependent. By contrast, the refereeing system should complement the "Blue Team," employing people of diverse backgrounds including representatives of state and local government, Congress, the legal profession, scientists, police, foreign policy experts, the media, etc. The referees will have the toughest job of all. Unlike judging a sporting event, there is no simple numerical scoring system to escape from the difficulties of performing penetrating analyses.

The "game" should be run many times in order to discover our weaknesses and strengths—and thus build our *national incident management system.* After three or four "games" have been played, sophisticated numerical weighting schemes, such as the Bennett-Saaty (discussed in the Technical Appendix), might be employed. *Fault-tree analyses,* and other mathematical tools, might be used to calculate downside costs, etc. When we reach this point, we will have arrived at a sophisticated stage.

There is a "chicken and egg" problem. Is the "game" to be played first and then develop the crisis management team? Or is the crisis management team to be formed, the team being subsequently tasked to construct and play "games"? While the organizational ideal of a *crisis management team* that does *gaming* may be appealing, the two concepts are interwoven. Thus, we must resort to an iterative procedure, guessing initially at the composition of the crisis management team and the rules of the game. After three or four iterations, the crisis management team and the "games" it plays should be clearly distinguishable.

What is the bottom line for *gaming*? The crisis management team is in the business of coordinating government operations, buffering the President and the senior-most officials from the moment-to-moment operational problems. Should a major terrorist incident occur, confusion must not reign. Thus, as far as possible, government's emergency response should occur in a preplanned context. The end products of gaming are sets of options to meet the more obvious sorts of scenarios, the crisis managers' full knowledge of government's emergency capabilities, and the ability to rapidly transform agencies (performing their normal functions) into emergency configuration. Once obtained, these skills must be *exercised*, otherwise the investment in gaming would grow stale.

With sufficient encouragement—and some resources—it should take two or three months to construct the first "game." Further, since the terrorism scenarios can be complex problems involving many agencies of government, "games" played about them should provide valuable insights into how government might deal with other crisis management problems.

DAMAGE LIMITATION

In the event that the government's bargaining strategy does not prove to be completely successful, measures must be taken to limit the potential physical, institutional, and psychological damage that the terrorists can inflict.

The havoc wrought by terrorists closely resembles the effects of natural calamities and accidents. We have seen industrial accidents spread deadly chemicals in a fashion any terrorist might well envy. (The 1976 industrial accident, releasing a highly toxic industrial agent, devastated a small city in Tuscany.) Earthquakes can outdo any bombing terrorists might threaten—even thermonuclear weapons. What terrorists can do is to increase the frequency with which we must endure such catastrophes, thereby making preparation against them more urgent. Moreover, terrorists hold out the threat of repeatedly induced catastrophes which accident and nature do not.

Resources developed to limit these effects and to restore the damage can be used to deal with industrial accidents, floods, earthquakes and storms. If logistical and emergency health care delivery were developed to meet the large-scale terrorist attack, much more could be done to alleviate human suffering in the event of industrial accidents or natural disasters. Therefore, preparations needed to cope with terrorist damage need not stand out like a "sore thumb." They can be included in the emergency preparedness efforts of all governments.

During a terrorist crisis, one of a government's most important responsibilities is to maintain public confidence in its ability to cope with all contingencies. As long as it can persuade its citizens that it has the ability to govern despite whatever concessions are made or physical damage is inflicted, the terrorists will be denied a major objective and government's leadership will be evident.

In order to limit damage, government should mobilize its resources to accomplish various functional tasks:

1. *Control.* The timely establishment of mechanisms for command and control of governmental resources to assure an efficient response to an incident, with adequate informational and decision-making provisions, designed to seize the initiative from the terrorists.
2. *Containment.* Emergency measures taken to delimit the terrorist act in a physical sense and to "decouple" it in a psychological sense from the intended political consequences. Actions to limit damage and provide emergency health care are included.
3. *Restoration.* Deliberate actions to conclude the incident and restore the situation, lasting until the situation is returned to normal and routine services are again available.

Unfortunately, damage-limiting actions cannot always be easily put into effect. However, because maintaining public confidence in the government is of supreme importance, appearance may often be more important than reality.

Controlling a Terrorist Act in Progress

We turn now to the questions of controlling a terrorist act in progress and of containing and restoring the damage done. For purposes of this discussion we distinguish two types of terrorist actions, the *hostage* action and the *surprise attack.* The essential difference is that the hostage-type action allows time for the government to "bargain" and devise tactics intended to improve the outcome. In the surprise attack, little can be done to control the situation; damage limitation and restoration are the primary concerns, but in the "hostage-type" actions, a threat is made and bargaining is attempted, providing the government with an opportunity to take initiatives toward controlling the outcome.

The hostage-barricade situation is an extremely fruitful area for the application of technology. The problems include getting information from behind the barrier, penetrating the barrier physically, and incapacitating the terrorists while limiting damage to the hostage. All of these are fairly well-posed technical problems subject to solution by physical and behavioral science techniques.

As an incident develops and the nature of the threat becomes manifest, highly specific and sophisticated technology may be applicable to control the outcome or contain the damage done, and it may well prove worthwhile developing very specialized technical resources to deal with certain types of likely terrorist incidents. Rapid availability in an emergency rather than ubiquity is the crucial factor determining usefulness of such resources. The possibility of rapid access to a wide variety of experts and equipment is crucial and the technical means of organizing such availability by various prearrangements and by the use of management information systems is an important technological aspect of combating terrorism. If, for example, a terrorist *does* threaten to use an exotic toxin, it then becomes important to be able to deal with it if it is carried out.

As previously noted, damage done by terrorists has everything in common with industrial accidents and natural disasters except frequency and intent, so only a strengthening of the systems required for such calamities and a shortening of the time required for the systems to operate appear to be indicated.

Medical Rescue as an Antiterrorist Measure

The public does not yet hold governments fully responsible for rescue after natural disasters, but demand is growing. Governmental responsibilities are being assessed and rescue operations dissected, although the resulting mortality is still regarded as inevitable and as an "Act of God." No such leniency, however, is guaranteed the "decision-maker" during and after a terrorist attack if efforts to save lives are inadequate or bungled. It is insufficient to merely remove the injured to overloaded existing municipal hospitals. The *public may expect special efforts on behalf of the health of victims of enemy action.*

The myths of overwhelming weaponry and the hopelessness of large disasters can be disproved by the research facts of modern medicine. A superior system of medical rescue can be devised to produce a higher salvage rate than is presently obtained.[13]

While it would be conceivable to justify a national emergency system purely as a counterterrorism measure, no such justification is necessary. The citizens of each nation have a right to protection of life and limbs, whether the etiological agent be a terrorist, an industrial accident or a natural disaster.

Technology has grown too complicated, populations too congested, and the incidence of regional medical emergencies too frequent to place sole reliance on the local community or the neighborly volunteer approach. Disaster planning for large events has been largely unsuccessful because it has been partitioned from the successful emergency medical systems which operate daily. The personnel disappear, become untrained and rehearsals tend to be unrealistic. Perhaps the necessity of counterterrorism will bolster the need for national emergency medical systems.

The topic of emergency health care delivery is not strange to government. It is receiving considerable attention, but possibly not enough. It is a complicated matter dealing with logistical and other management problems, resource allocation issues and communications. It involves training programs for paramedical personnel, stockpiling of equipment and drugs, and clinical research and evaluation objectives. Considerable technological development is also needed.

The Military Option

No discussion of the management of transnational terrorist incidents would be complete without exploring a military solution. It is clear that if negotiations fail, nations must be prepared to use military force. Yet few countries have an adequately trained or equipped paramilitary force that could deal with a fastbreaking crisis.

We think that a well-conceived, highly trained, and versatile international paramilitary force that is available to all is an idea whose time will come. The risks of tactical failure should be spread equitably among many nations. If acts of international terrorism are to be faced squarely, they must be viewed as international peacekeeping problems, not merely domestic law enforcement challenges. Individual nations should not be expected to bear the military and political burdens alone.

The military option, whether internationally implemented or not, must be an "on-the-shelf" ability. Lacking effective international cooperation means that the major powers will have to have some operational military force capable of mounting the sort of rapid and effective response exhibited by Israel at Entebbe and West Germany at Somalia. Improvisation with hastily assembled military units will only aggravate and confuse matters.

INTERNATIONAL COOPERATION

In many instances the efforts of one nation to thwart a terrorist threat may prove to be insufficient and international cooperation will be required. Irrespective of whatever political differences governments may have, they still share the common bond of being legitimate governing entities. They are still part of an established world order which some terrorists seek to disrupt. However, practical possibilities for cooperation are limited. This is in part due to the fact that there is no generally accepted definition of terrorism: one man's banditry is another man's liberation movement. Thus, seizure of an aircraft is an act of piracy or a flight for freedom, depending on political perspective.

Attempts to achieve agreement or consensus on practical approaches to terrorist threats should therefore avoid the definitional issue, so as to coopt as many potentially interested parties as possible. Rather than search for common definitions, cooperating states should focus on controlling specific acts already considered criminal under domestic law (e.g., kidnapping) and base their cooperation on generally recognized principles, such as protecting innocent third parties, and not accepting threats of mass national disruption.

Secondly, the extent of formal cooperation among nations varies with the subject. For instance, we might assume a high degree of unanimity between the US, Canada, Western Europe and Japan on the importance of protecting aircraft, airports, passengers and other transportation facilities against terrorists. Actual cooperation, however, such as their willingness to impose or be subject to sanctions in the event that agreements were not honored, is less certain. Perhaps only a few, even within this group, would accept limited sanctions or agree to impose them on others.

Effective counterterrorism action depends critically on intelligence. It requires that the states where terrorist acts are likely to occur, or whose citizens and property are likely to be victims, have timely warning in order to prepare themselves and others. Advance warning of terrorists' movements and plans and other information-sharing arrangements are of great importance. However, information-sharing, while desirable in theory, raises legal and moral problems that would need thinking through if an attempt were made to establish a sharing system. After all, the identification or tagging of citizens or resident foreigners to keep track of individuals whom police authorities see as potential terrorists can be used for a variety of unsavory purposes relating to local political disaffection but which bear no necessary relationship to international terrorism.

If like-minded governments were approached for intelligence data on terrorists and their mode of operation, such intelligence sharing would be best related to acceptable principles such as identification, extradition and prosecution.

Agreements relating to extradition and prosecution should, of course, seek to strike a delicate balance between encouraging nations to cooperate and actively resist terrorist threats, while still allowing sufficient room for tactical maneuvering during crisis situations.

One final point should be made; namely, arms control considerations are interwoven with terrorism. First, there is a generic concern about stability. Another important aspect of arms control is the problem of nuclear weapons proliferation. Some terrifying stability problems are evident when we think of many nations joining the nuclear club, but it is even more unsettling to think of subnational groups brandishing atom bombs.

There is an arms control initiative that can be taken, one which is specifically aimed at countering terrorism: inhibiting the sale or transfer of portable antitank weapons and surface-to-air rockets. These, and other weapons, should be strictly controlled. Little loss of competitive edge would occur if suppliers would unilaterally forgo the sale or transfer of such weapons. Certainly multilateral agreements would be better.

Formal agreements to counter terrorism are difficult to obtain. In all likelihood an informal arrangement will prevail. As the severity of the terrorist problem increases, so will the tendency for international cooperation.[14] An "old boys" network will be formed, just as the police, military and intelligence communities have done long ago.

A Program for Action

A basic message of the report is the need for prudence and planning in combating terrorism. Despite their possible severity, terrorist acts have been of limited intensity. Terrorism can thus be viewed as a malady low on a long list of more dreaded diseases. Unfortunately, however, the terrorism syndrome is inherently unstable. A slight qualitative change, even a terrorist's miscalculation, could have profound ramifications. Thus we come to the main point of the report. Without seeking a "shadow-government" solution, how can a viable counterterrorism program be developed in an environment controlled by the problems of the moment?

The answer is not obvious; it may not exist. But it is clear that a crisis team is needed to coordinate the federal government's activities at a time of a major incident. The team, which is the interface between the policy and operational levels of government, should be a part of a well-conceived civil emergency preparedness program. The opportunities for doing studies of the effects of resource interruptions, and actually gaining experience in emergency management, are plentiful under the aegis of civil emergency preparedness. Railroad strikes, fuel shortages, earthquakes and terrorist attacks—at root they are identical. Their physical character may differ greatly but to the crisis manager, who must allocate resources and who is constrained by time, logistics and politics, the problem is the same. If we are to realize the "last line of defense," a viable umbrella must be created, one which would be used frequently.

We are poorly prepared to deal with terrorism, especially the higher-order acts. Our capability to manage terrorist crises must be strengthened. We need to develop a strategy to increase the contribution the international community can make as well as a program of research on terrorist behavior, target hardening and the problem of restoration after attack. Among the actions to be taken are the following:

DEVELOP A NATIONAL INCIDENT MANAGEMENT SYSTEM

1. A crisis management team must be formed, preferably one which is a part of a viable civil emergency preparedness program, has immediate access to the highest level of government, and whose management role is set by pre-established authority.
2. The team must do contingency planning in order to refine negotiating strategies, determine resource and management information needs, and coordinate the operations of government at times of crisis.
3. The necessary standby arrangements for aircraft, communications, personnel and other resources must be made before the crisis. Further, a roster of experts and the means to summon them quickly is fundamental.
4. Consistent with the law, remotely accessible data bases concerning terrorist groups should be constructed for planning and operational purposes. (For predictive and incident management purposes, we need to maintain data bases on their tactics and operations, their weapons, and their organization and training.)
5. *International arrangements.* A vigorous international relations program to combat terrorism must be pursued: no safe havens and extradition agreements, multilateral controls on the transfers of antitank and antiaircraft weapons, and agreements for technical assistance and the exchange of intelligence.
6. *Military option.* Whether developed on a national level, or through cooperative international arrangements, large nations must have the specialized paramilitary ability to perform rescue operations such as those at Entebbe and Somalia.
7. *Technology.* Countering terrorism can only be accomplished by funding a vigorous research and development program. There are rich opportunities for behavioral and technological research. Even limited efforts could make dramatic contributions.

A CONCLUDING THOUGHT

Observing the behavior of modern terrorists, we are reminded of the world depicted in William Butler Yeats' poem, "The Second Coming," a world in which "the worst are full of passionate intensity while the best lack all conviction." To curb this behavior before it produces more serious sacrifices to the deities of apocalyptic destruction, architects of an effective counter-terrorism strategy must begin to *have* conviction—to care enough about the importance of their task to prevent the gratuitous waste of further killing.

Countering terrorism and managing incidents of it are not direct or fully prescribable tasks. One does not take a teaspoon of medicine every four hours to cure the scourge. At best, nations will be forced to live with a chronic disease, treat the occasional acute episodes symptomatically, and pray that its spread is containable.

To continue the metaphor, if the symptoms are treated too aggressively, both doctor and patient may die. If the disease frightens the doctor into submission, then the prognosis is congenital weakness. The malady infects us all and the statistics of morbidity and mortality worsen each time the least painful course of action is taken.

There is no doubt that mass annihilation is feasible—and resourceful, technically-oriented thugs are capable of doing it. Their leverage over nation-states is disproportionately high. But the day of mass destruction will be thrust upon us by ourselves; terrorists are as strong or as weak as society's fear of hobgoblins admit. Some thought and courage are all that lie between the usual perils of civilization and the spectre of self-inflicted carnage.

Notes

1. Terrorism is theatre. Even if terrorist groups lose public support, the terrorist may use the media, the public and governments to "play" to each other, each trying to outdo the others.
2. While the possibility that terrorists may acquire and use chemical, biological or nuclear weapons to cause mass casualties understandably causes the most concern, there is an *intermediate level of violence,* an order of magnitude greater than terrorist attacks seen thus far, but far short of the genocidal schemes that have attracted the media's attention, and still not requiring exotic weapons or specialized skills. Terrorists have already demonstrated their knowledge of explosives. Detonated at places of assembly—railroad and subway stations, bus terminals, aircraft—conventional explosives could cause heavy casualties and tremendous alarm. Several incidents producing fifty to a hundred deaths each, although well short of the mass murder scenarios, would bring terrorism into an entirely new dimension.
3. See the Technical Appendix for thoughts about modeling terrorism trends by analogy with epidemiological and ecological models.
4. An informative account of the connections between terrorist organizations may be found in Charles A. Russell's "Transnational Terrorism," *Air University Review,* 27, 2, January-February 1976. Other related

insights may be found in Millbank, D., US Central Intelligence Agency. *International and Transnational Terrorism: Diagnosis and Prognosis,* Washington, DC, 1976.

5. Because of the sensitivity of the subject we will not devote a section of the report to its discussion.

6. The conceptual bases for target hardening are simple; however, "cost-benefit" analyses and the details of technology are complex. Furthermore, a discussion of the "state-of-the-art" would be quite sensitive and in part classified.

7. One technique could be used to cause a closed-circuit television to sound an alarm if any motion occurs in a selected area of the picture. Although such a capability increases the cost and complexity of a surveillance system, it extends the number of cameras a single guard can monitor when the absence of motion is expected.

8. *Report to the Congress, United States Sinai Support Mission,* April 13, 1977.

9. The distinction between "strategic" and "tactical" is qualitative: a mere tactic to one may be a matter of strategic importance to another. Here, *strategic* concessions are those which, if revealed, would undermine either the political or financial stability of the government. By contrast, *tactical concessions are intended to limit shortrun damage and are not of a magnitude that would enhance the terrorists' leverage. The use of "bait money" to buy time and gain needed intelligence, techniques to wear down the captors during a drawn-out hostage-barricade ordeal, and false promises of safe passage are examples of tactical concessions. Such tactics can be risky and are often inherently deceitful. If they were published after the fact, we might have fewer courses of action to deal with a subsequent incident. Thus, in an operational context a proposed concession must endure the rigors of heated debate and policy-level decisions to assess whether it is "tactical" or "strategic."*

10. *Our discussion of the tactics of bargaining and substantive concession is not intended to be an endorsement of either; rather, at a time of crisis their consideration would be a matter of political reality. First and foremost, deterrence* should be the objective of all nations because the first publicly known concession may have a pronounced contagious effect. Yet, governments cannot afford to stand as rigid tin soldiers by refusing to concede to unimportant demands. The "game" between terrorists and government is not *zero-sum*—it is *cooperative* and it is rich with mixed strategies. When faced with the credible prospects of mass destruction, every concessionary move is *tactical*—and potentially *strategic.* In order of preference, enough time will have been borrowed to locate and disarm the terrorists, we will have succumbed to the extent of endowing the terrorists and becoming each other's hostage, or we will have conceded fully.

11. The details of present organizational arrangements are more elaborate than illuminating. They are steeped in statutory and bureaucratic precedent rather than being tuned to meet the external threat. In fair-

ness, however, as the terrorism problem becomes increasingly felt, "incremental" improvements are made. Progress is evident in the nuclear extortion and airline hijacking areas. Further, the Federal Preparedness Agency has developed the *Federal Response Plan for Peacetime Nuclear Emergencies (FRPPNE)*. We point out, however, that Canada's crisis coordination center, led by Robin Bourne of their Solicitor General's ministry, is among the world's best conceived incident management mechanisms.

12. There are a number of practical illustrations of using on-line management systems during crisis management situations. Some of the early developments occurred during the 90-day wage-rent-freeze of 1971. An on-line management information system called EMISARI became the matrix for the national and regional managers of the freeze. An extension of the system, called RIMS (Resource Interruption Management System), was used in conjunction with railway strikes and fuel shortages. (We will continue our discussion of this topic in the Technical Appendix.)

13. This point was discussed by Martin Silverstein in his *Medical Rescue as an Antiterrorist Measure,* prepared under the aegis of the present LEAA grants and delivered at the Seminar on Research Strategies for the Study of International Political Terrorism, Evian, France, June 1977.

14. As of the writing of this report, two well-publicized airplane hijackings occurred within a few weeks of each other: the first was that of a Japanese airliner, diverted ultimately to Algeria. Japan capitulated fully and Algeria "absorbed" the terrorists. In the second incident, a Lufthansa flight was diverted to Somalia. To mankind's benefit, Somalia cooperated with the West Germans, allowing them to execute a spectacular commando raid that saved the passengers' lives.

Technical Appendix: Additional Insights

In the main body of the report we discussed the importance of on-line management information systems as well as the virtues of "blackboard" exercises—gaming or simulation techniques intended for training and operations. Here, we continue our discussion of informational and computational aids to counter terrorism.

We rely heavily upon several . . . contractors' feasibility studies. . . . These studies include the efforts of Fogel[1] on modeling terrorist trends as analogs of "predator-prey" and epidemiological studies; Bennett's and Saaty's[2] structuring of terrorist incidents using a specialized "delphi" method; and Jenkins' and Waterman's[3] use of on-line heuristic, rule-based information systems.

While this appendix is devoted to a technical discussion of quantitative methods and computer-spewn heuristics, we emphasize (as we did in the main body of the report) that these methods are "tools" only. People in operational and policy positions make the crucial decisions—not computers. Our views of modeling vs. real-time situational behavior being understood, we proceed to substance: We discuss the question of predicting terrorist trends and levels of violence, speculating about possible epidemiological and ecological comparisons. Next, we deal with the structuring of an incident, especially its negotiational phase. We conclude with a discussion of heuristics and some comments on calculating downside costs.

PREDICTING THE LEVEL OF TERRORIST ACTIVITIES[4]

The efforts being expended on preparing suitable responses for terrorist incidents should be complemented by an attempt to forecast the level or type of terrorist activities. The mathematics of predictive epidemiology can be used with the terrorists treated as *infectives* entering populations with different levels of *susceptibles* (sympathizers), the contagion is "person-to-person" with the particular plans offered mutating—these being expressed in varying political terms and modes of attack. There is an incubation period before the symptoms of social disorder are observed (even before the contagion process appears openly).

The analogy with terrorism is clear. When placed in an unsympathetic population (generally unsusceptible), the outbreaks of violence are small, erratic, and soon dissipate of their own "weight." The "disease" only prospers in a sympathetic environment. This is much like cholera, wherein the disease always originates in a particular region of the world and propagates from there, being carried by individuals who are clearly traceable as they move from point to point.

Unlike cholera, meningitis is a high-carrier rate, low-case rate disease. That is, there is a relatively high percentage of individuals in the population who carry the disease organism in their nasopharynx (about 10% to 15%) and spread these organisms to other individuals as they breathe, cough, or sneeze. Humans are protected unless the disease organism can enter the bloodstream. In general, the incidence of meningitis is thought to be greater during times of public anxiety as, for example, during national mobilization (this being true across many nations).

By analogy, many individuals may have a strong desire to revise the political status quo. They spread this disease to other people. The level of susceptibility may relate to the general feeling of unrest and disenchantment, and yet, there may be few actual threats or outbreaks of violence because of prevailing pacifist beliefs or the highly suppressive practices of a government.

Epidemics of diseases take a different form; for example, the influenza organism mutates at a high rate so that the disease can spread within the same population that experienced a recent epidemic of this disease. In essence, the mutation has created new susceptibles.

By analogy, the idea of using violence to gain political ends is spread by modern technology through the press, television, and the mobility of those individuals who use personal appearance for the spread of their political doctrine. The same basic concepts are clothed in new garments to make them more saleable each time around. In fact, each new kind of violence is a "mutation" which can be spread as the techniques and weapons become more sophisticated and readily available within the population. For example, although it might be somewhat difficult to find an individual willing to use a rifle equipped with telescopic sight (such as Oswald), it might be even easier to find individuals willing to engage in larger-scale killing through the discharge of biological and chemical agents since these are released "impersonally."[5] By analogy, the population is becoming more dense, mobile, and susceptible—and may therefore be more ready to accept and propagate violence.

Predictive epidemiology has become a science only in recent years. It would be worthwhile to develop the analogy in detail and attempt to forecast the level of terrorism by modeling the collected data on the factors involved.

Still another model of terrorism is that of an *evolving process*. Here, the mathematical formulation might be drawn from studies of the fundamentals of natural evolution. Stochastic models have been developed which describe mutation and selection within a restrictive environment. Perhaps a sufficient correspondence can be found between the concepts or plans which are the basis for terrorism and the organisms which are evolving. Here, terrorist groups may be viewed as an emerging species being tested for their survivability in the social ecosystem.

Since there are reasons to believe that terrorist activities may become more prevalent in the future, it is useful to point out that modeling the many-predator/many-prey ecosystem demonstrated that, in general, such systems are less stable and never more stable than the analogous single predator/prey community. By analogy, the world power structure has evolved from the single center at the end of World War II to two centers with the development of the Soviet Union, to three powers with the development of China, and now to four and more as the resource cartels dictate their terms and accept their rewards. On the local scene, complex communities with separately recognizable competing centers of business and ethnic groups are likely to be less stable. The greater the diversity of political factions, the more the opportunity for terrorism by extremist groups and the greater danger to the stability of the "ecosystem."

STRUCTURING THE EVENT AT A TIME OF CRISIS[6]

The problems of uncertainty are exacerbated by the dynamic nature of many crises. Thus, with limited information and resources the manager may find it difficult just to keep up with rapid developments, let alone improve the overall picture of the situation.

During a crisis, not only does an involved manager suffer from poor information, but he has the problem of identifying the objectives he wishes to accomplish and ordering them by priority in accord with his limited resources.

Under crisis conditions the manager has relatively little time to analyze available alternatives (his own or those of an adversary) or to develop new capabilities. (If domestic and international tensions are to be mitigated with greater success, the important role of the "crisis avoider" must be recognized.)

The process of crisis management can be regarded as having the objective of convincing an opponent that the immediate and long-run costs of opting for, continuing, or increasing hostilities exceed the immediate costs of accepting an offer to resolve conflict that minimally promises face-saving opportunities to the leaderships.

Negotiations with an adversary rest, at bottom, on conveying to him the costs of opposition in terms of his own value system. (In many cases these may be opportunity costs; that is, costs attributable to lost or deferred opportunities.) Moreover, for our position to be credible to an opponent he must perceive that the costs we propose to meet in gaining our objectives are actually acceptable to us in terms of our value system.

A number of difficulties have been noted as being common to the management of crises: uncertainty, poor data-handling methods, too little data, too much data, inadequate communications, differing value systems, changing management objectives, political harassment, little planning, and insufficient time in which to learn. To this long list of conceptual difficulties must be added the psychological and physical problems of confusion and fatigue. Clearly, the successful crisis manager must be a versatile person—a resource allocator, a communicator, and an artful negotiator with a tough hide.

Although contemporary methods of systems analysis have been used in attempts to organize data and clarify options, they have generally been of little use in presenting an accurate picture of an opponent's values and perceptions. Since the crisis manager has few *given* measures of utility, he is forced to make highly subjective judgments even though he may benefit from available data and analytical models for allocating constrained resources. The point is that the crisis manager is forced to compare "apples and bananas."

But there are neither firmly established "pricing" rules nor a free marketplace from which to infer the "prices." Thus we come to the need to develop hybrid weighting schemes, such as *delphi methods,* which are useful for gaming and incident management. The inputs to a weighting scheme are subjective and its structural form is artificially linear. Nevertheless, the essence of "price" formulation is *fiat* or *feedback.* This can be accomplished in the context of an automated delphi technique, such as the EMISARI system which was mentioned in the main body of the report. Bennett and Saaty have developed a plausible weighting scheme, one which is interesting because of its ability to depict negotiating options at a time of crisis.

The Bennett-Saaty Model

Terrorist incidents are complex, multi-actor, mixed motive situations. The clarification of the structure of the incident is necessary to depict the constraints upon the actors' choice of strategies and is an aid to shaping government's initiatives to resolve the crisis on favorable terms. The means of clarification is the development of numbers that characterize relative value or weights, such as the relative value of possible management strategies or the relative importance of the "actors."

As Bennett's and Saaty's first step, comparison judgments were formed between pairs of activities. Examples of pair-comparison judgments are the actors' comparative importance in the incident, the actors' preferences regarding two objectives, the efficacy of two policies to further an objective, etc.[7]

The Bennett-Saaty numerical scale (shown . . . as Table 1) is obtained by asking a decision-maker to state: (a) which of two activities, in his opinion, is more important, and (b) his perception of the magnitude of that difference (expressed as a number on a given scale).

For example, consider the relative importance of the actors in the Munich incident. The actors were the Terrorists (T), German Government (GG), Israeli Government (IG), Arab World (AW), and Hostages (H). A possible pair-wise comparison of actors could then result in the following matrix:

	T	G	I	A	H
Terrorists	1	1	3	7	8
German Government	1	1	2	8	8
Israeli Government	1/3	1/2	1	5	8
Arab World	1/7	1/8	1/5	1	5
Hostages	1/8	1/8	1/8	1/5	1

Their method of characterizing the matrix of pair-comparison judgments is by its "eigenvector" of unit length corresponding to the maximum

Table 1.

Intensity of Importance	Definition	Explanation
1	Equal importance	Two activities contribute equally to one objective.
3	Weakness or importance of one over another.	There is evidence favoring one activity over another, but it is not conclusive.
5	Essential or strong importance.	Good evidence and logical criteria exist to show that one is more important.
7	Demonstrated importance.	Conclusive evidence as to the importance of one activity over another.
9	Absolute importance	The evidence in favor of one activity over another is of the highest possible order of affirmation.
2, 4, 6, 8	Intermediate values between the two adjacent judgments.	When compromise is needed.
Reciprocals of above non-zero numbers	If activity i has one of the above non-zero numbers assigned to it when compared with activity j, then j has the reciprocal value when compared with i.	See below.

"eigenvalue." Using this procedure the eigenvector that describes the relative importance of the actors in the Munich incident becomes:

Terrorist	.369
German Government	.369
Israeli Government	.176
Arab World	.50
Terrorists	.369

Such a procedure cannot possibly result in the "best" characterization of the matrix for "best" is a meaningful term only with respect to a given norm. But the characterization has the necessary properties: small changes in the matrix result in small changes in the "eigenvector" (continuity) and large changes in the matrix will significantly change the eigenvectors, etc.

The Bennett-Saaty method exploits the often limited room for negotiation, enabling government to design negotiating strategies. Obviously, no method can guarantee acceptable outcomes to all acts of terrorism. Rather, the scheme they propose can serve as a framework to guide negotiators. There are occasions in which the analysis prescribes "no concessions" and acceptance of the threatened damage, just as there are occasions when apparently complete concession (at least in the short run) is the wisest course. In short, negotiators should be armed with an available means to analyze the information they acquire about terrorists' motives, specific demands, and the costs of concessions.

Their method involves the construction of *dual hierarchies*. The relevant actors assign a set of operational modes and appraisals of the relative importance of each mode to each of their objectives. The relevance of each element which is a set of counter-demands or offers, is evaluated in a pair-wise manner. The second hierarchy pertains to the terrorists' perceptions of government and is difficult to prepare in advance. Judgments that quantitatively determine the hierarchal structure should be updated during the negotiations. The hierarchies are illustrated in Figure 1. . . .

A method of ratio scaling of the elements on each level of the hierarchy produces a quantified *prioritization* of demands and counter-demands and thus enables one to quantitatively measure the effect on "distances" between the "bottom-level" vector (by computing inner products among the prioritized vectors for alternative judgments or relative importance with respect to particular objectives). In a dynamic application, such as a terrorist crisis, vectors of demands and counter-demands can be prioritized to achieve *minimum cost to the government.* In other words, if the terrorists' hierarchy of values becomes approximately known, it is feasible for government to appraise alternative packages of concessions and counter-demands in a quantitative manner. The negotiators may, for example, concentrate on satisfying the terrorists' high-priority demands at the expense of others which are of relatively greater value to government. Or the negotiators may discover that only marginal changes in the relative importance of terrorists' grievances could facilitate convergence of the two parties' prioritized demands. Negotiators could then focus on attempts to influence the terrorists' most critical evaluations.

The Bennett-Saaty research generated a quantifiable structure, an updatable evaluation of the course of negotiations, enabling negotiators to allocate government's often scarce resources (such as influence) in order to alter the terrorist judgments. Thus, their computations help identify potential trade-offs, their analysis contributing to framing negotiations in a constructive fashion, to monitoring their progress and diagnosing obstacles along the way.

Bennett and Saaty applied their techniques to the analysis of three well-known terrorist incidents: the Hanafi Muslim seizure of three buildings in Washington in 1977, the Munich incident in 1972, and Tupamaro guerrilla terrorism in Uruguay in 1970 and 1972. In this last case they paid special attention to the 1970 kidnapping and killing of Dan Mitrione.

Figure 1.

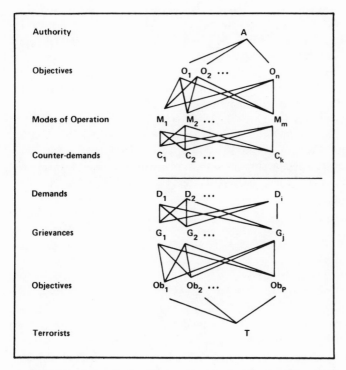

Before we conclude this section it is worthwhile pointing out that the Bennett-Saaty method is applicable to the problem of judging *threat-credibility*. Here, pair-wise judgments concerning scaling and "cost" must be made in the absence of meaningful measures of utility or a "marketplace." Obviously, this is not an ad hoc task—thought must be given to the problem ahead of time.

ON-LINE HEURISTICS

Crisis managers need checklists of "do's and don'ts" in times of strain.[8] The time for theorizing is over—what decision "rules" can be applied simply to guide government through a dangerous and largely unchartered labyrinth? We lift (in slightly paraphrased form) from the Waterman-Jenkins piece to shed light on the topic.

A heuristic model is a model of a situation stated in terms of heuristics (rules of thumb) which describe the dynamics of the situation. It is particularly useful for problem domains that are not well formalized and for which no generally agreed upon axioms or theorems exist. International terrorism is just this type of domain.

Heuristic modeling provides a requirement and a means for articulating the series of steps that lie behind the "intuitive" judgments made by analysts in reaching a particular conclusion. The requirements of machine analysis impose a new degree of rigor on analysts, lead to new questions, extract articulations about the theory and logic of terrorism, and point to new areas of exploration. In sum, it not only provides a useful tool for analysts to use but also aids them in formalizing their domain of study.

Three major assumptions are made. The first is that terrorist activities can be analyzed in a formal, rigorous fashion. The violence of political extremists, for the most part, is not viewed as a collection of mindless, irrational, and thus totally unpredictable events. It follows that certain rules of logic can be discerned by the experienced analyst. Patterns emerge which can be translated into "rules."

The second assumption is that although the domain of terrorism is obviously complex with each group and each incident unique, it is nonetheless believed that even a limited number of rules that prod thinking and formalize the domain will enhance analysis of the topic.

The third assumption is that heuristic models of terrorist activities can be formulated as rule-directed models. The limiting constraint here is the number of rules needed to adequately model the domain. This can be avoided to a certain extent by attempting to model only a small portion of the domain of international terrorism.

The primary objective of heuristic modeling is to determine the feasibility and utility of developing heuristic models within the rule-directed framework and to help the user make complex decisions in ill-specified domains containing large amounts of information that must be coordinated and used in a short amount of time. The secondary objective is to develop a demonstration model that performs interesting and useful deductions within the domain of international terrorism. Other objectives are:

1. to provide a method or procedure to stimulate new ideas and provoke new questions about the domain,
2. to provide a framework within which a high degree of analytic rigor can be imposed,
3. to provide a framework for decision-making that structures thinking and guides problem solving during a crisis situation,
4. to assist in the analysis and understanding of terrorist activities and groups,
5. to ultimately provide a predictive tool, one that can infer what will

happen in the near future or what the immediate effect of certain actions will be.

A *production system* is a set of rules of the form (condition, action), where the conditions are statements about the contents of the data base and the actions are procedures to alter contents. Waterman and Jenkins have developed RITA, a production system generating heuristics. The rules are left-hand-side driven; i.e., when all the conditions of a rule are true relative to the data base, the rule "fires," causing the associated actions to be taken. The goals, however, are right-hand-side driven. This means that the system is given a condition to make true, or, in effect, a question to answer through deductive inference.

A rule might be as follows:

IF: the political-ideology of the terrorist is not known

THEN: deduce the political-ideology of the terrorist.

The "deduce" action is a signal to process "goals" in an attempt to infer the desired information. The appropriate "goals" would have been constructed by a number of IF . . . THEN relationships that characterize the political-ideology of terrorists.

An example of the deductive inference of GOAL is as follows:

IF: the casualty level of the current-event is "high" or there is a campaign whose event-list is known

&   the name of the current-event is in the event-list of the campaign

&   the frequency of the campaign is "escalating" or the time-between-attacks of the campaign is "short"

THEN: set the public-opinion of the current-event to antiterrorist.

"Rules" and "goals" can be constructed by BUILD. BUILD might have constructed a RULE by the following set of questions and answers:

Question 1: What do you want to know about the event that you do not already know?

Answer 1:   I want to know the tactical-objective of the event and the political-ideology of the group.

Question 2: What do you think the tactical-objective might be? ("I don't know" is not acceptable.)

Answer 2:   Extortion.

Question 3: What do you think the political-ideology might be? ("I don't know" is not acceptable.)

Answer 3:   New left.

Question 4: What pieces of information would you need in order to validate or negate your answers?

Answer 4:   I would want to know the locale of the event, the target of the event, and the announced-purpose of the event.

Question 5:   What is a possible locale for extortion and new left?

Answer 5:   California.

Question 6:   What is a possible target for extortion and new left?

Answer 6:   Vital systems.

Question 7:   What is a possible announced-purpose for extortion and new left?

Answer 7:   Reduce utility rates for the poor.

Response: On the basis of your answers, I have constructed the following rule:

IF: the locale of the event is "California" and the target of the event is "vital systems" and the announced-purpose of the event is "reduce utility rates for the poor"

THEN: set the tactical-objective of the event to "extortion-specified philanthropic" and set the political-ideology of the group to "new left."

The system envisioned here first of all provides a straightforward way of proceeding toward a solution. It does this by asking questions about the episode already determined relevant by the experts. In other words, it produces demands for the most relevant information. It summons from its own memory the relevant judgments that have been made about similar groups or events in the past. Furthermore, it enables the users to explore various options by creating in the machine similar artificial events and changing various responses. The machine can then display likely outcomes to these events. Interaction between the users and the machine will cause them to examine their own conclusions and decisions in the same manner that it does for the analyst. In sum, the machine imposes a degree of discipline on the course of the discussion, asks the most relevant questions, provides the best judgments of expert analysis, and allows the users to explore viable options. It also sharpens the users' skills during the process. It is not essential that the system be entirely accurate or that its performance be flawless. Again, it is the interaction that leads to good sharpened answers, not the machine revealing them from a stored memory.

In addition to the usefulness of heuristic models in improving the skills of analysts working with the problem of internationl terrorism, it appears that minicomputers with heuristic modeling systems built into them may be extremely useful in the management of crisis situations. Terrorist actions, such as the hijacking of an airliner or the takeover of an embassy, frequently create a crisis situation to which the government must respond. The usual response is to assemble a task force or several task forces at different locations to deal with the crisis.

Such a system also has utility as a storehouse of judgmental information compiled by many expert analysts over a period of time. Indeed, it may be seen as a judgment retrieval system as opposed to a data retrieval system. This would add to the overall amount of expert opinion that is available, would allow interaction between experts at different times and in different locations, and would tend to ameliorate the effect of lost capabilities that result from rotation or unavailability of personnel.

CALCULATING THE DOWNSIDE COSTS

An aspect of a usable negotiation theory (or the wisdom of taking governmental actions in response to judgments about threat credibility) is the risk of failure and consequent losses. Analyses of incident management should include the expected cost of failure—in other words, the "downside costs" attributable to governmental initiatives. To borrow examples from other subjects, the economics of building a dam should account for its possible collapse and resulting liabilities. Similarly, Howard, Matheson and North[9] wrote about probabilistic considerations when deciding to seed a hurricane.

Such risk analyses require the construction of decision trees, setting out alternative actions, governmental responsibilities, possible damage, various probabilistic estimates, etc. Structuring the *event space* and the *decision tree* are useful exercises even when undertaken by themselves, but estimating the conditional probabilities is at best an "iffy" matter. Possibly, delphi techniques are important exploratory tools, providing high and low estimates of the probabilities and thus offering the possibility for limited sensitivity testing.

If our problems with terrorism increase, the legal and political aspects of governmental responsibilities will become all too evident. In our contingency planning efforts, we therefore should begin to account for the full downside costs of our potential actions. All too often this subject is treated as a painful afterthought.

Notes

1. Fogel, Lawrence J., *Predictive Antiterrorism,* Decision Sciences, Inc., April 1977.
2. Bennett, James P. and Saaty, Thomas L., *Terrorism: Patterns for Negotiations (Three Case Studies Through Hierarchies and Holarchies),* The Wharton School, Univ. of Pennsylvania, August 1977.
3. Waterman, D. A. and Jenkins, Brian M., *Heuristic Modeling Using Rule-Based Computer Systems,* RAND Corp., March 1977.
4. This section is paraphrased from the Fogel study referenced beforehand.
5. The same phenomenon has often been observed on the battlefield, soldiers

not identifying themselves with the act of killing when they are firing their weapons at barely identifiable human targets, but being quite shaken after experiencing close combat.

6. This section is drawn in part from the Bennett-Saaty study referenced beforehand. For a more detailed discussion of crisis management issues, see Kupperman, R. H., Wilcox, R. H., and Smith, H. A., *Crisis Management: Some Opportunities, Science,* Vol. 187, Feb. 1975.

7. Ordinarily one has difficulty in translating feelings and experiences into "numbers," saying how much more one activity influences a given objective than another. Furthermore, in order to assign meaningful numbers when comparing two activities, one needs to understand both activities and the properties they share with respect to (implicit or explicit) criteria for judgment.

8. The effect of emotional stress on the crisis management team, while providing intense motivation and concentration of effort, can lead to dangerously defective coping reactions. Recent studies of decision-making under emergency conditions have spawned a "conflict" theory of the decision process. (See Janis, I. L. and Mann, L., "Coping with Decisional Conflicts," *American Scientist,* Vol. 64 (Nov-Dec 1976).

9. Howard, R. A., Matheson, J. E. and North, D. W., "The Decision to Seed Hurricanes," *Science,* Vol. 176, June 1972.

Appendix 1

A Brief Technological Primer

Strong forces bind together the basic particles—*protons* and *neutrons*—that constitute the nucleus of the atom. Some of this binding energy is released when a neutron strikes a heavy nucleus and causes it to split, or *fission,* into two lighter elements plus more neutrons. The total mass of the products is slightly less than that of the original nucleus. This mass difference is converted into energy according to the relationship $E=mc^2$. The neutrons may, in turn, initiate other fissions. (Neutrons that have been slowed down by a *moderator* such as water or graphite are more likely to cause fissions.) Thus, a *chain reaction* can begin. In a nuclear reactor, the chain reaction is *controlled* to be just self-sustaining, with one of the extra neutrons, on the average, initiating a new fission. In a nuclear explosive, the chain reaction is carried on by fast neutrons in a multiplicative and uncontrolled mode. These different conditions—sustaining or multiplicative—depend on a number of parameters, including the quantity, chemical form, concentration, and geometrical arrangement of the *fissile* material and the amount, properties, and arrangement of the nonfissile material which is present.

Most materials, even when in pure chemical element form, contain a mixture of *isotopes*—atoms of the same element that have different numbers of neutrons in their nuclei and hence different masses.[1] Only a relatively few isotopes are fissile, and, in fact, only one fissile isotope occurs in nature—uranium-235, or, as it is usually written, U^{235}. Two other fissile isotopes are important in any discussion of nuclear power—uranium-233 (U^{233}) and plutonium-239 (Pu^{239}). These isotopes do not occur in nature, but are *bred* when the *fertile* nuclei U^{238} and thorium-232 (Th^{232}) absorb neutrons to become U^{239} and Th^{233}, and then undergo two successive radioactive decays to Pu^{239} and U^{233}.

The power reactors in common use today use uranium as fuel; the fissile concentration is well below that necessary for a nuclear explosive. Specifically, it is *impossible,* not merely impractical, to use a light water reactor (LWR) or a Canadian CANDU reactor uranium fuel in a nuclear fission explosive without an expensive and technologically advanced enrichment facility. . . .

Uranium fuel goes through many operations both before and after its use in the reactor. These operations constitute the nuclear *fuel cycle*. Figure 1 shows the fuel cycle for the most common reactor, the light water reactor (LWR).

From the mine, the uranium ore is sent to a mill where uranium is recovered from the ore in the form of an oxide. The next step, after conversion of the oxide to uranium hexafluoride, is *enrichment*. At the enrichment plant, the concentration of U ^{235} is increased from the naturally occurring value of 0.7 percent to about 3 percent. Most present-day enrichment plants use the gas *diffusion* process, but most new plants in the construction and planning stage will use the gas *centifuge* method. After enrichment, the uranium goes to a *fuel fabrication plant* to be formed into fuel elements which will be combined into fuel assemblies and inserted into the reactor.

After the fuel has been in the reactor for a time (typically several years), it contains too little uranium-235 and too many neutron-absorbing (and radioactive) fission products to be useful. The fuel is then removed and placed into pools of water for cooling. In an LWR, the *spent fuel* does not have to be reused, but it still has about 0.9 percent uranium-235, a higher concentration than occurs in nature, plus about 0.5 percent plutonium-239 which is bred from the abundant uranium-238. If it is deemed economical and desirable to recover the unused fissile material, the spent fuel will be sent to a *reprocessing plant*. There, the uranium and plutonium are chemically separated from waste products and (under present plans) from each other. The uranium may be reenriched while the plutonium is sent directly to a fuel fabrication plant. The plutonium is then mixed with uranium (both uranium and plutonium being in oxide form), to form *mixed oxide fuel*.

The fuel cycle for other reactors may differ in the necessity for, and nature of, the various stages in the light-water reactor fuel cycle just described. For example, the Canadian CANDU reactor uses natural uranium, and recovery of plutonium from its spent fuel is not at present economical. Hence, the CANDU fuel cycle excludes both the enrichment and reprocessing steps.

A future reactor concept is the *breeder*, a reactor that would create more new fissile fuel than it burns to produce power. Most development work has concentrated on the liquid metal fast breeder reactor (LMFBR), which will yield enough plutonium to refuel itself and excess plutonium to contribute to the fueling of new reactors. The breeder fuel cycle would eliminate the enrichment step but absolutely requires the reprocessing step.

All the reactors mentioned so far use uranium as a fuel, with fissile uranium-235 to produce power and with fertile uranium-238 to breed another fissile isotope, plutonium-239. Another fuel cycle may be based on the element thorium. The isotope thorium-232 is fertile and breeds fissile uranium-233.

Figure 1. Light-water reactor fuel cycle

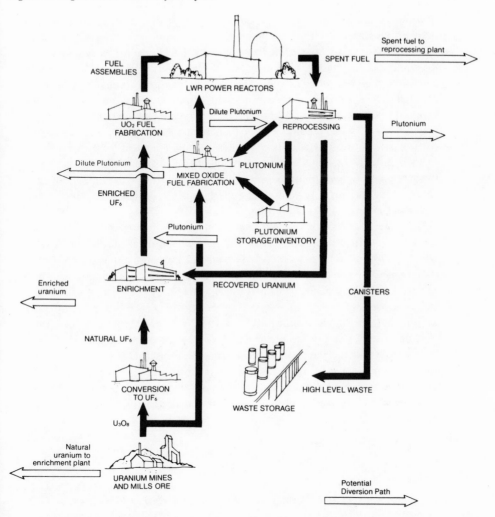

In most of the fuel cycle for commercial nuclear power reactors, the concentration of fissile fuel is low. By contrast, the concentration of fissile material in a nuclear weapon is quite high—typically pure plutonium, or uranium enriched to about 90 percent in the isotope uranium-235. . . . The object in designing a weapon is to initiate a chain reaction that will cause a large number of nuclei to fission in a very short period of time. This condition will be obtained only if a certain minimal amount of nuclear material called the *critical mass* is present. With less than this quantity, an explosion will never occur. No specific number can be assigned to the critical mass—it varies with a number of parameters, including, for example, the particular fissile isotope and its concentration and chemical form. A nuclear weapon initially contains one or more subcritical masses of fissile material. Detonation of the weapon requires a means of rapidly moving the subcritical mass or masses into a condition of supercriticality sufficient to produce a significant nuclear yield before it blows itself apart.

There are two basic methods of assembling the fissile material in a nuclear weapon. The first is to shoot two (or more) subcritical masses into each other. This is a *gun-type weapon.* The second is to surround a subcritical configuration of fissile material with high explosives and use them to compress the material into a supercritical mass. Such a device is called an *implosion weapon.*

Note that the highly concentrated fissile material required for weapons is exposed at only one portion of the nuclear fuel cycle described above—at the reprocessing and fuel fabrication plants and the transportation link between the two. These areas are thus the most vulnerable to the diversion of nuclear material from a power program to a weapons program. However, there are other possible crossovers between peaceful and destructive uses of nuclear energy that are not that direct and obvious. . . .

Notes

1. Isotopes are specified by the total number of neutrons and protons they contain and a symbol indicating the chemical elements. For instance, the isotope with 92 protons and 143 neutrons is uranium—235, or, as it usually written, U^{235} .

Appendix 2

Threats of Violence Against U.S. Nuclear Facilities

Licensed Nuclear Facilities (1969-1977)

	Date	Facility	Incident
1.	5/4/69	Illinois Institute of Technology	Pipe bomb found near reactor building
2.	9/11/70	Kansas State University	Bomb threat
3.	9/70	Wisconsin Michigan Power Company (Point Beach)	Dynamite found
4.	10/27/70	Commonwealth Edison Co. (Dresden)	Bomb threat
5.	11/10/70	Idaho State University	Bomb threat
6.	2/16/71	Yankee Atomic Electric Co. (Yankee-Rowe)	Bomb threat
7.	6/23/71	Purdue University	Bomb threat
8.	8/17/71	Duke Power Co. (Oconee)	Bomb threat
9.	9/18/71	VEPCP (Surry)	Bomb threat
10.	10/18/71	VEPCO (North Anna)	Bomb threat
11.	1/20/72	VEPCO (Surry)	Bomb threat
12.	3/13/72	General Electric Co., San Jose, CA	Bomb threat
13.	4/72	Florida Power Co. (Crystal River)	Bomb threat
14.	4/72	Duquesne Light Co. (Beaver Valley)	Bomb threat
15.	4/28/72	VEPCO (North Anna)	Bomb threat
16.	5/5/72	VEPCO (North Anna)	Bomb threat
17.	5/11/72	VEPCO (North Anna)	Bomb threat
18.	5/12/72	VEPCO (North Anna)	Bomb threat
19.	5/12/72	Duquesne Light Co. (Beaver Valley)	Bomb threat
20.	5/72	Florida Power Co. (Crystal River)	Bomb threat
21.	6/2/72	Iowa State University	Bomb threat
22.	6/30/72	Babcock & Wilcox Co. (VA)	Bomb threat
23.	7/4/72	Colorado Public Service Co. (Fort St. Vrain)	Bomb threat
24.	8/1/72	Gulf-United Nuclear Fuels Corp. Elmsford, NY	Bomb threat
25.	8/72	Southern California Edison Co. (San Onofre)	Bomb threat
26.	8/1/72	VEPCO (North Anna)	Bomb threat
27.	8/10/72	VEPCO (North Anna)	Bomb threat

	Date	Facility	Incident
28.	8/10/72	VEPCO (North Anna)	Bomb threat
29.	8/11/72	VEPCO (North Anna)	Bomb threat
30.	8/14/72	VEPCO (North Anna)	Bomb threat
31.	8/15/72	VEPCO (North Anna)	Bomb threat
32.	9/25/72	Metropolitan Edison Co. (Three Mile Island)	Bomb threat
33.	10/6/72	Nebraska Public Power District (Cooper Station)	Bomb threat
34.	10/20/72	Southern California Edison Co. (San Onofre)	Bomb threat
35.	10/31/72	General Atomic Co., San Diego, CA	Bomb threat
36.	12/72	Atomics International	Bomb threat
37.	12/29/72	Consumers Power Co. (Palisades)	Bomb threat
38.	2/5/73	Gulf-United Nuclear Fuels Corp. Elmsford, NY	Bomb threat
39.	3/15/73	Duke Power Co. (Oconee)	Break-in at fuel storage building (No material taken)
40.	3/23/73	Metropolitan Edison Co. (Three Mile Island)	Bomb threat
41.	5/3/73	Babcock & Wilcox Co., Lynchburg, VA	Bomb threat
42.	5/8/73	Babcock & Wilcox Co.,	Bomb threat
43.	6/19/73	Southern California Edison Co. (San Onofre)	Bomb threat
44.	11/5/73	Metropolitan Edison Co. (Three Mile Island)	Bomb threat
45.	11/16/73	Florida Power & Light Co. (Turkey Point)	Bomb threat
46.	1/6/74	Florida Power Corp. (Crystal River)	Bomb threat
47.	1/17/74	Rochester Gas & Electric Corp. (Ginna)	Bomb threat
48.	1/22/74	Florida Power Corp. (Crystal River)	Bomb threat
49.	3/11/74	Maine Yankee Atomic Power Co.	Bomb threat
50.	3/13/74	Pacific Gas & Electric Co. (Diablo Canyon)	Bomb threat
51.	4/17/74	Westinghouse Electric Corp., Columbia, SC	Bomb threat
52.	5/3/74	Consolidated Edison Co. (Indian Point)	Bomb threat
53.	5/17/74	Consolidated Edison Co. (Indian Point)	Bomb threat
54.	5/29/74	Baltimore Gas & Electric Co. (Calvert Cliffs 1)	Bomb threat
55.	5/30/74	Connecticut Yankee Atomic Power Co. (Haddam Neck)	Bomb threat
56.	7/15/74	Alabama Power Co. (Farley)	Bomb threat
57.	7/24/74	Southern California Edison Co. (San Onofre)	Bomb threat
58.	8/11/74	Commonwealth Edison Co. (Zion)	Bomb threat
59.	8/16/74	Consolidated Edison Co. (Indian Point)	Bomb threat
60.	8/26/74	Boston Edison Co. (Pilgrim)	Incendiary device detonated in public area

	Date	Facility	Incident
61.	9/4/74	U.S. Nuclear Corp., Oak Ridge, TN	Attempted fence breach
62.	9/7/74	Carolina Power & Light Co. (Brunswick)	Bomb threat
63.	11/1/74	Connecticut Yankee Atomic Power Co.	Bomb threat
64.	11/4/74	Boston Edison Co. (Pilgrim)	Bomb threat
65.	2/20/75	Pacific Gas & Electric Co. (Diablo Canyon)	Bomb threat
66.	2/23/75	Nuclear Fuel Services, Erwin, TN	Fence breach (No theft)
67.	2/25/75	Alabama Power Co. (Farley)	Bomb threat
68.	3/8/75	Commonwealth Edison Co. (Zion)	Bomb threat
69.	3/14/75	Mallinckrodt Chemical Works, St. Louis, MO	Bomb threat
70.	4/1/75	Philadelphia Electric Co. (Peach Bottom)	Bomb threat
71.	4/4/75	Wisconsin Michigan Power Co. (Point Beach)	Telephone line cut by rifle or pistol fire
72.	4/10/75	Northeast Nuclear Energy Co.	Bomb threat
73.	4/14/75	Baltimore Gas & Electric Co. (Calvert Cliffs)	Bomb threat
74.	4/16/75	Consolidated Edison Co. (Unspecified plant)	Bomb threat
75.	5/6/75	Jersey Central Power & Light Co. (Forked River)	Bomb threat
76.	5/13/75	Northeast Nuclear Energy Co. (Millstone 3)	Bomb threat
77.	5/27/75	Commonwealth Edison Co. (Zion)	Two shots apparently fired at security guard
78.	6/10/75	Georgia Power Co. (Hatch)	Bomb threat
79.	7/2/75	Kerr-McGee Nuclear Corp., Oklahoma City, OK	Attempted forced entry
80.	7/4/75	General Electric Co., (Vallecitos)	Bomb threat
81.	7/14/75	Carolina Power & Light Co. (Brunswick)	Bomb threat
82.	7/23/75	Nuclear Fuel Services, West Valley, NY	Possible arson, equipment storage barn
83.	8/21/75	Consolidated Edison Co. (Unspecified plant)	Bomb threat
84.	8/22/75	Northeast Nuclear Energy Co. (Millstone 1)	Bomb threat
85.	9/1/75	Commonwealth Edison Co. (Zion)	Bomb threat
86.	9/23/75	Carolina Power & Light Co. (Brunswick)	Bomb threat
87.	9/25/75	Massachusetts Institute of Tech.	Attempted forced entry
88.	9/26/75	Consolidated Edison Co. (Indian Point)	Bomb threat
89.	10/14/75	Westinghouse Electric Corp. Columbia, SC	Bomb threat
90.	10/17/75	Boston Edison Co. (Pilgrim)	Bomb threat

	Date	Facility	Incident
91.	11/3/75	General Atomics, Inc., San Diego, CA	Bomb threat
92.	11/4/75	General Atomics, Inc., San Diego, CA	Bomb threat
93.	11/8/75	Boston Edison Co. (Pilgrim)	Bomb threat
94.	12/2/75	Consumers Power Co. (Palisades)	Bomb threat
95.	12/8/75	Arkansas Power & Light Co. (Arkansas Nuclear One)	Bomb threat
96.	12/11/75	Allied-General Nuclear Services (Barnwell)	Bomb threat
97.	12/23/75	Duke Power Co. (Oconee)	Bomb threat
98.	12/23/75	Long Island Lighting Co. (Shoreham)	Bomb threat
99.	12/31/75	Jersey Central Power & Light Co. (Oyster Creek)	Bomb threat
100.	1/19/76	B&W Naval Nuclear Fuel Lynchburg, VA	Bomb threat
101.	1/22/76	Massachusetts Institute of Technology (MIT)	Bomb threat
102.	1/23/76	MIT	Bomb threat
103.	1/27/76	Three Mile Island 1 & 2 Metropolitan Edison Co. Goldsboro, PA	Intrusion
104.	1/30/76	MIT	Bomb threat
105.	2/3/76	Westinghouse Nuclear Fuel Facility Columbia, SC	Bomb threat
106.	2/4/76	Susquehanna Units 1 & 2 PA Power & Light Berwick, PA	Bomb threat
107.	2/26/76	Diablo Canyon Pacific Gas & Electric Co. Diablo Canyon, CA	Intrusion
108.	3/5/76	Brunswick 1 & 2 Carolina Power & Light Co. Southport, NC	Bomb threat
109.	3/5/76	Susquehanna Units 1 & 2 Pennsylvania Power & Light Co. Berwick, PA	Bomb threat
110.	3/8/76	Susquehanna Units 1 & 2 Pennsylvania Power & Light Co. Berwick, PA	Bomb threat
111.	3/9/76	Turkey Point Florida Power & Light Co. Florida City, FL	Bomb threat
112.	3/15/76	Sequoyah Nuclear Plant TVA Daisey, TN	Bomb threat
113.	3/16/76	Sequoyah Nuclear Plant TVA Daisey, TN	Bomb threat
114.	3/25/76	Purdue University West Lafayette, IN	Bomb threat

	Date	Facility	Incident
115.	3/25/76	Diablo Canyon Unit 1 Pacific Gas & Electric Co. Diablo Canyon, CA	
116.	4/6676	Millstone Units 1 & 2 Northeast Nuclear Energy Co. Waterford, CN	Bomb threat
117.	4/22/76	St. Lucie Unit 1 Florida Power & Light Co. Hutchinson Island, FL	Intrusion threat
118.	4/23/76	Turkey Point Units 3 & 4 Florida Power & Light Co. Florida City, FL	Bomb threat
119.	4/23/76	Grand Gulf Mississippi Power & Light Port Gibson, MS	Bomb threat
120.	4/26/76	Grand Gulf Mississippi Power & Light Port Gibson, MS	Bomb threat
121.	5/4/76	North Anna Units 1, 2, 3 & 4 Virginia Electric & Power Co. Mineral, VA	Bomb threat
122.	5/6/76	Diablo Canyon Units 1 & 2 Pacific Gas & Electric Co. Diablo Canyon, CA	Bomb threat
123.	5/7/76	North Anna Units 1, 2, 3 & 4 Virginia Electric Power Co. Mineral, VA	Bomb threat
124.	5/12/76	Zion Units 1 & 2 Commonwealth Edison Co. Zion, IL	Intrusion threat
125.	5/31/76	General Electric Wilmington, NC Fabrication Plant	Bomb threat
126.	6/2/76	Pilgrim Unit 1 Boston Edison Co. Plymouth, MA	Bomb threat
127.	6/3/76	Susquehanna Units 1 & 2 Pennsylvania Power & Light Berwick, PA	Bomb threat
128.	6/3/76	Nuclear Power Plants	Bomb threat
129.	6/7/76	Nuclear Power Plants in MA	Bomb threat
130.	6/23/76	Duane Arnold Energy Center Iowa Electric Light & Power Co. Cedar Rapids, IA	Bomb threat
131.	6/23/76	Nuclear Power Plants in States of Oregon or Washington	Bomb threat
132.	7/1/76	Joseph M. Farley NPP Alabama Power Company Dothan, AL	Bomb threat

	Date	Facility	Incident
133.	7/14/76	Peach Bottom Philadelphia Electric Co. Peach Bottom, PA	Bomb threat
134.	7/14/76	Northern States Power Co. Minneapolis, MN	Bomb threat
135.	7/16/76	Beaver Valley Duquesne Light Co. Shippingport, PA	Bomb threat
136.	7/18/76	Zion Units 1 & 2, IL Commonwealth Edison Co.	Automobile intrusion
137.	7/24/76	Prairie Island Units 1 & 2 Northern States Power Co. Redwing, MN	Intrusion attempt
138.	7/26/76	Farley NPP Alabama Power Co. Houston County, AL	Bomb threat
139.	8/3/76	Dresden Units 1, 2 & 3 Commonwealth Edison Co. Morris, IL	Bomb threat
140.	8/12/76	Turkey Point Florida Power and Light Co. Florida City, FL	Bomb threat
141.	8/22/76	North Anna Units 1 & 2 Virginia Electric & Power Co. Mineral, VA	Bomb threat
142.	8/25/76	Limerick Units 1 & 2 Philadelphia Electric Co. Pottstown, PA	Bomb threat
143.	8/31/76	North Anna Power Station Virginia Electric & Power Co. Mineral, VA	Bomb threat
144.	9/1/76	North Anna Power Station VEPCO Mineral, VA	Bomb threat
145.	9/2/76	North Anna Power Station VEPCO Mineral, VA	Bomb threat
146.	9/19/76	North Anna Power Station VEPCO Mineral, VA	Bomb threat
147.	10/3/76	Zion Unit 1 Commonwealth Edison Co. Zion, IL	Intrusion
148.	10/6/76	North Anna Power Station VEPCO Mineral, VA	Bomb threat
149.	10/6/76	North Anna Power Station VEPCO Mineral, VA	Bomb threat

	Date	Facility	Incident
150.	10/6/76	North Anna Power Station VEPCO Mineral, VA	Bomb threat
151.	10/7/76	North Anna Power Station VEPCO Mineral, VA	Bomb threat
152.	10/13/76	North Anna Power Station VEPCO Mineral, VA	Bomb threat
153.	10/14/76	North Anna Power Station VEPCO Mineral, VA	Bomb threat
154.	10/15/76	North Anna Power Station VEPCO Mineral, VA	Bomb threat
155.	10/15/76	North Anna Power Station VEPCO Mineral, VA	Bomb threat
156.	10/15/76	North Anna Power Station VEPCO Mineral, VA	Bomb threat
157.	11/3/76	North Anna Power Station VEPCO Mineral, VA	Bomb threat
158.	11/3/76	Waterford Steam Electric Station Unit No. 3 Louisiana Power & Light Co. Taft, LA	Bomb threat
159.	11/3/76	Waterford Unit No. 3 Louisiana Power & Light Co. Taft, LA	Bomb threat
160.	12/10/76	Calvert Cliffs, Units 1 & 2 Baltimore Gas & Electric Co. Lusby, MD	Bomb threat
161.	1/26/77	SC Electric & Gas Co., V.C. Summers Nuclear Station Unit No. 1 Summer, SC	Bomb threat
162.	2/6/77	U.S. Nuclear Corporation Oak Ridge, TN	Weapons discharge
163.	2/10/77	Westinghouse Electric Corp. Columbia, SC	Unspecified threat
164.	2/15/77	Arizona Public Service Corp. Palo Verde, AZ	Bomb threat
165.	2/22/77	Georgia Power Co. Hatch Baxley, Georgia	Weapons discharge
166.	3/3/77	Connecticut Light & Power Co. Millstone Waterford, CN	Bomb threat

	Date	Facility	Incident
167.	3/23/77	Arkansas Power & Light Co. Arkansas Nuclear One Russellville, AR	Bomb threat
168.	3/23/77	Arkansas Power & Light Co. Arkansas Nuclear One Russellville, AR	Bomb threat
169.	3/30/77	Pacific Gas & Electric Co. Diablo Canyon Diablo Canyon, CA	Bomb threat
170.	3/31/77	Louisiana Power and Light Co. Waterford Taft, LA	Three bomb threats
171.	4/1/77	Louisiana Power & Light Co. Waterford Taft, LA	Bomb threat
172.	4/6/77	Salem Nuclear Generating Station Salem, NJ	Bomb threat
173.	4/19/77	Public Service Co. of Colorado Ft. Saint Vrain Platteville, CO	Intrusion
174.	4/29/77	Long Island Lighting Co. Shoreham Brookhaven, NY	Bomb threat
175.	5/10/77	Long Island Lighting Co. Shoreham Brookhaven, NY	Bomb threat
176.	5/18/77	National Bureau of Standards Gaithersburg, MD	Bomb threat
177.	5/19/77	South Carolina Electric & Gas Co. Summer Broad River, SC	Bomb threat
178.	5/24/77	Allied Chemical Co. Metropolis, IL	Bomb threat
179.	6/1/77	Washington Public Power System Washington Nuclear Power Project Richland, WA	Bomb threat
180.	7/17/77	Consumers Power Co. of Michigan Palisades South Haven, Michigan	Weapon threat
181.	8/3/77	Consolidated Edison Co. of New York Indian Point Indian Point, NY	Bomb threat
182.	8/15/77	Commonwealth Edison Co. Braidwood Braidwood, IL	Bomb threat
183.	8/18/77	Rochester Gas & Electric Corp. Ginna Rochester, NY	Intrusion
184.	9/30/77	Mississippi Power & Light Co. Grand Gulf Port Gibson, MS	Bomb threat

	Date	Facility	Incident
185.	10/8/77	Vermont Yankee Nuclear Power Corp. Vermont Yankee Vernon, VT	Intrusion
186.	10/10/77	Visitors' Center at Trojan Nuclear Power Plant Prescott, Oregon	Bomb explosion
187.	10/29/77	Westinghouse Columbia, SC	Bomb threat
188.	11/4/77	Consolidated Edison Co. of New York Indian Point Indian Point, NY	Bomb threat
189.	11/6/77	Peach Bottom Atomic Power Station Peach Bottom, PA	Bomb threat
190.	11/14/77	Westinghouse Columbia, SC	Bomb threat
191.	11/22/77	Consolidated Edison Co. of New York Indian Point Indian Point, NY	Bomb threat
192.	11/25/77	Trojan Nuclear Power Plant Prescott, OR	Intrusion
193.	12/13/77	Quad-Cities Station Cordova, IL	Bomb threat
194.	12/23/77	Commonwealth Edison Braidwood Braidwood, IL	Bomb threat

Unlicensed Nuclear Facilities (1969-1977)

	Date	Facility	Incident
1.	3/24/69	Lawrence Research Lab., Berkeley, California	Arson attempt
2.	5/15/69	Lawrence Research Lab., Berkeley, California	Arson attempt
3.	5/17/69	Lawrence Research Lab., Berkeley, California	Arson attempt
4.	5/19/69	Lawrence Research Lab., Berkeley, California	Arson attempt
5.	6/9/69	Lawrence Research Lab., Berkeley, California	Arson attempt
6.	6/16/69	Lawrence Research Lab., Berkeley, California	Arson attempt
7.	6/17/69	Lawrence Research Lab., Berkeley, California	Arson attempt

	Date	Facility	Incident
8.	4/22/70	United Nuclear Corporation, New Haven, Conn.	Bomb threat
9.	6/12/70	Sandia Corp., Livermore, California	Bomb threat
10.	6/12/70	Goodyear Corp., Portsmouth, Ohio	Bomb threat
11.	8/6/70	Dow Chemical, Rocky Flats, Colorado	Bomb threat
12.	11/4/70	United Nuclear Corporation New Haven, Conn.	Bomb threat
13.	11/13/70	Dow Chemical, Rocky Flats, Colorado	Bomb threat
14.	12/23/70	Battelle-Northwest, Richland, Wash.	Bomb hoax
15.	1/12/71	Lawrence Research Lab., Berkeley, California	Bomb threat
16.	1/13/71	Lawrence Research Lab., Berkeley, California	Bomb threat
17.	2/15/71	Goodyear Corp., Portsmouth, Ohio	Bomb threat
18.	2/24/71	Bendix Corporation, Kansas City, Mo.	Bomb threat
19.	3/23/71	Lawrence Research Lab., Berkeley, California	Arson attempt
20.	4/15/71	General Electric Corp., Valley Forge, Pennsylvania	Bomb threat
21.	4/23/71	Lawrence Research Lab., Berkeley, California	Bomb threat
22.	5/12/71	Donner Laboratory, Berkeley, Calif.	Arson attempt
23.	6/14/71	Sandia Corp., Albuquerque, NM	Bomb threat
24.	6/19/71	Bendix Corp., Kansas City, Mo.	Bomb threat
25.	8/23/71	Westinghouse Astronuclear, Large, Pa.	Bomb threat
26.	10/13/71	United Nuclear Corporation New Haven, Conn.	Bomb threat
27.	10/25/71	Lawrence Berkeley Lab., Berkeley, California	Bomb threat
28.	10/31/71	Lawrence Berkeley Lab., Berkeley, California	Bomb threat
29.	11/5/71	National Accelerator Lab., Weston, Illinois	Bomb threat
30.	11/15/71	Los Alamos Scientific Lab., Los Alamos, New Mexico	Bomb threat
31.	2/5/72	Dow Chemical, Rocky Flats, Colorado	Bomb threat
32.	4/1/72	Monsanto Research Corp. (Mound Lab) Miamisburg, Ohio	Bomb threat
33.	4/13/72	Oak Ridge Operations Office, Knoxville, Tennessee	Bomb threat
34.	5/17/72	Lawrence Berkeley Lab., Berkeley, California	Bomb threat
35.	5/30/72	Babcock & Wilcox Corp., Lynchburg, Virginia	Bomb threat
36.	8/9/72	Savannah River Plant, Aiken, S.C.	Bomb threat
37.	12/7/72	Union Carbide Corp. (Y-12 Plant) Oak Ridge, Tennessee	Bomb threat
38	3/8/73	Lawrence Berkeley Lab., Berkeley, California	Bomb threat

	Date	Facility	Incident
39.	3/29/73	General Electric, Knolls Atomic Power Lab., Niskayuna, NY	Bomb threat
40.	4/16/73	Fast Flux Test Facility, Richland, Washington	Bomb threat
41.	4/22/73	General Electric, Knolls Atomic Power Lab., Kesselring Site, West Milton, New York	Fire
42.	5/30/73	Sandia Laboratory, Livermore, Calif.	Bomb threat
43.	6/25/73	General Electric, Knolls Atomic Power Lab., Niskayuna, New York	Bomb threat
44.	9/21/73	Stanford Linear Accelerator Center, Oakland, California	Bomb threat
45.	10/16/73	Bendix Corp., Kansas City, Mo.	Bomb threat
46.	10/21/73	Operations Office, Rocky Flats, Colo.	Bomb threat
47.	10/28/73	General Electric, Nuclear Energy Div., San Jose, California	Bomb threat
48.	12/31/73	General Electric Corp., Kesselring Site, West Milton, New York	Bomb threat
49.	2/20/74	Sandia Lab., Albuquerque, New Mexico	Bomb threat
50.	4/9/74	General Electric, Knolls Atomic Power Lab., Niskayuna, New York	Bomb threat
51.			
51.	4/11/74	Lawrence Livermore Lab., Livermore, California	Bomb threat
52.	4/17/74	Oak Ridge Operations Office (K-25 Area). Oak Ridge, Tennessee	Anonymous letter Bomb threat
53.	4/24/74	Iowa State University, Ames, Iowa	Anonymous letter
54.	4/30/74	Lawrence Berkeley Lab., Berkeley, California	Bomb threat
55.	4/30/74	Babcock & Wilcox Corp., Mt. Vernon, Indiana	Bomb threat
56.	5/21/74	Atomics International, Canoga Park, California	Bomb threat
57.	8/7/74	Washington Public Power System (#2 Site), Hanford, Washington	Bomb threat
58.	2/15/75	Sandia Corporation, Livermore, Calif.	Bomb threat
59.	4/4/75	Dow Chemical Corp., Rocky Flats, Colorado	Bomb threat
60.	5/16/75	General Electric Corp. (Kesselring Site), West Milton, New York	Bomb threat
61.	6/9/75	Lawrence Berkeley Lab., Berkeley, California	Bomb threat
62.	6/13/75	General Electric Corp., Nuclear Energy Division, San Jose, Calif.	Bomb threat
63.	6/23/75	Lawrence Livermore Lab., Livermore, California	Bomb threats (2)
64.	8/1/75	Lawrence Livermore Lab., Livermore, California	Bomb threat
65.	8/5/75	Airesearch Corp., Torrance, Calif.	Bomb threat
66.	8/6/75	Union Carbide Corp. (Y-12 Plant) Oak Ridge, Tennessee	Bomb threat

	Date	Facility	Incident
67.	8/9/75	Allied Chemical Corp., Idaho Lab.	Bomb conversation report
68.	9/1/75	Fermi National Lab., Batavia, Ill.	Bomb threat
69.	9/20/75	General Electric Corp., San Jose, California	Bomb threats (3)
70.	10/1/75	General Electric Corp., San Jose, California	Bomb threat
71.	10/3/75	General Electric Corp., San Jose, California	Bomb threat
72.	10/18/75	Monsanto Research Corp. (Mound Lab) Miamisburg, Ohio	Bomb threat
73.	10/24/75	Westinghouse Corp., Bettis Lab.	Bomb threat
74.	11/29/75	General Electric Corp., San Jose, California	Bomb threat
75.	12/7/75	General Electric Corp., San Jose,	Bomb threat
76.	12/15/75	Monsanto Research (Mound Lab), Miamisburg, Ohio	Bomb threat
77.	1/5/76	Fast Flux Test Facility, Richland, Washington	Written bomb threat
78.	3/18/76	General Electric, Knolls Atomic Power Lab, Windsor, Connecticut	Telephonic bomb threat
79.	3/24/76	Lawrence Berkeley Laboratory, Berkeley, California	Telephonic bomb threat
80.	7/2/76	Rockwell International Rocky Flats, Colorado	Telephonic bomb threat
81.	7/2/76	Sandia Laboratory, Albuquerque, New Mexico	Telephonic bomb threat
82.	1/27/77	Rockwell International Rocky Flats, Colorado	Telephonic bomb threat that did not materialize
83.	2/23/77	Union Carbide Oak Ridge, Tennessee	Possible pipe bomb outside of confines of facility
84.	3/30/77	FERMI Laboratory	Anonymous telephonic bomb threat that did not materialize
85.	4/28/77	Los Alamos Scientific Laboratory, Los Alamos, New Mexico	Anonymous telephonic bomb threat that did not materialize
86.	4/28/77	Rocky Flats ERDA Facility near Boulder, Colorado	Anonymous telephonic bomb message received by District Attorney, Boulder, Colorado that did not materialize

	Date	Facility	Incident
87.	7/8/77	Rocky Flats ERDA Facility near Boulder, Colorado	Anonymous telephonic bomb threat that did not materialize
88.	7/28/77	General Electric, San Jose, CA	Anonymous telephonic bomb threat that did not materialize
89.	8/31/77	Teledyne Wah Chang Plant, Albany, Oregon, subcontractor to B&W, Lynchburg, VA	Anonymous telephonic bomb threat that did not materialize
90.	9/13/77	Teledyne Wah Chang Plant, Albany, Oregon, subcontractor to B&W, Lynchburg, VA	Anonymous telephonic bomb threat that did not materialize
91.	11/8/77	General Electric, San Jose, CA	Anonymous telephonic bomb threat that did not materialize

Glossary

Breeder—A nuclear reactor that produces more fissile nuclei than it consumes. The fissile nuclei are produced by the capture of neutrons in fertile material. (See definitions below.) The resource constraint for breeder reactors is thus *fertile* material, which is far more abundant in nature than fissile material. These reactors have not yet reached commercialization. Fast breeders do not contain a moderator (see definition below) to slow neutrons down; i.e., fast neutrons are used. Thermal breeders do contain a moderator; i.e., slow neutrons are used.

Centrifuge—A rotating vessel that can be used for enrichment of uranium. The heavier isotopes of the UF_6 gas tend to concentrate at the walls of the rotating centrifuge.

Chain Reaction—A series of nuclear fissions, each one stimulated by a neutron emitted in a previous fission. A chain reaction occurs when at least one of the two or more neutrons released in a fission initiates another fission.

Critical Mass—The minimum amount of fissile material required to sustain a chain reaction. The exact mass varies with many factors such as the particular fissile isotope present, its concentration and chemical form and the geometrical arrangement of the material.

Dedicated Facility—A facility built indigenously (possibly clandestinely) in order to produce fissile material for nuclear weapons. It might be a plutonium production reactor, a uranium enrichment plant or a reprocessing plant.

Denaturing—A technique to render fissile nuclear material unsuitable for explosive weapons by mixing in other isotopes of the same element.

Diffusion—A technique for enrichment of uranium based on the fact that the lighter isotopes of a gas will diffuse through a porous barrier more rapidly than the heavier isotopes.

Diversion—The removal of material from some point in the commercial nuclear fuel cycle to use in nuclear weapons.

Enrichment—The process of increasing the concentration of one isotope of a given element.

Fast Neutron—A fast-moving, neutral subatomic particle. Neutrons are emitted when a nucleus, such as uranium-235, fissions.

Fertile Isotope—An isotope not itself fissile but that is converted into a fissile isotope, either directly or after a short decay process following absorption of a neutron. Example: U^{238} can capture a neutron to give U^{239}. U^{239} then decays to Np^{239} which in turn decays to fissile Pu^{239}.

Fissile Isotope—An isotope that will split, or fission, into two (or more) lighter elements plus extra neutrons when it is struck by a neutron.

Fission—The splitting of a nucleus usually into two or more lighter elements. The total mass of the resulting particles is less than that of the original atom, the difference being converted into energy.

Fresh Fuel—Nuclear fuel ready for insertion into a power reactor.

Fuel Cycle—The set of chemical and physical operations needed to prepare nuclear material for use in reactors and to dispose of or recycle the material after its removal from the reactor. Existing fuel cycles begin with uranium as the natural resource and create plutonium as a byproduct. Some future fuel cycles may rely on thorium and produce the fissile isotope uranium-233.

Fuel Fabrication Plant—A facility where the nuclear material (e.g., enriched or natural uranium) is fabricated into fuel elements to be inserted into a reactor.

Gun-Type Nuclear Weapon—A device in which gun propellants are used to move two or more subcritical masses of fissile material together to produce an explosion.

Implosion-Type Nuclear Weapon—A device in which high explosives surrounding a subcritical configuration of fissile material compress it into a condition of supercriticality to produce an explosion.

Isotopes—Atoms of the same chemical element whose nuclei contain different masses, even though chemically identical. Isotopes are specified by their atomic mass number, that is, the total number of protons plus neutrons, and a symbol denoting the chemical element, e.g., U^{235} for uranium-235.

Mixed-Oxide Fuel—Nuclear reactor fuel composed of plutonium and uranium in oxide form. The plutonium replaces some of the fissile uranium, thus reducing the need for uranium ore and enrichment. This is the form of the fuel that would be used in plutonium recycle.

Moderator—A component (usually water, heavy water, or graphite) of some nuclear reactors that slows neutrons, thereby increasing their chances of being absorbed by a fissile nucleus.

Multinational Fuel-Cycle Facilities (MFCF)—A concept for joint national ownership and management of certain steps of the nuclear fuel cycle—especially those steps that are particularly vulnerable to national diversion. Multinational reprocessing plants and spent-fuel storage facilities are currently under study.

Nth Country—A nation judged to have high potential of becoming a nuclear-weapons state—because of its technical and economic ability and its political motivations.

Neutron—Neutral particles which, together with protons, comprise the nucleus of an atom.

Non-State Adversary—Any individual or group that wishes to use destructive force to further its own goals.

Nuclear Fission Weapons—Devices that derive their explosive force from the energy released when a large number of nuclei fission in a very short period of time.

Plutonium-239 (Pu^{239})—A fissile isotope created as a result of capture of a neutron by U^{238}. It is excellent material for nuclear weapons.

Plutonium-240 (Pu^{240})—A fissile isotope whose presence complicates the construction of nuclear explosives because of its high rate of spontaneous fission. It is produced in reactors when a Pu^{239} atom absorbs a neutron instead of fissioning.

Protons—Positively charged particles which, together with neutrons, comprise the nucleus of an atom.

Reactor—A facility that contains a controlled nuclear fission chain reaction. It may be used to generate electrical power, to conduct research, or exclusively to produce plutonium for nuclear explosives.

Reactor-Grade Plutonium—Plutonium that contains more than 7 percent of the isotope plutonium-240. It is created in most power reactors under normal operating conditions, although the liquid metal fast breeder reactor does produce weapons-grade plutonium in one portion of the reactor.

Recycle—The reuse of unburned uranium and plutonium in fresh fuel after separation from fission products in spent fuel at a reprocessing plant.

Reprocessing—Chemical treatment of spent reactor fuel to separate the plutonium and uranium from the fission products and (under present plans) from each other.

Safeguards—Sets of regulations, procedures, and equipment designed to prevent and detect the diversion of nuclear materials from authorized channels.

Special Nuclear Material (SNM)—Plutonium, or uranium enriched in U^{235} or U^{233}.

Spent Fuel—Fuel elements that have been removed from the reactor because they contain too little fissile material and too high a concentration of radioactive fission products. They are both physically and radioactively hot.

Strategic Special Nuclear Material (SSNM)—Plutonium, U^{233}, or uranium enriched to 20 percent or more in U^{235}.

Spiking—A technique to deter theft of nuclear fuel by the addition of radioactive substances.

Thermal neutrons—Low energy, or slow moving neutrons.

Thorium-232 (Th^{232})—A fertile, naturally occurring isotope from which the fissile isotope uranium-233 can be bred.

Uranium-233 (U^{233})—A fissile isotope bred by fertile thorium-232. It is similar in weapons quality to plutonium-239.

Uranium-235 (U^{235})—The only naturally occurring fissile isotope. Natural uranium has 0.7 percent of U^{235}; light water reactors use about 3 percent and weapons materials normally consist of 90 percent of this isotope.

Uranium-238 (U^{238})—A fertile isotope from which Pu^{239} can be bred. It comprises 99.3 percent of natural uranium.

Weapons-Grade Plutonium—Plutonium that contains less than 7 percent of plutonium-240, an isotope that complicates the design of nuclear weapons.

Selected Bibliography

The obstacles facing those who set out to understand the problem of nuclear terrorism are confounded by the fact that they confront not one immense body of scholarly and popular writings, but indeed several. Contributions treating topics as varied as deviant behavior, terrorism, nuclear proliferation, revolution, nuclear physics, chemistry, and law enforcement are all likely to offer significant insight into the problem. Nor should the humanities be slighted, since many of the more insightful and even prescient contribucan be found in literature (for example the work of Albert Camus, Fëodor Dostoevski, and more recently Paul Theroux in *The Family Arsenal*). Therefore, what follows is a careful selection of contributions that offer a good beginning. For a more detailed bibliographic source on terrorism, the reader is invited to consult the editors' *International Terrorism: An Annotated Bibliography and Research Guide* (Boulder, Colo.: Westview Press, 1979). An excellent bibliography on nuclear proliferation can be found in Wohlstetter's *Moving Toward Life in a Nuclear Armed Crowd?* cited below. Robert Blackey has provided a thorough bibliography on revolution, *Modern Revolutions and Revolutionists* (Santa Barbara, Calif.: Clio Books, 1976), for those seeking yet a third perspective.

General Sources: Terrorism, Revolution and Nuclear Proliferation

Alexander, Yonah, and Finger, Seymour Maxwell, eds. *Terrorism: Interdisciplinary Perspectives.* New York: John Jay Press, 1977.

Arendt, Hannah. *On Violence.* New York: Harcourt, Brace & World, 1970.

____. *On Revolution.* New York: Viking Press, 1963.

Bell, J. Bowyer. *A Time of Terror: How Democratic Societies Respond to Revolutionary Violence.* New York: Basic Books, 1978.

Friedlander, Robert A. "Terrorism and Political Violence: Do the Ends Justify the Means?" *Chitty's Law Journal* 24 (September 1976): 240-245.

____. "Coping with Terrorism: What Is to be Done?" *Ohio Northern University Law Review* 5 (1978): 432-443.

____. *Terrorism: Documents of International and Local Control.* 2 vols. Dobbs Ferry, N.Y.: Oceana Publications, 1979.

Greenwood, Ted; Feiveson Harold A.; and Taylor, Theodore B. *Nuclear Proliferation: Motivations, Capabilities, and Strategies for Control.* 1980's Project/Council on Foreign Relations. New York: McGraw-Hill, 1977.

Gurr, Ted Robert. *Why Men Revolt.* Princeton: Princeton University Press, 1970.

Laqueur, Walter Z. *Terrorism.* Boston: Little, Brown and Company, 1977.

Nuclear Energy Policy Study Group. *Nuclear Power: Issues and Choices.* Cambridge, Mass.: Ballinger Publishing Company, 1977.

Thornton, Thomas Perry. "Terror as a Weapon of Political Agitation." In *Internal War: Problems and Approaches,* edited by Harry Eckstein, , pp. 77-99. New York: Free Press, 1964.

U.S. Congress. Office of Technology Assessment. *Nuclear Proliferation and Safeguards.* New York: Praeger Publishers, 1977.

U.S. Department of Justice. Law Enforcement Assistance Administration. National Advisory Committee on Criminal Justice Standards and Goals. *Disorders and Terrorism.* (Report of the Task Force on Disorders and Terrorism). Washington, D.C.: Government Printing Office, December 1976.

Walzer, Michael. *Just and Unjust Wars: A Moral Argument with Historical Illustrations.* New York: Basic Books, 1977.

Wilkinson, Paul. *Political Terrorism.* New York: John Wiley & Sons, 1977.

____. *Terrorism and the Liberal State.* New York: John Wiley & Sons, 1977.

Wohlstetter, Albert, et al. *Moving Toward Life in a Nuclear Armed Crowd?* Report to the U.S. Arms Control and Disarmament Agency. Los Angeles: Pan Heuristics, 1976

Specific Treatments: Nuclear Terrorism

BDM Corporation. *Analysis of the Terrorist Threat to the Commercial Nuclear Industry.* Report submitted to the Special Safeguards Study, U.S. Nuclear Regulatory Commission. McLean, VA.: BDM Corporation, September 1975.

Beres, Louis René. "Terrorism and the Nuclear Threat in the Middle East." *Current History* 70 (January 1976): 27-29.

____. "Terrorism and International Security: The Nuclear Threat." *Chitty's Law Journal* 26 (Marcy 1978): 73-90.

DeNike, Douglas L. "Radioactive Malevolence." *Bulletin of the Atomic Scientists* (February 1974): 16-20.

Dunn, Lewis A. "Nuclear 'Gray Marketeering.' " *International Security* 1 (Winter 1977): 107-118.

Frank, Forrest R. "Suppressing Nuclear Terrorism: A Modest Proposal." In U.S. Congress, Senate, Committee on Government Operations, *Export*

Reorganization Act of 1976, Hearings Before the Committee on S.1439, 94th Cong., 2d sess., June 1975. (Proposed treaty language for an international convention to suppress the theft or unlawful use of nuclear weapons or materials.)

Jenkins, Brian. *Will Terrorists Go Nuclear?* Santa Monica, Calif.: California Seminar on Arms Control and Foreign Policy, October 1975.

Kupperman, Robert H. "Treating the Symptoms of Terrorism: Some Principles of Good Hygiene." *Terrorism* 1 (1977): 35-49.

Lapp, Ralph E. "The Ultimate Blackmail." *New York Times Magazine,* February 4, 1973, pp. 13ff.

Larus, Joel. *Nuclear Weapons Safety and the Common Defense.* Columbus: Ohio State University Press, 1967.

McPhee, John. *The Curve of Binding Energy.* New York: Farrar, Straus and Giroux, 1974. (A highly readable, popularized presentation of Theodor Taylor's arguments.)

MITRE Corporation. *The Threat to Licensed Nuclear Facilities.* McLean, Va.: MITRE Corporation, September 1975.

Norton, Augustus R. "Terror by Fission: An Analysis and Critique." *Chitty's Law Journal.* In press.

_____. with the assistance of Martin H. Greenberg. *Understanding the Nuclear Terrorism Threat.* Gaithersburg, Md.: International Association of Chiefs of Police, 1979.

Rosenbaum, David M. "Nuclear Terror." *International Security* 1 (Winter 1977): 140-161.

_____, et al. *Special Safeguards Study.* Prepared for the U.S. Atomic Energy Commission in 1974. Excerpted in *Congressional Record,* April 30, 1974, p. S6621.

Willrich, Mason, and Taylor, Theodore B. *Nuclear Theft: Risks and Safeguards.* Cambridge, Mass.: Ballinger Publishing Co., 1974.

Willrich, Mason. "Terrorists Keep Out!" *Bulletin of the Atomic Scientists* (May 1975): 12-16.

U.S. Comptroller General. *Improvements Needed in the Program for the Protection of Special Nuclear Material.* Report to the Congress. Washington, D.D.: Government Accounting Office, Novermber 1973.

Index